A Performer's Guide
to Medieval Music

Music: Scholarship and Performance
Paul Hillier, general editor
Thomas A. Binkley, founding editor

Published in Cooperation with
Early Music América

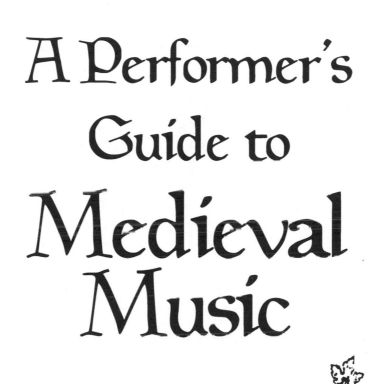

A Performer's Guide to Medieval Music

Edited by

Ross W. Duffin

Indiana University Press
Bloomington and Indianapolis

This book is a publication of

Indiana University Press
601 North Morton Street
Bloomington, IN 47404-3797 USA

http://iupress.indiana.edu

Telephone orders 800-842-6796
Fax orders 812-855-7931
Orders by e-mail iuporder@indiana.edu

The paper used in this publication meets the minimum requirements of American National Standard
for Information Sciences--Permanence of Paper for Printed Library Materials, ANSI Z39.48-1984.

Manufactured in the United States of America

Text set in ITC Garamond-Light
Titles in Goudy Medieval (MentorFonts)

Musical Examples set in Petrucci (Coda) for modern notation
Squarcialupi (Ross W. Duffin) for mensural notation
St. Meinrad (St. Meinrad Archabbey) for chant notation

Library of Congress Cataloging-in-Publication Data

A performer's guide to medieval music / edited by Ross W. Duffin.
  p. cm. — (Publications of the Early Music Institute) (Performer's guides to early
music)
  Includes bibliographical references (p.), discography (p.), and index.
  ISBN 0-253-33752-6 (cl : alk. paper)
  1. Performance practice (Music)—500–1400. I. Duffin, Ross W. II. Series.
  III. Series: Performer's guides to early music

ML457 .P475 2000
781.4'3'0902—dc21

                                        00-040968

ISBN 0-253-21533-1 (pbk.)

2 3 4 5 6 07 06 05 04 03 02

In Memoriam

Thomas Binkley

howard Mayer Brown

Barbara Thornton

Contents

<h1 style="text-align:center">PART 3
THEORY & PRACTICE</h1>

Preface

Ross W. Duffin

There has never been a book about the Middle Ages quite like this one. There have been books about instruments, about genres, and about places; there have been books about performing Baroque music, Renaissance music, and about performing both medieval and Renaissance music, but never one in which the focus has been entirely on the performance of music from the medieval period. The ultimate aim in producing such a unique volume is to foster more performances of medieval music—to bring the richness of those repertoires vividly to life for modern audiences—and to invite the participation of a wider circle of musicians in accomplishing that task. Two types of authors have been asked to contribute: scholars with strong interest and experience in musical performance, and performers with an abiding passion for learning and thinking about what they do. (In some cases, it is impossible to tell which is which.) Some authors have written eloquently about music near and dear to their hearts, while others, perhaps with little previous experience in writing, have generously shared insights achieved after years of working with the music and the instruments. In our various ways, we have all tried to weigh the historical evidence, meager as it is in many cases, and fill it in with our own observations about what has worked best for us in performance.

As a result, this book is rather more laden with historical background than most "how to" manuals, and rather more sprinkled with conjecture and "best guesses" than is typical for scholarly publications. Although definitive answers to many pertinent performance questions are frequently unavailable, our silence on such issues would almost certainly mean fewer performances and a perpetuation of the very situation we are trying to remedy. It would also mean the eventual loss of the beautiful and effective performance approaches evolved by many of these authors over a period of decades, a loss that in a small way, perhaps, would mirror the loss of the original performance traditions. Future generations may well choose to perform medieval music differently from the ways described or recommended in these pages, but at least they will not be totally ignorant of the thought that informs some of today's best performances.

This is not to imply that there is unanimity among performers and scholars as to how medieval music was performed or ought to be performed today. Far from it. Even within this book, authors express opposing views on such issues as the use of instruments in late medieval polyphony. That is as it should be. Things are rarely so absolutely clear as some writers have made them out to be—or genuinely believe them to be—and the unfortunate tendency to turn performance decisions into moral issues has plainly had a dampening effect on performance. No-one wants to be criticized for being "inauthentic" or worse yet, "musically immoral." But we are all, in a way, 'troubadours', seeking after beautiful, meaningful performances of this music, and we will not experience them if we are hesitant about performing.

The book is divided into three parts: Repertoire, Voices & Instruments, and Theory & Practice, each of which is subdivided into several chapters. The first section approaches the subject by genre, sometimes subdividing by geography, sometimes by chronology. Each repertoire chapter typically includes information on historical background, forms, language, notation, performance forces, and so on. The second section focuses instead on the performing forces, offering information on usage, surviving specimens and iconography, tuning, and technique. Thus, the first section might be used by those interested in performing certain repertoires and wondering how to go about it, while the second section could be consulted by those with certain performing forces and wondering how best to use them.

The book also includes a Select Discography. This is somewhat unusual, but as recording companies have recently discovered to their cost, CDs have a much longer life than previous formats, so older recordings that might have been of only referential interest in the past may indeed be available for purchase many years after their first appearance. There is also a Select Bibliography although for complete documentation readers will need to refer to the notes for the various chapters as well.

A further word is needed also about the chapter on voice. Since no medieval specimens survive, no depictions that can be measured, I thought it would be useful instead to have a more philosophical discussion involving one of the century's most respected and successful of singers of medieval music: Barbara Thornton. She was interviewed for this purpose by Lawrence Rosenwald, none of us suspecting at the time that the chapter would turn out to be such an important testament to her approach.

Several people have contributed mightily to the preparation of this book. Jeffery Kite-Powell has been especially helpful as general editor of the Early Music America series and as editor of the first book to appear, the *Performer's Guide to Renaissance Music*. Stewart Carter, author of the seventeenth-century volume, was a good soundingboard for ideas as we worked on our parallel projects. Herbert Myers, whose chapters occupy large portions of all three volumes, has been, as always, a fount of wisdom. Elizabeth Aubrey has not only written three chapters in the Monophony section, but also been a valued advisor for that portion of the book. Locally, Timothy Collins and Adam Gilbert read some of the chapters, R. Kent Quade, H. Christopher Wilson, G. William Milhoan, and my son David Simmons-Duffin assisted with the preparation of some of the musical examples and illustrations, and my mother, Eileen Duffin, cast her practiced eye in search of typos. Lastly, my wife, Beverly Simmons, Executive Director of Early Music America, spent many hours helping me prepare the final copy.

It has been exciting for me personally to see this book come together, although I would be lying if I gave the impression that coordinating a book with more than two dozen authors was "fun." So many of these authors are extraordinarily good at what they do, and to be able to assemble their collective wisdom and provide them with an opportunity to share what they know has been very gratifying. Not all chapters provide the same kinds of information (as they might have done with a single author), but the result, I believe, is stronger for offering so many highly-specialized points of view. Whatever shortcomings still exist in coverage, clarity, and presentation are my own responsibility.

Finally, a note about the triple dedication. Over the years that this book was being conceived and written, three people died whose work had an enormous impact on the performance of medieval music in our time: Thomas Binkley, Howard Mayer Brown, and Barbara Thornton. Thomas Binkley's recordings of medieval music with the Studio der Frühen Musik in the 1960s and '70s made whole new repertoires come alive again, and in fact, he was originally to have joined several of his former students and colleagues in contributing to this book. Howard Brown's passion for performance practice was wide-ranging over the Middle Ages and Renaissance, but he contributed especially to our understanding of trecento instruments, and it is significant that he chose to write the inaugural article in *Early Music* Magazine (1973) "On the performance of fifteenth-century chansons." The third dedicatee, Barbara Thornton, is a contributor to this book who passed away recently, after her chapter was complete but too soon nonetheless, considering the decades of life and career that should have awaited her. Along with her colleague and companion, Benjamin Bagby, her work directing and performing with Ensemble Sequentia over the last twenty years has been one of the most vital and important means of presenting medieval music to the world. The work of all of us herein represented has been touched in some important way by these three people.

A Performer's Guide
to Medieval Music

I. Sacred Music

1. Chant

William P. Mahrt

Gregorian chant is unique among all the genres of Medieval music, for it experienced a continuing cultivation through the whole period and has been sung ever since. The history of its performance, not to mention the varieties of its performance today, is more complex by orders of magnitude than is that of most other repertories. It has been the subject of some excellent discussions of the details of historical performance, with evidence coming from documentary, liturgical, and music-theoretical sources; the reader is recommended to seek these studies out.[1] Instead of replicating their method and content, however, this essay addresses the performance of chant in a broader context, dealing with a few fundamental issues which remain constant, regardless of the context of performance or school of rhythmic interpretation; this is followed by a summary conspectus of practical issues.

Principles of Chant Performance

How to perform Gregorian chant depends upon the purpose of the performance. Of all the repertories of early music, chant may be performed for the greatest variety of reasons, representing the broadest spectrum of historical, geographical, and systematic purposes.

A number of purposes are not primarily historical at all. One of these is in fact the principal rationale for the creation of chant in the first place—its singing as a part of a contemporaneous liturgical service—and it was ever so. A present-day Mass or Office sung in a medieval church makes use of a building whose principal structure may date from a specific historical period, yet that building contains additions, revisions, remodelings from various times since, and it often has hidden foundations that antedate the principal building, sometimes by several centuries. Likewise the same Mass or Office, sung principally in Gregorian chant—and this is still done as a viable liturgical observance—uses music from various historical periods, much of it stemming from as early as the first writing down of chant in the Carolingian era, with roots in oral traditions that may date back for centuries; but some of it may as well have been the creation of any century since.[2] The service is a coherent whole, nevertheless, since each piece was added carefully and knowingly to the received complex of pieces. Even so, the participants generally perform the pieces with little sense of their history. Paradoxically, then, the principal rationale for the performance of chant is not primarily a historical one.

While chant can be performed for a functioning liturgical service today, so it also can be performed as a viable aesthetic object outside the context of the divine service.

There are thus many purely musical objectives in singing chant, whether in or out of a liturgical service, musical reasons that no other repertory serves in the same way. I should like to single out three: unison singing, language, and mode.

There is a musical value in the singing of pure melodies which need no accompaniment, but rather, whose whole significance is contained in the single part, sung by every singer. This unison singing is a communal act that binds the singers in a common enterprise; because it is unison, the bond is most intimate, as Dante suggests in the *Purgatorio*.[3] In unison, the singers can perfect elements of tuning, timbre, diction, rhythm, and expression in common.

Another value is in the mastery of texts in a language that is ancient and yet has sufficient words cognate with our own to provide a foundation in something familiar. There is a musical value in experiencing the ways a melody can represent a text, which differ so remarkably from genre to genre of chant.[4] There is even a contrasting value in singing chants with prominent melismatic passages. The way in which a melismatic chant departs from the text without abandoning it, undertaking a purely musical development on a single syllable, is unique and beautiful; the shaping of the rhythm of the melismatic chant, however, is a greater challenge, since it depends less upon the rhythm of the text.[5]

There is a musical value in singing modal music; it is the historical antecedent of more familiar tonal music, and common elements give it a basis in familiarity; yet there are aspects of Gregorian modality that are new and even strange to a modern performer; the appropriation of these very aspects through performance provides an element of discovery and mind-stretching that is exhilarating and unforgettable. There are many other elements of the performance of chant that can be the occasion for discovery, particularly the things which entail some experimentation. These include the whole range of rhythmic interpretation, as well as the use of neumatic notation and singing from memory, all purely musical and experiential functions, essentially independent of history.

There are, nevertheless, also historical reasons for performing Gregorian chant. The historical position of Gregorian chant is unique: it was the first body of Western music to be recorded in notation; moreover, it has been a constant presence in Western musical history ever since, being performed alongside the newly-composed repertories of sacred music from the Notre Dame school through the Masses of Stravinsky, Poulenc, and Vaughan Williams. The performance of chant can thus function as a laboratory of music history. This includes many experiments, not the least of which is the challenge of essaying the rhythmic styles of the various periods, especially the earlier ones. A similar project is the exploration of the interrelationship of historical aesthetics and styles of performance; the notions of Romanesque, Gothic, and Renaissance as styles have important ramifications for chant performance. The music-historical laboratory can go so far as to recreate a performance of a historical liturgy, for example, Matins at St. Gall in the ninth century, interpreting the rhythmic style indicated by the sources in St. Gall notation, or a Mass at Paris in the thirteenth century, incorporating the organum of the Notre Dame school into the chant performance.[6] A more general experiment might be one exploring the basis of the earliest melodies in oral transmission, an experiment I have often done with a music history class:

> The students are given written text with no notation and taught to sing eight psalm antiphons, one in each mode, together with their psalm tones. They are then asked to classify and distinguish the antiphons by final, range, and reciting note, replicating in a small way the medieval classification of antiphons.[7] Invariably students rather unselfconsciously reinvent one or another type of neumatic notation in making aids to remember the melodies. A similar experiment asks them to memorize without notation a series of antiphons all belonging to the same melody type and invent a memory aid to distinguish the texts. This experiment generally shows the St. Gall notation to be a sufficient solution to the problem of how to remember the same melody set to varying texts.

In each of these purposes, there is an important relationship to how the chant was performed in a historical context, there is some sense of historical authenticity. But in each one, the relationship to a perceived historical antecedent is different. Indeed, for Gregorian chant, historical authenticity is a perplexing and complicated issue.

The paradox for the historical performance of Gregorian chant is that a strictly "historical" performance is unhistorical: at any given time in its earlier history, a time when its uses were almost entirely liturgical, the repertory in practice included pieces of great antiquity, new compositions, and everything in between, used side-by-side. Pieces of various historical vintages must have been performed originally in very diverse ways; yet I know of no historical evidence for performance which takes account of the respective historical styles of these pieces; one might rather assume that the prevailing style of performance at any given time pertained to all the pieces in the repertory.[8] Actually, the usual criteria for historical performance are ill-fitting. Most pieces are not principally the work of a single composer but are more likely the result of a collective compositional process ranging over a wide period of time. For the principal repertory, by the time the work had been written down, it may already have been the subject of considerable mutation; thus anything like the "original" version or intention cannot be determined—in fact, did not ever quite exist. Likewise, the pieces are not independent art music in the same sense as Baroque instrumental music is, or even, for that matter, as lyrics of troubadour or trouvère poets are.

The genesis of the music was as liturgical music; its characteristic styles arose as expressions of diverse liturgical functions. Any historically informed performance will better fulfill its own function, concert or liturgy, sacred or secular, if these differences are well understood.[9] This, then, is a more fundamental level upon which to base stylistic decisions: what functions the music served and how it served them in the context in which it was performed. While it is unlikely that the original context of performance can be reconstructed exactly, the enterprise might still well be one to understand the medieval context and adapt its elements according to the function of the present performance.

This is far from proposing that the notion of historical authenticity be abandoned; rather, it should be developed according to the demands of its material. Defining authenticity as fidelity to certain aspects of the work, I would propose four kinds: 1) historical, 2) analytic, 3) contextual, and 4) ontological. Each has its purpose and its limitations; together they should provide a set of keen tools for thinking about the appropriate styles of chant performance, as well as other types of performance.

1 **Historical.** The performance of a work takes account of the conventions, both technical and aesthetic, which were part of the current practice at the time of the conception of the work; this is the most commonly accepted meaning of "authentic performance." It has provided the conceptual basis for the revival of early instruments and a general sense of the differentiation of styles of performance appropriate to different repertories. It is invaluable in identifying suitable techniques for different styles of music, and when it incorporates such general matters as aesthetics, in realizing stylistic differences between works in performance.

The historical point of view requires some qualifications, though. Explicit principles of historical authenticity are of recent development and were not part of the consciousness of earlier periods. Outside the chant repertory, Renaissance ornamentation is a good example:

> The madrigals of Cipriano de Rore represented a development in the expression of text led to Monteverdi's definition of the *seconda prattica;* his settings of Petrarch texts in particular are models of intense and subjective expression of the poetry.[10] Dalla Casa's settings of Rore's madrigals are examples of the height of Renaissance ornamentation, providing one of Rore's voice parts with a virtuosic display that completely compromises the sensitive relation of music and text.[11] Without historical precedent, a modern performer would not have dared do this to a Rore madrigal. Yet, on the grounds of historical authenticity, it is justified, because it was done, it was received in its own time.

Thus principles of historical authenticity have to be qualified by matters of context and creativity. Still, historical authenticity is a crucial criterion for the performance of historical music and a substantial factor in the other kinds of authenticity.

2 **Analytic.** The performance of the work realizes its intrinsic musical parameters so that they achieve the greatest degree of internal coherence and effectiveness. There is a historical dimension to it, since an accurate analysis of a work is usually aided by principles of historical theory. In the case of chant, analytical matters include mode, text setting (especially placement of melisma), application of melodic formulae, and overall melodic structure, including identification of principal notes and their ornamentation.[12]

3 **Contextual.** The place and occasion of performance affects several broad, but rather intangible aspects of the performance, especially the elements of formality and interaction with the audience. The setting of a large formal concert calls for a formal style of performance, while the intimacy of a home calls for much less formality. The way in which elements of spontaneity play out, both in the intrinsic expression of the piece, in the ordering of the works performed, and in the response of the audience, differ importantly in such contrasting contexts; a liturgical performance differs markedly from both of these: its ritual setting is formal, but the interaction of performer and listener is intrinsic to its whole structure. Moreover, each of these contexts brings a different acoustical environment, which requires specific attention to tempo and sonority.

The difference between sacred and secular contexts is equally decisive. In a liturgical performance there is always a focal point which is beyond the chant—the text, the action, and even the direct encounter with the eternal.[13] Recordings of chant often betray an overly self-conscious attention to details of expression which draws attention to the performance in the absence of a sacred context. Concert compromises should not sacrifice that value of transcendence, but should rather keep in mind that, even without the theology and belief inherent in a liturgical context, the aesthetic experience of the transcendent can be accessible.

4   **Ontological.** The performance is faithful to the most fundamental sense of what the work is. For some chants, the identity of the work is in its text—for example, a hymn—whether a metric Office hymn, or a Mass "hymn" such as the Gloria or the Sanctus. But for others its identity is in its function, as demonstrated by the various settings of the same text below. Richard Crocker whimsically asks why we are always exhorted to consider how the music expresses the text, but never how the text expresses the music.[14] His question is most apt. The Gregorian propers of the Mass set the text in such a fashion that the music may be the more fundamental function, and the text the expression: the most fundamental aspect of these pieces is the sense of motion or reflection which the piece projects; the text, while essential, is the medium of this expression.

The genres of Gregorian chant arose within liturgical use, and their styles differ in ways which relate to their function in the liturgy. Their differences call for differences in performance, in what is emphasized in each genre—the text and its accents, the strong rhythmic style of some chants, the meditative quality of melismatic chants. By comparing and contrasting the musical styles of these genres, the basis for such differences in performance can be established.

This analysis is based upon two simple principles of text setting: 1) melodic placement—the position of melodic activity with regard to the accents of the texts; 2) melodic density,[15]—the number of pitches per syllable, usually distinguished as a) recitative (several syllables to a single pitch), b) syllabic (generally one note per syllable), c) neumatic (generally two or three notes per syllable), and d) melismatic (some syllables receive a large number of notes). These can be illustrated by two examples which highlight contrasting instances of the styles.

The first example illustrates melodic placement in the contrast of two recitative genres, the psalm tone and the versicle and response. When the verse is sung as part of the entire psalm—for example, in vespers—its psalm-tone formula takes into account the cadence of each half of the verse; after the recitation of most of the text on a single pitch, the pattern of accent which concludes the half-verse is articulated by a melodic turn emphasizing at least the last accent;[16] this melodic formula allows the text of the whole psalm to be chanted efficiently in an elevated tone of voice and speech-like tempo, since the entire psalter will be chanted in the course of a week. It provides a neutral but disciplined medium in which the text rather than the melody is the object of attention, yet the melody adumbrates something of the text, since it is dedicated to the cadence, that pattern of accents which defines the grammatical and rhetorical conclusion of the sentence. A different recitative formula is employed when there is a versicle and response in the Divine Office. This genre seems to serve as a large-scale punctuation in the course of a service; its purpose is not only in its text, but in the fact that it clarifies the structure of the service, as a kind of musical semicolon. Here a psalm verse is sung to a recitative formula which sets all of the text to a single pitch until, upon the last syllable (almost always an unaccented one), a melisma of eight notes occurs.[17] It is almost as if the melody had to wait until the text were finished; its musical effect is quite different from that of the psalm tone; instead of articulating something intrinsic to the text, it adds something decorative upon it, reflecting the function of the versicle and response as decorative, articulative. The difference between these two recitative genres is one of melodic placement—where the melodic activity takes place relative to the accent of the text: on the most important accents of the text, the cadence accents, or upon the last unaccented syllable as an "end-melisma." This distinction between placement upon accent versus ending syllable is fundamental to the distinctions between all the genres of Gregorian chant.

The second example is a lesson with melismatic responsory. At Matins a lesson is sung to a formulaic tone[18] and immediately followed by a melismatic responsory. For instance, on Christmas, a lesson from a sermon of St. Leo the Great is followed by the responsory *O magnum mysterium*.[19] The tone for the lesson simply articulates the middle of the sentence and the ending with turns of melodic cadence, leaving the rest of the lesson to be intoned upon a single pitch in a fashion similar to the psalm tone. The responsory which follows, however, treats the text in a very different way. There are just slightly more than three notes per syllable on average, but more remarkable is the use of end-melisma. The last unaccented syllables of "mysterium," "animalia," and "Virgo" bear melismas of eleven to thirteen notes each, giving a striking prominence to the ends of words. These suggest that the purpose of the musical piece itself is not just the delivery of the text or even a decorative use of the text, but rather that momentary departures from the text show the fundamental function of the piece to be more purely musical. An experiment can demonstrate the purpose of such pieces. Sing for a receptive audience (or congregation or class) a lesson followed by a responsory, and observe the listeners' state of mind. If the singing of the responsory is done properly—that is to say, beautifully, with a proper sense of elevated style—there will be absolute still in the room that indicates that the listeners have ceased completely to move and are no longer making the slight white noise which usually results from the unavoidable distracted motions made by any group of people; its complete absence indicates that their attention is highly focused; they are recollected; they are in a state of both repose and heightened attentiveness. This recollection has both spiritual and liturgical dimensions. Spiritually, it is a state of mind which is achieved by meditation upon something beautiful. Liturgically, it functions to complement the lessons: after having heard the lesson with many words set to few notes, whose meaning may require some assimilation, it provides a contrast, many notes, few words. The state of recollection includes an attentiveness by which the listener is then prepared to hear the next lesson. These distinctions between styles of text-setting clearly arose in liturgical contexts serving liturgical purposes. They are, however, an intrinsic part of the style of the work and can be as important a part of a concert as a liturgical performance, when the audience is prepared for it.

The range of text-setting from recitative to melismatic represents, then, a diversity of liturgical functions. This can be effectively illustrated by using one text as a basis for comparison.[20] The following genres set the text *Justus ut palma* with remarkable differences (see Ex. 1.1):

Ex. 1.1. Settings of *Justus ut palma.*

a. Antiphon[21]

Justus ut palma flo- re bit: sicut cedrus Libani multipli-cabi-tur.

b. Introit[22]

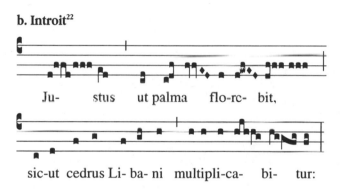

Ju-   stus   ut palma   flo-rc- bit,

sic-ut cedrus Li- ba- ni multipli-ca-   bi-   tur:

c. Offertory[23]

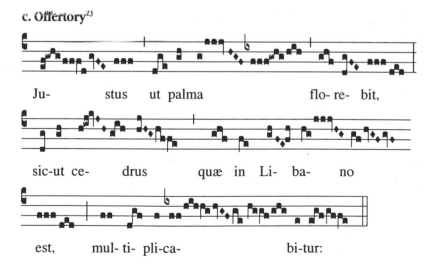

Ju-   stus   ut palma   flo- re- bit,

sic-ut ce-   drus   quæ in Li- ba-   no

est,   mul- ti- pli-ca-   bi-tur:

d. Gradual[24]

Ju- stus   ut palma flo-re-   bit: sic-ut ce- drus

Li-ba-   ni   mul- ti-pli-ca-   bi-

tur:

e. Alleluia[25]

Al-le- lu   ia

Ju- stus   ut pal- ma flo-

re-   bit, et si-cut ce-

drus multi- pli-ca-

bi-tur:

The single psalm verse (Ps. 91:13) is a paradigm of *parallelismus membrorum,* the characteristic poetic form of the psalm.[26] Though it is neither rhymed nor metric, it is nevertheless poetry in that its two halves are complementary complete statements, the second one often being a restatement of the first.[27]

The antiphon, largely syllabic, functions as a melodic refrain sung before and after the chanting of a whole psalm to a psalm tone; though its style is simple, its shapely melodic contours complement the neutral psalmody without unduly extending the performance. Were it less melodic, it would not be sufficiently distinguished from the psalmody which it complements; were it more elaborate, it would attract too much attention to itself and perhaps slow down the sequence of the psalms in performance.

The four propers of the Mass are more elaborate, but they also show significant differences between them. The introit can be described as neumatic, and as such stands half-way between the styles of the antiphon and the melismatic chants. Its liturgical function is to accompany a procession, the motion of all the ministers of the liturgy into the Church, moving to the altar and incensing it. For this it projects a sense of rhythmic motion, adding a degree of solemnity. The offertory accompanies an action, incensing the altar, but with not as much action of the ministers as the introit; it is the prelude to the most solemn part of the Mass, the canon, and so it projects a lesser sense of motion and a greater degree of solemnity. The gradual and alleluia, the melismatic chants for the Mass, have a function quite similar to that of the responsory of the Office, with the additional feature that the melismas of the alleluia are so extensive as to have their own internal melodic form. Thus the succession of gradual to alleluia creates a sense of climax, leading to the singing of the gospel, the high point of the liturgy of the word.[28] Similar comparisons and contrasts can be drawn between the tones for the lessons,[29] and for the prayers.

The Ordinary of the Mass has a different rationale; being texts which were repeated every time a Mass was sung, they required greater variety; for example, the number of settings of *Kyrie eleison* allows a stylistic diversity between the instances of this text, varying according to the solemnity of the day on which they are sung, from the simplest melodies for weekdays,[30] through the ordinary Sundays,[31] to major feasts,[32] and finally feasts of the Blessed Virgin.[33] Settings of the rest of the Ordinary follow similar patterns.

Another functional distinction can be fruitfully coordinated with the stylistic one, that of who sings each piece. The medieval liturgy was at one and the same time hierarchical and leveling. There was a sense that in the performance of the liturgy, everyone had a place, but each place was distinct from the others. This is particularly true in the details of the ordering of the life of the choir,[34] where the order of participation in the liturgy reflected the "orders" of the persons, what ecclesiastical rank each held; for example, lessons at Matins might be read by nine lectors, in ascending order, the last of which might even be the bishop. This sense of hierarchy is reflected in the fact that some texts are sung by bishop, some by priest, some by deacon, some by subdeacon, and some by cantors. Thus, the everyday singing of the liturgy reflected an unselfconscious celebration of an ordering of all persons.

On the other hand, there was a leveling effect, as well. The Rule of St. Benedict prescribes that the monks sit in choir in order, but only in the order in which they entered the community.[35] Those who came from noble families had no pride of place, but took their place alongside those of common origins. There is a musical correlative of this leveling effect, and it is in the psalmody. Though much of the liturgy was conducted by ministers whose place reflected a hierarchy, the singing of psalmody was based upon something more egalitarian: the psalms were sung antiphonally—by the choir divided in two equal parts, singing in alternation, verse by verse; this antiphonal performance applied to the Ordinary of the Mass as well. The practical benefit of this is obvious, in a day which may have included six or eight hours of singing, the division into two choirs would lighten the burden upon the voices by almost half. But symbolically, when it came to the bread and butter of the Divine Office, the psalmody, all were equal in its performance. Thus responsorial performances, in which celebrant or cantors are answered by choir reflect a hierarchical ordering, while antiphonal performances reflect an egalitarian one.

The aesthetic unity of any given service thus arises out of diverse but complementary functions and thus depends rather less upon historically differentiated styles. The important stylistic differences are functional and these functions are instructive about what the different effects of the music should be. Whether the chant is performed in the liturgy or not, these effects are somehow inherent in the styles of the pieces, and especially in the stylistic contrasts between pieces heard in close proximity. These principles can be realized in the reconstruction of a historical liturgy, in providing music for a contemporary sung liturgy, but also in non-liturgical contexts. The classroom is a place where singing of chant can easily be incorporated into the ongoing work of the class—a few minutes a day of singing from memory can illuminate several aspects of memory as well as of the nature of the repertory that was memorized. Likewise, in a concert, a cleverly constructed juxtaposition of pieces may successfully present the aesthetic functions of contrasting works.

The Practical Performance of Chant

In the most general terms the performance of chant must take into account two principal rationales—the linguistic and the harmonic, that is, the ways words shape the melodies, and the ways tones contribute to the beauty of harmonious pitch relations. These pertain to performance of chant no matter what school of rhythm is followed. Linguistic matters concern declamation, phrasing, and pronunciation.

Declamation. An important musical aspect of language is the declamation of the word rhythm. The accents of the Latin text for all three-syllable words are marked in the modern editions (the accent regularly falls on the first syllable of a two-syllable word), but such markings are not really necessary, for the melodies themselves teach where the accents belong. Moreover, singers whose linguistic experience is in a highly accentual language (like English) need to be cautioned that the basic treatment of a Latin accent must be a gentle caress, not a dynamic punch. In musical setting, accented syllables generally receive a higher pitch (particularly relative to the following syllable) or more notes; this treatment can be the basis for a sensitive projection of the substantive accents of the text. Still, singing rarely reproduces merely the natural rhythm of speech, but rather alters or subsumes it, sometimes exaggerating sometimes de-emphasizing. This process differs in general between the four styles of text setting described above, recitative, syllabic, neumatic, and melismatic, in relation to who sings them and what liturgical function they serve.

1 **Recitative.** The formulae for the singing of lessons (epistle and gospel of the Mass and the lessons of Matins) are the means of making a text sung by one person audible to a whole congregation. Their delivery should be rhetorical, the natural rhythms and rhetoric inherent in the text should be the basis for the style of delivery; accent and unaccent should play an important role, and the formulaic cadences, especially in the epistle tone, can emphasize the rhetoric. The psalmody of the Office, on the other hand is communal and meditative. The choir which sings the 150 psalms in the course of the week does not need to "bring out" the accents; rather the elevation of the voice and the ecstatic aspect of the psalmody tends to even out the syllables. Nevertheless, the text is primary in such a performance. The performance has to be rhythmic, ordering the entire group in singing together. Especially the alternation of sides of the choir and the measuring of the pause at the middle of the psalm verse must be orderly. The convention, as I know it, is that alternation between sides proceeds without a break. As one side sings its cadence, the other side picks up the rhythm and proceeds. The middle of the psalm verse, on the other hand is the point of a measured pause, sometimes measured silently by saying "Ave," or "Ave Maria," or even more, probably depending on the reverberation of the building.[36] It is necessary to provide regular, disciplined breathing for a long day of singing. I teach my singers to take a slow deliberate breath during the cadence of the opposite side, so that the beginning of the psalm verse is sung well supported; the measured pause at the middle provides for a similar breath. The psalmody is thus a substantial musical, vocal, linguistic, and even spiritual discipline. For my own chant choir, the singing of vespers has fundamentally changed the way we sing all of our chant, principally because of the recitative psalmody.

2 **Syllabic chants** require a different kind of performance. Here every syllable receives a discrete pitch, the higher pitches more frequently on the accents. It is quite necessary in such chants to give a little more weight to the accented syllables, not so much that they are perceived as longs and shorts, nor that they distract from the overall rhythmic and melodic shape and flow of the piece, but just enough to differentiate them.

3 **Neumatic chants.** The neumes require their own internal rhythms, which become the fundamental building blocks of the piece. Neumes were said to be a single stroke of the breath, so they must be treated as a single rhythmic gesture. While neumes of more notes tend to fall on accented syllables, the more neumes the piece has, the greater the tension exists between the simple rhythm of the text and the composite rhythm of the text plus neumes.[37]

4 **Melismatic chants.** Here the melismas can often fall on unaccented syllables, and the meditative purpose of such chants allows a fairly great disparity between text accent and the placement of melisma. It is important in such chants to maintain the integrity of the melisma—not allowing its individual notes to be

separated, but rather maintaining a balance between the integrity of the individual neumes and the overall contour and flow of the melisma.[38] Melismatic singing differs, depending upon how many are singing. A single soloist singing a melismatic verse has the ultimate control in shaping the performance of the melody; but two soloists have the greater challenge of shaping the melody together; the result can be more beautiful, partly because the coordination of two excellent singers requires more careful planning and execution, but also, just as when two dancers do exactly the same step in tandem, the artistry is more immediately apparent.

Phrasing

The chants have rhythm and melodic contour from the fact that they represent the comma, colon, and period of the text.[39] The structure of the melody derives in large part from the structure of its text. The psalm text is the paradigm, and its *parallelismus membrorum* results in chant melodies having an overall two-part structure. The preponderance of antiphons (psalm antiphons, introits, communions) and responsories (responsories for Matins, offertories, graduals, alleluia verses) have one central internal cadence at the dividing point in the parallelism. Just as in the psalm tone, which rises to its melodic peak, cadences there, and then descends to a point of repose at the end, so these more elaborate chants generally move to a principal cadence away from the final and back to its close. These midpoints are often marked in modern editions by the colon. Within each of these halves, there are smaller and smallest divisions of the text, each set to its own melodic curve and concluded by a cadence;[40] these often coincide with a comma in the text. The bars of the modern editions (full, half, and quarter) represent the levels of these divisions, and as a practical first step in articulating this kind of hierarchical linguistic structure, I recommend that at the full bar the cadence tone be held somewhat longer than the duration of two internal notes, and the pause that follows be about the same duration; at half bars I hold the cadence tone about two notes' duration with a comparable pause, and at quarter bars, just one. These points of articulation should then be adjusted and nuanced, according to their relative weight and conclusiveness, so that, just as in pronouncing prose, no two inflections are exactly the same. Likewise, this phrase structure must be projected in performance by attending to the quality of motion and intensity of singing which defines the melodic contours. As the contour of the melody rises the singers make a subtle increase of intensity, and as it falls a decrease; a slight increase and decrease of tempo can aid this supple shaping of the melodic contour. These changes cannot be made in an obvious way, such as to draw attention to themselves, but only to highlight the contour. Likewise, the intensity of the voice should be maintained at those cadences which are least final, and be relaxed more according to the strength and finality of the cadence.

The final performance thus arises from a complex of rhythmic factors: the rhythm of neumes, syllables, words, and phrases. The initial phrase of the introit *Da pacem* may illustrate this complex:

Ex. 1.2. *Da pacem*, first phrase.

Da pa-cem,	Do-	mi-	ne,	sus-ti- nenti-bus	te,	

| Main notes | D a | c | b | aG (aG) | F | GFE | D |

Neume rhythm

Word rhythm

Composite
rhythm

` = weaker beat, movement ´ = stronger beat, arrival`

Pronunciation

The pronunciation of the text is an interesting problem. "Church Latin" is essentially a modern Italian pronunciation.[41] It is, as well, a close approximation to a generalized European pronunciation (with the most marked exception being the soft c, which was generally pronounced *ts* rather than *ch*). But there is good evidence for quite varied national pronunciations, especially in the later Middle Ages, and even today a national pronunciation of Latin by German, or French, or English speakers can be easily identified by most listeners. Remarkably we are as reluctant to use a historic English pronunciation as the French are to use a French one. Moreover, there is good reason to work on the Carolingian pronunciation, since it is surely a significant component in the highly inflected rhythms of the first-generation notation.[42] Compromise pronunciations are traditionally made; the English, for example, have advocated continental vowels and English consonants.[43] A useful compromise musically is to modify the Italian vowels imperceptibly in the direction of the French; this can give considerable suppleness and agility in the singing.

Practical musicians may have to address specific problems of American pronunciation. Pure vowels are important, maintaining exactly the same sound for the entire duration of the syllable; such diphthongs as *Ky-uh-ri-e* or *Is-rah-ee-yel* and plosive pronunciations of t, p, and k should be avoided; a special case of the last is the current British aspiration following the k of Kyrie (approximating a German ch as in *ich*): *Khhy-ri-e.*

The harmonic rationale includes several matters of basic sound, which have important ramifications for the performance of chant: pitch, tuning, acoustics, and vocal technique.

Pitch

The notated pitches of Gregorian chant should not be confused with the absolute pitch of modern notation. While the medieval gamut[44] as a whole does represent fairly well the available notes of an average male singer including falsetto, its notated pitches in an absolute sense are not practical for the various modes. The normal range of any mode is about an octave, an easy range for singers without specialized vocal training. But the total notated range of the eight modes is nearly two octaves: *A-a* for the Hypodorian mode, and *G-g* for the Mixolydian.[45] It is inconceivable that some chants with an octave range should be sung nearly an octave higher than others. It is further inconceivable that pieces in Hypodorian on A should be sung a fifth higher than those in Hypodorian on D. It is much more likely that they should be sung in approximately the same octave.[46] As a rule of thumb, I set the reciting note at modern A, checking for unusually high or low passages, sometimes taking B-flat for the Phrygian mode, and then make adjustments if necessary; I also check that when two chants follow in succession their pitches are commensurate. All of this is probably obvious, but its ramifications for polyphonic music are often overlooked: the repertory of polyphonic music based on chant tenors was developed as an elaboration upon the chant repertory and most likely was ordered to the received pitches of the chant performances; thus the repertory is potentially as transposable as the chants themselves; the same is most likely true of the contiguous repertory which does not use a borrowed chant.

Tuning

Another concern about pitch is tuning. The Middle Ages taught Pythagorean tuning, a system with simple proportions for the intervals of the fifth (3:2), fourth (4:3), and whole step (9:8), i.e., these intervals are perfectly tuned. The major third, however, is not the acoustic third (5:4), but an interval appreciably wider, in a more complex proportion (81:64), and less consonant. In purely melodic music the integrity of the whole step is more important than the third—all whole steps should be the same. I have observed that my chant choir intuitively sings with this tuning. Pythagorean whole steps can be demonstrated easily: sing a succession of fourths and fifths with common tones:

F G G A A

C C D D E

If the fourths and fifths are perfectly tuned, the intervals C–D and D–E will be Pythagorean whole steps, and the interval E–F will be a Pythagorean half-step. The musical value of this tuning is that the whole steps are wide and robust and the half-steps are narrow and pungent; such narrow half steps tend upward and are part of the reason the notes E and B are weak or unstable.[47]

Acoustics

The acoustics of the room are an important aspect of chant performance. Churches from the Middle Ages generally are very resonant and contribute a support and fullness to the chant, as well as to the tuning. Performers should constantly be testing the acoustic of modern rooms and find those whose resonance is hospitable to chant. Unfortunately today's churches have been deadened for use with microphones, and many churches are now the least desirable places to sing.[48] Lobbies of banks, museums, and office buildings, even stairwells, sometimes repay investigation and experiment. Nevertheless, medieval buildings provide a focused acoustic which is quite different from the generalized resonance of a marble lobby. Experiment and speculation concerning the acoustics in English Gothic cathedrals has convinced me that the ceiling vaults play a crucial role in the acoustics of those buildings. The smaller lady chapels are an epitome of this principle: there, a few (sometimes only two or three) singers sang the daily Lady Mass. The acoustics of these chapels are ample for even such a small group, and may well be a factor in the sonorous character of much English polyphony. Moreover, this acoustic, as ample and full as it is, is clear and focused. Our speculation is that the Gothic rib vaults in the ceilings, with their nearly parabolic shape, focus the sound back to its source, giving optimum concentration of resonance with less delayed reverberation.[49]

Alternation

The performance of chant entails orderly alternation of various performers, whether between cantors and choir (responsorial) or the two sides of the choir (antiphonal), including as well the various liturgical functions, such as celebrant, deacon, etc. The most fundamental one is the cantors' intoning the first word or two of practically every piece, after which the choir completes the piece.[50] This has the practical function of setting pitch and tempo without reference to extraneous pitch sources. It also provides a cue to the listener about the solemnity of the day, since on the simplest days only one cantor intones, on Sundays and normal feast days, two, and on solemn days, four.[51] Responsorial forms are based upon alternation between soloists and choir, which establishes the overall formal rhythm of the piece; here soloists carry some of the most elaborate Gregorian music, in the verses of the graduals and alleluias, as well as the offertories;[52] their performance by two cantors in tandem can be exquisite. The repeat of the second half of the respond after the verse of the Matins responsories provides an interesting exercise in text reading, since this portion of the choir's text usually completes the meaning of the verse.[53] The performance of the alleluia includes a jubilus, an extended wordless melisma that falls to the choir after the text word has been intoned and repeated, and then often again as the conclusion of the cantors' verse. These repetitions could be multiplied and distributed among various elements of the choir, so that, for example, at Milan the alleluia on Quinquagesima Sunday included four statements of the alleluia, the verse, a repeat of the alleluia, and then several additional melodies from various locations.[54]

Antiphonal performance is intimately linked to the placement of the choir in choir stalls, where each side sits facing the other directly. The "gospel side" (that is, the north side in a church whose altar is at the east end) has priority, beginning the alternation, other things being equal.[55] In addition to the psalmody of the Office, its hymns as well as the Ordinary and the sequence of the Mass were sung antiphonally. It has the practical advantage of allowing the singers to rest their voices for half the singing, but it has an aesthetic value as well. It has a heavenly paradigm in the Old Testament—the two Seraphim crying out each to the other before the throne of God, "Holy, Holy..."[56] It delineates the lateral space before the altar of the church and creates a variety in the sound that might be called the first stereophonic music.

The schemes of alternation involve a musical and spiritual discipline, one suggested by the fact that in such schemes singers are also listeners. In order to continue the intonation of the cantors, the singers have to listen attentively. In fact, I tell the singers that they must sing mentally with the cantors, so that their entry is smooth and in tempo. Likewise, the melisma at the end of the melismatic verse of a gradual or alleluia must pick up and complete the sense of that text, requiring the singers to be singing along mentally. In antiphonal singing, the rhythm or regular alternation without a break between sides requires a similar attentiveness, but there is an additional role in psalmody: an old monk once told me that in singing the psalms, each side of the choir is ministering to the other, presenting the text of its verse for their meditation. Thus the participation of the choir in psalmody is as least as fundamental and intense when they are not singing. This suggests, in turn, that two different kinds of meditation are served by chant: the recollective meditation of listening, and the meditative activity of chanting.

Schemes of alternation are the basis for polyphonic music.[57] In the *organa* of the Notre Dame School, the parts of the responsorial chant assigned to cantors are set in polyphonic music, while the choir continues to sing what it traditionally sang in its performance.[58] Antiphonal performance is the basis of a large repertory of organ music—the organ Mass.[59] Here the chant for the Ordinary of the Mass, as sung antiphonally, is divided between choir and organ, the organ taking the leading role, i.e., replacing the gospel side of the choir. This actually explains the fact that the placement of the organ in medieval and Renaissance churches is often on that north side, as its liturgical function would dictate. Such alternation poses another problem of performance—the tempo of the chant should somehow be commensurate with that of the polyphony. I look for an actual proportion between the polyphony and the chant, something like one or two chant notes per semibreve of polyphony. Likewise, the historical style of the chant, insofar as can be estimated, should match. A ninth-century style is not suitable to a Notre Dame organum, nor is a Solesmes style appropriate to a Du Fay hymn.

Vocal technique

A monk once told me that in his monastery, every novice loses his voice within the first few months of singing the Divine Office. Only then does he learn to sing lightly and easily enough that his voice can sustain the extensive singing throughout the day. This suggests that the choral singing of chant might ideally be with a fairly light voice.

Optimizing the head resonance is quite consistent with the slightly forward vowels the French use.

The ethos of singing chant presents a challenge to a singer with modern training—it is communal and transcendent, it does not cultivate individual characteristics but incorporates the voice into a collective sonority and expression. It does not draw attention to itself or even to the specific piece, but rather turns the piece itself to a transcendent purpose. I take this to be the paradigm. Within the paradigm, there is considerable variation—solo melismatic chants employ a certain amount of virtuosity; the chants of celebrant and lectors require a sense of rhetoric. In the context of choral singing, however, several practical proposals might be made. A somewhat light sound, with vowels tending toward the head placement of the French will allow flexible singing and a sweet sound. In this style of singing, vibrato is not a problem—whether the singer's voice shows a modicum of a truly natural vibrato or not—this kind of singing will not support an exaggerated vibrato. The crucial matter is tuning. Some vibrato is in tune, i.e., well-centered upon the pitch, and some is not. A discrete well-centered natural vibrato that does not disrupt the tuning may not be objectionable.

There are a few demands the music makes upon the voice, such as ornaments and articulation. The quilisma is a quick, light note that can be sung with a tremolo I teach my singers to practice a slow reiteration of a note and then speed it up, something like the trillo (goat trill) of the seventeenth century. (It takes less than a minute to turn a choir into a herd of goats, and only another to refine the sound down to one light, ornamental note.) Chorally such a quilisma is subtle and expressive. The pressus is described as an intense note, one which can be sung with a vibrato. As a note of double duration intimately connected to the following lower pitch, it has an intense expression which can give spice and motion to solo chants, especially verses of graduals and tracts, and can contribute to a rhythmic vigor in choral chanting. Likewise, the reiterated notes (bistropha, trispropha) add rhythmic vitality to the ensemble—I prefer a slight impulse of the breath on such notes, rather than an actual break of the voice. While elaborate chants require an agility of articulation, the neumatic groupings require less articulation within neumes than between, a matter of considerable vocal skill.

Worthwhile experiments can be made in recreating the vocal technique of the Middle Ages; while they remain controversial, techniques similar to those still found in the Middle East today may ultimately provide sounds which explain the nature of some aspects of the melodies.[60]

Rhythm

The question of rhythm is likely to generate plenty of heat in most circles.;[61] I have placed other subjects first because I hold them to be substantial issues, while the specifics of rhythm pertain more to style and artistic finish. Over the history and geography of chant, the very indeterminacy of the rhythm has meant that national linguistic penchants and temperaments could give rise to indigenous rhythmic styles.

Chant performance in the earlier twentieth century was dominated by the Solesmes method.[62] It was originally a response to the tradition of singing chant in a chorale-style, in which each note received a substantial beat; accompaniments changed harmony every note. The remedy was to replace this with a theory of two or three notes to a beat. Its premise that the notes of the chant have a fundamental equality is one substantiated more by speculative rhythmic theory than by any historical evidence from before the high Middle Ages. Still, this work of Dom Pothier became a fundamental part of the tradition.[63]

Pothier's theory was given substantial refinement by Dom Mocquereau, a sensitive musician with substantial musical training as a pianist. His theory was an attempt to provide for rhythmic subtlety and nuance in so systematic a way as to provide for a unified method for the whole church.[64] From a perspective near the end of the milennium, Mocquereau's theories represent another historical style of performance. Yet, they have the weight of a lived monastic culture and a sensitive musical intelligence behind them—there is much to be learned from them. Learning to count groups of two and three notes, as well as considering rhythms of arsis and thesis, movement and repose, on several rhythmic levels can be a valuable discipline for a choir.

The fundamental equality of notes was challenged by the proportionalist theory of Vollaerts.[65] Reminiscent of classical metrics, this theory proposes that there are two fundamental durations, long and short, and they they can be deciphered by reading the earliest neumes together with the rhythmic signs. The result is a rhythm with somewhat free alternation of long and short values. The proofs of this theory have more coherence than would allow it to be easily dismissed out of hand. At this point, however, it has fallen out of favor, in large part because practical experiments have failed to produce aesthetically satisfactory results, the valiant efforts of some recordings notwithstanding.

A much more subtle reading of the apparent lengths in the neumes and rhythmic signs is found in the currently leading theory, represented by Dom Eugène Cardine, whose *Gregorian Semiology*[66] details a method of a sophisticated reading of the neumes and signs for strong nuances of a single fundamental duration. This can be heard in certain persuasive recordings.[67] A caution about this theory is that Dom Cardine is said to have believed no group of performers had grasped its proper performance, except for the schola he directed, for which he may now be reaping ample heavenly reward. I regret to say that rarely have I heard a performance based upon this work that I thought would sustain itself in regular liturgical usage.

All such theories are like advanced mathematics—ultimately significant, but you do not start with calculus before you can add, nor do you even develop the theory of calculus until you can do calculus. Begin with relatively even notes in neumatic groups and take good account of the rhythm of the text; this will give a satisfactory result that very likely reflects a performance the high Middle Ages. The earliest historical stages of chant rhythm can be the subject of experimentation and development. The best way is to begin with the notation of St. Gall neumes as represented by the *Graduale Triplex*: begin by performing each neume as representing a single musical gesture; incorporate the signs of length (t and -) as subtle lengthening of the note and the sign of shortness (c) as a slight quickening. Become independent of the square notation by teaching the pitches rote, looking at the staffless neumes alone. Then draw upon Cardine's *Semiology* for further refinements, of which there will be many. Always check the results against the yardstick: is it aesthetically satisfactory?

From the broadest vantage-point, then, there cannot be one historical practice of rhythm, but depending upon the purposes, several, from the most exacting reconstruction of a St. Gall performance to the relatively equal-note singing of a local congregation.

Historically-informed performances of Gregorian chant in modern times may thus be as inclusive of various styles as the history itself has been; their authenticity will not only depend on how they reflect history, but also on how they serve their purpose, an important aspect of which is how beautifully they are sung.

Notes

[1] David Hiley, "Chant," in *Performance Practice: Music Before 1600*, ed. Howard Mayer Brown and Stanley Sadie, Norton/Grove Handbooks in Music, pp. 37–54 (New York, 1989); James W. McKinnon, "Performing Practice, 2, i: Medieval Monophony, Sacred," *The New Grove Dictionary of Music and Musicians*, ed. Stanley Sadie (New York, 1980), XIV, pp. 371–73; Thomas E. Binkley, "Zur Aufführungspraxis der einstimmigen Musik des Mittelalters—ein Werkstattbericht," *Basler Jahrbuch für historische Musikpraxis* 1 (1977), 19–76; Lance Brunner, "The Performance of Plainchant: Some Preliminary Observations of the New Era," *Early Music* 10 (1982), 317–28; for an excellent introduction to the liturgical background of chant see John Harper, *The Forms and Orders of Western Liturgy from the Tenth to the Eighteenth Century: A Historical Introduction and Guide for Students and Musicians* (Oxford, 1991); a recent publication, which has already become the standard for chant, not the least for its extensive bibliography, is David Hiley, *Western Plainchant: A Handbook* (Oxford, 1993); the standard first source for Gregorian melodies is *Liber Usualis* (Tournai, 1963).

[2] For example, the commonly sung *Credo III* is from the seventeenth century; the simple *Salve Regina* from the eighteenth, and the proper chants for the Feast of Christ the King, from the twentieth.

[3] Canto XVI, lines 16-21; Dante Alighieri, *The Divine Comedy*, tr. & comm. Charles S. Singleton, Bollingen Series, 80; Vol. II, *Purgatorio* (Princeton, 1973), pt. 1, pp. 166-69.

[4] See the discussion of *Justus ut palma*, below.

[5] See the chapter "Gamut, Solmization, and Modes," below.

[6] For an introduction to establishing the order of a particular service see Harper, *Forms and Orders of Western Liturgy*, pp. 191–200.

[7] For example, that of Aurelian, *Musica disciplina*, chapters 10-17; see Aurelian of Reomé, *The Discipline of Music*, trans. Joseph Ponte, Colorado College Music Press Translations 3 (Colorado Springs, 1968), pp. 25-43.

[8] Even the revival by the monks of Solesmes, after it had established a style it proposed as ancient and normative, reduced more recent chants to that style, including the carol *Adeste fideles* (see *Variae Preces*, Tournai, 1901, p. 27) or the eighteenth-century *Salve regina simplex* (*Liber*, p. 279), supplying them with *episemas* and other subtleties derived from the era of St. Gall neumes.

[9] Paradoxically, it is from the heart of the sacred, liturgical use of the chant that one of the greatest obstacles to this understanding has come. The highly technical method of Dom Mocquereau, for all its virtues and beauties, has had, among some of its practitioners, the effect of evening out the performance of various chant styles, thus minimizing their differences and risking obscuring their liturgical functions.

[10] See Stefano La Via, "Cipriano de Rore as Reader and as Read: A Literary-Musical Study of Madrigals from Rore's Later Collections (1557–1566)" (Ph.D. diss., Princeton University, 1991).

[11] See Ernst Ferand, *Improvisation in Nine Centuries of Western Music: An Anthology with a Historical Introduction,* Anthology of Music 12 (Cologne, 1961), pp. 57–74.

[12] Christopher Lanz, when he was a student in my notation course, attempted to use the computer to analyse some Gregorian alleluia melodies and then to generate some new melodies based upon the analysis; he entered a number of parameters, without much success; then I suggested that he should enter the neumatic groupings, and that made the difference; the melodies generated were then quite plausible. In the process I noticed that the first notes of neumes were usually the structural pitches, while the others were more often ornamental.

[13] Dante touches upon attitude to a sacred performance in the *Purgatorio,* when he describes the pilgrims singing *Te lucis ante terminum* facing East with their eyes fixed upon the supernal spheres; *Purgatorio,* Canto VIII, lines 13–18; Singleton ed., 1, pp. 76–77.

[14] Richard Crocker, "Gregorian Studies in the Twenty-First Century," *Plainsong and Medieval Music* 4 (1995), 33–86, particularly pp. 43-48.

[15] This is a term adapted from Kenneth Levy, "Toledo, Rome, and the Legacy of Gaul," *Early Music History* 4 (1984), 57, where he uses the term "syllabic/melismatic density."

[16] *Liber,* pp. 112–17.

[17] *Liber,* p. 118.

[18] *Liber,* pp. 120–21.

[19] *Liber,* pp. 381–82.

[20] Peter Wagner first pointed out the range of the settings of this text in his *Einführung in die Gregorianischen Melodien: Ein Handbuch der Choralwissenschaft, III: Gregorianische Formenlehre: Eine Choralische Stilkunde* (Leipzig, 1929; reprint, Hildesheim, 1970), pp. 7–14.

[21] Wagner, *Einführung, III,* p. 11; see also the chapter "Gamut, Solmization and Modes," below.

[22] *Liber,* p. 1204.

[23] *Liber,* p. 1193.

[24] *Liber,* p. 1201.

[25] *Liber,* p. 1207

[26] The just shall flourish like the palm tree, like the cedar of Lebanon shall he be multiplied.

[27] For an extended discussion of this principle, see Robert Alter, *The Art of Biblical Poetry* (New York, 1985).

[28] See William Peter Mahrt, "The Musical Shape of the Liturgy, Part I: The Gregorian Mass in General," *Sacred Music* 102, #3 (Fall 1975), 5–13.

[29] See William Peter Mahrt, "The Musical Shape of the Liturgy, Part III: The Service of Readings," *Sacred Music* 103, #2 (Summer 1976), 3–17.

[30] *Liber,* p. 59.

[31] *Liber,* p. 46

[32] *Liber,* p. 28.

[33] *Liber,* p. 40

[34] See, for example, Frank Llewellyn Harrison, *Music in Medieval Britain,* second ed. (London, 1963), pp. 1–57 and *passim.*

[35] Chapter 63; see *The Rule of St. Benedict in Latin and English with Notes,* ed. Timothy Fry,

O.S.B., et al. (Collegeville, Minn., 1981), pp. 278–81.

[36] Oral communication of Mary Berry, who reported the statutes of St Alban's cathedral as specifying "Ave Maria, gratia plena, Dominus tecum" as the duration of the pause in the middle of the psalm verse.

[37] See the discussion of *Da pacem* below.

[38] It is in these melismas that the Solesmes principle of counting all chants in groups of two or three can be counterproductive, for often the melisma should be a single gesture of several notes.

[39] John of Afflighem, *De musica,* Chapter 10, in Warren Babb, tr., *Hucbald, Guido, and John on Music: Three Medieval Treatises* (New Haven, 1978), pp. 116–17; see also Calvin Martin Bower, "The Grammatical Model of Musical Understanding in the Middle Ages," in *Hermeneutics and Medieval Culture,* ed. Patrick J. Gallagher & Helen Damico, pp. 133–45 (Albany, 1989).

[40] A cadence in chant can be defined as the conclusion of a text segment with a formulaic melodic progression—the most frequent is a descending a second, the next a rising of a second (especially in the Phrygian mode).

[41] The rules for this pronunciation are found in *Liber,* pp. xxxv–xxxix. "Church Latin" is a modern creation, a significant component of the campaign of Abbot Guerranger of Solesmes, who on ultramontane grounds advocated Roman pronunciation as a sign of Catholic unity; but such an international pronunciation was advocated as early as Christoph Bernhard in the seventeenth Century; see Walter Hilse, tr., "The Treatises of Christoph Bernhard," *The Music Forum* 3 (1973), 20–21; for national pronunciations, see Harold Copeman, *Singing in Latin* (Oxford, 1990) and Timothy McGee, with A. G. Rigg and David N. Klausner, eds., *Singing Early Music: The Pronunciation of European Languages in the Late Middle Ages and Renaissance* (Bloomington, 1996), where Harold Copeman has provided the chapters on the national pronunciation of Latin.

[42] St. Gall notation, with rhythmic signs, as found in the *Graduale Triplex* (Sablé-sur-Sarthe, 1979), and especially such manuscript sources as Einsiedeln 121.

[43] See Frederick Brittain, *Latin in Church* (Cambridge, 1934).

[44] See the chapter "Gamut, Solmization, and Modes," below.

[45] That is, from A a tenth below middle C to G a fifth above it.

[46] I once asked a monk in a choir which sang without accompaniment how they set the pitch. He did not understand the question. He said, "like this," and began to sing a piece in a convenient range.

[47] I contend that Pythagorean tuning is also suited to the two-part counterpoint that is the structure of the three-part music of much of the fifteenth century: the points of repose are provided by perfect consonances, octaves and fifths, while the imperfect consonances provide the motion to the points of repose. These intervals function better when they are the less consonant Pythagorean sixths and thirds—they tend more strongly to resolution, and thus give the polyphony a greater sense of motion.

[48] Technology can provide a solution to such problems though not an inexpensive one. The Stanford Memorial Church once had an acoustic treatment which has been removed to reveal a beautiful oak ceiling, and the Church is now excellent for chant and polyphony sung by a small choir. Speech is easily audible throughout the church, though, because there are several speakers in every pew, and the system adds delay to each speaker appropriate to its distance from the microphone. The result is that the amplified speech is preserved from the exaggerations of a central speaker system; its amplification is nearly imperceptible, but clearly audible, and a natural resonant acoustic has been preserved for music.

[49] Tim Tatton-Brown, consulting archeologist for Salisbury cathedral, first suggested to me that it was the rib vaults with their near parabolic shapes which focused the sound. An experiment at Wells cathedral demonstrated the difference. A small group of singers

requested permission to test the acoustics of the Lady Chapel and were encouraged to do so, with the further recommendation to try the chapter house where concerts are held. The lady chapel had the typical ample, focused sound, but the chapter house had a nearly unbearable reverberation with no focus. This suggests that the acoustics of the lady chapel were probably very knowingly provided for its proper use. The chapter house, however, was rarely used for singing; we tried speech there, and found that when the voice was raised, everything carried, while *sotto voce* conversation did not carry at all—ideal for its use as well.

[50] This *incipit* for intonation is marked by an asterisk or a double bar in modern editions.

[51] "Rubrics for the Chant of the Mass," *Liber,* p. xv, gives basic rules for alternation in the Mass; such schemes were well in place by the high Middle Ages.

[52] See *Offertoriale triplex cum versiculis* (Sablé-sur-Sarthe, 1979).

[53] This kind of partial repetition, i.e., respond (A + B), verse, B of respond, is archetypal to medieval music, being found in such secular forms as the rondeau.

[54] Terence Bailey, *The Ambrosian Alleluia* (Englefield Green, Surrey, 1983), p. 25.

[55] This is similar to the designation of sides in the English tradition as decani and cantoris.

[56] See the responsory for Trinity Sunday, *Duo Seraphim,* in *Liber responsorialis* (Solesmes, 1895), pp. 418–19.

[57] See William Peter Mahrt, "The Musical Shape of the Liturgy, Part II: The Interpolation of Polyphonic Music," *Sacred Music* 102, #4 (Winter 1975), 16–26.

[58] Performers of organum should note in particular that the polyphonic music does not set the final word of the verse, and its text remains incomplete until the choir sings it in chant.

[59] See William Peter Mahrt, "The Musical Shape of the Liturgy, Part IV: The Function of the Organ," *Sacred Music* 104, #4 (Winter 1977), 3–18.

[60] See Binkley, "Zur Aufführungspraxis" (note 1); such experimentation has been undertaken by Timothy McGee.

[61] See the excellent chapter, "The Notation of Rhythm," in Hiley, *Western Plainchant,* pp. 373–85. Recordings are instructive as well; an initial comparison of performances of the Abbey of Maria Einsiedeln, conducted by Roman Bannwart, with those of Münsterschwarzach, conducted by Godehard Joppich, will suggest how wide the variation may be among groups which attempt a semiological performance; a comparison with the traditional performances by the Abbey of Solesmes, conducted by Joseph Gajard, or the more recent recordings of the same choir, directed by Jean Claire, or those by the Capella Antiqua, under Konrad Ruhland, should be sufficient demonstration of the breadth of possible performances. Recent recordings by secular groups, most notably Anonymus 4, show original interpretations of great integrity and artistry. For ongoing discography of chant, see the reviews of Jerome Weber in *Fanfare* and elsewhere.

[62] I once gave an entire semester course in Gregorian chant, dealing with some of the matters discussed in this chapter; at the end, a student said to me, "I took a course from Fr. X in chant and he didn't talk about any of this." What did he talk about?" "The rhythm." Not rhythm, but *the* rhythm.

[63] Joseph Pothier, *Les melodies grégoriennes, d'apres la tradition* (Tournai, 1880).

[64] André Mocquereau, *Le nombre musical grégorien, ou Rythmique grégorienne, théorie et pratique,* 2 vols. (Rome, 1908-1927).

[65] Jan W. A. Vollaerts, *Rhythmic Proportions in Early Medieval Ecclesiastical Chant* (Leiden, 1960).

[66] Eugène Cardine, *Gregorian semiology,* tr. Robert M. Fowels (Sablé-sur-Sarthe, 1983).

[67] For example, *Gregorian Chants for Advent and Christmas,* Münsterschwarzach Abbey, directed by Godehard Joppich (Christophorus 77567).

2. Organum

Alejandro Enrique Planchart

Prolegomenon: Some Matters of Early Terminology

Fritz Reckow begins his seminal chapter on organum in *Gattungen der Musik in Einzeldarstellungen* with the question, "is organum a genre?"[1] Even though he ultimately answers in the affirmative, the question is well posed, for organum began not as a musical genre but as a specific manner of performing chant and remained so for over half of its existence, not emerging as a genre until the second quarter of the twelfth century or even slightly later. The history of the term in its relation to music is tortuous and complex. In classical Latin it meant a small machine in contrast to the term *machina*, which referred to the larger architectural and military machines, so that if we spoke Latin today we would most likely refer to the automobile as a *machina* (as the Italians do) and to the toaster as an *organum*. Musical instruments, then, fell within the category of *organa* and instrumental music was called *organicum melos*.[2] Hence a number of writings of the eighth and ninth centuries that have sometimes been considered by scholars to refer to polyphony probably refer to instrumental music instead.[3] Similarly, prior to the tenth century the terms *symphonia* and *diaphonia* meant consonance and dissonance, but the intervals were still regarded as melodic motion rather than as simultaneous sound. In any event it is hardly surprising that writers on music seized on the term *organum* to refer to polyphony, since the ability to produce simultaneous sounds was one trait that musical instruments have but is all but impossible with the human voice.[4]

With the first unequivocal references to polyphony in the late ninth and early tenth centuries in the writings of Hucbald of Saint-Amand (d. 930),[5] and two treatises originating from his circle, the *Musica enchiriadis* and its *Scholica*,[6] we encounter a shift in the meaning of these terms. Organum and its derivates, *organicum melos, organizare, organizatio*, could still refer to instrumental music, but they also became the words that defined polyphony. Further, organum became a synonym of *diaphonia*, so that this term was also used to refer to polyphony, and though the theorists still use *symphonia* in the sense of consonance (now largely harmonic but still occasionally as a melodic interval), Hucbald seems to prefer the terms *consonantia* and *dissonantia* to refer to simultaneous sounds. Two centuries later, when the rise of florid counterpoint produced a sharp stylistic distinction between polyphony in which the different parts move at approximately the same speed and polyphony in which one voice presents elaborate melismas over a slower moving voice, a further terminological shift, almost as ambiguous as the one we encountered in the early tenth century, took place. Organum was still used as a general term for all polyphony, but in certain contexts it acquired a more restricted meaning referring to polyphony in which one or more florid parts are composed over a slow moving tenor, while the Latin term *discantus*, a translation of the

Greek *diaphonia*, became the term that defined polyphony in which the parts move at essentially the same speed.[7]

The Nature of the Repertories

Early organum and *cantus planus binatim*

With one notable exception, all the surviving polyphony between the *Musica Enchiriadis* and the writing down of the Compostelan and Aquitanian repertories in the twelfth century consists either of scattered pieces entered here and there in liturgical sources or as examples in music treatises. A good number of the examples seem to have been produced *ad hoc* for the treatises, a few are antiphons, and a notable one, used time and again in the *Enchiriadis* treatises is part of a *versus*.[8] This scattered repertory has been surveyed and inventoried by Marion Gushee, both in her dissertation and in later publications.[9] The picture that emerges from the surviving sources indicates that for the first hundred and fifty years of its existence organum was not something that musicians wrote down, but rather a set of procedures they learned through training and experience and then applied to the performance of certain chants on solemn occasions. In other words, *organa* were not what we today call "a piece of music," the "piece" was a gradual, and alleluia, a sequence, or what have you, and organum was a way of performing it.

The major exception to the absence of written sources for early organum are the 174 *organa* copied at the end of the tenth century and the beginning of the eleventh in one of the two tropers from the Old Minster at Winchester, Cambridge, Corpus Christi College, MS 473. The manuscript has only the organal voices without the plainsong upon which they are built, which were to be found in the gradual and antiphoners of the Old Minster, none of which survive. For some of the pieces, the alleluias, the melismatic *sequentiae*, the Gloria tropes and the Kyrie tropes, the melodies of the plainsong can be found in one or another of the two Winchester tropers (the alleluias in a fascicle added to CC 473 and probably copied in Canterbury), but even so both the *organa* and the plainsongs are written in staffless neumes without precise diastematy. Nonetheless, whoever wrote down these *organa* was clearly aware that, unlike the plainsongs, there was no reliable oral tradition to help with the reading of the polyphonic parts, and within the constraints of the diminutive size of the manuscript (146x92 mm) endeavored to suggest more clearly the intervals represented by the neumes through pockets of "local diastematy" and a liberal use of *litterae significativae*. Still, the Winchester *organa* were considered irrecoverable until the 1960s, when first Ewald Jammers and later Andreas Holschneider showed that the polyphonic parts written in Winchester appear to follow the rules described in the *Musica Enchiriadis* and in Guido d'Arezzo's *Micrologus de Musica*[10] for organum at the fourth below with considerable faithfulness. Holschneider also made a careful study of the plainsong traditions in England and could thus identify chant books where a good number of the plainsong melodies could be found in transcribable form and in versions presumably not far removed from those of Winchester. With this information in place and with a painstakingly detailed analysis of the notated *organa* and the contrapuntal style they represent he was able to propose not only a number of plausible reconstructions of this repertory, but open the way for other scholars to do so as well.[11] Still, attempting to reconstruct any of these *organa* is not for the inexperienced or the fainthearted, but a number of reasonable transcriptions have appeared in print and can be used by those interested in performing this repertory.[12] Probably no one should attempt a performance of any of the surviving examples of organum of the tenth and early eleventh century who has not made a determined effort to gain some experience in improvising the so-called free organum (actually organum at the fourth below in the thinking of the medieval treatise writers) as explained in the *Musica Enchiriadis* as well as the kinds of organum described in Guido d'Arezzo's *Micrologus*.

A stylistic shift in the nature of organum is indicated by the late eleventh- and early twelfth-century treatises such as the famous *Ad Organum Faciendum* preserved in the Ambrosian Library in Milan.[13] The organal voice, which in earlier *organa* lies mostly below the plainsong, is now regarded by the theorists to lie above the plainsong, but an increased emphasis on contrary motion between the polyphonic parts causes a considerable number of voice crossings. Another aspect of this new style is that the organal voice seems to be constructed by a rigid interplay of perfect consonances and contrary motion with the plainsong and becomes thus not so much a second melodic line as a very disjunct series of resonance tones associated with the melody of the plainsong.[14] What these treatises codify is what would become known as discant, that is, a two-voice framework that is both framework and surface in eleventh-century organum but becomes a "middleground" framework for all polyphonic composition until the end of the fifteenth century.

As in the case of tenth and early eleventh-century organum, examples of discant settings are found largely in the treatises, most of which transmit simple rules covering the organization of every possible melodic interval in the chant with the organal voice placed at every possible interval above the chant. Typical of this approach is the following set of rules from Anonymous 1.[15]

> If the chant ascends one step and the organum begins at the fifth, let it descend four steps and be with the chant. Conversely, if [the chant] descends one step, let the organum ascend four and be at the fifth:[16]

Ex. 2.1. Organum examples from Anonymous I.

The examples continue in this manner to cover every possible motion by the chant and every consonant starting point for the organum.[17]

Once more we realize that this type of organum or discant did not need to be written out, and what the treatises give is a set of rules for the proper improvisation of organum, rules that become extremely rigid in the writings of late eleventh-century theorists, giving the impression that there was little leeway for the performer in the choice of notes.

What repertories were ornamented with organum in the first century or so of its existence? For an answer to this question we have the extended collection of the Winchester Troper and the glimpses that the examples in the treatises give us. The *Musica Enchiriadis* and its *Scolica* provide a curious answer to this: the examples are taken from a fragment of the *Te deum*, a psalm tone, the *versus Rex caeli domine*, the antiphon *Nos qui vivimus* to Psalm 113 [*In exitu Israel*] which was the one psalm sung to the *tonus peregrinus*, two fragments of the writings of Martianus Capella, and the hymn *Gratuletur omnis caro*.

Thus it would appear at first sight that both choral (antiphons, psalms, hymns) and solo (*versus*) chants were sung with organum. Further, the presence of the fragments from Martianus suggests that some non liturgical works were also sung with organal voices added to the existing melodies.[18] Nonetheless, a closer examination of the repertories is suggestive. The chant categories used for the examples of the *Musica Enchiriadis* are strongly reminiscent of the types of works to be found in one of the oldest collections of music that survives from medieval France, manuscript *latin* 1154 of the Bibliothèque Nationale in Paris, a late ninth- or early tenth-century orational from the area of Limoges in Aquitaine that transmits verse songs closely related to the hymns, some proses, a number of *planctus*, and some of the *metra* from Boethius's *Consolatione Philosophiae* (which can be regarded as a counterpart of the fragments by Martianus in the *Musica Enchiriadis*) set to primitive Aquitanian neumes. In other words, organum has at the outset a strong association with the "new" forms of ninth-, tenth-, and eleventh-century music: *versus* or hymn, prose, and a few settings of late antique texts.[19]

The presence of antiphons, the *Te deum*, and a psalm tone among the examples in the *Musica Enchiriadis* suggests at first that not only soloistic chants but choral chants were sung in organum; but it is worth noting that the examples of choral chants in the treatise are restricted by and large to the strict parallel organum, a simple technique that would pose no problem for a *schola* and would require simply that singers pitch their voices at different levels when singing the chant. Whatever vogue the practice might have had in the early tenth century the *Enchiriadis* treatises are our only witness of it, no examples can be found in the extensive collection in the Winchester Troper. The practice merits a brief dismissive mention by Guido in the *Micrologus* as a hard-sounding procedure,[20] so that strict parallel organum was a relatively crude form of ornamenting the chant that seems to have gone out of style relatively quickly after the date of the first notices we have for it. But what the early tenth-century theorists considered organum at the fourth below with unison cadences, and which we call today "free" organum, seems to have been from the start associated largely with solo chants. At the time this included all the responsorial chants of the mass and the office, the proses and *sequentiae* in many centers, tropes to the ordinary and the propers of the mass, the final *Benedicamus domino* at the end of vespers and matins, and the repertory, related to the proses, of sacred verse songs which eventually led to the *conductus*.

It is therefore not surprising that the one practical source of late tenth-century organum that has survived is precisely a Troper, that is, a book that was a direct descendant of the *cantatorium* for the solo singers. The *organa* in the Winchester Troper cover virtually all the categories just mentioned except for verse songs. Genres sung in polyphony at Winchester included the following categories:

For the mass: Kyrie tropes, Gloria tropes (but not the Gloria melodies themselves), alleluias and tracts (!) but not the graduals, *sequentiae*, but not the proses. Later additions (early eleventh century) included introit tropes (for Easter only) and processional antiphons (which were soloistic). The manuscript was left unfinished and the *organa* to the *sequentiae* break off after only a few pieces. Had it been completed it most likely would have included *organa* to for the Sanctus and Agnus tropes.[21]

For the office: *Organa* for the responsories; not as is the case of the later Notre-Dame repertory for a single responsory in any given feast, but for all the responsories of those feasts for which organum was used, with an occasional organum for the invitatory at the beginning of matins.

What these categories of chant have in common is that they all call for singing by the soloists, the *cantores*, rather than the *schola*, but the settings are not, at first sight, exclusively for the soloists, since they include, for example, the responds of both the alleluias and the responsories, although we would have to know in detail the performance traditions at the Old Minster in Winchester before assuming that the responds of the alleluias were sung chorally there.

In any event, the few early eleventh-century *organa* that survive in practical sources from elsewhere are also settings of responsorial chants and thus largely soloistic music.[22]

Saying that these pieces were music for the soloists does not automatically imply that they were sung one to a part. The principal voice might in some cases have been sung by the *schola*, and even in the case of pieces sung by the *cantores* the rubric in the second Winchester Troper (Oxford Bodleian Library, Bodley 775) which has no *organa* indicates that the introduction to the Christmas Gloria trope (provided with an organum in the other troper) was sung by two singers: *Cantores gemini resonant haec verba canentes.* In the later repertory associated with the Cathedral of Notre Dame, the number of singers employed was determined not by the music but by the solemnity of the feast,[23] and the practice showed small variants from place to place. The very small amount of evidence we have suggests that even if the principal voice was sung by two to four singers (the numbers mentioned in a number of ordinals of the Middle Ages) the organal voice was most likely sung by one singer. In terms or present-day performance, singing the *organa* with only one singer to a part is probably the best course, since it allows the performers to deal more readily with matters of phrasing and intonation that are crucial to these repertories.

Examples of this relatively simple type of mostly two-part organum, largely note-against-note, survived in a number of centers well into the fifteenth century, largely as an improvised practice called in the fourteenth and fifteenth centuries, *cantare supra librum*, in which one or sometimes two voices were added to a given plainsong. A number of written examples of this procedure have survived, largely notated in chant books that contain otherwise no polyphony. During the fourteenth and fifteenth centuries the intervals between the plainsong and the organal (or rather discant) voice reflect the increased use of imperfect consonances as structural intervals, but otherwise the texture is identical to that of the examples of discant found in late eleventh- or early twelfth-century treatises. These written examples have seldom been published or studied in detail, and at first scholars called them "primitive polyphony," an unfortunate term that does an injustice to the simple elegance of many of the settings. More common now is the term *cantus planus binatim*, which describes their character more accurately, since both parts are notated in the sources in unmeasured chant notation.[24]

The treatises are largely silent on the performance of organum in the tenth and eleventh centuries, most likely because the authors did not see the organum settings as being much different from the chant itself. Thus the modern performer is well advised to perform such pieces as one would perform tenth- and eleventh-century chant, that is, as a *cantus planus*, where the notes all have essentially the same duration. There is some evidence that the chant was not performed very fast at the time,[25] already the tenth-century *Commemoratio brevis* calls for a deliberate performance of the psalm tones,[26] and even within this context the *Musica Enchiriadis* indicates that organum was performed slowly (*morose*).[27]

In terms of intonation the early organum probably made use of pure octaves, fifths, and fourths since medieval theorists are virtually unanimous in teaching a Pythagorean tuning. The imperfect consonances and the dissonances were also most likely carefully measured in terms of their distance from the principal voice, but for tenth- and eleventh-century organum and discant the dialectic of tension and resolution evident in twelfth-century polyphony and eloquently discussed by Christopher Page,[28] does not seem to be operating. In the parallel organum, even that with "free cadences" including the examples of the Winchester Troper, the cadential patterns are sufficiently varied and "unsystematic" as to suggest that the organal voice was still viewed largely as a replication of the chant. In the case of contrary motion discant, the polyphonic voices of the few surviving examples of eleventh-century discant can be startling to the modern performer in their melodic disjunctness and seemingly random motion, suggesting that the discant was at first viewed not as a melodic line per se but as a series of resonances above and below the notes of the plainsong. Under those conditions the widening or narrowing of imperfect consonances would have served no melodic purposes and the use of the most resonant version of any vertical interval, which may vary depending upon the vowel being sung should be used.

Phrasing in eleventh-century discant settings probably were viewed by their creators as following the phrasing of the chant itself. This is probably all the more the case with the earlier forms of parallel and "free" organum, where the organal voice has a far more defined melodic *ductus* than what one encounters in the discant voices of the eleventh-century repertory. The slight lengthening of cadential and precadential tones in the performance of chant in the tenth and the eleventh centuries finds a reflection in the fairly frequent use of ornamental neumes with one extra note relative to the chant in the *organa* of the Winchester tropers.[29] It is also an open question whether the slightly different neumation of the organal and the principal voices in Winchester (in the instances where we have a Winchester neumatic text for the principal voices) were intended to indicate subtle differences of phrasing between the two voices.[30] Nonetheless, we are still largely in the dark as to the kinds of performance information that late tenth-century neumes were intended to convey—information that was largely transmitted orally to the singers and was virtually never set down.[31] Thus modern performers dealing with these repertories need perforce to create their own interpretation of many of the signs. In the case of the Winchester *organa* a careful examination of the neumation of both voices reveals a fair number of rhythmic signs and the presence of certain regularities that probably indicated similar phrasings; but in the end, in the case of the early *organa*, the performer needs to "invent" his or her performance. The "modern" component of such an invention would ideally be a product of careful consideration of what can be known about the early *organa* and an artistic ideal, and the balance of all the elements will vary sometimes considerably from artist to artist.

Twelfth- and early thirteenth-century organum outside Paris

The twelfth century saw a momentous change in the nature of the repertories. For the first time since the end of the tenth century a considerable amount of polyphonic music was written down. The collections are not systematic but, as was the case of the Winchester troper, the polyphonic settings appear largely in the company of the "new" musico poetic forms, in this case the *versus* or *conductus*, as well as proses.

The new *organa* survive from two distinct regions, the region of Aquitaine around Limoges,[32] and Santiago de Compostela in northwestern Spain. The principal collections of polyphony are:

A. From Aquitaine
      London, British Library, additional MS 36881, 12c late
      Paris, Bibliothèque Nationale, *latin* MS 1139, ca. 1100
      Paris, Bibliothèque Nationale, *latin* MS 3459, 12c early
      Paris, Bibliothèque Nationale, *latin* MS 3759, 12c early[33]

B. From Santiago de Compostela
      Compostela, Archivo de la Catedral, MS sn, 12c middle.[34]

The repertories in these sources are related both stylistically and chronologically. It is not a matter of the same works appearing in various sources, although there is at least one piece in common between the Compostela manuscript and the Aquitanian sources, but rather in terms of both the kinds of pieces set to polyphony and the polyphonic styles in themselves.[35]

First of all we encounter a series of verse songs or *conductus* set in the Aquitanian sources in what is called today "successive" polyphony. For example, strophic verse songs that appear in the manuscript to have music written for the first two stanzas, instead of the more usual arrangement—common in sources of secular monophonic song—of the music under the first stanza turn out, upon close examination of the music, to be discant settings, where the music under the first stanza serves as the discant to the music set under the second stanza.[36] By and large such settings are relatively simple discant settings similar to what one encounters in the examples of the theory treatises. A second stylistic layer is represented by slightly more elaborate settings where a largely note-against-note texture has a number of passing tones in the organal voice, passing tones that sometimes develop into small melismas, most often at the approach of a cadence. Finally a third layer is represented by pieces where the organal voice has relatively extended and florid melismata, so that at times the plainsong moves in long sustained tones that function essentially as pedal points. This florid style provided the impetus for the terminological distinction noted above between discant and organum, a distinction first recorded in an anonymous treatise of the late twelfth century edited by Adrien de la Fage as follows:

> Between discantus and organum is this difference, that discantus answers its chant by the same number of notes always in some consonance, making the composition as unison, the organum on the other hand corresponds to the chant not through equality of notes but through infinite multiplicity and a certain wondrous flexibility.[37]

This same treatise contains what may be the first description of three-part polyphony, in which two parts are in discant and one is in organum,[38] but the example for this was never copied into the manuscript of the treatise; it appears, however, to describe well the piece of possible three-part polyphony in the *Codex Calixtinus*, the well-known *conductus, Congaudeant Catolici.*[39]

With the appearance of florid organum in the twelfth-century sources the problem of the rhythm of the parts is compounded by that of the coordination between the voices. This was clearly a problem even to contemporary musicians since even though the manuscripts of Aquitanian and Compostelan polyphony are written in what modern scholarship calls "pseudo score," the vertical alignment of the parts is not always clear and the manuscripts show contemporary efforts by scribes to indicate rough alignments by the use of vertical (or rather oblique) lines.[40] Rhythmic problems in these repertories have elicited a number of very different solutions from modern scholars and performers as well as long and sometimes acrimonious controversies that parallel largely the controversy concerning the rhythm of troubadour and trouvère music. These range from a rather rigid application of the modal rhythm of the thirteenth-century Parisian *organa* to the Aquitanian and Compostelan polyphony,[41] to interpretations based upon an essentially isosyllabic declamation of the text presented by Higini Anglès,[42] and as a "working hypothesis" by Leo Treitler,[43] to the suggestion that the notation did not indicate rhythm precisely because the music had a free non metric structure, which is proposed by Sarah Fuller.[44]

Treitler is undoubtedly correct in postulating that "the question for us is not 'how must they have sung this music?' but rather 'how can we sing it?'"[45] The notation itself seems to suggest the approach proposed by Fuller, since the free non metric rhythm was "traditional" at the time as the rhythm of all chant and singers must have been extremely comfortable with such an approach which probably did not preclude the cantors shaping the melismas as they considered it appropriate. The simpler, nearly note-against-note settings can easily be controlled by an essentially isosyllabic performance, and indeed most of these settings appear to be part of a tradition that led to the *conductus* of the Notre Dame school, where indeed recent scholarship suggests a fundamentally isosyllabic performance.[46]

In this respect, Karp's determinedly modal interpretations of the rhythm appear the most forced and least plausible; still his monumental work is well worth reading for it has much that is useful and enlightening concerning the contrapuntal style of these repertories, and his attention to every detail of the notation does have a salutary effect of making his reader far more sensitive to the possible nuances of what the scribes set down.

Anyone wishing to perform the Aquitanian and Compostelan *organa* may want to experiment with the rhythmic readings proposed by Anglès, Treitler, Fuller, and Karp, and also attempt to sing the pieces directly from the manuscript facsimiles without any further mediation, gradually building a sense of how to approach the flow of these works. This, in the long run, is the only way the individual performer can provide an answer to Treitler's second question mentioned above, which is, after all the principal question for a performer of any music.

The Parisian *organa*

The main repertory performers and audiences tend to think of when "organum" is mentioned is the enormous production of Parisian composers of the late twelfth and early thirteenth centuries known as the School of Notre Dame. This repertory was in use in Paris for well over a century,[47] and it was collected in two enormous anthologies copied in the city itself,[48] as well as exported to other French churches, to Italy, Spain, and to Scotland, where it seems to have spawned a number of imitations. Indeed, what may be the earliest surviving recension of this repertory survives in a late copy made in Saint Andrews in Scotland at the end of the thirteenth century.[49]

The Notre Dame repertory has been the subject of extensive studies since the nineteenth century, beginning with Edmond de Coussemaker and Wilhelm Meyer,[50] and Friedrich Ludwig's monumental catalogue raisonné of its sources.[51] Facsimiles of all the major sources are available,[52] and a considerable number of editions of the different repertories have been published, including a monumental edition of the entire organal repertory of the central sources now in progress.[53]

The Parisian *organa* and their related collections of discant *clausulae* fall clearly into two parallel cycles, an extensive one for two voices and a more restricted one for three and four voices. Virtually all we know about the genesis and authorship of these works comes from comments made by Anonymous IV, an Englishman who studied in Paris perhaps in the third quarter of the thirteenth century, and sought then to instruct his countrymen upon what he had learned and observed there.[54] It is Anonymous IV who mentions the names of Leonin and Perotin, tells us that Leonin wrote a *Magnus Liber Organi* later revised by Perotin, that Perotin supplied a number of discant *clausulae* for this repertory, credits Perotin with a number of compositions, including the two surviving *organa quadrupla*, and describes the contents of the polyphonic books in Notre Dame in terms that coincide quite closely with the contents of the diverse sections of the Florence manuscript, which is undoubtedly the one of the surviving sources that most closely reflects the cathedral's repertory precisely around the time when Anonymous IV was there.

For most of this century the two stylistic layers of the Parisian *organa* were viewed as representing a well-defined chronological succession, an early layer consisting of the two-voice *organa* and perhaps the simpler among the separate discant *clausulae* associated with Leonin and composed between ca. 1160 and 1190, and a second layer consisting of the tripla, the quadrupla, and the great majority of the discant *clausulae* associated with Perotin and composed between ca. 1190 and 1225. At this time we had absolutely no solid evidence of who Leonin or Perotin were, beyond the information provided by Anonymous IV, and none of the hypotheses associating the names with known historical figures (scholars did not even attempt to deal with Leonin, but concentrated on Perotin), were particularly convincing.[55] This situation changed drastically following the studies of Craig Wright, who has identified Leonin as an important canon of the cathedral and a well-known poet, and has provided the first plausible identification of Perotin as Pierre the succentor at Notre Dame.[56] In doing so he has also established that the entire organal corpus was indeed for the liturgy of Notre Dame and not, as had been proposed by Husmann, for several of the other Parisian churches.[57] At the same time, however, Wright's identification of the two composers (and we must remember that there must have been several others, some of whom are mentioned by Anonymous IV in passing) collapses much of the chronology, so that we can no longer assume that Leonin wrote no tripla and Perotin no dupla.

There is still, however, a relatively sharp distinction between the two layers of *organa*; it is a stylistic and technical distinction, and it affects the way a performer can approach this repertory. The *organa dupla* represent, so to speak, a later and more rational stage of the styles we encounter in the Aquitanian *organa* of the twelfth century. I say "more rational" because the Parisian composers restrict the *organa* to the soloistic intonation of the respond and the solo part of the verse of Graduals and Alleluias of the Mass, the Great Responsories at Matins and during the Vespers procession, and the *Benedicamus Domino* at the end of Vespers.[58] A twelfth-century treatise now in the Vatican Library, provides a clear insight on how the music of the *dupla* was composed. Its text reads like a virtual replica of the discant treatises such as that of Guy d'Eau, but the examples, rather than simple note-against-note discant progressions consist of a number of increasingly florid organal passages.[59] The examples, and the three complete *organa* appended to the treatise, belong to the same stylistic universe as the Notre Dame *organa*, even though the treatise itself is not from Notre Dame or indeed from Paris itself.[60] A simple example giving the first and sixth illustrations of one of the rules may suffice here:

> First rule: If the chant ascends by a second and the organum begins at the octave, let the organum descend by a third and it will arrive at a fifth, for example.[61]

Ex. 2.2. Examples from the Vatican organum treatise.

In any event, a glance at any of the *organa dupla* in the Notre Dame manuscripts reveals immediately enormously long florid passages, far more extensive than anything encountered in the Aquitanian *organa*, over held tones by the tenor. Alternating with discant passages where both voices move nearly note-against-note. The alternation of styles follows a relatively simple system: since virtually all the Notre Dame *organa* are settings of responsorial chants which contain extended melismas, the syllabic and neumatic sections of the chant were largely set in florid organum, called *organum purum* or simply organum by the theorists, while the melismata of the chant were set in discant.

It is for the discant sections of these *organa* that Leonin and his contemporaries devised the first rhythmic notation for polyphonic music. It is a contextual system based upon an alternation of longs and shorts in which the rhythmic value of the notes is expressed by specific combinations of the basic ligatures used to notate Gregorian chant. All the theoretical formulations of the system come from a much later period when what is known as modal notation was fully developed. At first the formulation might have been something like what follows:[62]

1. Measured breves are one beat, longs are two beats.
2. Values shorter than one beat or longer than two are beyond measure.
3. The rhythm proceeds by an alternation of longs and breves.
4. The last note of a ligature is normally a long, the penultimate note is normally a breve.
5. Rests following a group of ligatures normally derive their value from the penultimate note of the last ligature.
6. A long followed by another long is a long beyond measure.
7. A note that occurs where a long should occur is considered a long.

In the duplum, the rhythm is expressed by an patterned succession of ligatures; while the long beyond measure is the basic unit of motion for the tenor, it can be the sustained pedal of the *clausulae* in organum or, at its shortest, in a succession of longs of three beats, it produces the motion of the tenor in the *clausulae* in discant. The duplum in the sections in organum are often notated in ligature combinations that show no particular pattern. These passages seem to represent a continuation of the non-metric style of performance that obtains in the Aquitanian *organa*, and the remarks of the thirteenth-century theorists who discuss notation and rhythm in Parisian music appear to confirm the view that the unsystematically ligated passages over a held tone were performed with considerable freedom.[63] Example 2.3 presents the opening of one of the best-known of the Notre Dame *organa dupla*, the intonation of the Christmas gradual *Viderunt omnes.*[64]

Ex. 2.3. Organum duplum setting of *Viderunt omnes.*

Systems 1, 3-4, and 7-8 of the example present this kind of texture and are given thus with no indication of a rhythmic values for the duplum. The seventh system, however, is a discant *clausula*, in which the close rhythmic relationship between the two voices gives rise to a relatively sharp contrast between consonant and dissonant notes, and it is apparently this contrast that led composers to seek to produce and notate a clear rhythmic structure in the music.[65] At the same time the genesis of a metrical structure in these passages gave an even sharper definition to the theorists' concepts of consonance and dissonance.[66] In any event the ligation of the passage becomes entirely regular, particularly in the version of W 1, and it was through this use of ligatures that composers of *organa* gave rhythmic significance to the duplum part. The patterns of ligation and their rhythmic significance were codified by a number of thirteenth-century theorists with some difference among them.[67] The classification used most often by scholars today is that of Johannes de Garlandia and the theorists dependent upon him.[68] The ligation patterns and their rhythmic significance are given in Figure 2.1.

FIG. 2.1. Modal ligation and rhythmic patterns.

The discant sections of the Notre Dame *organa dupla*, in which patterned rhythm seems to have first developed, contain only music in what later theorists called modes one, two, six, and five. Of these mode two is very infrequent,[69] mode five is restricted to the tenors, and mode six appears most often as an ornamentation of mode one. Such is the case in the discant *clausula* in Example 2.3, where brief bursts of "mode six" open the entire *clausula* and close each of its half phrases.

The second, fifth, and ninth systems present a different texture. The tenor has a held tone, but the duplum shows the kind of consistent ligation pattern (albeit with the commonly found "shorthand" of using a five-note ligature in place of three- and two-note ligatures) that one would expect to find in a discant passage. These passages are what Johannes the Garlandia called "copula," which he defined as a style "between organum and discant," that is, where one of the voices behaves like a discant and the other like an organum.[70] The passages in copula are the other place in the repertory of *organa dupla* where one can find clear rhythmic notation in the duplum. In many of the copula passages, including the three in Example 2.3, the clear rhythmic organization is complemented by a melodic parallelism between half phrases, often with *ouvert* and *clos* endings.[71] This trait, though not essential to the copula, is found in a large number of *clausulae* in copula and, as Fritz Reckow suggests, it may be at the root of the large-scale phrase structure of the Perotinian tripla and quadrupla, where antecedent-consequent phrases are used with almost obsessive insistence.[72]

How is one to approach the singing of the organum *clausulae* in this style? An examination of the opening of *Viderunt omnes* may be useful. There is an opening "appoggiatura," where the scribe of W 1 has gone out of his way to indicate that the dissonant E is in this case a long note. In this and the dozens of similar opening in the repertory one can ask oneself if a dissonant opening is really intended or if the appoggiatura is to serve as an "intonation," with the tenor entering on the second F of the duplum. The reason behind such a question may be posed as follows, the repertory shows a strong predilection for cadential dissonance (cf. the endings of the third and tenth *clausulae*) not only in the *organa dupla* but in the tripla and the *conductus* repertory.[73] On the other hand in the entire repertory of *organa* tripla and quadrupla, virtually all of which open with a long simultaneity, there is not a single instance of an initial dissonance, and it is curious that such a dramatic gesture, which seems abundant in the *organa dupla* openings, was entirely absent in the tripla as written. And Anonymous IV writes:

> The first note [of the duplum] can be concordant or discordant, and it always begins shortly before the tenor, and the tenor begins with the second one, should it be concordant, or with the third.[74]

However, one should also consider that a great deal of stylistic change and change in taste may have taken place between the composition of *Viderunt* omnes and the writings of Anonymous IV.

The passage before the second rest in the *clausula* merely reiterates the octave with the tenor, while the next two passages move the duplum from the octave to the fifth. In the first of these two passages the end of the opening ligature in manuscript F is a consonant note, and the singer could choose to make it a long.[75] The following phrase essentially duplicates the gesture of the previous one but with no consonance at the end of the first of the first ligature, so that the singer is urged by the music to reach the final C rather quickly. Having sung that entire *clausula* the singer can reflect upon it and either do the last two phrases as two balanced gestures following the opening or dwell slightly on the consonant F's of the third phrase, thus creating a feeling of acceleration as the *clausula* ends.

The second *clausula*, written in copula, parallels the first. It has no introductory gesture but consists of two balanced phrases which twice move the duplum from the C that was the goal of the opening phrase to the F that starts the piece. The place of the "ritenuto" in the first *clausula* is taken here by a long ornamented with a *plica*, which theorists called a *longa florata*.[76] This note received some kind of ornament, either a melodic expansion, a repercussion, a trill, or even vibrato,[77] and the plica, a note written simply as an extra stem on the notehead and derived from the plainsong liquescence, probably carried over from that tradition a change in vocal production.[78] The effect of the *longa florata* is most likely to produce some kind of ritenuto in the middle of the *clausula*, so that the second *clausula* forms a pendant to the first, albeit with a different rhythmic organization.

The third *clausula* returns to *organum purum*. Melodically it summarizes everything that has happened thus far, going from F to C and back to F and landing on the second written simultaneity in the piece. Again, the ends of the ligatures provide points of consonance with the tenor and the duplum singer may consider then dwelling a bit longer on these notes. The ending of the *clausula* provides an interesting variant between W 1 and F: both sources end the *clausula* with a *longa florata* and a cadential dissonance (elongated by the scribe of W 1), but while the *longa florata* is at the pitch of the final consonance in F, in W 1 it is on the dissonant E of the final appoggiatura; the difference here is not trivial, as the effect of the passage is quite different in both versions.

On the evidence of the theorists, the sustained tenor should not be sung passively but should probably reflect its harmonic surroundings,[79] further, it is quite probable that the tenor singer paused together with the singer of the upper part or parts at the end of sections, perhaps, in the case of Example 2.3 at the end of every *clausula*. W 1, the organum fragment at Aberdeen,[80] and the relatively late Montpellier Codex,[81] have ways of suggesting this: Aberdeen and W 1 by repeating tenor notes at the beginning of systems and Montpellier by inserting rests or breath marks (*suspirationes*) far from where the tenor notes are on the page but coinciding with phrase ends in the upper voices.[82] In this case, given the cautions of a number of theorists concerning beginning of phrases on a dissonance,[83] it is quite possible that, if the tenor paused at the end of the second *clausula* it would not sound until the first F in the third *clausula* is reached by the duplum.

In discussing the first section of *Viderunt omnes* I have suggested a free and relatively fluctuating tempo even for the more strictly notated *copula*. This would apply even to sections in discant, and indeed there is no evidence of a *tempo giusto* for this music or any other thirteenth-century repertory. In fact, Anonymous IV has an extended discussion of what today we would call accelerandos and ritenutos:

> "One part proceeds after the manner of discantus, discussed above, and this proceeds by means of a pleasant manner with regards to time: slow, slower, and very slow, fast, faster, and very fast, moderate, more moderate, very moderate.[84]

And indeed, discant passages were thought of as moving slowly or moderately; *copula* passages, characterized by Franco as "a fast discant," moved faster, and organum passages moved even faster.[85] Anonymous IV cites the long descending melisma in the sixth *clausula* of Example 2.3, written in *currentes* (running notes) as an example of a passage that was to be sung very fast and evenly.[86]

The second and third layers of Parisian *organa*, consisting of the numerous two voice discant *clausulae* copied in W 1 and F, and the tripla and quadrupla composed by Perotin and his generation show little of the unpatterned rhythmic structure of the *organa dupla*. Instead, these pieces make use of virtually the full system of rhythmic modes, including mode three, where all the longs are beyond measure (i. e., ternary) and any note of less than three beats was regarded as a short. Mode three seems to have arisen from an elegant mode one pattern favored by Perotin, and present at the outset of his famous four-part setting of *Sederunt principes*:[87]

Ex. 2.4. *Sederunt principes*, by Perotin.

A. Reading in first mode

B. Reading in third mode

The example shows how the notation, in terms of its ligature pattern, could be read as either an "extended" mode one or as mode three. Since the work continues largely in mode one recent scholarship prefers that reading.[88] In any event, one of the curious consequences of the genesis of mode three from an extension of mode one was that the theorists, to complete the system produced its counterpart in mode four, but composers apparently ignored this. To my knowledge there is not a single work in mode four, which exists only in the theoretical literature.[89]

In the tripla and quadrupla, which virtually the full modal system is used, we meet nonetheless with hundreds of places where there are sudden modal shifts in a line, and moments of modal ambiguity, particularly around the cadences that mark the end of a group of phrases. Similarly, the ambiguities of the notation extend themselves to the rests, where the notation uses the same sign, a vertical stroke, to denote a measured rest, a breathing mark, or to warn the singer about a syllable change. The stroke is also found after every plica in the notation, even when it would be virtually impossible for the singer to pause or even take a small breath. In a large number of cases two or more rhythmic interpretations of the notation are equally plausible and an editor will not only have to make a choice but will seldom have enough space in the notes to the edition to describe all the possible alternatives.[90] Since facsimiles of all the major Notre Dame sources are now generally available it is always wise to compare any edition used with the facsimile, as the notation may suggest some alternatives that the individual performer may find more plausible or attractive. A number of professional ensembles perform this repertory directly from facsimiles of the manuscripts, and my experience is that students can learn relatively quickly how to become comfortable reading from facsimiles.

The relatively regular appearance of the tripla and quadrupla in modern transcription, with vast stretches of music in one or another of the modes can lull performers into a mechanical or driven approach. What we have from the thirteenth-century writers such as Anonymous IV suggests otherwise. As noted above, they speak about tempo fluctuations and regard them as particularly pleasing. Anonymous IV, with his fussy insistence on categorizing everything, describes, beyond the six rhythmic modes, six "irregular" modes and a seventh one that he calls a mixture of all the modes.[91] This seems an attempt to describe a flexible approach to the written rhythm and should warn performers that a rigidly metric approach to the notation, despite the apparent consistency that the tripla and quadrupla in their modern transcription, is probably not warranted.

The approaches to important cadences, both internal and at the end of the entire section, include, in the tripla and quadrupla, passages that appear to step out of the modal system of the mid thirteenth century and to hark back to earlier styles.[92] They also include passages with ornamental figures that suggest a relaxation in the tempo and the metric structure of the music.[93]

Performance forces

Even more than any of the earlier organum repertories, the Parisian *organa* are the province of the soloists within the body of singers at the cathedral, who were called *clercs de matines* at Notre Dame.[94] The polyphonic singers were also called *magistri organorum*.[95] While we do not always have accurate information as to who sang the Kyries, prose, and *Versus*, within the chant tradition of Aquitaine or

Compostela, the Parisian *organistae* set to music only the solo passages of the responsorial chants for the mass and the office. The cathedral's regulations specified the number of people who had to sing these chants (and by extension their polyphonic settings) for all of the feasts of the liturgical year, and these rules had nothing to do with the music but rather with the liturgical rank of the feast. Thus the *annuale* feasts required six singers, four for one of duplex rank, three to four for feasts of semiduplex rank, and three for a feast of nine lessons.[96] In the performance of the *organa*, most likely the upper voice or voices were sung by a solo singer, while the rest of the assigned singers took the tenor. This would allow for staggered breathing if necessary to prevent fatigue and allow the tenor to react to the polyphony in the ways described by the theorists.[97] The *organa* were performed entirely *a cappella,* since Notre Dame did not even have an organ until after 1300.[98]

Organum in England and other countries in the thirteenth century

The view of the Notre Dame repertory as a near monolithic central repertory, implied if not explicitly stated in the work of Friedrich Ludwig and other scholars earlier in this century, is no longer tenable. Despite the enormous loss of sources it is now clear that a number of centers in France imported some the Parisian repertory but also cultivated their own production.[99] In the same manner, the manuscript Madrid, Biblioteca Nacional, MS 20846, and the even later motet manuscript Burgos, Monasterio de la Huelgas, MS without number transmit works that are most likely of Spanish origin.[100]

Further, the copy of the Notre Dame *organa* in W 1 has two *organa* for Saint Andrew, the patron saint of Scotland, written essentially in a Parisian style but absent from the French sources, as well as an entire fascicle of *organa* for the Lady Masses that is clearly of insular origin.[101] In addition, later insertions within the main body of W 1, containing *organa* for the Sanctus and the Agnus, as well as the repertory of a fragment of the *Magnus Liber* found in Aberdeen with some local *organa* for the ordinary of the mass, indicate that in the British Isles there was a tradition of polyphonic settings of the ordinary of the mass, the alleluia, and the sequence (or prose) going back to the late tenth century.[102]

In any case, the largest surviving repertory of *organa* from outside France comes from the British Isles, largely in fragmentary manuscripts that still continue to turn up as pastedowns and binding material in British archives. A substantial collection of these works has now been edited by Ernest Sanders in a sound and reliable manner.[103] The English repertory, with its abundance of imperfect consonances, presents a very different musical profile from that of the Notre Dame *organa*. The large-scale formal structures that one finds in the Perotinian tripla and quadrupla seem to be largely absent (although echoes of them are heard in the English penchant for voice exchange), we do not encounter the relatively large wealth of third-mode writing one finds in Parisian music but rather what to our ears sounds like first mode, to the point that one wonders if the full Parisian modal system was ever of interest to English composers, despite the descriptions of it by

Anonymous IV. For continuity and drive the English works seem to rely on the sheer tension and richness of their largely "triadic" sonority, which would imply perhaps a tuning system slightly different from that which obtained in Paris. On the other hand, the ensembles that performed this music resembled in their composition those found on the continent, consisting largely of what today we would call low tenors and baritones,[104] so that in a sense, apart from matters of tuning that remain speculative in the absence of any clear documentation of any difference between France and England in this respect, the performance practices for insular *organa* are essentially the same as those we encounter for the French repertory.

Epilogue: The Notre Dame Conductus

The Notre Dame manuscripts, apart from the *organa* and motets, transmit an immense repertory of works called *conductus*, non liturgical devotional works ranging from one to four voices that are in may ways the direct descendants of the Aquitanian *Versus* tradition.[105] The polyphonic *conductus* are all discant settings of rhythmic poetry, in which all voices are essentially equal and there is, generally, no *cantus firmus*.[106] Since the Middle Ages theorists divide them into two categories, *conductus* with *caudae*, that is with extended melismatic passages, and *conductus* without *caudae*, where the text is almost syllabic.[107] The melismatic sections of the *conductus* with *caudae* are notated in reasonably clear modal notation in the Parisian sources and in W 1, but by its very nature, the notation of the *cum littera* sections is entirely unclear since the ligature context of modal notation is destroyed by the addition of text and the breakup of ligatures. This has led to a number of interpretations of the rhythmic structure of these pieces. Gordon Anderson, noting the existence of the so-called *conductus* motets in W 1 and Ma,[108] devised an elaborate manner of determining the mode of the *cum littera* section of *conductus* based upon the relationships that can be observed between the rhythm of the text and the music in the context of those works for which medieval versions with a clear rhythmic notation survive.[109] A similar approach is evident in the editions of *conductus* by Janet Knapp and Ethel Thurston, even though in both cases the editors present no extended explanation of their choices of rhythmic readings. These views have been sharply questioned by Ernest Sanders, who argues for a non-modal and essentially isosyllabic reading of the *cum littera* sections, in which each syllable receives the equivalent of a ternary long, with syllables before *caesurae* or at the end of the poetic line receiving sometimes the equivalent of a double long.[110] This view largely coincides with that proposed by Janet Knapp in an essay in which she revised some of her earlier views[111] and has the advantage of fitting well every surviving *conductus* without imposing upon this repertory rhythmic structures that postdate the origins of the repertory itself. At the same time it is worth noting that, on the evidence presented by Anderson, some of these *cum littera* sections of these *conductus* were being read in modal rhythm by 1300. In a few instances we do have *conductus* set entirely *cum littera* for which a contemporary modal reading survives. *Crucifigat omnes* provides a case in point,[112] the two lower voices are the final *cauda* of *Quod promisit ab aeterno*,[113] where it appears clearly notated in what came to be called mode 1. The text setting in *Crucifigat omnes* can be sung comfortably in that rhythmic pattern, but if we had nothing but the music for this piece it would be virtually impossible from the *cum littera* version of the notation to make a case for a mode 1 rendering.

Crucifigat omnes may serve as an illustration for another aspect of the *conductus* repertory, namely that pieces survive in different sources sometimes as three-voice works, sometimes as two-voice works, and often as monophonic pieces as well,[114] so that in the *conductus* repertory, as in the later motets, we encounter various scorings of a work sometimes with two scorings in the same source. The *conductus* is therefore a forceful reminder of the fluid nature of virtually all of the polyphonic repertory before 1300, something that runs counter to the modern view of "the piece" as some sort of art object fixed down in its essentials when set down in writing.

Notes

1   Fritz Reckow, "Das Organum," *Gattungen der Musik in Einzeldarstellungen. Gedenkschrift Leo Schrade*, ed. Wulf Arlt *et al.* (Bern, 1973), p. 434.

2   Note that in classical usage the Pythagorean term, *musica instrumentalis* meant what we today call music, whether it was vocal or instrumental, so that *organicum melos* filled a need when one had to specify music for instruments.

3   A convenient summary of these passages appears in Anselm Hughes, "The Birth of Polyphony" in *Early Medieval Music up to 1300*, New Oxford History of Music 2, ed. Anselm Hughes (London, 1954), 270-74.

4   But see Fritz Reckow, "Organum" [1972]. *Handwörterbuch der musikalischen Terminologie*, ed. Hans Heinrich Eggebrecht, 4 vols. (Wiesbaden, 1972-), where he makes an impressive philological case for the term also to include the human voice. I remain skeptical that tenth-century writers had the knowledge of Greek and classical Latin upon which Reckow's case rests.

5   *Huchald, Guido, and John on Music. Three Medieval Treatises*, trans. Warren Babb, ed. Claude Palisca, Music Theory Translation Series 3 (New Haven, 1978), p. 19 (107a/3).

6   See Nancy Catherine Phillips, "Musica and Scolica Enchiriadis: The Literary, Theoretical, and Musical Sources" (Ph.D. diss., New York University, 1984), and Bernard Schmid, *Musica et Scolica Enchiriadis una cum aliquibus tractatulis adiunctis*. Veröffentlichungen der Bayerische Akademie der Wissenschaften, Veröffentlichungen der Musikhistorichen Kommission 3 (Munich, 1981). The part of the *Scolica Enchiriadis* dealing with polyphony is translated in Oliver Strunk, *Source Readings in Music History from Classical Antiquity Through the Romantic Era* (New York, 1950), 126-38. For translations *Musica Enchiriadis*, trans. Léonie Rosenstiel, Colorado College Music Press Translations 7 (Colorado Springs, 1976), which should be used with caution because it is replete with errors and inaccuracies, and *Musica Enchiriadis and Scolica Enchiriadis*, trans. Raymond Erickson, ed. Claude Palisca (New Haven, 1995).

7   The classical meaning of *diaphoneo* is to sound discordantly or to disagree. In the world of plainsong, where all music is monophonic, it is easy to see how *diaphonia* comes to mean polyphony, and it is no coincidence that the rise of the Latin equivalent, *discantus*, in the late eleventh century, coincides with the shift from parallel to contrary

motion as the paradigm for contrapuntal motion (note how the word counter-point also reflects that). In non-musical terminology of the central Middle Ages *discantus* is used also to mean disagreement.

[8] The piece in question, *Rex caeli domine,* was published and discussed in Jacques Handschin, "Über Estampie un Sequenz," *Zeitschrift für Musikwissenschaft* 29 (1929-30), 11-12 and 19-20, and 30 (1930-31), 116-17, who regarded it as a prose. A correction of this view with much useful information about the earliest nature of organum appears in Nancy Phillips and Michel Huglo, "The *versus Rex caeli* -- Another Look at the So-Called Archaic Sequence," *Journal of the Plainsong and Medieval Music Society* 5 (1982), 36-43.

[9] Marion Gushee, "Romanesque Polyphony: A Study of the Fragmentary Sources," Ph.D. Dissertation (Yale University, 1965).

[10] See *Hucbald, Guido, and John on Music. Three Medieval Treatises,* trans. Warren Babb, ed. Claude Palisca (New Haven, 1978).

[11] See Ewald Jammers, *Musik in Byzanz, im päpstlichen Rom und im Frankenreich; der Choral als Musik der Textaussprache.* Abhandlungen der Heidelberger Akademie der Wissenschaften, Philosophisch-Historische Klasse; Jahrg. 1962, 1. Ab. (Heidelberg, 1962), and Andreas Holschneider, *Die Organa von Winchester. Studien zum ältesten Repertoire polyphoner Musik* (Hildesheim, 1968).

[12] Apart from the transcriptions in Holschneider, *op. cit.,* see also Alejandro Enrique Planchart, *The Repertory of Tropes at Winchester,* 2 vols. (Princeton, 1977).

[13] See Jay A. Huff, ed. *Ad Organum Faciendum and Item de Organo,* Music Theorists in Translation 8 (Brooklyn, n.d. [1969]).

[14] The classical example of this is the organal setting of the Kyrie "Cunctipotens genitor Deus," at the end of *Ad organum faciendum* (see Huff, *op. cit.,* p. 66) which has been included in numerous anthologies.

[15] "Tractatus de Consonantiis Musicalibus," in Edmond de Coussemaker, *Scriptorum de Musica Medii Aevi,* 4 vols. (Paris, 1864-76; repr. Hildesheim, 1963), I, p. 300.

[16] *Si cantus ascenderit unam vocem et organum incipiat in diapente, descendit quatuor et erit cum cantu. Et e converso, si descenderit duas, ascendat quatuor, et erit in diapente.* Note that the author uses a patently inconsistent terminology here referring to the ascent of one step and a descent of two [notes?] even though the example that follows makes the meaning unequivocal.

[17] The earliest of these treatises, with the most systematic set of rules (but no musical examples) is the short discant treatise appended to the *Regulae de Arte Musicae* of Guy d'Eu, published in Coussemaker, *Scriptorum,* II, pp. 191-92. This simple set of rules is repeated in a number of treatises up to the early thirteenth century, see Jane Knapp, "Two Thirteenth-Century Treatises on Modal Rhythm and Discant," *Journal of Music Theory* 6 (1962), 200-15.

[18] Indeed, Phillips and Huglo, "The *versus,*" p. 41, propose that perhaps organum began with secular music and is being regulated for use with liturgical music in the *Enchiriadis* treatises.

[19] See Jacques Chailley, "Les anciens tropaires et séquentiaires de l'école de Saint-Martial de Limoges," *Études Grégoriennes* 2 (1957), 163-88, idem, *L'École Musicale de Saint-Martial de Limoges jusqu'a la fin du XIe siècle* (Paris, 1960), pp. 74-78, and Hans Spanke, "Rhythmen- und Sequenzstudien," *Studi Medievali,* New Ser. 4 (1931), 286-320.

[20] *Hucbald, Guido, and John on Music,* p. 78.

[21] It is worth noting that the next oldest polyphonic source from the British isles, the eleventh fascicle of the famous Notre-Dame codex W 1 (Wolfenbüttel, Herzog-August Bibliothek, Helm. 628) transmits precisely organa to the Kyrie, the proses (*sequentiae* no longer being used), the Sanctus, and the Agnus.

[22] For example, the organa to graduals and responsories from Fleury in Vatican, Biblioteca Apostolica Vaticana, Reg. lat. 568, and Chartes, Bibliothèque Municipale, MSS 4, 109, and 130, see Holschneider, *Die Organa*, pp. 63-67, 172-81.

[23] See Craig Wright, *Music and Ceremony at Notre Dame of Paris, 500-1500* (Cambridge, 1989), pp. 100-02.

[24] See the example transcribed in Holschneider, *Die Organa*, pp. 180-81. Also Pierluigi Petrobelli and Cesare Corsi, eds., *Le Polifonie primitive in Friuli e in Europa: Atti del congresso internazionale Cividale del Friuli, 22-24 agosto 1980*. Miscellanea Musicologica 4 (Rome, 1989), and Petrobelli, ed., *Le Polifonie primitive di Cividale. Catalogo del Congresso internazionale: Le polifonie primitive in Friuli e in Europa* (Cividale, 1980).

[25] See the chapter on chant in this volume.

[26] *Commemoratio brevis de tonis et psalmis modulandis*, ed. Terence Bailey (Ottawa, 1979), pp. 102-07.

[27] Schmid, *Musica et Scolica*, pp. 38, 89, 97.

[28] Christopher Page, "Polyphony Before 1400," *Performance Practice: Music Before 1600*, ed. Howard M. Brown and Stanley Sadie (London, 1989), pp. 79-81.

[29] See Holschneider, *Die Organa*, pp. 124-25, for several examples.

[30] See, for example, the organa in Planchart, *The Repertory*, I, 310-24, where the principal voice survives in both of the Winchester tropers.

[31] See David Hiley, "Chant," *Performance Practice: Music Before 1600*, ed. Howard M. Brown and Stanley Sadie (London, 1989), pp. 42-44.

[32] For some time in the early part of this century the Aquitanian repertory was associated with the abbey of Saint Martial de Limoges mainly because the majority of the surviving sources came from the abbey's library, which was purchased in the seventeenth century by Colbert for the the Bibliothèque Royale (now the Bibliothèque Nationale in Paris). But the origin of the manuscripts is largely uncertain; they ended at Saint Martial on account of the aggressively acquisitive policies of the abbey's librarians in the twelfth and thirteenth centuries, a policy that led to the ultimate preservation of an astonishing number of chant sources from the Limousin, once the library was bought by Colbert and transferred to Paris.

[33] All four manuscripts are now available in facsimile editions as follows, *Paris, B.N. fonds latin 3549 and London, B.L., Add. 36,881*, ed. Bryan Gillingham, Publications of Mediaeval Musical Manuscripts 16 (Ottawa, 1987); *Paris, Bibliothèque Nationale, fonds latin 1139*, ed. Bryan Gillingham, Publications of Mediaeval Musical Manuscripts 14 (Ottawa, 1987); *Paris, Bibliothèque Nationale, fonds latin 3759*, ed. Bryan Gillingham, Publications of Mediaeval Musical Manuscripts 15 (Ottawa, 1987). The most important study of the repertory remains Sarah Ann Fuller, "Aquitanian Polyphony of the Eleventh and Twelfth Centuries," 3 vols. (Ph.D. diss., University of California at Berkeley, 1969).

[34] Two facsimiles of the manuscript have appeared, *Codex Calixtinus. Santiago de Compostela*, ed. Walter M. Whitehill and German Prado, 3 vols. (Santiago, 1944), and *Codex Calixtinus de la Catedral de Santiago de Compostela* (Madrid, 1993). The basic study of the music still remains Peter Wagner, *Die Gesänge der Jakobusliturgie zu*

Santiago de Compostela. Collectanea Friburgiensia, New Series 22 (Freiburg in der Schweiz, 1931).

[35] The Aquitanian repertory has appeared in three complete editions, Theodore Karp, *The Polyphony of Saint Martial and Santiago de Compostela*, 2 vols. (Berkeley, 1992), Brian Gillingham, *Saint-Martial Polyphony*, Musicological Studies and Documents 44 (Henryville, 1984), and Hendrik van der Werf, *The Oldest Extant Part Music and the Origin of Western Polyphony.* (Rochester, 1993). Four complete editions of the Compostela polyphony are available, van der Werf, *op. cit.*, Karp, *The Polyphony*, Whitehill and Prado, *Codex Calixtinus*, and Wagner, *Die Gesänge.* Karp's *The Polyphony* contains an extensive bibliography of studies on both repertories.

[36] The earliest notice of this procedure was by Judith Marshall in "Hidden Polyphony in a Manuscript from St. Martial de Limoges," *Journal of the American Musicological Society* 15 (1962), 131-44, with further identifications noted in Sarah Ann Fuller, "Hidden Polyphony—A Reappraisal," *Journal of the American Musicological Society* 24 (1971), 169-92.

[37] Inter discantum vero et organum hoc interesse probatur quod discantus equali punctorum cantui suo per aliquam semper consonantiam respondet aut compositionem facit unisonam; organum autem non equalitate punctorum sed infinita multiplicitate, ac quadam mira flexibilitate cantui suo concordat. In Adrien de la Fage, *Essais de diphthérographie musicale* (Paris, 1864; repr. Amsterdam, 1964), p. 360.

[38] La Fage, *Essais*, p. 361.

[39] There have been suggestions made that this piece is not really a three-part work but a two-part conductus with two alternate discants, but most scholars accept it as a three-part piece, see Karp, *The Polyphony*, pp. 131-32, for a summary of the arguments and references to the literature.

[40] A particularly problematic example is the verse song *Iubilemus, exultemus* in Paris, BN lat. 1139, fol. 41r, accessible not only in the facsimile cited above but as Plate XXI in Carl Parish, *The Notation of Medieval Music* (New York, 1957; repr. New York, 1978).

[41] This was suggested by Bruno Stäblein in "Modale Rhythmen im Saint-Martial Repertoire?" *Festschrift Friedrich Blume zum 70. Geburtstag*, ed. Anna Amalie Abert and Wilhelm Pfannkuch (Kassel, 1963), pp. 340-62, taken over in earnest by Theodore Karp in "San Martial and Santiago de Compostela: An Analytical Speculation," *Acta Musicologica* 39 (1967), and greatly expanded in *The Polyphony of Saint Martial* (cf. note 32).

[42] Higini Anglès, "Die Mehrstimmigkeit des Calixtinus von Compostela," *Festschrift Heinrich Besseler zum sechzigsten Geburtstag* (Leipzig, 1961), pp. 91-100.

[43] Leo Treitler, "The Polyphony of Saint Martial," *Journal of the American Musicological Society* 17 (1964), 29-42, and *idem*, "A Reply to Theodore Karp," *Acta Musicologica* 40 (1968), 227-9.

[44] Sarah Fuller, "Aquitanian Polyphony of the Eleventh and Twelfth Centuries," 3 vols. Ph.D. Dissertation (University of California at Berkeley, 1969).

[45] Treitler, op. cit. p. 40.

[46] See below. The same cannot be said for the florid organa, which show considerably less of a stylistic connection with the kinds of Notre Dame repertories where modal rhythm is employed unequivocally.

[47] See Rebecca Baltzer, "How Long Was Notre-Dame Organum Performed?" *Beyond the Moon: Festschrift Luther Dittmer*, ed. Brian Gillingham and Paul Merkley (Ottawa, 1990), pp. 118-43.

⁴⁸ Florence, Biblioteca Mediceo Laurenziana, MS Pluteus 29.1 [= F], facsimile in *Firenze, Biblioteca Mediceo-Laurenziana, Pluteo 29,1*, ed. Luther Dittmer, 2 vols., Publications of Mediaeval Musical Manuscripts 10-11 (Brooklyn, [1966-1967]), and Wolfenbüttel, Herzog-August Bibliothek, MS 1099 Helms. 1206 [= W 2] published in *Faksimile-Ausgabe der Handschrift Wolfenbüttel 1099 Helmstadiensis-(1206) W 2*, ed. Luther Dittmer, Publications of Mediaeval Musical Manuscripts 2 (Brooklyn, 1960). No extended study of the W 2 has appeared, but on F see Rebecca Baltzer, "Thirteenth-Century Illuminated Manuscripts and the Date of the Florence Manuscript," *Journal of the American Musicological Society* 25 (1972), 1-18.

⁴⁹ The source is Wolfenbüttel, Herzog-August Bibliothek, MS 677 Helmstadiensis 628 [= W 1], facsimile in *An Old St. Andrews Music Book (Cod. Helmst. 628)*. ed. J. H. Baxter. St. Andrews University Publications 30 (London, 1931; repr. New York, 1973), *Die mittelalterliche Musik-Handschrift W1*, ed. Martin Staehelin, Wolfenbütteler Mittelalter-Studien 9 (Wiesbaden, 1995), and see also Edward Roesner, "The Origins of W 1," *Journal of the American Musicological Society* 29 (1976), 337-80, and Mark Everist, "From Paris to St. Andrews: The Origins of W1," *Journal of the American Musicological Society* 43 (1990), 1-42.

⁵⁰ Edmond de Coussemaker, *L'art harmonique aux XIIe et XIIIe siècles* (Paris, 1865; repr. Hildesheim, 1964), Wilhelm Meyer, "Der Ursprung des Motetts: vorläufige Bemerkungen," *Nachrichten von der königlichen Gesellschaft der Wissenschaften zu Göttingen, philologisch- historische Klasse* 2 (1898), 113-45.

⁵¹ Friedrich Ludwig, *Repertorium Organorum Recentioris et Motetorum vetustissimi Stili*, 2 vols: I, A. *Catalogue Raisoné der Quellen. A. Die Handschriften, welche das Repertoire der Organa späteren Stils und das der ältesten Motetten in Quadrat-Notation geschrieben überliefern. B. Die Handschriften, welche das Repertoire der späteren Organa und der Motetten bis zum Ausgang des 13. Jahrhunderts in Mensural-Notation überliefern.* (Halle, 1910) II: *Vollständiges musikalisches Anfangs-Verzeichnis des systematich nach den Tenores geordneten Repertorium Organorum Recentioris et Motetorum vetustissimi Stili.* Halle, 1910 [Private complete printing without title page]. The official publication of Vol. II never took place, and after Ludwig's death the sheets of the 1910 edition with his handwritten corrections were issued. Revision of both volumes corrected by Friedrich Gennrich were issued in the series *Summa Musica Medii Aevi* (Langen, 1961-62) and a similar edition revised by Luther Dittmer appeared as Musicological Studies 7, 17, and 26 (Brooklyn, 1964-78). Easier to use, but by no means superseding the wealth of information in Ludwig's catalogue is Hendrik van der Werf, *Integrated Directory of Organa, Clausulae, and Motets of the Thirteenth Century* (Rochester, 1989).

⁵² See above, notes 48 and 49.

⁵³ The principal editions are: Gordon Anderson, ed., *The Latin Compositions of Fascicules VII and VIII of the Notre-Dame Manuscript Wolfenbüttel Helmstadt 1099 (1206)*. 2 vols., Musicological Studies 24 (Brooklyn, 1972-1976), *idem, Notre-Dame and Related Conductus. Opera Omnia.* 9 vols. out of 11 to date (Henryville, 1979-present), Heinrich Husmann, ed., *Die drei- und vierstimmigen Notre-Dame Organa: kritische Gesamtausgabe*, Publikationen älterer Musik 11 (Leipzig, 1940; repr. Hildesheim, 1967), Hans Tischler, ed. *The Parisian Two-Part Organa: The Complete Comparative Edition*, 2 vols. (Stuyvesant, 1988), Ethel Thurston, ed. *The Works of Perotin* (New York, 1970), *idem, The Conductus Collections of MS Wolfenbüttel 1099*, 3 vols., Recent Researches in the Music of the Middle Ages and Early Renaissance 11-13 (Madison, 1980), William

Waite, *The Rhythm of Twelfth Century Polyphony,* Yale Studies in the History of Music 1 (New Haven, 1954), a comprehensive edition of all of the Parisian organa, where the different redactions of the repertory in the each source will be presented, is in course of publication as *Le Magnus Liber Organi of Notre Dame de Paris,* Edward Roesner, general editor. 7 vols [planned] (Monaco, 1993-present). To date have appeared Vol. I, *Les Quadrupla et Tripla de Paris,* ed. Edward Roesner (1993), and Vol. V, *Les Clausules à deux voix du manuscrit de Florence, Biblioteca Mediceo-Laurenziana, Pluteus 29.1, fascicule V,* ed. Rebecca Baltzer (1995).

[54] His treatise, most likely lecture notes from his students, was the fourth anonymous treatise published by Coussemaker in *Scriptorum.* A reliable modern edition appears in Fritz Reckow, *Der Musiktraktat des Anonymus 4,* 2 vols., Beihefte zum *Archiv für Musikwissenschaft,* 4-5 (Wiesbaden, 1967), see also Jeremy Yudkin, *The Music Treatise of Anonymous IV: A New Translation,* Musicological Studies and Documents 41 (Stuttgart, 1985).

[55] For the situation as it stood even as late as 1985 see the entries on Leonin and Perotin in *New Grove Dictionary of Music and Musicians,* ed. Stanley Sadie, 20 vols. (London, 1980).

[56] Craig Wright, Leoninus, Poet and Musician," *Journal of the American Musicological Society* 39 (1986), 1-35, and *Music and Ceremony at Notre-Dame of Paris, 500-1500* (Cambridge, 1989), pp. 281-94. Scholars have generally accepted the identification of Leonin, but have resisted that of Perotin; but in fact the few new bits of archival information that have appeared since the publication of Wright's work only confirm his identification of Perotin.

[57] Heinrich Husmann, "St. Germain und Notre Dame," *Natalicia Musicologica Knud Jeppesen Septuagenario Collegis Oblata.* Ed. Bjorn Hjelmborg and Søren Sørensen (Copenhagen, 1962) pp. 31-36, "The Enlargement of the Magnus Liber Organi and the Parisian Churches of St. Germain l'Auxerrois and Ste. Geneviève du Mont," *Journal of the American Musicological Society* 16 (1963), 176-203, and "The Origin and Destination of the Magnus Liber Organi," *Musical Quarterly* 49 (1963), 311-30.

[58] See Wright, *Music and Ceremony,* pp. 258-67, and Roesner, *Les Quadrupla,* pp. lxvl-lxvii.

[59] See *Der vatikanische Organum-Traktat (Ottob. lat. 3025).* Münchner Veröffentlichungen zur Musikgeschichte 2 (Tutzing, 1959), and Irving Godt and Benito Rivera, "The Vatican Organum Treatise--A Colour Reproduction, Transcription, and Translation," *Gordon Athol Anderson (1929-1981) In Memoriam,* ed Irving Godt and Hans Tischler, 2 vols., Musicological Studies 9 (Henryville, 1984), II, pp. 264-345.

[60] See Wright, *Music and Ceremony,* pp. 336-38.

[61] Godt and Rivera, op. cit., p. 299.

[62] An extended discussion of a model for the emergence of measured music, which differs in some of its historical assumptions from the very schematic formulation presented here, is Edward Roesner, "The Emergence of *Musica Mensurabilis,*" *Essays in Honor of Jan LaRue,* ed. Eugene K. Wolf and Edward Roesner (Madison, 1990), pp. 41-74.

[63] Almost every thirteenth-century theorist discusses rhythm, though most deal with the later system of rhythmic modes. On the rhythm of organa dupla the most important theorists are Anonymous IV (see note 56 above) and above all Johannes de Garlandia. On this see *Johannes de Garlandia: De mensurabili musica. Kritische Edition mit Kommentar und Interpretation der Notationslehre,* ed. Erich Reimer, 2 vols. Beihefte zum Archiv für Musikwissenschaft 10-11 (Wiesbaden, 1972), and *idem, De Mensurabili*

Musica, trans. S. H. Birnbaum, Colorado College Music Press Translations 9 (Colorado Springs, 1978). A particularly thoughtful discussion of the problems posed by the rhythmic interpretation of this repertory is Ernest Sanders, "Consonance and Rhythm in the Organum of the 12th and 13th Centuries," *Journal of the American Musicological Society* 33 (1980), 264-86, while Jeremy Yudkin's "The Rhythm of *Organum Purum*," *Journal of Musicology* 2 (1983), 355-76, offers a detailed and imaginative, but in some ways implausible, interpretation of the writings of Garlandia and Anonymous IV on this subject. Edward Roesner, "Johannes de Garlandia on *Organum in Speciali*" *Early Music History* 2 (1982), 129-60, presents a detailed reading of Garlandia's rhythmic doctrine as it pertains to the performance of organum.

[64] In the example the upper ligature markings follow W 1 and the lower ones follow F. The notation "no" above or below a note or a sign indicates that the note or sign in question is not in the manuscript. Apart from the complete facsimiles of W 1 and F, the version of W 1 is available in a clearer facsimile as Plate XXVIb in Carl Parrish, *The Notation of Medieval Music*, rev. ed. (New York, 1959; repr. New York, 1978).

[65] Sanders, "Consonance and Rhythm," p. 271 and note 24.

[66] This point is made with particular cogency in Leo Treitler, " "Regarding Meter and Rhythm in the Ars Antiqua," *Musical Quarterly* 65 (1979), 524-88.

[67] On this see Gordon Anderson, "Magister Lambertus and the Nine Rhythmic Modes," *Acta Musicologica* 45 (1973), 57-73, and *idem*, "Johannes de Garlandia and the Simultaneous Use of Mixed Rhythmic Modes," *Miscellanea Musicologica* 8 (1975), 1-81.

[68] Reimer, *Johannes de Garlandia*, I, pp. 88-89, see also Fritz Reckow, "Proprietas und Perfectio; zur Geschichte des Rhythmus, seiner Aufzeichnung und Terminologie im 13. Jahrhundert," *Acta Musicologica* 39 (1967), 115-43.

[69] The presence of mode two in this repertory remains problematic. Ernest Sanders has proposed that mode two does not appear in any of the organa dupla in W 1 (Sanders, "Consonance and Rhythm," p. 276, note 26), but this ignores the extended mode two discant clausula on *Tamquam* in the Responsory *Descendit de caelis* (W 1, fol. 17v). To be sure, the version of the Responsory in F, fols. 65v-66r, has a simpler, first mode clausula relegated in W 1 to the section of separate clausulae (fol. 47r).

[70] Garlandia's term and his definition has caused a remarkable amount of misunderstanding in modern scholarship. The nature of copula and identification of passages in copula in the Patisian organa was finally established by Fritz Reckow in *Die Copula: über einige Zusammenhänge zwischen Satzweise, Formbildung, Rhythmus und Vortragsstil in der Mehrstimmigkeit von Notre-Dame*, Abhandlungen der Akademie der Wissenschaften und der Literatur, Mainz, Geistes- und Sozialwissenschaftliche Klasse 13. Jahrg. 1972 (Wiesbaden, F. Steiner, 1972), and Jeremy Yudkin, "The Copula According to Johannes de Garlandia," *Musica Disciplina* 34 (1980), 67-84.

[71] Reckow has called particular attention to this trait, and in "Das Organum," pp. 469-463, ties it stylistically to the estampie. Further, he hears in Perotin's large-scale structures, built upon antecedent and consequent phrases, an elaboration of the melodic and formal aspect of *copula*.

[72] Reckow, "Das Organum," 477-87, see also *idem*, "Processus und Structura. Über Gattungstradition und Formverständnis im Mittelalter," *Musiktheorie* 1 (1986), 5-29.

[73] Not all scholars agree in the interpretation of these cadential patterns as dissonant appoggiaturas (cf. Ernest Sanders, review of Roesner's *Les Quadrupla*, in *Notes* 52 (1995), 623-29) but the repertory of tripla and quadrupla as well as the three-part

conductus repertory do show a considerable number of places where the composer increases the level of dissonance considerably in the last gesture before a cadence.

[74]   Reckow, *Musiktraktat*, I, p. 88, ". . . prima potest esse concordans vel discordans, et semper incipit ante tenorem breviter, et tenor incipit cum secundo, si fuerit concordans, vel cum tertio"; Yudkin, *The Music Treatise*, p. 79.

[75]   The so-called rule of consonance in Garlandia and later theorists such as Franco of Cologne has caused considerable debate, cf. Ernest Sanders, "Consonance and Rhythm," pp. 268-74, dealing with earlier scholarship on this matter, and the exchange between Sanders and Fritz Reckow in *Journal of the American Musicological Society* 34 (1981), 588-91, as well as Yudkin, "The Rhythm of Organum Purum," pp. 373-74.

[76]   Reckow, *Musiktraktat*, I, 88. Also Franco of Cologne, *Ars Cantus Mensurabilis*, ed. Gilbert Reaney and André Gilles, Corpus Scriptorum de Musica 18 (Rome, 1974), p. 81, and Charles Atkinson, "Franco of Cologne on the Rhythm of Organum Purum," *Early Music History* 9 (1990), 11-13 and 21-23.

[77]   On the possible examples of *floraturae* see Edward Roesner, "The Performance of Parisian Organum," *Early Music* 7 (1979), 176-78.

[78]   See David Hiley, "The Plica and Liquescence," *Gordon Athol Anderson (1929-1981): in Memoriam von seinen Studenten, Freunden und Kollegen*, 2 vols., Musicological Studies 39, ed. Margaret Bent, Brian Gillingham, Irving Godt, and Hans Tischler (Henryville, 1984), II, pp. 379-91.

[79]   See Roesner, *Les quadrupla*, p. xcviii, citing Walter Odington and Anonymous IV.

[80]   Geoffrey Chew, "A Magnus Liber Organi Fragment at Aberdeen," *Journal of the American Musicological Society* 31 (1978), 326-43.

[81]   Facsimile in *Polyphonies du XIIIe siècle, le manuscrit H. 196 de la Faculté de Médecine de Montpellier*, ed. Yvonne Rokseth. 4 vols. (Paris, 1935-1939), I.

[82]   This was first noted by Roesner, "The Performance," p. 175.

[83]   See Roesner, *Les quadrupla*, p. xcviii.

[84]   Reckow, *Der Musiktraktat*, I, 83, Yudkin, *The Music Treatise*, pp. 74-75.

[85]   See Alejandro Enrique Planchart, "Tempo and Proportions," *Performance Practice: Music Before 1600*, ed. Howard Mayer Brown and Stanley Sadie (London, Macmillan, 1989), p. 130.

[86]   Reckow, *Der Musiktraktat*, I, 87-88; Yudkin, *The Music Treatise*, p. 79.

[87]   An extensive discussion of the rise of mode three from mode one and eventual developments later in the thirteenth century is Ernest Sanders, "Duple Rhythm and Alternate Third Mode in the 13th Century," *Journal of the American Musicological Society* 15 (1962), 249-91.

[88]   Thus in Roesner, *Les quadrupla*, p. 15. Husmann, *Die drei- und vierstimmigen Notre-Dame Organa*, p. 29, reads the opening as mode six, ignoring the deliberate absence of *quaternariae* ligatures in the passage. William Waite's unpublished transcription in mode three was adopted by a number of performers and is the version commonly heard in most recordings of the work.

[89]   The transcription of some *conductus* such as *Procurans odium* in a form of mode four in Janet Knapp, *Thirty-Five Conductus for Two and Three Voices*, Collegium Musicum [First series] 6 (New Haven, 1965), p. 34, is now acknowledged by Professor Knapp as a misreading. The same thing applies to all the examples of putative mode four *conductus* mentioned in Gordon Anderson, "The Rhythm of the *cum littera* Sections of Polyphonic Conductus in Mensural Sources," *Journal of the American Musicological Society* 26 (1973), 288-304.

[90] See, for example, the commentary in Roesner, *Les quadrupla*, pp. lxxxvii-lxxxviii, concerning just one passage in the Responsory *Descendit de caelis*.

[91] Reckow, *Der Musiktraktat*, I, pp. 84-85, Yudkin, *The Music Treatise*, pp. 76-77.

[92] Cf. for example, the end of the responsories *Descendit de caelis*, Roesner, *Les quadrupla*, p. 50, and F, fol. 15v, and several of the cadences in *Ex eius tumba*, pp. 174 and 176, and F, fols. 37v-38r.

[93] Cf. the end of *Pretiosus V. Athleta*, Roesner, *Les Quadrupla*, p. 155 and F, fol. 33r.

[94] Wright, *Music and Ceremony*, pp. 24-25, the soloists among them were given the name of "machicotus," a term as yet not fully explained, but which remained in use until the eighteenth century.

[95] Christopher Page, *The Owl and the Nightingale: Musical Life and Ideas in France, 1100-1300* (Cambridge, 1989), pp. 145-54.

[96] See Rebecca Baltzer, "Performance Practice, the Notre Dame Calendar, and the Earliest Liturgical Motets," *Das Ereigniß Notre Dame*, ed. Fritz Reckow (in press), and Wright, *Music and Ceremony*, pp. 338-44 with extensive documentation from Notre Dame and from the traditions of churches outside Paris as well.

[97] See Roesner, "The Performance," pp. 322-23, and *idem*, *Les quadrupla*, p. xcviii.

[98] Wright, *Music and Ceremony*, Chaper 4.

[99] See, for example David G. Hughes, "Liturgical Polyphony at Beauvais in the Thirteenth Century," *Speculum* 34 (1959), 184-200, *idem*, "The Sources of Christus Manens," *Aspects of Medieval and Renaissance Music. A Birthday Offering to Gustave Reese*, ed. Jan LaRue (New York, 1966; repr. New York, 1978), pp. 423-34, Wulf Arlt, *Ein Festoffizium des Mittelalters aus Beauvais in seiner liturgischen und musikalischen Bedeutung*, 2 vols. (Cologne, 1972), and Miroslav Perz, "Organum, Conductus und mittelalterliche Motette in Polen: Quellen und Probleme," *International Musicological Society, Report of the Eleventh Congress, Copenhagen, 1972*, 2 vols., ed. Henrik Glahn et al. (Copenhagen, 1974), pp. 593-97.

[100] See *Facsimile Reproduction of Madrid 20486*, ed. Luther Dittmer, Publications of Mediaeval Musical Manuscripts 1 (Brooklyn, 1957), *El Còdex musical de Las Huelgas (música a veus des segles XIII-XIV*, ed. Higini Anglès, 3 vols, Biblioteca de Catalunya, Publicaciones del Departament de Música 6 (Barcelona, 1931).

[101] See Edward Roesner, "The Manuscript Wolfenbüttel, Herzog-August Bibliothek, 628 Helmstadiensis: A Study of its Origins and of its Eleventh Fascicle," 2 vols. (Ph.D. diss., New York University, 1974), and Calvin Ray Stapert, "The Eleventh Fascicle of Wolfenbüttel 628: A Critical Edition and Commentary," 2 vols. (Ph.D. diss., University of Chicago, 1973).

[102] Geoffrey Chew, "A Magnus Liber Organi Fragment at Aberdeen," *Journal of the American Musicological Society* 31 (1978), 326-43, and Alejandro Enrique Planchart, "Communication," *Journal of the American Musicological Society* 31 (1979), 154.

[103] Ernest Sanders, ed., *English Music of the Thirteenth and Early Fourteenth Centuries*, Polyphonic Music of the Fourteenth Century 14 (Monaco, 1979).

[104] See Roger Bowers, "The Performing Ensemble for English Church Polyphony, c. 1320 - c. 1390," *Studies in the Performance of Late Medieval Music*, ed. Stanley Boorman (Cambridge, 1983), pp. 161-92. The ranges and layouts presented by Bowers in pp. 167-75 agree quite closely with what is found in the English repertories, of the previous century.

[105] Editions of this repertory include Janet Knapp, ed., *Thirty-Five Conductus for Two and Three Voices*, Collegium Musicum 6 (New Haven, 1965), Ethel Thurston, ed., *The*

Conductus Collections of MS Wolfenbüttel 1099, 2 vols., Recent Researches in the Music of the Middle Ages and Early Renaissance 11-13 (Madison, 1980), and Gordon Anderson, ed., *Notre-Dame and Related Conductus. Opera Omnia*. 9 vols. out of 11 to date (Henryville, 1979-).

[106] A few *conductus* are built upon preexisting monophonic tunes, for example, *Procurans odium* (F, fol. 226r-226v) where the lowest voice in the score is a contrafact of Blondel de Nesle's *L'amour dont sui espris* [cf. Hendrik van der Werf, *The Chansons of the Troubadours and the Trouvères* (The Hague, 1972), pp. 100-03], and *Veris ad imperia* (F, fols. 228v-229r), where the lowest voice is a contrafact of a Provençal *Dança, A l'entrada del tens clar* (van der Werf, *op. cit.*, pp. 98-99).

[107] See, for example, the classification implied in the listing of the Notre Dame music books by Anonymous IV, Reckow, *Der Musiktraktat*, I, 82, and Yudkin, *The Music Treatise*, p. 73.

[108] That is, three-voice single-texted motets built upon preexisting two-voice *clausulae*, which were sometimes copied (and presumably sung) without the tenor (that is, as *conductus*), but for whose rhythm we have a clearly documented version in the melismatic *clausulae*, as well as later copies of *conductus* in mensural notation.

[109] Gordon Anderson, "*Nove geniture*: Three Variant Polyphonic Settings of a Notre-Dame Conductus," *Studies in Musicology* [Australia] 9 (1975), 8-18, *idem*, "The Rhythm of the *cum littera* Sections of Polyphonic Conductus in Mensural Sources," *Journal of the American Musicological Society* 26 (1973), 288-304, "Mode and Change of Mode in the Notre Dame Conductus," *Acta Musicologica* 40 (1968), 92-115.

[110] Ernest Sanders, "Conductus and Modal Rhythm," *Journal of the American Musicological Society* 38 (1985), 439-69.

[111] Janet Knapp, "Musical Declamation and Poetic Rhythm in an Early Layer of Notre-Dame Conductus," *Journal of the American Musicological Society* 32 (1979), 383-407.

[112] Knapp, *Thirty-Five Conductus*, pp. 42-43, Thurston, *The Conductus*, II, 37-44.

[113] Knapp, *Thirty-Five Conductus*, pp. 85-88.

[114] F also transmits a large corpus of monophonic *conductus*, one of which, *Beata viscera*, is ascribed to Perotin by Anonymous IV.

3. Motet & Cantilena
Julie E. Cumming

Origins of the Motet

The origins of the motet resemble those of the sequence. Both arose out of a desire to embellish the liturgy by adding words to pre-existent music, but developed into independent genres in which complex formal structures were determined by the interaction of music and text. The motet emerged out of Notre Dame polyphony. The great two-part organa of Leonin and his contemporaries—and to a lesser extent the three- and four-part organa of Perotin—were constantly recomposed, modernized, and adapted. One of the most important ways of modifying an organum setting was to replace the discant sections, or clausulae, with new clausulae, or to replace a passage that had originally been written in organum purum with a discant clausula. We see this process going on in the different versions of the complete organa that survive; we also see it in sections of the Notre Dame manuscripts devoted to page after page of "substitute clausulae," brief discant passages made up of a chant fragment excerpted from one of the great organa and an additional upper voice. The number of these substitute clausulae—ten or fifteen settings of many different chant fragments from graduals or alleluias sung only once a year—suggests that the substitute clausulae began very early to exist as compositions, or at least as compositional exercises, independent of the great organa for which they were originally intended.[1]

The Notre Dame manuscripts also contain sections of discant clausulae with text added to the non-chant part or parts—texted clausulae, the first motets. The word "motet" is believed to come from the French "mot," meaning word—a motet is then, literally, a "worded" composition. The creation of the motet was originally as much a question of writing a text as it was of composing music, given the pre-existent clausulae. Recent research by Thomas Payne suggests that the first motets were in fact a collaboration between a composer, Perotin, and the poet Philip the Chancellor, around 1200.[2]

The tenor of the motet was a chant fragment from one of the responsorial chants that received organal settings; it carried its original text, sometimes just a syllable (such as "Do" from Dominus), sometimes a few words (such as "In seculum"). The added part, the upper part of a two-part clausula, was known as the duplum or motetus (because it was the texted voice). Untexted source clausulae can be found for most of the earliest motets; most have two voices, but there were also three-voice clausulae, as well as a few for four voices. These additional voices were known as the triplum and quadruplum.

There were three different kinds of motets. 1) The two-voice motet is the most basic type in the early thirteenth century, with a tenor and texted motetus. 2) The conductus motet is a three-voice piece in which the motetus and triplum phrase together, so that they can sing the same text at the same time (after the manner of all the voices of a conductus). The conductus motet could have been created by adding text to a three-voice clausula in which the duplum and triplum phrased together, or by adding a triplum that phrased with the motetus of a two-voice motet. 3) The double motet is a polytextual three-voice motet in which the motetus and triplum have different texts (hence "double"; the fragmentary text of the chant fragment in the tenor is not counted). If the duplum and triplum of the source clausula did not phrase together, then it was not possible to use the same text for both parts, and two different texts were required. The double motet could also be created by adding an independent triplum voice with its own text to a two-voice clausula. The double motet became the most common form of motet by mid-century.

The pitches of the tenor part were those of the chant fragment; this melody was often repeated, sometimes more than once. The rhythm of the tenor part generally consisted of a short rhythmic module that was repeated over and over. The phrasing of the upper parts played against the regularity of the tenor, alternately phrasing with the tenor part and against it. This tension between the regularity of the tenor part and the overlapping phrases of the upper parts is one of the defining features of the medieval motet.

Composers immediately began to embellish, expand, and experiment with the motet repertory. They would write a new, different text for the motetus voice in Latin, or, increasingly, in French. They would write a new text for the triplum of a conductus motet, or replace the old triplum with a new, independent triplum carrying its own text. Originally it seems that the tenor/motetus pair that had originated as a discant clausula remained constant, while texts and triplum parts were manipulated at will; but soon composers were writing new motetus voices and even composing new motets from scratch. They often used the traditional tenor melodies, but by the mid-thirteenth century they were drawing their tenors from multiple sources—from different genres of chant, and even from popular song. The texts of the upper voices had a broad range of topics, from serious devotional or theological contemplation to rowdy street songs. While Latin texts persisted, the majority were in French; the most common type of motet by mid-century was the three-voice French double motet.[3]

Notation and Rhythm

Notre Dame polyphony used modal notation: the pattern of ligatures indicated the rhythmic mode, the sequence of longs and shorts (longs and breves). This is a notational system very dependent on context, and there is much disagreement among modern scholars about interpretation of rhythm. The notation was developed for the massive organum settings of highly melismatic chants, in which text was virtually non-existent. One of the basic rules of chant notation was that all the notes in a neume or ligature were sung on a single syllable (in other words, you never change syllables in the middle of a ligature), and this rule remains in effect for ligatures until the end of the Renaissance. When a discant clausula (written in modal notation) was made into a motet, ligatures in the upper voices had to be broken up in order to correspond to the new syllabic text. Once this happened most of the evidence for the rhythm of those voices was destroyed. The modal notation of the tenor part is not changed, and a certain amount can be deduced from the relationships between the parts, and occasionally from the rhythm of the text. But the only way to be sure about the rhythm of the motetus and triplum parts of an early motet is to find the textless discant clausula on which it was based. A group of textless clausulae in the St. Victor Manuscript (Paris, Bibliothèque Nationale, fonds latin, 15139) has marginal annotations indicating the texts of the motets based on those clausulae. It has been suggested that the text was removed for the sake of clarifying the rhythmic notation, so that texted and untexted versions were used together in determining the rhythm of the motets. In many other cases the source clausula survives—but the rhythm of the early motet remains an area in which the performer has a great deal of leeway.

The invention of the motet, and the resultant breakdown of the system of modal notation, was one of the primary motivations for the creation of the system of mensural notation, in which duration is indicated by the shape of the note, rather than its place in a pattern of ligatures. After the early Notre Dame manuscripts the symbols for single pitches known in chant notation as *virga* (◄) and *punctum* (■) began to be associated with the long and breve respectively, and gradually fixed values came to be associated with ligature configurations as well. The patterns associated with the iambic second mode (♪♩♪♩♪𝄾) and related third mode (♩．♪♩♩．♪♩ 𝄾．) became especially popular in mid-thirteenth-century French motets. It was now possible to save parchment by abandoning the pseudo-score format of Notre Dame polyphony, and write out the parts separately in choirbook format, with the long-note tenor compressed into a line or two at the bottom of the page.

This primitive system of mensural notation was codified and expanded by Franco of Cologne, in the *Ars cantus mensurabilis* (ca.1280). Franconian notation made it possible to indicate fairly unambiguously the rhythm of all the parts in a motet, and to abandon the restrictive rhythmic choices of the modal system. Developments of notational style and manuscript format can be traced in the various fascicles of the Montpellier codex, a huge anthology containing motets from the beginning to the end of the thirteenth century (copied 1270-1300). [4]

The rhythm of the early motet was generally restricted to two note values, long and short (or breve) with the occasional duplex long (usually restricted to tenor parts). Longs and breves generally combined into what we would think of as compound meters, such as 6/8, 9/8, or 12/8, with groups of three breves duration making up the basic building block. The perfect long equals three breves, an imperfect long equals two, followed or preceded by a breve to add up to three. These values are generally transcribed according to a ratio of 1/16:

Duplex Long	◾	=	𝅗𝅥.
Long	◾	=	𝅗𝅥. (perfect); 𝅗𝅥 (imperfect)
Breve	◾	=	♩

There were occasional faster flourishes in values smaller than the breve, known as semibreves (♦) (notated in transcription as sixteenth-notes).[5]

Beginning in the thirteenth century we see the gradual introduction of smaller note values, resulting in the slowing down of the larger values. The new note value, the semibreve, was originally exactly that: half a breve, used as a brief melismatic flourish within a syllable. But then we start to see syllabic semibreves, which slow down the breve and long. This sometimes results in a different transcription ratio (depending on the editor). For some motets from the second half of the thirteenth century the transcription ratio is 1/8:

Long	◾	=	𝅗𝅥. (perfect); 𝅗𝅥 (imperfect)
Breve	◾	=	♩
Semibreve	♦	=	♩

When the semibreve becomes a value in its own right the predominantly ternary organization of longs and breves is extended to breves and semibreves, so that there are now three semibreves to a breve, and the modern transcription is adjusted accordingly (there are a variety of different approaches: triplets, time signatures of 9/16 or 9/8, etc.). There is some disagreement about when this triple division of the breve takes effect. In continental Franconian notation paired semibreves are generally transcribed as short-long, though some theorists of the time suggest the opposite.

The subdivision of the breve reaches its peak at the end of the thirteenth century in the motets of Petrus de Cruce. Here the breve can be divided into almost any number of semibreves (up to nine); all the semibreves can carry text. The approach taken in most transcriptions is to divide the semibreves equally into the breve (resulting in triplets, quintuplets, septuplets, etc.), but some scholars favor regularizing these subdivisions into multiples of two and three.[6]

Most scholars agree that the basic pulse of the medieval motet should be steady, an embodiment of "precisely measured" sound or time. At the same time theorists of Notre Dame polyphony describe certain kinds of rhythmic freedom: stretching of some values, reduction of others; rhythmic alteration as a kind of ornamentation.[7] Other theorists describe a ritard in the penultimate measure, as well as internal ritards, and longer pauses when all three voices of a motet have rests together.[8]

Performance Context

The origins of the motet raise questions about its performance context. Were early Latin-texted motets incorporated into the great Notre Dame organa? Some early motets are simply texted versions of discant clausulae that occur in these organa (while others are texted versions of independent substitute clausulae), and some of the motet texts are appropriate to the feast for which the chant tenor and organum setting were intended. Since we know, from the multiple versions in which we find the great organum settings, that they were constantly undergoing revisions, and because many scholars assume that the independent substitute clausulae were substituted into these organum settings, some scholars and performers conclude that at least some early motets were used the same way, i.e. they were inserted into Notre Dame organa. On the other hand, motets (like substitute clausulae) are found in their own sections of the Notre Dame manuscripts, and there exists no manuscript source of a complete organum setting in which a discant clausula is texted (i.e. in which a motet is included in the context of an organum). So the jury is still out on this issue.

It is clear, however, that most motets were performed as independent compositions, with no connection to the organa. Where and for whom were they performed? A variety of different kinds of evidence can shed light on these questions: the language and subject matter of the texts; the presentation in the sources; and mention of the genre in literary and theoretical writings.[9]

Texts

The texts of the thirteenth-century motet cover an astonishing range of subjects. Latin texts range from devotional sacred texts, to outright anticlericalism, to political commentary. French texts range from allegorical praise of the Virgin, to risqué seduction scenes, to street cries. This range of subjects suggests a range of performance settings. Some motets may have functioned paraliturgically, like conductus: they may have been sung during processions, at moments of great solemnity in the Mass (such as at the elevation of the host), or to fill in during the communion or offertory. Others, both French and Latin, with sacred and secular texts, may have functioned as a kind of clerical chamber music, performed by and for the singers of a cathedral or collegiate church, or as entertainment for meals and other gatherings for bishops and other high ecclesiastics. Still others, especially the French-texted motets, must have been performed in secular contexts, such as the courts of the king and the nobility.[10]

Manuscript Presentation

Motets of the thirteenth century are found in a variety of different kinds of manuscripts: large anthology manuscripts with sections devoted to all the major polyphonic genres of the time (such as the Notre Dame manuscripts); collections of motets; and chansonniers, manuscripts primarily devoted to monophonic song. The first two kinds of manuscripts are not too revealing with respect to performance. The last kind of manuscript is suggestive, especially since motets often appear in chansonniers with their tenors lacking. The modern view of the motet tends to focus on its creation: the essential thing about it is the pre-existent tenor and its organization, and the rest (motetus, text, triplum) is secondary. But from the point of view of a trouvère, or in fact, any member of a courtly lay audience, the two-part French motet looks like nothing so much as a trouvère song with accompaniment. From this point of view the essential element in the composition is the motetus voice and its text. Many French motetus voices quote popular "refrains" of the time, lines or couplets of text, or even text and music, that are found in French poetry and song of the period. All these facts suggest why at least some French motets could be transformed into monophonic songs by loss of their tenor parts: individual motetus and triplum voices would then be performed independently.[11]

Contemporary Discussion of the Motet

As Christopher Page has shown, some writers associated the motet with the "vainglorious and wanton pleasure" of trouvère lyric and dance song, while others state that it is too complex for the laity, and suggest that motets should be restricted to the "literati," the scholars and clerics of the University of Paris.[12] Clearly motets were performed in a variety of different contexts; they were also written in a many different styles. This was a large and multifaceted repertoire, with something in it to please almost everyone. We should recognize the potential appeal of the motet's subtlety and artifice.

Pitch and Performing Forces

There can be little doubt that all parts of Notre Dame organa were performed by virtuoso solo singers, without instrumental participation (the tenor may sometimes have been sung by more than one singer).[13] Early motets were presumably performed the same way, and there is reason to believe that motets were performed by unaccompanied vocal soloists throughout the Middle Ages. The almost textless tenor lines could have been vocalized, or sung to the syllables provided, with syllable changes strategically placed for structural emphasis or maximum effect. In a musical world that was still primarily monophonic, and an intellectual world that believed in the divinity of precisely measured ratios of small integers, it is no wonder that theorists of early polyphony stress the exact sizes of the different intervals. Solo singers are best equipped to adjust the sizes of their intervals, and to exploit, for example, the tension of the large Pythagorean third before its resolution to the perfect fifth.[14]

If we accept the ensemble of solo singers as a possibility for the performance of a thirteenth-century motet, some related questions arise. At what pitch were the motets sung? And what kinds of voices sang them? Scholars generally agree that there was no fixed pitch in the Middle Ages: the notated pitch was determined by location of the half steps in the diatonic system, and the desire to fit the parts onto the staff without ledger lines. The actual pitch would be determined by the comfortable ranges of the singers. In the thirteenth-century motet all voices are in approximately the same range, with a total range of about eleven notes. The tenor often has a more limited and slightly lower range than the other voices, but all the parts could be sung by the same person. There seems to have been some admiration for performers who could sing high; Christopher Page suggests placing the motets so that they lie somewhere between C and a', thirteen notes above.[15] Perhaps coincidentally, this range corresponds quite closely to the notated pitch of most motets. Given the scarcity of tenors in many performing organizations, however, I see no reason not to pitch the motets somewhat lower, in more of a baritone range. There is no evidence for the use of choirboys in polyphony until the early fifteenth century, and while countertenors or male falsettists may have existed during this period there is no need for them in the thirteenth-century motet repertory, given the limited range of most of the compositions. The motets may also be performed by women an octave or so higher. A late but important collection of Latin motets comes from the women's convent of Las Huelgas in Burgos, Spain; the music it contains was probably sung by the nuns. Women sometimes composed and participated in courtly song as well, and thus might have sung French motets in courtly contexts.

What about instruments? It has long been assumed that instruments were used on untexted lines or even passages (such as the caudae of conductus) in Medieval polyphony. Recent scholarship has come to distrust this automatic equation, and argues that many untexted lines were sung. But that does not mean that they could not also have been played on instruments; texted lines may have been played on instruments as well. Few instrumentalists could read musical notation, but they were probably very adept at learning and memorizing music by ear, and at composing or improvising new pieces in imitation of vocal music they heard. The most famous theorist of Notre Dame polyphony, Anonymous IV, mentions the use of a string instrument in connection with organum purum.[16]

There exist two sets of textless motets, possibly intended for performance on instruments: one in the St. Victor manuscript (discussed above), the other in the Bamberg manuscript (Bamberg, Staatliche Bibliothek, MS Lit. 115). The Bamberg pieces are primarily hockets based on the popular "In seculum" tenor, and it has long been assumed that hockets were instrumental works. On the other hand, hockets are also found remodeled as motets, so it is certainly possible that they (like textless clausulae), were sometimes performed by voices.

There is some evidence, however, to suggests that the hockets were instrumental. One of the Bamberg hockets is labeled "In seculum viellatoris." "In seculum" is the text of the tenor; "viellatoris" could mean "of the vielle player." This has been taken to indicate performance on vielle, though it could of course indicate that the piece was composed by a vielle player, and it is risky to extrapolate anything about the performance of other pieces from this example. It does suggest however that vielle players had some contact with the motet repertory. And hocket technique is referred to as *modus flaiolis* by one theorist, which could be a reference to the flageolet, a kind of recorder.[17] Other instruments that might have been involved include the organ (there are organ intabulations of fourteenth-century motets in the Robertsbridge Codex) and the harp (harpists were often musically literate, and some were composers).[18]

It is thus impossible to rule out the participation of instruments (especially vielle, organ or harp) in some performances of some motets. Instruments may have played tenor lines, or complete motets may have been performed as instrumental works. Nevertheless, performance by adult vocal soloists on all parts was probably the norm for the thirteenth-century motet in France.

PART II: THE ENGLISH MOTET, 1250-1350

The Notre Dame repertory was known in thirteenth-century England; one of the central Notre Dame sources, W1 (Wolfenbüttel, Herzog August-Bibliothek, MS 677), was probably copied at St. Andrews in Scotland. The eleventh fascicle includes some indigenous British two-part music for the Virgin. English motets are occasionally found in continental sources, and vice versa. Unfortunately no complete English manuscripts of polyphony survive between W1 and the Old Hall manuscript (London, British Library, Additional MS 57950), copied in the early fifteenth century. It appears that when earlier music went out of fashion in Medieval England the manuscripts were disassembled and used as binding material and flyleaves for new books. New manuscript fragments of English music turn up almost yearly in the bindings of account books, registers, collections of theological writings, and so forth. The surviving pieces are often fragmentary, and very difficult to make out. Much of the thirteenth-century repertory is found in the Worcester Fragments, a modern compilation of fragments believed to have come from Worcester cathedral. The fourteenth-century sources are even more various. While important studies of English medieval music were published more than thirty years ago,[19] only recently has there been a comprehensive attempt to publish large parts of the repertory,[20] and to establish bibliographical control over the hundreds of manuscript fragments now known.[21]

England developed an indigenous style of motet composition in the second half of the thirteenth century. While most English motets still resemble continental motets texturally—the rhythmic contrast between the tenor and the upper parts persists—some of the other defining features of the continental motet, such as cantus firmus and polytextuality, are not always present. There is a greater variety of constructive techniques, and the division between motet and conductus is much less clearly drawn.[22]

Some English motets use cantus firmi of the French type (i.e. a chant fragment), with tenor repetition. French chansons are also used as cantus firmi, somewhat more often than in France. Another English motet type uses an entire chant in the tenor without repetition. A wide spectrum of chants is used, including those for the Mass ordinary. The upper voices have one or two additional texts that comment in some way on the subject of the tenor cantus firmus; for this reason these pieces are sometimes called troped chant settings. In other English motets a new tenor part is created, called a pes. Two-voice motets are rare; most English motets have three or even four voices.

Structural techniques that are peculiarly English include isomelism (from "iso," same, and "melis," melody), in which repetitions in the tenor are accompanied by repetition of melodic material in the upper voices; and isoperiodicity, in which the phrases (periods) are the same length. These regular phrase lengths figure in two or more voices, usually offset, so that the phrases overlap. Neither of these techniques is completely absent from the continental repertoires, but they are exploited in new ways in the British isles.

The most important kind of isomelic motet is the motet with voice exchange, in which the two upper voices sing a phrase, then switch parts and then sing it again over a repeated phrase in the tenor, usually a freely composed pes. Voice exchange was a common feature of Perotin's three- and four-voice organum settings, but it was not otherwise used much in continental polyphony. It is closely related to the rondellus, an English form of conductus, usually in score format, in which three voices exchange parts (without a supporting tenor). This form dies out ca.1300, however, while the four-voice voice-exchange motet continues to flourish well into the next century. Most voice-exchange motets and rondelli have extensive textless passages and only one text, sung in one voice at a time. Motets built on a pes without voice exchange also generally repeat some material, with modified strophic forms and refrains. Striking large-scale voice-exchange motets from the fourteenth-century include *Thomas gemma Cantuarie* (about St. Thomas of Canterbury)[23] or *Hostis Herodes* (Epiphany).[24]

Isoperiodicity would later become an important element in French isorhythmic motets of the mid-fourteenth century, but it developed first in England, where it was less dependent on the rhythmic patterning of the tenor part. The majority of the surviving English motets of the fourteenth century are isoperiodic. In an English isoperiodic motet the phrases of two or more voices (of a three or four-voice motet) are the same length (e.g. 9 longs); the first phrases of the piece are different in each voice, however, so that the phrase endings do not coincide in the different voices. Many of these motets are for four voices with three individually texted voices over a tenor (e.g. *Petrum Cephas*).[25] Another type was dubbed by Lefferts the "duet motet with medius cantus," in which the slower-moving tenor is the middle voice, with isoperiodic outer voices singing in a rapid patter style in parallel imperfect consonances (e.g. *Rosa delectabilis*).[26]

Notation and Rhythm

Mid-thirteenth-century English music is written in modal notation very similar to that of the continent. There is compelling evidence, however, that the English preferred the trochaic, long-short, first mode rhythmic patterns to the iambic, short-long, second mode patterns becoming so popular on the continent at the same period.[27] The preference for long-short rhythms and the use of harmonies that sound "major" and "tonal" give English medieval polyphony a tuneful quality that is very appealing to modern listeners.

A distinctive English style of notation emerged in the 1260s, in which the breve is diamond shaped (like the continental semibreve). Franconian notation appeared in England ca.1300. Other English notational features that appear in the 1330s are the *signum rotundum*, a small circle preceding a semibreve to indicate that it is short, and *cauda hirundinis* (swallow tail), a double downward stem (♦) to indicate a longer semibreve. Fully developed French *ars nova* notation did not appear in England until after 1350.

Texts, Performance Context, and Performing Forces

The English motet invariably had a sacred Latin text, usually for a saint or for one of the important feast days of the church year. The structure of text and music were carefully correlated, and the upper parts were often related by rhyme or assonance. English polyphony, including the motet, seems to have been composed almost exclusively in a clerical milieu for use in church. Most of the surviving manuscript fragments with identifiable provenance are from monasteries. During the fourteenth century, however, the number of secular foundations and aristocratic chapels capable of performing complex polyphonic music increased noticeably, perhaps indicating that musical leadership had moved to centralized secular institutions. The conflicting evidence has resulted in a debate about the centers for musical composition and innovation.[28] It seems safe to suggest, however, that polyphony was cultivated first in the great monastic establishments, and then, increasingly, in cathedrals and court chapels.

Given the sacred character of the English motet repertory, there is little doubt that it was performed exclusively by voices, almost definitely by adult male soloists at a range comfortable for the singers involved. After consideration of the ranges and style of the various kinds of pieces in the repertory, Roger Bowers comes to the following conclusions:

English fourteenth-century polyphony appears to have been composed for performance by the resources available within small ensembles constituted according to a single standard plan. This plan predicated a membership of just four singers, comprising voices which corresponded roughly (in modern terms) to two altos, one tenor and one baritone; this ensemble performed its repertoire entirely *a cappella*.[29]

Some scholars find that Bowers puts his ranges a bit high.[30] But his basic point —that this was a repertory conceived by and for a rather specific performing ensemble—may be more true of medieval music in general than we have admitted up to now.

PART III: THE MOTET IN THE FOURTEENTH CENTURY

The motet was created in France in the thirteenth century, and the French motet of the fourteenth century dominates our idea of the late medieval motet. As we have seen, however, there was an alternative English tradition, which persisted well into the fourteenth century. There was also a local tradition of motet composition in trecento Italy. All three traditions—French, English, and Italian—trace their origins to the French thirteenth-century motet, and all of them share the basic texture of faster triplum and motetus over a slow-moving tenor (or occasionally tenor and contratenor). But the local traditions developed their own individual features in response to the different functions they fulfilled in different contexts, and to the preferences of different patrons, audiences, performers, and composers. I will discuss the individual features of the different local traditions, and then go on to consider the probable performing forces for all of them.

FRANCE

Notation and Rhythm

With the advent of *ars nova* notation around 1320 the scale and rhythmic complexity of the motet increased radically. There were two especially important new developments. A new note value was created: a subdivision of the semibreve, called the minim, which looks like a semibreve with the addition of an ascending stem (♩). Both triple and duple divisions were now possible at every level: the long could include three or two breves, the breve three or two semibreves, and the semibreve three or two minims. This greatly expanded the possible range of values and the difference in length between the biggest and smallest note values. The long could now contain as few as eight semibreves (with duple division all the way down) or as many as twenty-seven (with triple subdivision all the way down). Duplex longs and even triplex longs, later known as *maximae*, also occasionally made an appearance. The different combinations of subdivisions were known as mensurations; each mensuration had its own sign (though the signs are often omitted in the manuscripts). Triplum and motetus parts generally move in breves, semibreves, and minims, while the tenor continues to use primarily longs and breves, which can sound almost like pedal points beneath the faster upper voices.

The level of transcription in modern editions changes once again for music including minims. While some editions retain the 1/8 ratio for transcription (with sixteenth notes at the minim level), most French fourteenth-century motets are transcribed with a reduction of 1/4:

Minim	♩	=	♪				
Semibreve	◆	=	♩	or	♩.		
Breve	■	=	♩	or	♩.	or	♩.+♩. [♩:]
Long	▮	=	o	or	o.	or	o.+♩. (♩.+♩.+♩.+♩.)
						or	♩.+♩.+♩.+♩.+♩.+♩.

(depending on subdivisions at lower levels).[31]

Isorhythm

As in the thirteenth-century motet, the tenor was usually a fragment of a pre-existent chant (though many different styles and genres of chant were used). This collection of pitches is known as the *color*, and it was usually repeated, sometimes several times. The tenors of thirteenth-century motets were characterized by the repetition of a short rhythmic module (such as long-short-long); with the new notational possibilities of the fourteenth century these rhythmic modules became much longer and more complex. The repeated rhythmic module of the fourteenth-century motet is known as the *talea*, and there are often three or four taleae per color, although sometimes taleae and color overlap (with, for example, three taleae extending over two colores). This kind of tenor structure was dubbed isorhythm by modern scholars, because the tenor repeats the same rhythm over and over.

Phrase endings in the upper parts generally do not coincide with each other or with the ends of the taleae. On the other hand, the phrase lengths of the upper parts (after the first phrase) are often the same length as those of the tenor taleae, so that the triplum, for example, will end its phrase at the same point in each tenor talea. This is known as isoperiodic structure, which we have already seen in the English motet; in France, unlike in England, isoperiodicity is tied closely to the rhythmic structure of the tenor. Striking rhythmic features (such as hocket or syncopation) usually occur in the upper voices over a certain point in each tenor talea. The rhythmic structure of the tenor is therefore projected in the upper voices. As the fourteenth century proceeds, more and more of the rhythms of the upper voices are coordinated with the tenor talea, until in some motets the upper voices repeat their rhythms exactly with each tenor talea; this is known as panisorhythm. Pitch structures also sometimes correspond to the rhythmic structure of the tenor.[32]

Often the tenor talea will undergo some kind of mensural transformation, usually some kind of diminution, toward the end of the piece. This results in a sense of accelerando toward the end of the piece, as the tenor speeds up, approaching the level of rhythmic activity of the upper voices. Motets which emphasize this kind of mensural transformation are sometimes known as "mensuration motets."[33]

Texts and Performance Contexts

The isorhythmic motet appears in the first major fourteenth-century source containing polyphony, Paris, Bibliothèque Nationale, fonds français, 146, known to scholars of music as the *Roman de Fauvel*. The *Roman de Fauvel* is a satirical verse narrative by Gervais de Bus, completed in 1314, and found in many different manuscripts. One copy includes multiple musical interpolations. It was compiled by Chaillou de Pesstain by 1316, and this is the central source for early fourteenth-century polyphony.[34]

The musical interpolations are in many different styles and genres, but their texts are chosen or adapted to fit the subject and tone of the narrative in which they are embedded. Several of the isorhythmic motets in the manuscript are by Philippe de Vitry, a music theorist and prominent administrator at the French court. Some of his motets are satirical political commentaries; this admonitory political tone remains an important strain in the later fourteenth-century French motet. Sacred subjects (particularly saints and the Virgin) continue to be important; there are some laudatory political motets, and a few concerning music and musicians.

All but one of the motets attributed to Vitry (in the Roman de Fauvel and in later sources) have Latin texts, which becomes the norm for the motet. Only in the work of Guillaume de Machaut, a superb French poet as well as a composer, do we find a substantial body of French-texted motets, mostly about love. His motets are mostly preserved in great manuscripts devoted to his work, rather than in repertory manuscripts, and thus they appear not to have circulated as broadly as the Latin-texted motets.

The evidence concerning both the texts and their composers suggests that motets were performed primarily for private gatherings of intellectuals, especially university-trained clerics and French court officials, who appreciated the acerbic tone and the complexity of texts and music. French-texted motets may also have been performed in court settings along with chansons.

ENGLAND, 1350-1400

Very few late-fourteenth-century sources of motets survive in England, and those that do contain quite a few continental motets.[35] With the importation of French isorhythmic motets and *ars nova* notation in the second half of the century, the French style largely supplanted the indigenous forms of the English motet. Most of the late-fourteenth-century English motets are almost indistinguishable from contemporary French motets.[36] Some motets, however, seem to combine features of French and English style and notation.[37] A distinctly English approach to isorhythm would evolve from this fusion in the early fifteenth century (see below). The English still preferred Latin devotional texts, and there is at least one case in which a continental French text on love is replaced in the English source with a sacred Latin text.[38]

ITALY

The motet (or any other kind of written polyphony) does not seem to have been cultivated in Italy in the thirteenth century; until fairly recently it was believed that the motet was not composed in fourteenth-century Italy either. Recent research by Margaret Bent has, however, revealed a small but significant corpus of Italian trecento motets, primarily preserved in fragmentary manuscripts.[39] The early fifteenth-century motets of Ciconia came out of this fourteenth-century tradition. Italian motets were written in Italian notation, with the resulting musical opportunities and constraints.[40] Like English motets, they did not necessarily have pre-existent cantus firmi. The tenor part moves more slowly than the upper parts, but faster than the tenor of a French motet. Isorhythm did not develop, but some motets are characterized by a very symmetrical form: repetition of the rhythms of all the voices for the second half of the piece. This could be called a simple form of pan-isorhythm, but unlike the contemporary French pan-isorhythmic motet it requires no pre-compositional planning, since the tenor is freely composed, and mensural transformation is absent. The Italian motet often begins with imitation or echo imitation (where the first voice rests while the second voice enters), and it may derive some of its features from the caccia.

Texts and Performance Context

Italian motets usually have laudatory Latin texts about doges, princes, bishops, or saints. While many are polytextual, like the traditional medieval motet, some have a single text for both triplum and motetus parts. There are no admonitory texts after the French fashion, and the purely devotional texts of the English type are infrequent. Unlike in England or France, there is little evidence in fourteenth-century Italy for the cultivation of complex polyphony in ecclesiastical contexts. It seems likely that Italian motets were composed for use at court or in some civic ceremony.

Performing Forces and Pitch

As in the thirteenth century, fourteenth-century motets were probably performed primarily by voices. There is virtually no evidence for the use of instruments and voices together in church (other than *alternatim* performance with organ). For motets performed in church—the entire English repertory, and parts of the French and Italian repertories—vocal performance was probably mandatory.[41]

The overall range of the combined voices in the fourteenth century motet expands to more than two octaves, and there is much greater differentiation in range among the different parts than in the thirteenth century. This may have accompanied greater specialization of voice types and ranges. There is little evidence for the use of choirboys in the fourteenth century, but there is reason to believe that the upper parts of motets may have been sung by countertenors or adult male falsettists; alternatively the pieces may have been pitched low enough for high tenors to sing the upper parts.

Even in secular contexts the most difficult and complex motets were probably performed by the most literate and accomplished musicians of the time, adult male clerics employed as singers and composers. These same singers also sang secular polyphony.[42] It is not impossible, therefore, that some French (and possibly some Italian) motets were also performed by aristocratic or wealthy bourgeois amateurs, both male and female. We know that upper-class men and women performed secular music such as chansons and the Italian vernacular forms; why not motets as well? Many fourteenth-century motets work well with women on the triplum and motetus, men on the lower parts.

Similar arguments can be made to support the participation of instruments in the performance of motets in secular contexts. If a harp, vielle, or portative organ was involved in the performance of chansons, then perhaps they performed motets too. There is even stronger evidence for the performance of motets without voices by instrumental soloists or ensembles. Some motets from the *Roman de Fauvel* are found intabulated for organ in the Robertsbridge codex (London, British Library, MS Additional 28550), an early fourteenth-century English source written in Old German organ tablature. Philippe de Vitry's motets in particular turn up in almost every type of source in the fourteenth and early fifteenth centuries; it seems clear that they became classics, performed in every conceivable context and by every conceivable performance medium.

It is safe to conclude, therefore, that performing forces varied according to performance context. Vocal performance by adult male vocal soloists was the most likely possibility for all kinds of motet, and the exclusive medium for English motets. Women and instruments, however, may have participated in the performance of motets in secular contexts; and some motets, especially those of Philippe de Vitry, were probably performed by instrumental soloists (such as organists and, conceivably, harpists) or ensembles.

PART IV: THE ENGLISH CANTILENA, 1300-1430

The Notre Dame repertory using modal notation—organa, conductus, and early motets—is copied in score: i.e. the parts are written one above the other, with approximate vertical alignment. The ambiguity of the notational system (especially in the case of organum purum) made this necessary. With the development of mensural notation this form of notation was abandoned on the continent, in favor of choirbook format, which required less space on the page (especially in the case of long-note tenors). In England, however, score notation was retained well into the early fifteenth century for three-voice pieces with a single text sung at the same time by all parts (the text was written only once, under the bottom voice).

While English motets (and some Mass movements and other liturgical genres) were copied in choirbook format, the majority of surviving English polyphony from the fourteenth century is in score notation. Score format is used for every different kind of liturgical polyphony—Mass ordinary movements, propers, hymns, etc. Some of the pieces written in score format use a pre-existent chant in one voice; these pieces are often known as English discant (or descant) settings. Pieces in score format without chant are known as free settings or cantilenas.[43]

English discant is a method described in some English treatises for composing or improvising additional voices around a chant melody in a primarily note-against-note texture (the precise nature of the technique of English discant is much debated by modern scholars). Many of the simpler pieces in score format with chant resemble the kind of pieces that would result from the application of English discant to a chant cantus firmus.[44] Among the many different genres that use the technique of English discant is the polyphonic setting of chant antiphons in honor of the Virgin.

Free settings (or cantilenas) include settings of poetic texts that are difficult to assign liturgically: pieces with rhymed Marian texts in double-versicle sequence form (aa bb cc, etc.). They resemble short polyphonic sequences (and are sometimes called sequences).[45] But we would expect polyphonic sequences to be written for all the major feasts of the church year; the texts of these pieces are almost all Marian. Peter Lefferts calls this genre the "cantilena" in order to distinguish it from the sequence. An English cantilena, then, is a three-voice setting of a Marian sequence-like text notated in score. Most of these pieces are freely composed; there are, however, a few that use chant.[46] Lefferts has shown that the cantilena was developed in response to the desire for polyphonic music for the newer Marian devotions, especially the daily Lady Masses and, later, for the evening devotions following Compline known as Salve services. The cantilenas were used primarily as sequences and offertory substitutes, but also as hymn substitutes, and, later, as processional and votive antiphons for the Salve services. They also may have served as a kind of clerical chamber music.[47]

The precedents for the English cantilena go back to the early thirteenth century. In the eleventh fascicle of W1, the Notre Dame source from St. Andrews in Scotland, there is a collection of two-voice polyphonic music for Lady Mass, including both sequences and offertories with sequence-like texts. More direct functional and stylistic antecedents to the fourteenth-century cantilena are the three-voice English conductus and conductus-rondellus repertoires of the later thirteenth century.[48] In the fourteenth century the proportion of motets with Marian texts diminished substantially, and the cantilena became the primary Marian genre.[49] Most of these cantilenas have a more or less note-against-note texture, though some have a slightly more florid upper voice. There is a preponderance of 6-3 chords, with both parallel and contrary motion. Many of them have an F final; Ernest Sanders comments that "for sense of tonal direction, structural clarity, chordal richness and musical lyricism, these songs are not matched by any other medieval repertory."[50]

Prose antiphon texts in honor of the Virgin (including not only the four famous Marian antiphons, but quite a few others) appear alongside the sequence-like texts as early as W1. But polyphonic settings of these prose texts (with and without the associated chant melodies) appear more and more often toward the end of the fourteenth century and in the beginning of the fifteenth, while the use of poetic sequence-like texts declines (though never disappears: "Benedicta es celorum regina" or "Inviolata, integra et casta" are set by Josquin a century later). In the early fifteenth-century Old Hall manuscript both kinds of pieces—cantilenas and polyphonic antiphon settings—are found mixed together. With the increasing importance of the evening devotions after Compline, choir masters seem to have begun to use the cantilenas composed for Mass in the evening Salve services, alongside the growing numbers of polyphonic settings of prose antiphons.

Although the forms of their texts are different, the musical style of polyphonic cantilenas and antiphons are very similar, and increasingly both have a more florid upper voice over two lower voices in more or less the same range. In English sources these pieces are still usually copied in score format, but when found in continental sources they are always written in parts, or choirbook format. This repertory of early fifteenth-century English polyphonic cantilena and antiphon settings does not really have a satisfactory name. In England they were a genre distinct in style and text from the motet, and they are sometimes just called antiphon or sequence settings. My solution is to extend Lefferts's term cantilena to include the antiphons. The cantilena ca.1400-1430, then, is an English polyphonic setting for three voices of a Marian text. The text can be prose or poetry, and the music can be freely composed or use chant. Important composers of the cantilena include Power and Dunstaple, but examples survive by virtually every English composer of the period.

After the Old Hall manuscript, most early fifteenth-century cantilenas are found in continental manuscripts. When they appear in generically organized manuscripts they are found mixed in with the motets—not in their own section, and not with Vespers antiphons or sequences. It seems that the English cantilena, while distinct from the motet at home in England, was treated as a kind of motet on the continent. Why was this the case?

There was no polyphonic genre parallel to the English cantilena being composed on the continent in the fourteenth and early fifteenth centuries. Marian devotions were probably not as elaborate (witness the fact that Lady chapels, ubiquitous in England, are not a regular feature of church architecture on the continent), and monophony or improvised polyphony must have sufficed. When the English cantilenas arrived on the continent in the early fifteenth century, therefore, they fit no existing generic category. The closest genre was that of the motet—which resembled the cantilena in that it was also Latin-texted and functionally flexible. So for want of a better category, cantilenas were treated as, and thus became, motets.

Quite a few of the English cantilenas found in continental manuscripts lack attributions, or are simply marked "Anglicanus" or "De Anglia." But their style is very distinctive, and no piece that is securely attributed to a known continental composer can be confused with an English cantilena. Some of the English cantilena's distinctive features include: triadic opening figures; use of C and O mensurations (2/4 and 3/4); use of contrasting duet sections; a great variety of rhythms in the upper voice; and "panconsonant style," with extreme control of dissonance. Features of the English cantilena—its texts, its rhythmic variety, and its approach to harmony and sonority—would decisively affect the direction of the Renaissance motet on the continent.

PART V: THE MOTET IN THE EARLY FIFTEENTH CENTURY

While local traditions of motet composition remained relatively isolated during the fourteenth century (with the exception of French influence on English motet composition), conditions changed at the beginning of the fifteenth century. The English victory at the Battle of Agincourt in 1415 resulted in the English occupation of northwestern France.[51] The papal schism and the resultant series of councils convened to deal with it brought together ecclesiastics and political leaders from all over Europe, along with their musicians.[52]

Suddenly composers and performers from England, France and the Netherlands, and Italy were hearing each other's music. They were fascinated by the different varieties of motet, and wanted to try their hands at new kinds, while retaining pride in the virtues of their own compositional techniques. While the French, English, and Italian motet types of the fourteenth century persist, new varieties of motet also appear, primarily by composers from Northern France and the Netherlands. At the same time many French isorhythmic motets take on features characteristic of English or Italian motets. Guillaume Du Fay, the most important composer of the period, takes the lead in generic experimentation.[53]

In addition to motet types with the texture of the traditional medieval motet, almost half of the pieces in the motet sections of manuscripts from the early fifteenth century have a single upper melody line over supporting tenor and contratenor parts. The texture resembles that of the French chanson or the English cantilena, from which this new kind of motet probably descends. It has been called, among other things, the song motet and the cantilena. I will distinguish the two basic types of motets with the terms motet-style motet and cantilena-style motet. The motet-style motet retained some of the grander hieratic tone of Medieval polyphony; the cantilena-style motet was a more intimate or personal musical expression recalling the chanson or improvised polyphony.[54] Each type has several subsidiary varieties.

MOTET-STYLE MOTETS

Italian Motets

The most well-known Italian motets of the period are those of Johannes Ciconia. He was born in Liège, but he worked in Padua for the first decade of the fifteenth century and became, for all intents and purposes, an Italian composer. His motets, and those of his younger Italian contemporaries (such as Cristoforus de Monte, Antonius Romanus, and Antonius de Civitato), conform closely to the fourteenth century Italian style, though there is some experimentation with more complicated mensural notation. The scribe of the most important source of Italian motets of the period, Bologna, Civico Museo Bibliografico Musicale Q15, appears to have added contratenor parts to many of these Italian motets; modern performers should consider omitting these added parts in performance.[55]

English Isorhythmic Motets

The English isorhythmic motets of the fifteenth century, while still very influenced by French practices, have several distinctive style features, all exemplified in the motets of John Dunstable. Unlike most other motets of the early fifteenth century, the motetus voice is often lower in range than the triplum, and sometimes even goes below the tenor voice. The mensural transformation of the sections of these motets follows one or two strict patterns (6:4:3 or 3:2:1). Texts are devotional, sometimes pre-existent, and usually in honor of a saint, though the pieces may have been composed for specific state or church occasions.[56]

Motets by Composers from Northern France and the Netherlands

Isorhythmic motets

The isorhythmic motet remains one of the principal types of motet in the early fifteenth century. But now there is an even greater range of styles and approaches, from motets by French composers such as Carmen, Grenon, or Loqueville that resemble very closely those of fourteenth-century France, to the experimental works of Du Fay influenced by Italian and English models. The isorhythmic motets by composers who worked in Italy usually have laudatory political texts after the Italian model. For example, Du Fay's *Vasilissa ergo gaude* was written for the marriage of Cleofe Malatesta in 1420. As Margaret Bent and David Fallows have pointed out, it resembles an Italian motet in its use of two-part rhythmic structure, the subject of its text, and its use of a single text for both triplum and motetus. Like a French motet, however, it has a pre-existent cantus firmus and an essential contratenor voice. Du Fay's later isorhythmic motets (especially those found in Modena, Biblioteca Estense, MS alpha.X.1.11) continue to use laudatory political texts, but adopt a texture similar to the English isorhythmic motets, with a low motetus part. Proportional schemes resemble those of English motets (although they usually have four rather than three sections). Clearly Du Fay was drawing on his experience of all the contemporary motet styles and techniques.

Non-isorhythmic double-discantus motets

There exists a significant repertory of motets by composers from northern France and the Netherlands that retains the traditional texture of the medieval motet, but is not isorhythmic. I call these "double-discantus" motets, because triplum and motetus are equal in range and rhythmic activity, both taking the role of melodic discantus voices.[57] Precedents for such a motet style exist both in the early fourteenth-century English motet and in the Italian motet; we can think of these motets as new hybrids, combining features from a variety of repertories.

I have found that the double-discantus motets divide into two fairly distinct subgroups. The first is a small group of retrospective polytextual works, mostly by Humbertus de Salinis, with texts taken from thirteenth-century motets and conductus, or texts modeled on such texts in style and subject matter (complaints about the sins of the world, admonitory texts, etc).[58] More modest than isorhythmic motets, they often alternate texted and untexted sections after the fashion of thirteenth-century conductus. These motets seem to look back to the early days of the conductus and motet.

The second kind of double-discantus motet is characterized by the use of a single liturgical or biblical text, usually in praise of the Virgin. Although the composers of these devotional double-discantus motets are primarily from the Netherlands (Lymburgia, Arnold and Hugo de Lantins, and Du Fay), the musical style resembles the Italian motet, with echo imitation, a relatively active tenor part, and passages with imitative interchange and sequence in the upper parts. As in the case of the Italian motets, many of the contratenor parts appear to have been added by the scribe of Bologna Q15.[59] The texts, on the other hand, recall those of the English cantilena. Here we see Netherlandish composers setting English-style liturgical Marian texts to Italianate music.

CANTILENA-STYLE MOTETS

Just when the English cantilena arrived on the continent, continental Marian devotions, perhaps inspired by the English example, were on the rise. There was a new interest in polyphonic settings of Marian texts. English music was imported, copied into manuscripts, and performed all over Europe. Continental composers also began to write Marian cantilena-style motets. Because the English distinction between motet and cantilena did not apply on the continent, we see greater freedom in combining text types and musical types: cantilena-style motets were no longer exclusively Marian, but were also concerned with saints or even prominent rulers and ecclesiastics, while pre-existent Marian texts could receive motet-style (double-discantus) settings, as we have seen. There were several new continental varieties of cantilena-style motets.

Continental Chant Settings

A few works by continental composers seem to consciously imitate features of the English cantilena. They use pre-existent Marian antiphon texts, and full or partial chant paraphrase. Lymburgia's *Regina celi*, for example[60] begins with a chant *incipit* and paraphrases the chant in the superius, as do English settings by Power and Dunstaple. Du Fay's *Alma redemptoris* puts the chant in the tenor, also perhaps in imitation of English practice.

Declamation Motet

The most famous of the English cantilenas, then and now, is Dunstaple's *Quam pulchra es*. Like many fourteenth-century English cantilenas it has syllabic, note-against-note declamation of text in all parts. *Quam pulchra es* may have been the model for a small but important group of continental cantilena-style motets which use a similar declamatory style. Some of these pieces—*Quam pulchra es*, Du Fay's *Ave regina celorum I*, Grossin's *Imera dat hodierno*, and Arnold de Lantins's *Tota pulchra es* are among the most widely disseminated pieces of the period, appearing in practically every manuscript containing sacred music.

Cut-Circle Motet

A substantial group of cantilena-style motets that use the mensuration known as diminished perfect tempus (∅ or cut-circle, often transcribed as 6/4) are characterized by additional common features, such as melodic figures, florid writing, or fermata (corona) sections. None of those features can be associated with every one of these motets, but they occur in such variable clusters that we can understand this group of pieces as a category in which the members are related in a variety of ways, and features occur in various combinations. Well-known examples of the style include Du Fay's *Flos florum* and Brassart's *O flos fragrans*. About half of the cut-circle motets are Marian, but some are for saints and a few have laudatory texts, mostly for ecclesiastics in the Venetian orbit. Here we can see the function and tone of the cantilena expand to include subjects normally reserved for motet-style motets.[61] The composers of the cut-circle motets—Brassart, Du Fay, Lymburgia, Sarto, the Lantins, and Feragut—have similar biographies. All are northerners (from Liège or Cambrai) and most worked in Italy, where the motets were probably written. These composers must have known each other and each other's work; in these motets we can see them ringing changes on a similar theme.

Notation and Rhythm

Early fifteenth-century rhythmic notation is essentially identical in conception to the mensural system of the early fourteenth-century *ars nova*, but there are numerous modifications of detail. The most obvious change is the adoption in some manuscripts of white or void notation, in which the note-heads were hollow, rather than black: (▐ = ◫, ■ = □, ◆ = ◇). Coloration could now be indicated by black, full noteheads, rather than red ones. A new smaller value, the semiminim, became more common. It was notated with a flag or red coloration in black notation (♪), and a black notehead in white notation (♩). The numerous complexities of the late fourteenth-century *ars subtilior* gave way to a simpler melodic and rhythmic style. Signs of diminution and proportion become more common, however, and while it is generally agreed that mensuration signs provide information about relative tempo, there continues to be serious scholarly debate on this issue.[62]

The transcription ratio, even on the part of a single editor, can be 1/8, 1/4, or 1/2 (Besseler, for example, uses all three transcription ratios in his edition of Du Fay's motets).

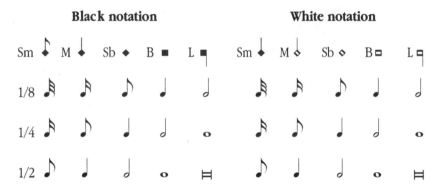

Different editors treat diminution and proportion signs differently in terms of transcription ratio, often changing it during the course of a piece in order to express a proportion in modern notation. Different voices in a single piece were often notated in proportional relationships as well, and an editor has to choose which voice on which to base the transcription, and adjust the others accordingly. These practices sometimes give a misleading impression of tempo relationships, however, and it is important to be aware of the transcription ratio and the original time signatures for all voices.

Performance Context

English motets and continental motets with devotional texts were probably performed in ecclesiastical contexts by clerics. They could have been performed as fillers or processionals at Mass or Office, or as part of special devotions for the Virgin such as Lady Masses or Salve services, or for other feasts, including those for saints.

Motets with retrospective critical or admonitory texts must have been performed in settings similar to those of the French isorhythmic texts, for private gatherings of intellectuals.

Many early fifteenth-century motets (especially isorhythmic and Italian motets) however, have laudatory political texts about a particular person and occasion. It is often assumed that these pieces were performed in public for the ceremony in which the person mentioned in the text took office. These assumptions deserve some scrutiny.

When were they performed? The laudatory tone of many fifteenth-century occasional motets is certainly appropriate for investiture ceremonies, and some motets make specific reference to investiture, such as Cristoforus de Monte's *Plaude decus mundi*, a motet on the investiture of Francesco Foscari as doge of Venice in 1423. But most of the surviving occasional motets are for individuals holding elective or appointed offices: doges, bishops, popes. The identity of the official is thus not known until the election, and the investiture often takes place shortly after the election, usually too soon to allow time for the creation of the text, composition, copying, and rehearsal of the motet. In theory the motets could have been composed ahead of time, before the election, with space for the appropriate name and other details to be inserted at the last minute. But in many cases, such as *Plaude decus mundi*, or some of the papal motets, the texts include specific details about the person praised in the motet, details that would have been difficult to work into the text at short notice. On the other hand, celebrations in honor of a doge, bishop, or pope often went on for some time after the actual investiture, and the anniversary of the event was also celebrated with some grandeur. In general it would be safer to take investiture as a *terminus post quem* for laudatory motets, rather than the date of composition or first performance.

Where were the motets performed, and for whom? I find it unlikely that motets were sung outside, where the performers would have been both invisible and inaudible. Some were surely sung in large churches and cathedrals. But motets, even occasional motets, were just as likely to be performed in a private chapel, or even in private apartments, for the pope, doge, or bishop, and a fairly select gathering of intimates, such as officials, courtiers, or distinguished visitors. The relevant audience were those who already had some power, whose actions and support made a difference. This group was small, well-educated, and close-knit. Some would have had practical listening experience, providing them with basic generic competence. These would have recognized the French, Italian, and English features of different pieces, and they would have been able to assess formality or intimacy of tone.

Performance Forces

As in the case of the earlier motet, the fifteenth-century motet was probably performed by adult male vocal soloists, at whatever pitch was comfortable. Several new developments in choral institutions, however, expand the performance possibilities. One was the beginning of choral polyphony, i.e. the use of more than one person on a part. The other was the use of choirboys in polyphony. Many choir schools were established in Italy during the early fifteenth century for the purpose of training boys.[63] Some pieces use alternating textures marked "unus" and "chorus," and some sections are marked "pueri." David Fallows has shown that polyphony was often performed with one or two adult male singers on the lower parts, and three to six choirboys or adult falsettists for the upper parts.[64] Modern performers using women instead of boys may want to adjust the numbers for the sake of balance, but they could keep this original voicing in mind.

Singers seem to have specialized in parts with a specific function, rather than simply a range: thus archival records mention that a certain singer was a "tenorista" or a "contratenorista"; if the "tenorista" was missing, you couldn't perform the piece.[65] Modern performers might learn to cultivate the different skills associated with these different roles: an experienced contratenorista was perhaps more flexible than a tenorista, with a wider range; he must also have been adept at tuning certain sonorities, such as thirds, or the middle voice in double-leading-tone cadences. The tenor, on the other hand, must have been absolutely solid in terms of pitch and rhythm, with perhaps a fuller tone.

What about the participation of instruments? Much of what was said of the earlier motet still applies to the early fifteenth century. Motets performed in secular contexts may well have been performed with instruments playing the untexted lines, and motets may have been performed by instrumental ensembles and soloists. There is one striking new development: the slide trumpet was invented around 1400. A number of Latin-texted compositions (Mass movements and motets) are found with parts marked "trompetta" or "tuba." There is some debate about whether these markings indicate that the voice is to be played on a slide trumpet, or simply that the music is written in imitation of a natural trumpet. Some of the parts do use repeated fanfare-like figures, but others do not. While the evidence is not conclusive, there is reason to believe that slide trumpets accompanied voices in some Latin-texted polyphony.[66] That may in turn have opened the door for more general participation of instruments with voices in Latin-texted music. On the other hand, there is no evidence for regular employment of instrumentalists in three of the major centers of polyphonic music (Rome, Cambrai, and Venice) during the fifteenth century.[67] So even though instruments may have performed with voices on special occasions, we must assume that most polyphony performed in church was sung *a cappella.*

Selected Facsimiles and Editions

General

Hüschen, Heinrich. ed. *The Motet.* Anthology of Music 47. Cologne: Arno Volk, 1937.

13th-Century French

Catalogues

Ludwig, Friedrich. *Repertorium organorum recentiuris et motetorum vetutstissimi stili.* Vol. I: Catalogue Raisonné der Quellen. Part I: Handschriften in Quadrat-Notation. 2nd ed. Musicological Studies 7. Brooklyn: Institute of Mediaeval Music, 1964. Part II: Handschriften in Mensural-Notation. Musicological Studies, 26. Brooklyn: Institute of Mediaeval Music, 1978.

Van der Werf, Heinrich. *Integrated Directory of Organa, Clausulae, and Motets of the Thirteenth Century.* Rochester: The Author, 1989.

Anthologies

Tischler, Hans. *The Earliest Motets (to Circa 1270): A Complete Comparative Edition.* 3 vols. New Haven: Yale University Press, 1982. Edition.

Idem. *The Style and Evolution of the Earliest Motets (to Circa 1270)* Musicological Studies 40. 3 vols. Henryville, PA: Institute of Medieval Music, 1985. Commentary.

Sources and Facsimiles

F: Florence, Biblioteca Laurenziana, MS Pluteus 29.1.
> Dittmer, Luther. *Firenze, Pluteus 29.1.* 2 vols. PMMM, 10-11. Brooklyn: Institute of Medieval Music, n.d. Facsimile.

W1: Wolfenbüttel, Herzog August-Bibliothek, MS 628.
> James H. Baxter, *An Old St Andrews Music Book (Cod. Helmst. 628) Published in Facsimile with an Introduction.* St. Andrews University Publications 30. Oxford, Paris: 1931. Facsimile.

W2: Wolfenbüttel, Herzog August-Bibliothek, MS 1099 (1206).
> Dittmer, Luther. *Wolfenbüttel 1099 (1206).* PMMM, 2. Brooklyn: Institute of Medieval Music, 1960. Facsimile.
>
> Anderson, Gordon A. *The Latin Compositions in Fascicles VII and VIII of the Notre Dame Manuscript Wolfenbüttel Helmstadt 1099 (1206).* Musicological Studies, 24. 2 vols. Brooklyn: Institute of Mediaeval Music, 1968. Edition.

St. Victor: Paris, Bibliothèque Nationale, fonds latin 15139.
> Thurston, Ethel. *The Music in the St. Victor Manuscript, Paris, Bibliothèque Nationale Lat. 15139.* Pontifical Institute of Medieval Studies, Studies and Texts. Toronto, 1959. Facsimile.
>
> *Die Sankt Viktor Clausulae und ihre Motetten.* Musikwissenchaftliche Studienbibliothek 5/6, ed. Friedrich Gennrich. Darmstandt and Langen bei Frankfurt. Second edition, 1963. Facsimile and inventory.
>
> Stenzl, Jürg. *Die vierzig Clausulae der Handschrift Paris, Bibliothèque Nationale Latin 15139 (Saint-Victor Clausulae).* Publikationen der schweizerischen Musikforschenden Gesellschaft Ser. II: 22. Bern, 1970. Transcription.

Mo, Montpellier Codex: Montpellier, Faculté de Médicine, MS H. 196.

> Rokseth, Yvonne. *Polyphonies du xiiie siècle. Le Manuscrit H. 196 de la faculté de Médecine de Montpellier*. 4 vols. Paris: L'Oiseau-Lyre, 1935-9. Facsimile, transcriptions, commentary.
>
> Tischler, Hans. *The Montpellier Codex*. Recent Researches in the Middle Ages and the Early Renaissance. 7 vols. in 4. Madison: A-R Editions, 1978. Transcriptions.

Ba, Bamberg: Bamberg, Staatliche Bibliothek, MS Lit. 115.

> Aubry, Pierre. *Cent Motets du XIIIe siècle*. 3 vols. Paris: A. Rouart, Lerolle, & Co., P. Geuthner, 1908. Repr. New York: Broude Brothers, 1964. Facsimile, transcriptions, commentary.
>
> Anderson, Gordon A. *Compositions of the Bamberg Manuscript: Bamberg, Staatsbibliothek, Lit. 115 (olim Ed. IV.6)*. Corpus Mensurabilis Musicae (CMM) 75. American Institute of Musicology (AIM), 1977. Transcriptions.

Hu, Las Huelgas: Burgos, Monasterio de Las Huelgas.

> Anglès, Higini. *El Còdex musical de Las Huelgas*. 3 vols. Barcelona: Institut d'estudis Catalans, Biblioteca de Catalonya, 1931. Repr. New York: AMS Press, 1977. Facsimile and transcription.
>
> Anderson, Gordon A. *The Las Huelgas Manuscript: Burgos, Monsterio de las Huelgas*. CMM 79. 2 vols. Neuhausen-Stuttgart: AIM, 1982. Transcription.

English Motet and Cantilena, 1250-1400

Sources and Facsimiles

Worcester Fragments

> Dittmer, Luther, ed. *Worcester Add. 68, Westminster Abbey 33327, Madrid, Bibl. Nac. 192 and Oxford, Latin Liturgical D 20; London, Add MS 25031; Chicago, MS. 654APPP*. PMMM 5-6. Brooklyn: Institute of Mediaeval Music, 1959 and 1960. Facsimile.
>
> Dittmer, Luther, ed. *The Worcester Fragments*. Musicological Studies and Documents 2. AIM, 1957. Transcription.
>
> Harrison, Frank Ll. and Roger Wibberley. *Manuscripts of Fourteenth-Century English Polyphony: Facsimiles*. Early English Church Music 26. London: Stainer and Bell, 1981.
>
> Summers, William. *English Fourteenth-Century Polyphony: Facsimile Edition of Sources Notated in Score*. Münchner Editionen zur Musikgeschichte, 4. Tutzing: Schneider, 1983.

Editions

Polyphonic Music of the Fourteenth Century (PMFC) 14. Ed. Ernest Sanders. *English Music of the Thirteenth and Early Fourteenth Centuries*. Monaco: L'Oiseau-Lyre, 1979.

PMFC 15. Ed. Frank Ll. Harrison. *Motets of English Provenance*. Monaco: L'Oiseau-Lyre, 1980.

PMFC 16. Ed. Frank Ll. Harrison, Ernest Sanders, and Peter Lefferts. *English Music for Mass and Offices (I)*. Monaco: L'Oiseau-Lyre, 1983.

PMFC 17. Ed. Frank Ll. Harrison, Ernest Sanders, and Peter Lefferts. *English Music for Mass and Offices (II), and Music for Other Ceremonies*. Monaco: L'Oiseau-Lyre, 1985.

The Fourteenth-Century Motet on the Continent

Sources and Editions

Roman de Fauvel: Paris, Bibliothèque Nationale, fonds français 146.

> Avril, François, Nancy Regaldo, and Edward Roesner. *Le Roman de Fauvel and Other Works: Facsimile with Introductory Essay*. New York: Broude Brothers, 1991. Facsimile, commentary.

PMFC 1. Ed. Leo Schrade. *The Roman de Fauvel, The Works of Philippe de Vitry, French Cycles of the Ordinarium Missae*. Monaco: L'Oiseau-Lyre, 1956.

PMFC 2-3. Ed. Leo Schrade. *The Works of Guillaume de Machaut*: Motets. Monaco: L'Oiseau-Lyre, 1956.

PMFC 5. Ed. Frank Ll. Harrison. *Motets of French Provenance*. Texts, with commentary by A.G. Rigg, in a supplementary pamphlet. Monaco: L'Oiseau-Lyre, 1968.

PMFC 12. Ed. Kurt von Fischer and F. Alberto Gallo. *Italian Sacred Music*. Monaco: L'Oiseau-Lyre, 1976.

Günther, Ursula, ed. *The Motets of the Manuscripts Chantilly, Musée Condé, 564 (olim 1047) and Modena, Biblioteca Estense, alpha.M.5,24 (olim lat. 568)*. CMM 39. AIM, 1965.

Ludwig, Friedrich, ed. *Guillaume de Machaut: Musikalische Werke*. 4 vols. Leipzig: Breitkopf & Härtel, 1926, 1954.

The Motet in the Early Fifteenth Century

Anthology

Reaney, Gilbert, ed. *Early Fifteenth-Century Music*. 7 vols. to date. CMM 11. AIM, 1955-1983.

Sources, Editions, Facsimiles

Bologna Q15: Bologna, Civico Museo Bibliografico Musicale, MS Q15.

> Cox, Bobby Wayne. "The Motets of MS Bologna, Civico Museo Bibliografico Musicale, Q15." 2 vols. Ph.D. dissertation, North Texas State University, 1977. Transcriptions and commentary.

Bologna 2216: Bologna, Biblioteca Universitaria, MS 2216.

> F. Alberto Gallo, ed., *Il Codice Musicale 2216 della Biblioteca Universitaria di Bologna*. 2 vols. Monumenta Lyrica Medii Aevi Italica III: Mensurabilia, no. 3. Bologna: Forni Editore, 1966-71. Vol. 1, facsimile; vol. 2, commentary and inventory.

Old Hall: London, British Library, Additional MS 57950.

> Bent, Margaret, and Andrew Hughes, eds. *The Old Hall Manuscript*. 3 vols. in 4. CMM 46. Rome: AIM, 1969-1973. Transcription.

Ox 213: Oxford, Bodleian Library, Canonici Misc. MS 213.

> David Fallows, ed. *Canonici Misc. MS 213*. Facsimile edition. Chicago: University of Chicago Press, 1995.

> Borren, Charles van den, ed. *Polyphonia Sacra*. London: The Plainsong and Medieval Music Society, 1932. Transcriptions.

Composers' Works

Brassart, Johannes. Keith Mixter, ed. *Johannes Brassart, Opera Omnia*. Vol. 2, Motets. CMM 35. AIM, 1971.

Ciconia, Johannes. PMFC 24. Margaret Bent and Anne Hallmark, eds. *The Works of Johannes Ciconia*. Monaco: L'Oiseau-Lyre, 1985.

Dufay, Guillaume. Heinrich Besseler, ed. *Guillaume Dufay, Opera Omnia*. 6 vols. CMM 1. Rome: AIM, 1951-1966.

Guillaume de Van, ed. *Guglielmi Dufay: Opera Omnia*. 4 fascicles. CMM 1. Rome: AIM, 1947-1949.

Dunstable, John. Manfred Bukofzer, ed. *John Dunstable, Complete Works*. 2nd ed., revised by Margaret Bent, Ian Bent and Brian Trowell. Musica Britannica, no. 8. London: Stainer and Bell, 1970.

Lymburgia, Johannes de. Jerry Haller Etheridge. "The Works of Johannes de Lymburgia." Ph.D. dissertation, Indiana University, 1972.

Ann Lewis, ed. *Johannes de Lymburgia: Four Motets*. Newton Abbot: Antico, 1985.

Power, Leonel. Charles Hamm, ed. *Leonel Power, Complete Works*. Vol. 1, Motets. CMM 50. AIM, 1969.

Notes

1   See Hans Tischler, "How were Notre Dame Clausulae Performed?" *Music and Letters* 50 (1969), 273-7.

2   Thomas B. Payne, "Poetry, Politics, and Polyphony: Philip the Chancellor's Contribution to the Music of the Notre Dame School" (Ph.D. diss., University of Chicago, 1991).

3   Tischler edits the source clausula and their related motets one above the other for comparison. See his *The Earliest Motets (to Circa 1270): A Complete Comparative Edition*, 3 vols. (New Haven, 1982). On French motets see Mark Everist, *French Motets in the Thirteenth Century: Music, Poetry, and Genre*, Cambridge Studies in Medieval and Renaissance Music (Cambridge, 1994); and Sylvia Huot, *Allegorical Play in the Old French Motet: The Sacred and the Profane in Thirteenth-Century Polyphony* (Stanford, 1997).

4   See Yvonne Rokseth, *Polyphonies du xiiie siècle: Le Manuscrit H. 196 de la faculté de Médecine de Montpellier*, 4 vols. (Paris, 1935-9) (includes facsimile, transcriptions, and commentary); and Hans Tischler, *The Montpellier Codex*, Recent Researches in the Middle Ages and the Early Renaissance, 7 vols. in 4 (Madison, 1978). For a new dating of the manuscript see Mary E. Wolinski, "The Compilation of the Montpellier Codex," *Early Music History* 11 (1992), 263-301.

5   See Edward Roesner, "The Performance of Parisian Organum," *Early Music* 7 (1979), 174-89.

6   See Margaret Bent, "Notation, III, 3: Western, c1260-1500," *The New Grove*, vol. 13, pp. 362-70.

7   See Roesner, "Parisian Organum," 174-89.

8   Christopher Page, "The Performance of Ars Antiqua Motets," *Early Music* 16 (1988),154-7; and Page, "Polyphony before 1400," in Howard Mayer Brown and Stanley Sadie, eds. *Performance Practice: Music Before 1600*, Norton/Grove Handbooks in Music (New York, 1990), p. 87.

9   For general discussion of the composition and performance of polyphonic music in Paris, see Craig Wright, *Music and Ceremony at Notre Dame of Paris, 500-1500*, Cambridge Studies in Music (Cambridge, 1989); and Christopher Page, *The Owl and the Nightingale: Musical Life and Ideas in France 1100-1300* (Berkeley and Los Angeles, 1990), chapter 6, "The Masters of Organum: The Study and Performance of Parisian Polyphony during the Early Thirteenth Century," especially pp. 148-54.

10   On the role of the Medieval motet see Christopher Page, *Discarding Images: Reflections on Music and Culture in Medieval France* (Oxford, 1993), as well as Huot, *Allegorical Play*, and Everist, *French Motets*. The phrase "clerical chamber music" is borrowed from Ernest Sanders; see "Cantilena and Discant in 14th-Century England," *Musica Disciplina* 19 (1965), 14, n.33.

11   See Richard Crocker, "French Polyphony in the Thirteenth Century," Chapter 13 of Richard Crocker, ed., *New Oxford History of Music*, vol. 2: *The Early Middle Ages to 1300*, 2nd ed. (Oxford and New York, 1990); and Page, "Ars Antiqua Motets," pp. 147-64. On "refrains" see Everist, *French Motets*.

12   Page, "Ars Antiqua Motets," pp. 147-48 and *Discarding Images*, Chapters 2 and 3.

13   Roesner, "Parisian Organum," pp. 174-75.

14   Page, "Ars Antiqua" and "Polyphony before 1400."

15   Page, "Ars antiqua," p. 154.

16   Page, "Polyphony before 1400," p. 92.

17   See Peter Jeffery, "A Four-Part *In seculum* Hocket and a Mensural Sequence in an Unknown Fragment," *Journal of the American Musicological Society* 37 (1984),16-19.

18   On the hocket, see Ernest Sanders, "The Medieval Hocket in Practice and Theory," *Musical Quarterly* 60 (1974), 246-56; and William Dalglish, "The Origin of the Hocket," *Journal of the American Musicological Society* 31 (1978), 3-20.

19   Frank Ll. Harrison, *Music in Medieval Britain* (New York, 1958, 2nd ed., London, 1963; repr. 1980).

20   Polyphonic Music of the Fourteenth Century (PMFC) 14-17: Ernest Sanders, ed., *English Music of the Thirteenth and Early Fourteenth Centuries*, PMFC 14 (Monaco, 1979); Frank Ll. Harrison, ed., *Motets of English Provenance*, PMFC 15 (Monaco, 1980); Frank Ll. Harrison, Ernest Sanders, and Peter Lefferts, eds., *English Music for Mass and Offices (I)*, PMFC 16 (Monaco, 1983); and Frank Ll. Harrison, Ernest Sanders, and Peter Lefferts. *English Music for Mass and Offices (II), and Music for Other Ceremonies*, PMFC 17 (Monaco, 1985).

21   William J. Summers, "English 14th-Century Polyphonic Music: An Inventory of the Extant Manuscript Sources," *Journal of Musicology* 8 (1990), 173-226.

22   The basic work on the English motet is Peter M. Lefferts, *The Motet in England in the Fourteenth Century* (Ann Arbor, 1986), but for a useful summary see David Fenwick Wilson, *Music of the Middle Ages: Style and Structure* (New York, 1990), pp. 273-87.

23   Frank Ll. Harrison, ed., *Motets of English Provenance* (PMFC 15).

24   Frank Ll. Harrison, Ernest Sanders, and Peter Lefferts, eds., *English Music for Mass and Offices (I)* (PMFC 16).

25   Frank Ll. Harrison, ed., *Motets of English Provenance* (PMFC 15).

26   Frank Ll. Harrison, ed., *Motets of English Provenance* (PMFC 15).

27   Ernest Sanders, "Duple Rhythm and Alternate Third Mode in the Thirteenth Century," *Journal of the American Musicological Society* 15 (1962), 249-91.

28   See Roger Bowers, "Choral Institutions Within the English Church: Their Constitution and Development, 1340-1500" (Ph.D. diss., University of East Anglia, 1975);

Christopher Hohler, "Reflections on Some Manuscripts Containing 13th-Century Polyphony," *Journal of the Plainsong and Medieval Music Society* 1 (1978), 2-38; William J. Summers, "The Effect of Monasticism on Fourteenth-Century English Music," in Marc Honneger and Paul Prevost, eds., *Actes du XIIIe Congrès de la Société Internationale de Musicologie, Strasbourg, 1982: La Musique et le rite Sacré et Profane*. 2 vols. (Strasbourg, 1986), II: Communications libres, pp. 104-142; .and Lefferts, *Motet*, pp. 9-13.

[29] Roger Bowers, "The Performing Ensemble for English Church Polyphony, *c.* 1320– *c.* 1390," Stanley Boorman, ed., *Studies in the Performance of Late Mediaeval Music* (Cambridge, 1983), p. 184.

[30] See Page and Andrew Parrott, in their response, "False Voices," *Early Music* 9 (1981), 71-2, to Roger Bowers, "The Performing Pitch of English Fifteenth-Century Church Polyphony," *Early Music* 8 (1980), 21-28. Bowers's reply appears following Page and Parrot in *Early Music* 9 (1981), 73-75.

[31] For editions, see Leo Schrade, ed., *The Roman de Fauvel, The Works of Philippe de Vitry, French Cycles of the Ordinarium Missae* (Monaco, 1956) (PMFC 1); Schrade, *The Works of Guillaume de Machaut* (Monaco, 1956) (PMFC 2-3), Frank Ll. Harrison, *Motets of French Provenance*, Texts, with commentary by A.G. Rigg, in a supplementary pamphlet (Monaco, 1968) (PMFC 5); and Ursula, Günther, ed. *The Motets of the Manuscripts Chantilly, Musée Condé, 564 (olim 1047) and Modena, Biblioteca Estense, alpha.M.5,24 (olim lat. 568)*, Corpus Mensurabilis Musicae 39 (American Institute of Musicology, 1965).

[32] See Sarah Fuller, "On Sonority in Fourteenth-Century Polyphony: Some Preliminary Reflections," *Journal of Music Theory* 30 (1986), 35-70, and "Modal Tenors and Tonal Orientation in Motets of Guillaume de Machaut," in Peter M. Lefferts and Brien Seirup, eds., *Studies in Medieval Music: Festschrift for Ernest H. Sanders. Current Musicology* 45-47 (1990), 199-245.

[33] See Ernest Sanders, "The Medieval Motet," in *Gattungen de Musik: Gedenkschrift Leo Schrade*, ed. Wulf Arlt et al. (Bern, 1973), pp. 497-573, and "Motet: I: Medieval," *The New Grove* vol. 12, pp. 617-28.

[34] For a facsimile and commentary, see François Avril, Nancy Regaldo, and Edward Roesner, eds., *Le Roman de Fauvel and Other Works: Facsimile with Introductory Essay* (New York, 1991); for transcriptions of the polyphony, see PMFC 1.

[35] See Lefferts, *Motet*, pp. 80-92.

[36] See, for example, *Sub arturo plebs*, ed. PMFC 5, and *Humane lingue* ed. PMFC 15.

[37] Examples include the predominance of thirds in *Inter usitata* and the *signum rotundum* in *Regne de pité*, see PMFC 17.

[38] Lefferts, *Motet*, pp. 190, 202-05, 279-80.

[39] See Margaret Bent, "The Fourteenth-Century Italian Motet," in *L'Ars nova italiana del trecento VI*, Atti del Congresso internazionale "L'Europa e la musica del Trecento," Certaldo, 1984, ed. Giulio Cattin and Patrizia Dalla Vecchia (Certaldo, 1992), pp. 85-125. For editions of some of these motets, see Kurt von Fischer and F. Alberto Gallo, eds., *Italian Sacred Music* (Monaco, 1976) (PMFC 12).

[40] See chapter 15.

[41] See Bowers, "The Performing Ensemble," and James T. Igoe, "Performance Practices in the Polyphonic Mass of the Early Fifteenth Century" (Ph.D. diss., University of North Carolina at Chapel Hill, 1971).

[42] See discussion of the chanson in chapters 14 and 17.

[43] Ernest Sanders, "Cantilena and Discant," 7-52, and William J. Summers, "The Effect of Monasticism on Fourteenth-Century English Music," in Marc Honneger and Paul Prevost, eds., *Actes du XIIIe Congrès de la Societé Internationale de Musicologie, Strasbourg, 1982: La Musique et le rite Sacré et Profane*. 2 vols. (Strasbourg, 1986), II: Communications libres, pp. 104-42.

[44] William J. Summers, "Fourteenth-Century English Music: A Review of Three Recent Publications," *Journal of Musicology* 8 (1990), 131-32.

[45] See Summers, "The Effect of Monasticism," pp. 113-14

[46] For a list of the 87 whole and fragmentary surviving fourteenth-century cantilenas, see Lefferts, "Cantilena and Antiphon," pp. 270-72. Many are transcribed in PMFC 17; others are found in the Old Hall manuscript.

[47] Sanders, "Cantilena and Discant," 14, n.33.

[48] Lefferts, "Cantilena and Antiphon," pp. 249-50.

[49] Lefferts, *Motet*, p.166.

[50] "Cantilena (i)." *The New Grove* vol. 3, p. 730.

[51] See Andrew Wathey, "Dunstable in France," *Music and Letters* 67 (1986), 1-36.

[52] See Manfred Schuler, "Die Musik in Konstanz während des Konzils 1414-1418," *Acta Musicologica* 38 (1966), 150-68.

[53] See Julie E. Cumming, *The Motet in the Age of Du Fay* (Cambridge, 1999), for a complete discussion of the motet and cantilena in the early fifteenth century.

[54] See Julie E. Cumming, "The Aesthetics of the Medieval Motet and Cantilena," *Historical Performance* 7 (1994), 71-83.

[55] See Margaret Bent, "A Contemporary Perception of Early Fifteenth-Century Style; Bologna Q15 as a Document of Scribal Editorial Initiative," *Musica Disciplina* 41 (1987), 183-201. Ciconia's motets are in Margaret Bent and Anne Hallmark, eds. *The Works of Johannes Ciconia* (Monaco, 1985) (PMFC 24); for other composers and pieces see Gilbert Reaney, ed., *Early Fifteenth-Century Music*. 7 vols. to date, Corpus Mensurabilis Musicae 11 (American Institute of Musicology, 1955-83), and Bobby Wayne Cox, "The Motets of MS Bologna, Civico Museo Bibliografico Musicale, Q15," 2 vols. (Ph.D. diss., North Texas State University, 1977).

[56] Margaret Bent, *Dunstaple*. Oxford Studies of Composers, no. 17 (London, 1981), and J. Michael Allsen, "Style and Intertextuality in the Isorhythmic Motet 1400-1440" (Ph.D. diss., University of Wisconsin, Madison, 1992).

[57] See also Robert Nosow, "The Equal-Discantus Motet Style After Ciconia," *Musica Disciplina* 45 (1991 [actually published 1995]), 221-275.

[58] Reaney, *Early Fifteenth-Century Music*, vol. 7.

[59] See, for example, the problematic contratenor of Du Fay's *Gaude virgo mater Christi*.

[60] Jerry Haller Etheridge, "The Works of Johannes de Lymburgia" (Ph.D. diss., Indiana University, 1972).

[61] See Julie E. Cumming, "Music for the Doge in Early Renaissance Venice," *Speculum* 67 (1992), 324-64.

[62] See Charles Hamm, *A Chronology of the Works of Guillaume Dufay Based on a Study of Mensural Practice*, Princeton Studies in Music, 1 (Princeton, 1964); Alejandro Planchart, "Tempo and Proportions," in Brown and Sadie, *Performance Practice*, pp. 126-144; and Anna Maria Busse Berger, *Mensuration and Proportion Signs: Origins and Evolution* (Oxford, 1993). For a new interpretation of cut-circle, tempus perfectum diminutum, see Margaret Bent, "The Early Use of the Sign Ø," *Early Music* 24 (1996), 199-225.

[63]   Giulio Cattin, "Church Patronage of Music in Fifteenth-Century Italy," in Iain Fenlon, ed., *Music in Medieval and Early Modern Europe: Patronage, Sources and Texts*, pp. 21-36 (Cambridge, 1981).

[64]   David Fallows, "Specific Information on the Ensembles for Composed Polyphony, 1400-1474," in Boorman, *Studies*, pp. 110-31, and Igoe, "Performance Practices," pp. 55-63, 75-94.

[65]   Fallows, "Specific Information," pp. 114-17.

[66]   See Heinrich Besseler, "Die Entstehung der Posaune," *Acta Musicologica* 22 (1950), 8-35; Vivian Safowitz (Ramalingam), "Trumpet Music and Trumpet Style in the Early Renaissance," Unpublished M.M. Thesis, University of Illinois, 1965; [Safowitz] Ramalingam, "The *trumpetum* in Strasbourg M222 C22," in Marc Honneger and Paul Prevost, eds., *Actes du XIIIe Congrès de la Societé Internationale de Musicologie, Strasbourg, 1982: La Musique et le rite Sacré et Profane*. 2 vols. (Strasbourg, 1986), II: Communications libres, pp. 143-60; and Chapter 27 below.

[67]   For Venice, see Jonathan Glixon, "Music at the Venetian Scuole Grandi, 1440-1540," in *Music in Medieval and Early Modern Europe: Patronage, Sources and Texts*, ed. Iain Fenlon (Cambridge, 1981), p. 204; for Rome and Cambrai, see Craig Wright, "Voices and Instruments in the Art Music of Northern France During the Fifteenth Century: A Conspectus," IMS, *Report of the 12th Congress, Berkeley, 1977* (Kassel, 1981), pp. 646-47.

4. Polyphonic Mass Ordinary

Alejandro Enrique Planchart

The Winchester Repertory

The earliest medieval polyphony for the Ordinary of the Mass was discussed briefly in the chapter on organum. It consists of the settings, set down at Winchester between 996 and 1006, of a number of Kyrie tropes and Kyries, as well as of Gloria tropes and the Greek Gloria.[1] Mentioning these pieces in the organum chapter I noted that the manuscript where they are copied, the famous Winchester Troper at Corpus Christi College in Cambridge, was left unfinished, and had the work been finished we probably would have in it organa to the Sanctus and the Agnus and their tropes as well. Since polyphonic Mass Ordinary settings are, as a rule, absent from Continental sources until the fourteenth century, but seem to be plentiful in what survives of twelfth- and thirteenth-century English sources, it maybe that such a tradition existed in England and Scotland, and can be traced to the Winchester school of the late tenth century.[2] In any case, it may be useful here to consider the differences between the Kyrie and Gloria settings in the Winchester repertory since these differences may affect what performers may choose to do if they decide to add organal parts to a performance of the Winchester Sanctus and Agnus settings. This is not an impossible task since the surviving Winchester polyphony shows close stylistic links to what the author of the *Musica Enchiriadis* views as organum at the fourth below.[3]

The oldest layer of the Winchester Kyrie repertory, which is the only one provided with organa, is exceptional for its time in that it consists entirely of true Kyrie tropes and of plain Kyries. The far more common Latin Kyries or Kyrie verses are absent from the original redaction and appear only as later additions in both Corpus Christi 473 and Bodley 775. The Winchester *organista* (most likely Wulfstan the Cantor) provided organa for both the tropes and the Kyrie melodies. This much can be determined by comparing the organal part with the principal voices, which survive in the main in both manuscripts. Unfortunately, because the melodies for most of the tropes (and the Kyries that go with them) are essentially unique to the Winchester repertory and do not survive in later sources, they cannot be reconstructed at all. Only the first trope and its Kyrie, the celebrated melody of *Te Christe rex supplices*, have principal voices that can be recovered and thus permit a reconstruction of the organa.[4] Several of the principal voices to the plain Kyries, however, do survive in sources that give them in transcribable notation and thus permit a reconstruction of the Winchester organa for them.

The Glorias present a different picture. Virtually all of the Gloria melodies and those of their tropes are recoverable, and thus they provide a solid foundation for a reconstruction of the organal settings. But as Andreas Holschneider discovered, the notation of the organal part becomes identical with the plainsong for the Gloria itself.[5] The first implication of this is that, of course, the tropes were soloistic and so was polyphony, so that in the choral sections of the Gloria the solo singers simply joined with the *schola* in monophonic song. The second implication is that, in Winchester at the end of the tenth century the entire Kyrie eleison was most likely the province of solo singers, a practice that is at variance with those continental centers for which we have some information, where the Kyrie tropes or the Latin verses were sung by soloists and the melismatic version by the *schola*.[6]

This, in turn, has some bearing in what one would do when adding a polyphonic part to the Winchester Sanctus and Agnus. The nature of the Sanctus tropes seems to suggest a treatment similar to what one encounters in the Glorias, so that only the tropes and certainly the one extended Osanna prosula found in the Winchester tropers would be provided with an organal part, while the official text would be sung in plainsong. The Agnus could be sung in the same manner, but in some ways they do resemble the Kyrie repertory at Winchester, and it is not impossible to see how they would have been sung by the soloists in organum throughout.

We must realize, however, that, from what we have left, this represents the tradition of Winchester alone. We have no written polyphony from anywhere else in Europe at the time except for a small fragment at Fleury, and none of it deals with the Ordinary of the Mass.

Continental Settings before 1300

The next kinds of evidence that we have for settings of the Ordinary of the Mass come from the treatises and from what has been described as "primitive polyphony."[7] The Milan treatise, *Ad organum faciendum*, has as one of its examples a setting of the Kyrie verse, *Cunctipotens genitor deus*, which is widely known because it has been used in countless anthologies of medieval music,[8] but it is perhaps one of the most graceless pieces to survive from the Middle Ages, and seems to be purely a text book example. Besides this piece there are, scattered here and there among late chant sources, simple settings of the Ordinary in two and some times three voices in *cantus planus binatim*. Many of these may be rather late examples, dating from the thirteenth or fourteenth centuries, but they are often elegant, euphonious, and unpretentious, and performers seeking early polyphonic versions of the Ordinary of the Mass would do well to give these works some attention.[9]

The Aquitanian polyphony of the twelfth and thirteenth centuries is devoid of settings of the Ordinary of the Mass, at least in terms of the sources that have survived. Not so, however, its Compostelan counterpart. The Codex Calixtinus transmits polyphony for two Kyries: the melody of Vatican Kyrie XII with the verses *Rex immense pater*,[10] and the melody of Vatican Kyrie IV with verses 1, 5, and 7 of *Cunctipotens genitor deus*, which a long liturgical tradition regarded as the Kyrie melody and verses most often associated with the Masses for an apostle. *Rex immense pater* is set in discant, while *Cunctipotens genitor deus* receives a florid setting.[11]

Polyphonic settings of the Ordinary of the Mass are absent from the central repertory of the school of Notre Dame, and only in the late thirteenth century do we meet with a few motets that use a Kyrie melody as their tenor as well as one on the *Ite missa est.*[12] But with a single exception these pieces are all secular works, and the exception is clearly a Marian piece with no obvious connection with the Mass. Indeed, these motets appear precisely at the time when Parisian composers are beginning to abandon the traditional repertory of motet tenors taken from the melismas of the responsorial chants, and are beginning to employ Marian antiphons as well as Rondeau refrains and dance tunes as a source for their tenors.[13]

British Settings, 1200–1400

In contrast to the French tradition, the English and Scottish sources of the thirteenth century present a very different picture. The eleventh fascicle of W 1, which contains a purely insular repertory, transmits an extensive collection of polyphonic music: the Masses of the Blessed Virgin, including seven Kyries with Latin verses, one Gloria with tropes, three Sanctus with tropes, and two Agnus Dei with tropes, all in two-voice discant settings.[14] Further, the main corpus of the manuscript, which transmits the Parisian organa, has a number of settings of the Sanctus and the Agnus in three-voice discant added in the folios originally left blank between the different sections of the Notre Dame repertory. Besides the repertory in W 1, a large number of thirteenth-century English settings of the Ordinary of the Mass has turned up in fragmentary manuscripts. Early on scholars dubbed this style the "Worcester School," since the first sizable fragments to be discovered appear to have originated at Worcester cathedral,[15] but a considerable number of other pieces has been discovered in the last two decades. Virtually the entire surviving repertory of late thirteenth-and fourteenth-century English Mass setting is available in a reliable modern edition.[16] In the sources late thirteenth- and early fourteenth-century English pieces are almost all notated in score with the text given only for the lowest voice. In this respect the presentation of these pieces resembles that of the conductus. The rhythmic and contrapuntal style of the music is very close to that of the conductus or else that of the mid-thirteenth-century motet,[17] although the rhythmic surface in virtually all pieces proceeds by unambiguous trochaic rhythms that are typical of English polyphony, which avoided both the second and third rhythmic modes. The thirteenth-century Ordinary settings make little use of what becomes almost a national trait in early fourteenth-century English music, namely voice exchange over a *pes* typical of the rondellus and the isoperiodic motet, but as the fourteenth century progresses such procedures begin to appear in some of the English ordinaries.[18]

English harmony, unlike that of the contemporary motet and conductus polyphony in France, is full of imperfect consonances—thirds and sixths—and seems to require a different approach to the tuning of the ensemble, away from the strictly Pythagorean tuning that Christopher Page feels is appropriate for French medieval polyphony, and closer to just intonation.[19] Judging from the ranges of the parts as written, virtually all thirteenth- and early fourteenth-century English polyphony requires an ensemble of tenors and baritones singing largely one to a part except for the passages in plainsong.[20] It is, of course, quite possible to use women's voices instead of men, and any ensemble which does any of this repertory should pick a pitch level where the singers can sing their parts easily and comfortably. The one combination that seems always to present problems is one where male and female voices are mixed. My experience is that in those cases one or more of the parts will lie too low or too high for some of the singers.

The kinds of Mass polyphony found in English sources in the thirteenth and early fourteenth centuries are almost entirely absent in contemporary French sources, but can be found, albeit in smaller numbers, in Spanish manuscripts, notably the large anthology copied ca. 1325 for the nunnery of Las Huelgas in Burgos, and in smaller sources and fragments copied elsewhere in the peninsula. The presence of such pieces in the Las Huelgas codex is telling because the manuscript contains, by and large, music from thirteenth-century Paris. Most of the Ordinary settings have no French concordances, however, but some of them appear in other Spanish manuscripts.[21] The two-voice settings in Las Huelgas seem to hark back to an older style close to that of *cantus planus binatim*, but the three-voice settings are very close to the discant one finds in the Parisian conductus and motets, and in this respect they differ in sonority from their English counterparts.

Given the very fragmentary state of the surviving English sources it is difficult to say with any assurance if relatively large collections of music for the Ordinary of the Mass were compiled in England in the late Middle Ages, but the little evidence that there is suggest that such collection might have been more prevalent in England than in the Continent. The surviving continental sources, for the fourteenth century, larger in number than those from England, consist mostly of collections of secular music. It is true that in Ivrea, Biblioteca Capitolare 115, and Apt Basilique de Sainte Anne 16 bis we have two relatively large collections of French Mass compositions from the end of the fourteenth century that reflect the international repertory of the Papal Chapel at Avignon, and indeed concordances to Mass movements found in these two manuscripts can be found throughout most of Western Europe.[22] Still, the existence of a source such as the Old Hall manuscript in England, a vastly more extensive collection of Mass music (albeit about a half century younger than Ivrea or Apt) which seems to date back in part to the final decades of the fourteenth century, suggests that the cultivation of polyphonic settings of the Ordinary of the Mass was more extensive in England than on the continent during the fourteenth century.[23]

Fourteenth-Century France

In France, and slightly later in Italy, polyphonic compositions for the Ordinary of the Mass begin to appear in the course of the fourteenth century essentially as isolated movements. The manuscripts that transmit them give the impression that the polyphonic ordinaries were thought of and thus copied in the same manner as the plainsong ordinaries had been copied in chant books for centuries, that is, with all the Kyries grouped together, then all the Glorias, and so on.[24] But it is precisely during the late thirteenth and fourteenth centuries that scribes began following the new Franciscan liturgy for the papal court and organizing the plainsong ordinaries into cycles consisting of the Kyrie, Gloria, Sanctus, Agnus, and Ite missa est.[25] This may have provided a model for composers writing polyphonic settings of the Ordinary, although one should note that the Credo, for example, was never part of the plainsong cycles, while in the case of early groupings of polyphonic movements composers seem to have regarded the two sections with long texts—Gloria and Credo—as suitable for pairing, and treated the Sanctus and the Agnus in a similar manner. The Kyrie remained an independent section for some time.

Much has been written suggesting that some of the early polyphonic "Mass cycles" were the product of scribal initiatives, that is, they were put together by the copyists, who would bring together pieces of different styles or even by different composers. And this is seen as evidence of a "tendency" towards the creation of unified Mass cycles. The evidence is however very ambiguous. One of the most celebrated cases, that of the "Mass of Tournai" provides no answer one way or another. The six independent polyphonic movements are the only polyphonic settings in the source that transmits them as a cycle and were intended for a specific ceremony, the Saturday Mass in honor of the Virgin. Thus it could well be that if the singers in the cathedral had wanted a larger repertory we would have had a manuscript with a series of Kyries, and series of Glorias, and so on.[26] On the other hand, some of the "composite" Ordinary cycles found in the early fifteenth century may be more than just the product of scribal initiatives and reflect actual performances by a given institution.[27] In the fourteenth century only a handful of composers seems to have thought of writing an entire polyphonic Ordinary as a single composition, and of those efforts only Guillaume de Machaut's *La Messe de Nostre Dame* survives complete. The Machaut Mass survives complete only because Machaut took pains to have his complete works copied in splendid manuscripts a number of times throughout his career, and a good number of these presentation copies have survived. Were we to rely only on the anthologies, as we do in the case of every other fourteenth-century composer, only one movement, the *Ite missa est* would be known to us.[28] Three other fourteenth-century composers are known to have written apparently complete Masses, Jehan Lambulet, whose work, known as "The Sorbonne Mass" survives incomplete,[29] and Jehan Vaillant and Royllart, whose Masses were listed in 1431 as being, together with Machaut's Mass, in a now lost manuscript at the Château de Quesnoy.[30]

In writing music for the Ordinary of the Mass, fourteenth-century composers in France had a number of polyphonic models at hand. The simplest of these models, and the one used almost exclusively by the English composers, was the conductus, leading to what Hanna Stäblein Harder calls "simultaneous style,"[31] which is, for example, the compositional strategy adopted by Machaut for the Gloria and Credo of his Mass (except for the "Amen" section of each movement).

87

A second, and equally obvious compositional strategy was that of the so-called isorhythmic motet, which allowed the appropriate liturgical plainsong to be used as the foundation of the polyphonic texture. Because of the length of the plainsong Glorias and Credos, composers avoided using them as the basis for motet-style settings of those movements, but such settings, using freely constructed tenors are plentiful in the surviving repertory.[32] English Mass movements composed along these lines are virtually unknown in the early and middle fourteenth century, but become relatively common in the early fifteenth[33] so that it would appear that the organization of Mass movements along the lines of the "isorhythmic" motet was a French contribution.

A third compositional strategy was to set the text of the Ordinary to a texture very similar to that evolved by French composers, and most likely by Guillaume de Machaut himself, for the composition of polyphonic secular songs. By the third quarter of the fourteenth century, this texture consisted most frequently of a melodic text-carrying voice [*cantus*] supported by a a tenor and a contratenor, which moved roughly in the same range as each other and had a slightly lower tessitura than that of the cantus.[34] Such a strategy has been called variously "discant style,"[35] and "cantilena" style.[36] At first blush it would be easy to see how such a song technique could be applied to the short text movements of the Mass, since for these the text setting in the cantus would approach the kinds of text setting one finds in much of the central and late fourteenth-century French song repertory. In the case of the Gloria and the Credo this would be less obvious, but as the ballade became more expansive in the hands of Machaut's successors, they had in it a model for a large-scale musical structure built along the lines of the song texture.

It will not do, however, to make too sharp a distinction in the Mass repertory between motet style and discant or cantilena style. The second seems to have evolved from the first and not only did it retain some of its traits, but composers seem to have returned to such motet-like procedures as mensural changes and the use of hocket when they used the discant or cantilena for Mass settings. One reason for this may be a matter of formal musical organization.[37] In the song forms it is the text that acts as the primary determinant of the large-scale shape of the piece; but with the Mass text, particularly in the case of the Gloria and the Credo which lack the obvious text repetitions of the Kyrie and the Agnus, or the parallelism and repetitions of the Sanctus composers seems to have turned to mensuration changes, and scoring changes (such as alternations of duos and full sections) as means of articulating the shape of the movements and eventually also as a means of interrelating several movements to each other.[38]

Fourteenth-Century Italy

The Italian repertory of fourteenth-century music for the Ordinary of the Mass, unlike the French repertory, survives in scattered sources, so that not until the comprehensive effort of Kurt von Fischer and F. Alberto Gallo did we have a clear picture of the extent and nature of the repertory; isolated works and fragments continue to appear as the contents of Italian archives are examined by scholars.[39]

On the basis of the surviving repertory there are some sharp differences with French and English music. The Kyrie was virtually ignored by Italian composers,[40] the Sanctus and Agnus, though not ignored, were not extensively set to polyphony. By and large the largest number of settings are those of the Gloria and Credo, often composed in pairs.

The earliest Italian polyphonic ordinaries were most likely improvised as *cantus planus binatim* but not necessarily written down. This is perhaps what was intended by the indications in the *Ordo officiorum* of Siena cathedral, written in 1215, by the indication "cum organo" appended to a number of the items listed.[41] Several surviving Italian Mass movements barely go beyond such a setting. They consist of two voices moving together, but written in Italian mensural notation with virtually no melodic ornamentation.[42] A Credo by Bartolino da Padova moves beyond this and approaches the kinds of two-voice texture one finds in the *trecento* madrigal, even though the ornamentation is quite modest.[43] More elaborate are pieces such as the Sanctus of Lorenzo Masini,[44] where the rhythmic surface resembles that of a full blown madrigal. In terms of counterpoint the piece has long stretches of virtual heterophony, where the two voices outline the same melody essentially in unison, but one of the voices provides a considerable amount of ornamentation while the other is entirely plain.

The anonymous three-voice settings as well as those attributed to Filipotto da Caserta and Matteo da Perugia inhabit a world halfway between the conductus and the texture one finds in the three-voice ballata settings at the end of the century. And in this respect their polyphonic texture is quite similar to that of French Mass sections that use the chanson format. This is hardly surprising, since in fact these movements seem to be the product of north Italian centers where the influence of French music was quite prominent at the end of the trecento. The settings by Ciconia and Antonio Zachara da Teramo approach the textures of the motet (in the case of Ciconia) and the polyphonic ballata (in the case of Antonio), several of whose pieces are built upon material derived from his own secular works.[45] In many of their works both men begin to use a systematic alternation of reduced and full textures, often coupled with mensural changes, as a means of organizing the movements. This will become a prominent feature of the Mass music by composers of the next generation. Further, in the music of both men, but particularly that of Ciconia, imitation and the reiteration of short motives begins to play an important part.

Finally there is in Italy a small but significant repertory of polyphonic Mass settings in what appears to be keyboard notation. The best known examples are the Kyrie and Gloria settings in Faenza, Biblioteca Comunale MS 117,[46] but a few similar settings in other manuscripts have been discovered relatively recently in Padua and Assisi.[47] These suggest the existence of a practice of singing the Mass using plainsong sections sung by the choir alternating with polyphonic settings for the organ. Not surprisingly, this is a north Italian tradition, and indeed among the earliest organ music that we have from northern Italy after the Faenza manuscript, the early sixteenth-century manuscript from Castell' Arquato, has also such "organ

Masses;"[48] and the tradition continues in the works of Claudio Merulo and the Gabrielis.

Cypriot Repertory

A final repertory of late fourteenth- and early fifteenth-century Mass music needs to be noted, and it is the rather extensive collection of music originating at the Lusignan court in Cyprus and now preserved uniquely in a single manuscript in the University Library in Turin.[49]

The manuscript itself must have been copied after November 1413, when Pope John XXIII granted King Janus of Cyprus to have an Office composed in honor of St. Hylarion, for the Office, in plainsong, occupies the opening folios of the manuscript.[50] It transmits three Glorias, seven Gloria-Credo pairs, and a four movement *cantus firmus* Mass (Kyrie-Sanctus) added later at the end of the manuscript. In many ways the style of the music belongs not so much to the fourteenth century but to the styles emerging in France and Italy in the early fifteenth century. Though one can make some distinctions between relatively simple pieces in simultaneous style (Gloria and Credo No. 6) and pieces overtly in the style of the motet (Gloria No. 1), most utilize a dense contrapuntal texture of near simultaneous motion in all voices but with sophisticated and subtle rhythmic differentiation of the parts. The four-movement cycle added at the end belongs in an entirely different tradition in that it uses a single *cantus firmus*, as yet unidentified, as the basis for each of the four movements, it thus belongs among the earliest examples of a cyclic Mass. Given that it is anonymous, and that it comes from a land as remote from England, the country that virtually all scholarship views as the *locus* of the rise of the *cantus firmus* Mass, it has received no attention from scholars or performers. This points to a serious historiographic problem with current ideas of center and periphery in terms of our view of the development of musical styles. That, and a certain reluctance to deal with anonymous works, which pose extra problems in securing geographic and chronological placement, has led to the virtual ignoring on the part of modern scholarship of a large and very important repertory of Mass music composed in the middle decades of the fifteenth century, apparently in Germany and Austria, along the lines of the English *cantus firmus* tradition. These works represent some of the earliest continental *cantus firmus* Masses and show extraordinary technical fluency and musical inspiration. And yet they had remained largely unnoticed until the recent work of Reinhard Strohm.[51]

Developments after 1400

Continental composers turned to the Ordinary of the Mass with greater frequency in the early fifteenth century. As noted above, Antonio Zachara and Johannes Ciconia composed a series of Gloria-Credo pairs that show important new developments in terms of the textures used and the attempts at a rational organization of the large-scale structure of the movements. Composers of the generations whose works begin to appear in sources from 1400 to 1430 appear to have followed the same patter as Ciconia and Zachara (as well as the Cypriot composers in the Turin manuscript) in favoring Gloria-Credo pairs. Still, the impression one gets from the surviving repertory is that polyphony for the Mass was not a common occurrence in the early part of the fifteenth century. For example, between the end of the Great Schism in 1417 and the death of pope Eugenius IV in 1447, the papal chapel, one of the most prestigious musical organizations in Europe, had a remarkably large number of composers among its members—far more than the chapels of popes of the fourteenth century or the succeeding fifteenth-century popes until the reign of Alexander VI at the end of the century—and yet, with the exception of Guillaume Du Fay, these men seem to have left very little music for the Mass. A list of known composers in the papal chapel in this period other than Du Fay, and their music for the Mass is as follows.[52]

Name	Mass Compositions Preserved	Years in Chapel
Arnold de Lantins	1 Mass, 2 Gloria-Credo pairs	1431-32
Barthélemy Poignare	1 Gloria	1425-33
Gautier Liebert	1 Lady Mass (with propers), 1 Kyrie	1429
Guillaume de Malebecque	No music for the Mass	1427/1431-38
Guillaume Lemacherier	1 Gloria, 2 Credos	1418-21
Jehan Brassart	3 Kyries (1 dubious), 2 Glorias, 1 Gloria-Credo pair, 1 Credo, 1 Sanctus, 1 Agnus	1430-31
Jehan Sohier	No music for the Mass	1443-1445
Niccolo Pietro Zacharia	1 Gloria	1420-24/1434
Nicolas Grenon	1 Gloria	1425-27
Pierre Fontaine	No music for the Mass	1420-28
Richard de Bellengues	No music for the Mass	1422-25/1427-28

Their contemporaries in other courts seem to have followed the same pattern. The extensive collection of early fifteenth-century music published by Gilbert Reaney simply confirms such a view.[53]

Compare these figures for the one member of the papal chapel in these years who seems to have taken up Mass composition in earnest, Guillaume Du Fay: 4 plenary Mass cycles (proper and Ordinary), 1 freely composed Mass, 1 requiem (lost), 4 *cantus firmus* cycles, 2 short Masses (KSA), 3 Gloria-Credo pairs, 3 Sanctus-Agnus pairs, 11 Kyries, 8 Glorias (one doubtful). This represents a drastic change in focus in terms of the types of repertory to which the composer paid attention, and it goes beyond the simple matter of our having considerably more music by Du Fay than by the other composers on the list. The amount of music for the Mass attributed to Gilles de Bins, called Binchoys, who apparently wrote no Mass cycles, is also well beyond what we have from the composers listed above or from those edited in Reaney's series.[54] There is, however, a considerable number of anonymous settings in north Italian and Swiss anthologies copied in the 1430s and 1440s, which appear to transmit an international repertory that reached northern Italy at the time of the councils. These include: Oxford, Bodleian Library, Canonici misc. 213,[55] Bologna, Biblioteca Universitaria, MS 2216,[56] Aosta, Biblioteca del Seminario Maggiore, MS 15 (*olim* A 1 D 19),[57] and Trento, Museo Provinciale d'Arte, Castello del Buon Consiglio MSS 1374 (87) and 1379 (92),[58] may represent compositions written in the first quarter of the fifteenth century.

The repertory of Mass music from the continental generation of Grenon, who is an almost contemporary of John Dunstaple,[59] even if one includes the anonymous music in the manuscripts just mentioned, shows little interest writing Mass cycles on a *cantus firmus*. The earliest continental cycles, such as the Reson Mass,[60] the Missa *Verbum incarnatum* of Arnold de Lantins, the Lady Mass of Reignault Liebert,[61] the *Missa Trumpetta* of Estienne Grossin,[62] and the Masses *Resvellies vous* and *Sancti Jacobi* of Du Fay,[63] reveal a wide variety of styles and compositional strategies. Some of the much-discussed techniques of unification are there—motto beginnings, similar alternations of texture and mensuration and similar cleffing and finals[64]—but far more important, as Strohm has argued, are the vitality and imagination that these works show in their approach to the formal and textural problems presented by setting the long prose texts of the Gloria and the Credo in opposition to the short texts of the other movements.[65] Most of these works, as well as the many isolated movements and pairs from the first half of the fifteenth century, adopt a style that often moves fluidly from a texture similar to that of the so-called isorhythmic motet to the chanson texture or the simple discant texture apparently pioneered by Du Fay in the 1420s and known as *fauxbourdon*.[66] In many of the isolated movements, particularly in Kyrie settings, the simple discant or chanson carries with it an elaboration of the plainsong in the top voice, a trait these settings share with antiphon, hymn, and sequence settings of this period and which was used as well by English composers of Dunstaple's generation in their antiphons and hymns, though virtually never in Mass settings.

It was English composers who apparently first extended the isorhythmic motet format to all the sections of the Mass. The purpose of this may have been twofold, first, the *cantus firmus*, acting as a regulator of the contrapuntal progressions provided a means of interrelating musically the different movements in ways that the composers apparently found interesting, and second, the emblematic possibilities of the *cantus firmus*, which had been used extensively in the motet repertory since the thirteenth century, allowed the composer to imbue a special liturgical or ceremonial significance to any given Mass setting. The first of these goals, resulting in what modern scholars view as musical unification, has been extensively discussed in the literature.[67] The second has been discussed only incidentally when the emblematic connotations of the tenors helps scholars with the dating or location of a work, even though with few exceptions we lack the knowledge of the circumstances that makes such attempts go beyond an educated guess.

In the English *cantus firmus* cycles, the driven, rhythmically nervous style of the motet upper voices gave way to a smoothly flowing rhythm that scholars have defined, together with the emphasis on imperfect consonances, as part of the *contenance angloise* which influenced Continental composers from about 1430 on.[68] Some of the earliest English cyclic Masses, such as John Dunstaple's now incomplete *Da gaudiorum praemia*, are strictly "isorhythmic" in the structure of each movements. But the majority of them, including Leonel Power's *Alma redemptoris mater*,[69] and the *Missa Rex saeculorum* attributed to both Dunstaple and Leonel,[70] show a flexible approach to the tenor, including some ornamentation and paraphrasing, a trait retained by later composer, particularly in the Masses for three voices.[71] The English tradition crystallizes in a series of anonymous Masses, most likely written in the 1430s and early 1440s, where the *cantus firmus* regulates not only the contrapuntal flow of the music but the structure of the movements independently of their text. These Masses show a structural plan that varies slightly from work to work, but which results in the Gloria and the Credo forming a closely related pair, the Sanctus and the Agnus another, with the Kyrie as either a separate entity or related to the Gloria and Credo. Works in this repertory include a group of pieces that apparently achieved a certain circulation on the continent, including the cycles on *Fuit homo missus*, *Salve sancta parens*, and *Quem malignus spiritus*, for three voices, and *Veterem hominem* as well as the famous *Missa Caput* that include a fourth voice below the tenor.[72]

The influence of the English *cantus firmus* Mass, despite the interest in English music that led to the wholesale copying of English works in France and Italy in the fifteenth century, does not make itself felt in continental works until the middle of the century, when we encounter Johannes Okeghem's own *Caput* Mass, closely modeled upon the English work,[73] Guillaume Du Fay's *Missa Se la face ay pale*, which reflects closely the English procedures in *cantus firmus* usage and in structural design,[74] and Juan Cornago's *Missa Ayo visto lo mappamundi*. Here one finds the same procedures in the three-voice Masses of the English composers, such as that on *Rex saeculorum*, applied with stunning originality not to a plainsong *cantus firmus* but to an early Neapolitan barzelleta that serves as the foundation for the work.[75] As noted above, among the early continental reactions to the English *cantus firmus* Mass there is a considerable number of Austrian and German works that remain still unavailable in reliable or useful modern edition.[76]

The mid-fifteenth-century four voice Masses, both in England and in the continent, still show the layering of the voices common to most of the earlier motet repertory, but the three-voice works, particularly those not built on a *cantus firmus*, begin to show an similarity of melodic motion in all the parts which is found indeed in the antiphon and hymn settings from the early fifteenth century on.[77] Much of what will happen with the Ordinary of the Mass between 1450 and 1475 is the gradual integration of the musical surface found in the freely composed three-voice

Masses and the four voice works on a *cantus firmus*, something that can bee seen in the later works of Du Fay, Okeghem, and Frye, and paves the way for the Mass settings of the next generation.

Performance Considerations

As twentieth-century scholars and performers became more and more interested in recovering the music of the Middle Ages as sounding music and not simply as notes on paper, the matter of what kind of an ensemble performed these different repertories then, and what kinds of ensembles can do it justice now has become increasingly important. The basic assumption that has never been questioned is that the singers of this repertory were all male although, given the traditions of church choirs known first hand to twentieth-century musicians, which are largely those that combine the voices of boys and men in single polyphonic texture, it was at first suggested that such a combination had been used for much of this repertory. As will appear below, such a conclusion is probably premature.

In any event, a purely vocal performance is not particularly hard to imagine for the compositions in simultaneous style or those that arose from the traditions of *cantus planus binatim*. After all, the underpinning of both styles, the thirteenth-century conductus and plainsong itself, are known to be entirely vocal styles. The textures of those pieces that took over the traditions of the motet, whether that of the *ars antiqua* as in the case of some of the English Mass movements of the early fourteenth century, or that of the *ars nova* and beyond as is the case of many of the French fourteenth-century Mass sections, as well as many by Ciconia, Antonio Zachara, and the composers of the Old Hall manuscript, present a problem in that the lower parts are almost always entirely without text and seldom have enough notes to accommodate even a complete grammatical phrase of the text that the upper voices are singing above them. Mass sections that adopt the texture of secular song, whether French or Italian, present essentially the same problem with their textless and heavily ligated lower parts. Thus suggestions for performance in editions even as recent as that of the Las Huelgas Codex by Gordon Anderson, assumed a combination of voices and instruments, where instruments were used for the textless parts and voices only for the parts with text. The same was applied to the Mass section that made use of the chanson format, for until the early 1980s scholars and performers alike assumed that the chanson repertory of the fourteenth and fifteenth centuries was performed most of the time by a combination of voices and instruments.

The archival and iconographic evidence that has come to light in the last few decades concerning not only the ecclesiastical institutions in the medieval cities, but the private chapels of a number of princes presents a very different picture. The choral institutions throughout Europe were relatively small, consisting of between four and twelve adult singers and between four and six choirboys when the church in question had a choir school. The papal chapel, which served as the model for most choral foundations on the continent, had an ideal number of twelve singers,[78] though it fluctuated from as few as five in the early 1430s to as many as sixteen later in the century.[79] Roughly the same numbers can be found in the Cathedral of Cambrai, where despite the fluctuating number of *petit vicaires* during the fifteenth century (the first century for which we have complete lists for several decades) the constitutions and official documents refer often to the "twelve vicars."[80] Cambrai is typical also in that it kept a choir school and the number of choristers was officially put at six (four in most other French churches), but a few other boys were also given instruction in music and appointed as choristers as places came open.[81] What obtained at Cambrai can be observed with little variation at Notre Dame in Paris,[82] Bruges,[83] and Brussels.[84] In the case of the courts, the best known and most thorough studies are of the Dukes of Burgundy, who had a considerable musical establishment from the end of the fourteenth century to the death of Charles the Bold in 1477.[85] There are extensive lists of chapel members, but virtually nothing about the ceremonies themselves, and the few descriptions of performances in the chronicles deal not with the liturgy but with special performances such as those that took place during the Banquet of the Pheasant.[86] There is, however, a relatively late document, an order for the chapel drafted during the first year of the reign of Charles the Bold, which details the numbers of singers to be used for each of the voices of a polyphonic composition. The document and its implications are discussed in a perceptive and useful essay by David Fallows.[87] It indicates that for polyphonic music the custom in the Burgundian chapel was to use about twice the number of singers for the top voice as for the lower parts, but when one considers that the top voice was sung by falsettists, and that in France, and at the time the document was redacted the French term "en fausset" was used as the equivalent of the Latin "voce submissa," it is clear that the larger number of singers used in the top part was probably intended to bring all voices into equal relief.[88]

Other courts whose musical establishments have been studied in some detail, though not always in terms of the Middle Ages are those of the Kings of Aragon in Barcelona and in Naples,[89] the Este in Ferrara,[90] the Sforza in Milan,[91] and the Dukes of Savoy in Chambéry and Turin.[92] In all of these cases, as with Burgundy, we have chapels numbering between twelve and twenty four singers, but virtually no information as to how many were used at any given performance. The same applies to the English choral institutions of the fourteenth and early fifteenth centuries despite the immense amount of information on them unearthed by Roger Bowers.[93] What Bowers has been able to determine, however, is the gradual changes in the range and the number of voices in English church music (including music for the Mass) in the course of the late fourteenth century and the early fifteenth century.[94]

The same applies to the performance of the ceremonial works such as the isorhythmic motets that provided one of the obvious models for the early settings of the Ordinary of the Mass. Even when we have a description as extended and detailed as that of the consecration of Santa Maria del Fiore in 1436, the descriptions of the music are written in terms so vague and general that it is impossible to determine even what forces were employed for a given piece.[95] From the music itself we can sometimes gather that, even though polyphony was the province of the soloists, the modern idea of "one on a part" solo singing was not really the norm at least in northern France in the case of composers trained in that tradition, since a considerable number of early and middle fifteenth-century works show some *divisi* in the parts, double notes that can hardly be considered alternatives. This is the case, for example with every one of the mature Masses of Du Fay and several of those by Okeghem, beginning with his *Missa Caput*, and even when the divisi are not immediately apparent, as in the case of the first three movements of Du Fay's *Missa Sancti Jacobi*, they are nonetheless there.[96] Much of the Mass music of the fourteenth and fifteenth centuries, as we are beginning to realize, was written not for performance *in choro* but for specific foundations, and the founders sometimes indicated how many people were to sing the work. It was the proliferation of such foundations early in the fifteenth century that led to a change in the status of singers of polyphony on the European Continent from that of itinerant journeymen to that of resident chaplains.[97] It appears that the compilation of movements that make up the *Mass of Tournai* was the result of such a foundation,[98] and the composition of Machaut's Mass and of Du Fay's *Missa Ave regina* were prompted by their composers' desire to set up a foundation in their own memory.[99] In his own will Du Fay requests that "nine of the better singers" perform his *Missa Sancti Anthonii de Padua*.[100] The size of the ensembles in the Low Countries at this time seems to be the same as what we find in France, and if the numbers of singers of polyphony in Cambrai and at the court of Burgundy can be used as a rough guide, the cathedrals and the courts of some of the princes had comparable forces.

The situation in Italy during the first half of the fifteenth century contrasts with that in France in that the ecclesiastical institutions, with the exception of the papal chapel, seem, by and large, to have employed fewer singers of polyphony, and this practice continued until the early fifteenth century,[101] so that one on a part singing would have been considerably more prevalent in Italy until the third quarter of the fifteenth century when the Medici, the Este, and the Sforza began assembling relatively large chapels.

Thus, for a modern performance, a small ensemble of between three or four and sixteen to twenty singers would be appropriate for most of the Mass music of the fourteenth and fifteenth centuries. A performance by adult males, with the upper voices sung by falsettists would accord with what we know was the practice at the time. Choirboys had their own special repertory and most often sang as a separate ensemble supported by one or two adult singers.[102] The use of women in place of the high falsettists, and a combination of men and women on high contratenor parts is a workable alternative and one used extensively by both professional and amateur ensembles on both sides of the Atlantic. My own sense in reading most of the arguments usually presented for the exclusion of women's voices from these repertories is that they have more to do with a long tradition of misogyny than with artistic or aesthetic matters.

Instrumental participation in polyphonic Mass music during the fourteenth and fifteenth centuries appears to have been very much the exception. Institutions such as the papal chapel and Cambrai cathedral excluded all instruments, including the organ, from their services. In churches and chapels where an organ was available there is little evidence that it was used in conjunction with composed vocal polyphony except in the case of alternation. So, the lower parts of much of the repertories discussed in this chapter, despite the absence of text and the sometimes disjunct nature of the melodic writing were, in all likelihood, vocalized, sung to fragments of the text, or sometimes, in the case of liturgically-derived *cantus firmi* sung to their own texts.[103] Still, there are occasional reports of the use of instruments in Masses,[104] and a few instances where the combination of the music itself, and archival evidence suggests instrumental performance of a *cantus firmus*, as is the case with Du Fay's *Missa Se la face ay pale* or Obrecht's *Missa Caput*.[105]

Matters of tempo and the interpretation of the mensuration signs are not exclusively problems of the Mass repertory of the Middle Ages, but in fact, the most vexing of these problems, the simple alternation between perfect time and some form of imperfect time in all voices is almost ubiquitous in the fifteenth-century Mass repertory in England and in the continent as well, and performers would be well advised to become thoroughly familiar with the problems presented by the succession of mensuration signs. The literature on these issues is vast and full of controversy, but recently two important studies have appeared that throw a great deal of light upon the problem and summarize much of the earlier research, Anna Maria Busse Berger, *Mensuration and Proportion Signs, Origin and Evolution*,[106] and Alexander Blachly, "Mensuration and Tempo in Fifteenth-Century Music: Cut Signatures in Theory and Practice."[107]

Notes

1. A complete inventory is given in Andreas Holschneider, *Die Organa von Winchester*, Studien zum ältesten Repertoire polyphoniker Musik (Hildesheim, 1968), pp. 41-44 for the Ordinary of the Mass.
2. In this context see Alejandro Enrique Planchart, "Communication," *Journal of the American Musicological Society* 31 (1979), 154.
3. See Chapter 2 above on organum.
4. This piece, as transmitted in Winchester, is an anomalous work and unique in the entire medieval repertory, see the discussion in Planchart, *The Repertory of Tropes at Winchester*, 2 vols (Princeton, 1977), I, pp. 249-54, and transcription, pp. 310-13.
5. Holschneider, *Die Organa*, pp. 102-03. Transcription of one Gloria in Planchart, *Repertory* I, pp. 314-24.
6. See Ulysse Chevalier, ed., *Ordinaire et Coutumier de l'église cathédrale de Bayeux (XIIIe siècle)*, Bibliothèque liturgique 8 (Paris, 1902), p. 296, and Joseph Pothier, "Kyrie 'Magne Deus potentiae'," *Révue du Chant Grégorien* 11 (1902-03), 19.
7. See Pierluigi Petrobelli and Cesare Corsi, eds., *Le Polifonie primitive in Friuli e in Europa: Atti del congresso internazionale Cividale del Friuli, 22-24 agosto 1980*. Miscellanea Musicologica 4 (Rome, 1989), and Petrobelli, ed., *Le Polifonie primitive di Cividale. Catalogo del Congresso internazionale: Le polifonie primitive in Friuli e in Europa* (Cividale, 1980).
8. These range from Willi Apel and Archibald T. Davison, eds., *Historical Anthology of Music*, 2 vols. (Cambridge, 1946-50), for decades the most influential such publication,

to David Fenwick Wilson, *Music of the Middle Ages: An Anthology for Performance and Study* (New York, 1990).

[9] A nearly complete inventory of sources containing this type of polyphony is available in Gilbert Reaney, *Manuscripts of Polyphonic Music 11th-Early 14th Century*. Répertoire International des Sources Musicales, B IV-1 (Munich, 1966), and Kurt von Fischer and Max Lütolf, *Handschriften mit Mehrstimmiger Musik des 14., 15. und 16. Jahrhunderts*, 2 vols., Répertoire International des Sources Musicales, B IV-3-4 (Munich, 1972).

[10] The piece is ascribed in the manuscript to Bishop Fulbert of Chartres but this is regarded as spurious by most scholars. If Fulbert had any connection with this piece it might be as the composer of the plainsong itself, not the organum or the Latin verses. The verses appearing in the Codex Calixtinus are found only in Spanish sources.

[11] Editions in Theodore Karp, *The Polyphony of Saint Martial and Santiago de Compostela*, 2 vols. (Berkeley, 1992), 2, pp. 223 and 228; Hendrik van der Werf, *The Oldest Extant Part Music and the Origin of Western Polyphony*, 2 vols. (Rochester, 1993), 2, pp. 207 and 212-13; Peter Wagner, *Die Gesänge der Jakobusliturgie zu Santiago de Compostela*. Collectanea Friburgiensia, New Series 22 (Freiburg in der Schweiz, 1931), pp. 121 and 123-24; and Max Lütolf, *Die mehrstimmigen Ordinarium Missae Sätze vom ausgehenden 11. bis zum 14. Jahrhundert* 2, pp. 36-37.

[12] See Hans Tischler *et al.*, eds., *The Montpellier Codex*, 7 vols. in 4, Recent Researches in the Music of the Middle Ages and the Early Renaissance 2–8 (Madison, 1978-85), Part 3, Nos. 261, 264, 267, 286, 293, 299, and 344.

[13] A glance at the index of works in the last two fascicles of the Montpellier Codex in Tischler, *Montpellier* 3, pp. vii-xi.

[14] All edited in Max Lütolf, *Die mehrstimmigen Ordinarium*, 2, *passim*. See also Edward E. Roesner, "The Manuscript Wolfenbüttel, Herzog-August Bibliothek, 628 Helmstadiensis: A Study of its Origins and of its Eleventh Fascicle," 2 vols. (Ph.D. diss., New York University, 1974).

[15] See Luther Dittmer, *The Worcester Fragments: A Catalogue Raisonné and Transcription*, Musicological Studies and Documents 2 (Brooklyn, 1957), and Ernest Sanders, "Worcester Polyphony," *New Grove Dictionary of Music and Musicians*, ed. Stanley Sadie, 20 vols. (London, 1980), 20, pp. 524-28.

[16] *English Music of the Thirteenth and Early Fourteenth Centuries*, ed. Ernest H. Sanders, Polyphonic Music of the Fourteenth Century 14 (Monaco, 1979), and *English Music for Mass and Offices (I)*, ed. Frank Ll. Harrison, Ernest H. Sanders, and Peter Lefferts, Polyphonic Music of the Fourteenth Century 16 (Monaco, 1983).

[17] See the remarkably motet-like *Sanctus Sance ingenite genitor* in Polyphonic Music of the Fourteenth Century 14, No. 65.

[18] See Margaret Bent, "A New Canonic Gloria and the Changing Profile of John Dunstaple," *Plainsong and Medieval Music* 5 (1996), 45-67. The numerous canonic pieces found in the Old Hall manuscripts and other late fourteenth- and early fifteenth-century English sources, if not true rondelli, retain much of the formal shape of the rondellus.

[19] Christopher Page, "Polyphony Before 1400," *Performance Practice: Music Before 1600*, ed. Howard M. Brown and Stanley Sadie (London, 1989), pp. 79-81. See also Chapter 40 below.

[20] Roger Bowers, "The Performing Ensemble for English Church Polyphony, c. 1320–c. 1390," *Studies in the Performance of Late Medieval Music*, ed. Stanley Boorman (Cambridge, 1983), pp. 161-92.

[21]   See Higini Anglès, ed., *El Còdex musical de Las Huelgas (música a veus des segles XIII-XIV)*, 3 vols., Publicaciones del Departament de Música de la Biblioteca de Catalunya 6 (Barcelona, 1931), 3, pp. 1-12, 20-37, and Gordon Anderson, ed., *The Las Huelgas Manuscript, Burgos, Monasterio de Las Huelgas*, 2 vols., Corpus Mensurabilis Musicae 79 (Rome, 1982), I, pp. 1-44.

[22]   See Andrew Tomasello, *Music and Ritual in Papal Avignon (1309-1403)*, Studies in Musicology 75 (Ann Arbor, 1983), pp. 123-50, idem, "Scribal Design in the Compilation of Ivrea Ms. 115." *Musica Disciplina* 42 (1988), 73-100.

[23]   Complete edition of the Music from Old Hall in Margaret Bent and Andrew Hughes, eds., *The Old Hall Manuscript*, 3 vols. in 4, Corpus Mensurabilis Musicae 46 (Rome, 1969-1972). See also Margaret Bent, "Sources of the Old Hall," *Proceedings of the Royal Musical Association* 94 (1967-68), 19-35, and idem, "The Old Hall Manuscript," *Early Music* 2 (1974), 2-14.

[24]   This is the organization to be found in Ivrea 115, in Apt 16 bis, in France, in Old Hall (where the Kyrie fascicle is lost) in England, and even in such a late source as Trent 93, copied in Tyrol after 1450.

[25]   See David Hiley, "Kyriale," *New Grove Dictionary of Music and Musicians*, ed. Stanley Sadie, 20 vols. (London, 1980), vol. 10, p. 311, with further bibliography.

[26]   The most extended study, showing the connection between the polyphony and the Lady Mass at Tournai, is Jean Dumoulin et al. *La Messe de Tournai*, Tornacum 4 (Tournai and Louvain la Neuve, 1988).

[27]   For a particularly striking case of this, involving music by two composers see Alejandro Enrique Planchart, "The Early Career of Guillaume Du Fay," *Journal of the American Musicological Society* 46 (1993), 357-60.

[28]   For an extensive and careful study of the Machaut Mass, together with a complete edition, see Daniel Leech-Wilkinson, *Machaut's Mass, an Introduction* (Oxford, 1990).

[29]   See Roland Jackson, "Musical Interrelations between 14th Century Mass Movements," *Acta Musicologica* 28 (1956), 54-64), the Mass has been edited in Leo Schrade, ed. *The "Roman de Fauvel," The Works of Philippe de Vitry, French Cycles of the "Ordinarium Missae,"* Polyphonic Music of the Fourteenth Century 1 (Monaco, 1956).

[30]   See Lawrence Earp, "Review of Daniel Leech Wilkinson, *Machaut's Mass: An Introduction* (Oxford, 1990)," *Journal of the American Musicological Society* 46 (1993), 296.

[31]   Hanna Stäblein Harder, *Fourteenth-Century Mass Music in France*, Musicological Studies and Documents 7 (Rome, 1962), pp. 17-18.

[32]   An easily available index of the surviving French compositions classified by style appears in Hanna Stäblein-Harder, *Fourteenth-Century Mass Music in France*, Corpus Mensurabilis Musicae 29 (Rome, 1962), pp. [i-iii], Nos. 44 and 47 of that edition present particularly elaborate settings of the Gloria and the Credo in motet style and may have been intended as a pair. They are copied in close proximity in the Ivrea manuscript.

[33]   Notable examples are the two originally complete but now fragmentary cycles by John Dunstaple on *Iesu Christi fili Dei* and *Da gaudiorum praemia*, see John Dunstable, *The Complete Works*, ed. Manfred F. Bukofzer, rev. Margaret Bent et al., Musica Britannica 8 (London, 1970), Nos. 15-17 and 69.

[34]   See Alejandro Enrique Planchart, "The Ars Nova and the Trecento," *Schirmer History of Music*, ed. Léonie Rosenstiel (New York, 1982), pp. 143-44, and Sarah Jane Williams, "Vocal Scoring in the Chansons of Machaut," *Journal of the American Musicological Society* 21 (1968), 251-57.

[35] Stäblein Harder, *Mass Music*, p. 9.

[36] Stäblein Harder, *Mass Music*, p. 17. On the uses of the term "cantilena" in the late Middle Ages see Ernest Sanders, "Cantilena," *New Grove Dictionary of Music and Musicians*, ed. Stanley Sadie, 20 vols. (London, 1980). Vol. 3, p. 729.

[37] See Reinhard Strohm, *The Rise of European Music, 1380-1500* (Cambridge, 1993), pp. 211-12.

[38] A striking example of these procedures is a Gloria-Credo pair by Dunstaple in *Collected Works*, Nos. 11-12. See also Andrew Hughes, "Mass Pairs in the Old Hall and Other English Manuscripts," *Revue Belge de Musicologie* 19 (1965), 15-27, and Philip Gossett, "Techniques of Unification in Early Cyclic Masses and Mass Pairs," *Journal of the American Musicological Society* 19 (1966), 205-31. But it is also well worth paying attention to the strictures against the obsession of early twentieth-century scholarship with "unification" in the Mass settings of the late Middle Ages raised by Reinhard Strohm in "Einheit und Funktion früher Meßzyklen," *Festschrift Rudolf Bockholdt zum 60. Geburtstag*," ed. Norbert Dubowy and Sören Meyer-Eller (Munich, 1990), pp. 141-60.

[39] The surviving pieces are collected and published in *Italian Sacred Music* and *Italian Sacred and Ceremonial Music*, Polyphonic Music of the Fourteenth Century (PMFC) 12-13, ed. Kurt von Fischer and F. Alberto Gallo (Monaco, 1976-1987).

[40] PMFC 12 has a single Kyrie, PMFC 13 has two, one of them a contrafact of Francesco Landini's ballata *Questa fanciulla amor*. Even composers working at the turn of the fifteenth century, like Johannes Ciconia and Antonio Zachara da Teramo, who were relatively prolific in terms of Mass compositions, apparently wrote only Glorias and Credos. See PMFC 13 and Margaret Bent and Anne Hallmark, eds. *The Works of Johannes Ciconia*, Polyphonic Music of the Fourteenth Century 23 (Monaco, 1985).

[41] See Kurt von Fischer, "Die Rolle der Mehrstimmigkeit am Dom von Siena zu Beginn des 13. Jahrhunderts," *Archiv für Musikwissenschaft* 18 (1961), 167-82.

[42] An example of this are the Anonymous Credos in PMFC 12, Nos. 10 and 11.

[43] PMFC 12, No. 13.

[44] PMFC 12, No. 15.

[45] See Nino Pirrotta, "Zacara da Teramo," *Music and Culture in Italy from the Middle Ages to the Baroque*, Studies in the History of Music 1 (Cambridge, 1984), pp. 126-44, and John Nadas, "Further Notes on Magister Antonius Dictus Zacharias de Teramo," *Studi Musicali* 15 (1986), 167-82.

[46] See Dragan Plamenac, "Keyboard Music of the 14th Century in Codex Faenza 117," *Journal of the American Musicological Society* 4 (1951), 179-201. The entire keyboard repertory of the manuscript is edited in Dragan Plamenac, ed., *Keyboard Music of the Late Middle Ages in Codex Faenza 117*, Corpus Mensurabilis Musicae 57 (Rome, 1973).

[47] See Giulio Cattin, "Il copista Rolando da Casale. Nuovi Frammenti musicali nell' Archivio di Stato [di Padova]," *Analecta Musicologica* 7 (1977), 14-41, and Agostino Ziino, "Un antico 'kyrie' a due voci per strumento a tastiera," *Nuova Rivista Musicale Italiana* 15 (1981), 628-31.

[48] See Knud Jeppesen, "Eine frühe Orgelmesse aus Castell' Arquato," *Archiv für Musikwissenschaft* 12 (1955), 187-205

[49] See Richard H. Hoppin, "The Cypriot-French Repertory of the MS Torino, Biblioteca Nazionale, J. II. 9." *Musica Disciplina* 11 (1957), 79-125. The entire manuscript is edited in Richard H. Hoppin, ed., *The Cypriot-French Repertory of the Manuscript Torino*,

Biblioteca Nazionale J. II. 9, 4 vols., Corpus Mensurabilis Musicae 21 (Rome, 1960-1963).

[50] Hoppin, The Cypriot French Repertory, I: i. The plainsong office is published in Richard H. Hoppin, ed., *Cypriot Plainchant of the Manuscript Torino, Biblioteca Nazionale J. II. 9*, Musicological Studies and Documents 19 (Rome, 1968).

[51] See for example *The Rise of European Music*, pp 423-24 and 530-39. A few other scholars have studied some of this repertory, notably Louis Gottlieb, "The Cyclic Masses of Trent Codex 89." 2 vols. (Ph.D. diss., University of California at Berkeley, 1958), Adelyn Peck Leverett, "A Paleographic and Repertorial Study of the Manuscript Trento, Castello de Buon Consiglio, 91 (1478)," 2 vols. (Ph.D. diss., Princeton University, 1990), and Rebecca Gerber, "The Manuscript Trent, Castello del Buonconsiglio, 88: A Study of Fifteenth-Century Manuscript Transmission and Repertory." (Ph.D. diss., University of California at Santa Barbara, 1983).

[52] One "composer" often mentioned, Jehan Vincenet, is eliminated. There is no evidence that the composer of the works attributed to "Vincenet," who worked for the court of Aragon at the end of the fifteenth century, is this man. The "Vincenet" in Aragon is actually the Savoyard organist Vincent du Bruequet. I am grateful to Prof. Pamela Starr who has identified him and allows me to publish this finding.

[53] Gilbert Reaney, *Early Fifteenth Century Music*, 7 vols. Corpus Mensurabilis Musicae 11 (Rome, 1955-1983), see also Charles van den Borren, ed., *Polyphonia Sacra: A Continental Miscellany of the Fifteenth Century* (Burnham, 1932; repr. College Park, 1963).

[54] See Philip Kaye, *The Sacred Music of Gilles Binchois* (Oxford, 1992).

[55] Now published in Facsimile with an introductory essay by David Fallows in *Oxford Bodleian Library MS. Canon. Misc. 213*, Late Medieval and Early Renaissance Manuscript in Facsimile 1 (Chicago, 1995).

[56] Facsimile, *Il Codice musicale 2216 della Biblioteca Universitaria di Bologna*, ed. F. Alberto Gallo, 2 vols. (Bologna, 1970).

[57] See Marian W. Cobin, "The Aosta Manuscript: A Central Source of Early-Fifteenth-Century Music," 2 vols. (Ph.D. diss., New York University, 1978), and Peter Wright, "The Aosta-Trent Relationship reconsidered," *I Codici musicali trentini a cento anni dalla loro riscoperta. Atti del convegno Laurence Feininger: La musicologia come missione, Trento, Castello del Buonconsiglio, 6-7 Settembre 1985*, ed. Nino Pirrotta and Danilo Curti (Trent, 1986), pp. 138-57.

[58] See Peter Wright, "The Compilation of Trent 87 and 92," *Early Music History* 2 (1982), 237-72, idem, *The Related Parts of Trent, Museo Provinciale d'Arte MSS 87 (1374) and 92 (1379): A Paleographic and Text-Critical Study*. Outstanding Dissertations in Music from British Universities (New York, 1989), and Tom Ward, "The Structure of the Manuscript Trent 92-1," *Musica Disciplina* 29 (1975), 127-47.

[59] By his own account Grenon was born in 1383, he died in 1456.

[60] See Charles Hamm, "The Reson Mass," *Journal of the American Musicological Society* 18 (1965), 5-21.

[61] Liebert was *magister puerorum* at Cambrai on and off from 1424 to 1438, he was dead by 1441. The Mass is edited in Guido Adler, ed., *Sechs Trienter Codices, erste-sechste Auswahl*, Denkmäler der Tonkunst in Österreich 14-15 (Vienna, 1900; repr. Graz, 1959-1960).

[62] Edited in Gilbert Reaney, *Early Fifteenth Century Music 3*, Corpus Mensurabilis Musicae 11 (Rome, 1966).

[63] On the Mass *Resvellies vous* see David Fallows, *Dufay*, 2nd ed. (London, 1987), pp. 165-68, on *Sancti Jacobi* see Fallows, *op. cit.*, pp. 168-73, but also Alejandro Enrique Planchart, "Guillaume Du Fay's Benefices and His Relationship to the Court of Burgundy, *Early Music History* 8 (1988), 128-29.

[64] Besides Hamm, "Reson Mass," cited above, a sensible overview of the standard approaches to these repertories in terms of musical and structural unity is found in Philip Gossett, "Techniques of Unification in Early Cyclic Masses and Mass Pairs," *Journal of the American Musicological Society* 19 (1966), 205-31.

[65] Strohm, "Einheit und Funktion," pp. 143-45.

[66] The literature on *fauxbourdon* and its relation to the English "faburden" is immense and often unenlighteningly contentious. The best general introduction remains Brian Trowell, "Faburden and Faux Bourdon," *Musica Disciplina* 13 (1959), 34-78.

[67] See Gosset, "Techniques," as well as Strohm, "Einheit und Funktion," cited above for important treatments of the subject, as well as Rob C. Wegman, "Petrus de Domarto's *Missa Spiritus almus* and the Early History of the Four-voice Mass in the Fifteenth Century," *Early Music History* 10 (1991), 235-304. The classic treatment of it is Edgar H. Sparks, *Cantus Firmus in Mass and Motet 1420-1520* (Berkeley, 1963; repr. New York, 1975).

[68] A cogent exposition of the traditional response to these stylistic traits is Sylvia Kenney, *Walter Frye and the Contenance angloise*, Yale Studies in the History of Music 2 (New Haven, 1964, but see also Philip R. Kaye, *The "Contenance Angloise" in Perspective: A Study of Consonance and Dissonance in Continental Music c. 1380-1440*, Outstanding Dissertations in Music from British Universities (New York, 1989), and see also David Fallows, "The *Contenance Angloise:* English Influence on Continental Composers of the Fifteenth Century," *Renaissance Studies* 1 (1987), 189-208, for a carefully considered reevaluation of the traditional views.

[69] Leonel Power, Missa *Alma redemptoris mater*, ed. Gareth Curtis (Lustleigh, 1982).

[70] Dunstable, *Collected Works*, Nos. 19-22 and 70.

[71] See in particular Walter Frye's *Missa Nobilis et pulchra*, in his *Opera omnia*, ed. Sylvia Kenney, Corpus Mensurabilis Musicae 19 (Rome, 1960). A better edition is in Gareth Curtis, ed. *Fifteenth-Century Liturgical Music III: The Brussels Masses*, Early English Church Music 34 (London, 1989).

[72] The first four (*Salve sancta parens* was eventually provided with a clumsily written fourth voice) are edited in Margaret Bent, ed. *Early English Church Music II: Four Anonymous Masses*, Early English Church Music 22 (London, 1979). The *Missa Caput* appears in Alejandro Enrique Planchart, ed. *Missae Caput*, Collegium Musicum Series I, 5 (New Haven, 1960; repr. Madison, 1967).

[73] See Manfred Bukofzer, "*Caput*: A Liturgico Musical Study," *Studies in Medieval and Renaissance Music* (New York, 1950), pp. 217-305. The work is available in Planchart, *Missae Caput*, and Johannes Okeghem, *Collected Works*, 3 vols., ed. Dragan Plamenac and Richard Wexler (New York and Boston, 1947-1992), II, No. 11, and Johannes Ockeghem, *Masses and Mass Sections I/1. Missa Caput*, ed. Jaap Van Benthem (Utrecht, 1992).

[74] In Heinrich Besseler, ed., *Guglielmi Dufay Opera Omnia*, 6 vols., Corpus Mensurabilis Musicae 1 (Rome, 1959-66), III, No. 1.

[75] Johannes Cornago, *Complete Works*, ed. Rebecca L. Gerber, Recent Researches in the Music of the Middle Ages and Early Renaissance 15 (Madison, 1984).

[76] See above, p. 90 and note 51.

[77] The two three-voice Masses attributed to Okeghem [Collected Works, I, Nos. 1 and 2] are good examples of this.

[78] Vatican, Biblioteca Apostolica Vaticana, MS Vaticanus Latinus 4736, fols. 83v-84r.

[79] The first important study of the constitution of the papal chapel was Franz X. Haberl, *Die römische 'Schola Cantorum' und die päpstlichen Kapellsänger bis zur mitte des 16. Jahrhunderts*, Bausteine für Musikgeschichte 3 (Leipzig, 1888, Reprinted Hildesheim, 1971), important later studies include Tomasello, *Music and Ritual*, Pamela Starr, "Music and Music Patronage at the Papal Court, 1447-1464" (Ph.D. diss., Yale University, 1987). Studies covering the papal chapel from the Avignon year to the end to the schism by John Nádas and Giuliano di Bacco and from 1417 to 1447 by Alejandro Planchart are in preparation. Some information on the papal chapel during this period appears in John Nádas and Giuliano di Bacco, "Verso uno stile internazionale' della musica nelle cappelle papali e cardinalizie durante il Grande Scisma (1378-1417): il caso di Johannes Ciconia da Liège," *Collectanea I*, ed. Adalbert Roth, Capellae Apostolicae Sixtinaeque Collectanea Acta Monumenta 3 (Vatican, 1994), pp. 7-74, and in Planchart, "The Early Career."

[80] Lille, Archives Départementale Du Nord, 4G 1086, No. 352: Bull of Eugenius IV, assigning the parish church of Casterlech to the office "of the twelve small vicars" at Cambrai. See also Craig Wright, "Performance Practices at the Cathedral of Cambrai, 1475-1550," *The Musical Quarterly* 64 (1978), 295-328.

[81] Lille, Archives Départementale Du Nord, 4G 7757 (fascicle of 1385-86), fol. 7v, expenses of livery "for the six choirboys," and for "little Hellin."

[82] Craig Wright, *Music and Ceremony at Notre-Dame of Paris, 500-1500* (Cambridge, 1989), pp. 20-21 and 24-25.

[83] Reinhard Strohm, *Music in Late Medieval Bruges* (Oxford, 1985), pp. 182-91.

[84] Barbara Haggh, "Music, Liturgy, and Ceremony in Brussels, 1350-1500," 2 vols. (Ph.D. diss., University of Illinois, 1988), II, pp. 700-46 with an immense amount of information cross-referenced to an alphabetical list in pp. 535ff.

[85] Craig Wright, *Music at the Court of Burgundy 1364-1419*, Musicological Studies 28 (Henryville, 1979), and Jeanne Marix, *Histoire de la musique et des musiciens de la cour de Bourgogne sous le règne de Philippe le Bon* (Strasbourg, 1939; repr. Geneva, 1972, and Baden-Baden, 1974).

[86] Henri Pirenne, *Histoire de la Belgique*, 4 vols. (Brussels, 1909-12), II, p. 256.

[87] David Fallows, "Specific Information on Ensembles for Composed Polyphony, 1400-1474," *Studies in the Performance of Late Medieval Music*, ed. Stanley Boorman (Cambridge, 1983), pp.109-59.

[88] See discussion in Alejandro Enrique Planchart, "On Singing and the Vocal Ensemble II," *A Performer's Guide to Renaissance Music*," ed. Jeffery Kite-Powell (New York, 1994), pp. 28-29.

[89] Maria del Carmen Gomez, *La música en la Casa Real catalano-aragonesa durante los años 1336-1432* (Barcelona, 1979), and Allan Atlas, *Music at the Aragonese Court of Naples* (Cambridge, 1985), and Alejandro Enrique Planchart, "Music in the Christian Courts of Spain." *Musical Repercussions of 1492: Encounters in Text and Performance*, ed. Carol E. Robertson (Washingon, 1992), pp. 149-66.

[90] Lewis Lockwood, *Music in Renaissance Ferrara, 1400-1505* (Cambridge, 1984).

[91] William F. Prizer, "Music at the Court of the Sforza: The Birth and Death of a Musical Center," *Musica Disciplina* 43 (1989), 141-93.

[92] Marie-Thérèse Bouquet, "La cappella musicale dei Duchi di Savoia dal 1450 al 1500," *Rivista Italiana di Musicologia* 3 (1968), 233-85, and Robert John Bradley, "Musical Life and Culture at Savoy, 1420-1450," 2 vols., (Ph.D. diss., City University of New York, 1992).

[93] Roger Bowers, "Choral Institutions Within the English Church: Their Constitution and Development, 1340-1500," (Ph.D. diss., University of East Anglia, 1975).

[94] Roger Bowers, "The Performing Ensemble for English Church Polyphony, c. 1320 - c. 1390," *Studies in the Performance of Late Medieval Music*, ed. Stanley Boorman (Cambridge, 1983), pp. 161-92.

[95] See Craig Wright. "Dufay's *Nuper rosarum flores*, King Solomon's Temple, and the Veneration of the Virgin," *Journal of the American Musicological Society* 47 (1994), 429-31, particularly note 64.

[96] See Alejandro Enrique Planchart, "Guillaume Dufay's Masses: A View of the Manuscript Traditions," *Papers Read at the Dufay Quincentenary Conference, Brooklyn College, December 6-7, 1974*, ed. Allan W. Atlas (New York, 1976), pp. 29-33.

[97] See Barbara Haggh, "Itinerancy to Residency: Professional Careers and Performance Practices in 15th Century Sacred Music," *Early Music* 17 (1989), 359-67, and also Strohm, *The Rise*, pp. 273-83.

[98] Dumoulin, *La Messe*, pp. 41-61.

[99] See Anne Walters Robertson, "The Mass of Guillaume de Machaut in the Cathedral of Reims." *Plainsong in the Age of Polyphony*, ed. Thomas F. Kelly. Cambridge Studies in Performance Practice 2 (Cambridge, 1992), pp. 104-12, and Strohm, *The Rise*, pp. 283-87, but also Alejandro Enrique Planchart, "Notes on Guillaume Du Fay's Last Works," *The Journal of Musicology* 13 (1995), 55-72.

[100] Fallows, *Dufay*, pp. 185-86, and idem "Specific Ensembles," pp. 117-20.

[101] See Albert Seay, "The 15th Century Capella at Santa Maria del Fiore in Florence." *Journal of the American Musicological Society* 11 (1958), 45-55, and Frank D'Accone, "The Performance of Sacred Music in Italy during Josquin's Time, c. 1475-1525," *Josquin Des Prez. Proceedings of the International Josquin Festival-Conference, 1971*, ed., Edward Lowinsky and Bonnie J. Blackburn (London, 1976), pp. 601-17.

[102] See Fallows, *Dufay*, pp. 179-81 and idem, "Specific Ensembles," pp. 120-31, Wright, *Music and Ceremony*, pp. 165 95

[103] See Gilbert Reaney, "Text Underlay in Early Fifteenth-Century Musical Manuscripts," *Essays in Musicology in Honor of Dragan Plamenac on his 70th Birthday*, ed. Gustave Reese and Robert J. Snow (Pittsburgh, 1969), pp. 245-51, Craig Wright, "Voices and Instruments in the Art Music of Northern France During the 15th Century: A Conspectus." *International Musicological Society, Report of the Twelfth Congress Berkeley 1977*, ed. Daniel Heartz and Bonnie Wade (Kassel, 1981), pp. 643-49, and Alejandro Enrique Planchart, "Parts with Words and without Words: The Evidence for Multiple Texts in Fifteenth-century Masses." *Studies in the Performance of Late Medieval Music*, ed. Stanley Boorman (Cambridge, 1983), pp. 227-52.

[104] See Wright, *Music at the Court of Burgundy*, p. 52.

[105] Alejandro Enrique Planchart, "Fifteenth-Century Masses: Notes on Performance and Chronology," *Studi Musicali* 10 (1981), 6-9 and 13-15.

[106] Oxford, 1993.

[107] Ph.D. diss., Columbia University, 1995. See also Chapter 38 below.

II. Non-Liturgical Monophony

5. Introduction

Elizabeth Aubrey

Our knowledge of how to perform the songs of the troubadours, trouvères, and Minnesinger, and other non-liturgical monophony, is hampered by the way that the music has been transmitted to us. A surprising number of the manuscripts of these songs do not contain music at all, but only poetry; not all of those that do contain melodies are reliable or complete. The surviving manuscripts are contemporary only with the latest composers, so their record of earlier music must be viewed with some skepticism. And the notation in which these songs were recorded is the barest sketch of what a performed melody would have entailed: much of it conveys no clear indication of the rhythms of the notes; it is completely silent on the question of who the performers were, whether a single singer, more than one singer, instrumentalists, or some combination. Furthermore, many songs survive in more than one version, often manifesting quite significant melodic differences; these differences may reflect choices or errors made by medieval scribes, or they may represent revisions made by composers or changes that came about during performance.[1]

The repertoires included in this section are marked by some fundamental distinctions, beginning of course with languages and their pronunciations, but also including genre, poetic and musical structure and style, dates, and cultural environments. The performers of some of the repertoires were members of the nobility, while the performers of other songs were itinerant musicians, secular clerics, court retainers, or bourgeoisie. Although there was a certain amount of borrowing among the repertoires, including *contrafacta* and translations of poems, for the most part the literatures were separate and autonomous and represent distinct cultural phenomena. For this reason, it is unlikely that we can find solutions to performance problems that can be applied universally.

But for all non-liturgical monophony, modern performers are faced with several similar questions. She or he must choose one of the extant versions of a piece and decide how faithfully to adhere to it; whether and how to ornament or improvise; how to interpret the rhythm; and what performing forces to use. While scholars cannot offer unequivocal solutions to these basic problems, a number of theories have been proposed, especially on the question of the rhythm of the melodies and on the propriety of using instruments. This Introduction explains what the main theories are, and the chapters that follow will deal with how the theories (or new ones) might be applied to each repertoire.

Rhythm

Without a doubt the difficulty of interpreting rhythm has proven to be the most frustrating problem of all, and sometimes the debate over how to find a solution has become acrimonious. The controversies have generated plenty of heat but little light for the performers, with the unfortunate result that musicians are sometimes reluctant to tackle non-liturgical monophony. It is important to realize that none of the proposed theories has been either proved or disproved, and that, given access to the original sources and other contemporary evidence, a modern performer can make decisions that are as well-informed as those made by modern editors.

Each of the rhythm theories uses paleographical, textual, musical, and extra-musical arguments for support. The paleographical evidence consists of the notation, most of which does not clearly indicate durations. Most of the manuscripts use the neumes of plainchant, which for lyric songs are typically arranged above the first strophe of the poem; most syllables have one or two neumes (each consisting of from one to three or four pitches—with an occasional melisma). Some French manuscripts contain a Franconian or pre-Franconian notation that conveys one of the six rhythmic "modes" that are associated with liturgical polyphony of the Notre Dame school, usually mode 1 (♩♪) or 3 (♩. ♪♩). The manuscripts that preserve the Old Galician-Portuguese *cantigas de Santa Maria* are unusual in that they use a somewhat irregular mensural notation that is not precisely modal, and whose interpretation is still disputed. The provenance of a manuscript is very important in considering the significance of the notation used, for mensural notation was not uniformly adopted all at once across Europe. A scribe in the Mediterranean region, for example, may not have known about a Parisian mensural notational system, or, even if he did, he may not have considered it appropriate for the songs he was writing.

The texts follow poetic rules that differ from language to language. In all languages, the poems are arranged by a regular rhyme scheme or by assonance. In the romance vernaculars the forms are governed by precise frameworks of numbers of syllables per verse. In Germanic languages, they follow successions of accent patterns. Poetry in the Middle Ages was considered to be closely allied to the discipline of music, largely because verse followed strict procedures that are comparable to the strict rules that governed musical consonances (according to Pythagorean numerical proportions). There are also some allusions in thirteenth-century music theory to an affinity between meters of classical poetry and the musical modes that take the form of repeated durational patterns. Music and poetry were inseparable, not only in a theoretical sense, but also in a practical sense in that, until the fourteenth century, lyric poetry appears almost always to have been sung rather than recited (when not serving a didactic or pedagogical purpose, e.g., as *exempla* for teaching grammar and rhetoric).[2] This fact is impossible to ignore, and it plays a significant role, albeit with widely divergent results, in all of the theories about musical rhythm.

The melodies themselves encompass a wide variety of styles and structures, and these features might convey some evidence about performance. A melismatic melody presents different problems in the interpretation of rhythm than does a syllabic one; a tune with several repeated phrases implies a different approach to rhythm than one that is through-composed; the rhythmic shape of a song with a double-cursus *lai* structure is conceivably different from that of a strophic song. The *cantigas de Santa Maria*, the Italian *laude*, and many French songs were later works, often characterized by fixed forms (especially ones with a refrain, like the *virelai*), which might mean that their rhythms were stricter than in other songs. On the other hand, the melodies of the troubadours and the so-called goliards, which more often than not have no repetition schemes, might have had rhythmic structures that were less strict or patterned.

External evidence has been brought to bear on the problem as well, some of which has to do with the cultural climate in which twelfth- and thirteenth-century non-liturgical monophony was created. The rise of lyric poetry coincided with the development of new forms of polyphony, including *organum, conductus*, and the motet. This is important not only from the standpoint of the emergence of a new rhythmic system and notations to convey it, but also as an indicator of the expansion of musical creativity of composers. It raises questions about the relationship between the new polyphony and the new lyric monophony, specifically whether or not they followed the same or similar rules of musical composition and performance. In the case of French monophony in particular, there are interrelationships that cannot be ignored, since composers often employed a secular melody as one of the voices in a polyphonic piece; some trouvères, notably Adam de la Halle, composed both monophony and polyphony. On the other hand, most lyric monophonic songs have no discernible relationship with polyphony, and it is conceivable that their manner of performance differed quite significantly.

There is also evidence that the different kinds of songs included within each monophonic repertoire required different kinds of performances. The *chansons, planhs, lieder*, and so forth, of the well-educated troubadours, trouvères, and Minnesinger were by and large intended for performance by and for the nobility at court, while *caroles, rondeaux, pastourelles*, and the like may have been more the province of the lower classes. The date of a song might also require a chronologically-specific approach, assuming that aesthetic tastes changed over time.

Another issue that has been raised with respect to rhythm is the effect that an oral tradition might have had on performance. Since nearly all of the extant manuscripts that transmit lyric monophony were produced after the middle of the thirteenth century (some much later, for example those of Minnesang), it is widely assumed that the songs were passed on mainly orally until at least the beginning of the thirteenth century, and perhaps even throughout the period when the surviving manuscripts themselves were written.[3] The fact that so many of the melodies manifest some significant differences among versions buttresses the hypothesis that singers were rather free (whether deliberately or unconsciously) in interpreting them. One might expect that the rhythm of a melody would aid in its transmission, but exactly how rhythm and oral transmission might have interacted is a matter of some dispute.

The theories and variations on theories that have appeared during the last century can be considered in three broad categories:[4]

1)   modal and mensural

2)   declamatory and free

3)   isosyllabic

Modal and mensural theories postulate that each melody has a discrete rhythm, measurable and proportionate. A modal theory suggests that the rhythm of a song falls into repeated patterns of longs and shorts, while a mensural theory requires a somewhat less predictable progression of longs and shorts that might or might not fall into strict patterns. The earliest proponents of the modal theory, Friedrich Ludwig, Jean-Baptiste Beck, and Pierre Aubry,[5] believed that the songs of the troubadours and trouvères should be considered part of the same tradition that produced Notre Dame polyphony, and that the patterns of the rhythmic modes described by Johannes de Garlandia, Anonymous IV, and other thirteenth-century theorists should be applied to lyric monophony as well. They pointed out that a number of Old French songs are transmitted in mensural notation that conveys modal patterns, and that these modes should be applied to all of the songs, including those that are given in non-mensural chant notation. Aubry, adopting an earlier argument of Paul Runge's,[6] argued in addition that French and Occitan texts embody accent patterns that can be translated into a rhythmic mode; Beck pointed out some flaws in this proposition, showing that verses in French and Occitan poetry did not necessarily have regular accent patterns, that duration (quantity) need not coincide with accent (quality), and that the melody can have a rhythmic mode that is in conflict with accents in the text.[7] Both Beck and Aubry produced editions of melodies that conform to one or another rhythmic mode, and for the most part these editions divulge neither how a specific mode in a piece was detected, nor whether there is any paleographical evidence to support it. Friedrich Gennrich adopted the modal theory for Minnesang; the most prolific modalist, his editions, articles, and books still dominate the secondary literature on lyric monophony.

Hans Tischler has championed a strict modal-mensural interpretation of trouvère songs, arguing with Aubry that the accents in the text should be used to help identify the modal patterns in the melodies. Tischler suggests that a melody need not retain a single pattern from beginning to end, but could embody changes in patterns, and would have been sung flexibly by a performer in any case.[8]

The advocates of free or declamatory rhythm do not argue that the melodies were arhythmic, or even that they were unmeasured. In the late nineteenth century Antonio Restori suggested shifting meters, including 2/4, 3/4, and 4/4, frequently treating melismas as ornaments; his interpretations often approach an isosyllabic style but with many exceptions.[9] Raffaello Monterosso offered similar interpretations in the 1950s.[10] Ewald Jammers has argued for a musical rhythm that is governed by the structures of both text and melody.[11] Motives, ligatures, repeated pitches, and other musical elements interact with text accents and rhymes to produce a rhythm that is not necessarily patterned (although in his scheme some songs might have a modal rhythm), yet not altogether free. The song as it is sung has a perceptible rhythm that is governed above all by the performer's understanding and interpretation of the song's structure. Jammers emphasizes the freedom of the singer in applying this theory, but it is a freedom tempered by internal structural features peculiar to each song.

The declamatory theory of Hendrik van der Werf gives almost complete freedom to the singer, who should be guided not so much by structural features, as argued by Jammers, but by the sound and sense of the text. He rejects the notion that monophony followed the same rules in performance as polyphony, but was perhaps more closely akin in performance to plainchant, as he implies by applying to secular monophony Johannes de Grocheio's description of the rhythm of ecclesiastical music as "not too precisely measured."[12] He suggests that the singer would sing the poem with the same rhythm with which he or she would recite or declaim it, giving each note more or less equal value, but dwelling on some syllables longer than others as an effective communication of the text would occasion. In his opinion, the melody is not an equal partner with the poem, but rather should be understood as being its vehicle, and should not embody rhythmic values that would obscure the poem; in fact, each stanza of a lyric poem, in van der Werf's view, might well necessitate a different rhythm for the melody.

Christopher Page lately has added weight to this theory, maintaining that the scribes of the late thirteenth century, in France at least, were concerned chiefly with helping perpetuate and record the new musical style of polyphony, with its notation that conveyed precise rhythmic patterns.[13] According to Page, if these scribes used notation that embodies these patterns to write monophony, this amounted to an anachronistic imposition of a mensural aesthetic that was foreign to the original character of the courtly lyric. Specifically, he asserts that Old French and Old Occitan courtly songs in the "High Style," including *cansos, complaintes, sirventes,* and the like, were originally free and unmeasured, while songs in the "Low Style," including dance songs, *pastourelles,* etc., would have been measured.

Taking yet a different lesson from the chant notation of most lyric monophony, and relying heavily on the traditions of twelfth- and thirteenth-century poetic theory, John Stevens has proposed that the melodies would have been sung in a manner that gave each syllable more or less the same time value, so that any two verses that contained the same number of syllables would occupy roughly the same amount of time.[14] In this isosyllabic theory, a neume with one note would be of the same length as a neume with more than one note, whose notes would be of equal value within the syllable. Given that some melodies have melismas over some syllables, which would be impossible to sing in the same amount of time as a syllable with only one note, Stevens allows that such an interpretation would require some flexibility. This is essentially the same theory offered earlier by Ugo Sesini in his study of one of the troubadour chansonniers.[15] But Stevens applies the method to all non-liturgical monophony, and he undertakes to support it by a far-reaching interpretation of late medieval poetic theory and practice.[16]

One variation on this theory is that the notes within a neume of two or more notes would not be of equal value, but would have long or short values depending upon the neume's shape, according to modal principles of the values of ligatures.[17]

Use of Instruments

The question of whether or not instruments were used to accompany lyric monophony did not arise until about twenty years ago. Before then, scholars and performers assumed that, judging from the presence of a variety of instruments in visual representations of performances of courtly music (notably illuminations in manuscripts that contain lyric songs), as well as the ample references to instruments in prose and poetic texts of the period, courtly songs quite probably were accompanied by instruments. Evidence of the acceptance of this assumption can be found in almost every modern recording of monophonic lyric, in which some—sometimes many—instruments accompany one or more singers.

Hendrik van der Werf was the first to argue strenuously that such an assumption is mostly wishful thinking, and that none of the evidence on which the supposition is based clearly states or proves that instruments were used to accompany courtly lyric.[18] Christopher Page has lent support and refinement to van der Werf's proposition by arguing that "Low Style" dances and pastoral songs were traditionally associated with instruments of every type, while "High Style" courtly songs would not have been accompanied.[19]

Defenders of the use of instruments have countered this challenge to traditional beliefs with several arguments. Vernacular songs are specifically associated with the fiddle (*viella*) by Johannes de Grocheio.[20] Furthermore, medieval authors did not make as fine a distinction among genres as is postulated by Page, and some references in literary works can be interpreted to refer to performance of courtly lyric songs on instruments (both with and without a singer). For instance, one song by the troubadour Albertet de Sestaro (PC 16,8) contains the following verses: "Peirol, violatz e chantatz cointamen de ma chanzon/los motz e.l son leugier" (Peirol, fiddle and sing my song gracefully, the words and the light melody.)[21] The paucity of such references could be construed as tacit approval or could even reflect the probability that the practice was so widespread as to make mention of it gratuitous.[22]

As meager and ambiguous as is the evidence about whether or not instruments were used, clues about *how* they might have been used are almost non-existent. If a performer decides to include instruments in a performance, she or he must choose what instrument(s) to use (strings, winds, percussion), how many, how often (throughout, at the beginning or end, or as an interlude between sections, possibilities for which there may be some support in Grocheio's treatise), and what exactly they should play (drones, simple unison on the melody, parallel intervals, etc.).

The addition of instruments in performance obviously changes the character of a song significantly. A drone, for instance, inevitably serves to establish some sort of "tonal" reference point that by its very presence defines some pitches as structurally important and others as ornamental or secondary—which the ear might hear very differently without the drone's presence. The addition of instrumental interludes interrupts the poem's flow, and because it is in a sense newly composed, alters the structure of the music. Whether or not musicians applied these procedures in the Middle Ages is perhaps not so much the issue as is the question of whether creating such "new" compositions in our day brings us closer to understanding and appreciating medieval monophony itself.

Definitive resolution of the instrument debate, which may now have supplanted that surrounding the problem of rhythm in its intensity, is unlikely. Almost forgotten in the discussion is a closely related question, that of the number of singers involved in a performance. The texts of some monophonic lyric songs are in a dialogue form, either between two authors, as in the case of a *tenso* or a *jeu parti*, or between two characters in a quasi-drama, as in the case of a *pastourelle*. Other songs have a refrain structure, which is commonly believed to point to some kind of solo-chorus performance. Direct sources are once again silent on this problem.

Other Issues

Other performance issues are common to all of the repertoires, and some guidelines are proposed in the sections that follow. One of the most important, alluded to at the beginning of this Introduction, concerns what manuscript source of the text and the melody one should use in preparing a performance. Some manuscripts are believed to be more reliable transmitters of songs than others, based on date, provenance, scribal skill, etc. Some manuscripts appear to be more trustworthy for their texts than for their music, or vice versa (as, for instance, when an Italian scribe copied a French text); some contain only fragmentary or incomplete records of a song; some are probably more reliable for some composers (late ones, for instance), than for others (such as earlier ones). A modern performer must learn how to choose a good modern edition (unless he or she has access to a facsimile or microfilm of a manuscript), as well as how to use it most effectively.

Performers then must consider how closely to follow the specific pitches and words found in a given source, or whether to improvise some variations, ornamentation, or other alteration of the received melodies. The most helpful information about what kinds of variations a performer might make is found in the different versions of melodies that happen to be transmitted in extant manuscripts. This in many cases can be a useful guide, but it is not always easy to extrapolate general performing techniques from a few examples. And there are large numbers of songs that we have received in only one version, so today's performer can only guess at appropriate improvisatory practices.

A related problem is how much of a song to perform. Strophic songs obviously consist of several stanzas, but some sources do not transmit all of them, nor is the order in which they are found always consistent. It is in any case reasonable to suggest that singing only one or two stanzas of a strophic song is not appropriate for medieval lyric, since most of the poets were concerned with a careful progression of sense and structure over the course of the entire poem.

Another difficulty is whether and which chromatic inflections a performer might add to the melody. Here the information is almost entirely paleographical, since medieval music theorists always discuss *musica ficta* in the context of polyphony, not monophony.[23] Some scribes indicated Bb, F#, and occasionally Eb and C#, and some did it more consistently than others. Other manuscripts, however, have no such indications. There has as yet been no thorough study of whether the rules governing the application of *musica ficta* to polyphony could be applied to monophony; such a study would have to involve an exhaustive catalogue of all of the manuscript indications of chromatic inflections, as well as a thoughtful consideration of the theoretical issues.[24]

For all of the repertoires studied in this section, the singer would do well to remember that a song came alive in the Middle Ages only when it was sung aloud; it was not an artifact studied in a library, but rather an important source of entertainment. A medieval singer was performing to an audience, and he or she no doubt tailored each performance to engage the attention and response of the listeners. This aesthetic should guide any decisions about text, melody, rhythm, and instruments today. Vernacular monophony is perhaps more difficult than other medieval music to communicate effectively to a modern audience, but the rewards of a successful performance are potentially worth the extra effort necessary to discover suitable and defensible answers to the questions posed here.

Notes

1 See Wulf Arlt, "Secular Monophony," *Performance Practice: Music Before 1600*, The Norton/Grove Handbooks in Music, ed. Howard Mayer Brown and Stanley Sadie (New York and London, 1989), pp. 55-78, for a discussion of some of the hermeneutical problems in studying the performance of medieval monophony. The question of whether any modern performance can be "authentic" or "historically accurate" is a complex philosophical one that should not deter singers from attempting their own solutions. (See Nicholas Kenyon, ed., *Authenticity and Early Music; A Symposium* [Oxford, 1988], for several essays on the problem.) Scholars have been able to establish some boundaries within which it seems likely that a medieval performance would have fallen; the difficulty lies in the fact that the boundaries enclose a somewhat wide spectrum of unknowns.

2 See Elizabeth Aubrey, *The Music of the Troubadours* (Bloomington, 1996), Chap. 3, "Poetics and Music."

3 Aubrey, "Literacy, Orality, and the Preservation of French and Occitan Courtly Songs," *Actas del XV Congreso de la Sociedad Internacional de Musicología, "Culturas*

musicales mediterráneo y sus ramificaciones," Madrid */3-10/IV/1992,* ed. Sociedad Español de Musicología, *Revista de Musicología* 16/4 (1993 [1996]), pp. 2355-2366.

[4] A fuller discussion of some of the theories described here can be found in Burkhard Kippenberg, *Der Rhythmus im Minnesang; eine Kritik der literar- und musikhistorischen Forschung*, Münchener Texte und Untersuchungen zur deutschen Literatur des Mittelalters, 3 (Munich, 1962). See also Aubrey, *The Music of the Troubadours*, pp. 240-54.

[5] The fracas over who exactly first devised the modal theory is one of the spicier episodes in the annals of musicology, but the commonly held notion that Beck and Aubry fought a duel over it, and that Aubry was mortally wounded, is a myth. See John Haines, "The 'Modal Theory', Fencing and the Death of Pierre Aubry," *Plainsong and Medieval Music* 6 (1997), 143-50.

[6] Aubry's theory first appeared in *La Rythmique musicale des troubadours et trouvères* (Paris, 1907). Runge had suggested deriving the rhythm of some Minnesinger songs from their texts, although he did not specify a connection with the Parisian rhythmic modes, in *Die Sangesweisen der Colmarer Handschrift und die Liederhandschrift Donaueschingen* (Leipzig, 1896).

[7] See his *La Musique des troubadours; étude critique* (Paris, 1910), pp. 46-52.

[8] See his introductory remarks in *Chanter m'estuet: Songs of the Trouvères*, ed. Samuel N. Rosenberg (Bloomington, 1981), pp. xxi-xxvi.

[9] Antonio Restori, "Per la storia musicale dei trovatori provenzali," *Rivista musicale italiana* 2 (1895), 1-22; 3 (1896), 231-60 and 407-51.

[10] Raffaello Monterosso, *Musica ritmica dei trovatori (con i tavola fuori testo e 28 esempi musicali* (Milan, 1956).

[11] In *Ausgewählte Melodien des Minnesangs: Einführung, Erläuterungen und Übertragung*, Altdeutsche Textbibliothek, Ergänzungsreihe 1 (Tübingen, 1963), pp. 29-67; see also his *Aufzeichnungsweisen der einstimmigen ausserliturgischen Musik des Mittelalters*, Paläographie der Musik, I/4 (Cologne, 1975).

[12] "Others, however, divide music into plain, or immeasurable, and measurable [music]; understanding by 'plain' or 'immeasurable', ecclesiastical [music], which is determined by many tones according to Gregory. By 'measurable' they understand that [music] which is effected by diverse sounds that are sounded and measured simultaneously, as in conductus and motets. But if by 'immeasurable' they understand music that is in no way measured—indeed totally said at will—their understanding is deficient, in that every operation of music and of any art whatever ought to be measured by the rules of that art. *If, however, by 'immeasurable' they do not understand 'measured' so precisely*, it seems that this division can remain." The Latin text is found in Ernst Rohloff, ed., *Die Quellenhandschriften zum Musiktraktat des Johannes de Grocheio, im Faksimile herausgegeben nebst Übertragung des Textes und Übersetzung ins Deutsche, dazu Bericht, Literaturschau, Tabellen und Indices* (Leipzig, 1967), p. 124, sentences 72-75: "Alii autem musicam dividunt in planam sive immensurabilem et mensurabilem, per planam sive immensurabilem intellgentes ecclesiasticam, quae secundum Gregorium pluribus tonis determinatur. Per mensurabilem intellegunt illam, quae ex diversis sonis simul mensuratis et sonantibus efficitur, sicut in conductibus et motetis. Sed si per immensurabilem intellegant musicam nullo modo mensuratam, immo totaliter ad libitum dictam, deficiunt, eo quod quaelibet operatio musicae et cuiuslibet artis debet illius artis regulis mensurari. *Si autem per immensurabilem non ita praecise mensuratam intellegant*, potest, ut videtur, ista divisio remanere" (emphasis added).

Van der Werf has articulated his theory most recently in "The 'Not-so-precisely Measured' Music of the Middle Ages," *Performance Practice Review* 1 (1988), 42-60. See a new edition and translation by Christopher Page of the sections in Grocheio's treatise dealing with secular song, "Johannes de Grocheio on Secular Music: A Corrected Text and a New Translation," *Plainsong and Medieval Music* 2 (1993), 17-41.

[13] *Voices and Instruments of the Middle Ages: Instrumental Practice and Songs in France 1100-1300* (Berkeley, 1986), pp. 73-76 and *passim*.

[14] *Words and Music in the Middle Ages: Song, Narrative, Dance and Drama, 1050-1350*, Cambridge Studies in Music (Cambridge, 1986), pp. 13-47 and *passim*.

[15] "Le Melodie trobadoriche nel canzoniere provenzale della Biblioteca Ambrosiana (R. 71 sup.)," *Studi Medievali*, nuova serie, 12 (1939), especially 53-101.

[16] See reviews of Stevens's book by Christopher Page in *Early Music* 15 (1987), 391-393, and Jeremy Yudkin, *Speculum* 64 (1989), 765-69.

[17] The inspiration for this comes from J.W.A. Vollaerts, *Rhythmic Proportions in Early Medieval Ecclesiastical Chant*, 2nd ed. (Leiden, 1960).

[18] See his *The Chansons of the Trouvères and Troubadours: A Study of the Melodies and Their Relation to the Poems* (Utrecht, 1972), pp. 19-21.

[19] Page, *Voices and Instruments*, *passim*.

[20] Rohloff, *Grocheio*, p. 136, sentence 139.

[21] See Joel Cohen "Pierol's Vielle: Instrumental Participation in the Troubador [sic] Repertory," *Historical Performance* 3 (1990), 73-77.

[22] See, for instance, Elizabeth Aubrey, "References to Music in Old Occitan Literature," *Acta Musicologica* 61 (1989), 118-120 and 131-132, and *The Music of the Troubadours*, pp. 254-62.

[23] Johannes de Grocheio specifically declares that *musica falsa* concerns polyphony, not monophony.

[24] Van der Werf, in *The Extant Troubadour Melodies* (Rochester, 1984), pp. 38-61, provides just such a list for troubadour songs, along with some discussion of the issue and some tentative conclusions.

6. Latin Monophony
Charles E. Brewer

Terminology and Background

Anumber of terms were used interchangeably during the Middle Ages to denote Latin songs: *cantio* (pl. *cantiones*), *cantilena* (pl. *cantilene* or *cantilenæ*), and *conductus* (pl. *conductus* or *conducti*). This variety of terminology is reflected in the diversity of types and styles of songs found in this repertoire, and whose poems cover a broad range of subjects, from drinking songs and erotica to serious political satires and deeply spiritual meditations.

In many earlier studies of medieval music, the repertoire of medieval Latin song is frequently associated with the semi-mythic "goliards." Though this term does occur in medieval sources, it appears that it frequently is used as a literary device or a general term of disparagement rather than a reference that can be directly related to the Latin poets of the Middle Ages. In fact, many of the poets, as much as they are known, were well-respected performers at court, including bishops (Stephen Langton), church and court officials (Peter of Blois), scholars (Peter Abelard, Gaulterus of Châtillon, and Philip the Chancellor), and some not entirely decorous (the "Archpoet").

The repertoire of extant medieval Latin song extends throughout the Middle Ages, and perhaps earlier, if neumed versions of Horace's odes in any way reflect earlier practices.[1] The first extensive repertoire comes from the Carolingian "renaissance" of the ninth and tenth centuries but most of this early repertoire, with only a few exceptions, is preserved in neumatic notation that does not show distinct pitches.[2]

The majority of the remaining songs stem from the twelfth and early thirteenth centuries and in many respects are associated with the increased activities of monastic, parish and cathedral schools and the new developing university centers. The most active centers of Latin song composition seem to have been in Aquitania, Normandy/England, and Paris.

By the end of the Middle Ages, Latin song was becoming more of a scholastic exercise. This is evident in the word games, such as acrostics, that are included in some of the *cantiones* from the Mosburg Gradual (1360).

Sources

The sources for medieval Latin song also present a variety of formats. In almost every instance, monophonic songs are copied along with polyphonic compositions. In some deluxe sources, such as the so-called "Florence" manuscript, the notation is a clear and elegant chant notation. Other sources, such as those associated with Aquitania (Paris, Bibliothèque Nationale, fonds latin 1139, 3719, and 3549; and

115

Ex. 6.1. *Argumenta faluntur fisice* (L 47).

Ar- gu - men- ta fa - lun - tur fi - si - ce, ru- unt
Dis- pu - ta- bat an - ti - cum se- cu - lum, si [Ma -

leges A - ri - sto - ti - li - ce, e - ner-
ri- a pre - sen - sit] ma - scu- lum; Chri- stus

va- tur vis ar - tis lo- gi - ce, sil- lo- gis - mi si - lent
mon strat hoc ver - bum gar- ru - lum, et vir- gi - nis non fran -

re - - - - tho - - - ri - ce.
git pes - - - su - lum.

R.
E- mi - cu- it, de- li - cu - it, quod la- tu- it in li - terra; ap-pa-ru - it,

pre- va- lu - it, quem ge- nu - it pu- er - pe-ra; et as - pe- ra que

ver - be - ra mi- na - ba-tur, per fi- li - um vis

vi - li- um tem- pe- ra - - - - - - - tur.

London, British Library, ms. add. 36,881) are less elegant and may represent more practical sources. An extreme type is represented by Cambridge, University Library, ms. Ff.i.17 (1), which is almost "impressionist" in its notation; this Anglo-Norman source was most likely a working personal *collectio* (notebook), rather than a clear reference manuscript, and its transcription into modern notation is rather difficult. Most of the central sources of medieval Latin song are available in facsimile (see below) and can easily be compared with modern editions.

Styles

Medieval Latin song exists in two basic formal patterns also found in liturgical lyric poetry: hymn (strophic) and sequence (paired versicles). A refrain (*reflexio*, often abbreviated *ref.* in text editions, or *repeticio*) can be added to either of these formal patterns.

As in the contemporary trouvère repertoire, a distinction between a "high" and "low" style can be seen in Latin song. The "high" style includes extended narrative songs, often with extended and elaborate melismas. The monophonic songs of the tenth fascicle of the "Florence" manuscript and a number of Anglo-Norman songs demonstrate this elaborate style. (See Example 6.1)

Ex. 6.2. *Dies ista colitur* (L 24b).

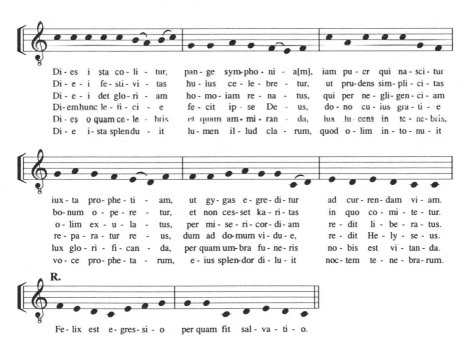

The "low" style is more clearly syllabic with clear melodic phrases and frequently has a prominent refrain, similar to other repertoires of dance songs.

Some of these refrain songs, such as the *rondelli* in the eleventh fascicle of the "Florence" manuscript, have been associated with medieval references to clerical dance. (See Example 6.2)

The medieval Latin song repertoire also served many different functions in the Middle Ages. The songs in the "high" style, whether elaborate spiritual songs or rambunctious drinking songs, were set pieces, music to be listened to as entertainment. The simpler songs may have served more practical functions, such as processional music within the liturgy or in liturgical drama, prefaces to readings within the service, substitutes for the *Benedicamus Domino* concluding certain masses and offices, or, in the case of the more risqué texts, clerical chamber music, perhaps even for dancing.

Performance Parameters

The various possible pronunciations of Latin during the Middle Ages are treated extensively and in detail by Harold Copeman.[3] Though much of this repertoire was truly international, its main centers were in Paris and Normandy/England, and, in general, "French" or "Anglo-Norman" Latin would be most appropriate.[4] Certain repertoires, such as the *cantiones* from the Mosburg Gradual in Munich, would more appropriately use a "German" Latin. Some recent recordings provide excellent examples of these different traditions, and some older recordings, especially of chant, will still use regional pronunciations that can be used as guides.[5]

Medieval Latin song, in common with other vernacular song, is also prone to various rhythmic interpretations in modern performance, as summarized in the introduction to this section. One important factor that would affect this repertoire more than others is the close connection with the performance of chant, especially in the more melismatic songs, which are very close in musical style to the responsorial chants, such as the graduals and alleluias from the Proper of the Mass, and great responsories of Matins. In the simpler songs, meter and rhythm may have been more prominent, and the current weight of scholarly opinion tends towards a type of syllabic equivalence, whether thought of as a loose fifth rhythmic mode or an isochronic syllabic style.[6]

A few songs survive in later manuscripts in a clear mensural notation, but the application of these rhythmic solutions retrospectively is still controversial.[7] The question of rhythm is further complicated since a number of monophonic songs also exist in polyphonic settings. Perhaps the most famous example is Philip the Chancellor's monophonic song, *Bulla fulminante* (L 5), whose tune was also used for the monophonic *Veste nuptiale* (K 81), and appears verbatim in the cauda for the three-voice conductus *Dic, Christi, Veritas* (C 3). In the polyphonic version, the rhythm is clearly notated using patterns of ligatures, but the single clearly notated manuscript of the monophonic *Bulla fulminante* does not indicate even basic rhythmic values. Rather than being an example of the general rhythmic practice of monophonic Latin song, it is possible that Philip the Chancellor only added a text to a preexistent rhythmic piece. In sum, a good performance will be the result of experimentation in order to discover a balance between the sound and rhythm of the poetry and the natural flow of the musical phrases.

Most modern editions reflect the preconceptions of their editors. Though readily accessible, the transcriptions by Gordon A. Anderson follow his rhythmic theories, but it is relatively easy, especially with the aid of a facsimile, to reconstruct a more neutral transcription. His edition, however, is invaluable for the annotated translations of virtually the entire Latin song repertoire preserved with music. The editions by Wulf Arlt and Bryan Gillingham primarily use a more neutral transcription style consisting of undifferentiated note-heads, as in Examples 6.1 and 6.2.

In connection with the earlier thesis that many of these poems were associated with dissolute and wandering scholars, at least two recorded performances have attempted to recreate a "drunken" performance of this repertoire. However, it seems more likely that the performance of these songs was taken as seriously as the performance of sacred or secular music in general during the Middle Ages.[8]

Most of the elaborate songs in the "high" style were probably solo songs, similar to most troubadour *cansos*, and probably should receive the same freedom in performance, especially in elaborate melismatic songs, such as Example 6.1. In the more syllabic songs, such as Example 6.2, especially the *rondelli* and other refrain songs, the style should be more controled. The alternation of a soloist singing the verses and a group responding with the refrain is occasionally indicated in a few rubrics found in the original manuscripts for these types of songs.

Selected Facsimiles and Editions

Facsimiles

Cambridge [Great Britain], University Library, ms Ff.i.17 (1). Publications of Mediaeval Musical Manuscripts 17, ed. Bryan Gillingham. Ottawa, Canada: The Institute of Mediaeval Music, 1989. Also includes a complete transcription of the manuscript in both neutral and measured form. This is sometimes referred to as the "Younger Cambridge Songbook."

Firenze [Italy], Biblioteca Mediceo-laurenziana, ms. Pluteo 29,1. Publications of Mediaeval Musical Manuscripts 10, 2 vols., ed. Luther Dittmer. Brooklyn, NY: The Institute of Mediaeval Music, *s.d.* This is frequently cited as either the "Florence" manuscript or simply "F" in discussions of this source.

London [Great Britain], British Library, ms. add. 36,881. Publications of Mediaeval Musical Manuscripts 16, ed. Bryan Gillingham. Ottawa, Canada: The Institute of Mediaeval Music, 1987.

Montserrat [Spain], Biblioteca, ms. I. Facsimile in Ma. Carmen Gómez Muntané, *El Llibre Vermell de Montserrat, Cantos y Danzas*, Papeles de Ensayo 5. Barcelona: Los libros de la Frontera, 1990. Includes a full study, facsimile, and transcription.

München [Germany], Bayerische Staatsbibliothek, hs. Clm 4660/4660a. Publications of Mediaeval Musical Manuscripts 9, ed. Bernhard Bischoff. Brooklyn, NY: The Institute of Mediaeval Music, 1967. The so-called *Carmina Burana*.

Paris [France], Bibliothèque nationale, fonds latin 1139. Publications of Mediaeval Musical Manuscripts 14, ed. Bryan Gillingham. Ottawa, Canada: The Institute of Mediaeval Music, 1987.

Paris [France], Bibliothèque nationale, fonds latin 3549. Publications of Mediaeval Musical Manuscripts 16, ed. Bryan Gillingham. Ottawa, Canada: The Institute of Mediaeval Music, 1987.

Paris [France], Bibliothèque nationale, fonds latin 3719. Publications of Mediaeval Musical Manuscripts 15, ed. Bryan Gillingham. Ottawa, Canada: The Institute of Mediaeval Music, 1987.

Editions

Anderson, Gordon Athol. *Notre-Dame and Related Conductus: Opera Omnia*, 9 vols. to date. Henryville, PA/Ottawa, Canada: The Institute of Mediaeval Music, 1979–1988. Vol. 6: monophonic songs from "Florence," fascicle 10; Vol. 8, *rondelli*; Vol. 7, monophonic songs in non-Notre-Dame sources, in preparation.

Arlt, Wulf. *Ein Festoffizium des Mittelalters aus Beauvais in seiner liturgischen und musikalischen Bedeutung*, 2 vols. Köln: Arno Volk Verlag, 1970.

Clemencic, René; Müller, Ulrich; and Korth, Michael. *Carmina Burana: Gesamtausgabe der mittelalterlichen Melodien mit den Sazugehörigen Texte*. München: Heimeran Verlag, 1979. The transcriptions in this edition are sometimes quite creative, but do not always reflect the music as it is actually preserved in medieval manuscripts.

Gillingham, Bryan. *Secular Medieval Latin Song: An Anthology*. Musicological Studies 60/1. Ottawa, Canada: The Institute of Mediaeval Music, 1993.

Notes

[1] The most comprehensive catalogue of later medieval Latin song, listing available editions and further bibliography, is Gordon A. Anderson, "Notre-Dame and Related Conductus: A Catalogue Raisonné," *Miscellanea Musicologica* (Adelaide) 6 (1972), 153–229; 7 (1975), 1–81. The reference numbers in parentheses that follow each title below are from this source. The monophonic repertoires are listed in Anderson's categories "K," "L," "M," and "N." There is at present no similar work for the earlier Latin song repertoires.

[2] A number of conjectural reconstructions can be found in Bryan Gillingham, *Secular Medieval Latin Song: An Anthology*, in the edition list above.

[3] In addition to Copeman's book, listed in the bibliography, he has participated in a number of articles on early Latin pronunciation in *Singing Early Music: An Introductory Guide to Pronunciation, 1250–1650*, ed. Timothy McGee et al. (Bloomington, 1996).

[4] In addition to the detailed discussions in Copeman, there is a short summary of medieval Latin pronunciation in this region in E.J. Dobson and F. Ll. Harrison, *Medieval English Song* (London, 1979), p. 321.

[5] The most readily available recording of medieval "French" Latin is Andrew Parrott's recording of Guillaume de Machaut, *Messe de Nostre Dame* (EMI Reflexe CDC 7 47949 2, 1984; reissued 1987). Most other performances of the Latin monophonic repertoire,

including those by Dominique Vellard and Emmanuel Bonnardot, Sequentia, and the Hilliard Ensemble, use a much more homogenized medieval Latin.

[6] On the question of rhythm, specifically in Latin song, see the following studies: Janet Knapp, "Musical Declamation and Poetic Rhythm in Notre Dame Conductus," *Journal of the American Musicological Society* 32 (1979), 383–407; Ernest H. Sanders, "Consonance and Rhythm in the Organum of the Twelfth and Thirteenth Centuries," *Journal of the American Musicological Society* 33 (1980), 264–286; John Stevens, *Words and Music in the Middle Ages* (Cambridge, 1986), esp. pp. 484–504.

[7] See Gordon A. Anderson, "The Rhythm of the Monophonic Conductus in the Florence Manuscript as Indicated in Parallel Sources in Mensural Notation," *Journal of the American Musicological Society* 31 (1978), 480–489. Anderson has also applied his theories to the transcriptions in the *Notre Dame Conductus: Opera Omnia*.

[8] The performance style in question can be heard on *Carmina Burana: Version originale*, Clemencic Consort (Harmonia Mundi France HMA 190336.38, 1975/1976/1978), and *The Feast of Fools*, New London Consort (L'Oiseau-Lyre 433 194-2, 1992).

7. Occitan Monophony

by Elizabeth Aubrey

Historical Background

The troubadours practiced their *art de trobar* between 1100 and 1300 in the Midi or Occitania, the area from Aquitaine and Limousin south and east through Provence, the south of present-day France. The troubadours traveled widely, particularly during the thirteenth century, and there is reliable evidence of the journeys of troubadours to Italy, the Iberian peninsula, France, Hungary, and on crusade to the Holy Land. Their songs were appreciated and imitated, receiving praise from Dante in the early fourteenth century, and serving as models for lyric songs in other languages.

The first several decades of the era of the troubadours were stable and prosperous ones, and the economic and cultural milieu of the Midi was in many ways the envy of Europe. This partly explains the vigor with which the clergy and nobility of northern France responded to the call of Pope Innocent III for a crusade against the Catharist heresy that had spread throughout much of Occitania. The Albigensian Crusade (1209-1229) became an excuse to despoil the rich resources of the region, and one of the far-reaching results was to scatter many of the troubadours into other parts of Europe, taking their songs and their mastery of the power of words and music with them.[1] Even though many of the troubadours continued composing until the end of the century, the culture of the Midi itself was profoundly affected by the Crusade and the inquisition that followed it, and the *langue d'oc* eventually became a regional dialect rather than a major European language. There was an attempt at revival, the self-styled *gai saber*, in the early fourteenth century in Toulouse and Catalonia, but its practitioners lacked the eloquence and creativity of the earlier troubadours.[2]

Manuscripts from the thirteenth and early fourteenth centuries transmit over 2000 poems by the troubadours, of which about 250 survive with melodies (a few of which are found with more than one musical setting, raising the total of extant melodies to 315).[3] Some of the most important manuscript collections of the songs of the troubadours were produced in Italy, Catalonia, and northern France. Of about 460 known troubadours (including about fifteen women, or *trobairitz*) whose poems survive, the music of only 42 (not counting the anonymous works) is extant. These 42 are generally admitted today to include most of the significant Occitan poet-composers, both in terms of the quality of their poetry and the size of their output.[4]

Language and Literature

The *langue d'oc*, often still called Old Provençal but now more commonly referred to as Old Occitan, is one of the romance languages, sister tongue of Old

French (the *langue d'oïl*), Italian, Spanish, Catalan, and Galician-Portuguese. Although all of the troubadours composed their poems in the standardized koine of *langue d'oc*, there are dialectal differences among the poems, ranging from limousin-influenced northern strains, to catalan-tinged southwestern varieties, to italianate southeastern dialects. The pronunciation of the language follows predictable patterns, more like Spanish or Italian than modern French. Its most subtle defining characteristic—and perhaps the most difficult for twentieth-century English-speaking singers—is its inflection, particularly word accentuation and the differences between open and closed vowels. A pronunciation chart can be a guide to learning the sounds, but in order to achieve the proper inflection of a complete verse or stanza, the singer will need to study the language itself, striving for understanding of the sense and flow of the poetry.

Old Occitan became the vehicle for the development of the earliest significant vernacular lyric poetry in western Europe. The poems are extraordinarily diverse in content, structure, and style. Contemporary theorists describe the poetry in the context of the art of rhetoric, one of the disciplines in the *trivium*. Rhetoric is concerned with eloquent expression which attempts to move an audience to a specific response, in the case of lyric poetry, emotions such as joy, pathos, sympathy, and anger. Different genres were developed to embody specific themes, love of a lady in the *canso*, lament over a loss in the *planh*, satire or complaint in the *sirventes*, a love dialogue in a rural context in the *pastorela*, intellectual or philosophical dialogue in the *tenso*, and so forth. Some early troubadours composed very obscure poetry, known as *trobar clus*, or "closed" style, in contrast to the more accessible *trobar leu*, or "easy" style.

Form

There are four elements of poetic structure in the troubadours' songs: number of verses, number of syllables per verse, rhyme scheme, and relationships among strophes. The first three elements customarily are graphed using lower case letters (upper case only in the instance of a textual refrain that recurs in all strophes) to indicate the same rhyme, and numerals to indicate the number of syllables in each verse. A prime (') indicates a paroxytonic (feminine) rhyme, i.e. one in which the accent falls on the penultimate syllable, and the final syllable is not counted, in contrast to an oxytonic (masculine) rhyme, in which the accent falls on the final syllable. For example, the first stanza of a *canso* by Bernart de Ventadorn has the poetic scheme a8 b8 b8 a8 c7' c7' d10 d10:[5]

> Ab joi mou lo vers e.l comens,
> et ab joi reman e fenis;
> e sol que bona fos la fis,
> bos tenh qu'er lo comensamens.
> Per la bona comensansa
> me ve jois et alegransa;
> e per so dei la bona fi grazir,
> car totz bos faihz vei lauzar al fenir.

The fourth element of poetic structure, strophe interrelationships, often is neglected by musicians today since the melody is the same for all strophes. The poem, however, often involves a complex and sophisticated progression of both structure and content from strophe to strophe. This is very important to keep in mind when performing the song, since omission of any of the strophes might violate the carefully conceived form and meaning of the poem. Most troubadour poems use a scheme in which all stanzas use exactly the same rhyme sounds. But sometimes a poet repeats rhyme words or sounds from stanza to stanza, or transforms them grammatically (as in the various forms of "comens" at the rhymes in the song by Bernart de Ventadorn given above), linking them in sometimes intricate and ingenious ways. One famous example of such complexity is Arnaut Daniel's sestina *Lo volgra ferm qu'el cor m'intra*, which has only six rhyme words (*intra, ongla, arma, verga, oncle, cambra*), which appear in a different order in each of the six strophes.[6] Some songs have a textual refrain consisting of a verse, part of a verse, or even one word, which recurs in all stanzas. Many poems end with a *tornada*, usually two to four verses, which follows the rhyme and syllable count structure of the concluding verses of the preceding strophes. These verses sometimes sum up the theme of the poem and often are addressed to a particular person (real or imagined)—a lady, a patron, or even a *joglar*.

The forms of the melodies of troubadour songs are not as easy to classify as the forms of the poems. There is no "regular" or "normal" form for a troubadour melody. Fewer than half of the extant troubadour melodies are in the standard ABABx form that characterizes the majority of the melodies of the trouvères. Furthermore, different manuscript readings of the melody for a single song often transmit versions that are structurally different. Although about one-fourth of the surviving melodies are through-composed, most of them involve some repetition of musical material, but generally with some kind of variation. Many melodies are held together by motivic interrelationships, incorporating such devices as transposition, sequence, motivic overlapping and linking, musical rhyme, and variation. Sometimes, ingenious interrelationships among motives bring about the subtle variation of a complete line, effectively transforming the phrase while maintaining its connection with others. The first three verses of Gaucelm Faidit's *Si anc nuls hom per aver fi coratge* (PC 167,52), for example, contain several motives that are modified and overlapped, making a simple graph difficult.

Ex. 7.1. Gaucelm Faidit (PC 167,52), X fol. 86v.

The traditional system for graphing musical structure in monophonic song defines musical phrases as coinciding with text verses, and the letters convey the relationships among the musical phrases. Repetition of phrases is designated by the use of the same letter, and slight variations can be indicated by means of prime and double-prime markings, or by superscript numerals.[7]

One type of song, which includes the *descorts* and *lais,* is not strictly strophic, but uses a "double-cursus" or paired-versicle structure. In this form, two or more verses are grouped together into larger units that make up the first half of a stanza, and this rhyme and syllable-count structure is duplicated in the second half. A graph of the verses and melody of such a song might look like:

abc	abc	de	de	fghi	fghi ...	xyz	xyz	rhymed verses
A	A	B	B	C	C ...	X	X	music

A song may consist of up to six stanzas of differing lengths and rhymes, and groups of identically structured verses within a stanza usually share the same melody.[8]

Special Requirements or Features

A modern performer needs to ponder not only what practices the singers followed when they sang the songs, but also to what extent the surviving melodies represent what the composers originally produced, and to what extent scribes changed (deliberately or by accident) the melodies in the process of writing them down. Each melody no doubt underwent some development during its life, which may have included revision by the composer, improvisation by singers, and conscious changes or unintentional changes or mistakes (a change is not necessarily an error) by a scribe. It is appropriate to assume, however, that the melodies that are transmitted are evidence of some kind of thirteenth-century aesthetic, whether it is that of composers, singers, or scribes, and that this aesthetic accurately represents to some degree the musical characteristics of a troubadour melody.

The main evidence we have for the roles that composers, singers, and scribes had in the production of the melodies resides in the variant readings that survive for about one-fourth of the tunes. A systematic study of the kinds of variants that exist, and of what they tell us about the composers, singers, and scribes, remains to be done.[9] But even some preliminary analyses and comparisons can lead a singer today to a few principles concerning what kinds of latitudes a singer might have exercised, particularly in the area of ornamentation and variation.

The act of performing aloud almost certainly resulted in changes in the melodies, whether intentional or unintentional, and it seems fitting that singers today be allowed a certain amount of freedom as they interpret the troubadours' songs. Upon repetition, a musical phrase might have been altered by filling in intervals, repeating notes, adding neighbor tones, rearranging pitches, or redistributing notes across syllables. Example 7.2 gives several extant examples of phrases that are repeated with such modifications.

Ex. 7.2. Marcabru (PC 293,35), W fol. 186v.

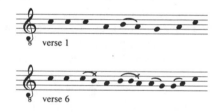

Albertet de Sestaro (PC 16,17a), X fol. 91.

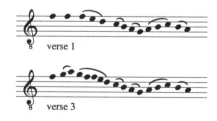

Arnaut de Marvuelh (PC 30,19), G fol. 33.

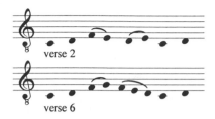

Folquet de Marselha (PC 155,10), G fol. 8v.

Folquet de Marselha (PC 155,22), R fol. 42v.

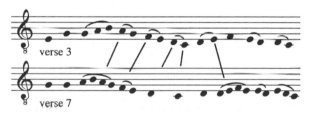

Singers today could make similar changes, but only after carefully studying many such variants in the manuscripts to learn the appropriate style (such variants do not resemble baroque-type divisions, for instance).

Choosing which extant version of a song to sing is another formidable task. The contents of the manuscripts represent many decades and regions of songs and troubadours, and their scribes reflected aesthetics and practices of their own eras and places.[10] The texts in the manuscripts vary as much as the music: some versions do not transmit all of the strophes, often strophes are found in different orders, words and verses are changed. Thus the theme of the poem might be developed quite differently from one manuscript to another. In general it seems advisable to use the reading of poem and melody that is given complete in one manuscript, although an argument can be made that poetry and music often traveled different paths in the Middle Ages, so a singer then, and today, might create a conflated version of a song from more than one source.

Notational Interpretation and Usual Transcription

Obviously the most problematic performance issue is rhythm. Exactly what the mainly rhythmless notations of the troubadour melodies were intended to convey will never be known for certain. Four large manuscripts are the primary sources for most of the extant melodies of the troubadours. Two of these sources were produced in the north and are considered to be among the most important repositories of trouvère songs; one of them might have been copied as early as ca.1240, the other probably ca.1270-80. The other two manuscripts were written in the south, one in Italy, and the other in Languedoc, both at the end of the thirteenth century. While northern scribes in the second half of the thirteenth century began experimenting with measured notations, there is no way of knowing when southern scribes began doing the same. A few of the melodies of the troubadours are written in one manuscript with distinguishable longs and breves, which means that some scribes at least were making an attempt by the late thirteenth century to capture more or less precise rhythmic values.[11] We cannot know for certain whether they were doing this in order to be faithful to a prevalent performance practice or were imposing a new aesthetic of mensural rhythm lately developed in the north in the context of polyphony (as Christopher Page argues).

Today's singer is forced to make his or her own educated judgment about which of the current rhythm theories to adopt, or perhaps to devise a new approach. There are, however, some problems common to all of the proposed theories about rhythm outlined in the Introduction above. All of them, in one way or another, assume that the poem is the source of rhythm for the melody. The modal theory says that there are accentual patterns in the text which should correspond with rhythmic patterns in the melody. The declamatory theory suggests singing the poem with the same rhythm that a speaker would use to recite the text without music. The isosyllabic theory gives every text syllable the same duration, regardless of the number of notes. In each of the theories, the melody does not have a rhythm of its own, but is essentially the vehicle for the poem. Furthermore, neither free declamation nor isosyllabism nor modal accentuation comfortably accommodates the many unstressed syllables in the troubadour songs that have four, five, or more notes; many musical phrases cannot be compressed easily into a metrical or syntactic mode dictated by the poetry.

Poets and poetic theorists of the thirteenth and fourteenth centuries spoke of a song as consisting of two elements, the words and the melody ("*los mots e.l son*"), implying the autonomy of the music as a distinct—and equal—element of the song. The melodies of the troubadours served the same rhetorical purpose that the poems did, and both together were regarded as sophisticated, integrated, and essential elements in the *art de trobar*.[12] A poem was said to have "good words" ("*bos mots*") not simply because it rhymed and scanned properly (this was the bare minimum), but also because of its eloquence of style. If a poem also had a "good melody" ("*bos sons*"), this was meant not only in a structural sense, but also in terms of its excellence of content. Most of the extant melodies seem to be carefully constructed following definable principles of musical composition, and as such they surely have their own inherent rhythm, even if it is inexact.[13]

There are three more or less complete editions of the melodies of the troubadours available today, and each of them embodies the theoretical bias of its editor. Friedrich Gennrich's work gives the melodies in modal or mensural rhythms; Hendrik van der Werf's supplies the pitches in noteheads without stems, even for the handful of songs that are transmitted in measured notation; the edition by Fernández de la Cuesta uses stemless noteheads too, but it also includes the neume shapes above the staves. None of these editions is a useful source for the texts. Only the Fernández de la Cuesta volume gives all of the strophes (edited by Robert Lafont), but the spellings have been modernized. A new anthology edited by Samuel N. Rosenberg, Margaret Switten, and Gérard LeVot contains complete texts and melodies of 34 troubadour songs, along with excellent translations; the music is given in stemless noteheads.

In a search for a practical rhythmic solution a singer should begin by examining the pitches of the extant melodies, carefully analyzing their structures, style, and variant versions, taken along with an appreciation for the interaction of music with poem. Characteristics of melodic structure and style, including such elements as repetition, phrase lengths, pitch goals, skeletal structures, motives, phrases, structures large and small, sequences, motivic and formulaic structures, and the function of individual pitches, might tell us something about rhythm. Even a declamatory performance would be based not so much on text accent and syntax as on melodic contour and structure, especially high and low points, pitch goals, phrasing, and the like. Sheer repetition—of phrases, motives, and strophes—gives a melody rhythm. The suggestion by van der Werf that different strophes of the same song might have entirely different rhythms seems implausible; even if singers exercised some flexibility in detail (as singers always do), it seems likely that all of the strophes shared a "macrorhythm" from strophe to strophe. Repeated verses (and perhaps repeated motives) within a melody surely had the same rhythm, regardless of the change of words.

Comparison of variant versions of a melody might lead to some possibilities for the duration of syllables. For example, pitches that are transmitted consistently in all readings might have been heard as more prominent, and hence perhaps were held longer or were accented; conversely, pitches that are in dispute among readings might have been less prominent and hence shorter. For example, the final cadence of Bernart de Ventadorn's widely disseminated *canso Can vei la lauzeta mover* (PC 70,43) indicates that D was accepted universally as the last pitch; further comparison of the extant versions (including *contrafacta*) also indicates that F often was lengthened on the last syllable:

Ex. 7.3. Bernart de Ventadorn (PC 70,43), final cadence.

R fol. 56v

W fol. 190v

G fol. 10

X fol. 47v and
Chigi fol. 78

O fol. 13v

FPn fr. 847 fol. 181 &
FPn n.a.fr. 1050 fol. 191v
(transposed down a 5th)

If a syllable has more notes in one version than in another, the syllable might have been sung longer in both cases. See, for example, the fourth syllable from the end in Example 7.3. On the antepenultimate syllable, one version (extant in two manuscripts) as E-D instead of E-C, suggesting that the E might have been stressed more than the other pitch. In analyses such as these, one cannot assume that there is an overall rule for all cases; on the contrary, the singer should study each melody on its own terms. Obviously, in the absence of variant versions, such considerations cannot be used.

The singer must understand the text—not just its meaning, but its structure and style as well—in order to convey it effectively to the hearers. The genre and topic can give an idea of tempo (a *planh* probably should move more slowly than a *dansa*, for instance). The poetic structure of verses, pauses (*caesuras*) within verses, rhymes, and strophes can be clues to a felicitous rhythmic interpretation. In the few songs that have measured notation, oxytonic and paroxytonic rhymes are treated quite distinctly: while oxytonic rhyme syllables are long, usually preceded by a short note, paroxytonic rhymes are always given the rhythm long-long. This is consistent with the principle expressed by contemporary poetic theorists that accent is important in the verse only on the rhyme word (and on the *caesura*, if there is one). See Example 7.4, in which the accented syllables are given in caps.

Ex. 7.4. Guillem Augier (PC 205,5), verses 17-18, W fol.186.

pos   li   plus   cor - TE - sa,   vol   sens   tort   au - SIR

(paroxytonic)   (oxytonic)

Instrumental Use

The songs of the troubadours can be quite effective when sung by a knowledgeable singer without any instrumental accompaniment. With a thorough understanding of the text and of the music, the sensitive singer will be able to communicate the theme and perhaps even some of the subtleties of the song to any audience.

A decision about whether or not it is historically defensible to use instruments for accompaniment receives little clear-cut guidance from late medieval sources. Some of the manuscripts that contain the songs of the troubadours show composers holding harps and fiddles (usually oval-shaped and always played on the arm) and small mandoras. These pictures tell us, at the very least, that such instruments existed in the thirteenth century, and that manuscript illuminators connected them with the *art de trobar*. Written accounts, including poetry, prose, and historical and didactic works, are replete with references to instruments and their use, and they could be used to support the idea that the lyric songs were accompanied.[14] Some troubadours were said to have traveled about with a *joglar* or two, who might have accompanied them when they sang. Other poet-composers were reported to have been good fiddlers themselves. In one famous instance, *Kalenda maia*, the melody was reported to have had its origin as an instrumental tune, which might imply that it had a measured rhythm to begin with; whether it retained this rhythm when Raimbaut de Vaqueiras composed words for it is, of course, unknown.[15]

Instruments such as fiddle, harp, small lute, pipe, and even bagpipe might be appropriate for use with songs of the troubadours, but there is no clue whatsoever in any medieval source about how any instrument might be used to accompany a troubadour song. Any accompaniment probably would not be very complicated, and should at the very least retain the basic shape of the monophonic tune. Professional musicians of the Middle Ages might have engaged in complex improvisation, but because the poetry of these courtly songs was central, the music certainly would not overshadow it. Very brief preludes, postludes, and interludes might be appropriate, as well as some simple elaboration, perhaps at cadence points or to highlight motives or variation; drones prove to be somewhat problematic in many songs in this repertoire, because it is often quite difficult—and perhaps dangerous—to determine a fundamental pitch (or pitches) in a melody. The most felicitous accompaniment, one that has the potential of being as elegant and expressive as anything more decorative, might be simply playing the melody with the singer; intensity, dynamics, timbre, articulation, and phrasing all can add profundity, shape, and sensual content to a melody. The overriding goal of the musicians should be to deliver the complete song—poem and melody—in as persuasive a way as possible.

Notes

1   See Elizabeth Aubrey, *The Music of the Troubadours* (Bloomington, 1996), pp. 1-5.
2   See Alfred Jeanroy, "Les *Leys d'Amors*," *Histoire littéraire de la France*, 38 (1949), pp. 139-233 for a history of this movement. In the late nineteenth century a new resurrection of literature in the *langue d'oc*, led by poet Frédéric Mistral, spurred the inhabitants of Provence to rediscover a pride in their cultural heritage, which sometimes expresses itself as a fierce chauvinism.
3   This number includes all songs in Old Occitan that are transmitted with complete melodies in thirteenth- or early fourteenth-century sources. The exact number of extant melodies has been in some dispute, because scholars have tried either to limit or broaden the definition of what a troubadour melody is. Thus, one of Friedrich Gennrich's purposes was to demonstrate the wide influence of the troubadour tradition, so he proposed the creation of some *contrafacta* after the manner of what he supposed was medieval practice, and he included these modern fictions, in a section called "Erschlossene Melodien," in his edition (*Der musikalische Nachlass*, full citation below in the Bibliography). On the other hand, Hendrik van der Werf chose to exclude from his edition songs that he considered suspicious because they survive in what he considers to be "late" (early fourteenth-century) sources (*The Extant Troubadours Melodies*, full citation in Bibliography). Others he omitted if in his opinion their formal structures (sequence-like, *virelai*-like) also betrayed late or external influence. On the basis of language, recent scholars have argued that at least six songs that were at one time considered to be part of the troubadour corpus have origins rather in the north. They include *A l'entrada del tens clar* and two others that survive with French or hybrid texts, and three songs that are known only as voices in motets and hence probably are not southern creations. See Robert A. Taylor, "*L'autrier cuidai aber druda* (PC 461,146): Edition and Study of a Hybrid-Language Parody Lyric," in *Studia Occitanica: In Memoriam Paul Remy* (Kalamazoo, 1986), II, pp. 189-97; and Elizabeth Aubrey, "The Dialectic between Occitania and France in the Thirteenth Century," *Early Music History* 16 (1997), 1-53.
4   See Elizabeth Aubrey, *The Music*, pp. 6-25.
5   PC 70,1 (refers to the index by Pillet and Carstens of the songs of the troubadours. See full citation in Bibliography). Ed. Martín de Riquer, *Los trovadores: Historia, literaria y textos*, 3 vols. (Barcelona, 1975), I, p. 392.
6   This device was imitated by a few later poets, including Dante and Petrarch. See Frank M. Chambers, *An Introduction to Old Provençal Versification* (Philadelphia, 1985), pp. 121-23.
7   See Elizabeth Aubrey, "A Study of the Origins, History, and Notation of the Troubadour Chansonnier Paris, Bibliothèque Nationale, f. fr. 22543" (Ph.D. dissertation, University of Maryland, 1982), pp. 147ff., for a graphing system that shows more motivic detail than the standard method. For further discussion of the use of motives, see Aubrey, *The Music*, pp. 184-94.

8   See Elizabeth Aubrey, "Issues in the Musical Analysis of the Troubadour Descorts and Lays," *The Cultural Milieu of the Troubadours and Trouvères*, ed. Nancy Van Deusen, Musicological Studies 62/1 (Ottawa, 1994), pp. 76-98.

9   See Elizabeth Aubrey, "Literacy, Orality, and the Preservation of French and Occitan Medieval Courtly Songs," *Actas del XV Congreso de la Sociedad Internacional de Musicología, "Culturas musicales mediterráneo y sus ramificaciones," Madrid 3-10/IV/1992*, ed. Sociedad Español de Musicología, *Revista de Musicología* 16/4 (1993 [1996]), 2355-66.

10 See Aubrey, *The Music*, chap. 2, "Transmission."

11 Ibid., pp. 247-54.

12 See Elizabeth Aubrey, "Genre as a Determinant of Melody in the Songs of the Troubadours and the Trouvères," *Historicizing Genre in Medieval Lyric*, ed. William D. Paden (Urbana, in press).

13 Ewald Jammers's complex theory about rhythm (*Ausgewählte Melodien des Minnesangs: Einführung, Erläuterungen und Übertragung* (Tübingen, 1963), pp. 29-67 is perhaps the most comprehensive in its inclusion of paleographical, textual, and, importantly, musical evidence. He has proposed the interaction of text and music on a structural level, which the singer must realize in the course of performance. Poem and music are closely interdependent in Jammers's system, though, so that a melody alone does not have an inherent rhythm.

14 See Elizabeth Aubrey, "References to Music in Old Occitan Literature," *Acta Musicologica* 61 (1989), 110-49.

15 This *razo*, or story, is quoted and translated in Aubrey, "References," p. 128. See Aubrey, "The Dialectic," pp. 40-52, for further discussion of this *razo* and its accuracy.

8. French Monophony
Elizabeth Aubrey

Historical Background

France was ruled in the late Middle Ages by strong dynasties, first the English Plantagenets, and then the French Capetians. The system of feudal allegiance that governed the aristocracy, even with its serpentine criss-crossing of interrelationships among counts, dukes, princes, lords, and king, helped give France a political and social unity that was lacking in the south. Paris was an important center of scholastic learning, and its cosmopolitan character distinguished it from the more provincial flavor of the Midi. Other urban centers, including Arras in Artois and Rheims in Champagne, looked to Paris for some of their intellectual and cultural inspiration.[1]

Monophonic music in the *langue d'oïl* differs in many ways from the music of the troubadours. In the first place, there is a much wider variety of genres. The vibrant indigenous musical-poetic tradition in Old French included not only the lyric songs and *lais* of the trouvères, which received much of their inspiration from the songs in Old Occitan, but also many anonymous works, including long narrative epic poems (whose music unfortunately does not survive), *jeux partis*, lengthy *pastourelles*, *rondeaux* and other dance songs, *refrains*, and musical insertions in dramatic and other extended works. Performance practices for each of these genres likely embodied different aesthetics that were closely tied to their function and intended audience.

Part of the reason for the differences between the monophony of the north and that of the south lies in the cultural and sociological distinctions between the two regions. The Midi was predominantly a rural culture whose class boundaries were not strictly demarcated, and whose *cansos, pastorelas, lais*, and *dansas* share an elegance and sophistication of language and style that appear to have appealed to a wide audience. France, on the other hand, was to a large extent still a feudal society with an increasingly powerful urban constituency. Class distinctions among the nobility, clergy, bourgeoisie, and servant groups are reflected more sharply in Old French genres, whose content and style differed according to the audience for which they were intended. The elevated language of *chansons* and epic songs, for example, was addressed mainly to the aristocracy, while dance *refrains, pastourelles, lais*, and *rondeaux*, belonged more to a popular audience.

Some scholars today describe the differences among these genres as "High Style" and "Low Style,"[2] or as occupying an "aristocratic register" and a "popular register."[3] Implicit in these delineations is not only an evaluation of differences in forms, styles, and language, but also of sociological function and cultural worth: where a song was performed, by whom, and for whom, are factors that help define it.

A third important difference between the songs of the south and those of the north is that the north was the center of extraordinary new developments in musical composition and notation, the effects of which monophonic music could not escape. Mensural notations that were created to express rhythmic values in the motet were appropriated by scribes for trouvère *chansons*. Some monophonic melodies of *chansons* and *refrains* turned up in motets—truncated, altered, excerpted, or fully intact—as one of the voices. At least two trouvères, Adam de la Halle and Jehannot de Lescurel, composed both monophony and polyphony, using the same type of poetry for each. The lines between monophony and polyphony thus were quite blurred, and it is difficult to sort out whatever differences there might have been in performance practices.

As might be expected from the rapid development of ways of writing music down, the north was much more interested in book production. Several scholars recently have described the second half of the thirteenth century in the north as a culture of literacy, when books became increasingly popular as a type of performance themselves.[4] Scribes expected their manuscripts to be seen and read, and music scribes became increasingly conscious of the semiotic implications of written notation.[5] Trouvères evidently welcomed the active involvement of scribes in the creation and preservation of their lyric songs.

A striking difference between the monophonies of north and south is that a great many more melodies survive for Old French songs than Old Occitan ones. Scribes recorded more than five times as many northern melodies, while only some 265 trouvères who were active in the twelfth and thirteenth centuries are known to us by name (in contrast to about 460 troubadours), and for almost all of them at least some music is extant. More than 4,000 lyric poems survive, and at least eighteen French manuscripts of the thirteenth and fourteenth centuries preserve close to 2,000 melodies for the monophonic songs of France.

Language and Literature

The *langue d'oïl*, or Old French, is the precursor of modern French, and except for some obvious spelling differences and some words that are no longer in use, a singer today who knows French should be able to become familiar with Old French fairly easily. A pronunciation guide will be necessary, since many of the sounds are different, but the pronunciation of Old French is somewhat more predictable than that of modern French. As with Old Occitan, there are some dialectal differences in the repertoire, notably that of Picard (the language of, for instance, Adam de la Halle's *Jeu de Robin et Marion*).

The *topoi* of the courtly songs are quite similar to those of the troubadour songs. But partly because the vocabulary of Old French was smaller than that of Old Occitan, the texts of the trouvère *chansons, jeu-partis, complaints,* and *lais* are more dependent on linguistic formulas. Although many laments and love songs of the trouvères are colorful and often emotional, most of them are not as earthy, diverse in imagery, or passionate as the best songs of the troubadours. There is no style comparable to the *trobar clus* of the troubadours in Old French lyric poetry.

The more popular songs, including *rondeaux, virelais, pastourelles*, dance songs, and *refrains*, comprise even simpler poetry, with even more formulas and conventional language.

Form

The poetic structures of songs in Old French vary to some extent with the genre. The strophic lyric songs are similar in structure to troubadour songs; the same principles of verse number, rhyme scheme, syllable count, and strophe interrelationships govern the songs,[6] with perhaps more predictability and regularity, and less variety of strophic linking devices. Strophic songs often have an *envoi*, extra verses at the end of the poem whose structure matches that of the concluding verses of the stanzas. The *lais* generally have the double-cursus poetic and musical structure that one associates with the Victorine liturgical sequence. Old French literature of the late thirteenth century saw the rise of the *formes fixes*, the *rondeaux* and *virelais*, which have strophic refrains of both text and music. These strict structures represent a new aesthetic, where poem and melody have matching structures, and where genre is defined in terms of form rather than content.

The regularity in the poetry of the courtly songs also characterizes their melodies, which usually contain repeated phrases in a ABABx pattern; through-composed melodies are relatively rare. The trouvères employed many musical formulas in their lyric songs, including intonations, cadences, and motives that mark caesuras.[7] In addition, many of the tunes have a clearly emphasized tonal center. The forms of the lyric melodies tend to be fairly stable from manuscript to manuscript, although there are many cases where different readings of a melody diverge significantly, especially after the first four verses. In general, the melodies of Old French songs are distinguished by a structural simplicity that endows them, more so than the troubadour melodies, with an autonomy apart from their texts. Where words and music seem to be closely integrated in the southern repertoire, so that each phrase of the poem requires a carefully matched musical phrase, in trouvère songs the music seems governed by an overall formal scheme that is not related to the content of the poem.

Special Requirements or Features

Because there are so many different versions of trouvère songs extant, one is faced with some difficulty in sorting out what the differences mean and which versions to trust. The manuscripts of trouvère melodies represent a significant diversity of origins, scribal practices, and contents. One manuscript, for example, the Cangé chansonnier, in general has many more chromatic inflections written in than the other manuscripts.[8] Some manuscripts contain melodies that are not at all related to the versions in most other manuscripts—in other words, are not "variant versions" in any sense but rather are entirely different melodies. Among manuscripts that do transmit variant readings, the melodic variants suggest some stability of important pitches on each syllable, while the details might vary. Such differences might be attributed to a practice of ornamentation by singers, and a systematic examination of such small-scale differences might yield some insights into improvisatory practices. Several such variants are shown in Example 8.1, the first verse of Gace Brulé's *Quant flours et glais et verdure s'esloigne* (RS 1779)[9] as found in four manuscripts. As can be seen, all of the versions have a common pitch on nearly all of the syllables (except the third), but details vary slightly.

Ex. 8.1. Variant versions of the opening of *Quant flours et glais* by Gace Brulé.

K fol. 70

M fol. 37v

O fol. 109

U fol. 8

Common pitches

In those cases where some or all of the verses have completely different musical content in different sources, it is impossible to say who is responsible for the creation of these unrelated versions, whether composers, singers, or scribes. But as in the case of the extant troubadour melodies, it certainly seems reasonable to suppose that whatever readings were written down in the thirteenth or early fourteenth centuries reflect the aesthetic at least of that period, if not of an earlier era.

Notational Interpretation and Usual Transcription

Rhythm is the most problematic of performance issues for Old French songs, and because the genres are more distinct in this repertoire, it is a more complex issue than for troubadour songs. A significant minority of the songs is given in Franconian or pre-Franconian notation, and these reflect the patterns of the Parisian rhythmic modes, particularly modes 1 (♩♪) and 3 (♩ ♪♩). Some scholars recently have argued that the measured notation found in some sources represents an aesthetic that grew out of the development of polyphony, and that "High Style" trouvère songs actually were sung with a free unmeasured rhythm. "Low Style" dances, *pastourelles*, and *refrain* songs, on the other hand, which may have been more closely associated with instruments, may have been sung with measured rhythm. Some manuscripts appear to support this theory because they use measured notation for some dance songs and unmeasured notation for some love chansons.[10]

A critical question, though, which is unanswerable with the present state of knowledge, is to what extent scribes could and did faithfully record the performance practices of music that stretched across one and a half centuries of time. Even in a period in which mensural notation was widespread, rhythmic notation was not always used in pieces where a measured performance was required. The "Manuscrit du Roi," for example, transmits readings of motet *dupla* in "rhythmless" trouvère notation, over tenors that have modal notation. Here obviously the absence of rhythmic notation does not mean the absence of precise rhythms, since the *dupla* of these motets would have to be sung with some sort of measured rhythm. It also is not known whether singers learned or sang directly from manuscripts, or whether they continued throughout the period to learn and sing mainly without the aid of written notation.[11]

Other evidence on rhythm, as difficult to interpret as that of the manuscript sources, comes from Johannes de Grocheio, the only medieval theorist who offers any significant commentary on medieval monophony.[12] His well-known warning that the word "measured" should not be understood "too precisely" has sometimes been applied to trouvère songs:

> Others, however, divide music into plain, or immeasurable, and measurable [music]; understanding by "plain" or "immeasurable" ecclesiastical [music], which is determined by many tones according to Gregory. By "measurable" they understand that [music] which is effected by diverse sounds that are sounded and measured simultaneously, as in conductus and motets. But if by "immeasurable" they understand music that is in no way measured—indeed totally said at will—their understanding is deficient, in that every operation of music and of any art whatever ought to be measured by the rules of that art [*cuiuslibet artis debet illius artis regulis mensurari*]. If, however, by "immeasurable" they do not understand "measured" so precisely [*non ita praecise mensuratam*], it seems that this division is able to remain.[13]

The music to which Grocheio refers here is plainchant, not trouvère song; moreover, it is not certain that the phrase "non ita praecise mensuratam" alludes to rhythm, since he precedes it with the comment that "every operation of music, and of any art whatever, ought to be measured by the rules of that art," a philosophical argument rather than a practical one.

Referring specifically to vernacular (i.e. French) music, however, Grocheio says that rounds (*rotundelli*) and the *cantus coronatus*, in his system the most noble of vernacular songs, should be sung slowly,[14] and that the latter "ex omnibus longis et perfectis efficitur."[15] Scholars have disagreed about what Grocheio means by this, because his wording is ambiguous. Most recent studies and translations suggest that "longa" and "perfecta" are more or less synonymous, meaning that only perfect *longas*, equivalent to three *breves*, are found in *cantus coronatus*.[16] The phrase could also means that *cantus coronatus* "is made from all sorts of longs, even perfect [ones]," which suggests that any kind of *longa* (including imperfect ones of two *breves*) might occur. Whatever Grocheio meant, it still it not clear whether he is saying that every individual note of such a song is equivalent to a long (whether perfect or imperfect), as some believe, or whether the overall meter of the song can be reduced to longs, as others have suggested. The language here, especially the verb "efficitur," is that of Aristotelian philosophy, and the context in which this passage is found is one in which Grocheio is attempting to explain the purpose and thematic content of such songs; whether he is describing a performance practice at all is highly questionable.[17]

There is no complete edition of French monophonic songs. Editions of selected songs have appeared, and as with the songs of the troubadours, each of them reflects the rhythm theory of its editor. Some of them (e.g. Beck, Gennrich, and Tischler), apply a modal or mensural interpretation to all songs, including those transmitted in non-measured notation. Others, notably van der Werf, give stemless noteheads for all songs, including those transmitted in measured notation. The 63 Old French songs in the recent anthology edited by Samuel N. Rosenberg, Margaret Switten and Gérard LeVot are mostly in stemless noteheads.

If there is mensural notation in a manuscript for one of the songs, it seems reasonable to follow it, even if the theory that this notation is a late addition to the music is true. "Late" in this instance still means the second half of the thirteenth century, when songs of the trouvères and other songs in Old French were in demand; the notation certainly reflects at least one medieval performance practice. The majority of the songs, however, are given in non-measured notation in the manuscripts, and while today's singers might attempt to apply metrical patterns to these songs, this should be done only if one is familiar with the rhythmic modal system. Perhaps a more valuable approach would be to conduct a detailed analysis of the Old French monophonic tunes that are transmitted in mensural notation, paying particular attention to how the rhythms interact with the text. If the choice is to opt for an application of the free declamatory theory (and such might also be appropriate even for songs that do survive in mensural versions), then it is even more critical that the singer be intimately familiar with the sounds, meaning, and structure of the poem.

One should not assume automatically, however, that the poem is of any particular help in making decisions about rhythm in this repertoire. As argued earlier, the meter of the poetry itself is not necessarily patterned. And in those songs that have mensural notation, long notes or notes that receive a stress at the beginning of a pattern do not always coincide with accented syllables, nor do short or unstressed notes always fall on unaccented syllables. For example, in this *romance* by Conon de Béthune, the notation is in the pattern of mode 3, but the accented syllables (shown in caps in the example), which do not fall into a consistent metrical pattern, do not always occur either on the first stressed note of the modal pattern, or on a long note.

Ex. 8.2. *L'Autrier avint* (RS 1574) by Conon de Béthune, O. fol. 74r-75.

1. L'au-TRIER a - VINT en cel AU - tre pa - IS
3. et la DA - me toz jors en son bon pris,

2. c'uns che-va - LIERS ot U - ne DA-me a - ME - a,
4. li a s'a - MOR es - con - DITE et ve - NE - e.

Furthermore, the mensural notation found in the manuscripts is not always consistently modal, so its interpretation is not always straightforward—it often does not seem to follow the modal rules carefully explained by thirteenth-century theorists like Johannes de Garlandia, Anonymous IV, and Franco of Cologne. But beyond this, if singers did derive metrical patterns from some principles inherent in the poems, as the modal theory suggests, these principles are not obvious today, and different singers (like editors) might arrive at different patterns.

Whatever the approach to rhythm, some general principles seem justifiable. First of all, since Old French melodies were relatively stable, at least as they are now transmitted, one might assume that rhythm contributed positively to this stability. The melodies were repeated many times, from strophe to strophe as well as performance to performance. They were also exchanged and borrowed freely, so that they had their own integrity, apart from a specific text; this integrity surely involved some kind of rhythmic shape. Structural coherence also contributed to their stability, no doubt, and this too may have been wedded to a rhythmic regularity. The large number of formulas in this repertoire undoubtedly was an aid in their transmission, and the formulas themselves might have carried a rhythmic as well as a melodic content.

Verse structures, including rhymes at verse ends and *caesuras*, probably should be articulated, and as implied above, the accentuation of the rhyme probably should be matched by elongation or stress in the melody. Repeated notes on one syllable probably should be read as elongation rather than reiteration, and syllables that have three or more notes in one version probably should be elongated in all versions. Analysis of the melody might lead one to sing identical or similar motives with the same rhythm, or to give notes that seem to be significant in some way a longer duration. Certainly exact repetitions of a musical phrase should have more or less the same rhythm.

Dance songs probably should have a regular beat, but the details must be worked out by experimentation. Other so-called "Low Style" songs, such as *refrains, pastourelles*, and pieces in the *formes fixes*, might also be given a regular meter, but for such songs transmitted in non-measured notation, the performers once again must experiment until a workable meter is found.

Instrumental Use

As with the songs of the troubadours, pictorial and literary evidence indirectly implies that instruments were associated in some way with monophonic songs in Old French. And as in the southern repertoire, the interpretation of that evidence is anything but certain.[18] Once again Johannes de Grocheio provides some clues about whether vernacular songs were accompanied by instruments, but some scholars recently have doubted whether the remarks of this late theorist (ca. 1300) can be applied to music that was waning by the time he wrote. After praising the vielle as the most powerful of instruments,[19] Grocheio asserts that good vielle players "introduce all cantus and *cantilena* and all forms of music in general."[20] In discussing antiphons in the Office, he mentions a "*neupma*," which he describes as "a coda or ending following the antiphon, just as an ending may be played on the vielle after a *cantus coronatus*...."[21]

There is no doubt that Grocheio associated this exalted instrument with the performance of trouvère songs. The language he uses may lead us to suppose that he is referring only to preludes and postludes, but his silence on the possibility that the fiddle might play the melody along with the singer should not be construed as a prohibition. The fact that his comments postdate the golden age of the lyric poet-composers is troublesome, particularly if it is true that his aesthetic was a new one, which the trouvères themselves would not have shared. There is no way of knowing the truth in this, however, and modern performers should not feel constrained by any particular dogma.

It might be significant that Grocheio mentions only the fiddle, and no other instrument, in connection with vernacular monophony. The little evidence that we have implies that mainly stringed instruments, perhaps including the harp and the lute, were associated with the courtly songs, and only rarely wind instruments or percussion. The more popular song types might have been sounded on flutes or bagpipes, perhaps with a pipe and tabor in accompaniment.

One further possibility with regard to performing forces concerns the *rondeaux, virelais*, and *refrains*, which in the view of many scholars have origins in popular dance types. Their refrain structures might have reflected a solo-chorus kind of performance, with a group of singers joining in the refrain for each strophe.

Notes

[1] See Mark Everist, *Polyphonic Music in Thirteenth-Century France: Aspects of Sources and Distribution* (New York, 1989).

[2] For example Roger Dragonetti, *La technique poétique des trouvères dans la chanson courtoise: contribution à l'étude de la rhétorique médiévale* (Bruges, 1960), and Christopher Page, *Voices and Instruments of the Middle Ages: Instrumental Practice and Songs in France 1100-1300* (Berkeley, 1986).

[3] Pierre Bec, *La lyrique française au moyen âge (XIIe-XIIIe siècle): contribution à une typologie des genres poétiques médiévaux*, 2 vols. (Paris, 1977-78).

[4] Sylvia Huot, in *From Song to Book*, has studied the carefully thought-out illuminations and decorations in many of the northern manuscripts, as well as their contents, layout, and rubrication, and has suggested that the chansonniers that survive were a type of performance in themselves, for the mind and eye as much as for the ear.

[5] See Christopher Page, *Voices and Instruments*; Mark Everist, *Polyphonic Music*; and Elizabeth Aubrey, "Literacy, Orality, and the Preservation of French and Occitan Medieval Courtly Songs," *Actas del XV Congreso de la Sociedad Internacional de Musicología, "Culturas musicales mediterráneo y sus ramificaciones," Madrid 3-10/IV/1992*, ed. Sociedad Español de Musicología, *Revista de Musicología* 16/4 (1993 [1996]), 2355-66.

[6] See the chapter on Occitan monophony above.

[7] See Jane Eckhardt McMullen, "Formulas in the Chansons of Gace Brulé: A Comparative Study of the Processes of Composition and Transmission in the Lyrics and Melodies" (Ph.D. dissertation, University of Iowa, 1989).

[8] See Theodore Karp, "The Trouvère MS Tradition," in *The Department of Music Queens College of the City University of New York: Twenty-Fifth Anniversary Festschrift (1937-1962)*, ed. Albert Mell (New York, 1964), pp. 25-52.

[9] "RS" refers to Gaston Raynaud's index of trouvère songs as reedited by Hans Spanke: *G. Raynauds Bibliographie des altfranzösischen Liedes, neu bearbeitet und ergänzt, erster Teil* (Leiden, 1955).

[10] See Page, *Voices and Instruments*, p. 17, Figure 2; see also pp. 73-74. See also Mark Everist, *Polyphonic Music*, pp. 204-05, and Hendrik van der Werf, *The Chansons of the Troubadours and Trouvères*.

[11] See Aubrey, "Literacy," and *The Music*, pp. 26-34.

[12] It should be noted that Grocheio's remarks are directly applicable only to French monophony, and not any other repertoire. He was a Parisian, writing for a Parisian audience. There is no evidence that he was familiar with the practices of any other vernacular literature.

[13] The full Latin text is found in Ernst Rohloff, ed., *Die Quellenhandschriften zum Musiktraktat des Johannes de Grocheio*, p. 124, sentences 72-75 (see above, Chapter 5, n. 12). See the new edition and translation of this and other passages on vernacular song by Christopher Page, "Johannes de Grocheio on Secular Music: A Corrected Text and a New Translation," *Plainsong and Medieval Music* 2 (1993), 17-41.

[14] "...in longo tractu cantatur...," Rohloff ed., p. 132, sentence 118b.

[15] "*Cantus coronatus* ...usually is composed by kings and nobles and is sung in the court of kings and princes of the land, so that their spirits may be moved to boldness and courage, to magnanimity and liberality, which all produce a good government. For this *cantus* concerns delightful and difficult material, like friendship and charity, and *is made from all sorts of longs, even perfect [ones].*" Rohloff, ed., p. 130, sent. 112-13: "Cantus coronatus...etiam a regibus et nobilibus solet componi et etiam coram regibus et principibus terrae decantari, ut eorum animos ad audiciam et fortitudinem, magnanimitatem et liberalitatem commoveat, quae omnia faciunt ad bonum regimen. Est enim cantus iste de delectabili materia et ardua, sicut de amicitia et caritate, et *ex omnibus longis et perfectis efficitur*" (emphasis added).

[16] Christopher Page translates this phrase, "it is composed entirely from longs—perfect ones at that" ("Grocheio," p. 24).

[17] See Aubrey, "Genre as a Determinant of Melody in the Songs of the Troubadours and Trouvères," *Historicizing Genre in Medieval Lyric,* ed. William D. Paden (Urbana, in press).

[18] See Sylvia Huot, "Voices and Instruments in Medieval French Secular Music: On the Use of Literary Texts as Evidence for Performance Practice," *Musica Disciplina* 43 (1989), 63-113.

[19] "And among all the stringed instruments that we have seen, the fiddle is considered to have the greatest power" Rohloff, ed., p. 134, sentence 137: "Et adhuc inter omnia instrumenta chordosa, visa a nobis, viella videtur praevalere."

[20] Rohloff, ed., p. 136, sentence 139: "Bonus autem artifex in viella omnem cantum et cantilenam et omnem formam musicalem generaliter introducit."

[21] Rohloff, ed., p. 160, sentence 255: "Est autem neupma quasi cauda vel exitus sequens antiphonam, quemadmodum in viella post cantum coronatum vel stantipedem exitus, quem 'modum' viellatores appellant."

9. Iberian Monophony

Manuel Pedro Ferreira

Historical Background

The Iberian Peninsula in the late Middle Ages (twelfth–fourteenth centuries) comprised a number of diverse, changing, and often conflicting political entities: expanding Christian Kingdoms in the North, shrinking Muslim Kingdoms in the South. Music from the Iberian South (the Andalus) has survived to a certain extent, but only through oral tradition (possible exceptions will be mentioned later).

The Christian North can be divided into two different areas. The first includes the Kingdoms of León (northwest, including Galicia, on the Atlantic coast; united with Castile in 1230), Portugal (west, originally southern Galicia, proclaimed independence from León in 1140), Castile (center) and Navarre (northeast, ruled by French nobility from 1234 onwards). The second area corresponds to the Kingdom of Aragon, in the east, united in 1137 with the Mediterranean County of Catalonia (linked to Occitania through language and religious culture). Given that the secular monophony of post-1234 Navarre properly belongs to the sphere of the *trouvères*, and that Catalonian troubadours are best studied in the context of the Occitan *canso*, no mention will be made here of these repertoires.[1]

The Iberian *cantiga* (the Galician-Portuguese word for "song") can be understood only as the result of cross-fertilization. In the twelfth-century, one of the largest and possibly the most cosmopolitan Christian town in the Peninsula was Santiago de Compostela, a famous pilgrimage center in Galicia. From the Compostela-centered North-West, a secular tradition of song-making in the local language (Galician-Portuguese), rooted in folk-song, was spread south and eastwards by Galician *jograis* (jongleurs). At about the same time (from 1135 onwards) Provençal and Catalan troubadours began to pay frequent visits to the royal and manorial courts along the Santiago route; the marriage of Alfonso VIII of León with Eleanor of Aquitaine in 1170 increased the influence of the Occitanic element in aristocratic circles. By the end of the century, an adaptation of the "high style" courtly song begun to be cultivated by Portuguese and Castilian noblemen who had personal links with the León court or close connections with the Aquitainian milieu.[2] This adaptation implied two important external differences: one was the use of the Galician-Portuguese language; the second was apparently the rejection of certain formal features popular in Occitania and the free refashioning of others to fit local taste. By the early thirteenth-century, the different traditions of song-making privileged by Galician jongleur and Iberian feudal lord had come together in a strong lyric tradition which was later to find increasing support from the Castilian-Leonese and Portuguese Kings.

Between 1220 and 1264, the Christian Kingdoms conquered most of the southern territories; the Muslim became confined to the far south, the Kingdom of Granada. These momentous political changes had little effect on secular Galician-Portuguese lyricism, but eventually allowed popular Andalusian music to influence Christian monody, specially in Castile, where it is found, refracted by northern practice, in some of Alfonso's *cantigas* to the Virgin.[3]

The Galician-Portuguese tradition of courtly song died away in the mid-fourteenth century, under the pressure of changing taste, plague, and social crisis; afterwards there is a vacuum in Portuguese poetic sources, and Galician poetry gradually fades away. Castilian language (today's "Spanish") began to be used in lyrical verse already in the thirteenth century, but it was in the second half of the fourteenth that it began to replace Galician-Portuguese in courtly poetry. No music survives for this early Castilian and post-1350 Galician poetry.

Language

Galician-Portuguese (or Galego-Portuguese) is the medieval ancestor of modern Galician and Portuguese. Derived from Latin, it was already a distinct language (i.e. a cluster of closely related dialects) in the ninth century. By the thirteenth century, in spite of slight differences between Galician and Portuguese ways of speaking, the language was in broad terms much the same, the more so in its poetic *koiné*, a supra-regional literary variety. The promotion of Castilian as the official language of the Leonese court, and then, from the fourteenth-century onwards, the forced Castilianization of Galicia's upper classes, hit the social status of the Galician language severely. In the meanwhile, Portugal's expansion towards the south and the use of Portuguese in the official documents favored its independent linguistic development.[4]

Galician had ceased to be a literary language by the fifteenth century, and was revived as such only from the nineteenth century onwards; it was outlawed under the Franco dictatorship. According to some authors, it eventually acquired the status of a co-dialect of Portuguese, or, according to others, that of a kindred, but different, language. Only very recently was it declared an official language in Galicia (now an autonomous region in Spain) where linguists and writers try hard to restore its prestige and overcome the pervasive influence of Castilian.

The Portuguese language was exported in the sixteenth century all over the world; it is spoken nowadays in Europe (Portugal and frontier sections of Spain where linguistic and political boundaries do not coincide), South America (Brazil), parts of Africa (Cape Verde, Guinea-Bissau, Sâo-Tomé e Príncipe, Angola and Mozambique), and a few places in Asia (Goa in India, Macau in China, East Timor). Portuguese may at first seem hard to learn, not so much because of its grammar (similar to that of Castilian), but because of its complex phonological system: for instance, instead of the five basic vowels found in Castilian, Portuguese has eight (in Brazil) or nine (in Portugal) "simple" vowels, to which one may add five nasal vowels and a few nasalized diphthongs. They read well on paper, but their pronunciation poses a challenge; diction coaching is therefore a necessity.

Furthermore, medieval Portuguese was not always pronounced like modern Portuguese. A few examples: the /o/ in "fremosa" was closed, not open; the /e/ in "Deus" was open, not closed; the digraph *ch* in "choran" was read /tsh/, not /sh/; the initial consonant of "cedo" sounded /ts/, not /s/; and the letter *z* in "prazer" before, and possibly also during part of the thirteenth century was pronounced /dz/, not /z/. Syntheses like Paul Teyssier's *Histoire de la langue portugaise,* or more specialized linguistic studies, should be consulted.

In Galician-Portuguese poetry, as in French versification, syllable-count stops on the last accented syllable; a seven-syllable line with masculine rhyme (7) is thus made equivalent to an eight-syllable line with a stress on the penultimate syllable (7'). Often a /r/, an /l/ or even an /n/ before a pause receives in actual speech a paragogic closed /e/ (sometimes spelled out in the manuscripts, e.g. mare, male); this allows some masculine rhymes to function as feminine rhymes.[5]

Genres

The main poetical genres in the Galician-Portuguese troubadour tradition are, on the secular side, the *cantiga de amor* ("love song," an aristocratic register) the *cantiga de amigo* ("boyfriend song," a bourgeois register, as the great Portuguese philologist Rodrigues Lapa calls it) and the *cantiga de escárnio* or *de mal-dizer* (satirical song with or without *equivocatio*). The religious *Cantigas de Santa Maria* include lyrical *cantigas de loor* and narrative *cantigas de miragre*. The Galician-Portuguese genres are defined not on the basis of form, but content. Nevertheless each genre exhibits a tendency to prioritize certain formal features.

The *cantiga de amor,* though heavily influenced by the Occitan *canso*—the most aristocratic of song genres—is generally shorter and often (in 52% of the cases) includes a refrain. It presents, in a rhetorical way, the poet's feelings towards a noblewoman (spoken of as his lady, *senhor*); the contents tend to be rather abstract and conventional. When it does not have a refrain, this kind of *cantiga* tends to be composed of three or four stanzas of seven decasyllabic lines each, divided by rhymes into four plus three lines; but in a majority of cases stanzas are reduced to four or five lines to allow the presence of a refrain occupying one to three lines (e.g., a stanza with four decasyllabic lines followed by a distich).

The *cantiga de amigo* seems certainly to be indigenous to the Iberian Peninsula; it is the most visible outcrop of the archaic European tradition of female-voiced song. In spite of its womanly character, the *cantiga de amigo* was composed and possibly sung by a man (a *jongleur*-composer could also teach his female companion to sing it). It was nevertheless supposed to convey the world of amorous feelings, thoughts, words and actions of a young woman in a domestic female environment, whether longing for her boyfriend, rejecting him, or somewhere in between. The poet tended to use an archaic technique known as "parallelism," which called for the presentation of the same idea in alternating lines, with slightly different wordings, the word-change being at the line-end (*coda*):

Ai ondas que eu vin *veer*,
se me saberedes *dizer*
　　porque tarda meu amigo sen min?

O waves that I came to see,
Will you not tell me
Why my lover tarries away from me?

Ai ondas que eu vin *mirar*,
se me saberedes *contar*
　　porque tarda meu amigo sen min?

The stanzas in the *cantiga de amigo* are short (two or four lines) and nearly always (in 88% of the extant texts) end in a refrain which includes one to three lines; the singer may have had relative freedom in rendering the refrain (which was not choral, though this has often been assumed).

The third most important genre in Galician-Portuguese lyricism is satirical, the so-called *cantiga de escárnio* (restrained or oblique satire) or *mal-dizer* (open satire, outright invective with frequent use of obscene words). Just under a third of the satirical *cantigas* (31%) include a refrain. No music survives for these texts; melodies taken from other *cantigas* can nonetheless be adapted to some of them for performance purposes, as has recently been proposed.[6]

On the whole, about 1680 secular Galician-Portuguese poems have survived. To these poems may be added 419 songs (preceded by an introductory poem) dedicated to the Virgin Mary, the well known *Cantigas de Santa Maria* compiled at the court of Alfonso X. One tenth of these religious *cantigas* are relatively short songs of praise written in a variety of forms (*cantigas de loor*), while the others narrate miracles and are normally longer (*cantigas de miragres*). All but seven of these *cantigas* include a refrain, which normally appears at the beginning; it is generally supposed to imply a choral performance. Only five of the *Cantigas de Santa Maria* have been transmitted without their music.

The Secular *Cantigas*

Unfortunately, most of the music for secular cantigas perished in the centuries that followed the demise of the tradition, around the year 1350. Only two documents are known to survive: the Vindel MS, a single, folded leaf written in the last quarter of the thirteenth century, found in 1913 by the Madrid bookseller Pedro Vindel, and which since 1977 has belonged to the Pierpont Morgan Library in New York (*M* 979); and the Sharrer MS, a fragmentary folio detached from a lost Portuguese songbook written ca.1300, found in 1990 by University of California Professor Harvey L. Sharrer in Lisbon's Arquivo Nacional da Torre do Tombo.

The Vindel MS includes seven *cantigas de amigo* attributed to the Galician jongleur Martin Codax (fl. ca.1250-60), one of them without music. Set in Vigo on the west coast of Spain, near the Portuguese border, the Codax songs seem to belong together as a cycle; their structural and rhetorical features lend further support to this view, which has been subscribed to by most scholars. The music, however, shows no trace of modal ordering.

The music is closely tied to the structural features of the poem: the regular strophic accents, the internal strophic contrast marked by the *coda*, and the opposition between strophe and refrain are all enhanced by melodic features. The songs tend to be in AA'B form, use a small compass (typically, a major sixth) and move mostly by step; the articulation of the text is syllabic or neumatic, melismas including generally no more than four notes (seven being the maximum). The music, despite a distinctive, rhetorically expressive character which sets it apart from other surviving courtly music of the time, is related to Gregorian psalmody and shares some formulaic vocabulary with the religious *Cantigas de Santa Maria*.

The Sharrer MS includes seven *cantigas de amor* by the Portuguese King Dom Dinis (1261-1325). His court was the last refuge of the Galician-Portuguese lyric tradition. The melodies, with ranges close to an octave, are unusually dense: at the very beginning they tend to be syllabic, but neumatic articulation then becomes the norm; the songs have, on average, three notes per syllable. Some of them follow an inverted-arch contour rarely encountered in Occitanian or French troubadour sources, in spite of musical influence from both traditions. Step-wise progression and melodic unisons are predominant, but thirds are given an important structural role. Most songs include repetition of musical phrases; the musical forms (sometimes unclear to us, due to the fragmentary state of the manuscript) seem to vacillate between the Occitanian *oda continua*, the Iberian solo refrain-forms, and the northern French repetitive forms. The structural archaism of some melodies, the repetition of conventional motives and melodic contours, and the traditional rhythmic style suggest a conservative compositional technique rooted in orality. The music displays special sensitivity to text-setting, being closely related, albeit in a subtle way, to the first strophe of the poems.[7]

The Religious *Cantigas*

The *Cantigas de Santa Maria* compiled in the court of Alfonso X, el Sabio ("the Learned") between 1264 and 1284 are, unlike the secular cantigas, mostly narrative, and their texts tend, also uncharacteristically, to adopt the formal features of the Andalusian *zajal* (*aa bbba [aa] ccca* etc.), a moorish song inspired by old Hispanic traditions. They nearly always call for a choral repeat of the refrain after each stanza, although it is not clear that this repeat was in every case maintained in performance; some of them seem to have dispensed with it altogether. Although composed in the Castilian court, their language is Galician-Portuguese, in keeping with the King's preference for the Galician-Portuguese language in his own secular poetry and with the presence at the court of a large group of Galician and Portuguese troubadours.[8]

The music of the *Cantigas de Santa Maria* (hereafter *CSM*) was notated in three codices. The first (Madrid, B.N. MS 10 069) comes from Toledo, hence its *siglum* *To. It includes 128 songs, and is a very early copy (ca.1275) of a manuscript written ca.1270 which contained the primitive collection of one hundred *cantigas*. In *To, this collection is enlarged with three appendices. The second codex is found in the Escorial Monastery (MS T. I. 1) and is generally referred to as *T (or E^2, or *e*);

it contains 194 *cantigas* and was meant to be the first volume of a two-volume luxury set, the second volume of which remained incomplete. It was probably written around 1280-84. The third codex, *E (or E¹), is also in the Escorial Monastery (MS b. I. 2) and was most likely written around 1283-85. It contains 407 *cantigas* (apparently 416, but nine are given twice) and represents therefore the final stage of the collection; but it is based, both from the philological and the musicological point of view, on less authoritative sources than *To and *T.[9]

Generally speaking, the melodies of the *CSM* are compatible with the standard Gregorian eight-mode system; according to Gerardo Huseby, there are only 43 *cantigas* (about one-tenth of the collection) that call for special modal categories or present unusual modal configurations.[10] Some melodic *topoi* are reminiscent of Gregorian chant. The melodic range tends to be comprised between a 6th and a 9th.[11] The melodic forms are normally of the *virelai* type: **AB** CC AB, **ABA'B** CDCD A''BA'B' or **ABCD** CDCD ABCD. The text articulation is predominantly syllabic, with occasional short melismas.

The music of the Marian *cantigas* has been described by Julián Ribera (1858-1934) as being essentially Arabic.[12] Higinio Anglès (1888-1969), in his monumental edition of the *CSM*, attacked Ribera's claim on solid musicological grounds.[13] The *CSM* might in fact be described as a mixed, Christian-oriented repertoire, as Anglès observed; but they also include, as Ribera suspected, some typical Andalusian traits, although not those pointed out by him

Medieval Andalusian music has both Hispanic and Arabic elements: Andalusian formal features are basically Iberian, while rhythmic features are basically oriental. According to recent research, the simple *virelai* form (types like **AA** BBAA or **AB** CCAB) probably corresponds to an old indigenous tradition later taken over and developed by Andalusian musicians; the Andalusian rondeau form (**AB** BB[B]AB) and possibly the rondeau-influenced, cyclical virelai (**AB** C[C]BAB) were developed in the Andalus. Most of the *CSM* exhibit a *virelai* form; over seventy of them adopt the Andalusian rondeau form, and seven more the cyclical *virelai* form.[14]

The Arabic rhythmic tradition has some superficial similarities with the French modal system, but it includes a few unusual, characteristic features: the large scale of some rhythmic cycles and periods, the use of syncopation, and the importance given to quaternary meter. It also uses dotted rhythm and quinary meter. In the *CSM*, there are more than twenty songs whose rhythm cannot be understood in terms of French modal theory, but make complete sense when confronted with Arabic rhythmic theory (Ex. 9.1a).[15]

Ex. 9.1a. *CSM* 109, *E, fol. 117.

Ex. 9.1b. *CSM* 424, *To, fol. 145.

Notational Interpretation and Usual Transcription

The Galician-Portuguese repertoire has been seldom discussed at length from the paleographical point of view and transcriptions do not abound, partly because of difficult access to the sources. The Vindel MS had been poorly reproduced in 1914 and could not be studied directly before 1977; a color facsimile and black-and-white enlargements were published in 1986.[16] The high-contrast, retouched facsimile of the musical notation in *To published by Ribera in 1922 is unclear and often unreliable;[17] the black-and-white, retouched facsimile of *E was published by Anglès only in 1964 and is not entirely faultless either;[18] the color facsimile of *T dates from 1979 but even there some details are not clearly visible.[19] Finally, the Sharrer MS was discovered only in 1990;[20] the first full photographic reproduction appeared in 1991, two years before a disastrous "restoration" washed out some music from the fragment.[21]

Before individual manuscripts are discussed, it should be stressed that they are contemporary or nearly contemporary with the authors who created the *cantigas*; their musical notation cannot be denied a certain historical authority. Recent research makes it clear that this notation, eccentric as it may be considered (in relation to Paris), does not lack inner logic and is musically satisfying.

The Martin Codax *cantigas* long presented a rhythmic riddle which most scholars evaded through chant-inspired note-equivalence (Tafall y Abad, Isabel Pope), imposition of pseudo-Arabic (Martínez Torner) or modal patterning (Friedrich Gennrich, J. A. Westrup) or simple note-head transcription (Ismael de la Cuesta). Higinio Anglès confronted the notation with subjective ingenuity, but having no access to the original, could not make complete sense of it and failed to notice that in the Vindel MS two different scribes copied the melodies. This is important, because the paramensural character of the musical notation (use of semibreve, breve and long, and of *c.o.p.* ligatures), which nonetheless displays some typical Iberian traits, allows us to see at least two different rhythmic styles. That corresponding to the first scribe (*cantigas* I, IV, V and VII) has been described as rhapsodic, due to the juxtaposition of rhythmic patterns and melodic *formulae* also found elsewhere, resulting in an irregular alternation of shorts and longs—a symptom of an archaic, oral-based composition process (Ex. 9.2a); the second scribe (*cantigas* II and III) appears closer to the aesthetics of modal rhythm (Ex. 9.2b).[22]

Ex. 9.2a. Codax, IV.

Ex. 9.2b. Codax, III.

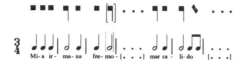

The rhythm of Codax's *cantigas de amigo* has nothing to do with that of the *cantigas de amor* by Dom Dinis. The notation in the Sharrer MS (derived from pre-Franconian notation, with Iberian traits) allows us to characterize Dinis's rhythmical style as generally slow, florid and iso-syllabic (Ex. 9.3); this fact, together with the high status of author and poetic genre, makes these songs unambiguous examples of *cantus coronatus* as it was adopted in Iberian troubadour circles.[23]

Ex. 9.3. *CSM* 6.

The notation in the manuscripts of the *CSM* belongs to two different types. The basic note-shapes are, in *To, the oblique and the square *punctum*; in *T and *E, the square *punctum* and the *virga*. The musical reality represented is the same (notwithstanding a few exceptions to the rule); but *To takes as its basis the basic note-shapes of the late variety of Aquitainian notation used in Iberian liturgical sources, while the notational repertoire of *T and *E has its roots in French square notation. Both kinds of notation are semi-mensural, yet while in the more archaic Toledo type there are, among the basic neumes, only five or six with a mensural meaning, the Escorial notation includes ten to fourteen mensural signs (Ex. 9.4). There are slight differences between the *T and the *E notation: the first is generally more reliable; unlike the latter, it shows a correct use of the *cum opposita proprietate* binary ligatures.[24]

Ex. 9.4a. Basic mensural signs in *To.

$$\blacksquare \quad \blacktriangleright \mathsf{F} \; (\mathsf{N}?)\} \; \mathsf{L}$$

$$\blacklozenge$$

Ex. 9.4b. Basic mensural signs in *T/*E.

$$\mathsf{1} \; \mathsf{J} \; \mathsf{J} \; \mathsf{L} \; \mathsf{T}(\blacktriangleright \; \blacktriangleright \; \mathsf{N}?) \; \mathsf{L}$$

$$\blacksquare \; \mathsf{U} \; \mathsf{N}(\mathsf{L} \; \mathsf{L} \; {}^\ast\mathsf{T}) \qquad\qquad \mathsf{B}$$

$$\blacklozenge \qquad\qquad\qquad\qquad \mathsf{S}$$

The melodies of the *CSM* were published in their entirety only once, in 1943 by Higinio Anglès (some transcriptions were later revised and re-published in 1958).[25] His is the standard musical edition used by most performers today. Anglès attempted to present a faithful modern translation of the original musical notation, which he at any rate took care to reproduce above the staves; whenever the manuscripts presented an unusual rhythmic profile, Anglès, unlike most scholars of his generation, did not let French modal theory hinder him. This, which we now see as his main strength, had the effect of casting a cloud over the seriousness of his work.

Anglès attempted to justify deviations from the French norm as instances of popular music, which was of course possible but not altogether convincing. His attitude was, as a matter of fact, impaired by a highly subjective stamp and the lack of a critical methodology. Besides, he gave priority in his transcriptions to the codex *E, which we now know is the least authoritative of the three extant musical manuscripts.

The transcriptions themselves are generally reliable, but not perfect, even if some subjectivity in the transcription is allowed for. Some pieces were interpreted in binary meter when nothing seems to justify it; not a few passages sound musically contrived, and that for no good paleographical reason. The notation above the staves is incomplete and sometimes incorrectly reproduced; and nine musical signs are wrongly transcribed (Ex. 9.5).[26] There is consequently room for improvement, assuming that we take the manuscripts themselves as our best historical witnesses and make an effort to understand their notation on its own terms.

Ex. 9.5. Incorrect mensural signs in Anglès.

Rhythm: *To ◗ ◖ ◗   *T/*E   ◖ ◢ ◣ ◤ (◿ ◣ *E)

Melos: *To/*T/*E   ◣═♩   ◣═♩♩

So, despite some notational ambiguity, typical of pre-Franconian systems, the collection of songs assembled by Alfonso X can be rhythmically transcribed with a reasonable degree of assurance. Already in Anglès's edition we could easily observe that the rhythm of the *CSM* is generally of the simple modal type, with frequent modal mixture (the combination of two modes is referred to by Anonymous IV and illustrated by the fifth mode of Lambertus). There are nevertheless special modal patterns (sixth mode of Lambertus), and also cases of quadruple meter which recall Andalusian music, rhapsodic rhythm (as in the *cantigas de amigo*), and iso-syllabic rhythm (sometimes of a florid nature, as in the *cantigas de amor*) (Ex. 9.6).

Ex. 9.6. Rhythmic patterns in the *CSM*.

Mixed modal rhythm (CSM 104)

*To, fol. 123
*E, fol. 113

Andalusian quaternary meter (CSM 100)

*To, fol. 156
*E, fol. 110-111

Sixth mode of Lambertus (CSM 288)

*E, fol. 258v

Rhapsodic/iso-syllabic rhythm (CSM 230)

*E, fol. 209v

Special Features

The *cantigas* by Dom Dinis are to be sung by a single male voice (including the refrains) as independent compositions. The *cantigas* by Martin Codax are to be sung by a single voice, but if possible as a complete cycle. This cycle may originally have comprised *cantigas* I to VI or possibly I to VII (VII being a coda); slightly later, the sixth song may have been dropped out. The seventh song, which was added in the Vindel MS by the first music scribe, may have replaced the sixth, which was left without music by both scribes. The sixth song can therefore be either recited (if the performer chooses to adhere to the poetic architecture of a six- or seven-song cycle) or skipped altogether in concert (if the late thirteenth-century version of the cycle with *cantigas* I-V and VII is adopted).[27] The performance of the complete cycle, a small musical drama, can be easily presented on stage as a theatrical event, provided that the singer can act properly. Other rhetorically correct alternatives are: cantigas I, IV, V and VII; cantigas II, III and IV. The pitch level in the modern transcriptions mirrors a medieval convention (acceptable final note, no sharps, flat only on B) and can therefore be changed at will, taking into account that the fourth cantiga should be sung in a relatively high register; the songs can be made tonally closer through transposition.[28]

The *CSM* seem generally to require soloist plus choir (in the refrain); but some of them (for instance: *CSM* 81, 83) are best performed by a single voice, and in a number of cases the repeat of the refrain after each stanza or at the end of the song is to be discouraged, since it would destroy the poetical *enjambement* or the poet's conclusion.[29] The performer should therefore pay special attention to the text in order not to be deceived by scribal convention. A different problem is the choice between different versions of the same cantigas. *To sometimes presents an older version; the comparison between the versions in *To and those in *T/*E can help the performer to gain some insight into melodic thought and stylistic change in the court of Alfonso (Ex. 9.7).[30]

Ex. 9.7. Contrast between *To and *E (CSM 162).

Instrumental Use

Galician-Portuguese medieval poetry and the musical iconography associated with it (in *T, *E and the Portuguese *Cancioneiro da Ajuda* of ca.1300) do not allow us to suppose that, as a general rule, the *cantigas* and instrumental performance belong together.[31]

This conclusion may sound odd, given that the early music movement has been particularly fond of instruments and the *cantigas*, specially those for Mary, seem to provide just the right context for them. Yet, although instrumental performance immediately followed by singing is explicitly described, there is not a single unambiguous reference in the secular poems to simultaneous instrumental accompaniment of the singing voice. We can thus presume that the aristocratic *cantiga de amor* was normally sung unaccompanied, and that the same kind of performance could extend to the *cantiga de amigo*. In this case, however, the bourgeois register of the genre, its close association to the professional jongleur, and the rich instrumental iconography of the *Cancioneiro da Ajuda* may lead us to suppose that instruments were allowed in its performance (probably not more than two at once).

In the *CSM*, the fact is that the famous musical illustrations in *E are a kind of instruments' catalogue with no obvious relation to the vocal performance practice of the *cantigas* (the illuminations include two rustic ensembles, two exotic instruments, and fourteen instances of wind-instrument playing that fail to portray any possible singing). It has been argued that in 1293, in the court of Sancho IV (the son of Alfonso X) there were twenty-five professional musicians known to us by name, amongst them eleven of Muslim origin, and that ten years before the reality could not have been much different; but twenty of these musicians fulfilled ceremonial and military functions playing percussion or trumpet, and none of them played any of the instruments which were most probably associated with the Galician-Portuguese poetry: the fiddle and the citole, followed by the psaltery and the harp.

We are thus left with one illumination in *E and three in *T that suggest some kind of instrumental participation in the vocal performance of the *CSM*. Two of these illuminations are associated with dance-forms performed out-of-doors; the two remaining suggest the participation of string-players in the informal transmission of the repertoire, either individually or in small groups of two or three. Taking into account the iconographical and historical evidence, the formal in-doors performance (in the court or in the church) of the *CSM* probably called for a trained choir and soloist, unaccompanied; young maiden singing together or one of them accompanying her own solo singing to castanets or tambourine are other possibilities. Thus, the performance of the *CSM* probably assumed different guises, depending on the kind of song and the kind of context provided; instrumental ensembles in excess of three musicians were probably used infrequently, and then only out-of-doors, for dancing.

Notes

[1] The Marian *ballada* "Los set gotxs recomptarem," written in the Catalan language except the refrain (critical edition in Mª Carmen Gómez Muntané, *El Llibre Vermell de Montserrat: Cantos y Danzas* [Barcelona, 1990]), should be studied in a wider geographical context, taking into account some textual and musical relationship with the *Cantigas de Santa Maria* (especially *CSM* 1 and 224).

[2] Manuel Pedro Ferreira, "Apresentação da lírica galego-portuguesa," in idem, *Aspectos da Música Medieval no Ocidente Peninsular* (forthcoming).

[3] See below the section on the religious *cantigas*.

[4] Clarinda de Azevedo Maia, *História do Galego-Português* (Coimbra, 1986).

[5] Celso Ferreira da Cunha, *Estudos de Versificação Portuguesa (séculos XIII a XVI)*, Paris, 1982, pp. 233-72.

[6] Manuel Pedro Ferreira, *The Sound of Martin Codax* (Lisboa, 1986), Appendix III.

[7] Manuel P. Ferreira, *Cantus coronatus: Seven cantigas de amor by Dom Dinis, King of Portugal and the Algarve* Vol. 1. (forthcoming)

[8] A complete English translation of the *Cantigas de Santa María* has been prepared by Kathleen Kulp-Hill as *The songs of Holy Mary by Alfonso X: a translation of the Cantigas de Santa Maria*, with an introduction by Connie L. Scarborough. Medieval & Renaissance Texts & Studies 173 (Tempe, AZ: Arizona Center for Medieval and Renaissance Studies, 2000).

[9] Manuel Pedro Ferreira, "The Stemma of the Marian Cantigas: Philological and Musical Evidence," in *Cantigueiros*, Vol. VI (1994), pp. 58-98.

[10] Gerardo V. Huseby, "The Cantigas de Santa Maria and the Medieval Theory of Mode" (Ph.D. diss., Stanford University, 1982), p. 238 ff.

[11] Ismael Fernández de la Cuesta, "Los elementos melódicos en las Cantigas de Santa María," in *Revista de Musicología*, vol. 7 (1984), 1-44.

[12] Julián Ribera, *La música de las Cantigas. Estudio sobre su origen y naturaleza* (Madrid, 1922).

[13] Higinio Anglès, *La música de las Cantigas de Santa María del Rey Alfonso el Sabio*, 3 vols. (Barcelona, 1943, 1958, 1964).

[14] Manuel Pedro Ferreira, "Rondeau and Virelai. Notes on the Music of the Andalus," originally written as an Appendix to Ferreira, *Cantus coronatus*.

[15] Manuel Pedro Ferreira, "Andalusian Music and the Cantigas de Santa Maria," to be published in Stephen Parkinson, ed., *Cobras e Som. Papers from a Colloquium on Text, Music and Manuscripts of the Cantigas de Santa Maria* (Oxford, forthcoming).

[16] Ferreira, *The Sound of Martin Codax*.

[17] Julián Ribera, *La música de las Cantigas. Estudio sobre su origen y naturaleza*. A few examples: in *cantiga* XX, the note over *pa deces* looks like a square punctum, but it is in fact a lozenge. In the original, the *cantiga* XXXVIII starts with a note with an upper stem on the left and a descending stem on the right, but this last stem is not reproduced in the facsimile. The *cantiga* LXV in the manuscript has a normal clivis over *ra zon*, and lozenges over *mira gre* and *cida de*; the facsimile suggests different notational shapes.

[18] Higinio Anglès, *La música de las Cantigas*, vol. 3. A few examples: in folio 6v (*CSM* 210), over *beeyta*, the c.o.p. stem in the facsimile is nonexistent, and the clivis over *da* had the stem erased by the medieval copyist. Folio 54r (*CSM* 30) has virga and punctum respectively over *sarmu do* and *nen*, while the manuscript itself has, for the same places, punctum and virga. Folio 62r (*CSM* 39) shows two clives over *ave o* and

mões teiro, but in the original the copyist wrote two descending ligatures *sine proprietate et cum perfectione*.

[19] Alfonso X El Sabio, *Cantigas de Santa María—Edición facsímil del códice T. I. 1* (Madrid, 1979).

[20] Harvey L. Sharrer, "The Discovery of Seven cantigas d'amor by Dom Dinis with Musical Notation," in *Hispania* 74 (1991), 459-61.

[21] Harvey L. Sharrer, "Fragmentos de Sete Cantigas d'Amor de D. Dinis, Musicadas—uma Descoberta," in *Actas do IV Congresso da Associação Hispânica de Literatura Medieval* 1 (Lisboa, 1991; repr. 1993 under the title *Literatura Medieval*), pp. 13-29. In this same volume the first musicological description of the fragment can also be found: Manuel Pedro Ferreira, "Relatório preliminar sobre o conteúdo musical do Fragmento Sharrer," pp. 35-42. Full color facsimiles and photographic details from before the "restoration" will be published in Manuel P. Ferreira, *Cantus coronatus*.

[22] Ferreira, *The Sound of Martin Codax*. See also Ferreira, "Codax revisitado," in *Anuario de Estudos Galegos* (1998), forthcoming [includes revisions].

[23] Ferreira, *Cantus coronatus*.

[24] These conclusions refer to the bulk of the MSS; in some *cantigas* a particular notational code may have been in use. For the latest research on the notation of the *CSM*, see Manuel Pedro Ferreira, "Spania *versus* Spain in the *Cantigas de Santa María*," in *España en la Música de Occidente. Actas del Congreso Internacional celebrado en Salamanca* (Madrid, 1987), vol. I, pp. 109-11; idem, "Bases for Transcription: Gregorian Chant and the Notation of the *Cantigas de Santa María*," in *Los instrumentos del Pórtico de la Gloria. Su reconstrucción y la música de su tiempo* (La Coruña, 1993), vol. II, pp. 595-621.

[25] Anglès, *La música de las Cantigas de Santa María*.

[26] Ferreira, "Bases for transcription." See also Ferreira, "Afinidades musicais: as *cantigas de loor* e a lírica profana galego-portuguesa," in *Festschrift G. Tavani* (forthcoming).

[27] The seven-song format occurs in both branches of the manuscript tradition (the sixteenth-century songbooks B and V and the Vindel MS), but in the Vindel MS, and possibly also in the medieval model for B/V, the seventh is an addition, which, together with the structural coherence of songs I to VI, suggests that the primitive version of the cycle did not include it. An alternative sixth-song format (*cantigas* I to V and VII) has been postulated on the evidence of the Vindel MS and a related marginal gloss incorporated into the text of V.

[28] Manuel Pedro Ferreira, "Codax, Martin," in *Diccionario de la Música Española y Hispano-Americana* (forthcoming).

[29] John G. Cummins, "The Practical Implications of Alfonso El Sabio's Peculiar Use of the Zéjel," in *Bulletin of Hispanic Studies* 47 (1970), 1-9; Stephen Parkinson, "False Refrains in the *Cantigas de Santa Maria*," in *Portuguese Studies* 3 (1987), 21-55.

[30] Manuel Pedro Ferreira, "Apresentação da lírica galego-portuguesa."

[31] Manuel P. Ferreira, *Cantus coronatus*.

10. Sephardic Song

Judith R. Cohen

Antiquity of the Tradition.

Sephardic music is actually not medieval, but for various reasons is often included in the performing repertoires of early music ensembles. Sephardim is the plural term (Hebrew plural form -im), which refers to Jews of Sefarad, an Old Testament place name traditionally interpreted as Iberia.[1] There is considerable debate about whether or to what degree their languages (Castilian, Catalan, Galaïco-Portuguese, etc.) differed from the peninsular norm(s) before the Sephardim left the Peninsula. The music of Judeo-Spanish ("Ladino") songs was not notated until the late nineteenth century, and the only reason to include it as an entry here is the popularity of the repertoire among performers of early music and the tendency to present it inaccurately as "medieval Spanish" or "medieval Sephardic." The information which follows is intended to provide information about how the repertoire has been performed since the time when it was first clearly documented—i.e. only in the past century. This does not necessarily mean that changes are inappropriate, but caution and respect should be observed: this is a living tradition, which, like any other, has substantially changed over the centuries, and presenting it as part of the early music repertoire would be misleading.

Terminology: Sephardic, Ladino, Judeo-Spanish, Romance

The term "Sephardic" traditionally means "(Jewish) from Spain" but has been popularly used to mean, roughly, "of non-western Jewish origin." Here it will retain its original sense. The term "Ladino" is often used to refer to the language of this song repertoire. This has been the subject of considerable controversy, but it is generally agreed among scholars that "Ladino" refers only to literal translations of Hebrew sacred texts into Spanish; i.e. it is not a vernacular language. Sephardim from the former Spanish zone of Morocco call their vernacular *haketía*, though they also speak standard peninsular Spanish (*castellano*). Sephardim from the former Ottoman Empire region refer to their vernacular as *djudezmo*, *ladino* or, simply, *spaniol*. The term *ladino* has become so popular in recent years that it is often used to refer to the vernacular language; scholars often use the artificial, but useful, term "Judeo-Spanish" to cover all these variations. *Romance* (pron. ro-*man*-ssé) can be loosely translated as ballad, or, more specifically, as a narrative poem consisting of an indefinite number of 16-syllable lines, each divided into two octosyllabic hemistichs, of which the odd ones are unrhymed and the even ones closed in assonance. Traditional singers use the term *romance* comparatively rarely. Moroccans usually say simply cantar (song), often with a qualifier (e.g. "song for swinging," "cradle song," "old song," "wedding song"). Ottoman Sephardim do refer to *romanzas* but their usage does not always correspond to the above definition. A large number of the songs commonly presented as *"romances"* or *"romanzas"* on recordings, are not, in fact, part of this genre. A *romancero* is a collection or corpus of *romances*.

Provenance of Texts and Music

It should be noted that the literary ballad form (*romance*) as such does not appear in Spain until the late Middle Ages–early Renaissance. Many Sephardic songs, particularly the lyric songs which form the bulk of most professional and semi-professional performers' repertoires, were composed well after the Expulsion from Spain, including several *romances* whose original forms do not predate the Expulsion. Though several scholars have studied the *texts* of those ballads (*romances*) which can be traced to Renaissance ballads and medieval epics, few musicologists have systematically investigated the possibility of actual survivals of early Spanish *melodies* in currently sung Sephardic song.[2] Etzion and Weich-Shahaq's findings suggest that, while complete melodies do not seem to have survived, certain similarities of musical style and structure between the Sephardic and the Renaissance Spanish ballads may be discerned after close scrutiny. There is no comparable musical repertory from the Middle Ages on which to base a systematic investigation, though the occasional resemblance, coincidental or otherwise, may show up in other medieval Hispanic genres. In the non-ballad Sephardic genres, a few wedding and lyric texts have survived, again without music[3]. Many of the current tunes are of undetermined origin. In the eastern repertoire, tunes can often be traced to popular Greek or Turkish melodies from the eighteenth century on; in the Moroccan repertoire, many peninsular tunes, again of comparatively recent origin, are found.[4]

Sources

In learning to perform any oral tradition, direct oral transmission or, at the very least, field recordings are the only reliable source; transcriptions cannot really help unless one already knows the tradition very well (as was the case, of course, when western music first began to be notated). For this reason, the anthologies available (some from collections notated by ear, without recording devices) are not recommended for learning purposes. If there is a local Sephardic community, its members may welcome serious visits from students interested in learning the tradition; if not, there are several fine field and semi-documentary recordings which have been made commercially available, and may be used as models (see discography). The serious performer may also request access to sound archives from individual collectors or institutions in Spain and Israel.

Performance Practice

The most traditional approach is *a cappella*, partly because women have been the main conservers of Judeo-Spanish song, and for various reasons (pragmatic, religious, etc.) they have not commonly used instruments. Harmonization is not traditional in Judeo-Spanish song: vocals are solo or unison (or octaves in mixed groups), and instrumentals are heterophonic. The Moroccan style is less melismatic than the older Ottoman style, which was highly influenced by local practice; however, many more recent Ottoman-area songs are based on popular western European tunes and sung very simply. Vocal style, technique, and timbre, more difficult to describe, are usually related to local practice. The women especially tend to sing in a fairly low tessitura (low alto range); it is quite rare to hear songs sung by a female voice in a high register, and this should be kept in mind when preparing songs for performance. The tempered Western scale is not usually used by older traditional singers. It is usually problematic for singers trained in Western concert music style, including those with early music background, to adjust their vocal style so that their renditions of Judeo-Spanish (or other traditional) songs are not only musical, but stylistically convincing, rather than incongruous. Here again reliable recordings are indispensable as models. If field recordings of Sephardic music are unavailable, documentary recordings of Spanish village music (for Morocco) or Turkish and Greek folk music (for the east) are useful.

Ballads are most often sung by women, solo and unaccompanied, though in the early decades of this century several highly accomplished Turkish Sephardic singers—mostly men—recorded *romances* with *oud* accompaniment. For wedding songs, women accompany themselves on various types and sizes of frame drums, held upright, with both hands playing. Paraliturgical songs, when not sung on a holy day or in the synagogue itself, are usually sung by men, who may use a traditional ensemble such as *oud*, and/or *kanun* and/or violin, as well as traditional percussion (*derbukka* [goblet drum] and frame drum).

Pronunciation varies (as does orthography), and, again, listening to documentary recordings is important. There are a few general characteristics, the most common being the absence of the modern Castilian lisped *c* (i.e. use English unvoiced *s* as in "Sam," not *th* as in "thug"); and *zh* (as in Eng. pleasure, leisure) instead of the guttural Spanish "jota" ("Bach"), except in certain words of Hebrew or Arabic origin. Judeo-Spanish is not, as some performers have assumed, pronounced like Portuguese, though in some Ottoman areas there are Portuguese-derived elements, such as final *sh* for *s* (e.g. "bushkash" for *buskas*, "you look for"). Again, it is best to base pronunciation on documentary recordings to account for regional differences.

New Performance Styles

Since the recent upsurge in interest in Sephardic music, a wide variety of performing styles has appeared. Sephardim themselves often use a combination of western and eastern instruments. Examples are: acoustic (or electric) guitar with Middle Eastern percussion; *oud* with western-style percussion; accordion, violin, small string orchestra with any of the above. One Sephardic musician in Turkey uses fretless acoustic and electric guitars to accommodate the microtonal *maqam* system. Only one performing group of Sephardic origin, at the time of writing, uses any early music instruments at all, and these were introduced by the group's one non-Sephardic member. For those who find it difficult to resist using replicas of early instruments, strings are the most closely related to traditional performance practice. Fretless vielles and rebecs—avoiding over-use of drones—and lutes played with a plectrum are the most appropriate choices. Percussion should be used with restraint, and not at all for ballads (except those few used as wedding songs); Middle Eastern technique should be studied. Frame drums with or without jingles, and sparing use of *derbukka* (*dombek*) are the best. Wind instruments are not traditionally used. The most important instrument—as in medieval music—is the voice. Moroccan songs, especially ballads and wedding songs, are typically sung with no breaks between couplets or stanzas. Ottoman wedding songs are sung straight through but ballads, when accompanied, usually when sung by men, may have typical middle-east style interludes, usually on the *oud*, between every few stanzas. Paraliturgical music, when accompanied, follows the latter pattern. However, again, the voice is paramount; improvisations are relatively brief, and to the point, rather than long and/or meandering.

Performers of non-Sephardic origin use eclectic and imaginative—if often inappropriate—combinations of instruments, and there is a very recent (and healthy) trend to become acquainted with reliable recordings. The term "authentic" has been deliberately avoided in this entry, as the original "authentic" style will never be recovered, and the current "authentic" style is probably too ascetic to invite many adherents. The best option for would-be performers is probably to study the available resources, and use their own good judgment and musical sensibility to arrive at interpretations which combine traditional and innovative elements, while being careful NOT to present the result as a historical or authentic rendition.

Selected Editions

COHEN, JUDITH R. "'Ya Salió de la mar': Judeo-Spanish Wedding Songs among Moroccan Jews in Canada," *Women and Music in Cross-Cultural Perspective*, ed. Ellen Koskoff, Westport: Greenqood Press, 1987:55-68.

HEMSI, ALBERTO, ed. Edwin Seroussi. *Cancionero Sefardí*. Jerusalem: Jewish Music Research Centre, 1995.

LARREA PALACÍN, ARCADIO DE. *Romances de Tetuán*. Madrid: Consejo Superior de Investigaciones Científicas, 1954, 2 vol, 1952.

LARREA PALACÍN, ARCADIO DE. *Canciones rituales hispano-judías*. Madrid: Consejo Superior de Investigaciones Científicas, 1954.

LEVY, ISAAC. *Chants judéo-espagnols*. London: World Sephardic Federation; Jerusalem: édition de l'auteur, 1959-73.

WEICH-SHAHAQ, SHOSHANA. *Musica y Tradiciones Sefardíes*. Diputación de Salamanca, 1992.

Discographies/Sonographies with Commentary

BUNIS, DAVID. in *Sephardic Studies: a Recent Bibliography*. Garland, 1981: early 78rpm recordings.

COHEN, JUDITH. "Sonography of Judeo-Spanish Song," *Jewish Folklore and Ethnology Review (JFER)*, 18/1-2, 1996: 95-100 and further entries in *JFER* fall-winter 1998; COHEN, JUDITH. "Sephardic Music: The Romance and Romanticization of Medieval Spain," entry in *Rough Guide to World Music,* 2nd edition, ed. S. Broughton, 1999: Vol. I: pp. 370-4.

Notes

[1] For history and general background of the Sephardim in Spain and Portugal, the Inquisition and expulsion, see Yitzhak Baer, *A History of the Jews in Christian Spain* (Philadelphia, 1961-66); Marc Angel, *La America: The Sephardic Experience in the United States,* (Philadelphia, 1983); Samuel G; Armistead *et al.*, *El romancero judeo-español en el Archivo Menéndez-Pidal (Catálogo-Indice de romances y canciones),* 3 v. (Madrid, 1978); Samuel Armistead and Joseph A. Silverman, "Sephardic Folk Literature and Eastern Mediterranean Oral Tradition," *Musica Judaica* 6/1 (1983-4), 38-54; José Benoliel, *Dialecto judeo-hispano-marroquí o haketía* (Madrid, 1977), pp. 1927-52; David Bunis, *Sephardic Studies: A Research Bibliography* (New York, 1981); Paloma Díaz Más, *Los Sefardíes* (Barcelona, 1986; English edition 1990, trans. George Zucker). Haím Vidal Sephiha, *Le Judéo-Espagnol* (Paris, 1986).

[2] See Judith R. Cohen, "Judeo-Spanish Songs in the Sephardic Communities of Montreal and Toronto: Survival, Function and Change" (Ph.D. diss., University of Montreal, 1989); Israel Joseph Katz, "The 'Myth' of the Sephardic Musical Legacy from Spain," *Fifth World Congress of Jewish Studies, IV* (Jerusalem, 1973); and, especially, Judith Etzion, and Shoshana Weich-Shahaq, "The Spanish and Sephardic Romances: Musical Links," *Ethnomusicology* 32/2 (1988), 1-38. For a specific melody, see Judith Cohen, "A Reluctant Woman Pilgrim and a Green Bird," *Cantigueiros* 7 (1995), 85-89.

[3] For these texts, see Margit Frenk Alatorre,

[4] See Edwin Seroussi, "The Growth of the Judeo-Spanish Folksong Repertory in the 20th Century," *Proceedings of the 10th World Congress of Jewish Studies* II (Jerusalem, 1989), pp. D173-80.

11. Italian Monophony

Blake Wilson

L ate medieval Italy was not *a* place, but many places, and just as individual cities like Florence often constituted a discrete cultural environment, so the musical repertories were probably just as manifold. But from a soundscape that certainly teemed with the songs of minstrels, *improvvisatori*, courtly singers, processing flagellants, and confraternity singers, each further subdivided by strong regional traditions of language and song, only a fraction survives in written form. The handful of monophonic ballate preserved in the Rossi and Squarcialupi codices belongs, in terms of literary, notational, and performing conventions, to the sphere of the Italian *Ars nova*. However, a significant extant repertory of Italian monophony of increasing interest to performers is the *lauda*.

The texts of these devotional songs are preserved in over two hundred surviving collections, but only two of these "*laudarios*," plus a handful of fragments, transmit musical notation, altogether a repertory of about 135 complete melodies. Like the cantigas repertory, the *laude* are sacred songs and were written down more or less at the same time they were being performed, but the most distinctive feature of the *lauda* repertory is the urban, mercantile, rather than courtly, aristocratic environment from which it emanated. We now know, in fact, far more about the immediate performing context of these songs than of the other monophonic repertories, for they were cultivated primarily by religious confraternities (called *laudesi* and *disciplinati*) in the burgeoning mercantile cities of late medieval Tuscany and Umbria, and their membership consisted primarily of artisans and merchants who kept detailed records of their *lauda*-singing activities and expenditures.

The confraternities were organized primarily by mendicant orders such as the Franciscans and Dominicans, and the intent of their urban ministry was to draw the laity away from the heresies that spread rapidly in the densely populated cities and into a more active role in the process of their salvation through such devotional activities as processing, ritual scourging, caring for the urban sick and poor, and *lauda* singing. Many *Lauda* texts bear the signs of the friars' anti-heretical preaching, but more typically they bristle with vivid and sensuous language and imagery that, like a good mendicant sermon, was intended to excite in the listener the extreme devotional states of praise or penance. The citizens of medieval Italy flocked to hear the charismatic friar-preachers, and something of their rhetorical power and persuasiveness surely informed *lauda* performances which, in many ways, were like sung sermons. This would explain why papal and episcopal indulgences were granted for the singing *and* hearing of *laude*.

The strategy of the friars in drawing the laity back into the church was two-fold: to render accessible and comprehensible to the laity the liturgy and liturgical practices of the church, and conversely to convert to spiritual ends the secular activities and mental habits of the urban laity. Like clerics, the *confratelli* conducted their own services within churches, before consecrated altars and altar paintings which they maintained in the dual role of chaplain and patron, but theirs was a vernacular, not a Latin, liturgy, and the core of the service was not Latin chant, but Italian *laude*.

Laudarios, like the two surviving musical collections from Cortona (Biblioteca del comune, MS 91; late thirteenth century) and Florence (Mgl1; Biblioteca nazionale centrale, Banco Rari 18; early fourteenth century) are confraternity service books, and are organized like Latin service books according to the church year (*de tempore*) and various saints (*de sanctis*). The music is copied in the square, non-mensural notation used to copy chant in the Latin books, and like the Florence manuscript, *laudarios* frequently contain elegant and colorful illuminations. Surviving statutes indicate that in preparing for a *lauda* service the company sacristan was to set up the proper lectern, candles, dossals, etc., and to locate the *laude* proper to that service (often determined by a bequest for a commemorative "*lauda* vigil" at which specified *laude* were sung in memory of a deceased member or relative). Ferial *laudarios* contained no music, but festal *laudarios* like the Florence Manuscript were placed on lecterns and used by the singers (*laudesi*), so that *lauda*-singing appears to have steered between the poles of written and unwritten traditions. Besides *lauda* singing, the services included prayers, readings, a candle procession and offering, a brief sermon by the company prior (usually the only cleric present), and, immediately following the singing, confession.

While the devotional activity of *lauda* singing was cast in a strong liturgical framework that certainly authenticated the spiritual aspirations of the laity, the friars also recognized the need to communicate with the laity in terms of the secular, urban, and mercantile environment in which the latter lived and worked. The latter is born out above all in the character and types of texts, melodies, and performing forces that were allowed to pass through the rood screens and into the cleric's sacred domain.

Text and Language

The medieval *lauda* repertory is distinguished by the pervasive application of the poetic scheme of the *ballata*. Originally a dance song with a choral refrain, the clearly secular *ballata* form was adapted to sacred texts during the later thirteenth century, and held fast in the *lauda* repertory to the end of the fourteenth century when it began to be displaced by a new array of poetic forms linked to an emerging polyphonic practice. In its strictest and most frequent form, the *lauda-ballata* consists of a two-line, end-rhyming choral refrain (repeated after each successive strophe), and a four-line, soloistic strophe comprised of *piedi* (two lines of identical versification and end-rhyme) and a *volta* (two lines that repeat the versification and, usually, music of the refrain). Rarely, however, do *laude* follow this *ballata minore* scheme strictly, and particularly in the Florence manuscript one finds not only more irregular line lengths, but the longer stanzaic forms of the *ballata mezzana* and *ballata maggiore* (see Ex. 11.2).[1]

The modern performer must decide, as did the medieval *lauda* singer, the number and order of stanzas from a given *lauda* to be performed. Some collections may transmit as many as the 54 strophes of *Magdalena degna da laudare* in the Cortona manuscript, and the widely different numbers of strophes preserved in various manuscript versions of the same *lauda* (e.g. for *Ave donna sanctissima*, 21 in Cortona, and 8 in Florence) indicate that the number and sequence of strophes probably varied among regions, companies, and individual performers and performances according to the exigencies of memory and context. The melody and text underlay of the initial strophe usually require minor alterations to suit subsequent strophes, but these are best worked out orally with the melody committed to memory and an understanding that no written form of a given melody was probably ever meant to be definitive.

Frequent irregularities and peculiarities in orthography, especially in the Cortona manuscript, reveal a repertory in transition: in transition from oral to written form, and an emerging vernacular in transition to becoming an established literary language. Since the Tuscan dialect of the Florence manuscript formed the basis of modern Italian pronunciation, these texts present relatively few pronunciation problems. More anomalous to the modern eye are the Umbrian texts of the Cortona manuscript, and Cyrilla Barr has set forth a short list of spelling habits which are of use to the modern performer in negotiating the few pronunciation problems posed by these short texts:[2]

1. Before p, b, and m, the n becomes an m, while before t and d the m becomes an n.
2. When c precedes a palatal vowel, it is written with the cedilla and pronounced as a sibilant, e.g. *merçede, dolçe*.
3. Common substitutions: g for c (e.g. *seguro* for *securo*), d for t (e.g., *emperadore* for *emperatore*), v or b for p (*savia* for *sapia*), e for i (and vice versa), ll for gl, and sc for g.
4. N or m frequently appears before -gn (e.g., *ongne*) without, however, altering its pronounciation.
5. Ecclesiastical Latinisms appear either in the form of Latin word endings such as *-entia* or *-antia*, or in whole words such as *juxta, lux*, etc.
6. Tonic o rarely becomes a diphthong (e.g., *fuoco* remains *foco, cuore* remains *core*, and *uomo* remains *omo*.

Music

Like the texts, the melodies of the *lauda* repertory range freely in style and character between chant and popular song, owing more perhaps to the latter. Examples 11.1 and 11.2 show how different two melodies (both dedicated to St. Dominic) can be. The first is syllabic and within the range of any male voice, and sounds like an austere processional song; the second demands control of a much wider range, and engages in an effusive and florid virtuosity that is characteristic of many *laude* found in the *sanctorale* section of the Florence manuscript.

Ex. 11.1. *San Domenico beato.*

Ex. 11.2. *Allegro canto.*

Al - le - gro____ can - to, po - pol cri - sti - a - no____

del gran - de__ san Do - me - ni - co,____

di tan - ti__ va - lo - ro - so ca - pi - ta - no.__

ca - pi - ta - no di mol - ti__ ca - va - lie - ri

fu____ sanc - to pre - ti - o - so,

che____ do - po Cri - sto l'an - no se - - - gui - ta - to;

e fu____ de li mi glior gon - fal - co - nie - ri,

quel____ fiu - me gra - ti - o - so,

che____ do - po Cri - sto si - a__ sta - to____ tro - va - to;

per lui__ è____ su - to spar - to et ri - pro - va - to____

o - gni per - ver - so he - re - ti - co____

che nel - la fe - de tro - vas - se lon - ta - no.

The two versions of the melody for *Ave, donna sanctissima* in Ex. 11.3 reveal the melodic plasticity of this repertory. Melodic intervals of a third or more might be filled in, and a variety of ornamental notes ranging from single anticipatory or appoggiatura-like notes to clusters of notes in stock formulae (abundant in Ex. 11.2 and other florid *laude* like it) might be applied. Entire phrases, including finals, might differ significantly, although this is not as common as once assumed. These written versions, in fact, must be regarded as attempts to notate several possible performances of a song that existed primarily in the world of oral traditions and memory, and that was constantly renewed and altered in performance according to a singer's circumstances, taste, memory, and ability. No definitive version of one of these songs exists or is even desirable, and a performer is probably closest to the spirit of the *lauda* when stock melodic gestures (which includes incipits and cadential formulae, as well as ornaments) are familiar enough to be spontaneously applied in performance. This melodic flexibility is useful in the performance of successive poetic strophes of a given *lauda*, where not only frequent differences in syllable count and accentuation must be accommodated, but rhetorical shifts in the poem delivered as persuasively as in a mendicant sermon.[3]

Ex. 11.3. *Ave donna santissima* in two versions.

It is precisely this melodic flexibility of the *lauda* repertory that argues against the application of rigid rhythmic schemes in performance. While Liuzzi's two volumes (see bibliography) are still valuable for their facsimiles and texts, his metric transcriptions are untenable and, in the case of the florid *laude*, absolutely fantastic. It would also be difficult to defend the application of the various rhythmic interpretations devised for modern chant performances in the secular and popular realm of the *lauda*. Rhythmic solutions to the performance of monophonic *laude* must be sought in the extra-liturgical environment of the late medieval Italian cities, where the possibilities ranged from unmeasured recitation to flexible mensural applications. Ornate, feast-day *laudarios* like the Florence Manuscript typically included an appendix with two- and three-part motets requiring mensural transcription and performance, so that the notational and performing conventions of this repertory would have been familiar to the confraternities. Rhythmic solutions might also be worked out keeping in mind that there is an ebb and flow to the melodic movement created both by the natural text accents and the strong pull of the tonic and notes of the tonic triad.

Notation and Transcription

The music and texts of the Florence Manuscript recently have been edited in a volume issued by A-R Editions (see bibliography), but the Cortona Manuscript still remains unavailable in a good critical edition.[4] Those wishing to prepare an edition from Liuzzi's facsimiles will encounter few problems reading original notation and text, but text underlay can be unclear (especially in the melismatic *laude*), and there are numerous scribal errors in both manuscripts with respect to clefs, custodes, and transpositions of melody. The Florence Manuscript is especially problematic, for sometime after its initial compilation the codex was damaged, the tops and sides trimmed and repaired, during which process the top musical staff on every folio was mutilated, the parchment restored, and the music recopied. The recopied music is, however, entirely corrupt, a fact which only the new A-R edition takes into account by proposing emended versions of these passages.[5]

This mutilation and corrupt reconstruction of the folio tops in the Florence Manuscript also provides insight into one of the puzzling aspects of the codex. For 50 of its 97 *laude*, the Florence Manuscript provides music (ranging from a single note to entire settings) for second and occasionally third strophes, and for 27 of these 50 *laude* the music for the additional strophes differs from that of the first strophe. This has been viewed as a challenging performance practice question, but the musical conflicts between first and second strophes in all but a very few of these 27 *laude* have been created by the corrupt reconstructions mentioned above. In other words, there is now no compelling evidence for any practice other than repetition for subsequent strophes of the music provided for the first strophe.[6]

The Cortona Manuscript suffered no such fate, though even here the would-be editor must watch for the scribal errors involving erroneous clefs, *custodes*, and transposition of repeated passages (the transposition is most often at the interval of a third or fifth).[7]

With the exception of the B♭'s in the last *lauda* of the Florence Manuscript (no. 108, which was copied at a later date), there is not a single accidental to be found in the extant musical sources. However, it is clear from those melodies surviving in transposed versions that some accidentals must have been applied in performance. Over half of the melodies in the Florence Manuscript have finals on d or f, and here especially it is often necessary to correct a melodic tritone with the occasional addition of a B♭ (Exx. 11.1 and 11.3), or to add the B♭ to the signature in most of the tritus mode melodies (Ex. 11.2).[8]

Performing Forces

Although women participated in the cultic life of the *laudesi* (though not the *disciplinati*) confraternities, and may have sung *laude* in more informal settings, the *laude* in the actual confraternity services (the "*lauda* vigils") were sung by men and/or boys. In a large and wealthy city like Florence, which supported at least a dozen *laudesi* companies during the fourteenth century, it is clear that the performing forces might vary from a single, unaccompanied solo singer at a modest company, to the ten singers, two rebec players, and players of lute, vielle, and organ retained in 1412 by the city's wealthiest confraternity, the Company of Orsanmichele.

Even during the fourteenth century, the Company of Orsanmichele seems to have retained instruments as well as relatively large numbers of singers (6-10), but most companies hired instrumentalists and more than one or a few singers only for special feast days. The instruments favored were "soft," indoor instruments associated with secular music, particularly those that allowed a performer simultaneously to sing and play (rebec, vielle, lute, harp, and organ), and it is clear that these were used to accompany *lauda* performances. One can only speculate, however, that the instruments were variously deployed to play drones, preludes, interludes, and postludes, to (perhaps heterophonically) double the melody, or to play simple kinds of improvised polyphony.[9]

The refrain form of the *lauda*, in conjunction with what we know about performing forces, suggests several performance possibilities. The oldest, pre-trecento practice, applicable to the Cortona Manuscript and continued into the early fifteenth century by smaller and more insular Florentine companies, was an alternation between congregational singing of the refrains and performance of the strophes by one or a few amateur singers drawn from company ranks. In Florence, at least, *lauda* singing became something of a business and profession in the early fourteenth century as the devotion grew in popularity, and increasing numbers of bequests were made for *lauda* vigils. The companies began to hire their musicians and draft contracts (which frequently revealed a concern with the quality of the singers), *lauda* schools (*scuole*) were established to polish congregational refrain singing, and *lauda* services revealed their own brand of liturgical pomp through the addition of instruments, extra singers, florid songs, ornate service books, and liturgical paraphernalia like painted candles and decorated altar cloths. The elegant Florence Manuscript, with its numerous florid *laude*, actually belonged to the modest Company of Santo Spirito, which in the early fifteenth century was still employing a single solo singer (one Antonio di Petro), an indication that singers throughout the city were expected to meet the technical demands of this repertory.

Whether a company hired one or more singers, the paid singers performed the strophes, either in alternation among them or in various combinations. Typically the music of the strophes is more technically demanding, with wider ranges, more florid passages, and longer, more complex phrases (see Exx. 11.1–2). The refrains, often employing F clefs, tend to be narrower in compass and within the range of most male voices, while the strophes usually shift to C clefs and exploit the higher register characteristic of late medieval timbre in general and Mediterranean singing in particular. Those *laude* with refrains as technically demanding as the strophes (e.g., Ex. 11.2) might well have been performed entirely by soloists (with individual singers on the strophes and all soloists participating in the refrains), and in any case this became the dominant performing practice in the larger Florentine companies by the close of the fourteenth century as *lauda* singing became increasingly professionalized.

A sensible role of the instruments in the *ballata* form would seem to be reinforcement of the choral refrains by all instruments present (if more than one), and a more discrete, soloistic use in the strophes (a singer and player were often the same person). But here as in other aspects of *lauda* performance the practice was undoubtedly variable and flexible, depending upon liturgical solemnity, company resources, local traditions, and the ability and availability of singers and instrumentalists.

Whether performed with one or ten singers, with or without instruments, the musical presentations of these vivid, narrative texts should be as dramatic and convincing as were the rhetorically flamboyant sermons to which the laity of the late-medieval Italian cities flocked.

Notes

[1]   A more extended discussion of the poetic forms employed in the *laude* of the Cortona and Florence Mss., including text-music correspondences, may be found in C. Barr, *The Monophonic Lauda* (see bibliography), chs. 3 and 4.

[2]   Ibid., 83-4. A good critical edition of the texts (like that of the Cortona Ms. by Varanini, et al.; see bibliography) also presents variant readings and spellings of given words, which can provide clues to pronunciation.

[3]   Melodic plasticity is also evident in the number of contrafacta in the *lauda* repertory, where a pre-existent melody has been fitted with a new text; for a comparative transcription of five such melodies (and a source of melodic variants that might be generally applied in the repertory), see Wilson, *Music and Merchants* (see bibliography), pp. 263-67 (though this now must be used in conjunction with the emended versions of the Florence melodies contained in the Wilson-Barbieri edition listed in the bibliography).

[4]   The best current and complete edition of the Cortona melodies is Martin Dürrer's *Altitalienische Laudenmelodie: Das einstimmige Repertoire der Handschriften*

Cortona und Florenz, 2 vols. (Kassel, 1996), though this should be used in conjunction with Theodore Karp's "Editing the Cortona Laudario," *Journal of Musicology* 11 (1993): 73-105, for important information about the Cortona melodies, and with the edition of the texts by Varanini, et al., since Dürrer provides no text beyond that actually underlaid to the music.

[5] These changes are discussed in the preface to vol. 1 of the edition, and are detailed and explained in the commentary with respect to each piece. A detailed analysis and discussion of the manuscript's idiosyncrasies is undertaken in B. Wilson, "Indagine sul laudario fiorentino."

[6] A more detailed discussion of this situation is provided in the preface to vol. I of the Wilson-Barbieri edition of the Florence Ms. (see bibliography).

[7] See Karp, "Editing the Cortona Laudario," where he provides many insights and clues on how to recognize and correct such scribal errors.

[8] Helpful in this regard is Dürrer, I, pp. 77-99.

[9] Possible models for such accompaniments are the two-part madrigals of Florentine trecento composers such as Lorenzo, Donato, and Gherardello; see Kurt von Fischer, "On the Technique, Origin, and Evolution of Italian Trecento Music," *Musical Quarterly* 47 (1961), 41-57. The relationship between the florid upper parts of these madrigals and the melismatic *laude* in the Florence Manuscript is explored in B. Wilson, "Madrigal, Lauda, and Local Style in Trecento Florence," *Journal of Musicology* 15 (1997), 137-77.

12. German Monophony

hubert heinen

Songs in German are attested from the mid-twelfth century on (though the transmission for most songs begins over a century later). Performance by sotto-voce reading for one's own amusement or even spoken recitation was arguably medieval reality; most codices of medieval German song contain only the text. However, the frequent internal references of the songs themselves to singing and internal definitions of them as combinations of words and melody (*wort unde wîse*) make it clear that the works were created to be sung.[1] Some of the scribes of texts transmitted without melodies must have known a sung version even though they as a rule were copying from a written exemplar. Since songs, as opposed to works in rhymed couplets, are almost always written in prose blocks, the best way to understand the strophic form, which was often complex, would be to sing it. Some scribes, to be sure, copied and altered with scant regard for the form, but most scribes showed a keen awareness of it. When on occasion they rewrote passages that they found defective in their exemplar, they replicated and even refined the strophic form. The melodies they knew may bear little or no resemblance to the original one, but the same is true of all melodies transmitted, as were most German and Romance ones, considerably later than they were composed.

Confronted with the embarrassment of riches in the troubadour and trouvère repertoire, the would-be performer of medieval German songs, especially minnesongs, the genre most loved by Germanist literary scholars, can only feel embarrassment. For the great literary names of the twelfth century such as Heinrich von Morungen or Reinmar der Alte there is little music transmitted with the texts, and that little is in neumes that give only hints at the shape of the melodies. For other minnesingers such as Albrecht von Johansdorf and especially Walther von der Vogelweide scholars have suggested Occitan and Northern French contrafacts to fill the gap. In addition, for Walther, there are a few melodies transmitted, mostly for his political songs, and other melodies ascribed to him but accompanying later didactic texts.[2] Friedrich Gennrich linked many of these melodies to known texts to allow modern audiences to experience the works of the masters as they were originally performed, as songs. In later publications, Gennrich seems to have forgotten that he originally made no claim that the texts and melodies he linked really belonged together. Subsequent scholars have generally occupied themselves with confirming or, more often, disputing the melodies' authenticity, though some new contrafacts have been proposed. Most recently, Anthonius Touber and his students have suggested additional new ones on the basis of a comparative database of Romance and German verse forms.[3]

Gennrich's original idea was perfectly sound: given the paucity of melodies for the songs with the greatest literary value, find medieval melodies to which they can be sung. To be sure, the songs' authors would rarely recognize their own creations, and their audiences would not believe their ears. Since, however, the only other alternative is to read the songs as written poems or perform them as spoken ones, why not make the best of a bad situation? For later singers, especially for Neidhart, and for other genres, such as the political and didactic songs, more music is transmitted. The richer transmission of melodies in the fifteenth century (and of apparently earlier melodies in the sixteenth) also opens up a wide range of poetic and melodic styles (including, in the songs of the Mönch von Salzburg and especially Oswald von Wolkenstein, polyphonic settings). Many modern anthologies gather what melodies exist.[4] Recent editions of individual singers or groups of singers as well as facsimiles of major manuscripts often include what music is available.[5]

The strophe seems to be the most important unit of the song; the medieval German word for a specific song was *diu liet*: the strophes. The earliest strophic forms we have for secular songs are similar to those for strophic epic verse: two long-line couplets, sometimes varied with inserted half lines. The melodies attached to both by scholars, though reconstructed from much later transmissions, apparently reflect heightened speech as they tend to arrive quickly at a recitation tone and stay there until they descend to a cadence marker. Another archaic form consists of a series of four-beat couplets, the meter generally used for narrative or expository verse. More elaborate strophic forms and melodies signal an influence of Occitan and French song. Most common is the *canso*, with a *frons* consisting of two *pedes* and a *cauda*. In German (using terms borrowed from the meistersingers of the fifteenth and sixteenth centuries), the *Bar* strophe consists of two parts. An initial melody (the first *Stollen*, usually two to four lines long, though sometimes longer) is repeated (the second), forming the *Aufgesang*. The *Aufgesang* is followed by a new melody (or, after a bridge or *Steg*, a repetition or variation of a *Stollen*), i.e., the *Abgesang*. Commonly the *Abgesang* is shorter than the *Aufgesang* but longer than a *Stollen*. A well-known relic of the *Bar* is Martin Luther's *Ein' feste Burg* (A Mighty Fortress). In addition to the archaic (long-line) strophe, the series of couplets, and the *Bar*, one finds a number of songs, often with internal references to a dance or to springtime festivities, in which the strophe is through-composed. Many of these songs suggest Latin models. The most elaborate form of song, but one for which a relatively large amount of music is preserved, is the *Leich*, which corresponds to the Latin *sequentia*, the Italian *istampita*, and the French and Occitan *estampie* and *descort*. The versicles of the *Leich* are often paired, but there is no fixed pattern of metrical or melodic structure.

In general, the extant melodies for German songs are sparsely decorated, with one note for each syllable being the rule. Melismatic decoration, to the extent it does exist, tends to occur on the off beat or to mark the cadences. Since Occitan and Northern French melodies for similar songs are often more ornate, the German sparsity may reflect a later simplification in transmission. For the strophic songs, melodies are generally given only for the first strophe. The *Leichs* tend to be less spartan in their use of melisma than the strophic songs.

Medieval German songs do not differ in their tonalities, melodic elements (except for decoration), or (except for archaic forms) basic strophic outline from Romance songs, which often served as sources or models for form, content, and melodies, but they definitely do in having a clear accent-based metrical structure.[6] Given the paucity of evidence for musical meters in German monophonic song codices until well into the fifteenth century, scholars have had, as they have in many cases for Latin and Romance, to rely on other evidence to establish them (or deny their existence). Some scholars posit musical meters based on the rhythmic modes described in some medieval treatises and utilized for motets; for the most part, the first and third rhythmic modes are chosen (♩♪ and ♩. ♪♩ with the first syllable receiving the accent). One of Neidhart's songs is transmitted in a fifteenth-century manuscript in mensural notation that suggests the first rhythmic mode (see below). A few assume an equal value for all notes, with an essentially arhythmic "hymnodic" performance. Even fewer still hold to a view popular earlier in this century that the songs can all be reduced to a musical four-beat line in two-four time. Most scholars today deny the music any independent meter, subordinating it totally to the verse meter (which is more plausible in German songs than in Romance or most Latin ones).[7] In editions based on this denial, bar lines are banned and the notes are presented neutrally (albeit sometimes in a manner that reflects ligatures). To a large extent, unfortunately, those who eschew musical meters also describe verse meters in a very approximate way, leaving performers with little guidance.

The basic verse meter for German songs is alternating, with an accented syllable followed by an unaccented one. However, it is not unusual, especially in the manuscripts, for an accented syllable (which must then be long) to be followed by another accent (which tends to be weaker) or for there to be more than one unaccented syllable between the accented ones. Most scholars assume that the accents follow one another at roughly equal intervals. For most songs, whether or not the verse line begins with an unaccented syllable (has an anacrusis) is optional, though some singers seem to have regularized this. More problematic is the question of the cadence, or end of the verse line (or half line). There may be as many as four different cadences: oxytonic (formerly "masculine"—a single syllable) and split oxytonic (two short syllables) cadences take up the first half of a measure; paroxytonic (formerly "feminine") cadence fills the measure; double-stressed cadence fills one measure and (with a secondary accent) the first portion of another. Both of the latter cadences require the first of the two syllables to be long. The distinction between long and short is a linguistic one. Unfortunately, length is rarely noted in the manuscripts. Those syllables are long that have a long vowel (a diphthong or digraph or, in normalized texts, a vowel with a circumflex over it) or that are followed by two or more consonants. All other syllables are short. The distinction is especially crucial at the verse boundary, since paroxytonic cadences do not correspond structurally to split oxytonic ones, and split oxytonic cadences may not be treated as double-stressed ones. A problem arises when one sings a song with an alternating meter in the first rhythmic mode. For example, the first line of the Neidhart song for which a mensural notation exists begins *Blôzen wir den anger ligen sâhen.* It fills five and a half "measures" if we assume, as I do, a double-stressed cadence; five, with paroxytonic cadence.

Ex. 12.1a. Neidhart's *Blôzen wir den anger ligen sâhen.*

Blô - zen wir den an - ger li - gen sâ – hen

The musical and verse meters match well enough, but the short syllable "li-" cannot fill a quarter note (lengthening it changes the meaning of "ligen"). One would need to either insert a eighth rest or stutter the "i" which, to judge from a few parodic songs, was sometimes done: there exist some songs (unfortunately without music) ostensibly sung by peasants where they are supposed to be singing something like "li-i-i-i-gen"—from which we might assume that an "untrained" singer confronted with having to produce a longish note (or a melisma) with a short vowel would stutter it. The parody could, of course, be poking fun at the melisma itself, as in Beckmesser's butchering of Walther's song in Wagner's *Die Meistersinger.* A more likely solution is the following:

Ex. 12.1b. Neidhart's *Blôzen wir den anger ligen sâhen.*

Blô - zen wir den an - ger li - gen sâ – hen

Actually, in the absence of mensural notation, modern literary scholars would be more likely to assign a duple rhythm to a song like this:

Ex. 12.1c. Neidhart's *Blôzen wir den anger ligen sâhen.*

Blô-zen wir den an-ger li - gen sâ – hen

To be sure, in accordance with their dialects, Heinrich von Veldeke, a twelfth-century minnesinger from present-day Belgium, and Heinrich von Morungen, another from Thuringia, may already have lengthened all short vowels followed by single consonants. By the end of the thirteenth century short syllables exist only in some southern parts of German-speaking areas. Few singers of the fourteenth and fifteenth centuries differentiate between "split oxytonic" and "paroxytonic" cadences (though the distinction between paroxytonic and double stressed cadences persists in folk songs to this day). By the time the Neidhart melody was written down in the fifteenth-century codex containing it, its underlying text would have been read with long syllables throughout.[8]

We need to remember that singers of monophonic songs sang *a cappella* or with the performer decorating his own performance with a harp, fiddle, or possibly a hurdy-gurdy. They probably had and used great rhythmic freedom (hurried or delayed the beat, extended or shortened the notes). Still, I assume, as do others, based on the essential fixedness of the verse meter, some degree of regularity to the beat. Some illustrations show other musicians accompanying a singer, and some songs appear to be dance songs; in such performances one would need a fairly steady beat.[9] Given a non-mensural notation and the usual alternating verse meter, most literary scholars attempting to perform a medieval German song would choose a duple rhythm. Surely, however, since from all accounts words were often set to preexistent melodies and even newly composed tunes would borrow from prior ones, triple rhythms were also available and utilized, whether or not they were directly linked to modal rhythms.

There are a number of songs in German in so-called medieval dactyls. Their underlying rhythm seems to come from a precursor of the *Ländler.* It cannot be explained except as a reflex of a melody. Though one can devise a variety of notations, a § measure works well. The first syllable (which must be linguistically long and capable of bearing a stronger stress than the following one) would be sung as a dotted quarter note and receive a strong accent. On the evidence of the manuscripts, although modern text editors often rewrite such variants, two syllables often replace the single one, in which case it would make sense to realize them as an eighth and a quarter note, with the eighth note being strongly accented. Following the initial syllable(s) we find two syllables, the first of which carries a secondary stress; the second half of the measure would have a lightly accented eighth note and a quarter note (which may itself be split). Though the text editors rarely allow it to stand, an occasional variant appears in the manuscripts and was surely intended by the singers: a single (linguistically long) syllable in place of the expected two; this would then be another, lightly accented, dotted quarter note. Songs in this form are often found in verses corresponding to Romance decasyllabics. Since many have a facultative anacrusis (that is, the line can appear with or without an initial unstressed syllable) and there can be, as we have seen, variations within the measure, the German verses are between nine and twelve syllables in length. As described, this form corresponds roughly to the third rhythmic mode (with the variations approximating a doubled second mode and something much like the fifth mode); however, I believe the rhythm, probably for a dance, was there before the rhythmic modes were developed as theory.

Ex. 12.2. Opening of Rudolf von Fenis, *Gewan ich ze minnen* (contrafact of Folquet de Marseille, *Si tot me soi*) in parallel "modal" and duple versions.

Few modern literary scholars do deal with the secondary stresses. Most read and realize the verses much like modern dactyls, with a single stressed syllable followed by two unstressed ones. In doing so, however, they ignore the striking stylization of language found in these songs. (If the verses are read, as it were, in waltz rhythm, why must the first syllable always be linguistically long?) More importantly, they ignore the variations, perhaps because editors have so commonly removed them. Very early on, German singers begin to utilze alternating and "dactylic" rhythms in a single song.

When performing medieval German songs it is helpful to refer to an edition that normalizes the texts for guidance in which vowels are long and which are short. Though purists might quibble, it is perfectly acceptable to use the modern German pronunciation of the vowel qualities (though not vowel length) with the exception of the diphthongs *ie*, *üe*, and *uo*. The first two of these are pronounced as short *i* or *ü*, followed by a schwa-like offglide; the third, as short *u* followed by a weak, open *o* offglide. It is especially easy to overlook the diphthong *ie*, since its orthography has survived in modern German to signal a long *i*. The diphthong *eu*, as in modern German *Freude*, is variously spelled *eu*, *öu*, *oi*, and *öi*. The diphthong *ei* (as in *ein*) may have had a higher initial vowel than its modern equivalent (which, despite its orthography, has the initial sound short *a*). The equivalent of modern German *au* (*Frau*) is generally variously spelled *ou*, *ouw*, *ow*, and also probably had a higher initial vowel, an open *o*, but the modern pronunciation is acceptable. Note that the digraph *iu* represents long *ü*. The consonants may be pronounced as in modern German with the following exceptions. Intervocalic *w* is a semivowel (like English *w*). Intervocalic *zz* and final *z* are pronounced like the German sharp *s*: *wazzer* = *Wasser*, *daz* = *das* / *daß*. Intervocalic *h* is always pronounced (in modern German it is silent), probably much like the *h* in English *hue*. Before *t* and *s*, *h* (as in *niht*, *sahs*) is pronounced like modern German *ch* (*ach*). Sometimes, especially in the manuscripts, final *ch* is spelled *h*: *ih*. The sound *pf* is also spelled *ph*. Scholars often carefully pronounce the initial combinations *st*, *sp*, *sm*, *sn*, *sl* as written, but they probably were spoken more like their modern German equivalents, i.e., with a lisped *s* (*Schlange*). The combination *ng* was pronounced as in English "finger," not as in German *Finger*. Double consonants were probably pronounced as such, as in modern Italian, but few scholars or performers try to do so. The orthography of the manuscripts is often wildly varied and not infrequently confusing. If at all possible, however, it is worth returning to them (at least to diplomatic editions of them), since so many literary scholars have ignored the freedoms singers must have enjoyed and imposed their own aesthetic sense of regularity of form and content on the texts they edit. Try to reproduce the dialect variants the manuscript suggests only if the song is by a roughly contemporary singer from the same general area; scribes often reflect their own dialect or the traditions of the scriptorium they trained in.

Authenticity is, from a literary scholar's perspective, preferable to modernization. After all, why perform medieval music if you want it to sound modern? However, in striving for authenticity, do not forget that all performers of medieval secular song, whether they were dilettantes or minstrels making their living from their songs, strove to entertain. They had to hold their listener's attention, especially since, from all the information we can glean from scant documentation, romances, and the songs themselves, they sometimes had to compete for it in a great hall or a courtyard filled with tellers of tales, jugglers, dancers, wrestlers, and the like. Even when there was less commotion, for instance after dinner, their performance had to create an audience for itself.[10] There were no "concerts" of medieval secular song; there was no captive audience. Singers sang directly to their listeners, they interacted with them, and they were probably in close proximity to them. They doubtless expected their listeners to catch every nuance, every catchy turn of phrase and witticism. We cannot easily replicate this situation, but we should at least make sure that the audience (and the singer) understands what is being said as well as appreciates the music and the manner in which it is presented. The music is rarely so complex, the melodies so compelling, that one cannot convey nuances of meaning, sarcastic asides, raptures, in each succeeding strophe (they may, but need not, occur at the same point). Brief summaries (or, even worse, mere titles) will not do. The audience needs to have the text available to them, preferably in bilingual, line-for-line translations. Some words of explanation before or after a performance might also help. These will be of no avail, however, if the presentation itself is not engaging and dynamic. The model should be not the concert soloist but the cabaret artist or the street singer. One can be too cute, but a modicum of overemphasis or even overacting is preferable to reverential, boring attempts at medieval authenticity.

Notes

[1] Hubert Heinen, "Making Music as a Theme in German Songs of the 12th and 13th Centuries," *Music and German Literature. Their Relationship since the Middle Ages*, ed. by James M. McGlathery, Studies in German Literature, Linguistics, and Culture 66 (Columbia, SC, 1992), pp. 15-32.

[2] Horst Brunner et al., *Walther von der Vogelweide: Die gesamte Überlieferung der Texte und Melodien. Abbildungen, Materialien, Melodietranskriptionen*, Litterae 7 (Göppingen, 1977), pp. 49*-100*, 312-58. See also Christoph Cormeau et al., eds., *Walther von der Vogelweide. Leich, Lieder, Sangsprüche* (Berlin, 1996). This edition includes most melodies transmitted under Walther's name, edited by Horst Brunner.

[3] James V. McMahon, *The Music of Early Minnesang*, Studies in German Literature, Linguistics, and Culture 41 (Columbia, SC, 1990), pp. 77-153 and "Works Cited," pp. 155-63. See also A. H. Touber, "Ulrichs von Lichtenstein unbekannte Melodie," *Amsterdamer Beiträge zur älteren Germanistik* 26 (1987), 107-18 and "Minnesänger, Troubadours und Trouvères im Computer, *AbzäG* 29 (1989), 243-49; as well as the overview of such efforts by Dominique Billy, "Répertoires métriques de la poésie lyrique médiévale," *sô wold ich in fröiden singen. Festgabe für Anthonius H. Touber zum 65. Geburtstag*, ed. by Carla Dauven-van Knippenberg and Helmut Birkhan, *AbzäG* 43-44 (Amsterdam, 1995), 49-78.

[4] Ewald Jammers, ed., *Ausgewählte Melodien des Minnesangs* (Tübingen, Niemeyer, 1963); Ronald J. Taylor, ed., *Die Melodien der weltlichen Lieder des Mittelalters*, 2 vols. (Stuttgart, 1964) and *The Art of the Minnesinger*, 2 vols. (Cardiff, 1968); Hugo Moser and Joseph Müller-Blattau, eds., *Deutsche Lieder des Mittelalters von Walther von der Vogelweide bis zum Lochamer Liederbuch* (Stuttgart, 1968); Ewald Jammers and Helmut Salowsky, eds., *Die sangbaren Melodien zu Dichtungen der Manessischen Liederhandschrift* (Wiesbaden, 1979); Max Schiendorfer and Karl Bartsch, eds., *Die Schweizer Minnesänger* (Tübingen, 1990); Margaret Lang and Walter Salmen, eds.,

Ostdeutscher Minnesang, Schriften des Kopernikuskreises 3 (Lindau, 1958); Wendelin Müller-Blattau, *Trouvères und Minnesänger* (Saarbrücken, 1956).

[5] Siegfried Beyschlag and Horst Brunner, eds., *Die Lieder Neidharts* (Darmstadt, 1975); Siegfried Beyschlag and Horst Brunner, eds., *Herr Neidhart diesen Reihen sang. Die Texte und Melodien der Neidhartlieder mit Übersetzungen und Kommentaren*, Göppinger Arbeiten zur Germanistik 468 (Göppingen, 1989); Karl Stackmann and Karl Bertau, eds., *Frauenlob (Heinrich von Meissen). Leichs, Sangsprüche, Lieder* (Göttingen, 1981); Wesley Thomas and Barbara Garvey Seagrave, *The Songs of the Minnesinger Prince Wizlaw of Rügen*, University of North Carolina Studies in the Germanic Languages and Literature 59 (Chapel Hill, NC, 1968); Franz V. Spechtler et al., eds., *Der Mönch von Salzburg. Ich bin du und du bist ich. Lieder des Mittelalters* (Munich, 1980); Karl Kurt Klein et al., *Die Lieder Oswalds von Wolkenstein*, 2nd ed. (Tübingen, 1975); Walther Brunner et al. (see fn. 2); Gerd Fritz, ed., *Abbildungen zur Neidhart Überlieferung I. Die Berliner Neidhart-Handschrift Rund die Pergamentfragmente Cb, K, O und M*, Litterae 11 (Göppingen, 1973); Ingrid Bennewitz-Behr, *Die Berliner Neidhart-Handschrift c (mfg 779)*, Göppinger Arbeiten zur Germanistik 356 (Göppingen, 1981); Helmut Lomnitzer and Ulrich Müller, eds., *Tannhäuser. Die lyrischen Gedichte der Handschriften C und c* (Göppingen, 1973); René Clemencic, Michael Korth, and Ulrich Müller, eds., *Carmina Burana: Lateinisch-deutsche Gesamtausgabe der mittelalterlichen Melodien mit den dazugehörigen Texten* (Munich, 1979); Helmut Tervooren and Ulrich Müller, eds., *Die Jenaer Liederhandschrift*, Litterae 10 (Göppingen, 1972); Ulrich Müller et al., eds., *Die Kolmarer Liederhandschrift der Bayerischen Staatsbibliothek München (cgm 4997)*, 2 vols., Litterae 35 (Göppingen, 1975); Hans Moser and Ulrich Müller, eds., *Oswald von Wolkenstein. Abbildungen zur Überlieferung I: Die Innsbrucker Wolkenstein-Handschrift B*, Litterae 12 (Göppingen, 1972); Walter Salmen and Christoph Petzsch, eds., *Das Lochamer-Liederbuch* (Wiesbaden, 1972).

[6] Some Latin songs have a regular pattern of accents. Dutch, Skandinavian, and Middle English verse has an accent-based meter similar to German. Slavic songs are also shaped by accentual meters.

[7] McMahon, pp. 42-59. Hendrik van der Werf did not intend his "declamatory rhythm to be understood as McMahon explains it on p. 58 (personal communication); his view is closer to that of Raphael Molitor (McMahon, p. 48) and Heinrich Husmann (cited McMahon, p. 158, but not discussed), i.e., that each note has an equal value and the rhythm is essentially free.

[8] Günther Schweikle, *Minnesang*, 2nd ed. (Stuttgart, 1995), pp. 156-68; Hubert Heinen, "*Minnesang:* Some Metrical Problems," *Formal Aspects of Medieval German Poetry*, ed. by Stanley N. Werbow (Austin, 1969), pp. 79-92. In this sketch I maintained, with the arrogance of ignorance, that the mensural notation (and the verse meter) of the Neidhart song suggested the second rhythmic mode. I was wrong.

[9] McMahon, pp. 60-71; Schweikle, pp. 54-58; Hubert Heinen, "Walther's 'Owe hovelichez singen': A Re-examination," *Saga og språk*, ed. by John Weinstock (Austin, 1972), pp. 273-86. I argue that Walther was objecting to a new fashion of accompanying songs with a hurdy-gurdy.

[10] McMahon, pp. 14-26, 71-73; Schweikle, pp. 113-15.

13. English Monophony
Paul hillier

I f fate had breathed just a little harder, it seems likely that the surviving corpus of medieval English lyrics, already skeletal in appearance, would have disappeared entirely. Nonetheless, the repertoire that remains offers musical substance out of all proportion to its size, encompassing a variety of genres, and including several pieces of particular beauty. To what extent this fragmentary condition represents the original total of notated English song, allowing for a few inevitable losses, or to what extent it is merely a small portion of a once substantial repertory which has simply been obliterated by time and circumstance, it is impossible to say. There are a number of points to consider, and the truth of the situation must probably reside in a mixture of each of them.

We must remember that the art of notated song, indeed of music generally, emerges from centuries of oral tradition, and the absence of manuscripts does not necessarily indicate the absence of vernacular song from the courts and monasteries of medieval England. It does however suggest the absence of a certain type of song and a certain tradition of performance—one that requires notation. Notation becomes necessary when composer and performer cease to be the same person; when the development of polyphony goes beyond the tradition of improvisation and beyond the bounds of memorization (though this was probably much wider than we generally realize) and thus requires a means of transmission: a notated musical score; and finally becomes necessary when preserving a work or repertory of works no longer, so to speak, in active service.

The situation for England is further complicated by the fact that, since the Norman Conquest, the language of courtly discourse remained French for a long period. The preparation of musical manuscripts was a costly and specialized practice which only suitably endowed institutions such as court chapels and monasteries could afford. So only very special circumstances would be likely to give rise to the preservation of songs with English texts.

To this situation—in addition to the normal wastages of time and a (to us) surprising indifference to music of the recent past—must be added the abundantly destructive work of English reformists during the reign of Henry VIII, which resulted in an immeasurable loss of art work, including of course manuscripts full of "Popish" music. We can very easily imagine that all kinds of innocent objects got caught up in this maelstrom, though it is hard to believe that any substantial collections of English lyrics, had there been any, would have been brutalized in the same way except by mischance.[1]

The repertoire that has survived, sometimes preserved in good condition, but sometimes purely by luck (on the inside of a book-binding for example), is gathered together in its entirety in the book *Medieval English Songs,* the texts edited by E.J. Dobson and the music by F. Ll. Harrison published in London in

1979.[2] Various individual items have been made available in other publications, both before and since, but given the practical purposes of this study I shall focus my attention on the songs as presented in this, the most readily available format, though not without criticism as will be seen.

While the songs as an entity do represent a haphazard collection, there is of course one unifying feature which must claim the attention of any would-be performer: the language.

English pronunciation has changed a good deal even since Tudor times, though it is rare to hear Tudor English used for madrigals and lutesongs, and of course it can reasonably be argued that, in that instance, the original words are close enough to modern English so that no adjustment need be contemplated. Be that as it may, the singer who approaches medieval English song simply *has* to acquire some understanding of the pronunciation and general mechanics of the language, to say nothing of the vocabulary which will require some translating.

An indifferent approach to the sound of middle English—particularly the use of modern vowels—will result in an indifferent, awkward rendition of the poetry and probably succeed only in giving it a fake charm, which is uninteresting to say the least; whereas in fact, the pleasure and challenge of this repertory lie as much in exploring the language as in any musical properties. Fortunately Dobson provides a pronunciation guide which will serve as the basis for developing one's own version of medieval English.

This last remark may raise an eyebrow or two, but it is, I believe, a necessary, albeit tacit, requirement of anyone who actually intends to perform this kind of music. It does not mean that we should ignore the guidelines that scholarship has established, and it is certainly not an invitation simply to invent a pronunciation. The basic rules must indeed be appropriately ingested. But it is not enough simply to follow the rules without noticing that they lead one's voice away from familiar patterns of intonation and voice placement, revealing a whole different range of color and nuance; it behooves the performer to listen carefully to what is happening and to try and get the feel of the language as a vehicle of communication. Only when there is a natural correspondence between the emotional tone of the text and its physical representation in sound, and moreover between the flow of information (meaning and grammatical implications) and its sonic realization, can the language actually be said to be authentic in any way.

This process is in truth not so very hard—it simply requires a little *time* for study and an imaginative application of the results so that the linguistic process can feel natural in performance. It is important to avoid letting the voice drop back (or forward) into its familiar modern setting, a danger which arises particularly when some words or syllables are stranger than others. There may be a tendency to give false emphasis to the less familiar elements, and at first the different vocal placement will probably make it hard to sing as fluently as normal. But this leads us on to one of the most important musical aspects of singing with an 'early' pronunciation, which is that there are certain things you can no longer readily do with your voice if you abandon the support system of modern singing techniques and allow the language to guide you. It would also be very useful if the singer has some experience of different English dialects. Today's "received pronunciation" (essentially a middle-class, toned-down version of what is heard on the BBC) is remarkably colorless when set against a broad regional accent; it has become too familiar and is too easily associated with "classical" singing; the would-be singer of medieval song must break away from this tradition. As a simple example, try declaiming any pop song of the past twenty-five years in a polite BBC pronunciation; the result is of course ludicrous! Not only are the words altered in various ways, but it becomes stylistically impossible to sustain except as farce. It is to avoid a similar degree of anachronism that we need to begin our approach to medieval song by working on a suitable pronunciation.

We shall now turn to the songs in more detail, dealing with them sometimes individually, but mostly by style or genre, the first of which we may describe as chant style. This includes the songs by St Godric and pieces such as "Worldes blis" and "Stond wel moder under roode." The transcription into modern notation avoids any rhythmic interpretation: that is to say, there is no suggestion of meter and all the notes appear to be the same length. I do not think that the editor wished to imply that all the notes should be exactly the same length, and certainly most experienced performers would give some degree of stress to the more important syllables and perhaps certain turns of phrase, especially at cadences; but this is precisely the area where no precise solution can be agreed upon and where the performer must focus considerable attention.

Ex.13.1 shows one possible interpretation of the opening of the first St Godric song in which some notes are clearly longer than others, but in which the underlying rationale is declamatory, taking its cue from the shape of the poetry mediated through the ebb and flow of the musical setting.

Ex. 13.1. "Sainte Marie" in declamatory style.

Ex. 13.2. "Sainte Marie" in 'equal syllable' style.

An alternative approach might begin by making each *syllable* approximately equal, pushing ahead slightly where the setting is syllabic ('moder Jesu Cristes') and being more expansive with melismas to avoid a sense of overcrowding:

A more purely syllabic song such as "Sainte Nicolas" can be sung in an equalist fashion (that is with all the notes the same length), and quite impressively too; but even here it must be stressed that the options are open. Experience and personal preference will lead the way. The more one sings such music, the less arbitrary this process appears as one develops an innate sense of articulating the text and allowing the music to breathe, without doing violence to either.

A similar range of possibilities (or challenges) faces the singer of "Worldes blis" which is clearly influenced by chant style and yet is strophic and has a strongly melodic (i.e. potentially song-like) character of its own: indeed, I would rank it among the finest pieces in the repertoire of medieval song in any language. The text-setting is a mixture of syllabic and neumatic elements with slightly longer melismas particularly on the penultimate syllable of certain lines. These florid elements do not underline stress, but rather frequently work against it, so that the singer is obliged to allow the melodic lines their full expressive potential in the abstract so to speak. The tune has a very well-defined shape rising to its highest point in the middle (line 5), cadencing furthest from the Final (G) in lines 7 and 8, from where it makes a sequence of descending patterns before settling down for the conclusion. At the same time we cannot ignore the forceful eloquence of the words: there are seven stanzas set to the same music; the tone of the poem, and the fact that the vernacular is used, ensure us that the message is intended to be communicated very directly to the listener. The singer will need to possess the text and lead with it from the front—rather than provide it from behind—clumsy, subjective descriptions which I hope will convey enough of what I mean without having to be taken too literally. This means that, like an actor, the singer will know what he is going to say (and what it all means) at the beginning of each phrase and stanza.

What can we say of vocal style? I believe it should balance the requirements of a fine line sung without vibrato (such as may be heard on any good chant recording) with the grainier residue that is obtained when the consonants and vowels are produced in close proximity to one another (as they are in speech) rather than kept well apart (as is the case in bel canto). Modern singers may need to resist the temptation to beautify their tone or to mask irregularities in the flow of its production!

Whatever solution is found regarding the relative length of individual notes (and certainly the fixed metric versions of yester-year are as remote as Villon's snows), it seems reasonable to insist that the result should be supple, and that therefore some notes will be lighter than others! In Example 13.3, the song's opening phrase is given in three slightly different ways, but in each case I have imagined that those pitches other than the first of each syllable are distinctly lighter than others, though not less distinct.

Ex. 13.3. "Worldes blis" in three possible rhythmic versions.

Although "Stond wel moder" is clearly affiliated with chant through its general melodic characteristics, it also offers the right singer a considerable dramatic range of utterance, provided this is kept within stylistic bounds. Structurally it is quite distinct from "Worldes blis," being a sequence: a series of paired verses in which the musical content varies from pair to pair. The sequence, allied with the secular lai, is a musico-poetic form of great subtlety, variety and, sometimes, length. In certain contexts this raises questions of instrumental collaboration which, fortunately, we can postpone at least as far as the next paragraph. "Stond wel moder" comprises a dialogue between Christ and his mother, and is set at the crucifixion. This dialogue, by its very nature, becomes intensely dramatic, even though by later standards it is deeply constrained by its own stylistic conventions. The challenge to the performer lies in fully realizing this oppositional content without doing violence to the music's integrity. It must be said that this is a piece which can very well survive an equalist interpretation (i.e. the notes can be the same length) provided the language is closely identified with and vividly rendered.

In any case, this is a powerful work which can speak to modern audiences with surprising immediacy. As a dialogue it can of course be rendered by two singers in alternation, though it is perfectly effective as a solo with the added challenge of subtly suggesting the difference between the two "characters."

Another powerful piece in the same genre is "Ar ne kuth ich sorghe non," sometimes known as "The Prisoner's Song." This is an English contrafactum of a Norman French lai, which is also printed in Harrison/Dobson, as is the more famous Latin counterpart, the *Planctus Ante Nescia* attributed to Godfroy de St Victoire. Harrison additionally provides a written out instrumental "improvisation" which seasoned performers will view with skepticism, the introduction especially so. This is not because of the presence of any particular pitches, right or wrong, but simply because it fixes what should belong purely to the moment of invention. It was no doubt intended simply as a suggestion of what might be done, and has been composed by someone with the authority of extensive experience in this period of music: nevertheless it is merely one idea, which, by being allowed to stand in print, asserts impossible claims to authenticity.

The use of a harp to support the voice is entirely borne out by historical evidence. The beginner should perhaps set out to use only the framework of fifths which are suggested beneath the tune itself and to flesh out further ideas based directly on the melody itself and working in conjunction with the singer, perhaps reiterating phrases just sung between each pair of stanzas. There are many other possibilities of course, but these can only be arrived at through a more protracted study of the period in question.

The same objection to printed improvisations may be lodged against the arrangement of "Miri it is." The melody is strong and can be accompanied, if necessary, by just two open-fifth chords (such as used by Harrison), though I am not convinced that it needs to be sung in a regular meter at the tempo of a jig which his book seems to suggest. The relative rhythmic character which Harrison indicates can be preserved perfectly well without applying a strict pulse, and in view of the song's brevity may be found more suitable: although there may well have been more stanzas originally, the fact is that only one remains to us and it seems inappropriate to try and make a substantial piece out of what is left. This is not to say that the tune cannot be rendered instrumentally, either as Harrison suggests or in some other way: but it does not have to be *sung* that way.

Another equally short piece (though its brevity has almost the force of a haiku) is "Fuweles in the frith," a lovely two-part song in descant style in which again the main melodic background seems to be plainchant. It may be contrasted with the gymel technique used in "Edi beo thu." Here there is clearly a main tune (and a very good tune at that) while the other voice is very much secondary in importance. Both voices may be sung, or the second voice can readily be played on any one of a number of historically appropriate instruments: harp, portative organ or vielle, for example.

Further use of gymel technique may be found in "Jesu Cristes milde moder," though in all other respects this returns to the style of "Stond wel moder" to which it is also related in verbal and musical content. Performance by two solo singers (rather than several to a part) will need careful preparation not only of the notes, but also the text, so as to achieve a mutual feeling for the details of pronunciation and the degree of stress and phrasing implied by the words. Even so, certain musical points will govern the interpretation, particularly the cadential intervals. Those that are more stable (the phrases which end with thirds moving onto a unison or a fifth) suggest to my ear more weight than those phrases which conclude on a third or sixth. This does not provide a recipe for interpretation, however! It is simply one means of getting beneath the music's fabric and differentiating between certain elements. Note that it is the middle phrase of each group of three that has the relatively unstable intervals.

The melodiousness of "Brid one brere" suggests that here the details of rhythmic transcription are essentially right. Certainly this is a very good tune and one likes to hear it played (separately) as well as sung—though again I find the imposition of a metronome speed burdensome, especially as I disagree with it! The nature of this melody suggests that, if the song is to be accompanied, then a heterophonic approach would be best; even the slightest of open chords is too constraining, and the ebb and flow of the tune can be nicely amplified by having several versions going on at once. This approach is encountered all too often as a *vade mecum* of medieval performance—but if I shy away from suggesting it elsewhere, here it seems entirely appropriate.

Another strong tune lurks in the slightly earlier and not so well known "Man ma longe lives weene." In this case the repetition of a C-C-C chord like an ostinato throughout the song can give this melody the foundation it needs. Whilst the rhythmic transcription again seems eminently appropriate, the singer may well choose to enjoy a few melodic flourishes and declamatory rhythmic variations, especially if set against a regular rhythmic background. I also find it musically stronger to add a breath measure at bar 9. The text is full of gorgeous expressions: "Er thu vall of thi bench/thi seen [sin] aquench" [Ere you fall off your bench, your sin a-quench]; "In wo ssel thi wele ti, in woop thi gli" [Into woe shall your wellbeing turn; into weeping your glee]; "Weil awei! death thee ssel throwe dun" [Well away! Death shall throw you down]. Have fun!

With its isorhythmic tenor and the extended melodic variation in its upper voice, the motet "Worldes blisse have good day/Benedicamus" transports us towards a different time and more sophisticated milieu than is generally evident in the earlier repertoire.

We have as it were bumped into the European mainstream—in particular the French courtly motet such as found in the Montpellier manuscript of the same general period (ca. 1300). The Tenor voice may indeed be played, though it is no longer unusual to suggest that it can be sung—vocalized to a neutral vowel is the most frequent recommendation. The vocalization of untexted voices in medieval polyphony is a subject that lies almost beyond the scope of this essay. It is a practice that has gained adherents in the past ten years or so amongst both scholars and performers, though quite what it involves is still open to much discussion. As a singer myself and for many years director of an a cappella vocal ensemble, I stumbled into this approach (as a purely practical means of co-opting additional repertoire to my purpose) long before it became a "topic." While I was delighted in due course to find myself borne along by the winds of musicology, I remain skeptical about bare vocalization on a single vowel. It may sound good, but to the singer it feels inadequate: and this is not evidence which should be simply tossed aside even though it is fraught with subjective dangers! While I am entirely convinced that a purely vocal rendition is extremely satisfying and musically convincing (and that alone is why I do it) it seems more likely that solmization syllables might have been used, or that part or all of the Cantus text would have been pressed into service. These methods have indeed been tried and proven in various quarters, but they carry an air of arbitrariness about them, and we still lack an agreed approach which carries conviction on all fronts. Editors, almost without exception, still avoid the challenge of printing out such solutions, preferring instead the discretionary suggestion "may be vocalized..." And who can blame them? The only way to get around this "locally" may be to find a kind musicologist who is willing to do in practice what he or she is not willing to commit to print.

Harrison's book concludes with a set of later songs, mostly two-part (for voice and instrument—though the suggested "viola" is now a redundant piece of pragmatism). Several of these are fine pieces of music ("Thy Yool, thys Yool" especially), though as they belong to a later musical idiom and pose relatively few questions of performance practice I will omit discussion of them here.

There remain three pieces to discuss, a song of the Annunciation, a Christmas carol, and the famous "Sumer" canon. The carol "Lullay; Als I lay" is perhaps one of the simplest songs in this collection for a small group of singers to approach, even if they have little experience with medieval music. Harrison's performance suggestions may be adopted directly, including the drone accompaniment which is indeed best sung softly (though surely by all available voices just as readily as two or three). To the inexperienced singer I would reiterate two important things: sing without bel canto/ vibrato and spend enough time on the pronunciation to feel at home with it as "language." There are one or two additional considerations to offer: the addition of an extra breath beat at measure 4 is a distinct possibility; in the middle of the piece a fifth could be added above the drone (moving in parallel to the suggested D and C); it is not necessary to articulate the rhythm given to the drone part in measures 8 and 9, simply move on to C where suggested and hold it; verses can be sung by two soloists in alternation; the piece gains in expressive power through longevity, and there is after all a story to be told, therefore consider singing all the verses, or at least more than half of them.

"Gabriel fram heven-king" is probably the most well-known item in the book apart from "Sumer is icumen in" thanks to Chaucer's mention of it in "The Miller's Tale." The number of different versions in which it survives also suggests that it was extremely popular in its own day too. Performers will naturally choose the version that suits their forces best, though I would make a plea here for choosing only one at a time! In this I am opposed to the practice of stringing several different versions of a piece together into one of those infamous sequences which mislead the public into thinking that medieval music is only good enough if served up as a mixed salad. The song tells a story and tells it very beautifully, and does not need dressing up in false variation. Although the three-voice version is best sung by three soloists (and is actually easier that way) it can be rendered by a small choir—though the basses should tread lightly above the stave.

Harrison offers various suggestions for performing "Sumer is icumen in" to which I would simply add that it could first be sung by a single voice (over the pes), before building to four and then six parts as suggested. Obviously choirs as well as solo groups can sing this piece perfectly well. I feel obliged to hint that solo voices are more effective—but in the end this is one of those pieces which attracts people to a style of music that they may not otherwise encounter. And so, the more the merrier, but don't stop there![3]

As I said at the beginning, those of us who take a special interest in early English music are lucky perhaps to have even these few songs. Nevertheless it *is* frustrating not to have more. And even though we can assume that Anglo-Norman and French repertoire would have been part and parcel of the aristocracy's musical fare, in the earlier English repertoire especially it is the Germanic character of the language that resonates so strongly and—for me at least—insulates these songs from the nearby continental repertoire. It is their very Englishness that attracts us to them, together with their very strong intrinsic musical value; and of course it is hard not to regret the lost body of songs to which these few so tantalizingly point.

Notes

1 But to the unlettered this distinction could hardly have counted for much.
2 I had the good fortune to work with both of these eminent scholars on several occasions and will always be in their debt for the generosity with which they offered me advice and instruction. The misgivings I voice here about certain details of presentation should not be allowed to mask the affection and admiration in which I hold their memory, nor should it discourage performers from putting the fruit of their labors to good use.
3 For a reconstruction of the original version of "Sumer is icumen in," see Ross W. Duffin, "The *Sumer* Canon: A New Revision," in *Speculum* 63 (1988), 1-21.

III. LYRIC FORMS POST 1300

14. French Ars Nova

Charles E. Brewer

Terminology and Background

The most significant differences between the lyric forms of fourteenth-century France and earlier French lyric are the consistent use of a clearly notated rhythmic and metric structure and the adoption of a limited number of poetic verse patterns. While earlier French song had occasionally made use of a mensural notation, and certain earlier genres, such as dance songs, were more likely to be metrically organized, the notational innovations associated with the *ars nova notandi* (new craft of notating) allowed composers to control a wide and varied palate of rhythmic possibilities. The possibilities of imperfect (duple) and perfect (triple) mensuration, as organized in the four prolations, provided for the basic combinations of rhythmic patterns that still remain as the fundamental rhythmic structures in contemporary music.

In the context of the so-called *formes fixes* of the fourteenth century, this meant that a composer could use a relatively stereotypical formal pattern, but still imbue each composition with a quite distinct musical character. However, this music was for the most part probably not expressive in any modern sense. In the so-called *Prologue* to his works, Guillaume de Machaut wrote:

> And Music is an art which likes people to laugh and sing and dance. It cares nothing for melancholy, nor for a man who sorrows over what is of no importance, but ignores, instead, such folk. It brings joy everywhere it's present; it comforts the disconsolate, and just hearing it makes people rejoice.[1]

It should be remembered that most evidence indicates that the courtly chansons of the thirteenth and fourteenth centuries were for entertainment, especially following the two main meals: *disner*, and later in the day, *souper*.[2] For a fourteenth-century listener or performer, there was not a sense that the music would create different emotions (as in the *Affektenlehre* [Doctrine of Affections] associated with music of the Baroque period), but that music could cure a melancholic temperament.[3]

Sources and Composers

The most significant early fourteenth-century source of French lyric is *Le Roman de Fauvel*, as edited by Chaillou de Pesstain, and preserved in Paris, Bibliothèque Nationale, fonds français 146, probably copied about 1317–18.[4] It has been suggested that the musical editor of this source was Philippe de Vitry, to whom a number of the motets have been ascribed, but the extent of his possible collaboration is unclear at best.[5] In any case, *Le Roman de Fauvel* is the first extensive source of French lyrics in the established poetic patterns of the *formes fixes*, including, *rondeaux, virelais, ballades, fatras,* and *lais.*[6]

Also included in *Le Roman de Fauvel* is a fascicle including the compositions of Jehan de Lescurel (d. 1304).[7] With the exception of one polyphonic rondeau (*A vous, douce debonaire*), his works are monophonic songs similar to the musical styles of *Le Roman de Fauvel*, and following the *formes fixes* of *ballades, rondeaux, virelais,* and *diz entés*.

Perhaps the most typical and exemplary composer of this period was Guillaume de Machaut (ca.1300–77).[8] As an influential figure in fourteenth-century literature, with royal patronage, he was to many other writers of the period, such as Geoffrey Chaucer, a model of contemporary poetry. His works are more completely preserved than any other medieval composer and poet, since he is known to have supervised the copying of manuscripts containing his complete poems and music—at least, up to the date of copying in each case.[9] The works of Machaut will provide the primary illustrations in this study of fourteenth-century French lyric forms.[10]

Individual works in the basic style of the French *ars nova* are also found in later manuscripts now in Ivrea (Biblioteca Capitolare, without signature), Chantilly (Musée Condé, ms. 564 [*olim* 1047]), and Paris (Bibliothèque Nationale, fonds français nouv. acq. 6771 [Codex Reina]), where the lyric forms are mixed with other genres, such as motets and other sacred music. There are also a number of smaller and fragmentary sources that provide insights into the wide diffusion of French musical influence. The music in these later manuscripts is more closely associated with the musical style termed the *ars subtilior*.[11]

Poetic Forms

The most important factor in the performance of fourteenth-century French lyrical poetry is that of established poetic patterns, termed the *formes fixes*. These patterns developed from thirteenth-century precedents into cohesive poetic / musical structures that were used through the end of the fifteenth century (a period of use at least as long as that of the sonata-form). Though the poetic and musical theory set the basic parameters, there is an infinite amount of variation possible between each individual example. It is important to note that in the fourteenth century, a division occurred between lyric poetry actually set to music (*musique artificiele*) and lyric poetry that exists only as texts (*musique naturele*).[12]

Overall, the general literary conceits of French lyric poetry in this period continue the thirteenth-century traditions of courtly love. As noted above, the performance context of these works seems to indicate that these poems were to be taken more as literary games and entertainments than serious and emotional texts. However, poets such as Machaut could endow these lyrics with wonderful variety and word play, and could even broach more religious subjects, as in the *La lay de la fonteine*, which combines an exposition of the Trinity with the praise of the Virgin Mary. An aspect of this literary play can be seen in Machaut's *Le Livre du Voir*

Dit (The Book of the True Poem), written late in his career. This is a literary correspondence between a younger woman, Peronne, and the elder poet, in which complete and fragmentary poems (often preserved in other sources with musical setings) are constantly exchanged and commented upon.[13]

There are two important contemporary descriptions of the *formes fixes* that should be consulted. The first is Guillaume de Machaut's *Remede de Fortune*, written in the 1340s, in which he gives actual musical illustrations of the basic *formes fixes* within the context of a longer love poem.[14] The illustrations include the following forms: *lai, complainte, chant royal, baladelle, ballade, chanson baladée* (= *virelai*), and *rondelet* (= *rondeau*).[15] The second is Eustache Deschamps' *L'Art de dictier*, which, following a preface on the seven Liberal Arts, is a purely literary description of the following forms: *balade, sirventes, sote balade, balade amoureuse, chanson royale, pastourelle, rondeau, virelai*, and *lai*.[16] Though these works delineate a wide variety of possible forms, the preserved musical settings are restricted to a few formal patterns.

Three of the most common *formes fixes* make important use of a refrain: the *virelai* (*chanson baladée*), the *ballade*, and the *rondeau*. The *virelai* may be closest to the dance songs from the thirteenth century, and an illumination in the *Remede de Fortune* preceding Machaut's example of this form depicts a *carole* (round dance).[17] Machaut's preferred term for this form, *chanson baladée*, probably refers to the addition of a refrain to a typical *chanson* pattern (aab). Though there are a number of possible verse patterns, the basic musical pattern remains the same. The use of upper case letters indicates a pairing of music and text in a refrain; lower case letters are musical phrases sung to varying text. In the case of the *virelai*, the opening musical phrase is used both for the refrain text and for the last lines of the varying stanzas. In the following, in reference to the musical pattern, the subscript letters indicate two cadential forms typical of this style: "o" = *ouvert* (open, 1st ending) and "c" = *clos* (closed, 2nd ending). The numbers in the verse pattern refer to the verse numbering most common in modern musical editions.

Virelai

Musical Pattern: A b_o b_c a   A b_o b_c a   A b_o b_c a   A

Verse Pattern: **1**   2   3   4   **5**   ...

Most of Machaut's *virelais* have three stanzas, though on a number of earlier recordings the later stanzas are often omitted. Partly this is due to the fact that only the first stanzas appear with the music in most modern editions, and given the complex nature of *ars nova* rhythmic patterns it is often difficult to read the music and look for the remaining text of the poem at the bottom of the page. For actual performance, it would be helpful to prepare an edition with all the text for all stanzas coordinated with the music.

The *ballade* is similar to the *virelai*, but its refrain occurs only between the varying stanzas of the poem. It appears to have been Machaut's preferred form, since there are over forty *ballades* with music, and two hundred preserved only as texts. There are two basic musical patterns for the *ballade* as found in the works of

Machaut, the *ballade simplex*, the most common form, and the *ballade duplex*. Both consist of two musical sections. In the "simple" *ballade*, a refrain is added to the basic *chanson* pattern, in which only the first section is repeated.

Ballade simplex

Musical Pattern: a_0 a_c b C $-$ a_0 a_c b C $-$ a_0 a_c b C

Verse Pattern: 1 2 3 4...[18]

In a number of fourteenth-century *ballades*, the refrain ("C") will often conclude with a musical rhyme, repeating all or part of the music from the *clos* ending of the first section ("a_c"); this is often termed a "rounded" *ballade*. In the *ballade duplex* (also referred to as a *baladelle*), the music of the second section is also repeated.

Ballade duplex

Musical Pattern: a_0 a_c b_0 b_c $-$ a_0 a_c b_0 b_c $-$ a_0 a_c b_0 b_c

In this form, the refrain is incorporated as part of the repeat of the "b" section.

As with the *virelais*, most fourteenth-century *ballades* have three stanzas, and most modern editions only place the first stanza under the music. One of Machaut's *ballades*, *Quant Theseus / Ne quier veoir*, actually has two separate texts, the first written by Thomas Paien and the second a response by Machaut, that share a common refrain, both of which are meant to be sung simultaneously in the manner of a polytextual motet.[19] Two of Machaut's *ballades* have three separate texts; the more direct of the two is, *De triste cuer / quant vrais amans / Certes, je di*, in which the traditional three stanzas of a *ballade* are sung simultaneously, sharing one common refrain.[20] The most musically complex of Machaut's *ballades*, is the canonic triple *ballade: Sanz cuer / Amis, dolens / Dame, par vous.*[21]

The *rondeau* is generally only a single stanza with a two-part refrain. Though musically it consists of only two sections (like the *virelai* and *ballade*), it has a much more complex "road map."

Rondeau

Musical Pattern: **A B** a **A** a b **A B**

Verse Pattern: 1 2 3 4 5 6 7 8

Some of Machaut's most complex musical games were formed by *rondeaux*, such as the famous *Ma fin est ma commencement*, in which the first section is sung in retrograde to create the second section.[22] Ex. 14.1 is a version of Machaut's second shortest *rondeau*, *Doulz viaire gracieus*, in which the A section consists of mm. 1–5 (to the fermata), and the B section includes mm. 5–12.[23] In verses 3 and 4, the performers would hold at the fermata and return to the beginning; only when the A section continues into the B section is the short melisma in the *Triplum* sung.[24]

Ex. 14.1. *Doulz viaire gracieus*, by Guillaume de Machaut.

One unusual *forme fixe* with refrain is not found among the works of Machaut, and in fact only four examples of the *fatras* are still known to exist. The *fatras* was a satirical, almost surrealistic poem consisting of a two-line refrain (the *fatras distich*) and an eleven-line stanza, the first line of which is the same as the first line of the refrain, and the last line of the stanza is the last line of the refrain.[25] As in the *rondeau*, there is a simple structure to the *fatras* stanza; each line of the form represents one or the other of the two musical sections.[26]

Fatras

Musical and Rhyme Pattern:	**A**	**B**	**A**	a	b	a	a	b	b	a	b	a	**B**
Verse Pattern:				1	2	3	4	5	6	7	8	9	10 11 12 13

The two earliest extant musical settings of a *fatras* are included among the insertions in *Le Roman de Fauvel*.[27] A *fatras distich* is also found as the tenor to a three-voice composition in Oxford, Bodleian Library, E. Mus. 7 (ff. 267v–288r / pp. 532–533): *Deus, creator omnium / Rex genitor ingenite / Doucement mi*

194

reconforte.[28] This tenor text is found among the *fatrasies* by Watriquet Brassenel de Couvin, who was active at the court of Philip VI from 1328 to *circa* 1340.[29] A text by Watriquet is also used in the only polyphonic setting of a *fatras distich*, which is found in the Wrocław *rotulus* (Wrocław, Biblioteka Uniwersytecka, rkp. Ak 1955 / KN195, *olim* I.Q.411 [Handschriftenfragmente 82]).[30] As in a *rondeau*, the two musical sections probably served through repetition to create a complete musical setting of the *fatras distich* and the eleven-line stanza.

Only one of the significant *formes fixes* is without refrain, the *lai* (sometimes also termed *descort*). Though it was still being discussed as late as 1392 in Deschamps *L'art de dictier*, it was not as popular a form as the ballade and rondeau. Basically, a *lai* was similar to the liturgical sequence, in that it is formed from constantly changing pairs of stanzas that are both sung to the same melody, which will occasionally use *ouvert* and *clos* endings.

Lai

Musical Pattern: a_0 a_c b_0 b_c c_0 c_c ...

Stanza Pattern: 1a   1b   2a   2b   3a   3b   ...

There is no poetic pattern or set number of stanzas for this form, except for the parallel structure. However, some *lais* show certain musical techniques that create more cohesive forms in the longer examples. For instance, the *lai, Talant que j'ai d'obeïr*, from *Le Roman de Fauvel*, has fourteen basic melodic sections, some of which are repeated twice, sections II and IV with *ouvert* and *clos* endings.[31] Section XIV of this *lai* is a literal repeat of the melody of section I, producing an overall "rounded" form, similar to the melodic rhyme in certain fourteenth-century *ballades*. This rounding is present in most of Machaut's *lais*, though in some of his later *lais* he will often transpose the initial melody up by a perfect fifth or down by a perfect fourth. In addition, in four of the *lais* Machaut uses different polyphonic techniques. In *En demantant et lamentant*, it appears that Machaut may have intended each group of three stanzas to be sung simultaneously to form a three-voice composition in three sections.[32] The *Un lay de consolation* appears to combine each half-stanza into a two-voice work.[33] The remaining two polyphonic *lais*, *Le lay de la fonteinne* and *Le lay de confort* both use different canonic techniques. In *Le lay de confort*, each of the twelve stanzas is a simple three-voice canon at the unison.[34] The musical style used to set the twelve stanzas of *Le lay de la fonteinne* is more complex, in that all odd-numbered stanzas are monophonic while all even-numbered stanzas are three-voice canons at the unison.[35] This *lai* is also rounded, so that the opening monophonic stanza returns in the twelfth stanza transposed down a perfect fourth as the melody for a three-voice canon.[36]

Rather than being a restriction on the creativity of a fourteenth-century composer, the basic formulas of these *formes fixes* appear to have stimulated a great variety of approach that most certainly delighted the imaginations of contemporary listeners and performers.

Musical Style and Notation

The musical notation of the fourteenth century in France was moving towards a clearly-defined system of note shapes and rhythmic organization that is generally termed the *ars nova*. The earliest sources, such as *Le Roman de Fauvel*, are not yet fully consistent as regards their rhythmic notation and this can occasionally result in divergent transcriptions, such as those by Wilkins and Gennrich of Jehan de Lescurel.[37] The later sources, including the so-called "Machaut Manuscripts" use a fully-developed notational system that was devised ca.1315-20 by two mathematicians, Johannes de Muris and Philippe de Vitry.[38] The basis of the *ars nova* notation, in its simplest terms, was the set of four prolations which produced four distinct rhythmic patterns equivalent to these modern meters: 9/8 (*tempus perfectum cum prolatione maiore*), 3/4 (*tempus perfectum cum prolatione minore*), 6/8 (*tempus imperfectum cum prolatione maiore*), and 2/4 (*tempus imperfectum cum prolatione minore*). The clarity with which the composers of the fourteenth century could notate rhythm lead to important compositional results, especially in the more elaborate use of syncopation and cross rhythms that could now be indicated without ambiguity. It is important to remember how significant this rhythmic innovation was to the fourteenth century, since it is a major element of the musical style which is sometimes overlooked in some modern performances.[39]

In general, most modern editions of this repertoire are serviceable, though each has its own editorial idiosyncracies. It is important to compare different transcriptions and take time to read the editorial prefaces and critical commentaries to find alternative solutions to occasionally ambiguous rhythmic passages. Again, for a performer, the fact that often only one stanza of a multi-stanzaic form is set to the music can be a significant problem that can only be solved by preparing an entirely new edition.

One performance issue that is not always clear in the main texts of the modern editions, is that compositions often underwent various transformations from manuscript to manuscript or as a result of a composer's revisions. A clear case of the latter that is not evident in the main texts of the modern editions is that the *ballade* illustration from the *Remede de Fortune, Dame, de qui toute ma joie*, was originally for two voices and only later did Machaut add a further two voices as possible alternatives.[40] In this case, the performers will have to decide upon the early version or any of the possible interpretations of the later version, but in almost every instance, throughout the repertoire of fourteenth-century French chansons, some experimentation with other scoring possibilities might provide interesting alternatives.

Perhaps the most confusing subject associated with *ars nova* notation is the inconsistent use of chromatic alterations and the editorial additions of alterations in the modern versions (so-called *musica ficta* or *musica falsa*).[41] The possible solutions for the fourteenth-century French lyric song range from the most conservative, in which an editor adds only those chromatic alternations necessary to avoid possibly blatant simultaneous cross-relations, to editions that freely add many chromatic alterations based upon various theories concerning fourteenth-century musical style. Often the questions of chromatic alteration are intimately linked with the analysis of the works in question. Given the uncertain knowledge of a number of aspects concerning fourteenth-century musical style, it is important that each work be newly studied in relation to its notation, harmonic and contrapuntal style before any final performance decisions are made concerning chromatic alterations.[42]

An example of this problem can be seen in music Ex.14.1. This *rondeau* is tonally quite ambiguous; though the first important cadence is on G, the final cadence of the two-part form is on B-flat. The manuscripts indicate a number of specific chromatic alterations, which are indicated on the staff. A number of other notes seem to require chromatic alterations, such as the f in m. 2 of the Cantus, to avoid an augmented octave with the explicitly notated F♯ in the Triplum. The chromatic alterations that seem necessary because of changes in the other voices are indicated by the chromatic signs above the staff. A number of other alterations are indicated above the staff within parentheses. These are alterations that are not required due to the musical structure of the piece or its original notation, but either help the composition move in a more consistent harmonic language or enhance the melodic direction.[43] These types of chromatic alterations and their method of notation vary from edition to edition. Ex.14.1 represents only one possibility.[44] In preparing a performance, it proves useful to try all of the possibilities and base any final decisions on subjective musical reactions.

Performance Parameters

The general consensus is that fourteenth-century lyric song was conceived as chamber music with only a single performer on each notated part. Though there was no absolute pitch, most French songs of the period have comfortable tessituras for singers around traditional modern pitch (a' = 440 cycles/second). For instance, Ex.14.1 could easily be sung by three tenors or sopranos, but it could as easily be sung at a lower pitch level by baritones or altos. However, in the *lais* of Machaut, though individual stanzas may have a melodic range of about a ninth, the overall range of the entire work can reach almost two octaves. This extreme tessitura raises important performance questions: were they sung by a single performer, by different performers in succession, or in some sort of group performance. The later possibility is implied in a miniature found in one of Machaut manuscripts before the *lais* (Paris, Bibliothèque Nationale, fonds français 9221, f. 16r), in which there are six singers depicted singing from a *rotulus* (roll) and by the existence of *Le lay de la fonteine* that alternates monophony and polyphony.[45]

There seems to be little doubt that much of the French fourteenth-century repertoire was meant to be performed using the so-called Pythagorean tuning, based on perfect fifths and octaves, and producing wide thirds and sixths compared to modern equal temperament.[46] This would be especially effective in a work such as Ex.14.1, whose opening sonority would sound positively raucous until it resolves in the second measure.

One more elusive question concerns the tempo for much of this repertoire.[47] The best general advice is to examine the note content of each piece, and examine any difficult syncopations and melismatic passages for the fastest tempo at which these may be performed comfortably and clearly. As music for entertainment, this was not music for virtuosos, but for dedicated amateurs and the court musicians.

The question of the pronunciation of Middle French is in some respects as speculative as that of any medieval language. Performers should study the available manuals on pronunciation and the numerous recordings of the repertoire.[48]

Perhaps the most problematic aspect of this repertoire is that frequently only one part is preserved with a complete text in the manuscripts. For instance, Ex.14.1 has the text copied only with the *Cantus*. The traditional solution has been to perform the untexted parts (frequently the tenor and contratenor) with instruments.[49] The principal difficulty with this solution is that there is little unequivocal documentation of the practice and the problem of which instruments are most appropriate.

In Jean de Meun's late thirteenth-century continuation to the *Roman de la Rose* (lines 21021–21041), there is a description of Pygmalion performing for the imaginary woman he has created, where he plays the portative organ and sings *Motet ou treble ou teneüre*.

> Then in a loud, clear voice full of great gaiety, he sang, instead of the Mass, songs of the pretty secrets of love. He made his instruments sound so that one might not hear God thundering. He had many kinds of instruments and, for playing them, hands more dexterous than Amphion of Thebes ever had. Pygmalion had harps, fiddles, and rebecs, guitars and lutes, all chosen to give pleasure.... He had excellent organs that could be carried in one hand while he himself worked the bellows and played as, with open mouth, he sang the motet or triplum or tenor voice.[50]

This passage clearly associates instruments and polyphonic music, but it does not specify if Pygmalion is singing one part and playing another simultaneously, or if he is singing and playing only a single part from a polyphonic composition.

Machaut himself mentions the possible performance of his *ballade, Nes que on porroit* (#33), with instruments in his *Le Livre du Voir-Dit*.

> I send you my book, *Morpheus*, which they call *La Fontaine amoureuse*, in which I have made a song to your order, and it is in the guise of a *rés d'Alemaigne*; and by God it is long since I have made so good a thing to my satisfaction; and the tenors are as sweet as unsalted pap. I beg therefore that you deign to hear it, and know the thing just as it is, without adding or taking away; and it is to be said in a goodly long measure; and if anyone play it on the organs, cornemuse, or other instrument, that is its right nature.[51]

Again, this passage does not clearly indicate that a polyphonic performance is being described.

There is a late reference to the performance of *teneur* and *contreteneur* on the *psalterium* by Jean de Gerson (d. 1429), in his allegorical poem, *Pratique du Psalterium Mystique*, but this might reflect changes in practice at the beginning of the fifteenth century: "Take [the psalterium], he said, and well set it [in music], in order to play it in sweet song with tenor and contratenor in order to enliven your bitter lament."[52]

Machaut included extensive lists of instruments in two of his longer poems: *La prise d'Alexandrie* and *Le Remede de Fortune*.[53] Again, however, these lists are not truly evidence that all of these diverse instruments performed in the courtly chanson.

The most common instrument used in modern performances of this repertoire is the vielle. However, there are a number of problems that recent research has brought forward concerning the use of this instrument in elaborate polyphony. The first is that of a flat versus a round bridge. A flat bridge, especially in conjunction with the tunings described by Jerome of Moravia would produce too many drones for a clear performance a single polyphonic line. There is some evidence from the fourteenth century for a slightly curved bridge and alternative tunings that would allow the performance of individual pitches and possibly this was one option.[54] The *Charivari* from the *Roman de Fauvel* (f. 34r), shows a single vielle surrounded by all sorts of percussion instruments, but the nature of this raucous post-nuptial ritual is not really applicable to the performance ambiance of the courtly chanson.

Another possibility, though again without significant documentation of its actual use in polyphony, would be the lute.[55] This would be capable of playing all the chromatic notes evident in this repertoire and also has sufficient range (as far as can be judged) to perform any part in a fourteenth-century French chanson.

The harp was perhaps the most common instrument used in courtly performances.[56] Though the majority of evidence seems to reflect the performance of monophonic song, the harp would have been capable of performing much of the fourteenth-century French repertoire, either as single parts or possibly even as intabulations of whole compositions. Machaut included an elaborate allegorical interpretation of this instrument in his *Dit de la harpe*, in which the twenty-five strings of the instrument are equated with the virtues of his lady.[57] He even writes concerning the harp that "of instruments it is the perfection" and it "... surpasses all instruments."[58] Christopher Page has noted that in the romance, *Cleriadus et Meliadice*, there is evidence both of an instrumental (harp) and a vocal performance of the same piece:

"As soon as Cleriadus entered his lodgings he demanded a harp at once.... When he was all alone, he began to compose the music for the song that Meliadice had sent him, and he succeeded so well that those who heard it sung afterwards said that they had never heard a better song. Afterwards, he put it on the harp and played for a long time."[59]

Later in the same romance:

"When the company had danced a good while to the minstrels, they began to dance to songs. So Cleriadus began to sing what Meliadice had written. A squire from his retinue held the tenor part for him and you may believe that it was good to hear, for [Cleriadus] sang better than anyone had ever heard before. When he had finished, he put a written copy of the song into the hands of Meliadice."[60]

Another strong possibility, suggested by the Gerson sermon cited above, is the *psalterium* (psaltery).[61] Like the harp, the psaltery could play distinct individual pitches and could have had the range necessary to perform even the lower parts of the French polyphonic chansons. The major difficulty with both the harp and psaltery, which is not present in the vielle or lute, is the lack of multiple chromatic pitches, though some authors, such as Page, Fulton, and Duffin, have suggested a nine-note octave that would include strings for both B♮ and B♭, though this would not account for all the manuscript accidentals or potential *musica ficta*.[62] In fact, the use of instruments can occasionally limit the editorial possibilities of chromatic alterations, which would not be the case with a vocal performance or with the use of a vielle or lute.

For a number of reasons, especially related to possible ranges and social associations, most wind instruments, with the possible exception of the flutes (both transverse and recorder like) and the ambiguous *douçaine* mentioned in a number of French poems from the fourteenth century, were unlikely to have participated in the performance of courtly polyphonic works.[63]

In summary, the use of instruments in this repertoire cannot be discounted, though it may have existed only in certain special circumstances, such as an entirely instrumental performance of a polyphonic work, perhaps involving only one single voice part and not the whole polyphonic structure.

There is equally strong evidence that polyphonic works were performed entirely by voices. This may have partly been due to an aesthetic view, based in Platonic philosophy and Augustinian theology, that the voice was superior to instruments since it could convey meaning. See, for example, the statement by Jacopus Leodiensis (of Liège) from early in the fourteenth century:

> Because truly, natural musical instruments [*e.g.*, the voice] are more perfect than crafted instruments [*e.g.*, flutes, organs, lutes, psalteries, vielles, *etc.*]. For craft [*ars*] imitates nature....[64]

A number of earlier writers sought to characterize the musical style of the untexted voices in the French polyphonic chanson as "unvocal."[65] However, Eustache Deschamps, implies that it is possible to sing a polyphonic composition without any words. This discussion is linked to his distinction between artificial music (musical compositions) and natural music (poetry).

> Similarly, *chançons natureles* are made delightful and embellished by the melody, and tenor, soprano and contra-tenor parts of artificial music. Nevertheless, each of these two [artificial and natural music] is pleasing to hear by itself. One can be sung by voice and by art without any words. Also the lyrics of the songs can often be recited in places where they are most willingly heard—even where artificial music would not always be performed, as among lords and ladies in private and secret.[66]

In certain instances, it is possible to set the words given with one voice part to match other, untexted, parts. Sometimes this might require breaking groups of notes ligated together into separate entities, or to break longer note values into smaller notes to accommodate a larger number of syllables. There is evidence that this was occasionally done with lower parts in the sacred repertoire, but it requires the performers to make decisions that radically affect the musical integrity of the original composition. Ex.14.1 represents this type of solution; by breaking the opening ligatures in the *Tenor*, it is possible to set the text editorially in all three parts.

One possibility that is rarely attempted is to perform the untexted parts of a polyphonic composition using traditional solmization and mutation techniques found in some medieval theory books.[67] However, the main objection to this technique is that while it would be very useful both as regards sightsinging and making modern editorial decisions concerning *musica ficta*, in performance it would create a second pseudo-text that would conflict with the main text of the composition.

Recently, the possibility of vocalization of voice parts has received more attention. The strongest advocate for the performance of untexted parts (especially tenors and contratenors) through vocalization is Christopher Page.[68] Based on his experiments, which can be heard in a number of his most recent recordings, Page advocates use of the sound [y] (similar to Modern French *tu*), since more "open" sounds tend to emphasize lower parts of the overtone spectrum that then cover up other texted parts.[69]

Men and women of all ages were probably equal participants in the courtly French chanson. As Page noted in the romance, *Cleriadus et Meliadice*: "And when they had danced their fill the minstrels ceased and they began to sing. There might you have heard men and women singing well!"[70] From the same source: "As soon as they were there the girls dismounted and the valets took the unicorns away; then the girls went off to one side and began to sing. Because of their beautiful song the instruments were commanded to be silent so that the girls might be better heard: all those who heard them, both men and women, said that they had never heard better singing in their lives."[71]

Overall, the most fruitful approach to this repertoire is that of experimentation. There is not sufficient evidence to make categorical decisions about what was or was not done in the fourteenth century. There are many possibilities, and each performance will be a unique event based upon the performers' decisions. The main point is to remember that these chansons were to entertain and cure melancholy.

Selected Facsimiles and Editions

Le Roman de Fauvel

Le Roman de Fauvel in the Edition of Mesire Chaillou de Pesstain: A Reproduction in Facsimile of the Complete Manuscript Paris, Bibliothèque Nationale, Fonds Français 146, introduction by Edward H. Roesner, François Avril, and Nancy Freeman Regalado (*New* York: Broude Brothers Limited, 1990).

Rosenberg, Samuel N. and Hans Tischler. *The Monophonic Songs in the Roman de Fauvel*. Lincoln: University of Nebraska Press, 1991.

Jehan de Lescurel (Jehannot de l'Escurel)

Complete Works. Edited by Nigel Wilkins. *Corpus Mensurabilis Musicæ* 30. Neuhaussen-Stuttgart: American Institute of Musicology / Hännsler Verlag, 1966.
Jehannot de l'Escurel: Balades, rondeaux et diz entez sus refroiz de rondeaux. Edited by Friedrich Gennrich. *Summa musicæ Medii Ævi* 13. Langen bei Frankfurt: *s.n.*, 1964.

Guillaume de Machaut

Musikalische Werke. Edited Friedrich Ludwig (vols. 1- 3) and Heinrich Besseler (vol. 4. 4 vols. 1926–43; *reprinted* Leipzig: Breitkopf und Härtel, 1954.
The Works of Guillaume de Machaut. Edited Leo Schrade. *Polyphonic Music of the Fourteenth Century* 2 and 3. Monaco: Éditions de l'Oiseau-Lyre, 1956. Reprinted in five volumes, edited by Stanley Boorman (Monaco: Éditions de l'Oiseau-Lyre, 1977).

Notes

[1] Guillaume de Machaut, *The Fountain of Love (La Fonteinne Amoureuse) and Two Other Love Vision Poems*, edited and translated by R. Barton Palmer, *Garland Library of Medieval Literature, Series A*, vol. 54 (New York, 1993), pp. 12–13: "Et Musique est une science / Qui vuet qu'on rie et chante et dance. / Cure n'a de merencolie, / Ne d'homme qui merencolie / A chose qui ne puet valoir, / Eins met tels gens en nonchaloir. / Partout ou elle est poie y porte; / Les desconfortez reconforte, / Et nès seulement de l'oïr / Fait elle les gens resjoïr."

[2] See Christopher Page, "The Performance of Songs in Late Medieval France: A New Source," *Early Music* 10 (1982), 442.

[3] This medicinal aspect was quite important to Machaut's "pupil," Eustache Deschamps; see his *L'Art de dictier*, edited and translated by Deborah M. Sinnreich-Levi (East Lansing, 1994), p. 61: "Musique est le derreneiere science ainsis comme la medicine des vij ars: car quant le couraige et l'esperit des creatures ententives aux autres ars dessus declairez song lassez et ennuyez de leurs labours, musique, par la doucour de sa science et la melodie de sa voix, leur chante par ses vj notes tiercoyees, quintes et doublees, ses chans delectables et plaisans..." (Music is the last science—the medicine of the seven arts. For when the hearts and spirits of men intent on the other arts elucidated above [the remaining six of the Liberal Arts] are fatigued and tired by their labors, music, by the sweetness of its science and the melody of its voice, sings its delectable and pleasing songs to them with its six notes, in thirds, fifths, and octaves).

[4] *Le Roman de Fauvel in the Edition of Mesire Chaillou de Pesstain: A Reproduction in Facsimile of the Complete Manuscript Paris, Bibliothèque Nationale, Fonds Français 146*, introduction by Edward H. Roesner, François Avril, and Nancy Freeman Regalado (New York, 1990).

[5] Edward Roesner in his extensive study of this question in the introduction to the facsimile edition (*Le Roman de Fauvel in the Edition of Mesire Chaillou de Pesstain*, pp. 38–42) concludes that the evidence for Vitry's collaboration in this project is "uncertain."

[6] The entire corpus of French song in *Le Roman de Fauvel* is published in Samuel N. Rosenberg and Hans Tischler, *The Monophonic Songs in the Roman de Fauvel* (Lincoln, 1991). In addition to transcriptions of all the songs, both Latin (with the exclusion of certain liturgical chants) and French, complete translations are included.

[7] The complete works can be found in two modern versions: Corpus Mensurabilis Musicæ 30, ed. Nigel Wilkins, (Neuhausen-Stuttgart, 1966) and *Jehannot de l'Escurel: Balades, rondeaux et diz entez sus refroiz de rondeaux*, Summa musicæ Medii Ævi 13, ed. Friedrich Gennrich (Langen bei Frankfurt, 1964).

[8] A convenient short biography and study is Gilbert Reaney, *Guillaume de Machaut*, Oxford Studies of Composers 9 (London, 1974). This should be supplemented with Reaney's article, "Machaut, Guillaume de," in *The New Grove Dictionary of Music and Musicians*, edited Stanley Sadie, 20 vols. (London, 1980), vol. 11, pp. 428–436. The most valuable reference on Machaut is now Lawrence Earp, *Guillaume de Machaut: A Guide to Research* (New York, 1995), which includes extensive studies of the musical sources, bibliography, and annotated discography.

[9] See Lawrence M. Earp, "Scribal Practice, Manuscript Production and the Transmission of Music in Late Medieval France" (Ph.D. diss., Princeton University, 1983) and Elizabeth Ann Keitel, "A Chronology of the Compositions of Guillaume de Machaut Based on a Study of Fascicle Manuscript Structure in the Larger Manuscripts" (Ph.D. diss., Cornell University, 1976).

[10] There are two complete editions of the works of Machaut that are generally used: *Musikalische Werke*, ed. Friedrich Ludwig (vols. 1- 3) and Heinrich Besseler (vol. 4), 4 vols. (1926–43; reprinted Leipzig, 1954) and *The Works of Guillaume de Machaut*, ed. Leo Schrade, *Polyphonic Music of the Fourteenth Century* 2 and 3 (Monaco, 1956). The critical commentary to the Schrade edition was only printed in a small edition and is available in only a few libraries. The Schrade edition has been reprinted in five volumes (without the critical commentary), edited by Stanley Boorman (Monaco, 1977); all references to Schrade's Machaut edition are to this reprint.

[11] See chapter 16 in this volume (Lucy Cross, *"Ars Subtilior"*) for further information on this repertoire and modern editions.

[12] This distinction is made by Deschamps, *L'Art de dictier*, pp. 60–67. A number of modern studies also deal with this distinction: Lawrence M. Earp, "Lyrics for Reading and Lyrics for Singing in Late Medieval France: The Development of the Dance Lyric from Adam de la Halle to Guillaume de Machaut," in *The Union of Words and Music*, ed. Rebecca Baltzer *et al.* (Austin, 1991), pp. 101–31; Christopher Page, "Machaut's 'Pupil' Deschamps on the Performance of Music," *Early Music* 5 (1977), 484–491; and John Stevens, "The 'Music' of the Lyric: Machaut, Deschamps, Chaucer," in *Medieval and Pseudo-Medieval Literature*, ed. P. Boitani and A. Tori (Cambridge, 1984), pp. 109–29.

[13] An imperfect edition of the poem was published as Guillaume de Machaut, *Le Livre du Voir-Dit*, ed. Paulin Paris (Paris, 1875). An edition by Daniel Leech-Wilkinson with a translation by R. Barton Palmer has recently been published (New York, 1998).

[14] See Guillaume de Machaut, *Le Jugement du roy de Behaigne and Remede de Fortune*, ed. James I. Wimsatt, William W. Kibler, and Rebecca A. Baltzer, The Chaucer Library (Athens, 1988). This edition also includes a complete edition by Baltzer of the lyric insertions on pp. 413–47.

[15] Schrade, vol. 3, pp. 32–43. The musical illustrations were also edited by Rebecca Baltzer in Machaut, *Le Jugement du roy de Behaigne and Remede de Fortune*, pp. 413–47, based primarily on the Machaut manuscript "C" (Paris, Bibliothèque Nationale, fonds français 1586), with a very useful set of critical notes on variant musical readings.

[16] See Deschamps, *L'Art de dictier.*

[17] This illustration is reproduced in Machaut, *Le Jugement du roy de Behaigne and Remede de Fortune*, as Miniature 27, following p. 452.

[18] Since the *ballade* is sung directly through the composition, without any unusual repeats, some modern editions, such as Schrade's Machaut edition, do not indicate verse numbers.

[19] Schrade, vol. 4, pp. 57–60. Concerning the polytextual motet, see chapter 3 in this volume: Julie Cumming, "The Motet."

[20] Schrade, vol. 4, pp. 47–48.

[21] The transcription of this work in the editions by Ludwig and Schrade is incorrect. A corrected version can be found in W. Thomas Marrocco and Nicholas Sandon, *Medieval Music* (London, 1977), pp. 157–59.

[22] Edited in Schrade, vol. 5, pp. 15–16.

[23] Machaut's shortest *rondeau* is *Puis qu'en oubli*, consisting of 7 measures; Schrade, vol. 5, p. 20.

[24] This piece is discussed in more detail below.

[25] A complete treatment of this genre is given in Lambert C. Porter, *La Fatrasie et le fatras: Essai sur la poésie irrationnelle en France au Moyen Age* (Paris, 1960), who does not mention the examples from *Le Roman de Fauvel*. See also Isidore Silver, "*Fatras*" in the *Princeton Encyclopedia of Poetry and Poetics*, edited by Alex Preminger (Princeton, 1974), p. 272; and Patrice Uhl, "La Poésie du 'non-sens' en français aux XIIIe et XIVe siècles. Diversité et solidarité des formes," *Perspectives Médiévales* 14 (1988), 65–70.

[26] The numbering scheme is that used in Rosenberg and Tischler, *The Monophonic Songs*, pp. 125 and 127.

[27] These are edited in Rosenberg and Tischler, *The Monophonic Songs*, pp. 125–27.

[28] See Peter M. Lefferts, *The Motet in England in the Fourteenth Century*, Studies in Musicology 94 (Ann Arbor, 1986), pp. 84–85. The motet is transcribed in Frank Ll. Harrison, *Motets of English Provenance*, Polyphonic Music of the Fourteenth Century 15 (Monaco, 1980), pp. 100–05; the texts, edited and translated by Peter M. Lefferts, are on pp. 192–93.

[29] See Porter, *La Fatrasie et le fatras*, p. 145.

[30] See Charles E. Brewer, "A Fourteenth-Century Polyphonic Manuscript Rediscovered," *Studia Musicologica* 24 (1982), pp. 9–11; the polyphonic *fatras*, *Amis loial vous ay trouvé*, is transcribed on pp. 14–15.

[31] Rosenberg and Tischler, *The Monophonic Songs*, pp. 59–70.

[32] See Margaret Hasselman and Thomas Walker, "More Hidden Polyphony in a Machaut Manuscript," *Musica Disciplina* 24 (1970), 7–16, including a complete revised transcription of the *lai*. Even in this *lai*, the melody of stanza 1 (sung with stanzas 2 and 3) is transposed down a perfect fourth to form the 12th stanza, though with different counterpoint when combined with stanzas 10 and 11.

[33] See Richard H. Hoppin, "An Unrecognized Polyphonic Lai of Machaut," *Musica Disciplina* 12 (1958), 93–104. Both Ludwig and Schrade print this work as a monophonic *lai*.

[34] Schrade, vol. 1, pp. 52–74.

[35] Ibid., pp. 39–51.

[36] The *lais* have certain specific performance problems that will be discussed below.

[37] See note 7 for further information on these two editions. The basic principles of this notation are described in Willi Apel, *The Notation of Polyphonic Music 900–1600*, fifth edition (Cambridge, MA, 1953), pp. 318–37.

[38]   See Apel, *The Notation of Polyphonic Music*, pp. 338–67.

[39]   Though quite beautiful in its own right, the performance of *Le lay de la fonteine* by The
         Hilliard Ensemble (*Guillaume de Machaut: Messe de Notre Dame / Le Lai de la
         Fonteinne / Ma fin est mon commencement*, Hyperion CDA 66358) is, in my opinion,
         too free in their interpretation of the rhythmic patterns in this work.

[40]   Compare Schrade, vol. 4, pp. 73–74, with Baltzer's transcription of the earlier version in
         Machaut, *Le Jugement du roy de Behaigne and Remede de Fortune*, pp. [428–29], and
         the critical notes on pp. 442–44. Baltzer suggests that even in four-voice works, such as
         the four-voice *Dame, de qui toute*, the additional parts are alternatives, and the best
         texture is actually only for three-voices, representing another possible solution for
         performers to experiment with.

[41]   See the discussion by Lucy Cross in chapter 37.

[42]   The classic studies of this issue include Margaret Bent, "Musica Recta and Musica Ficta,"
         Musica Disciplina 26 (1972), 72–100; Karol Berger, "Musica ficta," in *Performance
         Practice: Music before 1600*, edited by Howard Mayer Brown and Stanley Sadie (New
         York, 1989), pp. 107–125; Sarah Fuller, "On Sonority in Fourteenth-Century Polyphony:
         Some Preliminary Reflections," *Journal of Music Theory* 30 (1986), 35–70; Bettie Jean
         Harden, "Sharps, Flats, and Scribes: *Musica Ficta* in the Machaut Manuscripts" (Ph.D.
         diss., Cornell University, 1983); Jehoash Hirshberg, "Hexachordal and Modal Structure
         in Machaut's Polyphonic Chansons," in *Studies in Musicology in Honor of Otto E.
         Albrecht*, edited by John Walter Hill (Kassel, 1980), pp. 19–42; Andrew Hughes,
         Manuscript Accidentals: Ficta in Focus, 1350-1450, Musicological Studies and
         Documents 27 (Neuhausen-Stuttgart, 1972); Helmut Kühn, *Die Harmonik der Ars
         Nova*, Berliner Musikwissenschaftliche Arbeiten 5 (Munich, 1973); and Daniel Leech-
         Wilkinson, "Machaut's *Rose, lis* and the Problem of Early Music Analysis," *Music
         Analysis* 3 (1984), 9–28.

[43]   The three recordings of this work each reach slightly different solutions concerning
         these chromatic alterations: *Chansons, Vol. 2 (polyphony)*, Studio der frühen Musik,
         Thomas Binkley, director, EMI Reflexe CDM 7 63424 2 (1973; reissued 1990); *Le vray
         remède d'amour: Ballades, Rondeaux, Virelais, Motets et Textes dits*, Ensemble Gilles
         Binchois. Harmonic Records H/CD 8825 (1988); and *Machaut and his time: 14th-
         Century French Ars Nova*, Ensemble Alba Musica Kyo, Channel Classics CCS 7094
         (1994). Of the chromatic alterations suggested in Ex.14.1, only the two suggestions in
         parentheses on the last beat of m. 9 in the *Cantus* seem unnecessary, even though their
         omission produces parallel tritones leading to the perfect cadence at the beginning of
         m. 10.

[44]   For instance, Schrade's edition of this piece (vol. 5, p. 1), even includes a very unusual
         g♯ as *musica ficta* in m. 10 of the *Triplum* on the last eighth note. This has been
         omitted in Example 1.

[45]   This miniature is reproduced in *Die Musik in Geschichte und Gegenwart*, 16 vols.
         (Kassel, 1949–1979), vol. 2, col. 1037, and in Guillaume de Machaut, *La Louange des
         Dames*, edited by Nigel Wilkins (New York, 1973), facing p. 112.

[46]   See Christopher Page, "Polyphony before 1400," in *Performance Practice: Music before
         1600*, edited by Howard Mayer Brown and Stanley Sadie (New York, 1989), pp. 80–84.
         An experiment with performance of this repertoire in Pythagorean tuning can be heard
         in the French songs on *The Service of Venus and Mars*, Gothic Voices, Hyperion CDA
         66238 (1987). See also Chapter 40 below.

[47] For a general overview of this problem see Alejandro Enrique Planchart, "Tempo and Proportions," in *Performance Practice: Music before 1600*, edited by Howard Mayer Brown and Stanley Sadie (New York, 1989), pp. 126–144, and chapter 38, "Proportion and Tempo," by Alexander Blachly, in this volume.

[48] On early French pronunciation, see Jeannine Alton and Brian Jeffery, *Bele buche e bel parleure* (London, 1976); and *Singing Early Music*, ed. Timothy McGee (Bloomington, 1996).

[49] This is the case in the three recordings cited in note 41 with the exception that the Ensemble Gilles Binchois partially adopts the solution suggested below to break the ligatures of the *Tenor* and add the text from the *Cantus*; this version still uses a recorder to play the *Triplum*. The question of instrumental arrangements of fourteenth-century French repertoire is quite complex. The versions of works by Machaut that appear in the *Codex Faenza* may reflect more Italian practices than French. See chapters 33 and 35, on instrumental usage after 1300, in this volume.

[50] Guillaume de Lorris and Jean de Meun, *The Romance of the Rose*, translated by Charles Dahlberg (Princeton, 1971), p. 343. In this translation as figure 51, following p. 450, an illumination is reproduced of Pygmalion performing before the image, from Oxford, Bodleian Library, ms. Douce 195, f. 150v (dated 1487–1495), showing him playing a portative organ and with a rebec and harp on the table beside him.

[51] Translated in Piero Weiss, *Letters of Composers through Six Centuries* (Philadelphia, 1967), pp. 1–2.

[52] See Jean de Gerson, *Oeuvres complètes*, edited by Mgr. Glorieux, 10 vols. in 11 (Tournai, 1960–73), vol. 7 (1), p. 421: "Prens le, dit il, et bien le note / Pour y jouer en douce note / A teneur et contreteneur / Pour allegier ton amer pleur."

[53] For the passage from the *Remede de Fortune*, see Machaut, *Le Jugement du roy de Behaigne and Remede de Fortune*, pp. 390–93. The list from *Le Prise d'Alexandrie* is printed in Machaut, *Musikalische Werke*, edited by Ludwig, vol. 2, p. 53*.

[54] See Chapter 21 below by Margriet Tindemans and Mary Springfels in this volume. There is a short summary of this issue, concluding that the vielle was most likely limited to the monophonic repertoire, in Peter Holman, *Four and Twenty Fiddlers: The Violin at the English Court, 1540-1690* (Oxford, 1994), pp. 3–9. Concerning the question of alternative tunings, see Christopher Page, "Fourteenth-Century Instruments and Tunings: A Treatise by Jean Vaillant? (Berkeley, Ms 744)," *Galpin Society Journal* 33 (1980), 17–35.

[55] See chapter 25, "Lute, Gittern, & Citole," in this volume.

[56] See chapter 24, "Harp," in this volume.

[57] Karl Young, "The *Dit de la harpe* of Guillaume Machaut," in *Essays in Honor of Albert Feuillerat* (New Haven, 1943), pp. 1–20.

[58] Ibid., p. 10, l. 274: "Des instrumens est la perfection"; and p. 11, l. 283: "A la harpe qui tous instrumens passe."

[59] Page, "The Performance of Song," p. 446.

[60] Page, "The Performance of Song," p. 447.

[61] See Chapter 31, "Psaltery," by Herbert Myers in this volume.

[62] See Page, "Fourteenth-Century Instruments," p. 32, for possible alternative tunings for a psaltery. See also Chapter 17, note 27, in this volume.

[63] For a reference to the *douçaine*, see Machaut, *Le Jugement du roy de Behaigne and Remede de Fortune*, pp. 256–57, ll. 1605–06: "D'une belle vois, clere et saine, Plus

douce que nulle douçaine" (with a beautiful, clear, and rich voice, sweeter than any pan-pipe [*sic*]). See also Chapter 27 below.

[64] Jacopus Leodiensis (of Liège), *Speculum musicæ*, edited by Roger Bragard, Corpus Scriptorum de Musica 3, 7 vols. (American Institute of Musicology, 1955–73), 1, p. 54: "... verum quia naturalia instrumenta perfectiora sunt artificialibus. Ars enim naturam imitatur...."

[65] See Lloyd Hibberd, "On 'Instrumental Syle' in Early Melody," *Musical Quarterly* 32 (1946), 107–30.

[66] Eustache Deschamps, *L'Art de dictier*, edited and translated by Deborah M. Sinnreich-Levi (East Lansing, 1994), p. 65. For a more extensive discussion of Deschamps' significance for performance practice, see Christopher Page, "Machaut's 'Pupil' Deschamps on the Performance of Music," *Early Music* 5 (1977), 484–91.

[67] For further information, see chapter 36, "Gamut, Solmization, and Modes" by William Mahrt, in this volume.

[68] Christopher Page, "Going beyond the Limits: Experiments with Vocalization in the French Chanson, 1340–1440," *Early Music* 20 (1992), 446–59.

[69] In particular, Page recommends *The Medieval Romantics* (tracks 1, 3, 5, 7, 9, 10, 12, 14, 16, 17) and *Lancaster and Valois* (tracks 1, 3, 4, 8, 10, 14, 15, 16, 17).

[70] Page, "The Performance of Song," p. 443.

[71] Ibid., p. 444.

15. Italian Ars Nova
Alexander Blachly

When gauged by quantity alone, the surviving polyphonic music of the Italian *Ars nova* (trecento) falls short of that of fourteenth-century France but exceeds the impressively large corpus of English polyphony from the same period. Nearly all the trecento composers known to us by name have been identified as priests, clerics, or monks, mostly on the basis of their portraits in the Squarcialupi Codex.[1] It appears initially puzzling then that fourteenth-century Italian polyphony survives mostly as a secular art, such sacred works as there are constituting less than 15% of the total number we know in notated form.[2] Nino Pirrotta has accounted for this paradox by proposing that notated polyphony in fourteenth-century Italy represents only one element in a predominantly oral, improvisatory musical culture, both in the secular and sacred spheres.[3] In his view, improvisatory polyphony originated in the singing of liturgical music and continued to be cultivated in Italian churches long after those skilled in such practices turned their attention, under the encouragement of noble and middle-class patrons of the arts, to providing musical settings of vernacular poetry.[4] According to this hypothesis, the vernacular settings, as they became increasingly more elaborate, eventually required a fixed, notated form.

Like French polyphony of the time, most surviving Italian notated works have composer attributions. (In contrast, virtually the entire repertory of notated polyphonic music from fourteenth-century England is anonymous.) We might also note that whereas the treatises best describing early trecento notational features date from ca.1320 (Marchetus of Padua, Frater Guido), the earliest Italian musical manuscript to survive is from ca.1360 (the Rossi Codex).[5] All the other large sources are even later.[6]

An examination of the music leads to two inferences about the trecento repertory as a whole. First, it faithfully reflects general aesthetic principles that have long been considered characteristically "Italian": exuberance, spontaneity, and a penchant for striking gestures. (Contemporaneous English music, on the other hand, establishes its insular identity by an inclination to novelty, especially in connection with harmonic and sonorous effects; whereas French music exhibits features we might best describe as "rational" or "intellectual," with intricate and rigorous design often taking precedence over what is merely sensually attractive.) Second, trecento music frequently requires virtuoso performers; indeed, it seems, especially in its earlier stages, to have been composed, in part, *by* them. We cannot know if composers prior to the Rossi Codex wrote their music down, but presumably they did, since Marchetus was already explaining the Italian notational system by ca.1320. Nevertheless, like Pirrotta, Marie Louise Martinez has concluded that performers transmitted the earliest repertory not in notated form but orally, continually subjecting it to revision.[7] Thus, she understands the widely divergent forms in which works from the earliest phase tend to survive in different sources, sometimes even involving transposition to a different mode, as reflecting a process of change and revision exerted on the repertory by performers during the period between the putative date of composition of these works (ca.1340) and the forms in which they were entered into large anthologies more than two, three, or four decades later.

As already intimated, the music of the trecento (literally, the 1300s) spans a period that begins at some time around 1340; by ca.1410 it was over, having yielded to the *Ars subtilior* style of Matteo da Perugia and Anthonello da Caserta and, later still, to the new "international" style of Dunstaple, Du Fay, and their contemporaries. The Italian *Ars nova* divides into three phases that Leonard Ellinwood first accounted for by perceiving "three generations" of trecento composers.[8] This useful generalization could perhaps be more accurately focused on the evolution of genres, the first of which, cultivated by Maestro Piero (fl.1340-50), Giovanni da Cascia (da Firenze) (fl.1340-50), Jacopo da Bologna (active ca.1340-ca.1360), Vincenzo da Rimini (fl. mid-fourteenth century), and others, was the *madrigal* for two voices.[9] Also belonging to the first stage is the special type of *madrigal* known as the *caccia*. Like the contemporaneous French *chace*, the *caccia* normally features two voices in *fuga* (one chasing the other at a prescribed distance, while singing the same music). Also reminiscent of the *chace* are onomatopoetic effects that evoke barking dogs, chirping birds, or market cries, often by means of hockets. More like the *madrigal* than the *chace*, however, is the *caccia*'s third, supporting voice (the tenor) and the caccia's formal layout in tercet and ritornello.

The second stylistic stage reflects the activities of Nicolò da Perugia (fl. 2nd half of the fourteenth century), Bartolino da Padova (d.1405), and the Florentines Gherardello (ca.1325-64), Lorenzo (d. ca.1372), Donato (fl. 2nd half of fourteenth century), and especially Francesco Landini (d.1397), whose 154 works alone constitute about a quarter of the over six hundred surviving secular works. The Florentines' preferred form was the polyphonic *ballata*, not infrequently for three voices. Reflecting the adoption of many French notational and compositional devices, such works exhibit a more careful contrapuntal approach and a greater concern for intricate harmonic effects than is generally to be found in the earlier repertory of Jacopo, Giovanni, and Piero. In addition, the works of the second phase abandon many of the uniquely Italian notational features of the earlier madrigal.

The third and final stage of stylistic development, defined by the works of such composers as Grazioso da Padova (fl. later fourteenth century), Anthonello da Caserta (fl. 1390-1410), Johannes Ciconia (ca.1370-1412), Antonio Zacara da Teramo (d. ca.1413), Andrea de Florentia (d.1415), Paolo Tenorista (ca.1355-1436), Giovanni Mazzuoli (ca.1360-1426), Piero Mazzuoli (d.1430), Ugolino of Orvieto (ca.1380-1457), and by one of the treatises of the theorist Prosdocimus de Beldemandis (d.1428),[10] is retrospective in technique but forward-looking in sound. As in the *madrigale* of the first phase, the late Italian *Ars nova* revives the meters (*divisiones*) of the first phase as part of its concerted program of notational and compositional experimentation.

Little is known about the biographies of most trecento composers. Of those in the first phase, Filippo Villani[11] relates that before the death of Mastino Scaligeri II of Verona in 1351, Giovanni, Piero, and Jacopo competed against one another at the Veronese court in setting the same poems. In imitation of the troubadours' *senhal*, their pieces often hide the name "Anna," and sometimes other names, in the texts, as in the ritornello of Jacopo's *Un bel perlaro*: "ANNAvè, le donne chantando." The identity of Anna and the reason for references to her in madrigals, however, remains a mystery. An acrostic naming Luchino Visconti in the text of the motet *Lux purpurata radiis/Diligite justiciam* indicates that Jacopo had connections with the Visconti in Milan (as did Giovanni).

Landini has long been famous for having been crowned with the laurel wreath at Venice by King Peter of Cyprus upon the recommendation of a jury that included Petrarch.[12] He was also in the employ of the Veronese court and visited northern Italy from Florence, where there is evidence that he served as organist at the monastery of Santa Trinità (succeeding Giovanni in that position?) and then, from the 1370s on, as organist and *cappellanus* at San Lorenzo, where he was buried in 1397. Landini was blind from early childhood, a feature portrayed in his two known likenesses. Recognized not only for his skill as a player of organs but also for his knowledge of their design, Landini assisted in the construction of the new organs at Santa Reperata and Santissima Annunziata. The Florentine sources never identify Landini by his surname but instead by epithets such as "Franciscus de organis" or "Francesco degli orghanij."[13] Moreover, both known fourteenth-century pictorial representations of Landini show him holding a small organ. We will have occasion later to speculate on the significance of Landini's connection with organ for the performance of his vocal music.

Paolo Tenorista, who was a person of considerable status, served as abbot in absentia of the monastery of San Martino al Pino in the diocese of Arezzo from 1401 to 1428 and as rector of a small Florentine church known as Orbatello, and, according to Kurt von Fischer, probably played a decisive role in the compilation of the largest, most magnificent of the anthologies of trecento music, the Squarcialupi Codex.[14] Andrea de' Servi ("Magister Frater Andreas Horganista de Florentia") can also be identified as an important figure: from 1380 to 1397 he held the position of prior at the monastery of Santissima Annunziata in Florence, and from 1407-10 he was head of the Tuscan Servite Order.[15] He is also known to have collaborated with Landini in supervising the construction of the new organs of Santissima Annunziata and the Duomo and to have performed on the former.[16] Giovanni Mazzuoli degli Organi (Johannes de Florentia), who was organist at Orsanmichele beginning ca.1379 and held that position at the Duomo from after 1390 until 1426, also appears in the documentary record as a music teacher and builder of organs. (The final composer section of Squarcialupi was reserved for his music, but no pieces were entered; however, his songs survive in the palimpsest manuscript San Lorenzo 2211, where portions of them are recoverable.)[17] Similarly, we know the Benedictine prior and composer Bartolomeo da Bologna (fl.1407-ca.1430) to have been organist at Ferrara Cathedral.[18] From the foregoing, it can be seen that Landini, far from being the only composer of the Italian *Ars nova* to have a significant association with the organ, may on the contrary have been typical in this respect.[19] If such an association between composer and organ existed in the French and English traditions, on the other hand, it appears only sporadically in the surviving documentary record.[20]

The Notation

Any attempt to understand trecento music must include an effort to come to grips with its notation.[21] Fundamentally the system is not difficult, though it has numerous points of departure from fourteenth-century French practice, including the following: a six-line staff; the use of dots only for the purpose of separating notes belonging to one breve from those belonging to the next (comparable to French dots of division); downward-tending diagonal stems to indicate the lengthening of notes to which they are attached, comparable in effect to the *punctus augmentationis* (= *punctus additionis*) of the French system; signs of *divisio* (mensuration) written in each part at the beginning of each new section (these signs consisting of one of the following letters or sets of letters notated in the top space of the staff: .d. for *duodenaria*, .n. for *novenaria*, .o. for *octonaria*, .p. or .sp. or .y. for *senaria* perfecta (italica), .sg. or .g. or .i. for *senaria imperfecta* (gallica), .q. for *quaternaria*); two levels of semibreve for the *divisiones duodenaria* and *octonaria*; flagged stems on minims and dragmas to indicate duplets, triplets, and quadruplets; and one-note ligatures, consisting of two semibreves written close to one another to indicate a note held across from one breve to the next (across the bar-line in a modern transcription).

Of these features, only the use of two levels of semibreve in *duodenaria* and *octonaria* causes significant difficulties (for a diagram showing how semibreves relate to other notes in the system, see Chapter 38, "Proportions"). Marchetus of Padua in the *Pomerium* takes pains to argue against the use of any more stems on notes than absolutely necessary, thereby providing the rationale for the cumbersome and confusing two-tiered system of semibreves in early trecento practice.

"Longa" Notation

The scribes of all the known sources of trecento repertory after the Rossi Codex frequently modernize *duodenaria* and *octonaria* into so-called "longa" notation in order to make the music easier to read. Their method is straightforward enough: to eliminate two levels of semibreves, they rewrite breves as longs and major semibreves as breves, leaving minor semibreves and minims unchanged. Since four minims of what had been *duodenaria* or *octonaria* now equal a breve rather than a major semibreve, the new *divisio* is called *quaternaria*, by analogy with *duodenaria* (12 minims per breve), *novenaria* (9 minims per breve), *octonaria* (8 minims per breve), etc. It may be illustrated as follows:

Fig. 15.1. Duodenaria transformed into quaternaria in "longa" notation.

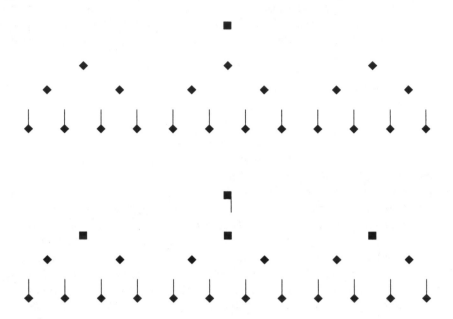

Fig. 15.2. *Octonaria* rewritten as *quaternaria* in "longa" notation.

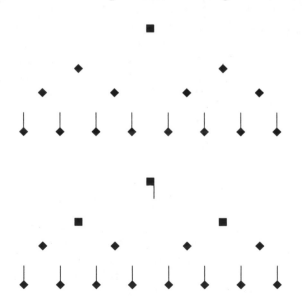

Unfortunately, in solving the problem of two levels of semibreves, the scribes who adopted "longa" notation created new and more intractable problems. In the old Marchettan system, the semibreves of *novenaria* and *senaria imperfecta* and the major semibreves of *duodenaria* and octonaria all had an equal duration. Thus, if *novenaria* were to be introduced for several breves in the upper voice of a madrigal notated in *octonaria*, the *novenaria* semibreve of the upper voice would equal the major semibreve of *octonaria* in the lower voice (three of the *novenaria* minims would equal four of the *octonaria* minims). While in the rewritten "longa" notation, the three *novenaria* minims still equaled four minims of "longa" *quaternaria*, they also equaled not the old major semibreve of *octonaria* but now its rewritten form, the breve of *quaternaria* (a disconcerting relationship to a performer or editor familiar with Marchetus's system). This is just the beginning of many inconsistencies the renotated versions of *duodenaria* and *octonaria* introduce; perhaps even more strange and seemingly impossible is that a semibreve of *novenaria* now equals a breve of rewritten *octonaria*. Such inconsistencies could and can still baffle a singer or editor unaware of the original notational forms. Perhaps partly in response to the illogical relationships introduced into trecento notation by modernizing scribes, composers began abandoning all multiple *divisiones* within a single work, with the exception of *senaria perfecta* and *senaria imperfecta*. No doubt, composers and performers alike found these two unproblematic, for they appear to have shared a minim of equal value, like the two corresponding mensurations of the French system—*tempus perfectum prolacio minor* and *tempus imperfectum prolacio maior*. Well before the final decades of the fourteenth century, the Italian theorists, perhaps also frustrated by the inconsistencies of "longa" notation, had begun claiming that all Italian *divisiones* shared a minim of identical value, as did minims of the four French *prolacions*. This of course ran counter to the teaching of Marchetus and, in the early fifteenth century, of the retrospective Prosdocimus de Beldemandis, both of whom emphasized the difference in value between minims arrived at by one level of semibreve (*novenaria* and *senaria imperfecta*) and those arrived at by two such levels (*duodenaria* and *octonaria*). Prosdocimus, like Marchetus, whose practice he attempted to revive, repeated the older theorist's assertion that four minims of *duodenaria* or *octonaria* equal three minims of *novenaria* or *senaria imperfecta*.[22]

One practical way a modern performer may by-pass the confusion introduced into Italian manuscripts by "longa" notation is mentally to reconstruct the original *duodenaria* or *octonaria*, recognizing that longs and breves of the new replacement *divisio* of *quaternaria* were not originally what they now appear to be but rather notes one level smaller. Recognition of the later scribes' practice helps also to understand otherwise perplexing statements like the following: "For the later trecentists, the French modus prevailed and the longa became the unit of measure for those compositions that were originally organized in *octonaria* and *duodenaria*."[23] By this arcane formulation, W. Thomas Marrocco attempts to describe the relatively uncomplicated scribal practice of re-writing *octonaria* and *duodenaria* in "longa" notation. To call the re-writing a "modus" notation (by analogy with thirteenth-century practice) may strike some as misleading, since the impetus for the notational revision comes not from a desire to center the system on longs, but rather to eliminate two levels of visually identical semibreves while keeping minims and minor semibreves intact.

Style

The style of trecento polyphony impresses the listener initially by its floridity, especially in works from the first and third phases; but even composers in Landini's generation show a fondness for flowing lines. As mentioned earlier, the repertory as a whole implies performance by highly skilled singers, even, on occasion, virtuosos. In contrast to the French *ballade* which it superficially resembles (with respect to their shared musical scheme AAB), the fourteenth-century *madrigal* normally opens and closes each major section with an extended and florid melisma, not infrequently preceded or followed by a long-held note or notes. Whereas the French style implies a relatively high degree of concern on the part of performers for controlling intricate vertical coincidences among the parts, or, to say this another way, for subjecting horizontal to vertical requirements, the early Italian style reverses these priorities. In the music of the first phase, especially, the subservient lower voice must follow any virtuosic license taken by the singer of the prime part. Undoubtedly as a result of this practice, the early Italian style shows a rather slow rate of harmonic change, in which harmonic events coincide with what Pirrotta has called the "larger rhythm." Pirrotta has also drawn attention to some of the startling melodic leaps one encounters in the trecento repertory, such as Andrea de' Servi's augmented octave in *Morrà la 'nvidia*.[21] As a more "primal" style, early trecento polyphony focuses on the pure sound of the words, nearly always opening major sections on a "good" vowel, such as "a" or "o." Indeed, the early trecento style can be said to be as much about verbal sound as about verbal meaning, since long melismas by their very nature tend to rob syllables of cognitive import.

As composer, Landini began his career writing two-voice madrigals in the Italian *divisiones* of *octonaria* and *duodenaria* (e.g., *Tu che ll' oper' altrui*), like the madrigals of Jacopo and Giovanni. He is among the first to attempt a polyphonic setting of the *ballata*, which had up to then, despite its formal similarity to the French *virelai* (AbbaA), been an exclusively monophonic, thoroughly Italian form. Landini's *ballate* exhibit the influence of the fourteenth-century French chanson not only in being cast polyphonically, but also in their preference for the *divisio senaria imperfecta* (equivalent to the *prolacion* of French music that soon would be indicated in the musical sources by the sign ₵). When French influence was strongest, during the era of Landini, Italian and French idioms show many signs of convergence. Landini's preference for the *divisio senaria imperfecta* signals such influence in the domains of melodic and contrapuntal motion. His cultivation in about a third of his *ballate* of three-part writing, often of considerable intricacy, also reflects a French orientation. Hand in hand with the adoption of French habits of musical thinking goes the loss of interest noted earlier in such native Italian features of style as the juxtaposition of contrasting *divisiones* within the various sections of a piece.

It would be a mistake, however, to imagine that Landini's style completely submerges Italian features. No matter how intricately "French" his music may appear, it always retains an identifiably vocal orientation with respect to flowing melodies and "natural" phrases. Several passages in Giovanni Gherardi da Prato's *Il Paradiso degli Alberti* (1389) describe performances of Landini's music in an idealized outdoor setting. Taken together they corroborate suggestions in the notated music itself of an ideal style of trecento performance. The accounts seem to imply, in the first place, that the first goal of the trecento composer was to move the listener rather than to charm and challenge the performer, as was the habit of French and English composers. We read in the third book of the *Paradiso*, for example, that when Francesco played his music on the organ for listeners gathered at the villa, "no one had ever heard such beautiful harmonies, and their hearts almost burst from their bosoms."[25] Later, in the garden, "much to the pleasure of all, and especially of Francesco, two young maidens appeared who danced and sang his *Orsu, gentili spiriti* so sweetly that not only the people standing by were affected, but even the birds in the cyprus trees began to sing more sweetly."[26] The fourth book recounts an occasion when, at sunrise, "a thousand birds were singing." Curious to see what effect Landini's music would have on the birds' behavior, those present requested the composer to play his organetto. As the music began to fill the air, the birds became silent for a moment, then "redoubled their singing."[27]

It is unlikely that Giovanni's account intends to be factual; like paintings of the time, it strives for a greater truth through allegory and symbolism than could be achieved by mere representation of the material world.[28] Thus, it can be no accident that Giovanni's idealized setting, with trees, flowers, maidens, and a cultured, appreciative audience, conforms to the *locus amoenus*, or ideal landscape, borrowed by trecento poets from the *Bucolics* of Theocritus and Virgil.[29] Even in Giovanni's "artificial" account, however, one may be struck by the two incidents involving birds. Admittedly, birds also figure in Boccaccio's bucolic evocations in the *Decameron*, but there they are not directly appreciative of human endeavors. Perhaps, then, Giovanni's birds are intended to remind the reader of the extraordinary effect Landini's playing had on all his listeners, whether human or animal.

Let us recall that Landini achieved his greatest fame in the fourteenth century as an organist; and though the pictorial and even Giovanni da Prato's evidence associates him with the organetto, the documentary record associates him instead with the church organ. The association also of so many other trecento composers with the organ reinforces the likelihood that what served in the trecento as the ideal of sound for art music generally may have been mellifluous roulades and gentle articulations sounding on the low-pressure, essentially chiff-less, bellows-driven, organs of medieval Italy.[30] If we are correct in surmising that the Italian organ reflects Italian musicians' ideal for vocal performance, trecento music, even in the fastest passages, must have been intended for a well-defined but essentially non-aspirated vocal production, which suggests that the "throat-articulated" style of fast-note singing characteristic in some circles of performers today misrepresents the original character of the repertory. This would also mean that the tuning system for trecento vocal music was based on the Pythagorean system advocated by Marchetus in the *Lucidarium*[31] rather than on the pure-interval tuning that gradually replaced the Pythagorean system in the course of the fifteenth and sixteenth centuries.

The Texts

A theoretical tradition beginning with Antonio da Tempo in 1332 and culminating with Gidino da Sommacampagna in ca.1384 associates poetry directly with music (an association not to be found in France until the end of the fourteenth century), but the trecento composers generally do not set poetry by the great poets of their time, especially Dante and Petrarch, or even Boccaccio, showing instead a preference for a lighter poetic style. Most Italian poetry tends to use various combinations of seven- and eleven-syllable lines.

Harmonic Language

Though music of the fourteenth century features sharper inflections than that of the fifteenth, with more unexpected melodic events and piquant intervals between voices, it conforms nevertheless with the principal formulations of contemporaneous theorists. Jan Herlinger has recently published the essence of these teachings as transmitted in the *Contrapunctus* of Prosdocimus de Beldemandis[32] (a teaching also handed down, in slightly different words, by other theorists, such as Antonio da Leno, Ugolino da Orvieto, and later writers):

In combinationibus perfecte consonantibus nunquam ponere debemus mi contra fa, nec e contra, quoniam statim ipsas vocum combinationes perfecte consonantes minores vel maximas constitueremus, que discordantes sunt.	In perfectly consonant intervals we ought never to place mi against fa or vice versa, because we would straightway make the perfectly consonant intervals minor [i.e., diminished] or augmented, which forms are discordant.

Herlinger shows how this seemingly generalized formulation can still lead to the solution of particular problems, such as that posed by Landini's *D'amor mi biasmo*. Here a notated c♯' in the upper voice coincides with an e♭ called for by the key signature of the lower voice, evidently resulting in an augmented sixth. Both Leonard Ellinwood and Leo Schrade allow at least one instance of this augmented sixth to remain in *D'amor mi biasmo* in their editions of Landini's works, and Carl Schachter has provided a verbal rationale for the decision.[33] As early as 1972, however, Margaret Bent had shown how the augmented sixth approach to the octave violates the theorists' prohibition of *mi contra fa* since the c♯' must be solmized as a mi, the d' it leads to will be a fa; whereas the e♭, representing a fa, must then lead to a d that will be a mi.[34] Because the augmented sixth leads to an octave solmized as *mi contra fa*, it consitutes an unacceptable interval. The notated c♯' in the upper voice consequently calls for a ficta e♮ in the lower voice.

Despite the control that the prohibition of *mi contra fa* might be imagined to exert on style generally, the trecento repertory exhibits many unusual melodic leaps and contrapuntal progressions. Thus, at the opening of Giovanni's famous madrigal *Nascoso el viso*, the specified c♯' in the upper voice in measure 2 may sound against f♮ in the lower voice because the momentary *mi contra fa* leads to an approach to the octave d-d' by way of the closest imperfect interval, the major sixth e–c♯', as required by Prosdocimus:[35]

Sed in vocum combinationibus imper-fecte consonantibus, sicut sunt tercia, sexta, decima, et huiusmodi, ponenda sunt etiam hec signa secundum quod oportet addere vel diminuere in ipsas reducendo ad maioritatem vel minor-itatem oportunas.... Illam semper su-mere debes que minus distat a loco ad quem immediate accedere intendis.

But in such imperfect intervals between voices—the third, the sixth, the tenth, and the like—these signs [sharps and flats] are to be applied to augment or diminish them so as to reduce these intervals to ajor or minor, as appropriate....
You should always choose that form which is less distant from the location you intend immediately to reach.

Whereas the augmented sixth leading to an octave lies outside the harmonic vocabulary of the trecento, other, initially stranger, effects do not Thus, we find in Landini's *O fanciulla giulia* a peculiar but not unpleasing dissonance on the beginning of an imperfect breve in m.3; an even more unconventional dissonance at the beginning of the second half of m.7; and similar dissonances on each half of m.28. At the end of the anonymous two-voice *Benedicamus Domino* from GB-Ob 229,[36] a g' sounding in the upper voice above a c in the tenor five measures from the end changes to a notated g♯' above the tenor's e one measure later, this major tenth leading to a final cadence a' above d. Such notated chromatic alterations of a single pitch are not infrequent occurrences in the trecento harmonic vocabulary.

Proportional Relationships among the Various *Divisiones*

We have mentioned already the most common relationships among the various *divisiones*. According to Marchettus, *duodenaria, novenaria, octonaria*, and *senaria imperfecta* all shared a (major) semibreve of identical value, at least in the earliest phase of the trecento repertory. From this starting point, the relationships of all other notes among Marchetus's four *divisiones* can easily be calculated. It remains then to account for the two mensurations Marchetus left out: *senaria perfecta* and *quaternaria*.[37] We might begin our search for the answer to one of these by noting that whenever we encounter *senaria perfecta* and *senaria imperfecta* in the same piece, they seem to share a minim of identical value. It might be reasonable, therefore, to assume that this was the standard relationship understood by trecento composers (and rejected only by Marchetus, for reasons explained elsewhere).[38] The relationship between *senaria perfecta* and the other *divisiones* can then be calculated as follows:

.p.　■　= .i.　■　= .o.　■　= .d.　2/3 ■

.p.　◆ ◆ ◆　= .i.　◆ ◆　= .n. ◆ ◆　= .o.　♩ ♩

.p.　◆　= .i.　◆ ◆

These are not extraordinarily difficult relationships for a performer to execute, but many of them require a double calculation, in which *senaria imperfecta* is used as a mental platform of transition. The change of speed between the tercet of Jacopo's *Aquil' altera*, notated in .o., and its ritornello, notated in .p., for example, can most easily be calculated by mentally subdividing the major semibreve of .o. (♩) into triplet minims (to get *senaria imperfecta*, the platform of transition) and then mentally regrouping these minims into three groups of two (to get *senaria perfecta*).

The situation with *quaternaria* is less clear. Of course, when it functions as a "longa" rewriting of *duodenaria* or *octonaria*, the performer need only mentally reconstruct the original notation to determine its intended relationship to the other *divisiones*. But when *quaternaria* is used as an independent mensuration in a piece that already has passages notated in *duodenaria* or *octonaria*, as does Paolo's three-voice *Benedicamus Domino*,[39] its meaning cannot be so easily ascertained. Presumably in this case Paolo does not intend for *quaternaria* to duplicate the *octonaria* heard earlier but instead to represent some contrasting mensuration, i.e., a contrasting tempo. Probably Paolo's *Benedicamus quaternaria* is meant to be somewhat slower than *octonaria*, so as to prevent the flagged minims at the end from being unsingably fast and also, paradoxically, so as to maintain a sense of increasing acceleration as the composer introduces four different *divisiones* in succession (see Example 15.1). Paolo's strategy in writing the tenor notes in chant notation (regardless of shape, all tenor notes are to be sung as breves), seems to have been to imply a constant against which all the *divisiones* are to be measured. Only with the appearance of *quaternaria* in the final section do we feel a necessity for this pattern to be modified, for to maintain constant tenor notes throughout the entire piece will necessarily reduce the final *quaternaria* to the *octonaria* of the opening, thus defeating the *accelerando* that seems to be the rationale for using the four different *divisiones* in the first place.[40]

Ex. 15.1. *Benedicamus Domino* **by Paolo Tenorista,** Paris, Bibl. Nat. 568, fol. 117 (after edition by von Fischer and Gallo).

Dances

We are fortunate in having 15 monophonic dances from the trecento, all preserved in a single source (Lo).[41] Not much is known about these works, certainly nothing of the dance steps they were presumably meant to accompany. Many of them consist of a series of repeated *puncta* of varying length (even within a single dance), each ending with an unlabeled *ripresa* supplied with both an "*aperto*" (open) and a "*chiuso*" (closed) ending. Four of the dances carry the label "salterello"; three are dance pairs, with the first section of two of them bearing a name—*Lamento di Tristano, La Manfredina*—and the second section labeled *rotta* or *troto*; and eight follow the manuscript heading *Istanpita*: *Ghaetta, Chominciamento di gioia, Isabella, Tre fontane, Belicha, Parlamento, In pro*, and *Principio di Virtu*.[42] F. Alberto Gallo has written that *Isabella* and *Principio di Virtu* were probably composed for the celebrations of the marriage of Isabella, daughter of King John II of France and Giangaleazzo Visconti of Pavia in 1360. (By this marriage Giangaleazzo became prince of Vertus in Champagne, and was known thereafter as the "conte di Virtù.")[43] The surviving descriptions of the performance of dance music often mention the vielle, in one case, four vielles playing at once,[44] other instruments only sporadically, although Boccaccio, in the *Decameron*, writes at one point: "...at [the queen's] command Dioneo picked up a lute and Fiametta a vielle, and began sweetly to play a dance. At that...the queen and the other women, together with two young men, made a circle and with slow steps began to dance the carol." Elsewhere, the *Decameron* describes the playing of a *stampita* on a *viuola*, the playing of another dance on the *cornamusa* (bagpipe), and the playing of a *ballatetta* on a lute. To what extent vielles might be expected to supply drones to support the notated melody is an open question, but perhaps a better case could be made for drones and/or drone effects in this repertory than for many other monophonic traditions in the Middle Ages. One striking feature of these works is the unusual flavor of the melodic scales they employ, which not infrequently traverse B♭ to F♯ or have unpredictable starting and ending notes: in "Belicha," the "*aperto*" ends on B and the "*chiuso*" on D, while the five *puncta* begin on A, D, C♯, and C♮, respectively.

Instrumental Participation

To what extent instruments participated in the performance of vocal works also remains unclear. In pictorial representations, it is not unusual to see scenes like the apse frescoes of San Leonardo al Lago near Siena, painted by Lippo Vanni: here the four panels show various groupings of instrumentalists and singers in what look to be possible performance combinations.[45] In all likelihood, however, no such groupings were known to Lippo Vanni, who, like his contemporaries, probably had little interest in depicting everyday reality. His representations of instruments may be of considerable value in establishing what contemporary instruments looked like, but they cannot be trusted to show standard performance combinations. Similarly, despite the mention of harps, bagpipes, lutes, recorders, psalteries, shawms, rebecs, and vielles by Prudenzani (*Il Solazzo*), Boccaccio (*Decameron*), and Giovanni da Prato (*Il Paradiso degli Alberti*), there is no way at present to know whether these instruments participated in the performance of polyphony with singers. Marrocco, in his edition of trecento secular music, is at some pains to fend off instrumental performance of the many melismas in the repertory, noting that in one source "the scribe often inserted vowels below the melismas every measure or two."[46] Similarly, Reinhard Strohm inveighs against an indiscriminate instrumental participation when he observes that recent research has led to "the recognition that practically every melody that was notated in the Middle Ages is singable, and that the instrumental drones, embellishments, 'improvised' tunes, the drumming, bellringing and other sundry noises as we know them from older recordings of early music can nowhere be found in the documents."[47] In the absence of any clear historical evidence, performers are left with a list of possible instruments, their imaginations, and their sensitivity to the character of any given piece.

Editions

Performers currently find at their disposal two complete modern editions of Landini's works;[48] two modern editions of all the other trecento secular repertory prior to Ciconia (one complete, one nearly so);[49] a complete modern edition of the contents of the Squarcialupi Codex;[50] two modern editions of the works of Ciconia;[51] and numerous editions of individual pieces. Signaling a welcome trend in musicology, publishers have issued facsimile editions of Lo,[52] FP,[53] the Lucca Codex,[54] the Rossi Codex,[55] the Squarcialupi Codex,[56] and the newly discovered Boverio fragments,[57] the last four of these in color. For any modern performer with the time, opportunity, and inclination to compare a published edition with photo-reproductions of its original source(s), the rewards cannot be overstated. Such a procedure immediately makes clear, in a way that no amount of explanation printed in the introduction to an edition can, just what the editor has included and excluded. To consider just one type of information: nearly every edition just listed fails to include the original letters indicating the *divisiones* that are to be found in nearly all the sources, usually relegating this information to the Critical Commentary, but often in an ambiguous form, e.g., "*Rhythm*: First section and Rit in .o."[58] (leaving unclear whether the sign ".o." is actually written by the scribe or whether the *divisio octonaria* has merely been inferred by the modern editor).

Pirrotta's procedure for indicating *divisiones*, at least for major sections of works, is to transcribe them under the following modern meter signs: 3*/4 = *duodenaria*; 9/8 = *novenaria*; 2*/4 = *octonaria*; 6/8 = *senaria* imperfecta; 3/4 = *senaria* perfecta; 2/4 = *quaternaria*. Fearing, however, that too many bar lines would give an inaccurate picture of the underlying "larger rhythm," he frequently groups bars together with formulations like 2 x 6/8, later in a piece reduced to 3 or 2 (meaning 3 x 6/8 and 2 x 6/8, respectively). The result is problematic, as even Pirrotta admits: "the good in this principle does not necessarily avoid the possibility that its application may in some cases apparently or even actually be open to discussion." Although he asserts that "this danger is less than that which it forestalls," the system, in fact, strikes many performers as difficult to use and thus as a barrier between the modern interpreter and the music as originally notated.

Marrocco employs similar modern meter signs as substitutes for the original *divisio* letters but does not employ Pirrotta's problematically grouped measures; his meter signs, however, have the drawback of failing to distinguish between *duodenaria* and *senaria perfecta* on the one hand and *octonaria* and *quaternaria* on the other: 2/4 = *quaternaria* and *octonaria*; 6/8 = *senaria imperfecta*; 3/4 = *duodenaria* and *senaria perfecta*; 9/8 = *novenaria*. Probably the best solution to the problem of transforming trecento notation into a modern score is that devised by Kurt von Fischer and F. Alberto Gallo in their edition of fourteenth-century Italian sacred music. Here minims are transcribed as eighth notes rather than sixteenths, and the modern meter signs show the original *divisiones* unambiguously: 12/8 = *duodenaria*, 9/8 = *novenaria*, 8/8 = *octonaria*, 6/8 = *senaria imperfecta*, 3/4 = *senaria perfecta*, 4/8 = *quaternaria*.

From the standpoint of performance/interpretation, the visual appearance of the original notation makes a radically different impression *vis-à-vis* intended performance manner and tempo from that of most modern editions. Because these latter nearly all reduce note levels by a factor of four,[59] every page tends to be dominated by sixteenth notes. While it may make little difference in the long run whether a performer learns a piece transcribed in eighths and sixteenths rather than in halves and quarters, eighths and sixteenths do seem to encourage the idea that trecento music should be sung as fast as humanly possible, an impression strengthened by some recordings of the trecento literature in which the performers appear to limit their artistic goals to the single preoccupation of executing hair-raisingly fast *fioriture.* (A careful consideration of the texts being set will illustrate the limitation, not to say the inappropriateness, of such an approach.)

In his edition, Pirrotta provides complete texts for the musical works only in the introduction, restricting the text underlaid beneath the music to the refrain words. Thus, the performer working from Pirrotta's publication must in effect "complete" a performing score from the elements printed separately in each volume, retrieving the non-refrain words from the opening pages and then underlaying them as best he or she can to the music printed later in the volume. For the performer, Marrocco's edition has a great advantage in this respect, since his publication prints all the surviving text for each piece under the music to which it is to be sung.

Ellinwood's edition of Landini and Clercx's edition of Ciconia are both hand-drawn, with unreduced note values, and both are now superseded by the more recent editions of Schrade and Hallmark/Bent, respectively. Johannes Wolf, like Ellinwood and Clercx, uses unreduced note values in his edition of the complete Squarcialupi Codex. His idiosyncratic editorial hand, evident throughout, will probably not be to the liking of most present-day performers.

Conclusions

Any effort to reconstruct in sound a repertory remote from us in time and culture obviously faces considerable difficulties. In seeking to get to the heart of the Italian *Ars nova* style, we are perhaps best off letting the trecento arts that come down to us relatively intact—painting, architecture, and literature—serve as spurs to our creative re-imagining. The sound of the medieval Italian organ may also, as mentioned above, provide an important point of reference. As with all vocal music, the starting point is the text. To disregard this most fundamental aspect of music for voices will virtually guarantee misunderstandings and misrepresentations. In the long run, perhaps the most important consideration for the modern performance of the trecento repertory is for those engaged in the endeavor to make themselves as sensitive as possible to the issues of importance to composers and performers in fourteenth-century Italy. It is from such present-day performers, in tune with the arts and personalities of the trecento as a whole, that we can expect performances that are at once more interesting, meaningful, and convincing.

Notes

1   Florence, Biblioteca Mediceo-Laurenziana, MS Palatino 87. See below, notes 7, 14, 19.
2   All of the surviving Trecento sacred polyphony has been published in F. Alberto Gallo and Kurt von Fischer, eds., *Italian Sacred Music*, Polyphonic Music of the Fourteenth Century, XII-XIII (Monaco, 1976-87).
3   *Music and Culture in Italy from the Middle Ages to the Baroque* (Cambridge, MA, 1984), especially Chapter 3, "Ars Nova and Stil Nuovo," and Chapter 11, "Novelty and Renewal in Italy, 1300-1600."
4   Despite its being an improvised art, some liturgical polyphony of the type inferred appears to have been notated and survives as what is known as *cantus binatim*. (Two examples are published as Nos. 26 and 27 in Polyphonic Music of the Fourteenth Century XIII). To support his claim that trecento composers moved into the secular sphere under the aegis of secular patrons, Pirrotta notes that the singing of madrigals was common both at universities and courts, as attested to in the *Paradiso degli Alberti*. See Nino Pirrotta, ed., *Il Codice Rossi 215/The Rossi Codex 215*, Introductory Study and Facsimile Edition (Lucca, 1992), p. 106.
5   Vatican City, Biblioteca Apostolica Vaticana, MS Rossi 215.
6   Florence, Biblioteca Nazionale Centrale, MS Panciatichiano 26 (FP), dating from probably after ca.1380-90; London, British Library, MS Add. 29987 (Lo), from the early fifteenth century; Paris, Bibliothèque nationale, fonds it. 568 (*Pit*), from ca.1400-10; Paris, Bibliothèque nationale, fonds nouvelle acq. 6771 (Codex Reina), from ca.1400-30; Florence, Biblioteca Medicea Laurenziana, MS Med. Pal. 87 ("Squarcialupi Codex"), from ca.1410-15; and Lucca, Archivio di Stato, MS 184 (Codex Mancini), from ca.1420-30.
7   *Die Musik des frühen Trecento* (Tutzing, 1963), cited by Brooks Toliver, "Improvisation in the Madrigals of the *Rossi Codex*," *Acta musicologica* 64 (1992), 165.
8   See Leonard Ellinwood, ed., *The Works of Francesco Landini* (Cambridge, MA, 1939), p. xii, where the composers are grouped as follows. First Generation: Giovanni da Cascia, Jacopo da Bologna, Bartolino da Padova, Grazioso da Padova, Vincenzo d'Arimino, Piero. Second Generation: Francesco Landini, Paolo Tenorista, Nicolò da Padova, Gherardello da Firenze, Donato da Firenze, Lorenzo da Firenze, Andrea da Firenze, Egidio, Guglielmo di Santo Spirito. Third Generation: Zacherio, Matteo da Perugia, Giovanni da Genoa, Giovanni da Cinconia, Antonello da Caserta, Filippo da Caserto, Corrado da Pistoia, Bartolomeo da Bologna.
9   In *Il Codice Rossi 215*, pp. 96f., Pirrotta cites the earliest known definition of the madrigal, by the anonymous author of the *Capitulum de vocibus applicatis verbis*: verba applicata pluribus vocibus—"words applied to several voices," i.e., polyphony itself. This in evident distinction to the *ballata* of the time, which Pirrotta concludes was monophonic and improvised. Some monophonic *ballate* survive in notated form, e.g., those of Lorenzo Masini.
10 *Tractatus practice de musica mensurabili ad modum Ytalicorum* (1412; rev. 1428); modern edition in *GS* III, 228-48; tr. Jay A. Huff, *Prosdocimus de Beldemandis: A Treatise on the Practice of Mensural Music in the Italian Manner*, Musicological Studies and Documents 29 ([n.p.]: American Institute of Musicology, 1972).
11 *Liber de origine civitatis Florentiæ*.

[12] Michael Long, "Trecento Italy," in James McKinnon, ed., *Antiquity to the Middle Ages: From Ancient Greece to the 15th Century* (Englewood Cliffs, NJ, 1990), p. 262.

[13] See Long, "Trecento Italy," p. 261.

[14] Kurt von Fischer (Squarcialupi commentary), p. 135 (see below, note 56).

[15] von Fischer, p. 142.

[16] According to Renato Lunelli, *Der Orgelbau in Italien in seinen Meisterwerken vom 14. Jahrhundert bis zur Gegenwart* (Mainz, 1956), Andrea dei Servi, Landini, Bartolomeo Lorini, and Tommasso di Bernardo Viviani also collaborated as a team in overseeing the construction of the new organ in the Cathedral of Santa Maria del Fiore in Florence around 1388. Bartomoleo and Tommasso were mostly involved in financial aspects of the project, Andrea and Landini in technical and artistic matters.

[17] See Frank D'Accone, "Una nuova fonte dell'ars nova italiana: Il codice di San Lorenzo, 2211," *Studi musicali* 13 (1984), 3-27; and John Nádas, "Manuscript San Lorenzo 2211: Some further observations," *L'Ars nova italiana del Trecento* 6 (Certaldo, 1984), 145-68.

[18] See Reinhard Strohm, *The Rise of European Music 1380-1500*, 139.

[19] Thus, it may not be entirely coincidental that in Simone Prodenzani's epic *Il Saporetto* of ca.1425, the fictitious musician Solazzo "plays Spanish and German tunes on the 'Flemish organs' ('organi framegni'), dance-tunes on bagpipe and lute, madrigals on the harp, and liturgical pieces as well as polyphonic chansons ('La harpe de melodie', for example) on the organ." Passage quoted from Reinhard Strohm, *The Rise of European Music 1380-1500* (Cambridge, 1993), p. 90.

[20] Though we know the names of many organists from the north, I know only a few northern composers from before 1500 who have been specifically associated with the instrument: Gilles de Bins dit Binchois (ca.1400-1460), who was hired as organist at Ste. Waudru in Mons in 1419; William Horwood (d.1484) of England, who is represented in the Eton Choirbook; and the Germans Johannes Lupi (in the service in 1440 of duke Frederick of Tyrol), Magister Conrad Paumann (d.1473), Paul Hofhaimer (1459-1537), Arnolt Schlick (ca.1460-after 1521), and Hans Buchner (1483-1538). For the major composers of the north in the fourteenth and fifteenth centuries, we cannot, as a rule, document a specific connection with the organ, with the possible exception of Du Fay, who stands beside a portative organ in the well-known portrait of him and Binchois together.

[21] Further discussion of the Trecento notational system is provided in Chapter 38, "Proportion," pp. 524-26.

[22] See Chapter 38, pp. 524-26, especially note 19 (p. 531).

[23] Thomas W. Marrocco, ed., *Italian Secular Music*, Polyphonic Music of the Fourteenth Century 11, p. xi.

[24] *The Music of Fourteenth-Century Italy* V, Corpus Mensurabilis Musicae 8 (AIM, 1964), p. ii.

[25] Quoted in Ellinwood, *The Works of Francesco Landini*, p. xv.

[26] Ibid.

[27] Ibid.

[28] For a discussion of Trecento art works, both representational and narrative, that are structured around numerical and allegorical conceits, see Nora Maria Beck, "Singing in the Garden: An Examination of Music in Trecento Painting and Boccaccio's 'Decameron'," (Ph.D. dissertation, Columbia University, 1993), esp. pp. 48-65.

[29] See Long, "Trecento Italy," p. 248.

[30] For the character of Italian instruments over the course of many centuries, see Corrado Moretti, *L'Organo Italiano, Seconda Edizione* (Milan, 1973).

[31] See Jan Herlinger, *The Lucidarium of Marchetto of Padua: A Critical Edition, Translation, and Commentary* (Chicago, 1985).

[32] "What Trecento Music Theory Tells Us," in *Explorations in Music, the Arts, and Ideas: Essays in Honor of Leonard B. Meyer*, ed. Eugene Narmour and Ruth A. Solie (Stuyvesant, 1988), p. 189. See also Herlinger's edition and translation of Prosdocimus's *Contrapunctus*, Greek and Latin Music Theory, Vol. 1 (Lincoln, Nebraska, and London, 1984), esp. pp. 74-77.

[33] Herlinger, "Trecento Music Theory," p. 188.

[34] "*Musica Recta* and *Musica Ficta*," *Musica Disciplina* 26 (1972), 74.

[35] *Contrapunctus* 5.6, as cited in "What Trecento Music Theory Tells Us," p. 186. The translation here is slightly modified.

[36] Modern edition in Polyphonic Music of the Fourteenth Century, Vol. XII, No. 26.

[37] Willi Apel, in *The Notation of Polyphonic Music 900-1600* (Cambridge, MA, fourth edition, 1953), p. 376, seems not to understand why Marchetus tries to sidestep *senaria perfecta*: it is precisely because if *perfecta* and *imperfecta* are allowed to share a minim of equal length, the perfect breve will, impossibly from Marchetus's premises, equal an imperfect breve.

[38] See previous note and also Chapter 38 below. The difficulty for Marchetus, from which there is no logical escape, is that equating the duration of minims in *senaria imperfecta* and *senaria perfecta* leads to the contradiction of an imperfect breve equaling a perfect breve. As Willi Apel has pointed out in *The Notation of Polyphonic Music*, p. 376, the theorist posits as the premise of his entire system the notion that the imperfect breve is one-third shorter than the perfect.

[39] Modern edition in Kurt von Fischer and F. Alberto Gallo, eds., *Italian Sacred Music*, No. 27; facsimile of unique source (F-Pn 568) in Apel, *Notation*, p. 379.

[40] I do not agree with the equations given by von Fischer and Gallo in their edition, which imply a constant minim throughout the piece. The equations in Example 15.1 above imply, on the contrary, that the major semibreve of *octonaria* is equal to the semibreve of *senaria imperfecta*, à la Marchetus, that the minims of *senaria imperfecta* and *senaria perfecta* are equivalent, à la French practice, and that, for the reason just explained, the minims of *quaternaria* at the end are slower than the minims of *octonaria* at the opening.

[41] London, British Library, MS Add. 29987; see below, note 49. All the dances in Lo have been published in a recent modern edition: Timothy J. McGee, ed., *Medieval Instrumental Dances* (Bloomington, 1989).

[42] All 15 are published in McGee.

[43] F. Alberto Gallo, *Music in the Castle*, trans. Anna Herklotz (Chicago, 1995), p. 54.

[44] McGee, *Medieval Instrumental Dances*, p. 26: "Vielle players are mentioned performing alone, in pairs, and, in one account, in four: 'Then the servants hurried and quickly took away the napery. Four minstrels of the vielle played a new estampie before the lady'."

[45] See Federico Ghisi, "An Angel Consort in a Trecento Sienese Fresco," in Jan LaRue, ed., *Aspects of Medieval and Renaissance Music* (New York, 1966), p. 308; cited in Alexander Blachly, "Review of Records," *Musical Quarterly* 55 (1971), 332.

[46] Polyphonic Music of the Fourteenth Century 6 (1967), p. xii, and Vol. 10 (1977), p. xiii.

[47] Reinhard Strohm, *The Rise of European Music 1380-1500*, p. 358.

[48] Leonard Ellinwood, ed., *The Works of Francesco Landini* (Cambridge, MA, 1939); Leo Schrade, ed., *The Works of Francesco Landini*, Polyphonic Music of the Fourteenth Century IV (Monaco, 1958).

[49] The nearly complete edition is Nino Pirrotta, ed., *The Music of Fourteenth-Century Italy* (Corpus mensurabilis musicae 8), 5 vols. (Amsterdam, 1954-64). W. Thomas Marrocco, *Italian Secular Music*, Polyphonic Music of the Fourteenth Century VI-XI (Monaco, 1967-78), includes all the Italian secular music of the fourteenth century not contained in Schrade's edition of Landini's works.

[50] Johannes Wolf and Hans Albrecht, eds., *Der Squarcialupi-Codex, Palatino 87 der Biblioteca Medicea Laurenziana zu Florenz* (Lippstadt, 1955).

[51] Suzanne Clercx, ed., *Johannes Ciconia: Un musicien liégeois et son temps*, Vol. II (Brussels, 1960); Anne Hallmark and Margaret Bent, eds., *The Works of Johannes Ciconia*, Polyphonic Music of the Fourteenth Century XXIV (Monaco, 1985).

[52] Gilbert Reaney, ed., *The Manuscript London, B.M., Additional 29987, A Facsimile Edition*, MSD 13 (n.p.: American Institute of Musicology, 1965).

[53] F. Alberto Gallo, ed., *Il codice musicale Pancciatichi 26 della Biblioteca Nazionale di Firenze. Reproduzione in facsimile* (Florence, 1981).

[54] *The Lucca Codex (Codice Mancini): Lucca, Archivio di Stato, MS 184 • Perugia, Biblioteca Communale "Augusta," MS 3065*, Introductory Study and Facsimile Edition by John Nádas and Agostino Ziino (Lucca, 1990).

[55] See above, note 4.

[56] *Il Codice Squarcialupi: MS Mediceo Palatino 87, Biblioteca Medicea Laurenziana di Firenze, Studi raccolti a cura di F. Alberto Gallo*, with introductory essays by John Nádas, Kurt von Fischer, Luciano Bellosi, Nino Pirrotta, Giuseppe Tavani, Giulio Cattin, Agostino Ziino (Florence, 1992).

[57] Agostino Ziino, ed., *Il Codice T.III.2: Torino, Biblioteca Nazionale Universitaria. Studio introduttivo ed edizione in facsimile* (Lucca, 1994).

[58] Marrocco, *Italian Secular Music*, Polyphonic Music of the Fourteenth Century 6, p. 173.

[59] Except Ellinwood's Landini edition, which reduces notes by a factor of two.

I would like to thank John Nádas for reading this chapter before publication and making many helpful suggestions for its improvement.   — A. B.

16. Ars Subtilior

Lucy E. Cross

The composers of the repertoire we now refer to as the *ars subtilior*, the "more refined art," have borne several different labels among music historians of the present era: "the post-Machaut generation," "mannerists,"[1] the "late fourteenth-century French" (owing to the preponderance of French-texted songs in the idiom), the "late fourteenth-century avant garde,"[2] and more recently the "International Gothic" by association with the "International Style" of painting emergent in France about 1380.[3] The musicologist Ursula Günther coined the term "*ars subtilior*," citing a number of uses of the word *subtilitas* by fourteenth- and fifteenth-century theoretical writers to describe the complicated rhythmic subdivisions, colorations, proportions, and syncopations characteristic of the style.[4] The term is an excellent one: it does not exclude the many Mass movements and Italian-texted works that display these techniques, and it would doubtless have been understood by fourteenth-century musicians in just the sense in which we use it.

The *ars subtilior* is a refinement of the *ars nova* and the term, like *ars nova*, refers to a style of rhythmic notation, although certain types of compositions and certain characteristic sonorities are associated with it. *Ars nova* was first described by Johannes de Muris with reference to the motet; *ars subtilior* too, applies theoretically to the motet, but most of the surviving representatives of the style are ballades or other secular songs in fixed form.

The music survives in three principal manuscripts: Chantilly, Musée Condé 564 (*olim* 1047); Modena, Biblioteca Estense Alpha M.5,24 (*olim* lat. 568 and often referred to as ModB); and Paris, Bibliothèque Nationale nouv. acq. fr. 6771 (usually referred to as the Codex Reina). These are supplemented by a few lesser or fragmentary sources. Of course their present locations do not correspond to the places where the music was written: from evidence in dedicatory ballades in the Chantilly MS, honoring Charles II ("the Bad") of Navarre (d.1387), King John of Aragon (d.1396) and Gaston Fébus, Count of Foix (1331-91), we know that Senleches, Solage, and Trebor were primarily associated with secular courts in southern France and northern Spain. The appearance of the name of Jean, Duke of Berry (1340-1416), too, would indicate either that the musicians travelled north, or that the Duke had negotiations or celebrations at southern courts. The Italians, Matteo da Perugia, Philipoctus and Antonello da Caserta, are assumed to have been active at Avignon where the popes resided for most of the century, and where the Antipope Clement VII based his schismatic see from 1378.

Ars subtilior notation is a mixture of French and Italian notations, which in the earlier part of the fourteenth century had been considered to be just as distinct as the two languages.[5] The nationality of the notation was inextricably bound to the type of text: if a composer set a French poem it would certainly be in one of the French fixed forms, and it would undoubtedly be set to music in French notation, even if he were an Italian. If the poem was a *madrigal*, a *caccia*, or *ballata*, it was in the Italian language and musically set in Italian notation, even if the composer were Johannes Ciconia of Liège. The notation of Machaut differed radically from that of Jacopo da Bologna, even though the shapes of their longs, breves, and semibreves were essentially the same, just as they used the same alphabet.

The *punctus divisionis* of the Italian idiom functioned as a demarcator of breve units, each of which could be subdivided into 4, 6, 8, 9, or 12 minims. In many ways it was what a modern bar-line is. The Italians did not use note-values that in modern notation would be tied over a barline, because a syncopation over the dot of division, from one breve to another, was impossible. The same *punctus divisionis* as used by French composers, however, had the capacity to move the complete unit over by a small value, or in other words, to insert a full unit, or a series of full units, amidst semibreves or minims. It thus became a *punctus sincopationis*. "Syncopation," said the early fourteenth-century treatise, *Libellus*, of Johannes de Muris (or perhaps, Philippe de Vitry), "is the division of any note value into separate parts which may be brought into relationship with one another again by counting off the perfect units that lie between them."[6]

French notation also used dots of addition (these are the only dots that have survived in our own notation), as well as coloration, which could shift meters "hemiolically" and prevent alteration or imperfection of selected note-values. It was also possible to create syncopations with coloration instead of dots.

What French notation lacked, however, were the myriad *semibreves caudatae* of the Italians, notes with tails, stems, double stems, flags to the right or left, oblique strokes, or curlicues, each of which could be used to represent a fixed value, not subject to alteration or imperfection. In the madrigal, *Ita se n'era a star*, of Lorenzo Masini, for instance, the following forms are found:[7]

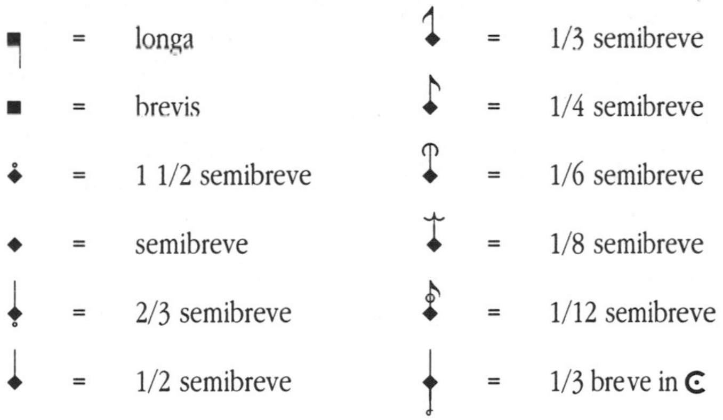
= longa
= brevis
= 1 1/2 semibreve
= semibreve
= 2/3 semibreve
= 1/2 semibreve
= 1/3 semibreve
= 1/4 semibreve
= 1/6 semibreve
= 1/8 semibreve
= 1/12 semibreve
= 1/3 breve in C

The values are fixed for only this piece of music; the dragma (double-stemmed) and flagged forms are found in other pieces with other significations.

Mixtures of French and Italian notation began to appear in the middle of the fourteenth century (all of Landini's *ballate* were conceived in French notation with an admixture of Italian tailed notes), but in the *ars subtilior*, the art of complicated notation is developed to its most extreme — to a point, it has been argued, not reached even in music of the twentieth century.

Often in the *ars subtilior*, a specific piece will exhibit a unique notational trick or novelty, so that reading the music has the quality of solving a puzzle. Jacob de Senleches is the master of this type: in *Je me merveil*, two voices have exactly the same melody sounding in canon, but written in different mensurations; in *En attendant esperance*, red notes which alter and imperfect other red notes, and black notes which alter and imperfect other black notes, are shuffled and scrambled together. Sometimes a song seems to be about itself: Senleches's *La harpe de melodie*[8] is a picture as much as a piece of music; and Matteo da Perugia's *Andray soulet* is a canon singing about being a canon. The song text may provide a clue to the musical reading, as in *En attendant esperance* ("look for perfection in your life, and perfections of red and black notes in this piece of music") or Matteo da Perugia's *Le greygnour bien* ("things are not what they seem").

This last piece, incidentally, has more distinct note-forms (16) than any other in the repertoire, even the anonymous motet *Sumite karissimi*, cited by Apel[9] as the "acme of rhythmic intricacy in the entire history of music" because of its syncopations. Despite the apparent trend toward the representation of fixed values with fixed shapes, however, it remains true throughout the *ars subtilior* that one form may represent two or more different values, or one value may be represented by two or more different forms.

Transcription into modern notation is at its most problematic in this repertoire, for many reasons. The very important visual aesthetic obviously has to be sacrificed: some pieces in the early fifteenth-century English "Old Hall" manuscript[10] are written – or painted – in as many as four different colors. Putting the parts in score has its casualties as well. But the travesty does most damage when proportional changes require messy triplet and duplet markings, and when syncopations of long duration have to be forced into modern measures, resulting in multitudes of tied values and misleadingly beamed groups of eighths and sixteenths. To a modern musician the beam and the barline always communicate a sense of meter or downbeat, exactly the sense that the *ars subtilior* syncopation proposes to displace. And though mixtures of metrical groupings by the relative weight or length of notes cannot be denied, those metrical groupings are often not simultaneous in all the parts.

Senleches's *Fuions de ci* is an outstanding example; a transcription of its beginning may be attempted in this way:

Ex. 16.1. Fuions de ci, by Jacob de Senleches.

This kind of studied detail in a transcription is quite impractical from the point of view of a music printer, and is to some extent an editorial imposition upon the performer (as all barlines are), but it is viable as a tool for rhythmic analysis of some of these pieces.

The entire *ars subtilior* repertoire of French-texted secular songs from the Chantilly, Modena, and Reina sources was published by Willi Apel in 1970.[11] The critical notes supply most of the necessary historical, literary, and technical information on individual compositions, but for an excellent general introduction to the style, Apel's preliminary selective edition entitled, *French Secular Music of the Late Fourteenth Century*,[12] has not been matched. It provides historical background, information about patronage and the occasions for which some of the pieces were composed, descriptions of the major manuscript sources, and analysis of musical forms, notation, and literary style, along with remarks and suggestions for performance. It also contains several plates of facsimiles in color, as does Apel's *The Notation of Polyphonic Music, 900-1600*.[13] It must be revealed, however, that some of the facsimiles have been retouched (the second note of the cantus of *Fumeux fume*, for instance, should be an F#).[14]

Apel's transcriptions sometimes include diagrams of the syncopations, which appear above the staff in small notes. They are characterized by long beams that reach over the whole phrase, connecting the elements of the full value that has been broken up by the syncopation, and barlines that separate the intervening units. These can be helpful, interpreted in terms of the medieval definition of syncopation quoted above.

The quality and sheer volume of Apel's work in transcribing the *ars subtilior* are monumental, but it would be disingenuous to expect every transcription to be correct: performers should be warned that some pieces, including Senleches's *En attendant esperance* and *La harpe de melodie*, contain fundamental errors.[15] In French Secular Compositions (1970), Apel departs from the accepted practice of placing editorial accidentals in every instance above the staff, sometimes supplying sharps or flats within the staff that are distinguishable as his own only by their slightly smaller than standard size. In any case, all given accidentals should be considered open to question.[16]

Because style of notation is the essence of the *ars subtilior*, and because not all transcriptions are quite accurate,[17] I recommend most emphatically that performers make their own transcriptions of pieces (to the extent that facsimiles of the originals are available), or at least try to imagine reconstructions of the originals from the transcriptions at hand. I know of no one, however, who has successfully sight-read from original notation any composition of the complexity typical of Senleches, or Anthonello, or Philipoctus. Such a feat is almost unimaginable. Scores are indispensable initially to show points of simultaneity, and to assure that all members of the ensemble are subdividing or multiplying a common time unit as they perform.

The harmonic or contrapuntal language typical of *ars subtilior* is not as "avant garde" as it has sometimes been made out to be. Sharps and flats are indeed incorporated to an unprecedented degree (e.g. Solage's *Fumeux fume*), but there are few unorthodox or deceptive progressions, and almost no direct chromaticism. The voice-leading, though it may be obscured by rhythmic complexity, is actually very smooth and standard, as a rule, except for some moderate extensions in vocal range and an occasional surprising interval. What problems arise in the area of *ficta*, therefore, are usually the results of scribal errors or editorial misreadings. In fact, the music of Machaut is far more angular melodically, and dissonant vertically —"chromatic" even—than that of any of his successors, even Solage, who was his closest imitator. In sound and performance, *ars subtilior* music reveals itself as typically French, and somewhat impressionistic. The appropriate air of nonchalance, even passivity, can be extremely difficult to achieve, as it requires a capacity in the performer to measure proportional units of time precisely, without beating.

Beyond its notational complexity, the *ars subtilior* repertoire poses a number of other unique challenges. Instrumentation is a serious problem: little iconographical evidence has been found for the existence of instruments that could play at the low pitch indicated by the clefs except, perhaps, for lutes and harps. Purely vocal execution may not be the answer, as it obscures the textural distinctions among parts, and as the song texts are nearly impossible to underlay to typical tenor (not enough notes) or contratenor (too many repeated patterns, rests, and skips) lines.[18] I would generally recommend a vielle or another sustaining instrument for the tenor, a lute, harp, or other lighter, agile sound for the contratenor (except where the contra movement resembles that of the tenor), and a very flexible attitude toward pitch level.

As in the music of Machaut, the presence of four parts does not necessarily indicate that a piece is intended to be done in four voices (Machaut's *De Fortune* sounds best in two). Indeed, the percentage of true four-voice works is probably higher later in the fourteenth century (many by Solage), but the performer ought always to regard dissonances and parallels as possible evidence that one of the participating voices is redundant. In any case, to play a contratenor and triplum (or second contra) simultaneously is often to reinforce a secondary rhythmic or harmonic element by doubling. In most fourteenth-century music, unlike Renaissance music, equal balance of voices is not desirable; the cantus, then the tenor, should predominate.

This imbalance, and the necessity for both reliability and trust on the part of each member of the ensemble, make performing works from the *ars subtilior* a musical and interpersonal experience without parallel, except perhaps for some pieces in modern styles. It separates sheep from goats, and almost always makes better musicians on both sides.

Editions

Apel, Willi, ed. *French Secular Compositions of the Fourteenth Century* (3 volumes, Corpus Mensurabilis Musicae 51-53, Rome: American Institute of Musicology, 1970). Contains the entire *ars subtilior* repertoire of French-texted secular songs from the Chantilly, Modena, and "Reina" sources.

Apel, Willi, ed. *French Secular Music of the Late Fourteenth Century* (Cambridge, Massachusetts: Medieval Academy of America, 1950).

Bent, Margaret, and Anne Hallmark, eds. *The Works of Johannes Ciconia* (Polyphonic Music of the Fourteenth Century 24, Monaco : Editions de l'Oiseau-Lyre, 1985).

Fano, Fabio, ed. *Le origini e il primo maestro di cappella: Matteo da Perugia* (Istitutzioni e Monumenti dell'Arte Musicale Italiana 1 (Parte prima di La cappella musicale del Duomo di Milano, Disegno generale di Gaetano Ccsari, Milano: G. Ricordi & Co., 1956).

Fischer, Kurt von, and F. Alberto Gallo, eds. *Italian Sacred and Ceremonial Music* (PMFC 13, Monaco: Éditions de L'Oiseau-Lyre, 1987). Contains *ars subtilior* Mass music, including the elaborate Glorias of Matteo da Perugia.

Greene, Gordon K., ed. *French Secular Music*, (PMFC 18-19, Monaco: Éditions de L'Oiseau-Lyre, 1981). Greene's editions contain the repertoire of the Chantilly manuscript, and differ from Apel's only in the reading of *ficta*.

Günther, Ursula, ed. *The Motets of the Manuscript Chantilly, Musée Condé 564, (olim 1047) and Modena, Biblioteca Estense, alpha M.5,24 (olim lat. 568)* (American Institute of Musicology, 1965).

Harrison, Frank Llewellyn, ed. *Motets of French Provenance* (PMFC 5, Monaco: L'Oiseau-Lyre, 1965).

Hoppin, Richard H., ed. *The Cypriot-French Repertory of the Manuscript Torino, Biblioteca Nazionale J.II.9*, (Rome: AIM, 1963). Contains several anonymous ballades in *ars subtilior* style, not included in Apel.

Hughes, Andrew, and Margaret Bent, eds. *The Old Hall manuscript* (CMM 46, American Institute of Musicology, 1969-73).

Notes

[1] Willi Apel, *French Secular Music of the Late Fourteenth Century* (Cambridge, MA, 1950).

[2] David Munrow, notes to *The Art of Courtly Love* (Seraphim SIC 6092, ca.1973), p. 14.

[3] David Fallows, article "Ars nova" in the *New Grove Dictionary of Music and Musicians*, vol. 1 (London & New York, 1980), p. 639.

[4] "Das Ende der Ars Nova" in *Musikforschung* 16 (1963), 105.

[5] For a contemporary theoretical source, see Philip E. Schreur, *Tractatus figurarum: Treatise on Noteshapes* (Lincoln, ca.1989).

[6] "Sincopa est divisio cujuscumque figure ad partes separatas que ad invicem reducuntur perfectiones numerando," See E. de Coussemaker, ed. *Scriptorum de musica medii aevi* 3 (Paris, 1864; repr. Hildesheim, 1963), pp. 34, 56.

[7] See Johannes Wolf, *Geschichte der Mensural-Notation von 1250-1460* (Leipzig, 1904; repr. Hildesheim, 1965), p. 311.

[8] Depicted on the cover of Richard Hoppin's *Medieval Music* (New York, 1978).

[9] *The Notation of Polyphonic Music, 900-1600*, Fifth edition, revised and with commentary (Cambridge, MA, 1961), p. 432.

[10] Transcribed and edited by Andrew Hughes and Margaret Bent, Corpus Mensurabilis Musicae 46, 3 vols. (Rome, 1969-73).

[11] *French Secular Compositions of the Fourteenth Century*, 3 volumes, Corpus Mensurabilis Musicae 51-53 (Rome, 1970).

[12] See note 1.

[13] See note 9.

[14] Apel, *French Secular* (1950), pl. 5.

[15] Richard H. Hoppin's edition of the latter in *Anthology of Medieval Music* (New York, 1978) is good.

[16] See my discussion of *musica ficta* in chapter 37 of this volume.

[17] For example, Günther's *Sub Arturo plebs* is the good one, as opposed to Harrison's, and the Fano edition has been supplanted by the more recent *PMFC* transcriptions.

[18] An untexted, vocalized rendition is possible, however.

17. Early Du Fay
Ross W. Duffin

Some authoritative music history textbooks, and therefore many of the people who once used those textbooks, are quite certain that Du Fay should be classified as a Renaissance composer. His mention by Tinctoris in the *Liber de arte contrapuncti* as a founder of a new style in the 1430s gives us a contemporary witness to that fact. And yet, in some ways, he is very much a composer of the late Middle Ages. He writes isorhythmic motets almost to the middle of the fifteenth century. He uses primarily the same lyric forms as Machaut (*ballade, virelai, rondeau*), and the preferred form of Landini (*ballata*). This "internationalism" confirms Du Fay as a prototypical Renaissance composer even though Johannes Ciconia preceded him as a Franco-Flemish composer carrying the notational innovations of the French *Ars nova* to Italy.[1] Du Fay was a master at experimenting within an established framework—as his late essays in the isorythmic motet genre demonstrate—and his early chansons are amazingly individual, especially considering the dominant conventions of subject matter and musical texture prevailing at that time. They stand as exemplars among the lyric works of the era.

Some of Du Fay's chansons are occasional pieces, written in honor of a specific patron or event; the majority are love songs. But within the conventional love song genre, a number of different types can be discerned. Some follow the traditions of courtly love as perpetuated in the ever-popular *Roman de la Rose* and extolled monthly in the Parisian "Court of Love." Some of these even refer to allegorical characters such as "Danger" and "Jealousy." Many are tied to a time of year, usually New Year's or Mayday.[2] A few of the lyrics show clear signs of having been written by Du Fay himself: *Craindre vous vueil*, for example, contains the enticing acrostic, "Cateline Du Fay" (Du Fay's mother's name was Marie, so Cateline may have been a lady friend), and *Ce moys de may* inserts the personal plea, "Karissime! Du Fay vous en prye." One song reprises an unconventional consolation on the death of a friend: "car une fois nous fault ce pas passer"—freely translated, "we all have to go sometime!" Only a handful of pieces have anything other than French text. Even some pieces composed explicitly for Italian patrons have French text, so it was clearly prevalent in the Italian court circles where Du Fay seems to have spent some of his early composing years.

Du Fay's French, barring a few archaisms, can be understood fairly well by anyone who knows modern French. The main difference is pronunciation, with sounds like [wɛ] for the combination "oi" or "oy" being one of the more obvious variants. Several convenient sources offer advice on the pronunciation of fifteenth-century French for singers.[3]

By far, Du Fay's preferred song form was the *rondeau*, with its intricate pattern of internal repetitions casting repeated text in a new light each time. This is one of the so-called "fixed forms" that he inherited from previous generations of French poets and song composers. It is important as a performer to memorize the "route" of such pieces, and I have found one easy way to accomplish that is by learning short English poems that illustrate the form. The English poet Austin Dobson (1840-1921) wrote a number of poems in old French forms and this is one of his *rondeaux*:[4]

A	In the School of Coquettes
B	Madam Rose is a scholar : —
a	O, they fish with all nets
A	In the School of Coquettes !
a	When her brooch she forgets
b	'Tis to show her new collar ;
A	In the school of coquettes,
B	Madam Rose is a scholar.

The two musical sections of Du Fay's *rondeaux* correspond to the "a" and "b" letters on the left, with capital letters denoting refrain text. For Du Fay, each musical section actually consists of two or three lines of poetry with the same number of musical phrases, and this is true for the other forms as well.

Du Fay's favored Italian form was the *ballata* which in fact resembles another French form, the *virelai*. It is normally strophic—the single strophe *virelai* became popular later in the century and was known as the bergerette—but the basic form can be seen in a single stanza. Here is a poem I wrote to illustrate the *virelai/ballata*:

A	I have written this song as a sort of *ballata*.
b	It did not take me long :
b	Did I do something wrong?
a	Even though it was fun it was no enchilada —
A	I have written this song as a sort of *ballata*.

The other main form Du Fay used was the *ballade*, which served mostly for occasional pieces such as odes and commemorations, but also for the odd love song and even the song of condolence mentioned above. Like the *virelai/ballata*, it is a strophic form, with each successive stanza following the pattern given below. The exception is *Se la face ay pale*, a *ballade* in which the setting for each stanza is through-composed. It is Du Fay's one fixed-form piece where the music does not follow the fixed form, and I wonder if that revolutionary characteristic may have contributed to its extraordinary fame. Below is a poem in the form of a *ballade*; I've given two stanzas in order to illustrate how the last part functions as a refrain. Some but by no means all *ballades* include an *envoi* which is a tag— a "parting shot."

But while Du Fay was a traditionalist in his choice of such forms, he was an innovator in the textures he created. For example, the four-voice *rondeau, Par droit je puis*, is a combination of the typical three-voice texture of the chanson

a	Should it be "Duf-I" or should it be "Duf-ay"?
a	Could you please reply as soon as yesterday?
b	I would even pay if the price is not too high.
C	Who knows the proper way? Certainly not I.
a	If you don't comply, the world won't end today,
a	And yet you can't deny we won't know what to say.
b	If Duf - I - ee's passé, I've friends who must know why—
C	Who knows the proper way? Certainly not I.
envoi	I'm asking you hereby:
C	Who knows the proper way? Certainly not I.

with that of the fourteenth-century Italian form, the *caccia*, in which the two texted voices are in strict canon with one another. In fact, so carefully worked out is this piece, that the two canonic voices between them create the cantus-tenor framework that is the contrapuntal basis of virtually every chanson from the period and that forms a perfectly acceptable minimum for successful performance. The other two voices serve merely to contribute to the harmony and to provide what I call "rhythmic counterpoint," a typical feature of Du Fay's music and one that sets him apart from most other composers of the time. The subtle syncopations and counter-accents applied to Du Fay's gracefully arching melodies provide one of the richest experiences in musical miniature from the whole history of music. His combination of French attention to rhythmic detail and Italian attention to melody was, in some respects, the genesis of the so-called international style of the musical Renaissance.

The notational system used by Du Fay for these works is unambiguous and, in fact, provides interpretational insights that do not always translate into modern notation. There is an excellent example of this in *Craindre vous vueil* but, in order to explain it, I need to give some notational background: the **O** mensuration corresponds most closely to, and in this repertoire is often transcribed as the modern meter 3/4, with a breve (▭) corresponding to a 𝅗𝅥 (imperfect) or a 𝅗𝅥. (perfect) depending on its context, a semibreve (◇) corresponding to a ♩, and a minim (𝅗𝅥) corresponding to a ♪ (there are more subtleties, but this will suffice to make the point). Occasionally, composers chose to replace two perfect breves (▭ ▭ = 𝅗𝅥. 𝅗𝅥.) with three blackened breves (■ ■ ■ = 𝅗𝅥 𝅗𝅥 𝅗𝅥) or their equivalent in blackened notation, causing a change of accent normally referred to as hemiola. This notational technique is known as coloration and is usually represented in modern notation by corner brackets. Finally, two consecutive semibreves (◆ ◆) may be replaced by a ligature (◣) which is usually represented in modern notation by a bracket above the ligated notes.

Now, the example: at the words "en quelque lieu que soye" in *Craindre vous vueil*, the reading of the top part in Heinrich Besseler's scholarly edition of Du Fay's songs is as follows:[5]

Ex. 17.1a. *Craindre vous vueil* after Besseler.

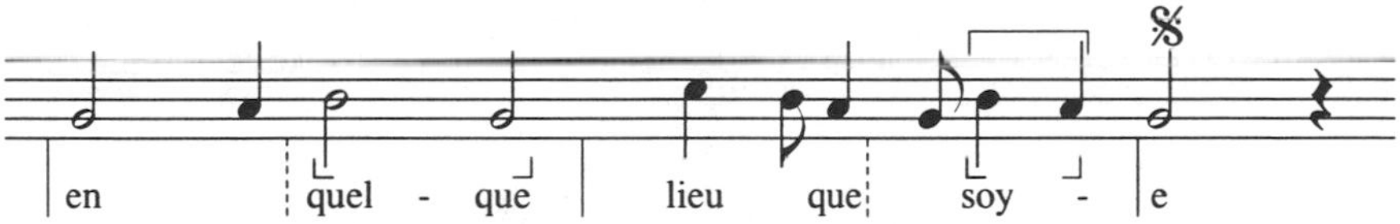

In its original notation, this passage reads:[6]

Ex. 17.1b. *Craindre vous vueil* after MS Can. 213.

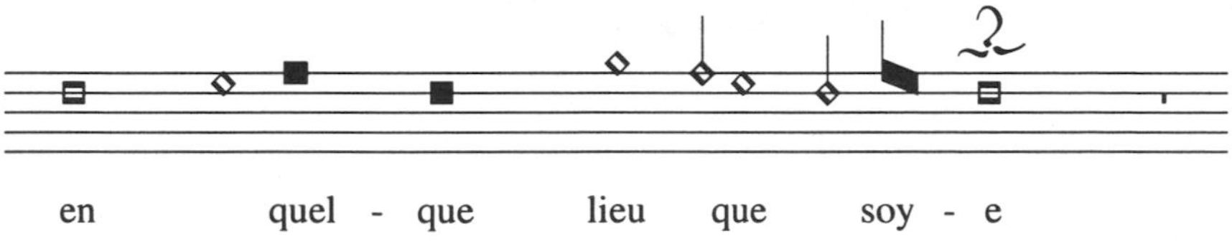

In modern notation, the passage is a paragon of accentual ambiguity. Barlines and dotted barlines imply accents in a confusing and even misleading way. In the original notation, we can see immediately that Du Fay is simply experimenting with the convention of hemiola coloration. He gives us the first two-thirds of a coloration pattern, interpolates a normal breve measure (one that displays a playful counter-accent), then completes the coloration pattern. The modern notation goes into contortions to try to represent what is in the original but is ultimately unhelpful; the original notation clarifies Du Fay's intentions. Nothing could be more important to the performer.

Unsuccessful as it is in this instance, at least the Besseler edition tries to represent the linear flow of this music by using *Mensurstriche*: barlines that go between rather than through the staves, allowing an uninterrupted path for the melody and rendering ties unnecessary. Congruent with this is the concept of "melodic-rhythmic flow," a performance approach to this music that has gained acceptance in some circles.[7]

Basically, melodic-rhythmic flow stipulates that barlines, non-existent in the original notation, have no impact on the patterns of stress in this music, and that the accents in any phrase correspond to the notes of longer duration or melodic prominence. There is some validity to this approach, and yet there are mitigating factors as well. EX. 17.2 gives the "a" section of Du Fay's *Ce jour le doibt* without barlines but with the perceived groupings and stresses dictated by melodic-rhythmic flow indicated by the small vertical lines above the staves:

Ex. 17.2. *Ce jour le doibt* excerpt

Some of these work nicely as counter-accents to the prevailing mensuration. Others seem to be contradicted by aspects of the notation beyond merely pitch and duration. Significant in this regard are the first line of text, indications of ligatures and coloration, and dots of division. Ligatures, after all, show groupings of notes and imply stress at the beginning, if anywhere, and dots of division are the closest thing in the fifteenth-century mensural system to modern barlines.[8] These show that while melodic-rhythmic flow is very useful as a way of thinking about individual lines as read by perfomers from the original parts, such accents may actually be contrary to what the performer thinks should be emphasized according to the visual impression of the individual line, particularly in modern notation, and even if the barlines are ignored. Moreover, it can be argued that accents derived without consideration of text, dots of division, and ligatures (not to mention what is happening in the other parts) do not represent the original notation very well. The pattern ♩ ♪♪♩ in 6/8 meter (**C**) might represent ♩ ♩ ♩ ♩ , which indicates a 3/4-like hemiola accentuation, but it can also represent ♩ ♩ . ♩ ♩ , which reinforces the metrical division instead. Again, this kind of interpretation cannot be derived from modern notation nor from the application of the theory of melodic-rhythmic flow, but it is obvious in the original notation and is a vital part of what makes Du Fay's music "tick."

Ornamentation, though important, is not as critical an issue for the performance of Du Fay's early chansons as it is for chansons of the later fifteenth and sixteenth centuries. There are written-out ornamentations in the Faenza Codex and the Buxheim Organbook, but these are florid and idiomatically instrumental, and not very applicable to vocal performance. Not that voices of the time were incapable of virtuosic singing—the texted melismas of *Resvellies vous* make that clear—but the *fioratura* in that instance are an integral part of the song, helping to glorify Carlo Malatesta whose wedding the song celebrates. Most of these chansons are love lyrics and would not be well served, in my opinion, by fancy diminutions, even though musicians of the sixteenth century did not hesitate to ornament love songs. What is indicated in existing ornamental passages and concordant readings are embellishment (or, at least, variant figuration) at cadences, occasional passing tones, and escape tones.

Typical cadential formulas that appear in Du Fay's early chansons include the ten shown in EX. 17.3. Small notes indicate common variants.

Ex. 17.3. Early 15th-century cadential figurations.

Aside from virtually interchangeable formulas like these, an ornament that may have had wide use in this repertoire is the escape tone and its close relative, the ornamented anticipation.[9] When faster notes appear—usually semiminims—they normally consist of pairs of passing tones (like those in the last formula above), ornamented anticipations (as shown in the third formula above), or escape tones (like the shortest notes in EX. 17.4 below), leading to the supposition that such figures are probably appropriate in similar situations elsewhere, even when they are not notated.[10]

Since about 1981, there has been a great deal of acrimonious debate surrounding the scoring of this repertoire, with a number of scholars maintaining that instruments did not take part and others maintaining adamantly that they did.[11] It is regrettable that this difference of opinion about a repertoire so dear to the hearts of the principals seemed to force each camp to extreme positions, reluctant to recognize validity in the arguments of the other side. It is equally unfortunate that the surge of musicological interest in the subject did not lead to a parallel increase in performances. If anything, the opposite has been true.

According to the *a cappella* view, instrumentalists had their own repertoire consisting of monophonic dances and monophonic song accompaniments, along with improvisation on *basse danse* melodies (like *Je suy povere de leesse*), and arrangements of polyphonic chansons. When this idea was first introduced, it seemed that fitting the words of the top part to the music of the untexted lower parts was the recommended way of using the voices. Later, some difficulties with that procedure were pointed out, leading to the view that untexted lower parts should mostly be vocalized.[12] Although the evidence for chanson performance practice is meager, there are descriptions of music-making as well as some manuscript indications that support all-vocal rendition, and performances of late-medieval repertoire by groups like Gothic Voices and Ensemble Organum have made it plain that it can work to excellent musical effect. However, there is some evidence to weigh against this as an exclusive practice.

This is not the place to re-examine in detail all of the evidence for chanson performance that has been scrutinized and written about over the last several years. Suffice it to say that there *are* references to the performance of sophisticated part-music by instruments, both in ensemble and as solo arrangements.[13] There are further references to instrumental accompaniment of chansons that could just as well refer to polyphony as monophony.

Thus, if instruments were indisputably playing chansons, why should they now be excluded only when they mix with voices, especially since the evidence is so slim? One statement against the use of instruments cited the rapidity of sound decay as forcing unnaturally fast tempos, and the softness as creating an imbalance with the voice or voices.[14] Such subjective musical criticism is perhaps understandable with the dearth of historical evidence, but it needs to be said in response that musicians of the next two and a half centuries seem to have had no problem with either the volume or decay of the lute in accompanying the voice. It is also true that players of instruments like the plectrum lute may have sustained notes by using the tremolo technique associated in more recent times with mandolin and balalaika or, more likely, by means of reiterations like so many of those already written into untexted parts in these works.[15]

So, while all-vocal performance remains an important possibility for these songs, a categorical banishment of instruments would seem to be unwarranted. Moreover, in Oxford, Bodleian Library, MS Canonici misc. 213, the central manuscript of Du Fay's early secular works, there is great care taken to underlay text in some voices and not in others.[16] In the typical three-voice texture, some pieces have text in all the voices, some in two of the voices, and some in just one. And the choice seems not to have been made due to considerations of space, which is adequate, nor due to scribal laziness, since some almost completely homophonic works, like *J'atendray tant* and *J'ay mis mon cuer*, have text underlaid in the tenor and contra parts where there would have been little question how to place the syllables in a texted *a cappella* rendition. While the texted/untexted relationship can be maintained by using singers to vocalize the untexted parts on a neutral vowel, the character of some of these parts lends itself so well to instrumental rendition that it seems a reasonable choice. Obviously, there are no definitive criteria for deciding what makes a part unsuitable for voice, or even whether *any* part is unsuitable for voice. It can be shown that there are "un-vocal" looking sections in, for example, Kyrie movements, where few would argue for instrumental participation, and there may have been singers who made a specialty of singing contra parts, however awkward vocally. But passages like the following from *He, compaignons* do not resemble most texted music from the time and, furthermore, look like they could have been designed for an instrument, with reiterations, fragmentations, and rapid changes of tessitura that suggest movement from one string or one harmonic to another.

Ex. 17.4. *He compaignons* (contra excerpt).

Another part that suggests an instrument is the lone untexted voice in the chanson, *Ma belle dame souverainne*. Here, the final phrase ends with ascending scalar motion, but the very last note is doubled at the octave below. With one performer to a part (the most likely disposition), this is not even possible for a singer;[17] with two singers, it is possible but extremely awkward for one of them; for a harp or a lute, it is a perfectly natural and easy doubling.

Ex. 17.5. *Ma belle dame souverainne* (contra excerpt).

Readers may be familiar with the *a cappella* recordings of late-medieval chansons by Christopher Page's ensemble, Gothic Voices, and other groups.[18] One of Page's more recent recordings, *The Medieval Romantics*, contains the somewhat understated but nevertheless unequivocal acceptance of the use of instruments in accompanying voices in this repertoire. Page says:"...the textless lines in fourteenth-century polyphony should...be vocalized or (less frequently, perhaps) performed upon instruments."[19] By this we may conclude that the most ardent advocate and eloquent practicioner of the exclusive *a cappella* view has changed his mind about the exclusion of instruments. David Fallows, distinguished Du Fay scholar and long an outspoken advocate of the *a cappella* position, has also seemed to pull back from his earlier stance.[20] This should help to lay the controversy to rest.

One last issue relating to text concerns the untexted sections at the beginning and sometimes the end of otherwise texted parts. The ones at the beginning are a problem because the first letter of the cantus text typically appears in the manuscript at the start of the first line, inviting the supposition that the text should begin immediately. Yet this is contradicted by the placement of the remainder of the first syllable which is usually under a note about four to six measures into the piece. The fact that the initial letters are frequently consonants, like "P" or "B," and that texted tenor parts with opening melismas place the entire first syllable after the melisma, suggests that these passages were not meant to carry text. It seems to work best to have them vocalized on a neutral vowel sound, like "ah" or the French "u," or [y].[21] This works for closing melismas as well, although some pieces, like *Resvellies vous,* call instead for a long melisma on the penultimate syllable of the text. Some performers use instruments to play opening and closing melismas, but this seems possible only where rests separate texted and untexted sections, thus facilitating performance by a single player/singer.[22]

This brings us to another aspect of the performance of these works: the instruments used, if any. The Renaissance preference, at least after 1500, is for a homogeneous sound with groups of similar instruments in a variety of sizes. From the Du Fay period, iconography suggests that the instrumental groupings are heterogeneous ensembles with instruments like those from the time of Machaut. There are some problems with this, however. It is never clear if instrumental groupings are shown in paintings because they are either "photogenic" or symbolic of something, or because they are representative of a real musical situation. Also, there is evidence that instruments of the same type were sometimes combined in performance. We know, for example, that recorders and douçaines (soft shawms) were sometimes purchased in sets of four, suggesting potential ensemble use. We also know that the Duke of Burgundy's two blind musicians were sometimes described as vielle players, sometimes lute players, sometimes rebec players, suggesting a pairing of whatever they were playing. Because untexted parts in Du Fay's chansons are often similar in character and range, a pair of identical instruments could perform them, as could two similar instruments such as lute and harp.

The choice of instruments is a complicated one. The vielle's participation in polyphonic music of this period has been challenged on the grounds that it had a flat bridge, which would make it suitable only for drones and heterophony. Enough curved bridges have been found in depictions now, however, to establish that it could have played a single line in a polyphonic piece.[23] Conjunct lines, such as the tenors of *La belle se siet* and *Je suy povere de leesse,* fit the vielle very well[24]—livelier parts less so. One further question about the vielle of the period, given what little we know about prevailing string technology, is whether it was capable of playing as low as the tenor c of many tenor/contratenor parts. Some tenor/contra parts descend only to f, however, and these would seem, even by conservative estimate, to fall within the range of a standard size vielle.[25]

Clearly, the range of tenor/contra parts was not a problem for either lute or harp. Plectrum lute is especially well-suited to accompanying singers in this repertory because of its wide, flexible range, and its ability to handle any and all chromatic inflections, both written and unwritten. Along with the keyboard, it is also the most likely instrument for solo arrangements of chansons even though, at this period, it was still played by plectrum rather than with the fingers.[26]

The harp's main problem, like the psaltery's, is the difficulty of playing chromatic inflections, although these can be achieved by using something hard (like a thumbnail) to stop the string near the tuning pins.[27] Thus, the harp tends to be better suited to tenor parts than contratenors, in view of the smaller likelihood of inflection at double leading-tone cadences, etc., in tenor parts.[28] The harp may also have had some priority in chanson performance, since harpers were sometimes composers or court *valets de chambre* and, as such, could be expected to have read both text and music notation, whereas some of the *menestrels* were probably illiterate.[29] This could mean that harpers were in charge of organizing the performance of chansons and other secular entertainments. The inability to read music was obviously not a great hindrance to musicians of the time, however, and does not mean that they were unable to perform sophisticated music. For one thing, the study of depictions of music-making suggests that performances were typically done from memory, and could well have been learned by rote, just as jazz musicians (and Suzuki violinists) commonly do today.[30] The Duke of Burgundy's blind string players obviously did not read music even though one of them seems to have been extraordinarily learned,[31] so if they were not improvising, they were playing parts that had been played or sung to them. Perhaps the harper's responsibilities included teaching the latest song to the virtuosic but illiterate musicians of the court.

Three other string instruments with a possible place in this repertoire are the gittern, rebec, and dulcimer. The first two are mentioned fairly frequently in contemporary accounts and work well on parts in the treble range, especially in combination with other string instruments. The small hammered dulcimer appears in depictions but it is not mentioned often and not much is known about its capabilities.

Wind instrumentalists, we know, took part in closed consort chanson performance. It is possible that they did some chanson accompaniment too, though not on shawms which are too loud to be combined with voices in music of this delicacy. But recorders and douçaines, the other instruments of the wind-playing minstrels, are possibilities. Recorders are frequently perceived by listeners as sounding an octave below their real pitch and, thus, even in the smallish sizes shown in fifteenth-century paintings, are capable of playing the many untexted tenors and contras that descend to f without creating unacceptable inversions with the cantus singer. Not everyone will agree with that assessment.

The douçaine could have played such parts at written pitch (at least, those parts that fall within the instrument's limited range) and may even have existed in sizes capable of playing the typical lower tenor/contra parts as well. It apparently combined with string instruments, too. We have, for example, more than one reference to an ensemble in Bruges consisting of lute, harp, and douçaine.[32]

The portative organ is an instrument associated with composers from Landini to Du Fay, who stands beside one in the famous depiction from Martin Le Franc's *Le champion des dames*, copied in 1451 and perhaps representing the meeting of Du Fay and Binchois at Chambéry in 1434.[33] With the size and range shown in most depictions, portatives would be suitable only for top parts, not for playing polyphonic arrangements.[34] Those arrangements must have been the property of the larger positive organ and the other developing polyphonic, or "perfect" instruments: lute, harp, clavichord, dulce melos, and even harpsichord. The Faenza Codex makes it plain that ornamented instrumental arrangements of chansons were done (whether for a duo or solo instrument is a matter of debate), and the Buxheim Organ Book even contains arrangements of some chansons by Du Fay and his contemporaries (although in a later ornamental style). Moreover, the unadorned keyboard score of *Ce jour le doibt* suggests, in contrast with the Buxheim selections, that solo versions of these pieces were not always embellished.

I have alluded once or twice already to the question of pitch. There was no standard that we know of for the early fifteenth century. Unaccompanied singers presumably found a pitch that was comfortable for everyone concerned and charged ahead. Ensembles of wind instruments probably settled on a transposition related to the pitches of their consort: since the instruments were likely pitched a fifth apart and the ranges of the written parts in this repertoire tend to be a fifth apart (that is, the tenor and contratenor share a range and the cantus is generally a fifth above that), it should have been quite straightforward. String instruments had greater apparent flexibility in transposition although as a spontaneous practice it must have been complicated somewhat by the unequal tuning. My guess is that such transpositions were mostly by fourth, corresponding to the most common interval between strings of most necked instruments.

As a rule, the pitch of this repertoire seems to work fairly well at the modern standard of A = 440 Hz. Not everyone will be able to perform every piece at that level without transposition, however, and it is not clear whether pieces written in, for example, an especially low tessitura are meant to be transposed up into the normal range or left where they are for special effect.[35]

The most important thing is for this exquisite music to be heard. Whatever it takes to accomplish that goal is worth trying.

Notes

[1] The most recent biography is *Dufay* by David Fallows (London, 1982). Additional information on Du Fay's early life and career can be found in Alejandro Planchart, "The Early Career of Guillaume Du Fay," *JAMS* 46 (1993), 341-68.

[2] Du Fay's *Ce jour le doibt* is a May song that could also have been written for the Court of Love, since it addresses a "prince d'amours."

[3] See *Singing Early Music*, ed. Timothy C. McGee *et al.* (Bloomington, 1996); Jeannine Alton and Brian Jeffery, *Bele buche e bele parleure* (London, 1976); Elizabeth V. Phillips and John-Paul Christopher Jackson, *Performing Medieval and Renaissance Music* (New York, ca.1986), pp. 284-286 (after Alton and Jeffery); *Guillaume Dufay—Chansons: Forty-Five Settings in Original Notation*, ed. Ross W. Duffin (Miami, 1983), pp. xv-xvi.

[4] *Collected Poems* (London: Kegan Paul, etc. 1914), p. 461.

---

[5]   *Guillelmi Dufay: Opera Omnia* 6, Corpus Mensurabilis Musicae 1, edited by Heinrich Besseler (Rome: American Institute of Musicology, 1964), p. 79. Actually, Besseler omits the coloration indication for the third and fourth notes. A new, corrected edition of this volume was issued by David Fallows in 1995.

[6]   For an edition in original notation, see *Guillaume Dufay—Chansons: Forty-Five Settings*, No. 1.

[7]   This approach was developed by Thomas Binkley and articulated by Timothy J. McGee in his *Medieval and Renaissance Music: A Performer's Guide* (Toronto: University of Toronto Press, 1985), pp. 20-26. Example 2 uses McGee's discussion to derive the groupings shown.

[8]   It is perhaps unfortunate for the melodic-rhythmic flow argument that *Ce jour le doibt* is one of the only chansons by Du Fay to exist in "keyboard score" with barlines after every breve: Vienna, Nationalbibliothek, Cod. 5094, fol. 148v. For a facsimile, see Theodor Göllner, "Notationsfragmente aus einer Organistenwerkstatt des 15. Jahrhunderts," *Archiv für Musikwissenschaft* 24 (1967), Abb. 2.

[9]   See the discussion in *Guillaume Dufay—Chansons: Forty-Five Settings*, xiii-xiv.

[10]   Escape tones appear also in *Bon jour, bon mois, Ce moys de may, J'atendray tant,* and *Je suy povere de leesse.*

[11]   Some highlights of this exchange include: Howard M. Brown, "On the Performance of Fifteenth-Century Chansons," *Early Music* 1 (1973), 2-10; Brown, "Instruments and Voices in the Fifteenth-Century Chanson," *Current thought in musicology*, ed. John W. Grubbs (Austin, 1976), pp. 89-137; Christopher Page, "Machaut's 'pupil' Deschamps on the Performance of Music: Voices or Instruments in the 14th-Century Chanson," *Early Music* 5 (1977), 484-91; Page, "The Performance of Songs in Late Medieval France: a New Source," *Early Music* 10 (1982), 441-450; David Fallows, "Specific Information on the Ensembles for Composed Polyphony, 1400-1474," *Studies in the Performance of Late Mediaeval Music*, ed. Stanley Boorman (Cambridge, 1983), pp. 109-59; Brown, review of "The Castle of Fair Welcome: Courtly Songs of the Later Fifteenth Century," Gothic Voices directed by Christopher Page (Hyperion A66194) in *Early Music* 15 (1987), 277-79; Fallows, "Secular Polyphony in the Fifteenth Century," *Performance practice 1: Music before 1600*, ed. Howard M. Brown and Stanley Sadie (London, 1989), pp. 201-21; Brown, "[Renaissance] Introduction," *ibid.*, pp. 147-66; Page, "Going Beyond the Limits: Experiments with Vocalization in the French Chanson, 1340-1440," *Early Music* 20 (1992), 446-59. Perhaps the earliest suggestion that all-vocal chanson performance was predominant for the Du Fay period is found in Craig Wright, "Voices and Instruments in the Art Music of Northern France during the 15th Century: a Conspectus," *Report of the Twelfth [IMS] Congress, Berkeley 1977* (Kassel, 1981), pp. 643-49. Some of David Fallows's contributions have been collected into the volume, *Songs and musicians in the Fifteenth Century* (Aldershot, Brookfield, 1996).

[12]   On vocalization of untexted parts, see Dennis Slavin, "In Support of 'Heresy': Manuscript Evidence for the *a cappella* Performance of Early 15th-Century Songs," and Lawrence Earp, "Texting in 15th-Century French Chanson: a Look ahead from the 14th Century," *Early Music* 19 (1991), 178-90 and 194-210; and Timothy J. McGee, "Singing without Text," *Performance Practice Review* 6 (1993), 1-32. It is interesting that one of the more recent *a cappella* recordings of this repertoire, the Hilliard Ensemble's *Sweet Love, Sweet Hope* (Isis CD 030, 1998), returns to the practice of texting of all parts.

[13]   Much of this information is summarized and discussed in Fallows, "Specific Information."

[14] See Daniel Leech-Wilkinson, review of Ensemble P.A.N. recordings in *Early Music* 22 (1994), 337-38.

[15] Reiteration may be what harpist/composer Jacob de Senleches had in mind in the performing direction "harpe toudis sans espasse blechier" (harp always breaking up [the notes] without waiting) for the untexted tenor part of his chanson, *La harpe de melodie* (Chicago, Newberry Library, MS 54.1, fol. 10).

[16] See discussion of "Text and texture" in Graeme Boone, "Dufay's Early Chansons: Chronology and Style in the Manuscript Oxford, Bodleian Library, Canonici misc. 213," PhD. diss., Harvard University, 1987, pp. 237-41. The manuscript has been published in facsimile as *Oxford, Bodleian Library: MS. Canon. Misc. 213,* with an introduction and inventory by David Fallows (Chicago and London, 1995).

[17] For example, the recent *a cappella* recording of this work by the Hilliard Ensemble (Isis CD030) ignores the lower note.

[18] See Select Discography for chapter 17.

[19] Hyperion CDA 66463, 1991.

[20] See his remarks in "Two Early Music Revolutions," *Early Music* 25 (1997), 564-65.

[21] The last is suggested as linguistically more appropriate in Christopher Page, "Going Beyond the Limits," 454-57.

[22] Du Fay's *He, compaignons* ends with such a passage in the texted voices, and in the cantus the last note is doubled at the octave as it is in the last contra note of *Ma belle dame souverainne,* cited above. This could mean that two singers were intended—not unreasonable for a convivial song—or it could suggest instrumental performance or doubling.

[23] The challenge came in Peter Holman, "Viols and Bridges," *Musical Times* 126 (1985), 452. Howard M. Brown responded in "The Trecento Fiddle and its Bridges," *Early Music* 17 (1989), 311-29. Holman countered in *Four and Twenty Fiddlers: the Violin at the English Court, 1540-1690* (Oxford, 1993), pp. 7-11.

[24] Because such conjunct tenors, like that for Binchois's *Filles à marier,* derive from monophonic songs, it has been suggested that they should always be sung, but the fact that they sometimes became part of the basse dance reportoire makes it clear that they could be performed instrumentally.

[25] Christopher Page interprets the fiddle tuning in the mid-fourteenth-century Berkeley treatise to be *c–d–g–c',* that is, notes in the octave below middle c. See "Fourteenth-Century Instruments and Tunings: a Treatise by Jean Vaillant? (Berkeley, MS 744)" *Galpin Society Journal* 33 (1980), 17-35. This would certainly be low enough to play most tenor/contra parts in Du Fay's early chansons, although we have no way of knowing how sounding pitch related to written pitch. See discussion below. Page also makes the point that this tuning would only make sense on an instrument with a curved bridge.

[26] *Jeloymors,* by Gilles Binchois, No. 17 (fol. 7r.)in the Buxheim Organ Book, bears the unique inscription, "In Cytaris vel etiam In Organis 3^m notarum" (for 'cithara' or even for organ). In view of German predilections, this probably refers to the lute rather than the harp. On this point, see Keith Polk, "Voices and Instruments: Soloists and Ensembles in the 15th Century," *Early Music* 18 (1990), 179-98, and *German Instrumental Music of the Late Middle Ages* (Cambridge, 1992), p. 137. Crawford Young makes the point that plectrum players can readily play up to four notes simultaneously in "On the Trail of Ensemble Music in the Fifteenth Century," *Companion to Medieval and Renaissance Music,* ed. Tess Knighton and David Fallows (London, 1992), pp. 143-45.

[27] I have found that it is sometimes useful to tune a harp with both B♭ and B♮, since both are part of the gamut, both occur frequently, and both are often shown in labeled paintings of tuned bells (also in the 17th-century harp depiction by Mersenne, on which see chapter 24c). This gives nine notes to the octave and makes scalar passages slightly more difficult but, overall, it renders unnecessary a great deal of accidental inflection and retuning from piece to piece. In "Fourteenth-century," p. 32, Chrisopher Page details several chromatic inflections given for the second drawing of the psaltery. He proposes these as alternative notes but they might just as well be chromatic notes to be tuned in the basic scale. Besides B♭ and B♮, they include E♭, F♯, and C♯. There is also the problem that a stopped note, inexpertly handled, can be conspicuously less resonant than the notes around it. The best results might be achieved with something metal attached to the finger, like a ring or a thimble. The nine-note octave method can be heard in Andrew Lawrence-King's performance of *Le gay playsir*, in *The Service of Venus and Mars*, Gothic Voices, directed by Christopher Page, Hyperion CDA 66238 (1987), track 10. An example of stopping the string is heard in *De ce que fol pense* on the same CD, track 4, at 2:06.

[28] It is interesting that in the recording cited in the previous note as well as in the same group's earlier CD, *The Castle of Fair Welcome*, Hyperion CDA 66194 (1986), there are a number of instances in harp performance where obvious cadential ficta is avoided and even manuscript accidentals are ignored.

[29] Chanson composers who served as *valets de chambre* for the Dukes of Burgundy from the late fourteenth century to about 1474 include Baude Fresnel (Cordier?) who played harp and portative organ, Jacques Vide, who played organ, and Hayne van Ghizeghem, who probably played lute. Mention must be made also of the composer Richard Loqueville, master of the choirboys at Cambrai during Du Fay's adolescence there, who is known to us as a composer and harpist, and Jacques de Senleches, mentioned in n.15 above, who was also a harpist and composer.

[30] On rote instruction of songs, see Lewis Lockwood, *Music in Renaissance Ferrara 1400-1505* (Cambridge, MA, 1984), p. 107.

[31] See Reinhard Strohm, *Music in Late Medieval Bruges* (Oxford, 1985), pp. 88-89.

[32] Strohm, pp. 81-82. The douçaine is an instrument that needs reviving and that would, I believe, find a valued place in the performance of this repertoire. With the fingering system of the one surviving douçaine—the Mary Rose "shawm"—a range of a tenth can be achieved, allowing performance of about half of the untexted parts in Du Fay's early chansons. For more details, see Chapter 27 below.

[33] Paris, Bibliothèque Nationale, f.fr. 12476, fol. 98.

[34] The combination of organ, lute, and harp appears in the same account cited by Strohm regarding the douçaine, above.

[35] On this point, see Kenneth Kreitner, "Very Low Ranges in the Sacred Music of Ockeghem and Tinctoris," *Early Music* 14 (1986), 467-79.

IV. DRAMA

18. Liturgical Drama
Timothy J. McGee

L
iturgical Drama offers the medieval music director the most extensive repertory for large-scale pageants and extravaganzas, involving soloists, chorus, instruments, costumes, staging, props, and sets. At the same time, there is also room here for a much smaller, simpler production, involving four to six singers, although they too should be costumed and staged. This is one of the few medieval performance areas that actually has material for which one can historically justify the presence of instruments other than organ in a sacred setting.

The earliest form of the Liturgical Drama, probably originating in the early ninth century, was the so-called *Visitatio Sepulchri*, the Easter Sunday morning visit to Christ's tomb by the three Marys: Mary Jacobi, Mary Salome, and Mary Magdalene. There are hundreds of manuscripts dating from the eleventh to the seventeenth centuries that record only this short scene, enacting the meeting of the three women at the tomb seeking Christ, the statement by the angel (or 2 angels) guarding the tomb that 'He has risen,' and the Marys' joyful response.

This basic Easter scene, the format that was most frequently produced during the Middle Ages, can be performed by itself with four or five singers (1 or 2 angels). On the other hand, there were also vastly expanded versions of this scene, with various elements added before and after the visit to the tomb,[1] and a modern performance would be historically correct to include either all or a selection of the additional material from any one of the more elaborate versions (providing, of course, that the visit to the tomb is included). Not all Liturgical Dramas are Easter Plays, and it is not even clear how closely associated with the liturgy many of the more elaborate plays really were. The following account will attempt to sort out the kinds of plays, their original function, and the way in which they can be reproduced within the bounds of what was probably their historical setting.

Easter Plays

The Easter Plays originated in conjunction with the sacred services of the monasteries. Before ca. 1100 they would have been associated with the procession of the *Collecta* ceremony, and performed in the cloister courtyard or at a side altar in the church. After 1100 the ceremony was gradually transferred to the end of the Matins Office, where it was performed just prior to the singing of the hymn *Te Deum laudamus*. If it is desired to perform the Easter Play within a *Collecta* context, the Tomb scenes should be preceded and followed by processional antiphons; the most frequently found are *Surrexit enim*, *Salve festa*, *Vidi aquam*, *In die resurrectionis, Sedit angelus,* and *Christus resurgens.*[2] If, however, the scene is to be placed at the end of the Matins ceremony, processional antiphons are not needed, but the modern director can select all or parts of the Easter Matins Office chants to precede the play,[3] and it should end with a choral performance of *Te Deum laudamus.*[4] Similar plays of relatively short duration, also intended to be performed in conjunction with Matins, can be found for Christmas and the Feast of the Annunciation.

The music for any ceremony deemed to be in conjunction with the liturgy should be performed by unaccompanied voices: soloists for the three Marys and angel(s), unison chant chorus for processionals, Matins items, and the *Te Deum laudamus.* Certainly by the time we have evidence of these plays we also have evidence of organum, and so the chorus can be assigned organum, in the style of whatever century is chosen, in the performance of the *Te Deum laudamus,* and any other chants chosen for choral performance. Also, to add more ceremony to the Matins enactment, it would be proper to begin to ring bells (church bells if that is where you are, or hand bells if in a concert hall), during the *Te Deum laudamus,* beginning at the line *Salvum fac populum,* and continuing to the end of the hymn. We know that some churches had organs in the late Middle Ages, and that they were played during services. Organs played preludes and 'intonations' (short introductory passages that set pitch for the choir), and interpolated hymns and other items during ceremonies, but apparently *never accompanied voices.*

For staging, the altar itself was considered in the Middle Ages to be a stylized version of Christ's tomb, and so a plain slab on legs with an altar cloth can be the entire set. Costumes for the Marys should be monks' robes, either Benedictine or Augustinian. In the medieval tradition, monks impersonated the three Marys by wearing their cowls over their heads. In modern performance of course, it would be satisfactory to use women (impersonating men impersonating women!), but the cowls should be worn up to keep the costuming correct. The angel (either sex!) should stand at the front of the 'tomb' and could be clothed simply in an *alb.* If two angels are used, one stands in front and the other behind the 'tomb,' or at either end of the altar. A staging of the simplest version would require the 'Marys' to separate themselves from the remainder of the choir of costumed monks, approach the angel at the altar, and after the exchange of dialogue with the angel, turn to the choir to intone an appropriate Easter antiphon for all to sing. As scenes are added to this basic core, the staging and props become more elaborate depending on what scenes are chosen.

The more elaborate productions

In some versions of the Easter drama, the Marys discuss amongst themselves how they will roll back the stone before approaching the tomb. In others, after hearing the news from the angel, they run to find two apostles to share their joy, and the apostles approach the tomb to see for themselves. These and other small scenes apparently were added in conjunction with the Matins placement of the drama, and always end with the *Te Deum laudamus.* The varieties of texts for these additional scenes, together with their manuscript sources, can be found in the study by Karl Young, but few of these intermediate-size versions have been published in modern transcription. In many cases the enterprising director, after consulting Young, will have to obtain an appropriate manuscript and edit it. Another possibility would be to extract the desired scenes from the wider selection of editions of the larger plays described below.

The most elaborate of the religious plays quite possibly were enacted completely outside of the liturgy, and therefore would not have been subject to the restrictions as mentioned above in terms of costuming, props, and the addition of instruments. Although all of the plays discussed below are usually referred to as 'Liturgical Dramas', most of them are found in sources containing miscellaneous and paraliturgical items, and other non-liturgical but sacred material. The very flimsy evidence that they had anything to do with the liturgy is that they end with the hymn *Te Deum laudamus*, the final item in the Matins ceremony. But that hymn was often sung outside of Matins when appropriate—as it would be in all of these plays. Simply the size of these dramas, some of which can last more than an hour, would suggest that they were probably independent productions, mounted for the education of the congregation, but completely outside of any connection with an actual liturgical ceremony. The logical result of this conclusion is that the large plays were probably not constrained to follow the traditions of liturgical practices, and therefore can be approached as independent dramas, with all the ceremony and freedom of that genre.

The Liturgical Drama best known to modern audiences is the thirteenth-century *Play of Daniel* owing to the successful enactment by the New York Pro Musica, which was recorded and published in a modern edition. It involves the well-known biblical story of the capture of Daniel and his survival in a pit of lions. A number of props are needed as well as a costumed cast of approximately 100 (or even more if a larger choir is available). The music in the original source provides a variety of monophonic melodic types, ranging from free-flowing melodies to regular metered marching songs, and including a conductus. There are a number of opportunities to interpolate additional music, especially processional pieces which could be vocal or instrumental. Ceremonies at the court of the king and queen would likely have included acrobats, jugglers, dancers, and an instrumental ensemble. This is clearly a story that presents myriad theatrical opportunities; it resembles the kind of story chosen four hundred years later for opera.

In the same category of large productions that can be filled out with instruments and other interpolated items are the ten plays from the so-called 'Fleury' Play Book, which contains, in addition to an extended *Visitatio Sepulchri*, four St. Nicholas plays, and five other plays on various biblical subjects. Two of these, *Ordo ad Representandum Herodem*, and *Ad Interfectionem Puerorum*, (*Play of Herod* and *The Slaying of the Children*), were combined as *The Play of Herod*, in a 1963 production by the New York Pro Musica, and also published. There are modern editions available of all of these 'Fleury' plays, but for those who might wish to make decisions from consulting the source, there are two published facsimiles of the relevant section of the manuscript.[5]

Directors should be aware of a few caveats concerning the relationship of available editions to what was probably performed in the Middle Ages. The first, and most problematic element is the rhythm of the music. With few exceptions, modern editors have subscribed to the turn-of-the-century theory of freely inventing rhythms according to a perceived textual rhythm—a theory now very much under attack. Notable for its adherence to what would seem to be the actual rhythmic values in the manuscript is David Wulstan's revision of W.L. Smoldon's edition of *The Play of Daniel*. But this edition is an exception, and unfortunately, short of doing extensive research into the more recent theories of interpreting the rhythmic values in chant notation and making a personal edition, there is little a modern director can do about this except to be aware of the whimsical nature of many of the rhythmic transcriptions.

Along the same lines but a bit easier to rectify, are the problems encountered with the interpolations of music in the various editions. The manuscripts themselves, with their seemingly free mixtures and variations on common scenes, support the idea of individual production enterprise; but there should be some contextual limits. While subscribing to the idea that the modern producer should feel free to use creative license in order to bring life and excitement to these productions, I would also suggest that close attention be given to historical verity. Most importantly on this score, any added material should be from the same century and geographical location as the basic material of the play if we are not to strain the limits of historical reproduction by indiscriminately mixing temporal and geographical styles into a general 'medieval stew.' If for artistic reasons it would seem proper to augment or supplement any particular scene, the interpolations should be both dramatically and historically believable: that is, the hymn, conductus, or motet should be chosen not only with attention to the relevance of the text, but also with care to see that the material was in existence during the time and in the general location of the basic play. For example, in supplementing a thirteenth-century play from southern France, the director should select the added material from thirteenth-century south-French sources. This type of historical integrity is not always observed in the available modern editions. The most frequently encountered error on this account is the use of the early fourteenth-century French dances in plays from all centuries and all European locations!

The use of musical instruments is one of the most perplexing problems in reproducing medieval music, and one for which assistance cannot necessarily be found in modern editions. Many of the modern editions were completed before much scholarly work had been done on early musical instruments. Consequently they often call for such anachronistic instrumentation as crumhorns in pre-16th-century plays, the instrumental equivalent of the problem of mixed musical styles mentioned above. Before making a decision the director should compare the suggestions in the edition with what is known about the popularity of instruments in the various areas and centuries.[6] If an extensive instrumental collection is available there may be no problem in choosing instruments, but this is rarely true and some compromises will be necessary. This is fine as long as the director is aware of what would have probably been the correct choice and the nature of the compromise. But the instrumentation suggested by the published editions may not be of help in this matter.

If instruments are to be added to the production of one of these large plays—and it is certainly not necessary for most of them—the other problem is what music they should perform. In the light of recent research, especially that by Christopher Page, it would probably be best to avoid as far as possible mixing instruments and voices at the same time. Instrumental preludes, postludes, and perhaps drones in conjunction with monophonic songs are probably historically correct, but performance of instruments in unison with voices, or as substitutes for some voices in polyphony, is probably not.[7] Instruments can be assigned dances, and monophonic and polyphonic material drawn from the contemporary vocal repertory, for use as processionals or background music in support of the dramatic action, as long as they play by themselves.[8] Since these dramas are to be fully staged, the music director will also need a large amount of assistance from an historically sensitive drama director and costume designer.[9]

In spite of all the problems and pitfalls mentioned above, Liturgical Drama production can be a richly rewarding experience. Bringing to life the oldest surviving music drama offers an opportunity to present a beautiful and attractive portrait of medieval culture, with its unselfconscious mixture of sacred and secular, in a way that no formal concert ever could.

Notes

[1] For an extensive discussion of the many versions, see Karl Young, *The Drama of the Medieval Church*, 2 vols. (Oxford, 1933, repr. 1967).

[2] Processional antiphons should be selected according to date and geography. For sources see the article "Processional," in *The New Grove*, vol. 15, pp. 278-81.

[3] The most convenient source for this material is the *Liber Usualis*.

[4] Also available in the *Liber Usualis*, but often included in modern editions of Liturgical dramas.

[5] Facsimiles of the MS are included in Thomas P. Campbell and Clifford Davidson, eds., *The Fleury Playbook: Essays and Studies*, Early Drama, Art, and Music Monograph Series 7 (Kalamazoo, 1985); and Giampiero Tintori, ed., *Sacre Rappresentationi nel manoscritto 201 della Bibliothèque municipale de Orléans*, Instituta et Monumenta Serie I, Monumenta 2 (Cremona, 1958). The photos in both publications unfortunately present problems: those in Campbell and Davidson are greatly reduced in size, and the Tintori photos are out of focus. The Greenberg and Smoldon edition of the "Play of Herod" includes photos of both of those plays.

[6] For an easy guide to instruments, see Timothy J. McGee, *Medieval and Renaissance Music: A Performer's Guide* (Toronto, 1985), Ch. 5.

[7] For an extensive discussion of this subject see Christopher Page, *The Owl and the Nightingale: Musical Life and Ideas in France 1100-1300* (London, 1989).

[8] For models and information about the technique of instrumental elaboration of vocal music, see chapter 35.

[9] For details concerning medieval drama production, costumes, and props, see works by Bevington, Collins, Smoldon, Tydeman, and Karl Young in the bibliography.

19. Vernacular Drama
David N. Klausner

Vernacular drama, that is, drama written in the language of the country of its production rather than in Latin, survives infrequently from the early and high Middle Ages. It survives in profusion, however, from the late Middle Ages and early Renaissance. With few exceptions, music is an integral part of these plays, though the musical director for a medieval play faces a number of problems. Before looking at approaches to these problems, however, it will be useful to consider generally the use of music in medieval drama. In the first place, our knowledge concerning practically all aspects of music in early drama is limited in one way or another. Stage directions, ranging from brief to elaborate, may give us some idea of where music is expected; characters in the play may refer to music in ways which assume its performance. Such references indicate where in the play music would be performed, and may give sufficient information to establish what kind of music would be expected. That, usually, is all we have. Often lacking is any indication of what music is to be played or sung, and with what forces. Some basic principles will help to fill in the gaps. For the most part, music in early drama fulfills one of three functions. First, music is used to indicate a change of location or action, or in some way to guide the audience's attention. The entry of a character of social or political importance, for example, is frequently signaled by a fanfare for pipes (shawms) or trumpets. Second, music is often used structurally to bridge a gap between scenes, to assist movement, or to cover an anticipated delay in action. Thus ascents and descents to and from Heaven in the biblical plays and miracles are frequently accompanied by singing. Finally, music can be used for dramatic purposes as an integral part of the play, defining a particular character (such as Mary Magdalene's worldly songs in the continental Passion plays) or scene (such as dances and songs in the secular plays). A clear idea of the function of music in a particular situation is a prerequisite to defining the kind of music required.

Information on the appropriate musical forces for a play may be contained in the stage directions and speeches of the play itself; where this is not the case, it is worth investigating the documentary evidence available concerning the play and others of its time and place. Documentary evidence is becoming more and more readily available and, although it is not always easy to use, its importance cannot be overstated. Instrumental music for the plays was always provided by professional musicians (with the exception of school and university plays); since they were paid by the sponsor (civic, ecclesiastical, court, guild), regular accounts were kept of the payments. Sometimes these accounts give us invaluable information on performing media; at minimum, they may tell us how many musicians were normally used[1]

Voices and Instruments

Vernacular drama was never liturgical, so the usual restrictions on the use of instruments did not apply. This is quite likely to have been the case even with performances of plays in church, as seems to have happened quite frequently, though the range of instruments used may well have been more restricted in church performances. There is no question that instruments were widely used in plays—documentary evidence in payments to musicians makes that quite clear, but several distinctions will help to clarify the ways in which instruments were used. First, I will assume a familiarity with the history of instruments themselves, so that proper instruments are used in their proper periods and places. Thus it would be as inappropriate to use a crumhorn for a performance of Adam de la Halle's thirteenth-century *Jeu de Robin et Marion* as to use a sackbut or a curtal for a fifteenth-century play.

Some questions may be asked of the play at hand which will help to guide the director towards the kind of music appropriate and its mode of performance. Was the play performed by amateurs or professionals? If by amateurs, it is likely to be one of the guild plays of the late Middle Ages, many of which were biblical in subject matter, or else one of the school or university plays of the early sixteenth century. The guilds frequently relied on the professional musicians of the city to provide instrumental music, and it is possible in some cases to reconstruct in a general way what kinds of instruments were at their disposal. Most civic musicians in England and Germany were principally shawm players, though it is clear that they also played other wind instruments, especially recorders and flutes, and, later in the sixteenth century, sackbuts, cornetts, and curtals. School plays used the boys and masters not only as actors but also as musicians, and the musical resources were correspondingly limited. Private instruction in music for the amateur would have been principally given in lute, viol, and occasionally flute. Thus four of the actors in the English school play *Wyt and Science* also play the viol.[2]

If, like some of the moral interludes of the late fifteenth century, the play was in the repertoire of professional players, it is likely that members of the company (rarely more than six) would have doubled as musicians as well, thus clearly limiting the scope of the music available. Here the instruments associated with the individual minstrel (rather than the civic ensemble) would be suitable: rebec, vielle, lute, recorder and flute, bagpipe, pipe and tabor. Most professional actors of the Middle Ages could probably sing (and dance) as well.

A second method of determining appropriate music lies in an understanding of the symbolism which developed around many of the instruments. Some of it is fairly obvious, such as the common association of trumpets or shawms with royalty and power. Music associated with heaven is almost always vocal, usually in the form of chant. The secular world was generally signified by the minstrel instruments. Richard III's "lascivious pleasing of a lute" had a long history, and the lute was a frequent accompaniment to fleshly passion and lust. Some of Mary Magdalene's songs in the German passion plays specify the accompaniment of a lute. Rustic scenes and shepherds would suggest bagpipes or pipe and tabor.

Bagpipes were also sometimes associated with lechery.[3] Recorder, rebec, and vielle have more generalized worldly significance.

Vernacular Plays in the High Middle Ages

The earliest vernacular plays which have survived are closely related to liturgical drama, and the appropriate performance practice would likely follow liturgical norms fairly closely (see the chapter on Liturgical Drama). For example, in both the eleventh-century Latin-Provençal *Sponsus* play and the great Anglo-Norman *Mystère d'Adam*,[4] all the sung passages are derived from liturgical usage, and thus would be most appropriately sung by a group of singers without accompaniment. The *Sponsus* play, which sets forth the parable of the wise and foolish virgins, opens with five strophes of sung Latin, with no indication of who sings them. Their sense is liturgical rather than dramatic, interpreting the coming play rather than merely introducing it, so it would seem most appropriate for the verses to be sung by a choir rather than by a character in the play.[5]

Two plays from around 1200 present a major problem. Jean Bodel's *Jeu de Saint-Nicholas* is as different from the Fleury St. Nicholas plays as possible.[6] Bodel, a native of the prosperous northern French town of Arras, likely wrote the play for a patron's day celebration for one of the civic confraternities dedicated to St. Nicholas, like the *Confrérie des clercs de Saint-Nicholas*. These celebrations involved feasts with lavish food, drink, and entertainment, so the atmosphere is very far removed from liturgy. Bodel sets most of his play in and around the tavern; professional musicians would have been involved in the feast, but what they played remains a problem, for our sources for the period are very limited. Some of the more rhythmic trouvère songs could be used as instrumental pieces, but a better solution might be to use some of the monophonic *conductus*, some of which may well have begun their lives as popular songs.[7] Possible instruments would include rebec and vielle, recorder and flute, bagpipes, tabor and tambourine. Like many liturgical dramas, the play ends with a general *Te Deum* which would be sung without instruments (except for the possible inclusion of bells from the verse *Salvum fac populum*). The anonymous play *Courtois d'Arras*, from about the same period, is very similar. It deals with the duping of a country lad with pretensions to courtly grandeur, and again takes place largely in a tavern.[8]

Arras must have been an interesting place in the Middle Ages; not only did it give birth to Bodel's very secular St. Nicholas play and the rollicking *Courtois d'Arras*, it was the home of one of the greatest dramatists of the age, Adam de la Halle. It is easy to misread Adam's two plays, however, for both of them give the impression on the surface by being rare medieval examples of folk drama. Nothing could be further from the truth. Both plays, *Le Jeu de Robin et Marion* and *Le Jeu de la Feuillée*, are highly sophisticated recreations of an imagined folk drama. Dance-songs existed throughout the Middle Ages, and song traditions dealing with rustic situations (*bergeries* and *pastourelles*) were as common in the thirteenth century as they were in baroque opera. Adam adapts these traditions for a courtly audience. I think it is important that *Robin et Marion* was probably not written for an audience in Arras at all. About 1283, Adam moved to southern Italy in the entourage of Count Robert II of Artois, as a part of the occupying army. He spent the remainder of his life at the Norman courts in Sicily and Naples, and *Robin et Marion* was written for this situation. It is, I suspect, an idealized vision of the northern French home they have left behind, and its bucolic delights have just a hint of sadness in them, of being out of reach, or too pretty to endure. Adam was also a celebrated composer (the music to *Robin et Marion* is found in several editions), and the play is unique in the extraordinary amount of music it contains. Adam did not compose his own music, though, but adapted traditional dances and tunes from Arras which would have been immediately recognizable to his expatriate audience. Professional musicians would certainly have been a part of the court, and the palette of instruments might have included any suggested above for Bodel's play as well as plucked instruments like the lute (in its medieval form) or psaltery. It is important to keep a distinction between the instruments associated with the rustics Robin and his love Marion (bagpipe, pipe and tabor, perhaps a small recorder) and the courtly would-be seducer (a lute would indicate his lecherous nature, but his overbearing qualities might find best expression in a shawm). The final dance could well be played in heterophony, using many of the instruments of the play.

Adam's second play, *Le Jeu de la Feuillée*, is not set to music. It is an elaborate and extraordinarily complex satire on social life in Arras which "of all medieval plays... comes closest to putting the real life of its contemporary audience on stage."[9] There are some sung lines in the play, but they are likely to be unaccompanied. "Incidental" music, if used, would follow that of Bodel's St. Nicholas play, especially in Adam's final tavern scene, though the dances of Paris, Ms. BN f. fr. 844c, and Montpellier, Ms. Bibl. Fac. Méd. H196 are of about the right period.[10]

Music, especially instrumental/dance music, for the plays of the twelfth and thirteenth centuries is hampered by the small size of the surviving repertoire, with the result that many plays are produced with inappropriate music (thirteenth-century French dances used for twelfth-century plays, late fourteenth-century Italian dances used for anything and everything). There are often better solutions. I have already suggested that conductus, especially monophonic ones, often have the flavor of dance tunes, and in some cases may even be derived from them. Secular tenors of motets can sometimes be extracted from their two- or three-part settings, given appropriate rhythms, and used as instrumental or dance tunes.

The *Miracles de nostre dame*

A fascinating repertoire of forty miracle plays survives from fourteenth-century France. They are not done often, but good performing editions are now becoming available and the plays pose some interesting musical problems.[11] All the plays were written for the annual festivities of the Goldsmith's Guild of Paris and were produced between 1339 and 1382. Although the guild was very wealthy, the plays are not overly complex and the most elaborate piece of staging required is the descent of the Virgin Mary from heaven to perform the miracle around which the narrative revolves, and her return to heaven at the end. The descent and ascent are accompanied in all the plays by two *rondeaux*, sung by the archangels Gabriel and Michael. There are clear indications in some of the plays that the *rondeaux* are sung, and not spoken, and the situation would seem to imply two part polyphony. No music survives with the plays, unfortunately.

There are, however, quite a few two-part *rondeaux* from the period, and one of these can usually be adjusted to fit the texts of the play. Seven of Machaut's *rondeaux* are in two parts, but perhaps more appropriate are the three anonymous pieces in Modena Ms. Bibl. Estense Lat. 568.[12] Setting the texts to the music requires an understanding of the *rondeau* form. All the songs in the *miracles* are either of the 8-line or the 13-line variety. Each song has only two rhymes (which I'll call a and b). The eight (or thirteen) lines need to be set to two musical sections (I and II). In the simpler, 8-line form, the first line (A) is repeated three times (as lines 1, 4, and 7). The second line (B) is repeated twice (as lines 2 and 8). The other lines (a, a', and b) are not repeated. The scheme is:

music:	I	II	I	I	I	II	I	II
text:	A	B	a	A	a'	b	A	B

The 13-line form is a bit more complex, requiring a first musical section twice as long, since it must accommodate two lines of text:

music:	I	II	I	I	I	II	I	II
text:	AB	B	ab	AB	ab'	b	AB	B

Although two sung parts would likely be the preferred performance practice for these angelic songs, one voice and an instrument (vielle or portative organ would fit best) is also a possibility.[13]

Biblical Plays in England

The four great cycles of biblical plays were likely composed during the fifteenth century, though in some cases they only survive in later manuscripts. Two of the cycles (York and Chester) were performed (at least in part) regularly over a period of between 150 and 200 years.[14] Thus, the first question that must be answered is where the performance will be set chronologically (in the range of—at minimum—mid-fifteenth to mid-sixteenth centuries), since it is important that the music derive from a relatively limited period of time, rather than ranging over the whole century-and-a-half. Many of the plays have specific indications of music which cause little difficulty: angels regularly sing Gloria in excelsis Deo while the shepherds sleep, and appropriate chant is indicated for Mary's ascension as well as Christ's resurrection. Although in a few cases, like the York play of The Assumption of the Virgin, polyphonic music is provided in the manuscript, it is frequently the case that the text of the chant will be given without the music.[15] If the required chant is a part of the Ordinary of the Mass or the Proper of the Mass for the Advent season, the Sarum versions are easily available in recent editions in the Antico Church Music series.[16] Less common liturgical chants can often be tracked down through the Index of Gregorian Chant.[17] For polyphonic settings of some texts from the early part of the period, the Old Hall manuscript is often useful, and some pieces in the collection work well instrumentally.[18] It is best to avoid settings by internationally-known composers like Dunstaple, or (for the French repertoire) Du Fay; when polyphonic settings were used in the plays, they were likely locally composed and relatively simple, like the York play settings already mentioned. If a polyphonic setting is required, it is perhaps better to have a colleague or graduate student who is working in medieval music compose a simple setting in the style of the period. Instrumental music again depends very much on the period chosen for the performance. For the fifteenth century, relatively little instrumental music survives with the exception of a small number of pieces like the Quene Note in Bodleian Ms. Digby 167.[19] The large and well-known repertoire of carols can be played instrumentally, though there is no evidence that this was a common practice. A relatively small body of texted music survives which can also be played instrumentally, such as the songs in Ms. Cambridge University Library Ms. 5943.[20]

Trumpets are often indicated for the entrances of royalty, but we have almost no information on what they may have played, for fanfares were traditional and were passed on from guild member to guild member without being written down. There are a few hints; the tenors of Du Fay's *Gloria ad modum tubæ* may afford a glimpse of the form of a simple fanfare. What limited evidence we have would suggest that they used no more than two or three notes. The texts of the biblical plays provide a wealth of references to musical instruments, suggesting the range of possible usage: trumpets, bells, flutes, psaltery, harp, viol, organ, regals, pipes, whistle, and tabor. Some of these terms are ambiguous: "flute" could refer to both recorder and transverse flute, as well as three-hole tabor pipe; "pipe" could refer to almost any instrument of the fipple-flute or double-reed groups, although its principal meaning seems to have been "shawm."

Practicality will guide the choice of instruments in many cases, and these choices need to take into account the well-known distinction between *haut* and *bas* instruments. For worldly royal music, including entry music for Herod, the standard *alta capella* band of two shawms (soprano and alto) and slide trumpet would be the most common choice. The slide trumpet can be replaced by a second alto shawm or, at least by the early sixteenth century, by a sackbut. Music of heaven is almost always vocal, but when instrumental music is needed for divine or earthly ecclesiastical scenes, a portative organ would be best. If audibility is a problem with a portative organ, regals can be used since they are frequently mentioned in the same situations, and were still considered *bas* instruments despite their carrying power.

It is perhaps most important to remember that none of the play texts gives us all the information we want, and often does not give it in the way we expect. There is some good evidence that at least some of the musical directions in the play texts are not so much prescriptive "directions" for future productions, as descriptive records of what was done on a particular occasion.[21] Thus, unless there is a specific dramatic or narrative reason for it (like the Gloria of the angels in the shepherds' plays), a specified piece of vocal music, whether chant or polyphony, can be replaced by another whose text is also appropriate to the situation. Conversely, it is important to take the exact meaning of the text into consideration when choosing music and performers; when one of the Chester shepherds remarks of the angel that he "had a mych better voyce then I have" (Chester Play 7, l. 406), it is assumed that this contrast will be clearly noticeable when the shepherds themselves sing shortly afterwards. There are also likely to be places where music will be useful in particular productions where it is not indicated in the play-text, and the director should not feel uncomfortable about including music in places where it is dramatically appropriate. Although music is rarely specified for the devils in the Harrowing of Hell plays, there is some evidence that the appropriate accompaniment for them was the antithesis of harmony, that is cacophony, and that percussion as well as noisemakers would be seen as suitable devil-music.

The Coventry Shearmen and Taylors' Pageant presents a special problem. Two songs survive with the play, one for the shepherds and one—the well-known Coventry carol—for the mothers of the Holy Innocents.[22] The manuscript was copied by Robert Croo, who dated his work 14 March 1534; the three-part music was added to the manuscript by Thomas Mawdyke on 13 May 1591 (the precision in dating is very unusual). We have no clear evidence when between these two dates the songs were composed, though they are certainly of the type of music which could have been written around the earlier date. The settings are for ATB voices and while this causes no problem with the shepherds, merely indicating that they need to be a countertenor, tenor, and bass, directors have been slow to draw the obvious further conclusion that the mothers were also played by men, at least in sixteenth-century Coventry.[23]

I have not discussed the late medieval passion plays of France and Germany, because with very few exceptions they are very long and very large, and the likelihood of a modern performance is correspondingly small. In some cases they do, however, provide extensive information on the musical forces (and in a few cases, the music) that was expected. Easily the most interesting of these is the elaborate passion play from Lucerne, performed at least eighteen times between 1453 and 1616. A considerable amount of documentation survives concerning the performance of 1583, largely collected by the director, Renward Cysat.[24] It is in these continental plays that the common stage direction "silete" often appears. This direction appears originally to have been a sung text, "Silete"—"Keep silent," but it soon became a direction for optional music to cover a change of scene or a delay in the action. So in the Mons passion play of 1504 we find, "If he is too long, silete." Similarly, the Valenciennes passion play (1547) notes a "place to play silete," clearly indicating an instrumental piece. It is also in these continental passion plays that we find another tradition not found in the English plays, that of setting nonsense syllables to monophonic chant (newly composed) to represent Jewish liturgical music. The large boards on which this chant was written for performances of the Lucerne play still survive in the municipal library. There is not necessarily any sense of parody in this tradition; the Jews' chant from Lucerne is often very beautiful.

Morality Plays and Interludes

Some of the morality plays and interludes, which remained popular from the fifteenth century until quite late in the sixteenth, seem to have been the property of small professional companies, most of whom earned their livelihood by traveling. Lacking the municipal waits of the cycle plays, their music must have been for the most part restricted to the musical talents of the members of the company and (perhaps) an attendant instrumentalist. With few exceptions the musical requirements of these plays are very limited. Many of the morality plays and interludes have more elaborate musical requirements, though. One is Wyt and Science, already mentioned, which requires actors who can play the viol and sing. This is a school play, however, not a professional play, and is a good example of the importance of information concerning the original sponsorship of the play.[25] A second would be the monumental Castle of Perseverance which, because of its size could not possibly have been a professional play.[26] Castle has extensive musical requirements, though its stage directions are not very helpful on the subject. The size of acting area required to contain its five scaffolds and central castle would seem to indicate that something equivalent to the continental "silete" must have been used regularly to accompany movement about the stage. Castle dates from the first half of the fifteenth century, and the sources I have already mentioned for that period are useful in this case as well.[27] Wisdom (also known as Mind, Will, and Understanding) provides some interesting problems.[28] In addition to the five singers who accompany Anima, the play calls for three dances, each representing a perversion of one of the three powers of the soul which give the play its alternate title). Trumpets are specified for the dance of maintenance, bagpipes for the dance of perjury, and a hornpipe for the dance of lechery.[29] Unfortunately we have no sources for dance music from the time of the play, about 1460. Some vocal music can be used, such as the songs in Cambridge University Library Ms. 5943 mentioned above. Another possible solution would be to use Italian dances of the period, since Italian dances seem to have traveled quite far from their homeland (especially if the present location of manuscripts is at all relevant).[30]

Providing music for vernacular plays of the Middle Ages, whether secular or religious, requires as much understanding of the theatrical conventions of the period as possible coupled with a high degree of imagination. Perhaps the most important rule to remember is that transference between locations as well as between time periods is rarely justifiable. Performing conditions and musical traditions were different between Chester and York, not to mention between York and Paris; similarly what was played in 1450 may very well not be what was played (or sung) in 1500. Only where there is some clear evidence of related (or parallel) traditions can we use information from one place and time to illuminate another. This is not intended to discourage potential music directors for these plays; practical solutions to all the problems in these plays can be found, though many of them will be based more on imagination than on any clear surviving evidence.

Notes

[1] A useful survey of music in German passion plays is Ernst Schuler, *Die Musik der Osterfeiern, Osterspiele und Passionen des Mittelalters* (Kassel, 1951). The documentary evidence for England is being published in the series *Records of Early English Drama* (Toronto, 1977–) in which nineteen collections have so far appeared in seventeen volumes. The series covers all references to performers from the earliest records to the closing of the theaters in 1642. Much useful material can be found in Peter Meredith and John E. Tailby, *The Staging of Religious Drama in the Later Middle Ages: Texts and Documents in English Translation*, Early Drama, Art and Music Monograph Series 4 (Kalamazoo, 1982), esp. pp. 152-59 on music, and pp. 173-75 on dance.

[2] The most convenient edition of John Redford's *Wyt and Science* is in David Bevington, *Medieval Drama* (Boston, 1975), pp. 1029-61.

[3] See Chapter 28 below.

[4] d'A. S. Avalle, *Sponsus: Dramma delle Vergini Prudenti e delle Vergini Stolte* Documenti di Filologia IX (Milan and Naples, 1965). The text alone is given in Karl Young, *The Drama of the Medieval Church* (London, 1933), vol. 2, pp. 362- 64. *Le Mystère d'Adam* survives in a thirteenth-century manuscript, but was likely written somewhat earlier. It is also known as *Le Jeu d'Adam* or (as in the manuscript) *Ordo representacionis Ade. Le Mystère d'Adam*, ed. P. Aebischer (Paris: Minard, 1963). I have not taken into consideration here plays which are incomplete to the extent of being unperformable, like the Spanish *Auto de los Reyes Magos*, or the Anglo-Norman *Seinte Resureccion*.

[5] This suggestion has also been made by Richard Axton, *European Drama of the Early Middle Ages* (London, 1974), p. 102.

[6] *Le Jeu de Saint-Nicholas de Jehan Bodel*, ed. A. Henry (Geneva, 1981). The Fleury St. Nicholas plays are discussed in the chapter on Liturgical Drama.

[7] A good example is in W. T. Marrocco and N. Sandon, *Medieval Music* (London, 1977), p. 62, #13.

[8] *Courtois d'Arras*, ed. E. Faral (Paris, 1911).

[9] Axton, *European Drama*, p. 158.

[10] The surviving dance repertoire is collected in T. J. McGee, *Medieval Instrumental Dances* (Bloomington, 1989); the Paris dances are on pp. 57-70, the Montpellier dances on pp. 121-23.

[11] The standard edition of all forty plays is Gaston Paris and Ulysse Robert, *Les miracles de nostre dame par personnages*, 8 vols. Société des anciens textes français (Paris: Didot, 1876-93). A good modern edition of two of the plays is Nigel Wilkins, *Two Miracles: La Nonne qui laissa son abbaie, Saint Valentin* (Edinburgh, 1972).

[12] All three are edited by Willi Apel in *French Secular Music of the Late Fourteenth Century* (Cambridge MA, 1950), pp. 132-33.

[13] For a further discussion of the musical aspects of these plays, see Nigel Wilkins, "Music in the fourteenth-century *Miracles de Nostre Dame*," *Musica disciplina* 28 (1974), 39-75.

[14] The N-Town cycle has not been shown conclusively to derive from any particular city, while the fourth, the Towneley cycle, may well not have been intended for performance as a cycle at all. For much fuller discussions of music in the cycle plays, see Joanna Dutka, *Music in the English Mystery Plays*, Early Drama, Art, and Music,

Reference Series, 2 (Kalamazoo, 1980); Richard Rastall, "Music in the Cycle Plays" in *Contexts for Early English Drama*, Marianne Briscoe and John Coldewey, eds. (Bloomington, 1989), pp. 192-218; and in particular, Richard Rastall, *The Heaven Singing: Music in Early English Religious Drama* (Cambridge, Rochester, 1996). The standard editions of the cycles are: Richard Beadle, *The York Plays* (London, 1982); R. M Lumiansky and David Mills, *The Chester Mystery Cycle* 2 vols. (London, 1974, 1986); Martin Stevens and A. C. Cawley, eds., *The Towneley Plays,* 2 vols. (London, 1994); Stephen Spector, ed., *The N-Town Plays,* 2 vols. (London, 1991).

[15] The music for the York play is edited by Richard Rastall, *Six Songs from the York Mystery Play "The Assumption of the Virgin"* (Newton Abbott, 1985).

[16] *The Use of Salisbury: The Ordinary of the Mass*, ed. N. Sandon LCM1 (Newton Abbott, 1984); *The Use of Salisbury: The Proper of the Mass from Septuagesima to Palm Sunday* (Newton Abbott: Antico 1991); *The Use of Salisbury: The Masses and Ceremonies of Holy Week* (Newton Abbott, 1996). The Sarum (Salisbury) usage would certainly be appropriate for southern England; and the York usage which would be more appropriate for plays from the north can be found in *Missale ad usum insignis ecclesie Eboracensis,* ed. W. G. Henderson, Surtees Society vols. 59-60 (Durham, 1874); *Breviarium ad usum insignis ecclesie Eboracensis,* ed. S. W. Lawley, Surtees Society vols. 71, 75 (Durham, 1879, 1883), and *Manuale et processionale ad usum insignis ecclesie Eboracensis,* ed. W. G. Henderson, Surtees Society vol. 63 (Durham, 1875).

[17] John R. Bryden and David G. Hughes, *An Index of Gregorian Chant* 2 vols. (Cambridge MA, 1969).

[18] *The Old Hall Manuscript,* ed. Andrew Hughes and Margaret Bent, Corpus mensurabilis musicae 46 (Rome, 1969).

[19] A convenient edition is Brian Trowell, *Invitation to Medieval Music,* vol. 3 (London, 1976), pp. 31-32.

[20] These have all been published in excellent performing editions by Richard Rastall, *Four French Songs from an English Song Book* (Newton Abbott, 1976); with Ann-Marie Seaman, *Six Fifteenth-Century English Songs* (Newton Abbott, 1979); *Four Songs in Latin from an English Song Book* (Newton Abbott, 1979); with Ann-Marie Seaman, *Four Fifteenth-Century Religious Songs* (Newton Abbott, 1979).

[21] See, in particular, Peter Meredith, "John Clerke's Hand in the York Register," *Leeds Studies in English,* n.s. 12 (1981), pp. 245-271, and David Mills, "The Stage Directions in the Manuscripts of the Chester Cycle," *Medieval English Theatre* 3/1 (1981), 45-51.

[22] The manuscript of the play was destroyed in a fire in the Birmingham Free Library in 1879; our only source now is the edition published by Thomas Sharp in 1825. See *Two Coventry Corpus Christi Plays,* ed. Hardin Craig (London, 1957).

[23] For an extensive discussion of these two carols and their performance, see Richard Rastall, *The Heaven Singing,* sections 2.6 and 3.4.

[24] Much of Cysat's information is included in M. Blakemore Evans, *The Passion Play of Lucerne: An Historical and Critical Introduction* (New York, 1943). Other well-documented passion plays were performed at Bourges, Mons, and Valenciennes.

[25] For English plays, information on the auspices under which a play was originally performed can be found in Alfred Harbage, *Annals of English Drama, 975-1700: An Analytical Record of All Plays, Extant or Lost,* second ed. rev. by S. Schoenbaum (London, 1964).

[26] The most convenient edition is in Bevington, *Medieval Drama,* pp. 796-900.

[27] The songs in British Library Ms. Egerton 3307 are also useful for this period. See Gwyn McPeek, *The British Museum Manuscript Egerton 3307: The Music Except for the Carols* (London, 1963).

[28] The best edition is Mark Eccles, *The Macro Plays* (London, 1969), pp. 113-52.

[29] We don't know precisely what a hornpipe is, but I suspect it is a bone flute or recorder, like the fourteenth-century one excavated at Keynsham, Somerset, in 1964. Several makers have made working replicas of this instrument. A small recorder makes a good substitute. It might also be a pibcorn, a single-reed instrument with horn pieces at each end, though this does not seem to have been very widely distributed.

[30] Early Italian dances were collected by Ingrid Brainard in *The Art of Courtly Dancing in the Early Renaissance*, 1st preliminary ed. (West Newton, MA: by the author, 1981). Two of the major treatises on dancing have been printed with translations: Fabritio Caroso, *Nobilità di dame*, ed. Julia Sutton (Oxford, 1986), and Guglielmo Ebreo da Pesaro, *On the Practice or Art of Dancing*, ed. Barbara Sparti (Oxford, 1993). Several English dances ca.1500 have been found in a manuscript in the Derbyshire County Record Office and have been published with a facsimile of the manuscript by David Fallows, "The Gresley Dance Collection, c. 1500," *Research Chronicle of the Royal Musical Association* 29 (1996), 1-20.

V. The Voice

20. Poetics as Technique

Barbara Thornton[†] & Lawrence Rosenwald

BT:

I'd like to start by saying something about the title I've given this interview, since it's probably not the title most readers would expect for an interview with a musician. But it is the right title here, since Sequentia's mode of music-making is not only radically different from "common practice" because the pieces of its repertoire are found in manuscripts with notations dating from up to one thousand years ago, but also because a fundamentally different world view is implied in the music of the Middle Ages. What immediately comes to mind is the name the Middle Ages gave to a musical creator: In the twelfth century one equivalent name for "composer" was *trobador*, a word whose root is *trobar* in Old Occitan (the language of medieval Occitania, now in South-western France, related to Catalan) and was chosen to describe the well-documented, master poet-musicians who are credited with founding vernacular "art song" in our culture.

This word can be variously translated as "finder," "searcher," "inventor," and is closely related to the medieval idea of "creativity" as such. In view of the fact that medieval musics were, in all performance aspects, oral traditions, we often look more to authoritative sources (treatises) which deal with performance-oriented "sciences" for guide-lines to our research than we do to contemporary treatises on music. (In the Early and High Middle Ages music treatises often concerned themselves with highly theoretical and abstract ideas rather than actual, sounding music.) Disciplines which one could call the performance-oriented sciences were rhetoric (Dante: "Rhetoric is the science guiding the embodiment of a poetic idea") and its corollary, memorization. Those sciences in addition to music which drew on the tenets of rhetoric were poetry, oration, preaching, theater, all forms of entertainment, and all literary activities. Much more than we can imagine in our era, all "literate" forms of culture were essentially vocal, and only for documentary purposes carried out in the written mode. In light of what we read about disciplining the mind and spirit through rhetoric and memorization, we learn that our idea of creativity is considered a function of the soul, and that its virtue is in its "image-forming" energy (*virtus custoditiva, virtus memorialis*). A creative soul has much of this energy, and busies itself with feeding on images (what we would call listening and interiorizing, in other words, memorization) so as to be able to learn to produce images that others may consume. (This process is not so very different from learning to sing classical Indian music or the way musicians learned jazz earlier in this century.)

The measure of the effectiveness of image-energy is memory. Simply put, if one can invariably remember a certain image (a poem, an oration, a sermon, a riff, a song, etc.), that image, and the person who retained it, are both possessed of sufficient creative energy to keep themselves alive. The more such living ideas one is able to store in one's "inner library" (*Bibliothek*, or *Apothek*, or *cellula, cubicula, thalamus*), the more material is available for contemplation, augmentation, and eventually, the construction of new, unheard-of images within one's own soul. (These matters are discussed in Aristotle's *De Anima*, and Augustine's *De Musica*, which, paradoxically, deals with texts, and are admirably related to the discipline of memorization in Mary Carruthers' book, *The Book of Memory*.[1])

In this context we can see why poetics (in the medieval definition: the musical arrangement of words), and music (the harmonious arrangement of proportions of movement) are to be considered the stones with which a singer or player can build up the edifice of a performance. The trobador, in his very title, had an even more dynamic function than being the architect of a composition: he was a pathfinder. He worked out in the open imagination and charted with each song a new and infallible system, a heuristic system, intended to stimulate the inner and outer senses into an actual experience of word and tone. (In Latin tradition *inventio* refers to retrievable schemes for reconstituting an experience, a sensation, or image: "heuristic trails into the space of memory"—Mary Carruthers.) Our claims for nineteenth-century art song may actually be the same, but the poetics of the two repertoires are very different.

This rather complex way of approaching the repertoire is meant to clear the air right away of simplistic attitudes towards our earliest, most "primitive" repertoires. A session at the piano for the melody, and a little bit of "text-work" (usually no more than reference to a poor translation), is not going to suffice for comprehension and communication.

LR: You say, "our claims for nineteenth-century art song may actually be the same." Could you elaborate on that a bit? I mean, students studying that repertory in a conservatory don't usually think about how Goethe composed poems or how Schubert composed the setting of them.

BT: True, but people in Schumann's and Schubert's time were thinking about poetry. An evening of Schubert's music could just as easily be described as an evening of Goethe's poetry in some cases. Schubert's musicales were, by him and his friends, not considered concerts of classical music—they were evenings of contemporary music. They were fun, pleasure, stimulation, being part of a "scene." Music, when it's real, is always part of a "scene" which entails more than just musical pitches and having a career. If we don't see historical repertoires in this way, we ask the wrong questions, just as if we didn't belong in the scene. Without the life which goes along with music in our imaginings, our approaches seem sterile and beside-the-point.

LR: Got it. So then, since you've established why you begin where you do, can you talk more about how that works?

BT: It works through the grammar of music, the grammar of text—these are the building blocks of poetics and rhetoric. These are the concerns of the practising musician because they are the basic techniques for building up images within one's self and sending them off in performance to impregnate others.

When we look at the cadres of society where "official" music was created (music which reached manuscript form), we invariably see that developed intellectual traditions existed simultaneously with musical ones. The roots of poetry and music were the same in such circles, and reached far back into Antiquity. Most of the wisdom of tradition had been preserved in verse form (this is true of all ancient cultures). As I said, in the eyes of the ancient and medieval thinkers poetics and music deal in proportions intended to stimulate the soul in various ways—the study of the laws which govern these relationships was considered a most precious heritage. (Augustine, *De Musica*: *Musica bene modulandi scientia*, music is the science of measuring motion; to do this well, bringing into harmonious proportions. "It is easier to discern in words whatever numbers prevail in all motion of things.") This meant that verse composition, whether deadly serious or frivolous, was an essential cultural expression, not a sentimental entertainment as art song has become in some instances. The way in which each era uses verse—measured speech, measured song—can indicate fundamental things about its contemporary character, especially when seen in the context of its past. Let us say a tenth- or eleventh-century monastic poet writes some pieces in the spirit of Virgil or Sappho (as we can still witness in the thirteenth-century collection known as *Carmina Burana*); he has, first and foremost, created something contemporary, but in his homage to an "immortal" from ancient times, he has passed his model's aura along to the next generation as well. How do we know he was drawing on Virgil? How do we know what he invented himself? We know Virgil's works by heart—we know his meters, his vocabulary. We know in a flash if our tenth-century poet is using a meter in earnest or in jest. And the music was simultaneously always contemporary, yet always drew from the ancient pool of modal associations. This is how a musico-poetic "scene" was built up over the centuries. We have to feel part of that scene in order to perform the music; otherwise we miss the point of most compositions. (See examples 20.1 and 20.2.)

Ex. 20.1. *Levis exsurgit Zephirus*. Anon. Cambridge Song Book.
Germany (tenth century), ed. George Whicher,[2] tr. George Whicher and Barbara Thornton.

Levis exsurgit Zephirus	Lightly rises the Westwind,
et sol procedit tepidus;	the sun warms up;
jam terra sinus aperit,	Now the earth bares herself
dulcore suo diffluit.	and meltingly offers up her sweets.
Ver purpuratum exiit,	Spring comes forth in purple,
ornatus suos induit;	adorned in rich robes,
aspergit terram floribus,	scatters flowers about the land,
ligna silvarum frondibus.	the leaves of the wood multiply.
Struunt lustra quadrupedes	Each beast digs his den anew,
et dulces nidos volucres;	each sweet bird builds his nest;
inter ligna florentia	among the trees of the wood
sua decantant gaudia.	echoes the cries of joy.

Quod oculis dum video
et auribus dum audio,
heu, pro tantis gaudiis
tantis inflor suspiriis.

All this passes before my eyes
and with my ears I seem to hear;
Alas, the more they rejoice,
the more I am given over to sighs.

Cum mihi sola sedeo
et hec revolvens palleo
sic forte caput sublevo,
nec audio nec video.

When I sit musing alone,
my cheeks grow pale;
If I suddenly raise my head,
I hear nothing, see nothing.

Tu saltim, Veris gratia,
exaudi et considera
frondes, flores et gramina;
nam mea languet anima.

You, quickening grace of Spring,
hear me and nurture those
leaves, flowers, and seeds:
as for me, I languish in my soul.

Ex. 20.2. *Chanson do.il mot*. **Arnaut Daniel** (twelfth century), text edited by Pierre Bec, translated by Pierre Bec and Barbara Thornton.

Chanson do.il mot son plan e prim
farai puois que botono.ill vim,
e l'aussor cim
son de color
de mainta flor,
e verdeia la fuoilla,
e.il chan e.il braill
son a l'ombraill
dels auzels per la broilla.

I will make a song of words plain and prime
because the twigs are now in bud,
and the highest tops
are coloring
with countless blossoms,
and the leaves are turning green,
and the songs and cries of birds
in the shadows
are heard throughout the grove!

Pelz bruoills aug lo chan e.l refrim
e, per so que no.m fassa crim,
obre e lim
motz de valor
ab art d'Amor,
don non al cor q.em, tuoilla;
que si be.is faill,
la sec a traill,
on plus vas mi s'orguoilla.

Throughout the grove I hear their song & refrain;
and, so that no one can reproach me,
I labor and file away
at precious words
with the artistry of Love, (from which
I haven't the heart to ever extract myself;)
For if Love should ever fail me
I will still follow her trail,
even if she prove more prideful than I am!

Petit val orguoills d'amador
que leu trabucha son seignor
del luoc aussor
jus el terraill
per tal trebaill
que de joi lo despuoilla;
dreitz es lagrim

Pride in a lover is of little value
for it easily topples its lord
from the highest place
down to the earth below with such sufferings
as to strip him of all his joy;
It serves him right
if he weeps,

et arda e rim	burns, and cracks
qi'n contra Amor janguoilla	who complains against Love!
Ges per janglor no.m vir aillor,	It is not that I turn, complaining, away from
bona dompna, ves cui ador;	you, my Lady, whom I adore,
mas per paor	but , in fear of being discovered (by others)
del devinaill,	so that I tremble with joy,
don jois trassaill,	I give no outward sign of my desire;
fatz semblan qe no.us vuoilla;	Never did we have our joy
c'anc no.ns gauzim	from that which they (others, slanderers)
de lor noirim;	had to offer —
mal m'es que lor acuoilla.	It would be difficult to welcome them now!
Si be.m vau per tot a es[t] daill,	So if it seems that I welcome you "inside-out,"
mos pessamens lai vos assaill;	my thoughts are assailing you THERE!
q'ieu chant e vaill	For I sing and I am strong
pel joi qe.ns fim	by the joy which we felt,
lai on partim;	THERE where we parted:
mout sovens l'uoills mi muoilla	and so my eyes often grow moist
d'ira e deplor	with the suffering, and the tears,
e de doussor,	and the tenderness,
car per joi ai qe.m duoilla.	for I have such joy from my sorrow!
Er ai fam d'amor, don badaill,	In truth, I have no sorrow from a love which makes
e non sec mesura ni taill:	me groan this way, and I follow no measure or meter—
sois m'o egaill!	I wish to be rewarded in kind! —
C'anc non auzim	knowing that it has never been told,
del temps Caym	since the time of Cain,
amador meins acuoilla	of a lover less possessed
cor trichador	of a treacherous
ni bauzador;	or deceptive heart;
per que mos jois capduoilla!	And so my joy is consummate!
Bella, qui qe.is destuoilla,	My Beauty, whoever else may turn aside,
Arnautz dreich cor	Arnaut runs straight ahead,
lai o.us honor,	THERE, to honor you,
car vostre pretz capduoilla!	for your valor is consummate!

LR: That's very helpful, but I'd like to press you a bit more, because it's hard to take what you say emphatically enough. Ordinarily, that is, when we start to think of text and music, we start by thinking of them as separated and then we think, either a musician comes along who reads some text and does something to that, or the reverse; and our habits of thought make music and text separable, and it's hard to change the language enough to make them inseparable. So I was wondering whether you could elaborate your point in relation to a particular example.

BT: Well, let's consider the invention of the form known as the sequence.

According to legend, these syllabic songs with wholly original texts were created using the pitches of the *jubilus* (untexted final melisma of an Alleluia chant) sometime between the seventh and ninth centuries. An entirely new poetic form (characterized by a very un-Gregorian structure AA BB CC etc.) was superimposed upon the old and beloved chant formulae (which carry not only deep musical, but also deep verbal associations). The performer-listener hears the new message projected upon the old music principally through the new proportions of the new poem. This creates not only a new meter, but a new arrangement of the pitches he knows as a chant as well as his own body. One can imagine, then, what an intense experience it would have been to hear sing such a composition for the first time, and how much room for "*ruminatio*" (ruminating: inner chewing of text and music) would also be yielded with time. With such a close relationship between "audience" and creator, aspects of technique gain enormous significance. There is significance in the number of syllables per poetic line, how the lines combine to make a strophe, and how strophes march along in time to command attention and memory. A performance cannot communicate these essential things in a composition if it is ignorant of them, or, more importantly, itself unmoved by them. The creator shows the way into the space of the piece, the living interpreter must make the journey. In its day, all this was achieved without notation. Having never or rarely seen a text or notes written in separate form, the medieval musician was never obliged to think of them as two separate things. (See Example 20.3.)

Ex. 20.3. *Planctus Cigni* (ninth century), ed. Paul Klopsch, tr. Paul Klopsch and Barbara Thornton.

1	Clangam, filii, ploratione una	Let resound, my sons, a lamentation
2 a	Alitis cygni, qui transfretavit aequora.	of a winged swan who journeyed across the open sea;
2 b	O quam amare lamentabatur arida	O how bitterly he lamented the firm
3 a	Se dereliquisse florigera et petisse alta maria;	flowering ground he left behind in order to fly across the high ocean:
3 b	Aiens: 'Infelix sum avicula, heu mihi, quid agam misera.	He cried out, "Unhappy bird that I am! Woe to me, what shall I do in my misery?
4 a	Pennis soluta Inniti lucida non potero hic in stilla	My feathers are not mighty enough to bring me towards the light in this dampness!
4 b	Undis quatior, procellis hinc inde nunc allidor exsulata.	And battered I am by storms; thrown here and there, exiled.

5 a	Angor inter arta gurgitum cacumina. Gemens alatizo intuens mortifera, non conscendens supera.	Pressed down towards the foaming crests of waves, winging I sigh, my eye turned towards the death-bringer;
5 b	Cernens copiosa piscium legumina Non queo in denso gurgitum assumere alimenta optima.	I see copious schools of fish — I am not in such denseness able to take this excellent nourishment.
6 a	Ortus, occasus plagae poli, administrate lucida sidera.	O Rising (East) and Falling (West), heavenly poles! — send the guidance of your bright stars!
6 b	Sufflagitate Oriona, effugitantes nubes occiduas.'	Call upon Orion to clear away the clouds of the West!"
7 a	Dum haec cogitarem tacita, venit rutila adminicula aurora.	As silently he thought these words, the redness of dawn came to help;
7 b	Oppitulata afflamine coepit virium recuperare fortia.	Held up by a breeze he began to regain his force.
8 a	Ovatizans iam agebatur inter alta et consueta nubium sidera.	Exalted he was borne between the sea and the trusted Milky Way,
8 b	Hilarata ac iucundata nimis facta penetrabatur marium flumina.	Now made joyful and delighted he dived into the floods of the sea.
9 a	Dulcimode cantitans volitavit ad amoena arida.	Singing in sweet tones he flew to beloved land.
9b	Concurrite omnia alitum et conclamate agmina:	Come all you multitudes of birds and raise your voices together:
10	'Regi magno sit gloria.'	"Glory be to the great King!"

LR: As I hear you say this I'm beginning to see why you teach the way you do.[3] A lot of your teaching works on what happens before the music starts, and you don't exactly make it easy for people to get to the stage of performing.

BT: Yes, we try to teach in a manner fitting to oral tradition. At the same time we admit to and compensate for the fact that we aren't actually able to limit ourselves to such transmitted knowledge. Naturally, compared to a music tradition which sets a premium on sight-reading, our way of working seems very indirect. The goal of working in the oral manner, however, is not just to get the music learned—far from it. It is intended to stimulate the imagination. A singer who sings without the imagination in gear, in our repertoires at least, is not giving of him or herself, is not communicating. As I am trying to make clear, within oral tradition, imagination is THE medium for knowledge. The process of turning knowledge into wisdom is tradition, *ruminatio*, practice (a medieval attitude, of course). It is generally acknowledged that ultimately this is a very mysterious process and needs lots of time. This is something present-day people don't have in abundance.

LR: Look, there's a question I want to ask you about this, though it's a bit off the topic, and that is, how did you ever manage to develop this way of working? At some point you were a kid doing nineteenth-century music like everyone else, and now you, unlike practically everybody else in the universe, are doing what you do. What happened?

BT: That's a good question, but not easy to answer. Relative to our way of trying to communicate these repertoires to the public have been the processes of developing a common musical language with our colleagues performing with us. These communal experiences, most analogous to the original contexts for these musics, have been crucial in effecting my own transformation from a standard-repertoire singer to a medieval one. It should also be said that my long-standing partnership with Benjamin Bagby is the single most important element in the process. The transition has taken a lot of effort and led me into many blind alleys. Human interaction always brought me back to something worthwhile. For myself, it involved trying to build up a different emotionalism (we will discuss this later) in something of a vacuum. There were many points at which I had to confront old musicianly assumptions—even finding out they were there at all was often the main problem. The willingness on the part of my friends and associates to experiment and try things out that couldn't be proven created a handful of theoretical and practical certainties that I could build on. Take this idea that there is a music of poetry: it was a long time before I could rely on a true belief based on my own experience that such a thing can be dealt with technically and communicated to others. There were some important turning points which indicated to me that such things really do exist.

LR: When you say "[your] own experience," do you mean particular moments when the idea of the "music of poetry" got embodied?

BT: Yes, hearing certain singers, certain actors; hearing people respond to certain experiments. Think of a written play as a score—what do actors rehearse? Not syllables, but emotions. The actor trains emotions and unleashes them in performance. What is the matrix for the focusing of his whole person? The written words. He does not need notation to tell him how to work his magic upon the text, he needs to train his focus.

LR: And in a way, when you make singers work just from text with neumes, you're placing them precisely in an actor's position.

BT: Absolutely. I want them to have the same freedom as actors by giving them the right kind of matrix. Monophonic song should be as much of an improvisation upon a given text as an actor's. Would you be interested in attending the performances of an actor who gave his soliloquy in the same way every night? You know that the same series of words is going to be spoken, but what is going to happen with them? What is the experience of the words going to be?

LR: I'd like to take what you've said so far as a general account of "interiorizing" medieval music, to use the word you like, and to proceed to a more particular question, namely, what does it mean to interiorize the medieval music of particular nations, of particular national image-patterns and what you call national "humors"?

BT: There are perhaps a couple of concrete ideas to hang on to when thinking about national images or "humors," and, of course to be true to tradition, a good deal of subjectivity, as well. In our repertoires linguistic grammar determines a lot. It, too, was in Antiquity and the Middle Ages considered a discipline of the soul capable of creating motion within the soul, and its training led to an even greater mastery: that of rhetoric. When we speak of singing as being potentially as vital and communicative textually as an actor's speech, we are touching upon the potencies of rhetoric. The Christian Saint Augustine was a professional classically trained rhetorician before he converted and became an important Christian writer. From such figures, and from treatises on the subject, we learn that rhetorical training was rigorous, and the responsibilities great of those who had this as a profession, be they secular potentates or churchmen.

Briefly stated, rhetoricians exercized the art of moving and persuading their listeners. Like modern advertisers, they were slick, and effective, and left nothing to chance. In the High Middle Ages a revival of interest in the powers (as opposed to the theories) of rhetoric took place, and we find in monophonic songs of the time many earmarks of the rhetorician's craft. These powers are reflected in the music as well as in the poems.

If we accept this premise, then we come a step closer to understanding the technical intentions of creators within various traditions. It leads also to the idea that every language has, by virtue of its grammatical make-up, and sonorous properties, not to mention its collective undertow, its own unmistakable rhetoric. Poet-musicians are expected to gain influence upon the souls of listeners through *motio*: vibrations, perceivable to soul, of a strong enough sort to be stored in memory. If each language can be said to have its own natural rhetoric effect, then it must generate its own images as well. Its humors are perhaps its sensualities—how percussive, how wet or dry or run-on or accented or pitched it may be. Building up images instead of clichés, we can slowly start to assemble a feeling for language's deep undercurrents. All these elements need to be conscious to a performer. The consummate rhetorician knows in his body the feel of all these elements, and he conjures them up within himself according to the scheme he has invented in advance of actually delivering them. Only in this way can he be certain of his effect.

It's important to note, by the way, that this approach can be applied to instrumental interpreters as well—knowing in advance what one's rhetorical effect must be, and clarifying to one's self what the units of expression are going to feel like in mind and body.

It has recently been said that medieval music and its texts live in a state of indifference towards one another. Why, goes the argument, can a German text be superimposed upon a French melody with impunity (as was often done in the early years of Minnesang tradition, for example)?

Ex. 20.4a. *Under der Linden*, **by Walther von der Vogelweide** (twelfth century), tr. Barbara Thornton.

Under der linden	Under the lime tree
an der heide,	on the open field,
dâ unser zweier bette was,	where we two had our bed,
dâ mugt ir vinden	you still can see
schône beide	lovely broken
gebrochen bluomen unde gras.	flowers and grass.
vor dem walde in einem tal,	On the edge of the woods in a vale,
tandaradei,	tandaradei,
schône sanc diu nahtegal.	sweetly sang the nightingale.
Ich kam gegangen	I came walking
zuo der ouwe:	to the meadow,
dô was min friedel komen ê.	my love already was there.
dâ wart ich enpfangen,	And he received me,
hêre frouwe,	Blessed Lady,
daz ich bin sælic jemer mê.	the joy of that will last.
kust er mich? wol tûsentstunt:	Did he kiss me then? A thousand times, at least,
tandaradei,	tandaradei,
seht wie rôt mir ist der munt.	look now, how my mouth is red.
Dô hât er gemachet	Then he made
alsô rîche	a lordly
von bluomen eine bettestat,	place to lie in, all of flowers,
des wirt noch gelachet	There's a good laugh there
inneclîche,	even now
kumt jemen an daz selbe pfat.	for anyone coming that way:
bî den rôsen er wol mac,	he could tell, by the roses,
tandaradei,	tandaradei,
merken wâ mirz houbet lac.	just where my head lay.

Daz er bî mir læge,	If anyone found out,
wessez iemen,	God forbid, he lay by me,
nu enwelle got, sô schamt ich mich.	I'd be ashamed.
wes er mit mir pflæge,	What he did with me there
niemer niemen	may no one ever
bevinde daz, wan er unde ich,	know, except for him and me
und ein kleinez vogellîn,	and one little bird,
tandaradei,	tandaradei,
daz mac wol getriuwe sîn.	which will not say a vord.

Ex. 20.4b. *Contrafactum* in the *Minnesang* tradition of *Under der Linden*
(Walther) / *En mai au douz tens* (Anonymous French).

This was unquestionably a common practice, but no one should for a moment
think that these two versions imply the same rhetorical (not to say emotional) event!
To me, this practice does not indicate indifference of text to music, but rather the
liberality of the art which respects the separate identity of each element, expecting the
two to combine with new results every time. The elements are infinitely flexible but,
within themselves, always obey their own rules: the grammar of music, the grammar
of text. Without awareness of the intended effects of each of the elements, the new
whole created of the parts cannot be appreciated in its very specific identity.

LR: Could you talk more about that? It's not that what you've said is unclear, but I
know from my own experience that in trying to differentiate the genius of one
language from the genius of another it's really, really hard to see and to experience
where that genius is located.

BT: To experience what you are talking about I think that singers must make a
whole-hearted commitment to the language they are singing. By this I don't mean one

absolutely must to run off to Spain for 15 years in order to sing in Spanish; rather it means that much time should be devoted to coaxing the feel of language to come deeply into sensual consciousness and memory. Part of the singerly gift is doing just that, so language-enjoyment must surely be a pre-requisite to singing of all types and periods. The process of making a language one's own can be brought a step further when the singer becomes the poet, for all practical purposes. The very act of inventing the ideas, grammatical units and sentences of a sung language can become second nature within the context of a given song. This is what we mean by the song being a path: the singer's imagination is the leader along that path, and the path issues out of the feeling of the language in the singer's own mouth. Before one's own mouth has embraced the ideas, nothing of communicative value can come out of it.[4]

LR: This phrase "the singer's own mouth" is very evocative; it implies that what a singer knows with is the mouth rather than the mind, but also that it's the singer's own mouth and no one else's.

BT: Naturally, it is helpful to have actually lived life in another language than one's own to build up identification with another's reality. Learning language, like learning music, is an exercize in oral transmission in belief, only it encompasses every aspect of life. Outside of real human contacts and identifications there are perhaps some difficult and esoteric ways to move the psyche into something new. In any case, the psyche of the singer must confront the psyche, or genius, of language.

LR: So, to put coarsely what you've put elegantly, you have to confront not just the discrete characteristics of a language—its sounds, say, as defined by the International Phonetic Alphabet—but also its inner life, what you're calling its "genius."

BT: Brute superimposition of mere characteristics of language upon the sensitive tissue of a medieval melody renders something grotesque. Clearly experiencing the underlying currents of language enables us to experience the deep music and to instinctively give a melody its appropriate force of line. There are singers with uncanny abilities to hear and render such linguistic music. Some have it to a pronounced degree for certain languages, and not for others. Perhaps one should always start to work on this process where the affinities are strongest. Some have a dramatic gift, a lyric gift, and so forth, and the strength of these gifts should be also used in service of the genius of language. The mesh created between text and music in the medieval world is so fine that it needs to be kept alive with active imagining at all times. That is what we mean when we say the singer is not only re-constructing the piece, but re-composing it as he goes along. He is so active in this process that his own poetic soul moves the performance, his poetic core has met the poetic core of the work. It is for this reason that a) there is "scanty" indication of performance mode in medieval notation (a notation I would certainly challenge in the transmission of some monophonic repertoires), and b) one comes to a satisfying result in some repertoires only after a process that resembles that of originally composing it. This is very challenging, ultimately, and very rewarding.

Instrumentalists in this tradition are quite literally in the position of composers, in that, if there is some pride in their art, they are going to want to learn the styles of these repertoires so thoroughly as to be able to create their own pieces. As a contributor to a sung composition, an instrumentalist functions literally as a poet—scrupulously weighing each contribution against the overall effect, searching for *le mot juste* for each situation, waiting in heightened anticipation to be ambushed by inspiration. Poetic technique only makes sense to the poetic soul— otherwise it is only technique—numbers, syllable counts, repetitions, rhymes, games, tricks. The poetic soul knows how to unite the myriad levels of detail by feeling through them.

LR: If I'm following you rightly, one of the things you mean by "the poetic soul" is an agency that puts all the details in place. You want the singer to be immersed in all the detail—the detail of technique, the detail of language, everything—and then you need something we might call a poet to say, "this is how to make choices in this world of detail, this is what is important and unimportant, this is the poem within the poem." But could you say a little more about the relation between the poetic soul and the singer's other faculties?

BT: In a sense the musical field is characterized by the idea of discipline. One feels in an undifferentiated way that the Middle Ages exude an aura of stability through discipline, yet there is a great deal of high spirits and freedom involved as well. To reach a fine focus for performance there is some delicate balance (exemplified in the music itself), which between observing basic rules and engaging in intense flights of imagination makes it possible to reach the depths and heights within ourselves as described in the works we sing. This is very different from trying to build something up within yourself based on secondary information. Even the tradition of writing about these matters in the original times was couched in language appropriate to the speculative disciplines, not to our practical needs. This is why we go to treatises on rhetoric and memory for our needs.

LR: Could we return for a while to the question of how, practically, the singer is to work? I mean, let's say a singer comes to you and says, "Barbara, please, I want to sing this piece, tell me what I have to do?"

BT: I usually say, "don't ask me that."

LR: But the singer persists, and you feel some obligation, and so...

BT: I guess the very first step towards practical work is recitation, and I think recitation is most effective in a group situation: the reciter is forced to become more communicative, the listener is encouraged to be critical, and if there is successful communication, the reciter can sense it right away. I am trying again to emphasize that more personal, communal contexts need to be created for working on medieval music because all written media are inadequate. One can always try to set up "oral transmission" for one's self: study groups, music ensembles, book clubs which deal with medieval poetry, informal collections of like-minded medieval nerds. There are many levels of analysis (via what we have been calling poetic technique), which should be made sensible to the ear first, that can and should be carried out without aid of pen or pencil within a group.

After technique comes rhetoric—this too can be practiced in a group. If there is doubt as to the tone of a work, one can exercise one's actorly skills and try various approaches. It is painful to note how many deadly earnest present-day performances are visited upon what are actually ironically clever, light pieces. So, it is important to know exactly what tone is implied in a piece through thorough acquaintance with it. One should also have a clear image of which public (even an imaginary one) the author had in mind, and play to that public. Let's say, hypothetically, that a piece was created for performance at a high-ranking cleric's sumptuous residence after an important feast, ca.1200. Is this hard to imagine? What would the modern equivalent be— performing, as we once did as students, for a private banquet attended by the executives of the pharmaceuticals industry? All these aids to the intellect, imagination, and senses are more reliable than starting with a preconceived idea of what the music is going to sound like. "Music in the Middle Ages sounded nasal," we were told many years ago. It must be obvious now why such statements represent the height of absurdity.

To really become one with a piece, memorize it. Wouldn't one memorize a Schubert song? A Rossini aria? The evidence pointing to the necessity of memorization in many of these repertoires is overwhelming. This is the best way to follow its path, interiorize its techniques, and to free the voice from cares.

LR: So it's through this route, and not by some short-cut, that the singer can come into relation with "national humors and images."

BT: It usually takes one successful experience with this way of working to initiate a long process. Eventually, this builds up to the feeling that one can actively participate in the tradition. Once one has sensed how a form or a specific technique has truly determined performance choices, working by comparison can begin. Let us take an example from the Parisian Notre Dame School, early thirteenth century. In the same manuscript in Florence where many large polyphonic works are to be found, there exists a fascicle of single-voice pieces: they are long, and constructed in many sections. Their structures are sometimes unclear. Several of them are laments (Lat. *planctus*), but even this concept is enlarged to include political, personal, cosmological subjects. The Latin is both simple and obscure. The modalities are impossible to catalogue, and they sometimes make no sense as what we would call melodies. Their logic is seemingly totally divorced from the logic of the strophes. After a great deal of study and experimentation, the reasons for all the disharmony among the elements become clear: this is a collection of highly rhetorical laments in greatly elevated style (whose every oratorical flourish can be cited in pseudo-Cicero or Geoffrey de Vinsauf) and it stands outside of every other type of song known to us. It represents a tradition in and of itself.

Ex. 20.5a. *Jerusalem, Jerusalem,* ed. and tr. by Gordon A. Anderson.

I.
Iherusalem, Iherusalem,	Jerusalem, Jerusalem,
Que occidis et lapidas,	Who kills and stones (the prophets),
Quamdiu gentes perfidas	How often hast thou suckled
Lactabis, mater libera?	A treacherous people, 0 mother free?
Contra promissum littere	Against the promise of the Law
Regnat heres adultere,	The heir of an adulteress rules;
Ridet Agar adultera	The adulteress Agar laughs
Legis in improperium,	At the reproach of the Law,
Quia risus fidelium	Because the smile of the faithful
In luctum mundo vertitur,	Is turned into grief on earth,
Dum lapsu gravi labitur	When by a heavy fall falls
Henricus, heres libere.	Henry, heir of a free woman.

II.
O pessima	O most wretched
Conditio mortalium,	Condition of men,
Dum lacrimantur filium!	When they mourn their son!
Nondum repente lacrima	But Death, not yet satiated,
Resolvit nos uberrima	In sudden grief turns us again
Mors in meroris flumina,	Into the waters of sorrow,
In lapsum matris labimur.	And we are overwhelmed in the mother's fall.
Ad Mariam convertimur,	We turn to Mary,
Stellam de qua tot lumina	The star from whom so many lights
Nostris scintillant seculis,	Have illuminated our age,
Quod virtutum carbunculis	For powerless, we leave
Obtusi nos excedimus,	These jewels of virtues,
Et pio planctu plangimus,	And with holy dirge give vent to grief,
O gratiosa domina.	O gracious mistress.

III.
Mira loquar: cecidit	Allow me to speak of wonders:
Sol in oriente,	The sun fell in the East,
Casus solem concidit	And its falling made the sun sink
In hoc occidente,	In this Western world,
Illa lampas Campanie,	She the lamp of Campania,
Mater Maria gratie,	Maria the mother of grace,
In qua tot luminaria	In whom so many luminaries,
Noctis et umbre nescia,	Not knowing darkness or shadow,
Tot stelle laudis luxerant,	In whom so many stars of praise shine,
Quod oculi mortalium	Because the eyes of mortals
Tante virtutis radium	Had not seen in widowhood
In vidua non viderant.	The ray of such virtue.

IV.
Quid est homo quod iactitas	What is man; Why make yourself prominent,
Et quibus mundo militas?	And for what do you strive in this world?
Forma, genus, divitie	Form, race, riches,
Valent ad epitaphium;	All go well for an epitaph!
Corpus, quod nutris hodie,	That body which today you nourish,
Cras fiet cibus vermium.	Tomorrow will be food for worms.
Ecce, nostra conditio!	Behold, our condition!
Vide, ne vacet dextera,	See that your right hand be not empty,
Quia decurso stadio	Because when the course is run
Mortem sequuntur opera.	Your works go on after death.

Ex. 20.5b. *Jerusalem, Jerusalem* (opening) (Florence, Plut. 29.1, fol. 434r).[5]

Ex. 20.5c. *Jerusalem, Jerusalem* (opening) diplomatic version by Sequentia.

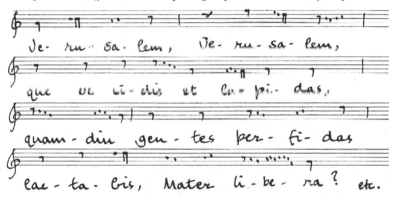

Ex. 20.5d. *Jerusalem, Jerusalem*
neumed version by Sequentia.

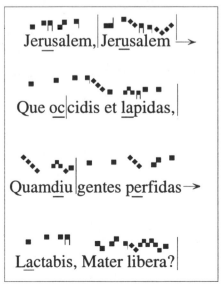

Upon realizing this, all further experiments are undertaken within a closed system. We gather impressions, techniques, colors which will all serve to further the specific artistic aims of this single body of works. Within the repertoire we establish poles: the longest piece, the weightiest piece, the finest images, the most beautiful mode, our favorite piece, the piece we don't understand at all. Within the manuscript tradition we set up poles: this is the most rhetorical repertoire; which is the most measured?

Ex. 20.6. *Verbum patris humanatur* (Cambridge, Univ. Lib. MS Ff.I 17., fol. 7), ed. Benjamin Bagby, tr. Barbara Thornton.

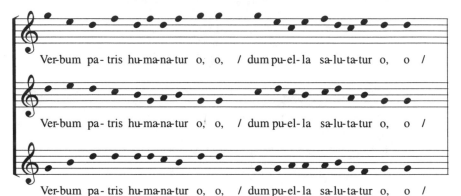

* ms: g'

1. Verbum patris humanatur o, o,
   dum puella salutatur o, o
   Salutata fecundatur,
   viri nescia.
   Eya, Eya, nova gaudia.
2. Novus modus geniture, o, o
   et excedens vim nature o, o
   dum unitur creature
   creans omnia. Eya...
   etc....

The word of the father is made flesh, Oh, Oh!
when the news is brought to the maiden...
Saluted, made fruitful,
not knowing a man...
Eya! Eya! New joy is ours!
A miraculous birth...
beyond the power of nature...
when creator and created are
united in one person...
etc....

There is great skill demonstrated in all areas of Notre Dame composition—what is the skill demanded of a short line, of a long weighty line? Who would have performed the *planctus?* Who the *rondelli?* What are the skills involved in writing *conductus* which, like some amphibious animals, one minute behave like measured poetry, the next have entered pure contemplation in the form of extended melismas on a single vowel? How unlike the monophonic *planctus* they are in searching for a broad palette of modal coloring through polyphony. Or are perhaps the *planctus* trying to do just that through monophonic means? Would all of these dimensions and nuances be available to us if we started with the assumption that Parisian music of the thirteenth century had this or that fixed association, rhythmic system, sound, or characteristic?

Let us say that we have some experience with these Notre Dame repertoires behind us, and are now confronted with songs from the Jena Lieder Manuscript, a large collection of German song from the late thirteenth and fourteenth centuries. Same century—same artistic goals? It might take a while, but eventually we would establish that the Jena Lieder Manuscript contains very little real love poetry. In fact, to understand the texts, one needs quite a bit of Biblical knowledge. There was a great deal of Biblical erudition in the Parisian *planctus* as well—are the repertoires similar? In some senses, yes; in some important senses, no. A courtly song written in the vernacular in the thirteenth century has a fundamentally different rhetoric than a Latin song springing from a clerical milieu in that time. Yet both repertoires rely heavily on a vocalist's rhetorical art and on the Bible. Seen against the backdrop of a repertoire we have already investigated, the "national" characteristics of German song start to emerge—humor, sharpness and audacity of images; adoption of many points of view, many personae; fearless directness. So how would our direct, clever, theologically sophisticated German professional musician influence and harangue his public! Yes, I said professional musician—he lives off his song (we are told this over and over again). His psychological relationship to his audience is going to be quite different from that of the sheltered cleric. We feel that difference in psyche in everything about the *Spruchdichter* (wandering moralist poets), including their "modernity"—lively poems, clear structures which vary widely from poem to poem, ingenious story-telling...so ingenious, you want to throw your money at the man—and that is just what he had in mind! Are there not modern musics with all these typically German characteristics which might be inspiration to listen to? With a specific agenda in mind relative to specifics of repertoire, one is no longer just engaging in superficial imitation if one uses a modern style as an aural guide to something unfamiliar. In all cases of exploration and comparison, allowing the process to take its time is important because jumping to conclusions is usually a direct result of our simple ignorance.

LR: I see what you mean, I think. I sometimes tell my students that there are two approaches to understanding America: through the abstract concept of democracy and through the concrete skills necessary to maneuver in traffic and not get killed. In your case, the general character of national poetry and music is much harder to grapple with than are the things you're talking about—you're asking people to think about how person X in country Y would make a speech to get money or votes, and with that kind of specificity the whole task is contracted, made manageable—and it's also part of what I take it is important to you, part of a relation between one human being and another.

BT: This comment of yours makes me think of how intense and rewarding teaching these repertoires is, and how very unorthodox. The more I involve myself with this music, the more I treasure the performer's role, the performer's world. I want to be a performer, not an authority—these are two separate identities in the medieval world. The authority (*auctoritas*) writes from the highest viewpoint with the aim of establishing steadfast truths and principles. Though I have mentioned often that we look to practical treatises for practical guidelines, the musical treatises of the period provide the underlying philosophical ground for everything we do, and we move entirely within that context, acknowledging it freely. This is the function of *auctoritas*: to remain in contact with the "higher spheres," as exemplified by Pythagoras, Aristotle, Plato, Augustine, Boethius, Cassiodorus, etc. As a performer, I wish to embody the philosophies of the art naturally, almost unconsciously; other than that, I am a collection of techniques, observations, and experiences. In a teaching capacity I think of myself as a transmitter: I pass on the material in human, not written form. I supposedly thereby stimulate the imagination (mine included). With what? With the poet's images and the musician's music; only to the extent that my imaginings help the original material are my personal images of any importance. Principally, the goal is to reach and "empower" the independent imagination of the other person. Once it is operative, the hunt for the poet's path and the life of his images is shared equally. There is definitely competition involved—who comes back with the most valuable prize, the richest and most powerful idea? High standards benefit everybody. Were I to stand in front of a group of people and expound to them on German, French, or Latin style, I would first of all lose my own inner flexibility which allows me to reopen such questions every day. Secondly, our hunt would become mere killing. We would find ourselves surrounded by a pile of carcasses and skins—trophies to our intellects carrying little value to anyone else.

LR: So there are two reasons, really, for not laying down the law for your students. One is that it just doesn't work; the other is that it's at odds with what you call your own "inner flexibility."

BT: I cannot take away a student's own hunt for meaning in the material, nor can I create it. Nor should I put myself in a position, by playing *auctoritas*, of depleting my own imaginal energies. Look to the poems themselves, and learn to feel, feel, feel through modes—you will find the elated, disappointed, consummated, frustrated traces of other people looking for "poetic truth." You will find the best possible company for your quest. These are the tracks and traces to follow. I try to teach how to see the tracks, how to hunt with them.

LR: We're coming close to a question I'd meant to ask you, about the role of emotions in this process, and I'd like to put the question in an extreme way. It seems to me there are two common ideas about emotions in performance, neither of which I take it you have. One idea imagines the singer saying, "well, what this poem says is that I am a man in love," and proceeding on that basis to assimilate or interiorize that emotion. We might call this the Stanislavsky method of doing troubadour song. The other idea you can see in the work of those who generally treat medieval song as a formal construct, with emotion absent or secondary. As I said, clearly you don't subscribe to either of these ideas; but where between them would you position yourself?

BT: Once more to the issue of establishing principles: Whenever one confronts *auctoritas*, one should be made aware of what gods, or what world order are being served by the pronouncements set forth. In the past, authoritative writers themselves made this abundantly clear—in fact it was their avowed purpose to uphold a Divine World Order with their "sciences." Nowadays, what is being upheld is a personal view of what "scientific truth"—another aspect of the nineteenth century ripe for a fundamental overhaul—must be. In lieu of a universal there reigns a personal world order in most present-day tracts, and it is strenuously being upheld at all times,—but it is obscure because it is not scientific to acknowledge that one is actually serving something else, and therefore never stated outright. It is there, nonetheless, and has to be ferreted out. Until one divines which individual forces are being maintained by a given writer's view, our view of the Middle Ages will be in service of those same, unclarified forces. What are the gods which inspire an author to the reductionist attitude that 1000 years of verse composition has no more elevated contribution to make than a collection of numerical constructs? (Perhaps I first encountered this manner of literary criticism in the works of James Hillman; sometimes it can be mis-applied, as well.)[6] Isn't it more likely that these constructs are contributions to a much greater whole? Wouldn't it be more helpful for us to have help in understanding the greater whole so we could appreciate the roles of the various parts clearly and have them organized in our minds?

Both the first and second approaches you mention impose a middleman between the work of art and the performer. In both cases, the performer is saved the wear-and-tear of truly identifying himself with what he is doing. This vacuum is then heralded as "emotionally exciting" in the first case, and "scientific," or "pure," or "accurate" in the second.

In support of my plea for real emotions in medieval song, it might please the reader to read the poems I have included here:

Hildegard von Bingen (twelfth century); from *O splendissima gemma*, tr. Barbara Thornton.

O resplendent gem,
and unclouded beauty of the sun
which was poured into you,
a fountain springing from the Father's heart which is His only Word,
through which He created the prime substance of the world
which Eva greatly troubled.
For you the Father fashioned this Word as mankind, and therefore you are that
luminous matter through which this selfsame Word breathed forth all Virtues,
just as in the prime substance he brought forth all creatures.

Bernart de Ventadorn (twelfth century); the second strophe of the song *La dousa votz ai auzida*, tr. Barbara Thornton.

Indeed, a man has a vile life
if his dwelling is not in joy;
likewise is he who does not direct
his heart and desires towards Love,
since all that exists abandons itself
towards joy, sounds and sings with it:
meadows and hedgerows and orchards,
heathlands, plains, and forests!

Heinrich von Meissen (fourteenth century), called "Frauenlob" (*In Praise of Woman*); from Chapter 12 of *Frauenleich*, sung by "The Woman"; tr. R. Rossbacher and Barbara Thornton.

I am a richly-rooted meadow;
My blossoms are all pregnant;
Their shimmering liquid redolent with scent carries a bright yellow color!
Ai! Such a swift-flowing stream drenches my blossoms so that they, as desired, might
        burst forth as the wheat in its season;
Thus we are nourished in God's mysteries. I threshed, I milled, I baked tender bread,
        not hard when I spread it all with oil—
thus it remains sweetly soft.
I am the throne which the Godhead never fled since he slipped inside of me.
My plow plows utterly straight!
I, God; She, God; He, God—I forget no one; I, the Father-Mother, He was, truly, my
        Mother-Father— and this is true,
I was born, I suffered, broke Death, exerted myself as was expected;
I went, I came, I, Adelheid, Eagle of Virtue. He did not suffer, my Engelmar.

These poems, the melodies of Bernart de Ventadorn, Hildegard von Bingen, Frauenlob's *Leich*—are these really intended to be sung with emotional distance?

In every one of these cases, there are immensely clever number constructs in play, but they serve the emotions; and the emotions, in their turn, serve larger concepts, as well. Robert Edwards, speaking of such matters in his book, *Ratio and Invention*, makes the following statement: "Intelligible structures locate meaning in larger relations."[7] Medieval cosmology is set up to allow infinite relations, infinite emotions. What is the emotionalism which informs this music? There is, first and foremost, nothing limited about it. There are no contemporary emotions which have to be left out. There is no reason to sing more softly, play more dully, or feel less stimulated. The emotionalism of medieval music is grounded in the medieval world-view, however, which in some respects, but certainly not all, differs from ours. One thing which might be revealing is to look at some of the people who created the music of the long, "learned" tradition; many of them would have carried different titles than "musician" in their day. Some were very influential churchmen, philosophers, bishops, cardinals, abbots and abbesses, theologians, master teachers, diplomats, cantors; lettered people brilliant in Latin or in the vernacular (men and women). Some were politically prominent, landed aristocrats; some were in charge of powerful institutions such as libraries, monasteries, cathedrals; some were disaffected, idealistic intellectuals. There were emperors, kings, counts, as well as the sons of bakers, musicians, petty nobles. (The daughters tended to be of high birth.)

What they had in common was their education (Bible, classics, commentaries, liturgy, fables, stories, "literature," liberal arts), and their unquestioning participation in a cosmos known, and proven throughout the centuries, to operate according to stable metaphysical laws. Even the most hard-bitten intellectual in this era saw his intellect as a function of soul, within the context of World-Soul. The intellect had a very high function, it is true—it was there to receive and distribute Divine Light, as insight, enlightenment. It was through the assiduous disciplining of all these soul-functions I have been talking about that a medieval intellectual might come to the masterful stage of being able to create new texts and music. Within such a universal, human manner of educating the mind, mastery of the whole spectrum of human experience could be expected. These are very high claims for medieval emotionalism, but they are based on the high estimation of the human soul in the Middle Ages. The soul was, of course, also thought to be a dark and unknowable thing, subject to gross passions. Whereas the medieval creator may have had a view of the cosmos which presupposes a harmonic collaboration among its parts, he was as well-acquainted with the dissonances, both inner and outer, as we are today. Clashes which occur between one's ideals and reality were just as infuriating to medieval people as they are to us; death, birth, struggle, infirmity, human love and divine love concerned them passionately. The kind of process-oriented work on medieval repertoires I am advocating actually teaches, with time, what it feels like to live within such an intact world-view, which was, after all, the stated intention of many of these works in the first place. They were intended to communicate universal harmonies then, and they still do now!

There are times, of course, when one experiences something like a break-down in trying to get to the correct emotionalism for a piece: one's modernism, or post-modernism, just doesn't seem up to the job. But then it can happen that one's "innate medievalism" (belief in the world-view?) rises up from within one to save the day.

LR: For example?

BT: I suppose a good example would be my original confrontation with the music of Hildegard von Bingen. In those days, I was not very well equipped to understand her art. I tried to break into her world through many doors, but they remained shut to me for a long time. I took the time to sing, recite, look at her miniatures, read her works, but nothing helped me to feel her music. I perpetrated several analytical operations upon her modes and melodies—to no avail. I finally began a process which was so arduous and tedious that it is no wonder I had tried everything else first: I compiled a lexicon of her words in their musical settings—in E-mode all of the 3rd person singular verbs, all the proper nouns, all the gerundive phrases, etc. Likewise for D-mode, C-mode, etc. (I was probably influenced in this by a sinologist friend, Rudolf Ritsema, in his work with ancient Chinese texts.) I divided them into groups corresponding to the way she had divided up the cosmos: Heavenly, Infernal, Earthly, etc. Areas which had special interest for me—the natural world, the feminine world—seemed to have had special interest for her, for she took particular care in her tone-settings of words of these genres. I discovered there was a "place" within this cosmos for every idea, and that every modal gesture contributed to this gigantic matrix of meaning and tone. One merely had to know where to locate one's self at any given moment. If a rhetorical event is cast in the Heavenly, Earthly, or Infernal, one must be aware of its manner and usage; if a mode is being used in conjunction with or in conflict with its own nature, this knowledge will affect one's thinking and performance. As in modal improvisation, the use of every pitch can be brought into conscious relationship with every other and still sound spontaneous. A certain style of thinking goes along with the setting of priorities. You see, one cannot "play" the medieval person who feels all these—one must feel it one's self.

I learned to think in dynamic spatial arrangements, in colors, in simultaneous dimensions (writings on memorization are rife with words referring to memory as a space.) I grew to the realization that the notational system used for her music is not inadequate at all, but rather is ideally suited to communicating the plasticity of the music and language as she conceived them. Most surprising of all, having learned to think in spatial, simultaneous relationships I was freed from my judgmental and rigid attitude towards her spirituality. Using this kind of imagination not only opened her world to me, but the worlds of other creators from medieval and ancient times which had been too daunting to me beforehand. Since then, I feel that I need not so much to be armed with knowledge as to be initiated into techniques for making my way into the various spheres of meaning, especially if they are initially puzzling to me.[8]

LR: In this particular case, then, the way in was by way of what elsewhere in this conversation you've been calling technique, by way of analytically figuring out how the thing was put together. You came to the work, it seemed repellent—that's a stronger word than you used, I know—and rather than turn away from it you said, "how is this constructed?"

BT: Yes, analysis can be a very powerful tool, as long as we make it part of a creative, not a reductionist, process. If I discover a technique which reveals things about one piece, it will not necessarily work for another piece, even from the same time or place or author. With every experience I increase the hoard in my bag of tricks (other medieval images for memory: hoard, bag) in case I need to apply them again.

LR: A question just occurred to me: would you say that the singer coming to medieval music has to learn new emotions?

BT: Based on the experiences I had with Hildegard's music, I would say that I did learn to feel new things, and to feel comfortable in a new universe. What I "knew" previously about this universe did not prepare me for the myriad and differentiated feelings that were available. I didn't remotely understand living imagination—the energy which gives texts and music real power. Each new image, or each new guise an image receives, is like learning a new emotion. One may even have very conflicting emotions about a single image. In contrast to our polarizing way of regarding things, a negative feeling can be stored peaceably alongside of a positive one in the memory vault without their disturbing one another. Images and memories can accumulate in this way to enrich emotional experience, not blot it out altogether just because it is negative in its nature.

LR: There's a sort of counterpoint in this conversation—counterpoint in a musical sense, obviously—between matters apparently pertaining to technique and matters apparently pertaining to feeling, and I wondered whether I could ask you to talk a bit more about one matter pertaining to technique, namely notation. You talked before about the really remarkable powers of Hildegard's notation, and I noticed this morning how central that notation is to you when you teach Hildegard's music. I also noticed you prepare your own editions, if that's the right word, of her music, and that does set you apart from other people dealing with this repertory—to your advantage, I think.

BT: I am grateful for the training I had in medieval notation—it is one of those "grammars" one needs when putting together the big picture. It is another insight into the conditions surrounding the creation of a piece, and, more importantly, into the specific creature the piece is intended to be. It is important to know, in all notational systems, which aspects of the actual aural experience have been included and which have been left out. It is valuable not to take a confrontational attitude toward the notation of a piece— better to say, "This notation is for me, it speaks to me. What does it say?" One tries to be rigorous in observing what is specifically said through notational means, but, again, they indicate only one of several levels of composition to be taken into consideration. (It is sometimes extremely hard for present-day musicians to accept that fact—that the notation he sees before him is not the prime commander.) We have learned to think in these notations, if need be. We use them to express our musical ideas, independent of known manuscripts. We treasure all the small signals they provide us, and which might be overlooked by others, as they are usually left out of even the most up-to-date transcriptions.

Hildegard von Bingen's notation (NOT invented by her), is one which retains a number of "neumatic" shapes, and therefore contains a certain amount of interpretative information (relative length of syllable, of line movement, ornamental aspects). As in neumatically notated Gregorian chant, we are aware that the notator works very carefully at this level. By utilizing the signs skillfully, the whole sense or oratorical thrust of a line of text can be made evident—even in its theological point of view. One of our mentors in these matters, the semiologist Godehard Joppich (whose work with Gregorian Chant can be heard on Archiv records) once said to us, "I learned more theology from neumes than from ten years of seminary in Rome!"

If we are in a position to say, "This is our music," about medieval repertoires, we are also saying, "This is our notation," which is true. There is no substitute for our notation. We learned to think about the music through these notations (in lieu of having masters)—how should we now think of alternatives?

Pl. 20.1. Hildegard, *O Splendissima gemma* (Dendermonde, St. Peters & Paulusabdij MS Cod. 9, fol. 154r).[9]

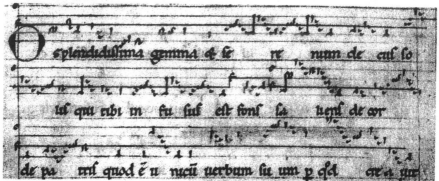

LR: If I'm understanding you rightly, you're not saying that working from original notation is a better way of doing something that working from transcription would be a worse way of doing. You're saying that notation is not a better way of doing something; it is the thing that one is doing.

BT: Yes, and this brings us to the issue of authenticity. I feel it is very unauthentic to perform with the point of view which says, "I am now going to perform someone else's music from long, long ago, not my music." As an audience member I would want to say something like, "Well go home and find out what your music is and then come back." The biggest "aha! sensation" of my entire medieval endeavor was to realize that it was just as hard to gain mastery of medieval tradition for a medieval person as it is for me. (It is just as hard to gain mastery of Baroque or Classical or Romantic tradition, for that matter.) The building blocks in medieval tradition are known and available. They are stable principles which won't go away. If you want to train yourself in them, you can create medieval music. If you practice the rules of discantus, you can improvise authentic medieval polyphony. If you interiorize medieval modes in your heart and soul, you can create recitations. You can consider yourself vulnerable at any time to be criticized on the grounds of taste and degree, which presumably spurs you to refine yourself further, but you would have no reason to doubt your authenticity. Most criticisms of medieval music start rather unreasonably way back at square one by setting the whole enterprise into question, or polarizing discussion around utterly secondary considerations.

LR: There's a question I've often wanted to ask you that I think is related to this, namely, why do you always perform all the text of a sung poem? I've tried to think whether anyone else ever performs the whole of a sequence, or a trouvère song, or a middle English homily, and I can't come up with many examples; but I know you always do, and I know it's a point of principle, and I see that point of principle as related to the point of principle about notation.

BT: Would you go to a film that stopped in the middle? The feature film—that is a form in our culture that we have interiorized perfectly. We are willing to sit beyond three hours watching a film, as long as we get to see the end. Our expectations run between 1 1/2–3 hours—anything radically different from that disturbs us. Barring extreme antipathy to a film, no normal person walks out until he has experienced its full form. No normal member of a troubadour circle would be satisfied with the performance of a troubadour song until he had heard all of its seven strophes. These seven strophes had all the clues, blind alleys, suspense, and clever endings of a modern detective story. Naturally, if the performer is moving along the surface of this experience, is not aware of the decorations, details, tones and intensities of color, or of his rights to certain freedoms within the structure, the audience is going to have an experience of seven strophes which discredits the archaic form itself (if it is unaware that interest is lacking in the performer, not in the form).

About that word "archaic," by the way—the most archaic "form" I can think of is actually the most rigorous and the freest at one and the same time, and that would be the long winter's night filled with epic recitation. The twelfth-century troubadours developed a canon for canso of seven strophes. Whereas the trouvères used all kinds of strophe lengths, composers of the thirteenth and fourteenth centuries started experimenting with miniature forms. The late medieval Sequences are often longer than the original ninth-century variety. Somehow I think formal experiments have to do with deep levels of perception (as Plato said about geometry being the most instinctive way to recognize the principle of form), not with attention-span.

LR: That reminds me of a wonderful point that Milman Parry makes. He's writing about Homer as oral poetry, and in the course of his argument he notes that among the living singers of oral poetry he's worked with the worst thing you can say about a singer is that he's shortened the song. You don't get reproached for having lengthened it. [10]

BT: Oral literature or musical poetry was surely to the medieval person what film is to us, or books were to generations previous to ours. The best thing about the oral way is that it is much more participatory for the audience, and much more dangerous for the performer. It's strange, really. Medieval strophic songs can be really baffling, and some particularly insensitive remarks have been made about them by some scholars. Yet in living memory in the British Isles and in the southern United States, or in Brittany and France, some of the most breath-taking singing of syllabic or melismatic strophic song could still be heard. The interplay between the "rigidity" of literal repetition of a melody, and all the variations and adaptations which must take place for the progression of ideas and sound to take place, make it a most subtle poetic art.

Entering into the form of a piece is a little like knowing whose house you are in. You can see how each room is decorated, what color predominates, how much space there is, how many objects there are, what feeling you get; you stay in each room for a while, then you leave it and go to the next and start all over again.

LR: Stanza in Italian means "room," right?

BT: Yes, yes!

A strophe is called, by Dante (and by us), a stanza, and stanza means "room." When one creates a strophe by virtue of its syllable count, and number of lines, and weight and rhythm of those lines, and the quality (heavy-set, light-weight, masculine, feminine, noble, inane) of the rhymes, one has, in effect, decorated that room in specific shades, with specific objects set here and there, with a certain balance of light and shade. This should make it clear what a challenge and indescribable pleasure it is to be made responsible for the complete decoration plan for seven consecutive rooms that must be so aesthetically and vividly appointed as to implant memories and emotions into anyone who comes into them through song.

LR: That's beautifully said, I think. It makes me think that when people hear this music without understanding the forms, they do not know that they are missing something—they are not aware of what they are *not* doing.

BT: If language has psyche or genius, then surely form does as well, coming from that world which Plato says is so profoundly recognizable to soul. Once again, the performer's psyche and the very specific psychological experience implied by a form have to come into contact with one another. In this way he is able to "occupy" the space he intends to create it around his listeners as he is performing. Think of a very "archaic" form, the Sequence : AA BB CC DD, etc. What architecture corresponds to such a form, which knows no developments as such, no build-up, no let-down? To me it evokes a medieval cloister—walking endlessly around a medieval cloister with columns and sculptures at the capitals; stopping to examine each one at one's leisure. This one shows Daniel in the lions' den, the next one shows Christ appearing to Mary Magdalene in the garden. Why are they shown in succession? Are they related? There will be many opportunities to regard everything in detail, to see everything in relation, in proportion if the piece is well-interiorized—no need to be in a hurry and decide upon an interpretation.

The sequence in its earliest manifestation presented a highly concentrated art which, at the same time, communicated this blessed sense of contemplative leisure (extolled in monasteries as *otiosa*). With time it proved to be a very flexible and durable form, indeed: as courtly entertainments (twelfth-century French and Latin *lais*); vehicle for long laments or long visionary journeys (Peter Abelard's *Plancti*, extended pieces in Notre Dame and Las Huelgas Codices, etc.); Bible stories (Lay of the New and Old Testament, thirteenth-century France); as the basis for a full-fledged instrumental tradition (thirteenth-century French *notae*); and as elaborate late-medieval German mystical tapestries of music and meaning (the *Leichs* of Frauenlob, Wilde Alexander, Regenbogen, etc.). Just as the Roman temples were based on the Greek, and the Paleo-Christians took up these sites for their first basilicas, and the Carolingians and twelfth-century builders took the remains to erect their magnificent churches and monasteries, and the Gothic architects made pointed arches out of the Romanesque round, so the venerable, old psychological spaces of form were forever undergoing renovation.

Perhaps it is now clear why a five-strophe song presents a fundamentally different experience from a seven-strophe one; why a line of eleven syllables is so distinct from a jaunty, five-syllable line. In the fourteenth century the composer's freedom to invent a new form for every piece was abandoned in favor of the *formes fixes: rondeau, virelai, ballade.* This put the onus of invention into other areas for ambitious poet-musicians. A new sense of concentrated rhythm went together with a new type of measured music.

LR: And knowing such things, hearers will be aware of certain things; and not knowing such things, they won't be.

BT: And they never will be aware if performers decide that the true experience should be edited out or pre-digested.

My initial commitment to early music in general had to do with not settling for an experience in music that was not intended. The pioneering virtuosi of historical music-making demonstrated a lot of courage in their day, insisting on the use of gut strings, uncommon tunings, smaller ensembles, etc. to serve what they perceived as unmutable artistic intentions of their repertoires. Every musician in every era of music-making has had to battle the trends of fashion. You know how the cliché goes—those with the courage to be out of fashion are also the ones able to see ahead a bit, to prepare listeners' imaginations for more demanding experiences. Perhaps it is also very authentic to be moving in and out of favor all the time.

And it is not right to reduce certain repertoires of the twelfth century which love rich imagery and long-winded rhapsodic styles to the scale of certain thirteenth-century pieces which love miniature and intense confusion. There may be room for taking medieval repertoires into the realms of modern sensibilities—it is done all the time, but usually not stated openly and passed off as something medieval. Such a juxtaposition seems very vague and unsatisfying to me. I am interested in finding and acknowledging the "innate medieval-ness" (which might ultimately gain another name entirely) in myself and others, and I'm not put off if it takes a lot of time and effort.

We, as performers, cannot ultimately know or judge what our portion of the whole experience really is. As performers, we are not looking for judgments anyway. We are pushing, generally, for more participation and less distancing in all aspects of music-making.

Notes

[1] Mary Carruthers, *The Book of Memory* (Cambridge, 1990).

[2] George Whicher, ed. and tr., *The Goliard Poets: Medieval Latin Songs and Satires* (Cambridge MA, 1949), pp. 26-27.

[3] LR: This interview was conducted in Vermont, at a workshop Barbara was giving on Hildegard von Bingen; I'd spent the morning and afternoon watching the workshop, and the interview followed directly on the afternoon session.

[4] LR: In a note to me, Barbara wrote "this sounds very biblical, sorry." I agree that it sounds very biblical, but I don't think there's anything to be sorry about.

[5] Facsimile from *Firenze, Biblioteca Mediceo-Laurenziana, Pluteo 29,1,* 2 vols., ed. Luther Dittmer (Brooklyn: Institute of Medieval Music, ca.1967). Used with permission.

[6] James Hillman is a psychologist interested in myth; his work helps us to understand, to use Barbara Thornton's words, the "greater whole" to which "numerical constructs" might be

contributing. Hillman's *Emotion: A Comprehensive Phenomenology of Theories and Their Meanings for Therapy* (Evanston, 1961) is his first and most explicit work.

[7] Robert Edwards, *Ratio and Invention* (Nashville, TN, 1989), p. 3.

[8] For an analytical scheme for Hildegard von Bingen's *Ordo Virtutum*, see Barbara Thornton, "Hildegard von Bingen's *Ordo Virtutum*: Die Rekonstruktion eines Mysterien-Dramas aus dem 12. Jahrhundert," ed. Herbert Henck, *Ansätze zur Musik der Gegenwart* 4 (Neuland, 1983/4), pp. 182-83.

[9] Facsimile from *Hildegard of Bingen: Symphonia harmoniae caelestium revelationum*, ed. Peter van Poucke (Peer: Alamire, 1991). Used with permission.

[10] Milman Parry, *The Making of Homeric Verse: the Collected Papers of Milman Parry*, ed. Adam Parry (Oxford, 1971).

VI. Bowed Strings

27a. The Vielle before 1300

Margriet Tindemans

The terms viella, vidula, fidula, vielle, fedylle, Fiedel and many others were used in the Middle Ages to describe any stringed instrument played with a bow. No standard shape, pattern, tuning or technique were implied. It came to be used as a more specific name for the instrument we now know as the "medieval fiddle" or "vielle."

Historical Background

It is thought that bowing originated in Central Asia. From there it is thought to have spread via the Arab countries and via Byzantium. Spanish and southern Italian sources depict bowed instruments as early as the tenth century. By the middle of the eleventh century bowing was known in most of Northern Europe. Because at first the names vidula, fidula, fydyl were used in such a generic way to describe any bowed instrument, it is hard to tell when exactly the "medieval fiddle" we are dealing with here came into use. It appears in sources from Southern Europe and from Byzantium in the eleventh century. Literary texts confirm that the twelfth-century troubadours used fiddles.

No instruments survive from the period. The earliest extant fiddle is in the Corpus Domini monastery at Bologna. It dates from the fifteenth century. The body and neck are carved out of one piece of wood; part of the soundboard is supported by a bar, but it does not have a soundpost.

When trying to reconstruct earlier instruments we have to rely entirely on visual and literary sources. These reconstructions can at best be educated guesses. Too many obstacles stand in the way of accurate copies. The painter or sculptor may not have been acquainted with the instrument to the degree necessary to depict it accurately, nor may he have wanted to do so. He may have had aesthetic or symbolic reasons to include a fiddle in his work of art, or to elaborate and enlarge some parts of the instrument without regard to proportions and measurements that interest us. He may not have had the means technically to present us with the aspects that are so important to modern players of the fiddle: the curvature of the bridge, how the strings were fastened, how the bow hair was attached to the stick. All these elements are very hard to discern, even on a twentieth-century photograph, let alone on a twelfth- or thirteenth-century painting or sculpture. Furthermore, literary accounts that mention fiddles rarely deal with technical matters or issues of performance practice in an indisputable way.

Because of the scarcity of source material, it is not possible to make a clear distinction among the various medieval string instruments. We assume that the rebec or rubeba commonly had a pear-shaped body, and that the crwth was a bowed lyre. The medieval fiddle most often appears as an oval shape, sometimes with indented sides, giving it a figure-eight shape, with a separate neck. Up to 1300 the neck seems to have been unfretted. It usually has 4 or 5 strings and is seen played on the shoulder or the chest like a violin, or between or on the knees like a viol. In this position it is often combined with an underhand bow-grip. Similarly shaped instruments could be played in either position. No distinction is made in size or shape between instruments played on the shoulder, or between the knees. In the twelfth century slightly larger instruments, played viol-like, seem to have been preferred, while in the thirteenth century smaller instruments, played on the shoulder, are more frequently seen. Some German manuscripts show the fiddle played across the chest, held by a strap. It is possible that this was the way German fiddlers played, but it could also be that this trend was started by one painter, who happened to have been copied by many later artists.

Pl. 21a.1. Fiddles played between the knees and at the shoulder (detail)
English, ca.1215-20. The Pierpont Morgan Library, New York, M.791, f. 170.

No two instruments are quite alike, and again one must hesitate to take measurements and proportions from paintings and sculptures too literally. As there was no standard shape or size there was probably a large variety. Issues such as social and financial status of the player would have had an influence on the quality, shape, size, and technical possibilities of an instrument.

Pl. 21a.2. Oval fiddle played at the shoulder (detail)
English, ca.1215-20. The Pierpont Morgan Library, New York, M.791, f. 170.

Some fiddles are very ornate, with painted sides or inlaid wood and jewels, or even woodcarvings. It is good to keep in mind that just as there are many different qualities in violins nowadays, there must have been quite a difference in quality in medieval fiddles as well. Much would have depended on the status of the player, whether he was a professional at court, a nobleman or -woman, a cleric, or a lowly jongleur entertaining the country folks.

The vielle usually has C- or half-moon shaped soundholes, although F-like holes are also seen, as well as clusters of small holes arranged in patterns. The top or soundboard may have been flat. However, if it had been slightly bent or carved, one would not be able to tell so from a painting. A twelfth-century relief in the Walraff-Richartz Museum in Cologne, Germany, shows an instrument with a top that seems bent or carved, but the artist may have merely wanted to round off the edges of his relief.

Since no instruments from the period survive nothing can be said with certainty about the use of soundposts. My practical experience is that most instruments with a flat top do not survive very long before the top caves in under the pressure of the strings, even under the relatively low tension of gut strings, unless the top has some kind of heavy cross bracing, or the instrument has a soundpost. Balkan string instruments, possibly descendants of medieval instruments, typically have a bridge with one elongated foot. This foot reaches through the soundhole to the back of the instrument and so fulfills the function of a soundpost. An additional argument for soundposts may be found in the sixteenth-century lira da braccio, which may be the most directly related instrument to the medieval fiddle. It has the same large oval shape, a flat back, and a string running parallel to the other strings but off the bass side of the fingerboard. And the lira does have a soundpost. I think it reasonable to assume that at least some medieval fiddles might have had something functioning as a soundpost—in itself a very simple technical device, and one not very difficult to make.

Separate tailpieces and fingerboards are found on some instruments but not on all. In some depictions, the tailpiece seems to have feet, combining the functions of stringholder and bridge; but not all instruments have a fingerboard. It is not clear whether this was an inaccuracy on the part of the artists or an accurate representation. It is possible to play fiddles without fingerboards, especially if only one or two strings are used to play melodies, while the other strings are used to play drones. On some folk instruments the strings are stopped not by pressing the fingers down, but by pushing the nails against it from the side. This technique can be used without separate fingerboards.

Sometimes a drone string runs alongside the instrument, over the bridge but off the fingerboard. This string could be played with the bow or plucked with the thumb of the left hand. Pegboxes are not common: pegs are usually inserted in holes in a pegdisc, either from above or from below. A scroll- or sickle-like shape is used if lateral pegs are used. The number of strings can be from two to six. However, several writers confirm that the five-string fiddle was considered the best. Visual sources sometimes suggest that strings were paired, as on a lute. Strings were generally made of gut (mostly sheep gut) or silk. Frets are found only after 1300.

Most instruments appear with a bridge. The question whether it is flat or curved is very difficult, if not impossible, to answer, but continues to puzzle many twentieth-century players of the medieval fiddle.[1] A flat-bridged instrument allows one to play all strings at once, thus producing a four- or five-note chord, depending on the number of strings. The top or bottom string can be stopped and played separately, if the indentation on the sides of the instrument or the height of the bridge allows it. The middle strings cannot be stopped without stopping all or at least more strings at once since any pressure will put them below the point where the bow can touch them. The result is a sound very much like that of a symphonia or hurdy-gurdy: a continuous drone with one or two melody strings with fairly limited range. The pitch of the drone strings determines the mode or key the fiddle plays in. A slight curve gives the player the choice to play strings separately or two or three at the same time. It does not restrict the mode or key that can be used. It would have been very hard for a medieval painter to depict a slightly curved bridge. A full front view of the instrument will not show a curve even if there is one. Modern photographs of fiddles show that at certain angles the curve is not visible: the bridge appears as a straight line. A bridge does not have to be very curved to allow some string separation. Another possibility is that a bridge might have been flat on top but allow for different string heights by changing indentation: see Fig. 21.1. This kind of "curve" would not show up on any kind of painting. A third possibility is a bridge with slots where strings could "rest." They could be lifted off the bridge and back on, when needed. This type of bridge shows up in later paintings, but it is possible that it was in use earlier. However, it is beyond the scope of this chapter to delve too much into such a complicated matter. We will return to the implications of flat versus curved bridges on tuning and repertory in the paragraph on tuning.

The bow or "fydylstyk" was originally just like a bow used with an arrow: a stick with horsehair attached to it in such a way that the stick was bent and the hair tight. The hair might have been attached by means of a knot either through a hole in the stick or on the side. No frogs were necessary because of the extreme curve of the stick. Pressure on the hair could be adjusted by placing the thumb on the hair. Using an underhand grip it would have been no problem adjusting the hair tension.

Fig. 21.1. Vielle Bridges.

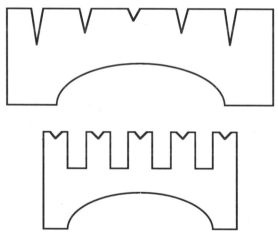

Technique

As mentioned above, two ways of playing the fiddle existed side by side, regardless of size and shape of instrument. Playing the instrument on or between the knees is a very comfortable technique for viol or cello players. It frees up the left hand, but ties the player down since it can only be done sitting down (although in some pictures the instrument seems to be played hanging from a strap around the neck). Although frets do not appear on fiddles until after 1300, they might be helpful to beginning fiddle players and can always be taken off later if so desired (like training wheels!). Placing the instrument on the shoulder or chest (as in Renaissance violin playing) has the advantage that the player can stand and move around. This is a good technique for anybody with violin or viola experience. The shape and size of the instrument and of the player's body should determine which technique is more comfortable.

In general the bow is held further away from the frog than a modern bow because of the different balance and weight distribution. Again, no definite rules can be given. Fiddle players should be prepared to do a certain amount of experimenting to find what works best for them.

Tuning

The only source for the tuning of the medieval fiddle is Jerome of Moravia's *Tractatus de Musica*, written around 1300 for the use of *fratres ordinis nostri vel alii:* (brothers of his own order or another one). His chapter on the "rubeba" and the "viella" read as an instruction book for the well educated, interested in learning about the fiddle that was capturing the imagination of many clerics and students. He gives the following three tunings:

1.	*d*	*G*	*g*	*d'*	*d'*
2.	*d*	*G*	*g*	*d'*	*g'*
3.	*G*	*G*	*d*	*c'*	*c'*

These do not represent absolute pitches but relative pitches and correspond to the ranges most commonly used in written sources of vocal music. What we do know about the techniques of string making in the Middle Ages and later makes it hard to imagine the lowest string having had a very focused sound tuned to *G* (wound strings were not used until the seventeenth century), especially when stopped. If we take into account that *G* was merely the lowest note possible, not an absolute pitch, and if we assume the lowest string to be tuned high enough to sound good, the highest string, especially in the second tuning, would be stretched beyond breaking point. Possibly the lowest string was only used as a drone string, or, as Christopher Page argues, strings might have been arranged in pairs like the double strings of a lute. *G* and *g* would be an octave pair, and *d' d'* or *c' c'* unison pairs. Stopping the octave pair *G g* would pose some problems for intonation since their very different thickness would place intervals in slightly different places on the fingerboard. But then, that might have been a sound acceptable or even enjoyable to a medieval ear.

The second tuning gives the widest range and, as Jerome says, it is the one "necessary for secular and all other kinds of songs, especially irregular ones, which frequently wish to run through the whole hand."[2] The peculiar placement of the *G* string between *g* and *d* again points to the use of that string as a drone string, but does not exclude its use as a stopped string. With this placement a *G* drone can be played continuously with a scale from *d* to *d'*.

When Jerome is talking about "running through the whole hand," is he talking about the Guidonian hand? This would indicate a very wide range indeed, wider than most medieval vocal or instrumental music. Could he be indicating that in this tuning the player could play a scale from *G* to *d"* without interruption? This seems possible although whether it would be useful to have that capability in music from this era is another question.

The irregular songs he mentions are probably those that do not adhere to the rules of the modes. The anonymous *Tractatus de cantu mensurabili* describes irregular music as "rustic or layman's music, which observes neither modes nor rules."[3] One would expect to find these kind of songs more in secular than in sacred repertory.

The third tuning is the most unusual one because of the interval of a seventh between the *d* and the unison pair of *c'* strings. It is not possible to play an uninterrupted scale without shifting into higher positions on the middle string. We do not have any information about position shifting until much later (sixteenth century). It would have been much easier with the "viol" way of holding the instrument, since the left hand does not have to support the instrument. With the "violin" way, shifting might have been used on the highest string, but it seems unlikely that it would have been used on middle strings. This tuning does provide ample possibilities for the accompaniment of epic songs and some lais though, since these usually have melodies with a fairly limited range. Christopher Page gives this as the only surviving example of an "epic" melody:[4]

Ex. 21.1.

Au - di- gier, dit   Raim- ber - ge,   bou- se vous di.

While Jerome's *Tractatus* is a very important document, it is equally important to remember that it is only one source, and that what he says does not apply to all periods and regions. Confirmed by other sources on the tuning of plucked string instruments is the principle of tuning in concordances, i.e. combinations of fifths and fourths. The treatise *Summa Musice* gives directions to suggest that *d a d' g'* would work as a good tuning for four-string plucked instruments. (The top string would be stopped to produce a concordant *a'*).

On the flat-bridged vielle the tuning would have had to be in consonances, since all strings would always have sounded at once. This would have limited the use of the instrument to one tonal center. Within limits it would have been possible though to alter the tuning of the instrument without changing the strings : the tuning *d G g d' g'* could be adjusted to *d A a d' a'* or to *c G g c' g'* without too much trouble.

Given the lack of standardization in shape and technique, as well as in use and social context of the fiddle it seems reasonable to assume that many different tunings were in use. Jerome certainly seems to indicate that even the same player would use different tunings depending on the repertory. I encourage all modern players of the medieval fiddle to experiment with different tunings: if the fiddle is played predominantly with one singer (possibly the fiddle player him- or herself) it can work to adjust the pitch to whatever suits the range of the singer best (adjustable G) as long as no instruments with fixed pitches (wind, keyboard) are used.

It is very useful in the repertory before 1300 to have a drone string in solo playing as well as for accompaniment. This can be achieved by using a re-entrant tuning such as Jerome's *d G g d' g'* tuning, or by using a tuning with a pair of unison strings such as *d a d' d' g'* or *d g g d' g'*. All these tunings provide the opportunity to play a continuous drone with a scale of approximately an octave, a range very well suited to most medieval repertory. With Jerome's second tuning *d G g d' g'* or a similar tuning it is possible to drone, but the drone would alternate between *g*'s and *d*'s. This tuning also makes it easier to produce an even scale, since no strings have to be skipped over as is necessary in the tunings with unison pairs when going from one of these strings to the next one up or down.

Because few modern fiddle players accompany epic poetry exclusively, Jerome's third tuning with its limited range may be less useful, unless more than one instrument can be used.

Finally, Jacques de Liege reports that instrumentalists divide a tone into two unequal semitones. This would seem to indicate that instrumentalists knew and used Pythagoras's tuning and distinguished between a major and a minor semitone.[6]

Repertory

Johannes Grocheio, writing in Paris ca.1300, says that "the viella is capable of playing every kind of cantus and cantilena, and every musical form."[7] He is not alone in his praise: more writers mention the fiddle as the most popular instrument since it can play every form. Based on Grocheio's descriptions the following repertories can be distinguished:

Sacred

Indications are that fiddles played many kinds of sacred music. They do seem to have been used at least in some churches: Magister Lambertus (ca.1270) complains of fiddles creeping into church use.[8] Anonymous IV (thirteenth century) on the other hand mentions the fiddle as one of the instruments that can double singers in organum.[9] It is certain that they played a part in non-liturgical settings: fiddlers are praised for the Kyries they performed; a famous story that crops up in the Galician Portuguese *Cantigas de Santa Maria* (*Cantiga* 8) as well as in Gauthier de Coinci's *Miracles de Nostre Dame* has the Virgin Mary attach a burning candle to a fiddler's instrument because he played so beautifully before her altar;[10] there is an account of at least twelve fiddlers being present when Edward I knighted his son, among them Tomasin, the prince's own fiddler.[11] Sacred pieces could include hymns, Mass movements, sequences, *conducti*, and maybe polyphony as well.

Secular

Grocheio implies that fiddlers played every secular form, and he distinguishes further:

cantus gestualis   chanson de geste, epic songs

cantus coronatus   he is probably talking about the more refined trouvère songs, but we may include here settings of courtly love texts by troubadours, trouvères, and Minnesänger, as well as Latin songs, and political and satirical *conducti.*

cantus versualis   strophic songs, related to the *cantus coronatus,* but less excellent. This group might include the *lai,* a form which uses formulaic melodies, clearly organized in sections. Melodies and sections are often repeated twice or more. It is mentioned as an instrumental form in many literary texts, but there are no purely instrumental examples.

cantilena   the more popular forms, often with refrains, including *rondeau, rondellus,* or *rotunda;* all with returning refrains, including *stantipes, estampie,* or *ductia*

The estampie is the only purely instrumental form of which we have examples, albeit from the fourteenth century. Each phrase is repeated, first with an open ending, then with a closed ending:

A   open ending (*ouvert*)

A   closed ending (*clos*)

B   open

B   closed

C   open

C   closed etc.

Each pair of phrases is called a *punctum.* The *ductia* is thought to be a shorter and lighter, maybe less complicated version of the *estampie.*

Grocheio's implication that fiddlers played all vocal music should be taken to heart by all modern players. There is no better way to familiarize oneself with the repertory than by playing it. Since fiddle players—even if they were musically literate—did not perform from music, their repertory is not written down (with the exception of a few estampies and dances). This leaves modern players with the task of re-inventing their own, using vocal music as model and inspiration.

Useful addresses for people interested in the medieval fiddle

The Viola da Gamba Society of America has many fiddle players among its members and occasionally has information in its newsletter. Many summer workshops include classes on medieval fiddle. Early Music America publishes a listing of workshops every year, and maintains current addresses for many instrument makers.

Makers

Medieval Fiddles	*Medieval Bows*	*Strings*
Christopher Allworth	Ralph Ashmead	Boston Catlines
Carl Dennis	Lyn Elder	Damian Dlugolecki
Richard Earle	Harry Grabenstein	Daniel Larson
Lyn Elder	Daniel Larson	
Daniel Larson		

Notes

[1] Scholars find it controversial as well: See the discussion in Peter Holman, "Viols and Bridges," *Musical Times* 126 (1985), 452; Howard M. Brown, "The Trecento Fiddle and Its Bridges," *Early Music* 17 (1989), 311-29; and Holman, *Four and Twenty Fiddlers: The Violin at the English Court, 1540-1690* (Oxford, 1993), pp. 7-11.

[2] See Christopher Page, "Jerome of Moravia on the Rubeba and Viella," *Galpin Society Journal* 32 (1979), 90-91.

[3] See Christopher Page, *Voices and Instruments of the Middle Ages* (London, 1987), p. 268, n. 6.

[4] For a more detailed description and discussion of Jerome's tuning see Page, "Jerome of Moravia," pp. 77-98, and *Voices and Instruments*, pp. 62-66, 126-33.

[5] See Martin, Gerbert, *Scriptores Ecclesiastici de Musica* 3 (St. Blasien, 1784; repr. Hildesheim, 1963), p. 214.

[6] See Roger Bragard, ed., *Jacobi Leodiensis Speculum Musicae* 6, Corpus Scriptorum de Musica 3 (American Institute of Musicology, 1970), p. 146. For further details on aspects of Medieval tuning, see Chapter 40 below.

[7] See the discussion of Grocheio's comments in Page, *Voices*, pp. 196-201. The treatise itself is printed in E. Rohloff, ed., *Die Quellenhandschriften zum Musiktraktat des Johannes de Grocheio* (Leipzig, 1972).

[8] Edmond de Coussemaker, ed., *Scriptorum de Musica Medii Aevi* 1 (Paris, 1864), p. 253. See the discussion in Mary Remnant, *English Bowed Instruments from Anglo-Saxon to Tudor Times* (Oxford, 1986), p. 87.

[9] See Jeremy Yudkin, *The Music Treatise of Anonymous IV: A New Translation*, Musicological Studies and Documents 41 (American Institute of Musicology, 1985), p. 38 line 45:8, p. 80, line 88:20.

[10] Quoted in Page, *Voices*, pp. 176-77, 191-94.

[11] See Remnant, *English Bowed Instruments*, p. 98.

27b. The Vielle after 1300

Mary Springfels

In order to come to an understanding of the changing role of the fiddle in late medieval music-making, scholars have looked at images, read poetry, romances, plays, and chronicles, and visited archives; to a lesser extent they have examined the music itself. Our daunting task as performers is to try to absorb this mass of non-musical information and make sense of it for ourselves. We must then apply our imaginations to the "facts" and bring them to artistic life.

Many scholars of medieval music have preferred to specialize in a particular medium in their pursuit of information about performance practices: Christopher Page[1] works with written materials from France—romances, sermons and treatises; Keith Polk,[2] Craig Wright,[3] and Richard Rastall[4] in archives; Mary Remnant[5] and Ian Woodfield[6] in musical iconography. Other historians are generalists: the late Howard Mayer Brown dealt with a tremendous amount of material drawn from throughout the Middle Ages and Renaissance; his greatest contribution to the history of fiddling is his exhaustive study of trecento Italian painting.[7] Another generalist is Reinhard Strohm, whose *Rise of European Music* is essential reading for any musician interested in the performance of fifteenth-century music. Generalists help us to put musical sources in their proper cultural context, having consulted art, literary, and social historians of the Middle Ages. The literary scholars Christopher Kleinhenz, Paul Gehl, and Sylvia Huot have also done wonderful work on our behalf.[8] This chapter is primarily a summary of recent scholarly work on instrumental performance practices in the late middle ages.

The great questions we twentieth-century fiddlers need to ask concern our repertoire and how it was played. What is our evidence? How broadly can it be applied?

Italy

Northern Italy is unquestionably the most rewarding place in which to begin a study of the late medieval fiddle. During the fourteenth and fifteenth centuries, "viola" was the word applied to all mid-sized bowed instruments, irrespective of shape or fittings. The viola is the most frequently painted musical instrument in Italy from about 1350 through the first decade of the fifteenth century. It also appears in all kinds of literary and archival sources. Well over 600 paintings of musical instruments were thoroughly catalogued and analyzed by Howard Mayer Brown in his *Catalogus*. He intended to expand his study to include manuscript illuminations and sculptures, but did not live to complete this monumental project. From a close examination of these images, performers can get a relatively complete idea of what trecento violas looked like, who played them, and on what occasions.

Viola body types range from a waistless oval to a curvaceous guitar-shape. Crucial details of fittings, i.e. tailpieces, bridges, fingerboards, frets, nuts, and strings, are often missing or indecipherable.[9] However, there is enough detail to postulate several types of viola: Oval instruments have long tailpieces which sometimes incorporate bridges. Occasionally these have separate, curved bridges, which support from three to five strings; the fifth string is almost invariably a "bourden" string which runs off the bass side of the fingerboard. The necks of these instruments can sometimes be fretted. Oval violas tend to be large, though string-lengths can vary considerably, depending on the placement of the bridge. Waisted violas can have a great variety of string and bridge arrangements, from conventional curved bridge and tailpiece to a flat, presumably fixed bridge. This bowed-guitar style of instrument can have as many as six strings on the fingerboard. Most trecento violas are of an elongated oval shape, with very slight waisting, and their necks seem to be fretted only rarely.

Trecento violas are most commonly played on the shoulder, with the chin on the instrument rather than down on the arm, or strapped across the body in the German manner. On infrequent occasions the instrument is played viol-style.[10]

Who played the viola? According to iconographic evidence, "angel musicians," mythical and allegorical characters, noble amateurs, every kind of minstrel, and even the occasional saint.[11] Angel violists played for God, Christ, various sanctified persons, and especially the Virgin. She is serenaded by fiddlers at her wedding, the nativity of her Son, her assumption and coronation. Instrumentalists most often play for her while she sits enthroned with the infant Christ on her lap.

In recent years there has been a resurgence of scholarly interest in medieval religious confraternities.[12] In Italy there were two principal types, the *laudesi* and the *disciplinati*. By the fourteenth century, both sorts of confraternity had amassed considerable wealth, and had become important patrons of religious art, drama, and music. A great many of the frescoes and panel paintings with musical subject matter were commissioned by these societies to adorn their chapels, or to serve as objects of devotion. The singing of *laude* was central to confraternal worship services, processions, and religious dramas. Starting around 1340, the most important Florentine confraternities began to hire professional singers and instrumentalists to perform on festal occasions. Organ, lute, harp, viola, and rebec appear most commonly in the archives. Instrumentalists were often hired in pairs; they were players who had sometimes worked together for many years and who frequently belonged to the same family. These documented groupings of two to three players and/or singers are entirely in agreement in time and location with groupings of angel musicians in Florentine and Sienese paintings. I am convinced that many devotional images were idealized but essentially realistic portrayals of the performance of *laude* in the later trecento period.

Instrumentalists stop appearing in Florentine confraternal archives around 1450. In Venice, on the other hand, the viola was used in confraternal rites throughout the fifteenth century.[13] Gentile Bellini's famous painting of the Corpus Christi procession of the Scuola Grande in 1496[14] is consistent with the late fifteenth-century accounts of that confraternity. At the head of an ensemble of six singers (five men and one boy) are three musicians; a harpist, violist, and lutenist. It is absolutely clear that this group is playing and singing simultaneously. Three of the singers are carrying meticulously painted partbooks; while to my knowledge the music has not as yet been identified, it is doubtless a polyphonic lauda.

In general, confraternities had very conservative musical tastes. In fact, only a few societies in Florence are known to have performed polyphony. Blake Wilson feels that the instrumental performance of devotional polyphony was limited to lay services. However, there is some bizarre and tenuous evidence that *ballate* were occasionally sung and played at certain moments in the mass in the early fifteenth century. A Russian monk who attended the Council of Florence in 1438 described a solemn mass attended by the Pope. Winds played at the Elevation; vielles and other instruments played as the Pope ascended his throne.[15] This report is given weight by the account of an extravagant Christmas Eve Vespers service in Simone Prudenzani's early fifteenth-century sonnet, *Il Saporetto* (sonnet 28):

> At Vespers—it was the very solemn feast of Christmas eve—
> All were there where each of the singers came
> Some to play and some to be in the chorus.
>
> At the beginning, Solazzo stayed with the *tenoristi* and carried the *biscantar*
> Then he had to play the organs
> For he had been begged to do so by all.
>
> No *stampita* was heard there
> Except ordinary church ones
> Like antiphons and other church music:
>
> *Christe redemptor* in different manners,
> *Magnificat* next without interruption,
> *Benedicamo* and then some joyful melodies,
>
> Like the one called *Alba columba*.
> Next they served up *Doi angilette*,
> *Aura chiome* next was done.
>
> I can promise you the church resounded
> When he did *Li gran desio* with other musical selections
> Without pause...[16]   *tr. Christopher Kleinhenz & Paul Gehl*

The repertoire of *ballate* played here in a chapel on the organ resembles the secular pieces to be found in the *Faenza Codex*. The viola or harp could also have supplied music for such occasions.

Trecento paintings illustrate noble amateurs of both sexes playing the viola in consorts with other soft instruments—particularly the lute or psaltery. Minstrels of all kinds perform for processions, weddings and banquets, and dances. In addition, courtly musicians also play in their masters' chambers, to promote sleep and emotional or physical fitness.

Alberto Gallo, in a recent essay on music in the Visconti courts[17] has examined the lovely illustrated versions of the *Tacuinium sanitatis*, prepared for members of that family in the second half of the fourteenth century. The *Tacuinium sanitatis* is a medieval health handbook translated from Arabic into Latin in the thirteenth century. Amongst all the herbal remedies is a section on music, included by virtue of its crucial role in the maintenance of good health. In the Visconti versions, healthful music is divided into three types, in the manner of Boethius. "Cantus" is illustrated by men and boys singing chant. "Organare cantum vel sonare" (accompanying a song or playing music) is depicted by a fiddler, a singer, and an organist making music together. Another illustration of the same text shows an organist who might be singing, a fiddler and a wind-player (mute shawm?). The third musical category, "Sonare et balare," is exemplified by men and women dancing in a line to a shawm and bagpipe.

The Visconti courts at Milan and Pavia fostered an international musical scene of great sophistication. Their library at Pavia contained a collection of French motets and a book of treatises (now in the collection of the Newberry Library) that includes a schematic transcription of Senleches's *Harpe de Melodie*. A goodly number of polyphonic pieces in the Italian style celebrate the lives of members of the Visconti family. The close Visconti connection with musical high culture leads me to speculate that the "Organare cantum vel sonare" illustrations in their *Tacuinium sanitatis* could be taken to mean any kind of secular music, monophonic or polyphonic.

Purely literary accounts of music-making, like paintings, need to be approached with caution; they are, after all, fiction. Keeping this in mind, Boccaccio's story of Minuccio d'Arezzo (*Decameron*, Tenth Day, Sixth Story) is probably a fairly accurate portrait of a fiddler/singer of some status.[18] His role as a self-appointed go-between has a long literary history. What is important for us to know is that, in 1350, Minuccio composed courtly love poetry, set it to music, and sang and played it on the viola.

Of even greater interest to us is Prudenzani's account of fiddling in *Il Saporetto* (sonnet 35):

> With the viola he did a May song,
> *Rosetta che non cambi mai colore,*
> *Je suis nafres tan fort, Dolze sapore,*
> *Comme partir de te me posso maio.*
>
> *D'amor languir* and then *El dolce raggio,*
> *O rosa bella* which gladdened my heart,
> *Lesgiadra donna*, and then *Donna d'amore,*
> *Un fior gentil del qual m'ennamodraio.*
>
> *Questa mirabel donna Margherita*
> *Con Lagrime bagnandome nel viso,*
> *Deducto se'*, and he did *Se la mia vita,*
>
> *Custiei sirebbe bella in paradiso,*
> *Non credo donna, O giemma incolorita,*
> A part by Ciconia was also seen there.

Solazzo appears to be playing the viola as a solo instrument. It could also be that he is playing and singing, or that he is being accompanied by an unnamed *tenorista*. But, to me, the evidence is strongest that he is simply playing the melodies of popular new pieces. We have no way of knowing whether violists embellished tunes in the style of the *Faenza Codex*. It seems most likely that a bowed string player would have played fewer notes, but might have added chords or drones. Zacharia's *Rosetta,* the first of Solazzo's viola songs, seems actually to be suggestive of this practice.

Ex. 21b.1. Zacharia's *Rosetta*, Paris BN nouv. acq. 4917, fol.21v-22, mm.1-9.

In other episodes of *Il Saporetto,* Prudenzani is careful to describe polyphonic playing:

> He played the *cetera* (citole?) and *pifar sordi* (mute shawms) to tenors.[19] With a trio of *rubebe, rebechette* and *rubecone* pieces by Landini were played.

Regarding instrumental performance of vocal part-music outside of Italy, Nigel Wilkins[20] quotes a fourteenth-century poetic source which declared that "although one (normally) sings motets, ballades, virelais and rondeaux, and lais, [they] performed them on all kinds of instruments, with movement of fingers, or percussion, or wind."[21] Informal, self-accompanied polyphony appears frequently in French and English literary sources: In *The Romance of the Rose*, Pygmalion sings and plays a motet on the organ. In Chaucer's "Miller's Tale," the clerk of Oxenforde sings *Angelus ad virginem* to the accompaniment of the "gay psauterie."

There are many important lessons to be learned from Prudenzani's *Il Saporetto.* Alas, at no point does Prudenzani ever describe a vocal and instrumental performance of a secular song. Solazzo performs *ballate* on a variety of instruments. Fiddlers in particular should notice that this particular kind of vocal music made up a large part of the bowed-string repertoire, but that these pieces were not necessarily always played polyphonically. Sometimes one part (probably the contratenor) was omitted, as in sonnet 25, where Solazzo plays two of the three parts of Jacopo a Bologna's *Aquil'altera* on the harp. In the *Faenza Codex*, three-part music is also reduced to two parts for the organ. For a particularly popular piece like *Rosetta*, there can be multiple "authentic" performances. This *ballata* was a two-part vocal composition, a three-part mass-movement, a highly embellished organ piece, and a viola solo.[22]

In summary, the Italian violist's repertoire was large and varied, and an impressive amount of it is still available to us. In addition to the list of songs given by Prudenzani, there are the *Faenza Codex* pieces, which can be adapted to the idiom of the viola, and the dances and *istanpitte* from the Manuscript London BL Add. 29987.[23] During the course of the fifteenth century, the viola experienced a decline in popularity as a courtly instrument in Italy and elsewhere in Europe. However, it enjoyed a considerably longer long career as an accompanying instrument for the recitation of epic stories. In Italy, a stringed instrument played with the *chantari,* singers who in the fifteenth century specialized in the outdoor performance of Arthurian legends. In France, the fiddle had always been associated with the recitation of *chansons de geste.* Evidently this ancient tradition persisted throughout the fourteenth century. In 1377, at Beauvais, *chansons de geste* were performed at Christmas, Easter, and Pentecost. The reciters were expected to appear at these events with a book of words and a fiddle.[24]

The fiddle was also played uninterruptedly throughout the fifteenth century as a part of the musical expression of lay piety. In 1487, Johannes Tinctoris declared that the viola and rebec were his favorite instruments, and that their sweet sounds inspired religious contemplation.

> For these reasons I would rather reserve them solely for sacred music and the secret consolations of the soul, than have them sometimes used for profane and public festivities.[25]

We fiddlers should therefore explore, as solos and in soft consorts, the monophonic and polyphonic *laude* of the fourteenth and fifteenth centuries, as well as processional hymns and even the rather conservative motet repertoire associated with confraternal use. These are available in a number a facsimiles and modern editions.[26]

Flanders

In Flanders, as in Italy, scholars have been able to trace an enduring tradition of devotional minstrelsy.[27] "Zangers and vedelers" performed for a banquet associated with the procession of the Holy Blood in Bruges in 1391. In the great commercial cities of Bruges and Ghent, wealthy merchants and tradesmen formed confraternities which commissioned polyphonic music for religious festivals and made use of minstrels for feasts and other ceremonial occasions. There were important lines of economic communication between Italian and Flemish trading centers; the famous Luccan businessman Arnolfini (immortalized in the brilliant Van Eyck portrait) worked extensively in Bruges and commissioned Flemish polyphony to take back with him to Lucca. The painter Hans Memling belonged to the brotherhood of "our Lady of the Snow," which "fostered music most actively in the third quarter of the fifteenth century."[28] His angel musicians may have been portraits of the musicians who played for ceremonies he attended. Memling's fiddles, because of their beguiling wealth of detail, are the most commonly copied and played instruments today. However, they are unusually small, and their "crenelated" bridges[29] seem to be unique to Flanders. (Mary Remnant has come up with the ingenious notion that the purpose of the crenelation was to allow the player to disengage strings easily.) Several other sorts of fiddle were painted in Flanders, in many of the same shapes we shall see throughout Europe. Oval shapes are less common. Because manuscript illuminators were heavily influenced by Parisian and English manuscripts, we frequently encounter instruments based on types established by the Limbourg brothers, and square, boxy instruments associated with the Bedford Master. We also find bowed guitars. I am not aware of anyone who has attempted to copy fiddles depicted by the Van Eycks. The fascinating instrument in the Ghent Altarpiece was overpainted at least once and, therefore, is suspect as a model. The fiddle in The Triumph of the Church Over the Synagogue is equally mysterious: it is very large, has six strings, and some kind of integrated bridge-tailpiece. The neck cannot be seen. The bow is enormous.

Pl. 21b.1. Fiddle (detail) from *Mary, Queen of Heaven* (ca.1485), by the Master of the St. Lucy Legend. National Gallery of Art, Washington, DC, Samuel H. Kress Collection, 1952.2.13.

The only late fifteenth-century account of bowed string playing in Flanders comes from Tinctoris:

> Nor must I pass over a recent event, the performance of two Flemings, Charles and Jean Orbus, who are no less learned in letters than skilled in music. At Bruges, I heard Charles take the treble and Jean the tenor in many songs, playing this kind of bowed viola so expertly and with such charm that the viola has never pleased me so well... Accordingly the viola and the rebec are my two instruments; I repeat, my chosen instruments.[30]

By Jean and Charles Orbus, Tinctoris meant Jean and Carolus Fernandez, who were Castilians of long residence in Bruges. Their repertoire included a motet by Agricola.

Over the course of the fourteenth century, Flemish cities had become important international centers for minstrelsy. The Carmelites supported minstrels' schools in Bruges.[31] Ghent held a school in 1378, and Brussels hosted minstrels at the end of that century.

Minstrels must have been at least partly responsible for the swift transmission of music to all parts of Europe, through attendance at *scholae* which convened during the Lenten season. Minstrels were used as couriers, bringing documents or information from court to court. We also know that important patrons played host to visiting artists." German fiddlers were ubiquitous throughout the continent during the later middle ages. Herman Hans di Henequin was on Gaston Fébus's payroll. Henequin was sent to a minstrels' school in 1381 in the company of Jacomi—presumably Senleches, the great composer and harpist.

What would Fébus's fiddler Henequin have played in the 1380s? Making cautious use of Prudenzani's *Saporetto* (which bears some uncanny relationships to Froissart's accounts of music-making at the court of Gaston Fébus), I would suggest that he functioned primarily as a soloist, or part of a duo, most likely with another fiddler or harper. He could easily have played *ballades, rondeaux,* and *virelais* by Machaut, Senleches, or Solage in one to three parts, depending on whether one of the players was also a *menestrier à bouche* (singing minstrel). He may have also known some older music, since troubadour and trouvère melodies were still being copied and collected at the time. Henequin might also have belonged to a religious confraternity: in Apt in 1377, an Anequin "who plays vyolla" was paid for his participation in a processional drama for Corpus Christi.

France

The role of the fiddle in the musical culture of late medieval France is difficult to assess. Iconographic sources, music theory, and literature when studied in tandem give us the impression that the instrument (here called the vielle) was at the height of its popularity around 1300. It would appear that the use and prestige of the vielle began a slow decline in the later fourteenth century. After about 1430, it is rarely seen in pictures, nor is it mentioned often thereafter. In my perusal of vielles in French paintings—mostly Books of Hours painted between 1300 and 1450—I have found that they enjoyed moderate popularity.[32] Most instruments drawn before 1360 have the typical variety of shapes, ranging from oval to slightly waisted. It must be kept in mind that, on the whole these images are so minute that any serious analysis of structural detail is almost impossible. Towards the end of the century certain artists, notably the Parement Master, began to paint bowed guitars.[33]

Paintings from 1300-1350 show the vielle in a variety of roles: accompanying solo and social dancing; playing for processions and banquets. Distinct instrumental groupings are not often represented, with the exception of the popular David and his musicians. (These players are dressed as minstrels and play soft instruments, especially lute and psaltery.) Angel musicians begin to appear more often and in larger numbers in the second half of the century. Iconographical subject matter resembles that of Italian artists and may have been strongly influenced by them. In this context, the vielle is often grouped with the portative organ, harp, lute, and transverse flute. These representations may have some grounding in reality. Newly-discovered evidence adds considerable weight to the theory expressed by Reinhard Strohm that

> Street pageants, living pictures and mystery plays were also the models for the most popular iconographic genre of the era: *angels concerts.* Angels, acted by children could perform almost any kind of music. Together with prophets, they could form

complete ensembles for vocal polyphony. If the script of the pageant required them to play and display unusual instruments, these could be bought or made... Many confident statements about the unreliability of iconographic evidence may need reexamination.[34]

Kenneth Kreitner has found that records of Barcelonan Corpus Christi processions in the early fifteenth century include detailed descriptions of instrumentalists costumed as angel musicians. At a banquet

> ...in came the *entremes* of the eagle and ten players of stringed instruments dressed in white robes, and with the masks, crowns and wings of angels."[35]
> *Llibre de Solemnitats*, January 14, 1440

Later in the evening, the same musicians (still in angel costume?) played for dancing.

An archival source which links fiddles with the performance of devotional music in Northern Europe comes from the Court of Burgundy in 1383:

> A plusieurs menestrels, vieleurs et chanters qui pour jours ont joue et chante devant madame et ses enfens environ la feste de toussains dernierement passe....[36]

> (To several minstrels, vielle players and singers, who played for days for Madame [the Duchess] and her children around the last Feast of All Saints....)

England

Close cultural ties between England and France persisted throughout the fourteenth century despite the Hundred Years' War. Thus most of Mary Remnant's superb organological study, *English Bowed Instruments from Anglo-Saxon to Tudor Times* is applicable to both nations. In addition to manuscript illumination, Remnant analyzes late-medieval stained glass and sculpture, media better preserved in England than in France. From sculpture she has deduced that earlier fourteenth-century fiddle bodies were carved from a single piece of wood. By the beginning of the next century she notes the presence of overlapping edges, evidence of a more "modern" method of construction.

Three-dimensional images have also revealed that apparently flat, guitar-shaped bridges can be tall and not necessarily glued to the table of the fiddle, rendering the strings more bow-able. Remnant gives at least three clear examples of curved bridges and a number of types of flat bridge. She also discusses various ways in which flat bridges can be made to function melodically as well as chordally, and she copes bravely with the unsettling question of double bridges, as well. Several examples of fretted fingerboards are given. Interestingly, Remnant associates frets with shifting. Two of the fretted necks she illustrates are quite long, and frets extend to their limit so that the player would have to shift in order to use them. Frets establish a fixed intonation, a factor more crucial to ensemble than solo performance; they also limit the musician to one tuning system at a time; finally, frets facilitate sustained chordal playing. In discussing tuning, she summarizes Jerome of Moravia's three systems, suggesting that his third tuning— *G G d c' c'*

—might work best on instruments with flat bridges. Tinctoris suggested tuning a three-stringed instrument in fifths, and a five-string tuning of "fifths and unisons," by which he could have meant something like *G d d a a*, giving the fiddle two courses and a single string, or a combination of fourths and fifths, such as *C G c g c*, assuming that Tinctoris may have meant octaves for unisons. Both tunings are intriguing.

Remnant devotes a chapter to what she calls the "medieval viol," which she feels has distinct characteristics—aside from how it is held—that set it apart from the fiddle. Her most striking example is also her most recent, the "Bologna Cope," which dates from around 1320. On it a fiddler and a "violist" are both represented. The "viol" is large and resembles a cornerless cello. I have found an example of a vielle played viol-style in a Parisian illumination of the late fifteenth century, and another, only partially visible, from a French manuscript source from about 1390.[57] I have also looked at a number of Italian instruments, played in both ways, that do not conform to the ordinary models; most of these are Florentine or Sienese, and there are enough of them to discourage their dismissal as artists' fancies. I would rather call them exotica; real instruments that were either experimental or of non-European origin. This is a classic problem of nomenclature: there is only one vague, generic word for too many instruments!

English Royal household records show the presence of fiddlers at court from 1272 to 1423.[58] Merlin the violist was a minstrel of the Queen's in 1307. Peter and Nicholas of Prague, "fiddlers," appear at court in 1327, as does Hanekin (the same Henequin that entertained Gaston Fébus?). A fiddler with the immortal name of Counce Snayth shows up in the archives beginning in 1399. The last record of his employment is in 1423; fiddlers are not mentioned by name thereafter until the reign of Henry VIII, by which time "fiddle" meant "violin." However, many musicians were simply listed on the payrolls as minstrels; we have no idea what they played.

This is a typical archival problem. Keith Polk has shown that in late medieval Germany, lutenists and even shawm players doubled on the fiddle. If they appeared on payrolls associated with their primary instrument, the doubling instrument would not necessarily show up; certainly a goodly number of instrumentalists have been hidden from view in this way. (There is also the story of Guillaume Racine, who was a fiddler for the Valois court of John II around 1355. Guillaume decided to become a priest and, having taken orders, sang a Mass for his former patron.[59] There is no reason to believe he burned his fiddle after his career change.)

Germany

In Germany the word *Geigen* can mean several things: At the beginning of the fifteenth century, the term referred to any bowed stringed instrument, including the rebec, for which there was no specific German name. By the end of the same century, the *Grosse geigen* refers to large, fretted, bowed instruments that are played viol-style. The *vedel* referred to the instrument we think of as the fiddle, viola, or vielle [40]

Polk's investigations have revealed that civic instrumental ensembles began to increase in number during the second half of the fourteenth century, and that by ca.1380, virtually every town in south Germany had a small, liveried wind band, usually consisting of two shawms and a slide trumpet. During most of the fourteenth century, string players found employment in private courts. Nevertheless, Polk discovered that "archival documents reveal a continuous string ensemble tradition through the fifteenth century," and that fiddles "seem to have been as popular as any other instrument at this time in Germany, though it seems that the 'vedel' as a solo instrument had passed from the scene by 1420 or so." [41] Ensemble groupings of the period gradually expanded from two to four parts; the documents themselves seem to prove that the fiddle did not survive to be part of a four-part consort. Two and even three fiddles played together up until 1400. After that, the combination of lute and fiddle becomes common.

The German standard of playing and instrument-making was so high that German instruments and musicians seemed to be ubiquitous by the end of the 1300s. German players of the viola begin to show up in Italian documents as early as 1425. [42] While it is thus clear that German minstrels abroad mastered an international repertoire, what they played at home remains largely to be explored. We do know if there was a rich German tradition of native art and popular monophony throughout the period. As Reinhard Strohm has said: "There would be plenty of material for a history of German song in the late Middle Ages. The fifteenth-century sources are more numerous than appears from any published discussion of them." [43] Certainly the fiddle would have played a major role in the performance of such material.

Conclusion

The fiddle played a central part in all kinds of music-making throughout the period 1300-1400. Even while it was losing status as a courtly instrument after about 1425, it maintained an important position among guildspeople as an instrument appropriate for devotional music. At the very end of the fifteenth century, its contours—both physical and musical—became blurred; the instrument disappears into a crowd of emerging instruments, *lire da braccio* and violins.

The repertoire of the fiddle was vast, including songs, *laude,* hymns, motets, epic poetry, estampies, and dances. Christopher Page has demonstrated that the relationship of any melodic instrument to the performance of polyphonic song literature is ambiguous, at best. [44] If one relied exclusively on literary sources, it would be easy to conclude that singers and instruments did not collaborate in the performance of part-music until the beginning of the sixteenth century. What the written materials *do* make clear is that instruments played vocal music in a number of ways: ensembles played in consort; polyphonic instruments—harp and keyboards—played arrangements idiomatically suited to them; fiddles played solos or tenors for other instruments. It is worth noting that, frequently, the *only* documented descriptions of performances of specific pieces from the polyphonic vocal repertoire are in instrumental renditions, as, for instance, Solazzo's performance of the "arpa di melodia" on the organs, or Ciconia's *O Rosa Bella* on the viola.

Pictures and archives supply a mass of information about performance practice. Treatises can be interpreted variously, depending on how they are placed in the context of the other evidence. We are learning that devotional images provide us with reliable information about instrumentalists. The numerous flocks of painted European angel musicians can give us a fair idea of the sizes and shapes of fiddles, and with what other instruments they might have played. These and the less-common pictures of secular music-making allow us to make a strong case for accompanied singing. Archives tell us that the important courtly and confraternal patrons of polyphony—at Foix, Avignon, Milan, Pavia, Bruges, and Florence—were also the most important patrons of minstrelsy. Instrumental virtuosi at the top of their profession, like Landini, Paumann, the Fernandez brothers, Senleches, and Pietrobono, enjoyed a relatively high social status. Landini and Paumann were also important composers of polyphony; there must have been many other minstrel-composers whose names are lost to us, or disguised.

With the notable exception of the Bellini painting of the Venetian Scuola Grande, it is difficult to prove that fiddles played part-music with voices. On the other hand, it is in my view counter-intuitive to posit that all groupings of voice-plus-two or more instruments (like the trio in the *Tacuinium Sanitatis*) invariably performed monophony. Nevertheless, the literary sources *do* suggest strongly that the most typical courtly performances of partsong were either all-vocal or all instrumental. We twentieth-century fiddlers will be enriched by a thorough exploration of these fascinating alternatives to instrumentally accompanied vocal performance.

Notes

[1] Christopher Page, *Voices and Instruments in the Middle Ages* (Berkeley, 1986), and *The Owl and the Nightingale* (Berkeley, 1989).

[2] Keith Polk, "Vedel and Geige—Fiddle and Viol. German String Traditions in the Fifteenth Century," *Journal of the American Musicological Society* 42 (1989); "Instrumental Music in Urban Centres of Renaissance Germany" *Early Music History* 7 (1987); *German Instrumental Music of the Late Middle Ages: Players, Patrons and Performance Practice* (Cambridge, 1992).

[3] Craig Wright, *Music at the Court of Burgundy, 1364-1419: A Documentary History* (Henryville, 1979).

[4] Richard Rastall, "The Minstrels of the English Royal Households," *RMA Research Chronicle* 4 (1964).

[5] Mary Remnant, *English Bowed Instruments from Anglo-Saxon to Tudor Times* (Oxford, 1986).

[6] Ian Woodfield, *The Early History of the Viol* (Cambridge, 1984).

[7]   Howard Mayer Brown, "The Catalogus: A Corpus of Trecento Pictures with Musical Subject Matter," *Imago Musicae The International Yearbook of Musical Iconography* 1-5, ed. Tilman Seebass (Durham, 1984-88).

[8]   Christopher Kleinhenz and Paul Gehl have translated the musical sonnets of Prudenzani's *Il Saporetto* and two of the ballate in *Il Solazzo* (unpublished to date); Sylvia Huot, "Voices and Instruments in Medieval French Secular Music: On the Use of Literary Texts as Evidence for Performance Practice," *Musica Disciplina* 43 (1989).

[9]   See Howard Mayer Brown, "The Trecento Fiddle and Its Bridges," *Early Music* 17 (1989).

[10] Millard Meiss, *French Painting in the Time of Jean de Berry. The Fourteenth Century and the Patronage of the Duke* (London, 1968), plates 18, 21.

[11] Saints Ginesius and Ranieri are shown playing a variety of soft instruments. See Brown, "Corpus," nos. 22, 23, 26, 453 (particularly interesting) and 455.

[12] Blake Wilson, *Music and Merchants. The Laudesi Companies of Republican Florence* (Oxford, 1992); Cyrilla Barr, *The Monophonic Lauda* (Kalamazoo, 1988); *Crossing the Boundaries. Christian Piety and the Arts in Italian Medieval and Renaissance Confraternities,* ed. Konrad Eisenbicher, (Kalamazoo, 1991); Ronald Weissman, *Ritual Brotherhood in Renaissance Florence* (New York, 1982).

[13] Jonathan Glixon, "Music and Ceremony at the Scuola Grande," in *Crossing the Boundaries.*

[14] Howard Mayer Brown, "On Gentile Bellini's Procession in the Piazza San Marco, 1496," *IMS Report of the Twelfth Congress,* ed. Daniel Heartz and Bonnie Wade. Payments were made in 1446 to players of the harp, lute and violeta for Corpus Christi Processions. In 1497 the Scuola paid two lutenists, one harpist and three viola players for their participation in the procession. For a good look at the instruments, see Edmund Bowles, *La Pratique Musicale au Moyen Age* (Geneva, 1977), plate 126.

[15] James Igoe, "Performance Practices in the Polyphonic Mass of the Early Fifteenth Century" (Ph.D. diss., University of North Carolina at Chapel Hill, 1971). Examples are given from 1438 and 1450.

[16] Simone Prudenzani, *Il Saporetto,* ca. 1400. ed. Santore Debenedetti (Turin, 1913).

[17] F. Alberto Gallo, *Music in the Castle* (Chicago, 1995), Ch. 2, "The Visconti Library."

[18] Howard Mayer Brown, "Fantasia on a theme by Boccaccio," *Early Music* 5 (1977), 324-39.

[19] See discussion of the cetera in chapter 25, and of the doucaine in chapter 27.

[20] Nigel Wilkins, *Music in the Age of Chaucer* (Cambridge, 1979).

[21] A similar example is from the *Roman du Compte d'Anjou:* "...others perform on the fiddle songs, rondeaux, estampies, instrumental dances and dance tunes..." trans. Wilkins, *Chaucer,* p. 130.

[22] Gilbert Reaney, ed., *Early Fifteenth Century Music* 6, CMM (Rome, 1977). No. 1 is the two-part vocal piece and two keyboard versions from the Faenza Codex, No. 12, "et in terra Rosetta," is a three-part mass movement with an added contratenor.

[23] Gilbert Reaney, ed., *The Manuscript London, BM Add. 29987,* MSD 13 (Rome, 1965) (facsimile). For a recent transcription of the instrumental materials, see *Medieval Instrumental Dances,* ed. Timothy J. McGee (Bloomington, 1989).

[24] Wilkins, *Chaucer,* p. 126.

[25] Johannes Tinctoris, *De Inventione et usu musicae,* tr. Anthony Baines, in "Fifteenth Century Instruments in Tinctoris's De inventione et usu musicae," *Galpin Society Journal* 3 (1950), 25.

[26] For modern editions of laude, see F. Liuzzi, *La Lauda e i primordi della melodia italiana* (Rome, 1934). The rythmic transcriptions are not nearly so valuable as the facsimiles. G. Varanini and L Banfi, eds., *Laudario di Cortona* (Venice, 1987). Blake Wilson, ed., *The Florence Laudario*, Recent Researches in Music of the Middle Ages and Early Renaissance 29 (Madison, 1995). Giulio Cattin, ed., *Italian Laude and Latin Unica in the MS Capetown Grey*, CMM 76 (Rome, 1977).

[27] Reinhard Strohm, *Music in Late Medieval Bruges* (Oxford, 1985; rev. 1990), p. 67.

[28] Ibid., p. 48.

[29] See the bottom example in Figure 21.1 in this volume.

[30] See Baines, "Fifteenth-century," p. 24. Another account of the fiddle comes from a Spanish literary source, the *Libro de Buen Amor* by Juan Ruiz, 1343, ed. Juan Corominas (Madrid, 1967). At the solemn feast of Easter, Arabic and Western instruments were mixed: the "strident" Moorish fuitar, the lute, the Spanish guitar, the "loud" rebec, and the bowed viola, which "gave forth sweet rhythms, sometimes soothing and sometimes lively, with dulcet, full, clear, well-turned sounds that gladden and please everyone." In a later passage, the narrator declares that the fiddle was not suited to Arabic songs, nor were the guitar or hurdy-gurdy. Ruiz goes on to describe "French-style concert" in which the psaltery, harp and Moorish rebec made merry: "The Organs recited chansons and motets, with the lowly jester intermingling." Nigel Wilkins has made a study of the close musical relationships between Aragon, Foix and Avignon during the late fourteenth century in "The Post-Machaut Generation of Poet-Musicians," *Nottingham Medieval Studies 12* (1968). The "French-style concert" may reflect this connection.

[31] For an excellent account of minstrels' schools, see Wilkins, *Chaucer*, ch. 5, "Minstrels." There were several schools held just for fiddlers: in Malines in 1328 and 1368, for example.

[32] No musical iconographer has yet assembled a catalog of northern European paintings with subject matter. The most useful books by art historians for our purposes are Millard Meiss's classic works on late medieval French painting. *French Painting in the Time of Jean de Berry: The Late Fourteenth Century and the Patronage of the Duke* (London, 1969); *French Painting...The Boucicaut Master* (London, 1969); and *French Painting: The Limbourgs and Their Contemporaries* (London, 1974). For more detailed reproductions of the Limbourg images, see Raymond Corelles and Johannes Rathoffer, *Illuminations of Heaven and Earth* (New York, 1988). For the early fourteenth century, see Lilian C. Randall, *Images in the Margins of Gothic Manuscripts* (Berkeley, 1966). The most thorough iconographic studies of later medieval music-making are Edmund Bowles' *Musikleben im 15. Jahrhundert*, Musikgeschichte in Bildern 3/8 (1977), and *La Pratique Musicale au Moyen Age*. There is also a valuable unpublished dissertation by Margareth Owens, "Musical Subjects in the Illumination of Books of Hours from Fifteenth Century France and Flanders" (Ph.D. diss., University of Chicago, 1987).

[33] Meiss, *Patronage*, pl. 80.

[34] Strohm, *The Rise of European Music*, p. 306 and n.128.

[35] See Kenneth Kreitner, "Music in the Corpus Christi Processions of Fifteenth-Century Barcelona," *Early Music History* 14 (1995). Kreitner includes a checklist of paintings with angel-musicians from 1350-1480. Fiddles are the fourth-most frequently painted instrument, preceded by the lute, shawm, and harp. The basic source for medieval and Renaissance Spanish painting is C.R. Post, *History of Spanish Painting*, 14 vols. (Cambridge, MA, 1930-66).

[36] Wright, *Burgundy*, p.29.

[37] Meiss, *Patronage*, pl. 180. Angel musicians form a solid tapestry behind an enthroned Virgin and Child. The fiddler is easy to miss; it is in a collonaded space to the left of the Virgin. For another vielle played on the knee, see Glynne Wickham, *The Medieval Theatre* (Cambridge & New York, 1974), pl. 26.

[38] Rastall, "Minstrels..."

[39] Gordon K. Greene, "The Schools of minstrelsy and the choir school tradition," *Studies in Music* 2 (1977), 33.

[40] Keith Polk, "Vedel and Geige," pp. 505-06.

[41] Ibid., p. 504.

[42] Polk, "German String Traditions in the Fifteenth Century," pp. 531-33. On pp. 522-23, Polk makes a strong case for the performance of polyphony by instrumental ensembles at the end of the fifteenth century.

[43] Strohm, *The Rise*, p. 500.

[44] I would be remiss in not including at least a short list of writings on the issue of instrumentally accompanied secular polyphony: Christopher Page, "Machaut's 'Pupil' Deschamps on the Performance of Music: Voices or Instruments in the Fourteenth Century Chanson," *Early Music* 5 (1977); Page, "The Performance of Songs in Late Medieval France," *Early Music* 10 (1982); Howard Mayer Brown, "The Trecento Harp," *Studies in the Performance of Late Medieval Music*, ed. Stanley Boorman (Cambridge, 1983); David Fallows, "Specific Information on the Ensembles for Composed Polyphony," *Studies in the Performance*; Brown, "The Trecento Fiddle and its Bridges," *Early Music* 17 (1989); Page, "Going beyond the Limits: Experiment with Vocalization in the French Chanson, 1340-1440," *Early Music* 20 (1992). Finally, I would urge early musicians to read Reinhard Strohm's assessment of this question, which is woven throughout *The Rise of European Music*.

22. Rebec

Sterling Jones

General Description and Historical Background

The rebec is a bowed stringed instrument rather small in size generally in the shape of a half-pear, that is, a curved back carved from one piece of wood which gradually tapers toward the neck so that the body and neck of the instrument become one piece along with the pegbox which contains lateral pegs. Earliest pictures of the instrument show a flat pegbox with vertical pegs like those in pictures of fiddles. In its usual form the rebec has three strings tuned in fifths with no frets, although there are some pictures of rebecs with frets.[1]

The rebec has this shape in common with the *rabâb* and *lyra* which are still played in north African[2] and Balkan countries today. These instruments first made their appearance in Europe as far back as the eleventh century. Although the word rebec does not generally appear in literature before about 1300, the instrument can be frequently identified in artwork much earlier in association with words such as *lira* or *lyra*, and *gigue*. If the rebec was related to the *rabâb* and *lyra* which were played in a downward position, that is, on the lap or knee, it departed from these instruments in that it was generally played in an upward position on the shoulder or neck. This is evident, for example, in comparing the artwork of Spain where the Moorish *rabâb* appears in the miniatures of the late thirteenth-century *Cantigas de Santa Maria* manuscript played in a downward position, and where rebec-type instruments appear in the artwork of north Europe played in an upward position.

Iconography

No rebec specimens have survived from this early period, but rebec-type instruments appear frequently in artwork such as manuscript illustrations in the form of initial and border illuminations in psalters and Bibles, on capital and tympanum sculptures, choirstall and roofbeam wood carvings, and stained glass windows of cathedrals. Fig. 22.2 is a detail from a pictorial representation of secular music, taken from an English psalter manuscript.[3]

Fig. 22.1. Detail from a twelfth-century English Psalter.

Tuning

The only tuning reference for a rebec-type instrument of this early period is given by Jerome of Moravia, in his *Tractatus de Musica* written in Paris between 1280 and 1300. He said the "*rubeba*" was tuned to c and g; this might have referred to the moorish *rabâb*, a two-stringed instrument which for centuries was tuned in fifths, and still is today. Even though three strings are the most frequent, some instruments in the iconography show anywhere from one to five or six strings. The earliest known picture of a rebec in an English source dating from about 1050 shows an instrument with four strings.[4] One can only conjecture as to how such instruments were tuned, but keeping Jerome's reference in mind some form of fourths, fifths and/or octaves was likely. Three-string rebecs of this period might have been tuned *g d'g'*, or a fourth higher— *c'g' c"* (or *d"*).[5]

Usage

The rebec can be used for any repertory of this early period which fits its descant or alto range, and with transposition this can include many possibilities: doubling upper voices in the motet repertory or even playing the tenors if the pieces are high enough, playing the instrumental hocket (*In seculum*) repertory, performing inprovised preludes, interludes, and postludes in the monophonic song repertory. As a high-range instrument it is perhaps less useful in bourdon or drone-type accompaniments for songs, although this type of usage is possible if it is combined with other instruments. Using a short bow on strings of short length produces a quick-responding sound. This makes the rebec adept at playing fast-moving parts. The rebec is very useful in the early instrumental repertory such as the *estampies* and *danses royales* found in the Paris Bibl. Nat. f. fr. 844 MS. Rebecs sound good, played together, as documented by references to the two German *gigatores* who played at the Court of Edward I.[6] One thinks here perhaps of the three two-part English Ductia pieces found in the British Library, Harley MS 978.

The following is an example of how the rebec can perform alone, making use of its open strings as an accompaniment to a monophonic dance melody (Ex. 22.1):[7]

Ex. 22.1. Possible rebec "arrangement" of Salterello from BL MS Add. 29987.

AFTER 1300

Historical Background

After 1300 various derivatives of the word *rabâb*, mentioned above, such as *rubube, rubebe, rybybe, ribible,* begin to appear in literature and all probably referred to a rebec-type instrument. Later, in the fifteenth and sixteenth centuries words such as *rabec, rebequin, rabecca, rebicchino, rebekke,* etc. were used. It has been conjectured that the r-b-c form of the word may have come from a shortened form of *rabé griego,*–the Greek *lyra*.[8] Johannes Tinctoris in his *De Usu et Inventione Musicae* (ca.1487) refers to the fiddle and the rebec as his chosen instruments, preferring to reserve their use for sacred music rather than profane festivities.[9] This indicates that the rebec was used for all kinds of music, both sacred and secular. A number of rebec players are listed as minstrels at the early Tudor court.[10]

As the rebec gave way to the violin in the sixteenth and seventeenth centuries, its social status declined, being played mainly by street musicians and beggars. Nonetheless, a rebec player still appears among well dressed society along with a curtal and lute player accompanying singers in a Flemish painting from the early decades of the 17th century.[11] The instrument was saved from extinction by being transformed into the *pochette* (see below) or kit, the dancingmaster's small fiddle which remained in use into the eighteenth century.

Specimens and Iconography

One typical instrument of the lira-type dating from the Middle Ages has survived,[12] and a rebec-type instrument seems to have been formed into an Italian *violeta* dating from the fifteenth century.[13] Several rebecs have been preserved from the seventeenth or eighteenth century.[14] Even though few instruments have survived, detailed depictions are nevertheless quite abundant in various paintings, frescoes, and drawings.[15] Drawings of rebecs appear in sixteenth-century German publications where they are called *klein Geigen*, or small three-stringed *Handgeiglein* without frets.[16] In the Martin Agricola publication of 1529 there are four sizes of instruments shown, all clearly with rebec shapes (Fig. 22.2).[17]

Fig. 22.2. Four sizes of rebec shown by Martin Agricola (1529).

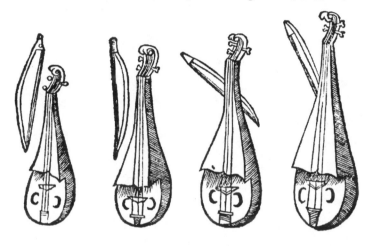

This reflects the established tendency by then of having families of instruments such as viols (*gross Geigen*) and later those of the violin, also called *Geigen*. Difficulties in the mixture of terminology become evident in Michael Praetorius who used *rebecchino* as a synonym for the violin, whereas the illustration of a rebec was described as a small *pochette* (*Kleine Poschen/Geigen*).[18] The present-day colloquial word for violin in Portuguese remains *rabeca*.

Tuning

Martin Agricola (1529) gives three tunings for the four sizes of *klein Geigen* with three strings, and the pattern of fifths is evident: for the descant g d' a', the alto and tenor c g d', and the bass F c g. These intervals in the 1529 edition are derived from his discussion on how to tune the instruments beginning with the highest string a' on the descant tuned "so high, but that it does not break" (so hoch / das sie nicht zureist).[19] Thus it seemed not to have been a matter of exact pitch, although the comment could also concern the choice of appropriate string-thickness for the given pitch. Excluding the Martin Agricola publication, there seems to be little other contemporary pictorial evidence of rebec-type instruments large enough to cope with the low bass tuning, even though fairly large instruments can be seen in earlier illustrations.[20] As the name *klein-Geigen* suggests, they were smaller instruments. A practical tuning today for a rebec copy of "normal" size with three strings would be $g\,d'\,a'$ or $c'\,g'\,d''$; and with four strings: $g\,d'\,g'\,d''$, or $g\,d'\,a'\,e''$.

Usage

As noted above, Johannes Tinctoris (ca.1483) stated his preference for the use of the rebec in sacred rather than profane music—a clear indication that the instrument was used in both kinds. Overlooking the fact that there were tenor and bass rebecs as described by Martin Agricola (see above) the most commonly used rebecs in use today for early music performance are those of the descant or alto range. Although the tone quality can differ greatly among rebecs, as it must have done in earlier times, they do have in common a distinctively nasal, high-pitched, even shrill quality to their sound, terms also used earlier to describe the rebec. They can also have a sweet sound which must have been that quality which appealed to Tinctoris.[21] All these aspects make the rebec useful in adding a distinctive color to upper parts either alone or with voices. Good examples can be found in the fifteenth-century Burgundian repertory of Guillaume Du Fay and Gilles Binchois where top parts often have non-texted preludes, interludes, or postludes. Singers sometimes prefer to sing these florid passages. This often works well, but many of these are definitely instrumental in character and work nicely on rebec whereby the player can continue playing when the voice enters.[22] Some of these pieces even have an added triplum such as Du Fay's *Pour l'amour de ma doulce amye*, which is a very suitable part for rebec. Rebecs combine well with plucked instruments such as lute and harp, combinations seen frequently in pictures. As mentioned above, rebecs also sound good when played together.

Technique

Anyone with violin-playing experience will have few problems taking up the rebec. Players with Baroque violin experience will already have learned to hold an instrument without the help of a chin rest plus shoulder pad, and will be used to playing on a shorter string length (ca.32.5 to 33.5 cm) with little vibrato and with more articulate bowing—all aspects which apply to rebec playing as well. It must be said, however, that the Baroque cliché of using the *messa di voce* bowing technique is not generally applicable in performing medieval and Renaissance music.

A rebec is best held against the left side of the chest at about armpit level. One of the first problems is that, because of its round body-shape, the instrument tends to turn with any movement of the left hand. Placing the end of the instrument directly at the armpit can prevent this. A small piece of unpolished leather can be attached to the end of the rebec to help obviate the turning problem. The leather can be attached to the end pin or placed under the string material holding the tail piece. If the rebec is constructed with a flat top and a low bridge with not much curvature, there can be the problem of hitting the sides of the instrument with the bow. Widening the distance between the strings on the bridge can help this problem. A higher bridge can also help, but in general, a better tone quality is achieved when the bridge is not too high.

The best kind of bow is one which is not too long, but not too light. This seems to be confirmed also in the iconography, although a few bows appear to be very light. As mentioned above, a short bow combined with a high-pitched, short string length produces a crisp, quick-responding sound which is well suited to active parts.

For playing the rebec up (shoulder, chest, armpit) the use of upper positions for the left hand is for all practical purposes not possible and not really required. Returning to first position by means of the hand-crawling method is difficult because of the tapered shape of the neck and problems of holding the instrument stable. However, by holding the neck high allowing the instrument to gravitate downward even this technique is possible with practice. Those who play rebec in the 'gamba' position on the leg (as in *rabâb* or *lyra* playing) do not have this problem, and there is sufficient evidence for this playing position in southern Europe, especially in Spain,[23] and in present-day Balkan countries. When holding the instrument in the upward position a few notes can be added to the first-position playing range by using fourth-finger extension on the top string.

Care, Maintenance, and Supplies

Care and maintenance of a rebec is hardly any different from that for any other type of bowed instrument. The bridge must remain straight, for in the process of tuning it tends to lose its perpendicular very easily, especially on instruments with flat tops. If they remain slanted they can warp; if they tip and fall under pressure of the strings, they can break. As usual for any bowed string instrument the bowed area of the strings and the bow hair should not be touched, as any oil will cause a spot which will not sound. Once rosin is well applied to a bow only small amounts are needed thereafter. If too much rosin accumulates on the strings the sound can be greatly inhibited and the rosin should be removed with a clean cloth.

Gut strings should be used for upper strings and even quite good quality roped gut (catline) can now be purchased for the lower g and c' pitches. Often, time-consuming experimentation is needed to find the right strings for an instrument, but it has become simpler since one can now order specially made strings for specific string lengths and pitches. If shortcuts have to be used the following can work, for example, on a rebec tuned c' g' d'' with a string length of about 34 cm. (bridge to nut): c'— wound violin or viola d', g'— half-length gut bass viola da gamba d', d''— gut violin e''; for g d' a' tuning, gut and wound violin strings are a substitute.

Conclusion

One wonders how many dance-band musicians today, when they speak of "playing a gig" (playing a musical job), are aware of associations going back to medieval times: gigue, a lively dance form in 6/8; *Geige*, German for violin and, earlier, for rebec; *gigue*, synonym for the medieval rebec—all having associations with dance at some point in history. Yet the rebec played a dignified role in serious music as well, as its appearance in religious art testifies. Its use then was as versatile, and its history as extended as that of the violin in later centuries.

Notes

[1] See M. Remnant, "The Use of Frets on Rebecs and Medieval Fiddles," in *The Galpin Society Journal* 21 (1968), 146. Other works on the history of the rebec include: Werner Bachmann, *The Origins of Bowing* (London, New York, Toronto, 1969); Anthony Baines, "Fifteenth-Century Instruments in Tinctoris's De Usu et Inventione Musicae," *The Galpin Society Journal* 3 (1950), 19-26; Nicholas Bessaraboff, *Ancient European Musical Instruments* (New York, 1941, 1964); David D. Boyden, *The History of Violin Playing from Its Origins to 1761* (London, 1965; reprint 1967); Howard M. Brown, "Instruments" The New Grove Handbooks in Music: *Performance Practice, Music before 1600* (London: 1989), pp. 15-36; Henry G. Farmer, "Rebab," *Die Musik in Geschichte und Gegenwart* 11 (Kassel: Bärenreiter, 1960), pp. 79-83; Brigitte Geiser, *Studien zur Frühgeschichte der Violine* (Bern and Stuttgart, 1974); Christopher Page, *Voices and Instruments of the Middle Ages* (Berkeley and Los Angeles, 1986); Christopher Page, "An Aspect of Medieval Fiddle Construction" *Early Music* 2 (1984), 166-67; Bernard Ravenel, "Rebec und Fiedel—Ikonographie und Spielweise," *Basler Jahrbuch für Historische Musikpraxis* 8 (1984), 105-30; Mary Remnant, *English Bowed Instruments from Anglo-Saxon to Tudor Times* (Oxford, 1986); Mary Remnant, "The Diversity of Medieval Fiddles" *Early Music* 3 (1975), 47-51; Mary Remnant, "Rebec" *The New Grove Dictionary of Music and Musicians* 15, ed. Stanley Sadie, 635-38; Dora Rittmeyer-Jselin, "Das Rebec," *Festschrift Karl Nef zum 60. Geburtstag* (Zurich, 1933); Wilhelm Stauder, *Alte Musikinstrumente in ihrer vieltausendjährigen Entwicklung und Geschichte* (Braunschweig, 1973).

[2] See Ruth Davis, "Arab-Andalusian Music in Tunisia," *Early Music* 24 (1996), Ill. 1, pp. 423, 430.

[3] St John's College Library, Cambridge, MS B. 18, fol. 1 dating from the second quarter of the twelfth century.

[4] M. Remnant, *English Bowed Instruments from Anglo-Saxon to Tudor Times* (Oxford, 1986), p. 31, illustr. plate 2.

[5] Ibid., pp. 35-36. Remnant gives an overview of possibilities as to how three- to six-stringed instruments might have been tuned.

[6] Ibid., pp. 39, 83.

[7] Jerome of *Moravia* in his *Tractatus* mentions the use of a bourdon string in consonance with notes produced on other strings.

[8] H. G. Farmer, "*Rebab*," in *Die Musik in Geschichte und Gegenwart* 11, p. 80.

[9] Johannes Tinctoris, *De inventione et usu musicae*, Naples, ca. 1487, trans. Anthony Baines, "Fifteenth-Century Instruments," p. 25.

[10] See Fiona Kisby, "Royal minstrels in the City and Suburbs of Early Tudor London: Professional Activities and Private Interests," *Early Music* 25 (1997), 199-219.

[11] See Beryl Kenyon de Pascual, "Two Contributions to Dulcian Iconography," *Early Music* 25 (1997), 417-18.

[12] Excavated at Novgorod and now in the Institute of Archaeology of the Academy of Sciences, Moscow (see *New Grove* 15, p. 636).

[13] M. Tiella, "The Violeta of S. Caterina de' Vigri," *The Galpin Society Journal* 28 (1975), 60.

[14] The Heyer collection, formerly Cologne, now in Leipzig.

[15] Fra' Angelico (1387-1455): *Musician Angel*, Museo S. Marco, Florence; Gerard David (1450/60-1523): *The Virgin and Child*, Kunstmuseum Basel; Giovanni Bellini (†1516): *The Virgin and Child*, Accademia, Venice; Maître de Morrisson (15th/16th c.) *Virgin and Child*, Musée Royaux de Beaux-Arts, Brussels; Francesco del Cossa (ca. 1436-78): *Month of April*, fresco in Schifanoia Palace, Ferrara; Hans Holbein (the elder 1460/70-1524): *Drawing with Rooster and Rebec,* Öffentliche Kunstsammlung Kupferstichkabinett, 1662.202, Basel.

[16] Sebastian Virdung, *Musica getutscht* (Basel 1511); Martin Agricola, *Musica instrumentalis deudsch* (Wittenberg, 1529); Othmar Luscinius, *Musurgia seu praxis musicae* (Strassburg, 1536); Hans Gerle, *Musica Teusch* (Nürnberg 1532, 1537, 1546). On Virdung, see Beth Bullard, trans. and ed., *Musica getutscht: A Treatise on Musical Instruments (1511) by Sebastian Virdung* (Cambridge, 1993). On Agricola, see William E. Hettrick, trans. and ed., *The 'Musica instrumentalis deudsch' of Martin Agricola: A treatise on musical instruments, 1529 and 1545* (Cambridge, 1994).

[17] Agricola mentions and illustrates another type of *klein-Geigen* with four strings tuned in fourths, with frets. See Hettrick, pp. 47-49.

[18] *Syntagma musicum* II (Wolfenbüttel, 1619).

[19] See Hettrick, p. 49.

[20] By comparison, if the smallest rebec in Agricola's illustration had a string-length of about 33 cm. then the largest rebec would have one of about 49 cm., a very large instrument to play in an upward position on the shoulder.

[21] For more on the aesthetic judgments of Johannes Tinctoris, see Rob C. Wegman, "Sense and Sensibility in Late-Medieval Music," *Early Music* 23 (1995), p. 299.

[22] See also the discussion in Chapter 17.

[23] See I. Woodfield, *The Early History of the Viol* (Cambridge, 1984).

23. Symphonia
Robert Green

General Description and Historical Background

*S*ymphonia is currently defined as a generic term for the early hurdy-gurdy.[1] It shares this meaning, however, with a number of other terms including *organistrum*. Although Christopher Page has shown these two terms to be virtually synonymous as used in medieval times, there are those who would like, for the sake of clarity, to maintain a distinction between them.[2] Formerly, the term *organistrum* was applied to the earliest form of hurdy-gurdy, which had three strings and was played by two musicians, one of whom turned the wheel while the other operated the tangents which stopped the strings. It was associated in some way with the church. In contrast, the term *symphonia* was applied to a smaller instrument, played by one player, and associated with secular music. The many terms used to describe the hurdy-gurdy in the first years of its existence create serious problems when examining the sources in order to determine which instruments were used in particular circumstances.[3] The many shapes and sizes which one finds in the first centuries of its existence, indeed throughout its history, further complicate the distinctions between them.[4] It seems useful for the purposes of the following discussion to maintain the distinction between the terms *symphonia* and *organistrum*, recognizing the limitations of this usage.

In the past, some writers concluded that the hurdy-gurdy originated in Arab countries and entered Europe through Spain, as did so many other instruments.[5] A close study of the sources shows that in fact the instrument originated in Northern Europe, perhaps Germany, around 1100 and made its way into other countries sometime before 1200.[6] The *organistrum* was probably used in monastic circles to learn chant. At present there seems to be no evidence that it actually played a part in church services. It combined the general concept of the monochord with the bowed sound derived from new instruments such as the rebec which were then making their first appearance in Europe. The use of a wooden wheel to produce a sustained sound, however, seems to be an invention entirely of European origin.

In the thirteenth century, smaller instruments played by one person made their appearance. Their advent was accompanied by much experimentation. The sliders which required both hands of the player were replaced with keys which could be operated by the fingers of the left hand while the right hand turned the crank. These keys begin to appear on the side of the instrument opposite the player. The wide variety of shapes suggests that builders made attempts to improve the acoustic properties of the instruments.

In secular music, the *symphonia* was probably used to play dance music and, in aristocratic circles, to accompany monophonic songs.

Surviving Evidence

The many forms of hurdy-gurdy in the period 1100-1300 are depicted in sculpture, such as the doors to churches, and in manuscripts.[7] In addition, there are many literary references which provide some idea, though meager, of how the instrument functioned in society. Concerning the *organistrum*, there is considerable description in theoretical treatises concerning its tuning. These treatises have their origins almost entirely in German-speaking countries. On the other hand the many stone representations on churches come from France and Spain. Notable are the figures on the façade at Santiago de Compostela, sculpted by Magister Mateo about 1188. The *organistrum* is positioned in the center of the ensemble suggesting that it functioned as a leader.

Pl. 23.1. Organistrum from a medieval codex no longer extant.
(reproduced by Martin Gerbert in *De cantu et musica sacra* 2 [1774], pl. 32).

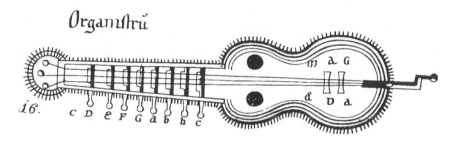

Representations of the *symphonia* are often found in manuscript illuminations, as well as in sculpture. Most famous is the representation of two players in the manuscript which contains the *Cantigas de Santa Maria*. In contrast to the earliest form, the later instruments come in a variety of shapes and sizes. Some are shaped like boxes; others are merely smaller versions of the early instruments. Since these instruments were used primarily for secular purposes, there is no verbal description of them.

Pl. 23.2. Pair of hurdy-gurdy players from the *Cantigas de Santa Maria*.

Tuning

The descriptions of tuning in theoretical manuscripts give the melody string of the instrument a range of an octave (*C-c*) with both a *b♮* and a *b♭*, nine notes altogether. It seems likely that this range was maintained in the smaller instruments, since the melodic ranges in sacred and secular music was virtually the same. The drones would most likely have been tuned to *C* and *G*, although any mention of these is curiously omitted from any description.[8] Sources discussing the *organistrum* all describe Pythagorean tuning as the basis for setting the tangents much as described for the monochord.[9]

Usage

The *symphonia* can be used much like the other bowed strings in playing monophonic music, the difference being the continuous drone. Obviously, the appropriateness of the drone depends on the melodic properties of the piece. The *symphonia* can be used to play interludes between verses and to accompany the singer in unison, perhaps with a more ornamented version of the melody. The illustration in the *Cantigas* of two players seems to suggest a situation similar to this. One musician sings the melody, probably accompanying himself in unison, while the other player listens carefully in order to learn to play the melody himself. The association with vocal music emphasizes the melodic properties of the instrument. In spite of the mechanical nature of the hurdy-gurdy, it is capable of great melodic sensitivity. The *symphonia* is also very effective in dance music.

AFTER 1300

Historical Background

After 1300, the *symphonia* permeated every level of society. For the first time, there are references to the instrument as played by blind beggars.[10] At the same time there are many literary and iconographical references to the use of the instrument in more polite contexts. Unfortunately, the hurdy-gurdy appears too often in paintings with supernatural and religious subjects. The reason for this is that the instrument took on many symbolic references.[11] *The Garden of Earthly Delights,* painted about 1490 by Hieronymus Bosch (ca.1450-1516), stands out in its detailed representation of the hurdy-gurdy. Clearly, the instrument possesses a vibrating bridge. This painting provides the first example of this device which creates the buzzy articulation so characteristic of later music. This device is often used by players today in medieval dance music. While recognizing the anachronistic aspects, it is nevertheless very effective in this repertory.[12]

Treatises by Virdung (1511) and Agricola (1528) provide representations of the hurdy-gurdy but little detail.[13]

Technique

One of the most difficult problems for the player who wishes to incorporate the *symphonia* into performances of medieval music is finding a good instrument. Many makers produce a small boxlike instrument which resembles those found in the *Cantigas* manuscript. Proportionally, these instruments tend to be smaller than the visual evidence suggests. The hurdy-gurdy is the most mechanically complicated medieval instrument, and it must be constructed with great precision. Further, the player must make many adjustments himself. The balance between the sound produced by the drones in relation to the melody, for example, is a matter of personal taste. Supplies include raw cotton (not the treated variety found in the drugstore) which is used to wrap the strings.

The hurdy-gurdy is unique in that it has a continuous tradition going back to medieval times. A good instruction manual, even though it may focus on modern folk music or the Baroque literature, can provide many useful tips for technique and maintenance. Modern fingering as described in these manuals is useful, because it makes possible great rapidity of execution, rivaling the other bowed strings.[14]

Notes

[1]   Christopher Page, *Voices and Instruments of the Middle Ages* (Berkeley, 1986), p. 150.

[2]   Christopher Page, "The Medieval *organistrum* and *symphonia:* 2 Terminology," *The Galpin Society Journal* 36 (1983), 71-87. Christian Rault, *L'Organistrum* (Paris, 1985), pp. 24-26, arguing that Page's proof is not convincing, maintains that the original meaning of the term *organistrum* referred to the instrument with two players. Later, it became a *mot fossile,* applied indiscriminately to any hurdy-gurdy.

[3]   Susann Palmer, *The Hurdy-Gurdy* (London, 1980), for example, assumes the term vielle (or viele) as used in medieval sources refers to the hurdy-gurdy in situations which clearly mean a fiddle.

[4]   See Susann Palmer, *The Hurdy-Gurdy,* pp. 22-30, for a classification of the different shapes which the instrument has assumed over nearly ten centuries.

[5]   For the most complete exposition of this theory, see Marianne Bröcker, *Die Drehleier: Ihr Bau und ihre Geschichte* (Düsseldorf, 1973), pp. 38-43.

[6]   See Christopher Page, "The Medieval *Organistrum* and *Symphonia:* A Legacy from the East?," *Galpin Society Journal* 35 (1982), 37-44; Christian Rault, *L'Organistrum,* pp. 29-36, supports Page and provides some new insights into the same sources.

[7]   Christian Rault, *L'Organistrum,* pp. 29-36, provides a list of fifty-one sources of this type prior to 1300. There is also an index of all twelfth- and thirteenth-century representations of the hurdy-gurdy in sculptures, pp. 153-66.

[8]   The drones found on the organistrum, together with the slider mechanisms and tangents which stopped the strings, may pose the most difficult practical problem to solve in a definitive manner from the existing evidence. Did the tangents stop all three strings, two strings, or only one string? If all three strings were stopped, the result would be parallel organum as described in the *Musica Enchiriadis.* On the other hand, would chant have been sung against a continuous, unchanging drone? It is also

possible that all the above options were open. Christian Rault, *op. cit.*, has explored the mechanical problems associated with all these possiblities.

[9] See Rault, pp. 120-22, for a discussion of tunings in the sources.

[10] Susan Palmer, *The Hurdy-Gurdy*, p. 72, cites Mathieu de Gournay, *Chronique de Bertrand du Guesclin* and Corbichon, *Proprietaire des choses* (1372), as associating the instrument with blind beggars.

[11] Kahren Jones Hellerstedt, "Hurdy-Gurdies from Hieronymus Bosch to Rembrandt" (Ph.D. diss., University of Pittsburgh, 1981), discusses the representation of the instrument in paintings for the pruposes of instruction. For example, the instrument's association with blind musicians leads to "the blind leading the blind."

[12] Pascal Lefeuvre, "La vielle & roue: 800 ans d'evolution," *Trad* 28 (May/June 1993), 10-13, argues the philisophical case for the full use of the modern instrument when playing medieval music. He asserts without supporting evidence that the appearance of the vibrating bridge can be dated as early as the fourteenth century.

[13] Sebastian Virdung, *Musica getutscht* (1511). See Beth Bullard, trans. and ed., *Musica getutscht: A Treatise on Musical Instruments (1511) by Sebastian Virdung* (Cambridge, 1993); French translation and notes by Christian Meyer (Paris, 1980). Martin Agricola, *Musica instrumentalis deudsch* (1528) bases his references on Virdung. See translation by William E. Hettrick, (Cambridge, New York, 1994).

[14] Doreen Muskett, *Method for the Hurdy-Gurdy* (Piper's Croft, Bovingdon, 1979) is unquestionably the most useful modern method in English.

VII. Plucked Strings

24a. harp

herbert W. Myers

O f all medieval instruments the harp is perhaps the most ubiquitous; it is certainly one of the most universally recognized musical symbols of the period. Its origins and early development in Europe are still somewhat shrouded in mystery, but it is clearly depicted in European art from the eighth century onward. The European harp is generally (and invariably, after the twelfth century) of the variety known as the "frame harp"—that is, one composed of three elements: body, neck, and forepillar. The body is an elongated resonating cavity, always running rather vertically and held close to the player's own body in European harps; to it are attached the lower ends of the strings. The neck carries tuning pins, around which the upper ends of the strings are wound. The forepillar acts as a brace between the far end of the neck and the lower end of the body, counteracting the pull of the strings; harps lacking a forepillar (as in the case of many non-European varieties) are called "open harps." (It has been suggested that the absence of a forepillar in some pictures of European harps up to the twelfth century may be more apparent than real, resulting from artistic carelessness; when, as in the case of the earliest harps, the forepillar is straight, it is sometimes hard to distinguish the lines representing it from those representing strings.) From about the eleventh century the harp acquires some of the graceful curves that, with many variations, will characterize it for the rest of its life: typically the neck curves inwards, in the direction of the pull of the strings, while the forepillar curves outwards. Bodies often appear to be fairly massive, sometimes appearing to bulge upwards towards the pull of the strings. There is tremendous variation in decoration. Often there is a zoomorphic finial at the joint of the neck and forepillar; sometimes a mouth adorning the end of each element appears to swallow the beginning of the next. There is also a large variation in proportions, although through the fourteenth century the three elements tend to be about equal in length, producing a fairly squat overall shape.

This in broad outline describes the "romanesque" harp, so dubbed by Curt Sachs to distinguish it from the "gothic" harp developed in the fifteenth century. The latter is familiar to many from the paintings of the Flemish masters (such as Jan van Eyck and Hans Memling) whose depictions of angel musicians have appeared on countless Christmas cards. From early in the century we see evidence of the elongation of the body and forepillar—presumably to accommodate longer bass strings—producing a taller, slimmer outline. (Occasionally we see evidence of an alternative method of providing for longer basses: opening out the angle between neck and body, lengthening the forepillar and resulting in a so-called "high-headed" design.) At the same time the forepillar (often quite outcurved on earlier harps) was somewhat straightened and was carried upwards beyond the joint with the neck, terminating in an ornamental, horn-like protrusion; an answering protrusion was often to be found further back on the neck. Both forepillar and neck were often deeply fluted, evidently in order to reduce mass while retaining strength; the flutings also serve to emphasize the graceful curves. The body was both narrow and quite shallow, expanding rather minimally towards the bottom. The result of these modifications is (visually speaking) an extremely well integrated design; the gothic harp appears to the casual eye to have been made of a single piece of wood.

This appearance is, of course, somewhat deceptive; for strength, the grain of the wood must run generally parallel to the length of each principal element, requiring the joining of separate pieces. But in one sense the appearance is quite genuine, for all three elements (including the body or soundchest) were made of a single type of wood. This means that the active acoustical surface—the belly—was, like the rest of the instrument, of hardwood (though the particular species of wood varied among instruments). The soundchest was not so much constructed as carved, being made up of two hollowed-out planks joined at the edges to form an enclosed cavity. Its cross-section (as viewed from either end) was often a flattened oval; three surviving examples from around 1500 (in Eisenach, Nuremberg, and Leipzig) have the latter form, and it is depicted clearly by Hieronymus Bosch in his famous *Garden of Earthly Delights* in the Prado, Madrid. However, many pictures show that the cross-section could also be rectangular or almost so, with a flat back and either flat or bulging belly. (A flat back is a definite advantage when one wants to lay the harp down.)

The choice of hardwood as belly material has considerable acoustical significance, for it is inherently much stiffer than the softwood (spruce or pine) employed for the bellies of the more recent types of harps with which we are familiar (and, indeed, for the bellies of most other stringed instruments, bowed or plucked, from the Middle Ages to the present). The stiffness of the hardwood belly, coupled with its small surface area, makes for a very inefficient resonator, particularly for bass frequencies. However, the fifteenth-century builder had quite an effective solution to this problem: "bray pins" (also known simply as "brays"). These are L-shaped wooden pegs that serve both to anchor the gut strings in the belly (much as modern guitar bridge pins do) and to touch them a short way along their vibrating length, imparting a buzzing quality that amplifies and prolongs their sound. They are most efficient at this in the bass, where the excursions of the strings when vibrating are greatest—and where, as we have seen, their amplifying effect was most needed. They are clearly depicted in art works from early in the fifteenth century, through the sixteenth, and into the seventeenth; they also figure in illustrations of harps in musical treatises (notably the *Dodecachordon* of Glareanus, 1547 (see Fig. 24a.1), and the *Syntagma musicum* II of Praetorius, 1619). In addition, they are to be found on several surviving instruments (including two of the three mentioned above; the Eisenach example has lost them, it seems). Mersenne (*Harmonie universelle*, 1636) calls them *harpions* and claims that they had gone out of fashion in France; however, they are still present on some later seventeenth-century harps, and their use on the Welsh harp continued into the nineteenth century.[1]

Fig. 24a.1. Glarean's diagram of a harp with bray pins from *Dodecachordon*, 1547.

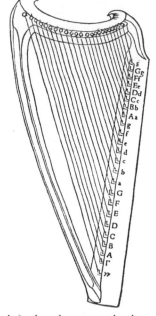

One might be tempted to regard the use of brays as but one of the available options (or a mere fad among certain players) but for the evidence that the nasal quality they impart was then considered characteristic of harp timbre. In more than one European language the verb "to harp" came to imply a buzzing quality. For instance, in the lute book of Vincenzo Capirola (ca. 1517) we are advised to make the frets of the lute almost touch the strings, so that they will "harp."[2] Similarly, in describing a newly invented keyboard instrument, Sebastian Virdung (*Musica getutscht*, 1511) says, "This is just like the virginals, except that it has different strings (of sheep gut) and nails which make it 'harp'..." Such references continue through the Renaissance: *Arpichordum* was the name of a stop often applied to Flemish muselars, being a batten (carrying metal hooks) placed next to the bass part of the bridge; it could be moved to bring the hooks close to the vibrating strings, causing them to buzz. Praetorius uses the expression *harffenierender Resonantz* (harping sound) to describe the buzzing effect of both this stop and the peculiar bridge of the trumpet marine, even claiming that the term had this buzzing connotation for the common man. Finally, "harp" was the name of a renaissance organ stop consisting of regal pipes (which also, of course, buzz). Given all this evidence for the use of brays throughout this period, it seems odd that they have been so generally rejected by modern builders and players. Some have suggested that they might have been turned on and off at will, like an organ stop—an idea that makes sense only until one has experienced the tedium of getting them to work, one by one, evenly and effectively on an actual instrument; this is not labor thrown away lightly!

As to the use of brays before the fifteenth century there is very little evidence; the written sources are quite silent on the subject. When string-anchoring devices are depicted on earlier harps, they tend to be round studs, sometimes of a different color (and hence material) from the wood of the body. (Brays, by contrast, often show up as little rectangles, usually of the same color as the rest of the harp and aligned parallel with the body; only when a painting is large enough to provide fine detail can one see the shanks of the brays poking into the holes of the body.) Brays would seem acoustically less necessary on earlier harps, too. Although the available evidence would point to the same hollowed-out construction from hardwood for the romanesque as for the gothic harp, the soundchest of the former is proportionately larger; at the same time, it was probably not expected to respond to pitches as low as the basses of the gothic harp, making it altogether an adequate resonator without the amplifying effect of the brays.

Both the romanesque and gothic harps were strung normally in gut, although horsehair and silk were occasional (but rare) alternatives. Developed in the second half of the thirteenth century and coexisting with these Continental harps was the wire-strung Irish harp, which represented a completely different concept of tone and performance. Elegant in its own way, it was much more robustly constructed. As with the romanesque harp, the joints between its members, rather than being disguised, were emphasized by ornamentation. Its massive soundchest was hollowed out completely from behind to make a deep trapezoidal box, whose "lid" then constituted the back of the chest. This back was left removable to allow access to the inside for attaching the brass strings, which were held in by toggles, never brays. (This remarkable chest often served the itinerant bard as a sort of suitcase.) The string holes in the soundchest were reinforced against wear by inset metal "shoes." Irish harpists traditionally played with sharpened fingernails, in contrast with the players of gut-strung harps who used the fleshy part of the finger. The strong, prolonged, and bell-like tone of the Irish harp demanded an elaborate system of damping by the fingers. The use of the Irish harp was known to Continental audiences during the Middle Ages through the activities of Irish bards, who swarmed over Europe; Dante (probably incorrectly) considered it the ultimate prototype for the harp he knew.

It should be mentioned that the so-called "Celtic" and "Troubadour" harps offered by modern harp companies are a complete fiction as historical (or at least medieval) instruments. Having evolved from some nineteenth-century designs, they generally preserve in their smaller format the acoustical and playing characteristics of the modern concert harp. They are commonly provided with "hooks"—bent wire devices set into the neck of the harp that can be turned quickly by hand to raise specific strings by a semitone—or levers that accomplish the same purpose. Hook harps were an invention of the late seventeenth century and represent one of the first stages in the mechanical development leading to the modern pedal harp.

Medieval harps appear from pictures to have varied greatly in size and number of strings, some having as few as six or seven and some as many as thirty. Pictures are obviously not very reliable in this regard, ranging from the obviously schematic to the apparently photographic. Writers are more dependable, naturally, but rarely have anything to say on the subject; three exceptions are the twelfth-century troubadour Guirot de Calanson who recommends seventeen strings, the fourteenth-century poet Machaut who (in the *Dit de la harpe*) compares his lady's twenty-five virtues to the twenty-five strings of his harp, and the early fifteenth-century cleric Jean de Gerson who (in his sermon *Puer natus est nobis*) mentions that the harp has twenty strings. Fragments (consisting of neck and forepillar) of an elaborately carved ivory romanesque harp from ca. 1400 survive in the Louvre; the neck was originally pierced for twenty-four tuning pegs but was given a twenty-fifth as an afterthought. Of the three surviving gothic harps mentioned above, the

Eisenach and Nuremberg examples have twenty-six strings and the Leipzig, twenty-five. It is hard not to link these instruments with the common sixteenth-century tunings for this type of harp that specify a range of *F* to *a″* or *c‴*, twenty-four to twenty-six notes; the same range is still given by Praetorius (*Syntagma musicum* II, 1619) for what is basically the same size and style of harp, suggesting finally that these tunings are close to "actual" (as opposed to nominal or "conceptual") pitches.[3]

Treatises throughout the medieval and early Renaissance period confirm that the basic tuning of all harps was diatonic—that is to say, there were regularly only seven notes to the octave.[4] At the same time, there is some evidence that the medieval minstrel retuned his harp constantly for different pieces and maybe even during pieces; we often see the tuning key held "at the ready" in early depictions. It is not until the sixteenth century, however, that we find clear evidence of both dissatisfaction with the harp's lack of chromaticism and experimentation with ways to overcome it; even so, the diatonic, single-strung harp remained standard until the end of the century.[5] Even the simple expedient of adding just one note (such as B♭) to the octave was resisted; Martin Agricola (*Musica instrumentalis deudsch*, 1529 and 1545) still gives B♭ and B♮ as alternative tunings for the same string in each octave. (His xylophone—*Strofiedel*—by contrast includes *both* notes in each octave.)[6]

Specific information on medieval harp technique is quite scanty. Iconography suggests the use primarily of the thumb and first two fingers; this is borne out in later written sources which indicate that the use of the ring finger was then innovative. (The use of the little finger is still avoided in modern technique.) Early depictions of Continental harps imply indifference as to which hand played uppermost; later ones more consistently show the right hand taking the treble and the left, the bass (as in modern playing); in traditional Irish (and Welsh triple) harping, the rôles of the hands are reversed. Thus the harp was always a "two-handed" instrument; it would seem as improbable to restrict it to a single line as to so restrict a keyboard instrument (with the obvious exception of the organetto).[7] In fifteenth-century pieces, therefore, the harp can easily handle two voices or even play an intabulation of the complete texture (*ficta* willing, of course—although one defensible solution to the *ficta* problem is to ignore it). The combination of harp and plectrum lute would seem particularly apt for this repertory, the lute's chromatic flexibility complementing the harp's limitations.

A fine general work on the harp is Roslyn Rensch's *Harps and Harpists* (Bloomington and Indianapolis: Indiana University Press, 1989; this is a revised and updated version of her earlier book, *The Harp*). Also useful is the entry "Harp" in the *New Grove Dictionary of Musical Instruments*. Howard Mayer Brown's "The trecento harp," *Studies in the performance of late mediaeval music*, Stanley Boorman, ed. (Cambridge: Cambridge University Press, 1983), pp. 35-73 is a marvelously thorough investigation of the instrument and its place in one limited geographic area and time frame. Recordings of bray harps are extremely rare; one of the few is to be found on the CD *Forse che si, forse che no* by the Ferrara Ensemble, directed by Crawford Young (Fonti Musicali—Atelier Danse, fmd 182,

1989); it is track 11, "Giove" by Domenico da Piacenza, performed by Debra Gomez. A gothic harp with working brays on just a few bass notes is to be heard on the *Harp Collection* (Amon Ra CD SAR36, 1989) by Frances Kelly, second piece on track 4.

Notes

[1] See Robert Hadaway, "The Re-creation of an Italian Renaissance Harp," *Early Music* 8 (1980), 59-62.

[2] I am grateful to Ray Nurse for pointing me to this reference.

[3] Praetorius's reference pitch—his *Kammerton*—seems to have been about a semitone above modern.

[4] For a review of modern discussions of the evidence see Howard Mayer Brown, "The Trecento Harp," *Studies in the Performance of Late Mediaeval Music*, Stanley Boorman, ed. (Cambridge, 1983), pp. 35-73 [specifically p. 46, fn. 36, and p. 50].

[5] Already in 1511 some form of triple harp was said to be in use in England, according to the theorist Johannes Cochlaeus (*Tetrachordum musices*, Nuremberg, 1511; translated and edited by Clement A. Miller, American Institute of Musicology, Musicological Studies and Documents 23, 1970, p. 30). A two-rank harp (with parallel string planes) is shown in one Spanish illustration from the late fourteenth century (Mary Remnant, *Musical Instruments: An Illustrated History from Antiquity to the Present* (London, 1989), Ill. 8). Adding extra strings is such an obvious invention it probably took place more often than it was documented; however, the impediment it imposes to a fluent technique evidently outweighed its advantages in the opinion of most players for a long time.

[6] See also the diagram by Mersenne as Figure 24c.1.

[7] See Curt Sachs, *The History of Musical Instruments* (New York, 1940), p. 264, for a couple of early references to two line playing on the harp.

24b.Imagining the Early Medieval harp
Benjamin Bagby

Everyone has his own ideas, usually corrupt, about the Middle Ages. (Umberto Eco)

One of the strangest aspects of performing a music we have decided to label "medieval" is that the quantity of iconographical information about instruments and the debates on performance practice are rarely matched by the quality of actual music-making. Among today's passionately dedicated players of medieval instruments (and not a few singers), many seem confronted with a feast of information and opinion which they cannot convert into useful musical nourishment. As a result, coherent and thoughtful schools of playing have been slow to emerge, whereas superficial imitations of non-European musical traditions are hailed as "innovative research." We risk arriving at a permanent state of indigestion as less dedicated players mindlessly begin to copy the performances and recordings of others, creating something which seems reassuringly like a tradition, but which merely completes a self-referential circle. What is the missing element which might allow us to nourish ourselves as musicians so that *ratio* and *anima* can work in harmony with hands and ears? Where is the missing link between information and intuition?

The following are personal reflections on these questions, specifically as related to the use of the medieval harp. Since scholarly sources of information about the harp are relatively easy to locate, I will limit my narrative to the current state of my own relationship with this small instrument and its potent musical voice. If my ideas are corrupt, as Prof. Eco assures us they probably will be, I hope they might at least nudge a few brave players to find out for themselves, the hard way, how the harp can sing again for us today as an authentic musical instrument.

I'll begin with a passage from a story which delighted courtly European audiences in the thirteenth century:

> do begunde er suoze doenen
> und harpfen sô ze prîse
> in britûnischer wîse,
> daz maneger dâ stuont unde saz,
> der sîn selbes namen vergaz.
> dâ begunden herze und ôren
> tumben unde tôren
> und ûz ir rehte wanken.
> da wurden gedanken
> in maneger wîse vuer brâht...
>
> jâ sîne finger wîze
> die giengen wol ze vlîze
> walgende in den seiten.
> si begunden done breiten,

daz der palas voller wart.
dane wart ouch ougen niht gespart,
der kapfete vil manegez dar
und nâman sîner hende war.

("He played such sweet tones and struck the harp so perfectly in the Breton manner that many who stood or sat nearby forgot their own names; hearts and ears began to lose touch with reality, like mesmerized fools, and thoughts were awakened in many ways...With determination and agility his white fingers went into the strings, so that tones were created which filled the whole palace. And the eyes were not spared either: many who were there intensely watched his hands.")[1]

This passage, excerpted from what is arguably the most famous description of a harp performance to have survived from the Middle Ages, is single-handedly responsible for my own involvement with the instrument. When I read it for the first time, I was like a listener at Tristan's performance: my "thoughts were awakened in many ways." Without ever having touched a harp before in my life, this scene made perfectly clear to me the essential nature of the instrument, its power over hearts and senses, and the magic role it still embodied in the collective memory of Gottfried's early thirteenth century courtly audience. I felt that it must be possible to experience the essence of such harp playing in our own day.

And yet, the passage offers very little of what we would call "useful historical performance information" about the instrument; its specific tuning, materials, size, playing technique, and the pieces being performed are all shrouded in mystery and vagueness. We are not even sure if the harp performance described here reflects contemporary practice, or if it is the poet's idealization of some dimly-perceived, mythical courtly yesteryear.

We know only that the player is an attractive 14-year old boy, Tristan of Parmenie, a charming stranger of noble bearing who has arrived at the castle of King Mark of Cornwall. One evening after the meal, the boy is enchanted (to put it mildly) by the playing of a Welsh harper entertaining the royal audience, and after a certain amount of adolescent squirming he begins asking well-informed questions about the music. Of course, the Welshman lends him the instrument to see what he can play, and we learn that "it fit his hands perfectly" (any player who has ever borrowed a stranger's harp knows that this is a good sign). Tristan, the boy-harper with perfectly-formed white hands, first does a bit of expert re-tuning: a ritual of self-assertion common to this literary genre, since clearly he has his own personal repertoire of pieces, each of which will require specific string configurations and tunings (and besides, what harper ever accepts another's tuning?). This is followed by a series of warm-up passages and preludes which are strangely sweet, so that word begins to spread that magic is being created and the whole household comes running to hear. The harp and the harper, now one, begin to play so sweetly that everyone falls under their spell during the ensuing performance, which includes instrumental *lais* as well as accompanied singing in four languages. Later, while answering questions posed by his royal host, Tristan confesses that he studied harp with Welsh masters for seven years, and that he plays a variety of other instruments as well.

Assuming that Gottfried, a cultured man of his time, is describing not an idealized, imaginary past but a musical experience known to him and his contemporaries, what then exactly did Tristan play that evening and how did he play it? What was the Welshman's harp like? How did those listeners differentiate between playing styles and repertoires, between Breton and Welsh harping? And most important: How can two hands, touching a limited number of tuned strings attached to a resonator, achieve a state of the soul in listeners such as Gottfried has described?

It is this last question which should intrigue us as musicians: when we can answer it for ourselves, we will have begun to find a modus and a voice in our own time for this small instrument which once moved the hearts of northern Europe.

But where can we look for help? Almost 800 years have passed since that Tristan scene was written down, and everyone involved with it has oozed through the gene-pool several dozen times, their instruments turned to dust, the pieces they played and sang never put in writing (or if they were, no direct record survives). Of the musical traditions which once enthralled their listeners, most have been forgotten, and of those which might have survived, all were certainly mixed and remixed many times, subjected to the effects of "cross-over," "fusion," "improvement," popular culture, travel and adaptation, so that we can hardly label any current European harp tradition as the genuine inheritor of the Welsh, the Bretons, or any other medieval harpers.

And yet musicians today do play something confidently called "the medieval harp," in ensembles, as soloists, and as singers; builders offer a wide variety of instruments reconstructed from sculpture or painting, and the medieval harp is the object of philological and iconographical studies. Clearly, somebody is interested, somebody knows where to look, knows what to do, and harps are being heard far and wide.

But we are surely fooling ourselves if we think we have re-created medieval harp music or playing techniques. How can we reconcile what we read in an account such as Gottfried's with the blandness of melody-cum-arpeggio playing we have come to accept today as medieval harp? Is this something one would have to study years with a Welsh master to achieve? When is the last time you became a mesmerized fool and forgot your name listening to a "medieval" harper? What is it we have so fundamentally misunderstood, in our noble positivist search for an authentic medieval harp and its music?

I believe the answer lies in our vision of what the instrument is and how it might function; and the answer also lies in the language we use, or do not use, as musicians. These two issues are related; let me tell a story of how they came together for me.

Some years ago, as I was becoming increasingly frustrated with the seemingly limited spectrum of my instrument (actually, the instrument was just fine; I was the limited one), I realized that I was one of the unquestioning inheritors of an ill-defined contemporary usage called "medieval harp," which is actually a Neo-

Victorian concoction of delicate melodies played above arpeggiated chords. Somehow I had failed to grasp the imaginal riches offered by Gottfried which had inspired me to pick up the instrument in the first place. I could not make the connection between my instrument and its essential nature.

In looking for advice and inspiration, I examined the playing traditions of modern-day European folk harps as well as the literature on medieval harp

What could be learned from folk harps? The contemporary folk-harp scene is mostly a world of relatively large instruments (except that in comparison with the concert harp they seem small) performing chordally-harmonized versions of old tunes, with much of that "old" stuff dating from the seventeenth and eighteenth centuries. The inheritors of Tristan, in Ireland, Scotland, Wales, Brittany, and elsewhere have reconstructed and carried on their own beautiful and venerable traditions, but they are traditions which have accommodated enormous changes in the harp's function in musical society, in the way tunings are employed, in playing technique, and in the music being played (these last two owing a great deal to Baroque and later harp traditions); they scarcely contain any remnant of Tristan's long-since diluted genetic material.

Pl. 24b.1. King David playing harp (detail) English, ca.1215-20. The Pierpont Morgan Library, New York, M.791, f. 170.

Scholarly literature on harps provided plenty of iconographical evidence,[2] scraps of information, and some conjecture, often intriguing but difficult to apply to actual playing; even the best research presents little more than a fascinating smorgasbord of juicy tidbits which leaves the practical harpist just as hungry as before. Unfortunately, the language needed by scholarship is not the language of music-making. And so while looking for enlightenment I found myself coming up against an army of careful formulations which left me wishing for a language which musicians can understand, one which would give imaginal sparks such as the one I imagine Tristan received from his venerable Welsh masters. However, in examining the research on the harp, I was able to perform one very simple and wordless investigative task: to take a long look at the visual nature of the harp as it was when Gottfried saw and heard it, in the late twelfth and early thirteenth centuries. Since no instruments from this period have survived, we are obliged to consult manuscript depictions and sculpture. This yielded images of an instrument much at variance with the medieval harps we find in our own concert venues: the harps on the knees of medieval minstrels, and even King David, are very small instruments. On the average harp, the number of strings is quite limited, so that an instrument with 15 strings would have to be considered a super deluxe model, with 10 to 13 strings being more common (this string count is often based on the number of tuning pegs depicted). In comparison, even the smallest modern folk harp boasts many more strings than this, and most reconstructions of medieval harps, designed by their builders to satisfy the demands of folk, Baroque and modern harpists, have more than 15 strings, with 21 strings not uncommon. In addition to this, the spacing between the strings, as observed in medieval harp depictions, is quite wide by our standards. We ask ourselves: how could medieval harpists have been satisfied with so few strings? Would not more strings allow for more variety and virtuosity? And finally this: the dimensions of medieval harps (corpus size and string length), measured against average medieval body size, generally would not allow for the effective resonance of a bass register and certainly not more than a few tones below middle C. Gerald of Wales, writing about the Irish harp in his *Topographia Hibernica* in ca.1185, attests to this fact when he mentions "the duller sound of a thicker string"[3] in contrast to the brighter-sounding, thinner strings. The highest and the lowest notes would be the weakest, and the resonant strength of the instrument, its true voice, would come from its center: a group of 8-10 strings. What kind of music comes out of such an instrument?

Clearly, a small harp whose middle strings are optimally resonant is not the sort of instrument which invites a technique based on melodies played above arpeggiated chords. There simply are not enough strings to effectively cope with the necessary division of hand-function except for one or two chords, and the natural resonance of the instrument would generally work against a successful sound. An image for Tristan's harp began to emerge in my mind.

Researchers could not play the instrument for me, and the people who really knew how to make harps sing were playing other kinds of music on larger, much later instruments. So there I was, a frustrated "early musician," looking in vain for access to the hidden world of a delicate, 13-string instrument perched silently on my knee.

And that's when fate arranged for a book to fall into my hands. It was not about the medieval harp; in fact it was not even about harps at all, and it had nothing to do with Europe. It was Paul F. Berliner's *The Soul of Mbira*, a fascinating study of the small, hand-held instrument played in numerous African societies, but particularly by the Shona people of Zimbabwe. The mbira, which typically consists of a number of tuned metal tongues attached to a resonator-gourd and played with the thumbs and fingers, has a venerable history as a solo and ensemble instrument, with a rich tradition of spiritual associations. As I began to read descriptions of mbira music-making and the instrument's function, musically and socially, something sounded vaguely familiar: the descriptions of this strange, non-European instrument "fit my hands perfectly," a spark jumped between this book and Gottfried's and I realized they were using the same language to describe something very similar.

To observe the communicative effect of this language on other musicians, I tried an experiment: during a meeting of historical harpists at which I was scheduled to speak, I informed the audience that I had "discovered a book about the medieval harp" and, replacing the word "mbira" with "medieval harp," I read aloud several passages from Berliner's study. The looks on their faces said it all: Finally, someone who speaks our language! (try this experiment yourself with the passages from Berliner's book which follow). The audience of hungry musicians understood immediately the kinds of musical experiences and techniques that were being described, and they could viscerally grasp how those "harps" would sound, how the hands would move, how a music played on so few "strings" could work magic, and what that music could be. By way of comparison, I also read aloud passages which were indeed about the medieval harp, from several musicological studies whose authors had a very different agenda. Obvious to all of us in that room was the confrontation with a language musicians do not speak or process very well. It was imaginally unrelated to our experiences as harpists; instead of guiding our hands to the strings, it gave our minds yet another piece of interesting, indigestible information to help us postpone the decision to pluck the first string.

What did we hear in Berliner's book that struck such a resonant note? It was his eloquent description of an intact instrumental (and vocal) tradition within a tribal society, and a detailed musical analysis based upon intimate contact with masters and their students: we hear them speak to us directly, in a language every musician would understand, just the way we would expect to learn any instrument ourselves under ideal circumstances. We learn how the players think and feel about their instruments, how they function, how boys learn to play, how they describe their techniques, repertoires, and the role of the mbira in the spiritual life of their people. Their language is clear and unequivocal.

But how can we justify analyzing descriptions of the twentieth-century mbira traditions of the Shona to understand the harp playing of a 14-year-old white boy in medieval Cornwall? Is this not just another case of the "superficial imitation of non-European traditions" which I criticized earlier? No, and here's why: I am principally interested in finding a spark which will ignite our imaginal feel for the *function* of the medieval harp, to give us a new musical perspective for the instrument's role in our hands; but under no circumstances do I hear mbira music resonating in King Mark's castle, nor am I planning to transcribe mbira riffs for the harp. I would simply like to examine, in this brief space, what the Shona masters can teach us about our own lost art.

Why the mbira instead of an African harp? Is not Africa the continent with the greatest variety of harps and performing traditions in the world, played by people in over 50 cultures?[4] The simple reason is that Prof. Berliner was captivated by the mbira, and his book made ideas about the mbira accessible. Detailed studies of African harps would surely provide yet more welcome input, but the essential differences would not be that great. The mbira is an instrument which functions in a similar way to the harp as I have described it: a small instrument with a limited number of sounding elements (metal keys) attached to a resonator, played by both hands. Each individual sounding element, and each group of elements, has a particular name and function, and the player feels an enormous sense of companionship, even dialogue, with his resonator. It is played as a solo instrument and in ensembles, and often the player sings as well. The repertoire of pieces is personalized by each master or group, and young people must memorize their particular patterns, through long years of dedicated study with teachers and observation of older players, before being considered mature members of the tradition. People playing and listening to mbira music are regularly transported into altered states of consciousness (remember the "mesmerized fools"?), and the greatest players have a shamanistic power within Shona society. The similarities with the harp as described by medieval authors are astonishing.

Based on what we learn about the mbira, even superficially as described here, what image can we make of an instrument which has a limited number of sounding elements, and how might this apply to the harp?

Briefly summarized, Berliner's study describes an instrument of patterns and structures which can be endlessly varied: "Shona mbira music consists of a continuous stream of subtly changing musical ideas; its texture is like a fabric of tightly interwoven melodic/rhythmic lines that interact with each other...."[5] so that "...the complexity of the mbira's music often gives the impression of more than one instrument being performed."[6] The complexity of what the listener (including the performer) hears often seems unrelated to the actions of the hands, which are combining relatively simple two or three-note patterns in such a way as to create an illusion:

> ...musicians themselves observe that a single mbira can produce the effect of two or more instruments being played simultaneously. One explanation for the apparent complexity of the music lies in a phenomenon known as 'inherent rhythms.' Inherent rhythms are those melodic/rhythmic patterns not directly being played by the performer but arising from the total complex of the mbira music. They are the product of the psycho-acoustic fact that the ear does not perceive a series of tones as isolated pitches, but as a gestalt.[7]

This kind of patterned playing has a characteristic which is particularly eloquent: irregular or chance shiftings of finger patterns (we used to call them "mistakes" in conservatory) can yield openings into new registers of the mode, new patterns, and ultimately inspire the player to develop an idea in a different way than was originally planned:

> The origin of other new compositions is unanticipated discovery in performance. While playing a sequence of pitches, for instance, a musician sometimes reaches for a particular key but misses it, hitting another instead...Such accidents during the performance of mbira music can lead to the creation of new versions of older pieces or to new pieces altogether.[8]

And this situation arises partially from the nature of the instrument: "...Because of the limited number of pitches on which mbira pieces are based...changes such as the substitution of one or two pitches in a melodic sequence can cause whole new phrases to appear...."[9] The importance of this function is seen as an aspect of the instrument's intimate relationship to the player:

"Other musicians...personify the role of the mbira in the performance of mbira music. In this context the mbira is said to be capable of making musical suggestions to the player during the performance of an mbira piece. If as the musician plays a particular finger pattern he inadvertently strikes a different key than the one for which he has aimed, it is not necessarily viewed as a mistake. Rather, if the mbira player likes the new pitch he can interpret it as the mbira's suggestion for the next variation and can incorporate it into his performance."[10]

These descriptions resonate in the words of the American jazzman Clark Terry: "One object of jazz is to redefine 'mistake'. There are no mistakes *per se*. The trick is to find graceful exits from unexpected situations. The only inexcusable error is not swinging."

Tuning of the instrument is also an important aspect of the mbira and is essential to the nature of each player's identity with his repertoire: "The tunings that players of mbira dzavadzimu adopt either as individuals or collectively as members of the same group can vary considerably, and players differ greatly in their commitment to a particular tuning."[11] Shona players use the word *chuning* to refer to "...a number of interrelated aspects distinguishing the overall sound of certain mbira from that of others. These include tone, sound projection, pitch level, tuning, variation within octaves...."[12] In many medieval descriptions of harp performance we read about a harper changing the tuning of his instrument.[13] Tristan is not alone in this story-telling convention, and there's a reason for it: In a patchwork of musical societies which knows no common practice but can best be described as clannish or tribal, it would make sense that each player, coming from a different master and a different milieu, would bring along a personal as well as a clan repertoire, with the personalized modal tunings needed to realize those pieces. Tristan was acutely aware that the Welshman's *chuning* would make it impossible to play his own pieces, and as he re-tuned to establish his own *chuning*, the listeners were already falling under his spell.

In twelfth-century Wales or Cornwall, just as in the Shona lands of Zimbabwe today, it was this spell which proved music's power in a tribal society, and the almost magical function of instruments, be they a small harp or an mbira. And as the player creates a world of beautiful illusion, he must himself be transported, letting the instrument speak to him and lead him, so that "...many who stood or sat nearby forgot their own names." Or, as Berliner tells it:

> The mbira player, enveloped by the sound of the music, entranced by its repetitive, cyclical nature, and captivated by its subtle variations, may find his state of consciousness transformed. Several performers reported that playing mbira music made them feel 'dreamy' or 'sleepy.' Another player remarked that the effect of playing mbira was sometimes like that of smoking marijuana, and once, after I had been playing the mbira with a great deal of force, I was jokingly warned by other mbira players that I would one day be found wandering in the forest, *not knowing my own name.* [italics mine] Furthermore, non-musicians among the Shona sometimes imitate mbira players by staring blankly into the space before them, totally absorbed in their own thoughts....[14]

Tuned to enhance a given piece's special mode, its *chuning,* the small medieval harp with its few strings can actually serve as a huge repository of melodic gestures which bounce around one another in seeming complexity, creating tones which "fill the whole palace"; as the hands perform a series of simple, varied patterns, crossing and re-crossing ("many who were there intensely watched his hands..."), a texture can be created which mesmerizes the listener and the player as well with its inherent rhythms. Anyone who has gazed at illuminations from such manuscripts as the Book of Kells knows the power of pattern, repetition, illusion and the weaving of simple elements into a complex whole. Even Gerald of Wales knew the feeling, when he described the Irish harpers, who "...the more their concealed art delights them, the more luxuriously they caress the ear so that the greatest part of their art seems to conceal the art...."[15]

I feel that this imaginal, densely-patterned world belongs to our search for "medieval" instruments more genuinely than the dainty melodies with chordal accompaniment and other such techniques which colonized the harp several hundred years ago and haunt it still. But we can reclaim that world and in doing so rediscover the magic of a medieval instrumental tradition. We will gain a music that is our own, that has been within us all along.

Notes

[1] Gottfried von Strassburg, *Tristan, nach dem Text von Friedrich Ranke* (Stuttgart, 1980), lines 3588–97 and 3601–08 (English translations by Benjamin Bagby).

[2] See Martin van Schaik, *The Harp in the Middle Ages: The Symbolism of a Musical Instrument* (Amsterdam & Atlanta, 1992).

[3] J.F. Dimock, ed., *Girardi Cambrensis Topographia Hibernica,* Rolls Series 21:5 (London, 1867), pp. 153-54. English translation: Hibberd/Page; see Christopher Page, *Voices and Instruments in the Middle Ages* (Berkeley, 1986), pp. 229-30, 153.

[4] Sue Carole DeVale, "African Harps: Construction, Decoration and Sound," in *Sounding Forms: African Musical Instruments,* ed. Marie-Therese Brincard (exhibition catalogue), American Federation of the Arts (New York, 1989), p. 53. See also Philippe Bruguière *et al.,* eds., *Song of the River: Harps of Central Africa* (Paris: Musée de la Musique with the assistance of the Société d'Ethnologie, Nanterre, 1999).

[5] Paul F. Berliner, *The Soul of Mbira. Music and Traditions of the Shona People of Zimbabwe* (Berkeley, 1978), p. 53.

[6] Ibid., p. 52.

[7] Ibid., p. 88.

[8] Ibid., p. 87.

[9] Ibid., p. 98.

[10] Ibid., p. 128.

[11] Ibid., p. 60.

[12] Ibid., p. 61.

[13] See also Page, *Voices,* pp. 112-14.

[14] Berliner, p. 131.

[15] Dimock, p. 154.

24c. Playing the Late Medieval harp

Cheryl Ann Fulton

Recreating the sound of the late medieval harp is an exciting challenge to today's performer. The nature of the performance then, as now, depends largely upon the skill and inclinations of the performer, the technique, as well as musical originality and creativity, and the nature and quality of the harp itself. Precise information about exactly what harps played in this period is sparse. The majority of it comes from indirect sources such as paintings and poetic accounts. Since the harp during this period also had great symbolic significance, as, for example, in the instrument's association with the biblical King David, care must be taken in deriving practical applications from iconographical and written evidence.[1] Asking the right questions becomes far more important than producing definitive, correct answers.

One of the first questions that needs to be asked is what kind of harp is most appropriate for the music of this period? If the intention is to try to meet the music on its own terms as much as possible, an attempt must be made to find the best reproduction of a harp from this period. This includes considering preferences in various geographic areas. Recent research has shown that the bray harp was probably used far more frequently than is evident in modern performances.[2] On the other hand, the wire-strung harp, the clarsach, should perhaps take precedence for music from the British Isles. The structural characteristics of the harp influence the required techniques as well as the musical language and style. In the area of improvisation the harps themselves have much to say and reveal to the players. The instrument itself, a bray harp, wire-strung harp or gut-strung harp without brays, should play a major role in influencing the choices a performer makes.

A performer may choose to perform this music on a much later style of harp and attempt to apply appropriate performance practice and stylistic ideals, but even the most learned and skillful attempt cannot compare to using the best possible harp for the given music. Beyond this, the performer must try to understand the music as much as possible in the same way as a musician from the period. For musicians trained in later music this can involve a conscious recognition and analysis of set physical and mental patterns influencing the player's approach to both the music and the instrument. For example, studying rudimentary medieval music theory and rhetoric can influence the performer's fundamental approach to the music.

There are no intact harps surviving from this period. And with the exception of the Robert ap Huw manuscript (on which, see below),[3] there are no technique tutors, no pieces designated as harp pieces, and no indications in the music as to what a harp could or should play. Despite this lack of specific information, there is an abundance of helpful information to be found in theoretical treatises of the time, a careful study of the notation, iconographical sources, narrative and poetic accounts and descriptions, and the music itself.

Structure and Stringing

Structure

Most harps depicted in fourteenth- and early fifteenth-century paintings are single strung. One piece of iconographical evidence shows that experiments with multiple rows of strings began at least as early as the fourteenth century.[4] The tall, slim gothic shape is the most common, built with a light construction as contrasted with the shorter, much heavier build of the metal-strung harps. Generally the harps from this period could have been strung with anywhere from 10 or 11 to 25 or 26 strings.[5] They range in size from lap harps about two feet tall to harps about four feet high.

Some of the harps appear to have a box type construction, a three-sided body with a flat soundboard, and others a carved body construction, a body hollowed out of one piece of wood with a carved soundboard on top. Beginning attempts at copying iconographical sources were often unsuccessful because the very narrow, small boxes did not produce an adequate sound. Research into the use of bray pins has helped to solve part of this mystery and the construction of carved body harps with paper thin but strong soundboards has resulted in harps with very slender bodies but having a tone capable of good projection.[6]

Many of the 15th century harps depicted do appear to be equipped with bray pins.[7] These bray pins serve the double function of holding the string in the soundboard and can also be turned and delicately positioned to touch the strings in such a way that a buzzing sound results.[8] The bray pin changes the timbre and increases the volume of the sound produced. Paintings that show the gothic harp being played in an ensemble with loud instruments become understandable if the harp used is taken to be a bray harp. Bray pins can also be "turned off" and used simply as string pins.

String material

Documentary evidence suggests that most harps used in Europe during this period were gut strung.[9] Metal strung harps, some with strings said to be made of gold, were associated with the Celtic countries, particularly Ireland and Scotland. Horsehair strings were used later on Welsh harps and could have been used earlier as well. For the purposes of this chapter we will consider only the use of gut strings.

Today's performer has the choice of nylon or carbon fiber strings as well as polished and unpolished gut. Although nylon and carbon fiber strings are less expensive and more durable, they do not provide an adequate substitute for the tone quality and feel of gut strings. Polished gut strings are generally better, last longer and produce fewer false strings than unpolished gut strings which tend to fray easily, wear out and go false more quickly.

String Spacing

A wide range of string spacings appears in iconographical sources. The spacing may be partially a function of whether the harp is being played with the flesh of the pads, or with the nails. Wire-strung harps, which are played almost exclusively with the nails, tend to have a much closer string spacing than gut strung instruments played with the finger pads.[10] Spacing is also related to the desired range and harmonic curve of the neck of the harp. Since no standard can be determined for harps of this period, it is advisable to play on a harp with comfortable string spacing, which allows for a firm, full, yet gentle contact with the string. One should not have to play on the very tip of the finger with a shallow, superficial touch, but should be able to have the string cross over the pad comfortably.

Stringing system

From the sixteenth century to the present day the majority of harps worldwide have been strung with a basic, eight note to the octave, major scale system. Even triple and double harps, with their additional chromatic rows, have their diatonic rows strung based on this premise.[11] This stringing, naturally, reflects the practical and stylistic requirements of the music from these periods.

One of the earliest diagrams depicting a diatonic octave stringing of the harp is given in Virdung's *Musica getutscht* (1511). The earliest full description of a specific diatonic octave tuning for the harp is given in Lanfranco's *Scintille di musica* (1523). He says of the harp: "...its tuning consists of eight tones, since from octave to octave (always returning to the repetition) the high tones derive from the low ones, as can be considered by these fifteen strings noted by the singing syllables, which can be found on them naturally." A diagram designates the first fifteen strings of the harp as: Bass ut (tone), re (tone) mi (lesser semitone) fa, sol, re, mi, fa ut, re, mi, fa, sol, re, mi, fa. He also notes that if the lowest string is C fa-ut the Bs will be natural, if from F fa-ut the Bs will be flat. The importance here is the emphasis on the sequence of tones and semitones, which results in what we now conceive of as a major scale.[12]

These two diagrams strongly suggest that a diatonic tuning with eight notes per octave was used on medieval harps.[13] Although some harps certainly were strung with eight notes to the octave, both of these examples show how this stringing was derived from tetrachords and hexachords. More importantly, both diagrams are being used to illustrate Greek music theory. The harp in the Berkeley MS is described as being composed of a heptachord and a tetrachord producing an eleven-note range (labeled *a b c d e f g a b c d*) said to have been devised by Teulex of Egypt.[14] Therefore these examples can be used to support the idea of approaching the stringing of the harp from the basis of hexachords and tetrachords and not eight-note, diatonic scales. Diatonic tuning therefore in this context can refer to either a harp strung with B♮ only, B♭ only, or both. Chromatic tunings would imply the tuning in of any notes outside the hexachord system.

Much of the music from 1300-1450 which a harp can play requires that both B♭ and B♮ be easily available. The other commonly required *ficta* notes are F♯, C♯, G♯ and E♭. If the harp is strung according to the notes of the gamut, with separate strings for B♭ and B♮, other accidentals can be obtained by fretting (see below). Not only does stringing the harp in this manner provide the harpist with the basic notes most frequently needed, but it also takes the harpist into the realm of the hexachord system. So, for example, a 22 string-harp could be strung as follows: *c d e f g a b♭ b c'* (middle c) *d' e' f' g' a' b♭ ' b' c'' d'' e'' f'' g'' a''*.

A seventeenth century source gives one of the best illustrations of tuning the single-row harp according to the hexachord system.[15] Marin Mersenne, in his monumental treatise, *Harmonie universelle* (Paris, 1636) includes descriptions of the harp in two Propositions from the *Book of Instruments*. For Mersenne the triple strung harp is the "normal" harp, but in *Proposition XXIV, Chapter 3*, to explain the shape, tuning, range, and use of the harp, he also discusses a single-strung gothic harp:

> I have added yet another illustration of a single row harp so that we may consider the way in which the old bray pins made the strings buzz in an unpleasant way, as well as the [reasons for] the 23 intervals of the 24 strings that make up the 24-note range, because the numbers that are to the right of the shell explain them (the intervals). [See Figure 24c.1.] One also notices between the strings the names that the Greeks gave to each string in their literature. The letters above the lines are taken from Porphyre and other ancient Greek authors. However, I have placed the letters from our regular scale above the tuning pins so that it can be understood from that one figure how Guy Aretin related the letters of the Latin alphabet to the Greek strings. The strings next to which I have not placed the Greek word εσωζ were mobile. This word means immobile; thus, the strings bearing that sign always stay at the same tone on the instruments, whereas all the others can be raised or lowered depending on the differences in styles and kinds of pieces.
>
> The musicians of this century change all the strings by adding flats in all sorts of keys. They do, however, almost always keep a few tones unchanged: for example, the principal strings of the mode they are in. These they call "modals," as I have mentioned elsewhere. Hence, one may conclude that this harp can be used to learn a great deal of music that has come to us from the Greeks as well as modern music. [16]

Perhaps the most important aspect of Mersenne's comments concerning the single-row harp is that he considers this harp completely in the context of the hexachord system. His reference to Guy Aretin (Guido d'Arezzo) makes this connection perfectly clear, and the harp is shown strung according to Guido's gamut including separate strings for B♭ and B♮. Mersenne also describes the retuning of the single-row harp. According to the old system, he reports, eight notes—G ut, A re, D sol re, B♮ (mi), C fa ut, F fa ut and B♭ (fa) according to the diagram—were constant and all the other strings could be changed as needed.[17]

Fig. 24c.1. Mersenne's diagram of a harp with B♮ and B♭.

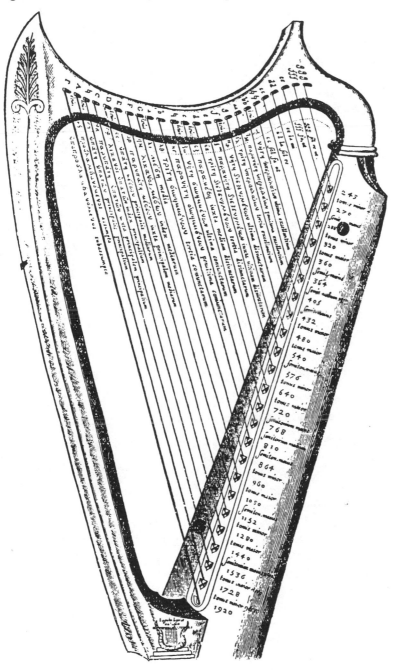

Tuning and Temperament

After deciding whether to string the medieval harp according to the hexachord system or not, other necessities and options must be considered. First is temperament; how is the harp actually going to be tuned? Treatises from this period overwhelmingly advocate the Pythagorean tuning system. In practice, however, although generally a fairly strict Pythagorean tuning is preferable, some adjustments occasionally need to be made. The best notes to begin a tuning from are *c, g,* or *d* depending on the range of the harp. It is best to tune the lower/middle register first and then tune the octaves above and below. A Pythagorean tuning for the harp starting on g could be done as follows:

> *g* up a perfect fifth to *d'*
> *d'* down a perfect octave to *d*
> *d* up a perfect fifth to *a*
> *a* up a perfect fifth to *e'*
> *e'* down a perfect octave to *e*
> *e* up a perfect fifth to *b*
> *g* up a perfect fourth to *c'*
> *c'* down a perfect fifth to *f*
> *f* up a perfect fourth to *b♭*

For a harpist beginning to explore medieval music, the use of a strict Pythagorean tuning, with pure fifths and very wide thirds, helps to wake up the ears![18] Such a tuning also encourages a harpist to think and feel in linear terms, to feel dissonances in a linear context and the tension and release in melodic cadences.

Retuning, Scordatura, and Fretting

A crucial point in relation to the gamut is to remember that pitch was not fixed. Transposition was a common and frequently used means, both in sacred and secular music, of staying within the system. So for example, if a harpist is playing in mode 8 with a final on F, the harp must be tuned with E♭s and B♭s. By tuning E♭s for this purpose the harpist is not using *musica ficta*, but is playing a transposed mode. In this way the syllables and whole- and half-step relationships remain the same, but the final of the mode or the actual vibrating pitch of a named note can be variable.

In his book Voices and Instruments of the Middle Ages, Christopher Page includes several translations from medieval poems which contain some of the earliest descriptions of the retuning of the harp. Two are from the thirteenth-century romance *Tristan en prose*:

> ...Take this harp (said Iseult), and tune it according to the music for your lines....The harper... then began to tune it according to what he knew would be necessary for the music he was about to perform.[19]

> Tristan takes the harp and begins to tune it in his way and after his fashion...[20]

Another 13th century poem, *Lumiere as Lais* (1267) by Pierre of Peckham, gives an excellent description of the flexibility of the tuning for the harp:

> One may change the settings
> By tuning different notes,
> And by different arrangements
> Of variously placed semitones.
> By this means
> There is diverse tuning in the harp.[21]

Another issue in tuning is the use of scordatura. Different choices for whole and half steps can be made for different registers of the harp. For example a 22 string harp could be tuned as follows: $C D E F G A B\flat B c d e f g a b c' c\sharp' d' e' f\sharp' g' a'$. From this example it can be easily seen that many choices are possible.

Another example of retuning is found in the above mentioned Robert ap Huw manuscript. According to harpist William Taylor, "Robert ap Huw's repertoire requires five tunings for the harp, with lengthy appendices giving lists of pieces to be played in specific tunings. Other tunings are possible (and illustrated), but are seen as less important. The tunings, while not necessarily always yielding straight diatonic scales, derive from an orthodox Guidonian framework."[22]

A practical consideration for both retuning and the use of scordatura, however, is that in a modern concert hall, even the best of harps can only take so much retuning in one evening before they become unstable and impossible to tune precisely. Therefore in choosing the pieces for a program a minimum of retuning should be used.

Accidentals, particularly at cadences, may also be played by using the technique of fretting. Fretting is a technique that was documented in the 16th century and is a still used in many traditional harp techniques today. It is most definitely an option in the period under consideration, especially on harps built with light construction, a wide enough neck, no bridge pins so the string falls directly from the string pin to the soundboard, and light string tension. Fretting involves pressing the string against the neck of the harp under the tuning pin to raise the pitch a semitone. If playing on the right shoulder the harpist can use the following methods:[23]

- use the left hand thumb to press the string against the neck and pluck the string with the right hand.
- press with the thumb of the left hand, play the raised note with the right hand while plucking lower notes with the third or fourth fingers of the left hand.
- reach over the top of the neck with the right hand and press one or two strings against the neck and play the string(s) with the left hand.
- press the string with the index finger of the left hand and pluck the string with the left hand thumb.
- use the tuning key or some other devise to press the string instead of a finger.

Another method of shortening the string to raise it a semitone is to push the string towards the belly of the harp just above where the string enters the soundboard. This technique can be somewhat more problematic and difficult than fretting on the neck.

Articulation and Fingering

Articulation is a way of grouping or relating notes to each other to delineate music phrases. It is as much involved with the space—the silence—between each note, as with the notes themselves. In a rhetorical context George Houle says, "Articulations are sometimes explained as a means of producing an instrumental equivalent to pronunciation that can be subtly and infinitely varied to fit different music circumstances."[24] Not only an intellectual understanding of articulation, but also a physical ease with a variety of articulation patterns, is essential to effectively communicate subtle phrasing. Perhaps the most fundamental aspect of articulation and fingering is the ability to create good phrasing by subtle agogic accents and weight shifts, not by dynamic contrast and stress.

On the harp, weight must be felt with regard to "horizontal gravity." On the lute, by contrast, the function of plucking or strumming the strings occurs in a natural relationship to gravity. Strong or long articulations are most easily executed by plucking or strumming down with gravity and weak or short articulations by plucking or strumming up against the pull of gravity. On the harp the same shifting of weight can be used, but in a horizontal field with motion going towards the column or coming in towards the player. Because this is an artificial relationship to natural gravity, this weight shift can be felt and used as strong and weak in both directions. So, for example, when plucking a single string the player can start with the thumb plucking towards the column with a long or strong beat followed by the second, index finger plucking the string again back towards the player with a shorter or weak articulation. It is also possible to start with the index finger playing a long, strong note plucking in towards the player, followed by the thumb playing a weak note releasing and moving towards the column. The feeling can be compared to the ebb and flow of waves in the ocean. This fingering can be extended to play melismas and scales, ascending and descending, with long and short articulations. Different passages, depending primarily upon what precedes or follows the given passage, require different choices as to which pattern to use: thumb for a long stroke, second finger for a short one or vice versa. Many variations of this basic fingering pattern are possible, including alternating the second and third fingers on short notes with the thumb on long notes, but the principle remains the same.

Choices in fingering do not need to be rigid and can even change from performance to performance. The study of fingering is more essential to the performer's understanding of articulation than to the actual fingering used. Now, as then, fingering choices can be highly personal, but the stylistic requirements of the music must be understood and honored.[25]

Conclusion

The practical considerations of obtaining an appropriate late medieval harp, stringing it and tuning it are only the beginning. The next daunting task is to approach the music and discover how to use the harp in both monophonic and polyphonic, composed and improvised music of the period. The instrument itself, however, will have much to teach and show the receptive player. A delicate balance between authenticity/historical accuracy on the one hand, and originality and vital, creative expression on the other, must be established and nurtured. As Arnold Hauser says of the medieval epic, "The poems have their own legend, their own heroic history: works of poetry live not only in the form the poets give to them but also in that which they are given by posterity... every serious attempt to interpret a work from the point of view of a living present deepens and widens its significance."[26] The medieval harp, when played with a sensitivity to and knowledge of its original place and time, as well as its timeless beauty, can join past and present in living harmony.

Notes

1. For an excellent discussion of this issue, see Martin van Schaik, *The Harp in the Middle Ages: the Symbolism of a Musical Instrument* (Amsterdam, Atlanta, 1992).

2. S. Ron Cook, "The Presence and Use of Brays on Gut-Strung Harp through the 17th Century: A Survey and Consideration of the Evidence," *Historical Harp Society Bulletin* 8 (1998), 2-39.

3. Although the manuscript is dated 1613, the music evidently dates largely from the 15th century. This manuscript provides exercises for a fingernail technique which makes precise and detailed use of damping techniques. Although outside the scope of this chapter, much work has been done in this important area by harpist William Taylor.

4. The harp in a triptych dated 1390 from the Piedra Monastery, Madrid, shows a small Romanesque style harp with two rows of strings, 14 strings on the visible left side.

5. Guillaume de Machaut (1300-1377) describes a harp strung with 25 strings in his poem *Dit de la Harpe*.

6. The medieval harps, both the gothic and *Cythara Anglica* models, built by historical harp builder Rainer Thurau of Wiesbaden, Germany, exemplify these characteristics and are among the finest medieval harps being made today.

7. S. Ron Cook's extensive list of iconographical sources is available through the Historical Harp Society.

8. Later Welsh sources equate the sound of the bray harp with the buzzing of bees. See Cook, "The Presence."

9. See Christopher Page, *Voices and Instruments of the Middle Ages* (Berkeley, 1986), Appendix 4, String-materials in the Middle Ages, pp. 210-42.

10. In 1460, the theorist Paulus Paulirinus describes a gut-strung harp, probably a bray harp, being plucked with fingernails. See Judy Kadar, "Some Practical Hints for Playing Fourteenth and Fifteenth Century Music," in *Historical Harps: Theoretical and Practical Aspects of Historical Harps*, ed. Heidrun Rosenzweig (Basel, 1991), p. 130.

11. Speculation about possible chromatic, single-row, seventeenth-century wire-strung harps exists. The sister strings used on some Irish harps is also a known tuning that

differs from a straight diatonic octave tuning. See Ann and Charlie Heymann, "*Clairseach*: The Lore of the Irish Harp," *Eire Ireland* 26 (1991), 82-95.

[12] For more on the gamut and modes, see chapter 36. Among theorists, I recommend *Brevis summula proportionum quantum ad musicum pertinet* and *Parvus tractatulus de modo monachordum dividendi* by Prosdocimo de Beldomandi, ed. and tr. Jan Herlinger (Lincoln and London, 1987).

[13] From *Breviarium regulare musicae* (England, ca.1400) Bodleian Libr. at Oxford, Bodley 842, f.66v and *The Berkeley Manuscript* (French, ca.1350-75). See Oliver B. Ellsworth *The Berkeley Manuscript. A New Critical Text and Translation* (Lincoln & London, 1984).

[14] Christopher Page says of this diagram, "Fortunately the second harp in the manuscript is straightforward. Its eleven strings are tuned to a diatonic series: *a b c d e f g a b c d*. The number of strings has probably been reduced for ease of drawing; Machaut mentions twenty-five...." The number of strings quite clearly corresponds precisely to the description in the text. The relationship, if any, of this harp to the harp described by Machaut is unclear. See Christopher Page, "Fourteenth-Century Instruments and Tunings: a Treatise by Jean Vaillant? (Berkeley, MS 744)," *Galpin Society Journal* 33 (1980), 31. The heptachord was devised by Terpander of Lesbos who added a seventh string to the six strings representing the natural hexachord to establish a correspondence to the seven planets.

[15] I thought I had "invented" the system of stringing the harp in this way in 1978. In 1980, after using this system with great success for almost two years, when doing research on the triple harp, I discovered Mersenne's diagram and was excited to have some historical confirmation.

[16] Marin Mersenne, *Harmonie universelle* (Paris, 1636), pp. 169-71. Translations of Mersenne's texts by Charles Pearo in consultation with Cheryl Ann Fulton. Mersenne's discussion of instruments has also been translated in Marin Mersenne, *Harmonie universelle: The Books on Instruments*, trans. Roger E. Chapman (The Hague, 1957).

[17] He says that his contemporary musicians, however, make more extensive changes but still keep a few constant pitches. He also indicates that by the early 1600s the buzzing sound of the "old" bray pins was still known but not in fashion. He does not, however, describe how the brays created the buzzing sound as he said he would.

[18] The use of an electronic tuner with variable temperament settings including Pythagorean may be advisable for harpists not familiar with or accustomed to temperaments other than equal temperament. Many might be surprised to find that their perception of a fifth is far from perfect! Further discussion of medieval tuning can be found in Chapter 40.

[19] Ibid., p. 112.

[20] Ibid., p. 114.

[21] Ibid., p. 116.

[22] Personal communication with the author.

[23] See also Kadar, pp. 125-28.

[24] George Houle, *Meter in Music* (Bloomington & Indianapolis, 1987), p. 85.

[25] For example, a modern pedal or folk harpist whose fingers are primarily trained and accustomed to playing triadic chordal arpeggios and even, equally articulated scales will have mental and physical habits which neither easily apply to late medieval music nor facilitate an appropriate technique on historical harps.

[26] Arnold Hauser, *The Social History of Art*, Vol. 1 (New York, 1957), p. 167.

25. Lute, Gittern, & Citole

Crawford Young

Introduction

The significance of lute music in music history has, in recent decades, taken on more importance. Only proportionately small areas of this wide topic have gained some accessibility, however; and the lute—once the celebrated queen in the art of instrumental music—takes but a most humble place in the eyes of the music historian.[1]

After reading the opening remark from Oswald Körte's 1901 study, *Lute and Lute Music up to the Mid-16th Century*, we may well ask whether anything since then has changed in terms of what we know of the earlier history of the lute and related instruments of the lute family, in particular before 1500. The answer would have to be yes, and yet in many ways the early Renaissance or—even more so—the medieval lute has remained elusive (both as a subject of music history and focus of modern early music performance) than the later Renaissance or Baroque lutes. Why has this been the case? Although hardly any actual instruments have survived, we do not lack depictions of lute-types in the visual arts of the Middle Ages. We seem to lack lute music, however, in the form of tablature before the end of the fifteenth century, and it is only recently that lutenists and musicologists have begun to understand that the previously "hidden" repertory of fifteenth-century music for solo lute and lute duo is in fact accessible to those who are willing to reconstruct this repertory from sources other than tablatures.

It is not until the thirteenth century that we begin to find practical information about the family of medieval lutes. This is consistent with a new trend in describing or depicting instruments for their own sake, as it were, rather than simply as obligatory and rather abstract illustrations to Bible commentaries. The thirteenth century sees the first descriptions about contemporary practical music making (including instrumental playing) from Jerome of Moravia and Johannes de Grocheo, who were connected with the cutting-edge musical life of late thirteenth-century Paris. In the fourteenth century, the number of works of visual art with more or less realistic depictions of musical instruments dramatically increases. Lute-type instruments are found much more in the fourteenth century than in the thirteenth, and considerably more appear in the fifteenth.

How may the different members of the medieval lute family be classified, and how were they classified during their own period?

Classification

Modern research has been slow to find a consensus regarding both clearly defined forms and modern historical names of medieval instruments.[2] A profusion of phonetic spellings, in different languages, within different kinds of sources, plus a lack of labeled depictions of instruments, has caused confusion for latter-day scholars. Although there is, upon close examination, a clearly discernible, consistent terminology for the mainstream chordophones of the Middle Ages, our starting point for classifying these instruments will not be name, but physical form; after a brief classification by form, we can proceed to terminology, and then to further questions related to performance practice, especially playing technique and repertoire.

Generally speaking, most medieval depictions of chordophones give us at least two aspects of an instrument's basic form: the shape of the soundbox seen from the front, and the length of the neck relative to the size of the sound chamber. We can begin with these two bits of general information to classify any lute-type image: (1) round (or oval) form versus non-round (or waisted) form and (2) long-necked versus short-necked. The frontal form of the sound chamber may be taken to imply what sort of back the sound chamber has (basically round or flat). A round form would usually imply a rounded back (that is, a bowl carved from one piece or built up from ribs), whereas a shouldered form would point to a flat-back construction. Note that these are general tendencies only, not fixed, black-or-white rules. Using, then, the criteria of the frontal form of the soundbox, type of pegbox and type of neck-joint (seen frontally), it is possible to classify chordophones into the following generic orders :

A = Pear-shaped frontal form

A1:   Instruments with a straight pegbox, bent back at a 90-degree-or-less angle to the neck; the neck is joined at the body either in a sloping, gradual joint or at a clear, cornered intersection of neck and body. The back is rounded, built up (ribbed) construction.

A2:   Similar to A1 but somewhat smaller with a sickle-shaped pegbox and gradual neck joint. Rounded back, one-piece (carved) construction.

B = Non-pear-shaped frontal form

Instruments with straight or in-curved sides, shoulders with or without ornaments, a tail projection, often trefoil, to which strings are fastened. The pegbox can be sharply angled back from the fingerboard, sickle-shaped, or nearly flat; body depth depends upon pegbox form: angled-back pegbox = increasing body depth towards pegbox with "spine" (with thumb-hole) connecting body to pegbox; flat pegbox = "fiddle construction." Construction: one-piece (carved), wooden frets. Lower bouts rounded, pointed or ornamented like upper shoulders.

Types A1, A2, and B are "mainstream" medieval plucked instruments and are referred to in modern English as "lute," "gittern," and "citole" respectively. While it is outside the scope of this article to offer an exhaustive list of medieval references to members of the lute family from the earlier Middle Ages through the late fifteenth century, a short representative selection of terms used for lute, gittern, and citole follows:[3]

A1 = "lute"

leüz	*Roman de la Rose* (before 1285)
leüs	*Cleomadès* (ca.1285)
leuto	*L'intelligenza* (late 13th–early 14th c.)[4]
leü	*Remede de Fortune* (ca.1340)
laud	*Libro de buen amor* (ca.1330)
luth	*La Vieille* (14th c.)
leuto	*Il Paradiso degli Alberti* (ca.1425)
lutene	Arnaut de Zwolle (ca.1445)
cithara	Paulus Paulirinus (1459-63)
lyra	*Musica practica*, Ramos de Pareja (1482)
"*lyra populariter leutum dicta*"	Tinctoris (1480s)

A2 = "gittern"

gitere	*Blancheflour et Florence* (ca.1270)[5]
quitarres	*Roman de la Rose* (before 1285)
kitaires	*Cleomadès* (ca.1285)
chitarre	*L'intelligenza* (early 14th c.)
chitarra	Dante (ca.1300)
quiterna	*Die Minne Regel* (1404)
quinterna	Paulus Paulirinus (1459-63)
lira	Berkeley, MS 744, p. 52 (ca.1375)
guisterna	Bibl. Nat. MS 7378 (14th c.)
guisterne	*La Vieille* (14th c.)
chitarino	Pietrobono dal chitarino (mid-15th c.)[6]
ghiterra	Tinctoris (1480s)
quinterne	Virdung (1512), Agricola (1536)

B = "citole"

citola	*Daurel et Beton* (late 12th c.)
citole	*Li Biaus Desconeus* (13th c.)
situla	*Flamenca* (1225-50)
citole	*Blancheflour* (ca.1270)
zitol in	*Der Renner* (13th c.)
sitol	*Kyng Alisauder* (bef. 1300)
ceterare	*L'intelligenza* (ca.1300)
cetera	Dante *Paradiso* (ca.1300)
zitolin	*Der Renner* (ca.1300)
cistole	*La Vieille* (14th c.)
cetula	Tinctoris (1480s)

Although the term *mandora* or even *mandola* has sometimes been confused with *gittern* in twentieth century research, the problem of gittern terminology is now resolved.[7] Unlikely to be conclusively resolved, however, are a handful of other terms that seem to be related to gittern names: *guitarra morisca* and *guitarra latina* (Spanish, ca.1330), *morache, guiterne moresche* and *guiterne latine* (French, middle third of fourteenth century), and *quitara sarracenica* (Latin treatise, ca.1300). The terms *guiterne latine, guiterne moresche*, their Spanish versions, and *morache*, are found in just a few fourteenth-century sources, and Laurence Wright has pointed out that these sources are related.[8] Because of the apparent lack of any medieval Eastern Mediterranean or Arabic source documenting the presence of the gittern, it is possible that *guitarra latine* and *guiterne latine* refer to this instrument (so well known in Italy, for example), in which case *guitarra morisca* and *guiterne moresche* might refer to the lute. Alternatively, these names could refer to different types of gitterns, or possibly *guitarra morisca / guiterne moresche* were used in reference to an instrument found in a few French fourteenth century marginal drawings, with, apparently, a skin top, rounded back(?), narrow neck which is longer than a gittern's, and sickle-shaped peg box.[9] Closely related to *guitarra morisca / guiterne moresche* is the term *quitara sarracenica*, which comes from Johannes Grocheo (whose Latin treatise also mentions *cithara* and *lyra).*[10] *Quitara sarracenica* could here mean lute, following the logic outlined above; given what is known about the mainstream instruments used in Grocheo's milieu (Paris, ca.1300), it could otherwise perhaps refer to the gittern (what it most likely did *not* indicate was the citole). Grocheo's *cithara* likely means harp and *lyra* perhaps rebec. To further complicate matters, we find *guiterne, leü, morache,* and *cytolle* in Machaut's *Remède de Fortune,* so it would seem here that *guiterne* and *morache* are two different instruments, also that *morache* is not the same as lute *(leü).*[11]

We cannot conclude a brief discussion of plucked instrument terminology without mentioning a few other terms. *Viola,* having related variants such as *viüela de pendola* (*Libro de buen amor,* ca.1330) and in later general usage, *viola da mano,* seems to have been especially in Mediterranean areas a generic term for B-type instruments which could be bowed or plucked. Because of the word's similarity to *vielle* and even *viol, viola* is often quickly assumed to mean a bowed instrument, yet one suspects that the plucked version was more common than has been hitherto understood by *viola.* Since Antiquity, the Greek/Latin term *cithara* has been the fundamental historical term for plucked instruments, and from this term came both gittern and citole name forms.[12]

To summarize:

- A1: *lute* and related names; *cithara* used exceptionally
- A2: *gittern* and related names; possibly *guiterne latine, guitarra latina, quitarra sarracenica*
- B: *citole* and related names; possibly *viola* and related names

Lute

A pre-fifteenth-century lute is generally spoken of as a fretless, short-necked instrument with four (or possibly five) double-courses. Tenth-century Spanish sources provide us with early depictions of 'ud-like lutes and long-necked instruments, but the stylization of most tenth, eleventh and twelfth-century images offers little precise information regarding anything but the most basic details.[13] If surviving works are a reliable indication, the number of representations of lutes increased substantially in the thirteenth century and continued to increase in the fourteenth and fifteenth centuries. Pre-fourteenth-century lute depictions continue to be 'ud-like, with short-necked fretless instruments having a gradual neck-body joint. Long-necked lutes occur less frequently and have clear neck-body joints; some, as shown in the ninth-century Utrecht Psalter, are fretted.

Pl. 25.1. Spanish miniature (1220) showing lute and tanbur (?)or citole (?) (New York, Pierpont Morgan Library, MS M. 429, f. 112r.).

Body shapes of medieval lutes are variable, some rounder, some more oval, but these were all variations upon a handful of basic designs. As outlined by Henri Arnaut de Zwolle, ca.1445, one begins with a circle (symbol of perfection), includes a circle within a circle (the rose, another symbol of perfection), and derives all measurements (for example, diameter of body, length of body, length of neck to length of body) using circle-generated geometrical constructions.[14] Despite the care which he takes in showing these geometrical relationships, we rarely, if ever, find a representation of a lute in the visual arts that perfectly matches Zwolle's plan. Should we then discard his plan as having little or nothing to do with "reality"? On the contrary, he shows us the constructional idea upon which every lute made of wood, glue and sheep gut was based, each "human-made" instrument being by definition a variation upon this ideal. An analogy could be made with the authority of the Boethian interval system in medieval music theory: while there was a consistent, absolute set of proportions, based upon a tradition going back to Boethius, in actual practice, each singer/instrumentalist must have sung or played with a certain amount of variation within the system so consistently outlined by the treatises which survive.

Tuning

The tuning of the lute is reasonably well documented only from the last quarter of the fifteenth century. The earliest sources which provide information about lute tuning are the following, all presumably from the 1480s and 90s:[15]

1. Ramos de Pareja's *Musica practica* [16]
2. Johannes Tinctoris's *De inventione et usu musicae* [17]
3. Cambridge, Trinity College, MS 0.2.13, f. 97v [18]
4. Elio Antonio de Nebrija's *Vocabulario espanol-latino* [19]
   (fingerboard diagrams)
5. Venice, Bibl. Nazionale Marciana, Ms. Lat. 336, coll. 1581, f. 1 [20]
6. Kassel, Landesbibl. und Murhardsche Bibl., 2° Ms. math. 31 [21]
   (tablature staff explained with note names)
7. Bologna, Bibl. Univ. Ms. 596 HH. 2ª (for six- and seven-course *viola da mano*) [22]

The above tunings are summarized as follows (only **relative pitch** is given):

Fig. 25.1. Lute Tunings

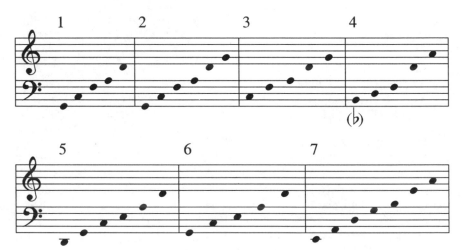

A survey of these tunings yields a few interesting observations. The Kassel MS and Ramos de Pareja indicate that five-course lutes could have the third between the second and third courses, or between the third and fourth courses. [23] Both give the lowest string as *gamut*, which brings up the questions of notating sounding pitch and actual lute size in the fifteenth century. In the late thirteenth century, Jerome of Moravia had given vielle tunings with *gamut* as the lowest string, which of course does not mean a fixed pitch in the modern sense. By the 1490s, however, it seems likely that a large five-course lute could have had such a low string, and that the pitch reference could be taken more literally. Further, it is interesting that the disagreement over where to place the third comes only from sources for five-course lute that use *gamut* to describe the lowest string. A lute player who could read from notation on, say, a five-course lute in G would have an easier time reading lower lines on a larger lute if the third were in the same place as on the higher instrument (i.e., between the sounding *a la mi re,* second course, and *F fa ut,* third course), whereas one who had memorized pieces on the G–lute would have an easier time using the same fingerings on the larger lute, having the third in the same place between the third and fourth courses. Another interesting tuning is hinted at by Nebrija, who describes a fifth between the top two courses and possibly another fifth between the bottom two (fourth and fifth) courses.[24] Nebrija's tuning seems to imply a variation on a standard five-course G–tuning. The G–tuning has *C fa-ut* as its lowest (fifth) course, and extending the instrument's low range by lowering the bottom string a tone must have occurred to many a lute player. Likewise, extending the upper range by tuning the highest string up a tone is equally a possibility.

Praetorius (1619) stated that "die lauten haben anfangs nur vier Chor mit doppelten Sàiten, als *c f a d'* gleich wie eine Quinterna gehabt: hernacher haben sie oben noch einen Chorsäiten darzu erfunden, als *c f a d' g'*."[25] This information regarding the early four-course lute does not accord, however, with the thirteenth-century treatise *Summa musice*, which states that fingerboard instruments "are tuned in the consonances of octave, fourth, and fifth," i.e., there is no mention of a third.[26] Modern players, following the lead of Thomas Binkley in the 1960s and early 70s, have used a fourths tuning with a fifth on the bottom (i.e., *d a d g'*) for the pre-fifteenth-century (four-course) lute. Binkley also experimented with the "New Persian tuning" described in the works of Henry George Farmer *(c d g a)*.[27]

No stage in the thousand-year history of the lute in Europe saw as dramatic an evolution in the instrument as was seen in the period ca.1400–1490. Fundamental changes during this period included an increase in the number of strings which expanded the lower range, a change of technique from plectrum to finger play, a change of playing position from standing to sitting, and changes in the basic size of the instrument, both the body and the length of the neck relative to body size. It is of course easier to determine by when these changes had been assimilated than it is to isolate when they first began, but the main point here is that the lute was increasingly becoming (as the keyboard had already become) an instrument suited for self-contained polyphony.

Playing Technique

Before the fifteenth century, if we base our conclusions upon depictions in the visual arts, the lute was most often played standing. More than ninety percent of the drawings, paintings, sculptures, and miniatures illustrate this position, and the context of most depicted performances would, according to the conventions of social conduct, allow only this and not a seated position. In the few instances where the player is seated, for example in a fresco in the church of San Lorenzo in San Gimignano (ca.1375), the instrument is still held up on the chest rather than placed upon the player's lap. Such an "against-the-chest" playing position allows the player to walk around, and is consistent with the typical short-necked lutes of the thirteenth and fourteenth centuries. Straps, cords, or other means of artificial support, seen occasionally in paintings of the sixteenth and later centuries, are rarely encountered before 1500, possibly because if one learned to play standing, one held the instrument and played without worrying about how difficult it was. Lutes of this period were fretless, and the short neck seen in many pre-1400 depictions would suggest that the player's left hand remained more of the time in first position than higher up the neck.

This is consistent as well with being able to support the instrument while standing without the help of a strap.

At least one, and possibly two, fundamental changes in hand position seem to have occurred in the first half of the fifteenth century, probably earlier than later. Up to this time, the right-hand position for lute players is not unlike the hand position of a scribe holding a quill, and very similar to the right-hand position of Trecento psaltery players; Paulus Paulirinus (ca.1460) comments that the psaltery is "plucked with a quill held in the hand like a lute" (indeed both the lute and the psaltery may typically have been doubled by the same musician in fourteenth-century Italy).[28] The lute plectra most often depicted throughout the Middle Ages and early Renaissance are feathers, likely, as with writing quills, goose feathers.

We cannot know for sure which specific kind of feather is shown in any given picture, and each player must decide by trial and error which type of feather works best. In the author's experience, alternating up and down plucking becomes difficult or impossible when the plectrum is too bulky and stiff; this observation, on the other hand, provides no real information about what actually was done in the fifteenth century. While other kinds of material—parchment, horn, bone, wood, even metal?—may have been used to make lute plectra, broader, larger (wooden?) plectra, sometimes with a trefoil on the upper end, are shown in the hands of citole players (see below), and the lute and gittern are shown with finer, thinner plectra. The present writer has used plectra made from ostrich feathers, which can be finely worked to be flexible yet strong. The use of ostrich feathers in the fourteenth or fifteenth centuries as plectra can of course not be documented; to be sure, they were available to the well-to-do as clothing ornaments, yet this in itself says nothing about their use as plectra. Yet two of the earliest preserved treatises on plectrum playing, albeit for *mandoline* (and no fewer than three centuries after the age of Pietrobono) specify ostrich feathers as the plectrum of choice: "The quill must not be stiff, but on the contrary, carved very thin."[29] While it would be foolish to attempt to draw a direct line of tradition between these sources and medieval/early Renaissance plectrum lute technique, they are products of a well-established, well-tried, and well-thought-out school of plectrum playing.

Pl. 25.2. Detail of Angels with gittern and lute (?) by Giovanni Biondo (1380s) (Walker Art Gallery, Liverpool).

Detailed depictions of plectra sometimes show a further intriguing aspect, namely multiple tips or points on the end of the plectrum which is not in contact with the strings (see Pl. 25.2; a few paintings also show multiple tips at the string-contact end). This may indicate that multiple feather shafts were held or bound together, possibly for increased strength and loudness; alternatively a long piece of gut string or other material may have been folded to give a double thickness. In the few cases where multiple tips are visible at the plucking end of the plectrum, a speculative question arises: Could plucking the strings with rapid multi-attacks have given more "presence" or projection to the sound in an acoustically challenging situation?[30]

Representations of lutes being played in the fourteenth and fifteenth centuries usually show the instrument being plucked close to the bridge, and this would produce the bright, nasal tonal color common to other instruments, and perhaps of the voice, in medieval music. It is difficult to accept the argument occasionally heard that painters placed the plucking hand far back by the bridge in order to leave the rose fully visible. In the later fifteenth century, as more players used a finger-only technique, examples can be found of a higher, over-the-rose right hand placement (as one illustration, see Lorenzo Costa's *Concert* [ca.1488], National Gallery, London).

The development of finger-style plucking has been rather oddly portrayed in nearly every work on the subject of fifteenth-century lute. Plucking the lute with the bare fingers should not be understood as a new development from the time of Tinctoris's writing ca.1480. It should also not be regarded as a new development of the mid- or early-fifteenth century. It had always been another possibility for plucking a string, albeit much less often heard of or depicted in the visual arts, but it found a new context and usage with the advent of two and three-part counterpoint as lute repertoire. The comment of Howard Mayer Brown echoed countless "histories of lute technique" before and after his own formulation: "The new technique (finger technique) enabled performers to play polyphonic music on their instruments."[31] Polyphonic playing can, in fact, be achieved with a combination of plectrum and fingers, or with plectrum alone, and a depiction of a lutenist playing a fretted lute (perhaps even an unfretted instrument) with a plectrum is not necessarily an indication that he or she is playing monophonically. The most reasonable assumption is that for the fifteenth century and possibly for the last quarter of the fourteenth, "plectrum polyphony," normally on a fretted lute, *was* possible and *was* practiced.

Frets

The approximate period 1400–1430 was a pivotal one for the lute, for any visual records we have of the instrument datable before ca.1400 show a fretless instrument, while sources roughly after 1400 show a fretted instrument. Although both Sachs (1920) and Geiringer (1923) pointed this fact out, it has only slowly been accepted by modern performers of medieval music.[32] Geiringer claimed that the "Madonna del Belvedere" of Ottaviano Nelli (Gubbio, Church of Santa Maria Nova), dated 1403, held the distinction of being the earliest source for a fretted lute, but this writer's examination of the painting yielded a fretless instrument. Possibly the earliest example of a lute with frets is in an apparently original, unrestored fragment of an altar painting by Giovanni Biondi now in the Walker Art Gallery in Liverpool (see Pl. 25.2). This painting, thought to date from the 1380s, shows two angels, one playing a gittern (back turned to the viewer) and the other playing what seems to be a lute. I say "seems to be" because the pegbox is not visible, and this would be an important feature in identifying the instrument as a lute and not a second gittern. However, the body shape and shoulder profile would point to this instrument being a lute rather than a gittern. In any case, there are two pairs of frets which are visible on the fingerboard. A much clearer depiction of a fretted lute is in the *Coronation of the Virgin* by the Sienese artist Sassetta, in the Louvre (ca.1430). Assuming that this is not the earliest depiction, and projecting somewhat backwards to allow for the iconographical convention to take hold, it would seem that at least a few late-fourteenth century lutes were candidates for being played with frets.

Pl. 25.3. *Coronation of the Virgin* by **Sassetta (ca.1430)** with early 15th-century lute (Louvre).

What about temperament? Here we encounter a few problems, the first being the accurate representation of fretted fingerboards in paintings. In general, depictions are rarely precise in this regard (even when they are otherwise highly realistic), and it would seem that artists did not particularly care about realism in accurate fret measurement. A second problem is that, on a fretted instrument, multiple strings share the same fret, and medieval music is based upon a scale with unequal semitones. Pitch inflections can be achieved by sliding a fret higher or lower, but this then results in a compromise for pitches on other strings which use the same fret. Fretted instruments that use a wide variety of chords and modal transpositions have little choice but to move toward equal temperament, and by the late fifteenth century, music theorists were beginning to acknowledge that the chant-based tuning system was problematic for ensembles with fretted instruments.

Paired frets present an interesting problem of interpretation with fourteenth and fifteenth-century lutes and gitterns. The well-known *Investiture of St. Martin* in the Lower Church of the Basilica of St. Francis in Assisi (ca.1325) shows a gittern with fret pairs, and the Madonna and Child of Sassetta now in the Louvre, mentioned above, contains a lute that also features paired frets. These two sources showing "paired frets" are by no means unique. Have the painters given an accurate rendering of the instruments, or have their memories (or models) deceived them in regard to the frets? The Martini instrument seems otherwise consistent with the body of contemporary visual sources, and other details—binding, inlays, string thicknesses—have been carefully dealt with by the artist. It would seem to be a reasonable assumption that the artist has painted a fret system actually used in his time or earlier. How might such double frets have functioned?

One might be tempted to explain them as early examples of double-tied gut frets, which they indeed may be. There are, however, at least two other possibilities. The first would allow a choice of lower or higher intonation for all fretted notes, while the second possibility would produce quite a different sound than one expects from a lute. This sound, or better said, "sound color," is similar to the sound of the bray-pin harp, of the drum with a snare, of a triangle with rings, of a fiddle bow with bells attached to the end, of the tromba marina with the vibrating bridge; it is a buzzing sound which intensifies the projection and rhythmic profile, especially of an otherwise "soft" instrument. In a relatively noisy acoustic (for example, a dance or procession outdoors) or ensemble, an instrument with such a device becomes more present, more "hearable."[33] A similar interpretation, focusing upon the sound of the bray-pin harp, has been suggested for the passage with the verb *arpiza* in the instructions of the Capirola lutebook: "the closer the fret is to the strings it makes the strings of the lute sound like those of the harp and the instrument sounds better."[34] Buzzing frets on a lute create the impression of enhanced sustain after a note is plucked, and so this reading would seem to go along with Capirola's insistence on the importance of *tenuto* or legato playing for the sake of the counterpoint. On the other hand, the successful setting of the frets to achieve a consistent buzzing on each string at every fret has eluded this writer's efforts until now, and perhaps a consistent buzzing could indeed be more easily achieved by installing a pin (*Nagel*) under each string at the bridge.

Surviving Lutes

To my knowledge, no surviving lutes can reliably be dated before the sixteenth century (see below regarding a surviving gittern and a surviving citole). Occasionally proposed as a candidate for a surviving fifteenth-century instrument is the so-called "Witten lute," formerly owned by Laurence Witten II in Connecticut and now in the collection of the Shrine to Music Museum in Vermillion, South Dakota.[35] This is a small five-course instrument with ivory ribs. Its form, rose design, narrow neck-depth, and inlaid ornaments where the fingerboard meets the soundboard all speak strongly of a sixteenth-century origin (or later); indeed it would be an ideal instrument for playing diminutions in a late-sixteenth-century "broken consort." Altogether more believable as somewhat closer to the fifteenth-century style is the body of the instrument attributed to Laux Maler, now in the Instrument Collection of the Kunstmuseum in Vienna, which the museum dates at ca.1520. Although the soundboard of this instrument is most likely not original, the back, made of yew, certainly seems to be. The construction is marvelously light, feather-weight, and therein lies one answer to why so few lutes of this period survive.

Lute Function

It is easy to generalize, yet frustratingly difficult to pin down exactly what sort of musical function the lute had before 1400. Sure are two general functions: accompaniment of the voice, whether monophonic or polyphonic music, and playing dance music. Contemporary references mentioning the lute are unspecific: in Boccaccio's *Decameron*, for example, "Emilia cantasse una canzone dal leuto di Dioneo aiutata" (Emilia sang a song with the help of Dioneo's lute). In general it is difficult to find clear traces of soft-instrument ensembles in the fourteenth century, and more difficult still to identify examples of instrumental polyphony. Even so, given the solid identification of known singer-composers of polyphony—such as Jacob Senleches—as instrumentalists (Senleches played the harp), it would be short-sighted to presume that an instrumental ensemble performance of polyphonic music was unheard-of in the fourteenth century.[36] Further, representation of the lute-gittern pair in fourteenth-century French and German art is so consistent that one cannot help but wonder whether this could suggest practical usage (= duo performance = polyphony) rather than simply an iconographic convention symbolizing the plucked instrument family.[37] The best documented soft-instrument ensemble during the late fourteenth and fifteenth centuries was the duo format, often lute with gittern, harp, fiddle, portative, or second lute.[38]

Lute Repertoire

Reference was made in the opening paragraph of this study to the lack of attention the pre-1500 lute has received from modern players. Central to this relative lack of interest has been the lack of repertory for the instrument, yet this repertory is, to a great extent, retrievable; more specifically, it is available to those who are willing to take the time to learn how to arrange appropriate music for the lute. It cannot be overemphasized that in order to "get close" to late medieval or early Renaissance lute music, we must do today what our predecessors did then: learn to "set" pieces to the lute, to "realize" polyphonically a *cantus firmus*, to "arrange" a *bassadanza*, to intabulate vocal polyphony for solo or ensemble rendering. Accomplished lutenists were expected to be able to do these things. They studied model pieces and undoubtedly learned by imitation. Whether we prefer to name their music-making "improvisation," "memorized composition," "sight-reading," or something else, professional musicians of the fifteenth century were composer-arrangers as well as instrumentalists or vocalists. The repertory for the fifteenth-century lute is all around us, in every notated form but "lute tablature" (with the exception of the few tablatures from the end of the century).

In searching for models for arranging vocal music for lute, a great help is provided by the so-called keyboard sources of the fourteenth, fifteenth, and earlier sixteenth centuries. Documents continue to come to light that suggest certain links between two instrument families, lute and keyboard. A manuscript now at the Gesamthochschul-Bibliothek in Kassel, presumably from the late fifteenth century, shows a careful drawing of a five-course lute, with an explanation of its tuning and notation given from a reference point of what is now referred to as "keyboard tablature."[39] Another source (now in Bologna) shows a similar proximity of "keyboard" and "lute" (actually viola da mano) notation, and there are two sources, the so-called *Buxheimer Orgelbuch* and *Lochamer Liederbuch*, associated with one of the most famous polyphonic soloists of the fifteenth-century, lutenist-organist Konrad Paumann; these show tantalizing hints that what has hitherto been considered keyboard notation was in fact read equally well by lutenist-keyboardists. A possible further lute-keyboard link is the treatise of Henri Arnaut de Zwolle, ca.1445, where the construction plan of various keyboards and lute are given.

Fifteenth-century Germany was the home of the well-educated merchant-class citizen, which was often synonymous with "musical amateur"; the rise of the self-taught musician (lutenist) was in part dependent upon the printing revolution. In the mid-century, the lute was still foremost an instrument of professionals like Paumann or Pietrobono. Yet by the time Tinctoris had written his treatise (ca.1480), the lute was fast becoming the fashionable instrument *par excellence* for the musical pursuits of amateurs. One could accompany one's own or a friend's singing, one could participate with other instruments in soft polyphonic music, one could play solo intabulations of vocal compositions and perhaps ornament them, and one could also provide music for the dance. This last function is traditionally one of the strongest for lute-family instruments in general; any plucked chordophone, after all, is a kind of melodic percussion instrument.

Gittern

Closely related to the lute in form and playing technique is the gittern. This instrument—according to the number of surviving depictions and taking Europe as a whole—was more common than its larger relative in the thirteenth and fourteenth centuries. As was true for the lute, thirteenth-century Spain provides the earliest body of depictions of gitterns. The gittern was referred to in a fourteenth-century narrative, the *Libro de Buen Amor* (ca.1330) as being "unsuitable for Arab music," possibly because it was, unlike the lute, a fretted instrument; it is interesting that this instrument is often shown in close proximity to an unfretted lute in Trecento paintings with angel musicians. A century and a half after the *Libro de Buen Amor*, Tinctoris said the gittern was "invented by the Catalans" and that it "is used most rarely, because of the thinness of its sound. When I heard it in Catalonia, it was being used much more often by women, to accompany love-songs, than by men."[40]

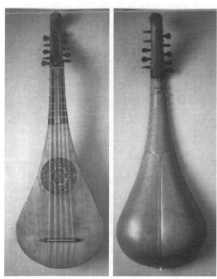

Pl. 25.4. Gittern from the Wartburg Collection. Photo by Crawford Young.

Surviving Gitterns

The instrument that Tinctoris heard cannot have been fundamentally different from the existing gittern (*quintern*) in the Wartburg Collection in Germany, thought to date from about 1450. As a typical fifteenth-century example, this unique surviving example has ten strings (= five courses), whereas the pre-fifteenth-century version is usually seen with four courses, less commonly with three. The Wartburg *quintern* is thought to have been made in Nürnberg in the middle of the fifteenth century, and it displays an astonishing level of workmanship, yet it is also a "player's instrument," showing apparent traces of plectrum wear on the soundboard.[41] One-piece, robust construction, small size, and portability allowed the gittern to be heard in many social situations, including, as mentioned by Chaucer, in taverns.[42]

Gittern Function

As we have seen above in Tinctoris's remark, the gittern could provide vocal accompaniment. The sixteenth-century French translation by Alexandre le Macon of the *Decameron* reads "si tu veux aporter ta guyterne, et que tu chantes un peu avec elle de ses chansons amoureuses..." (if you want to bring your gittern, you can sing some love songs with it).[43] Similarly we find the passage "singe with the giterne" in *Piers Plowman* (ca.1400).[44] It was also an ideal instrument for playing dance tunes: "joué d'une gisternei qu'il avoit pour faire esbatre et dansier plusieurs jeunes gens" (account roll of 1399 in du Cange); "suon di molto dolzi danze di chitarre e carribi smisurati" (*L'Intelligenza*). Pietrobono was called "dal chitarino," apparently being a virtuoso on the gittern, and was a singer as well.[45]

The emphasis on vocal accompaniment for this instrument brings up a question: For which kinds of songs? If polyphonic, which line did the gittern play? A reasonable answer would be that the instrument found its use generally in secular song accompaniment, both in monophonic and polyphonic music of court and popular entertainment. Indeed for a more rustic setting it is easier to imagine melodic doubling (at the unison or octave), a complementary melody ("tenor"), or chordal accompaniment, remembering that the last can mean strummed chords or "broken" chords that hint at counterpoint. Instrumental elaboration of a pre-given vocal melody with a second instrument providing lower line(s) was surely already in the fourteenth century a function of this instrument for those musicians with proper training in polyphonic art music, and the gittern, like both the lute and citole, was a popular "soft" instrument to play dance music of all kinds. The common lute duo of the fifteenth century very likely featured a small lute (=gittern) and a larger one, that is, a five-course gittern with the top string at *c″*, for example, and a five-course lute with the top string at *g′* (or a fourth lower). Such a duo would have had access, through transposition, to the range of the three parts of most vocal music of the fifteenth century.

Citole

The most fascinating member of the medieval lute family is, in many ways, not the lute or the gittern, but the citole. It has been perhaps the most misunderstood member of the medieval lute family. Tinctoris reported that the Italians invented it, yet in some form it seems to be present already in Carolingian Psalter illumination, and in the late twelfth and thirteenth centuries it was more often found in church sculptures of Christian Spain than in Italy. Like the gittern, the citole was deemed "unsuitable for Arab music" in the *Libro de Buen Amor*, ca.1330, perhaps because it, too, had frets, and possibly because of a certain identification, as a *cithara*, with Christian symbolism (as found in the tradition of Psalm commentaries; related to this, the lower end of the citole was often given an ornamental projection in the form of a *fleur-de-lys*, the Christian symbol of purity).[46] Tinctoris gave the impression that it had a lower status than the lute, being "only used in Italy by rustics," yet in Italian fifteenth-century painting, for example, it was associated with lofty figures of Antiquity, sometimes being the cithara of King David, or of the Muse Terpsichore, or of Venus:[47]

> The statue of Venus, glorious for to se,
> Was naked, fletynge in the large see,
> And fro the navele doun al covered was
> With wawes grene, and brighte as any glas.
> A citole in hir right hand hadde she,
> And on hir heed, ful semely for to se,
> A rose gerland, fressh and wel smellynge;
> Above hir heed hir dowves flikerynge.[48]
>
> (from Chaucer, *The Knight's Tale*)

The iconography of the citole is astonishingly rich, a kind of microcosm of medieval art itself; this is because of its strong association with two of the main themes of medieval art, Classical Antiquity and the Bible. Two examples of citoles may provide us with a glimpse of the instrument's iconographical background.[49] The first is the only surviving (fourteenth century) medieval citole, now owned by the British Museum. This instrument features, at the lower end, the trefoil projection (purity) mentioned above. At the other (pegbox) end, a dragon's yawning mouth threatens to swallow up the neck of the citole. Here we are reminded of the Elders of the Apocalypse tuning their *citharae* from the Book of Revelation, who wait for the Final Judgement to begin: to Heaven or to Hell? Early Christian commentators remind us that the *cithara* symbolizes Christ's Cross (since it is made of wood, roughly in the form of a cross) and His Agony (tension of strings made of flesh). Pastoral, bucolic scenes marvelously carved on the side of the instrument remind us of Classical Antiquity, as does the citole's medieval association with shepherds and with the dance, also a point of tension ("worldly," "temptation") with the Christian moralistic view. The citole's form, too, points to the Antique *cithara*, with well-defined shoulders and a prominent stringholder at the bottom; unfortunately, the British Museum instrument no longer has its original top, but some English depictions of fourteenth-century citoles show a Star-of-David rose (Old Testament connection), and this citole may well have once had a large plectrum carved with matching motifs, reminiscent in form of the large kithara-plectra of Antiquity.

A second example which provides clues to the citole's identity comes from an intarsia ca.1500 in the Church of Monte Olivieto outside of Siena. The association with King David is especially obvious thanks to the instrument's proximity to a page of music, the lauda *Verbum caro factum est*. Citoles, or *cetulae* (Tinctoris) occur in a number of such inlaid choir stalls in fifteenth-century Italian churches, and they also seem to have had an association, as a kind of "monochord" (or rather, "polychord") with the demonstration of proper musical proportion and measurement. As such, they were the *citharae* of Boethius and Pythagoras.

The citole's documented period of use, according to depictions in the visual arts and literary references, may be sketched as follows:

Fig. 25.2. Citole Prevalence

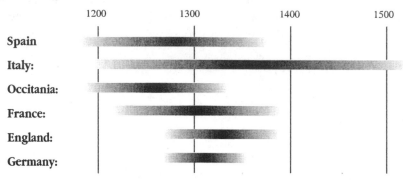

This sketch of the chronology of the citole is in conflict with previously published interpretations, such as "the citole is never to be seen in Italian pictures from the thirteenth and fourteenth centuries."[50] To be sure, there are not nearly as many Italian sources from the thirteenth and fourteenth centuries for the citole as for the gittern, but already in the late twelfth century there is a citole shown in the relief carving of King David and his musicians in the Baptistry at Parma, and there is a set of sixteen Elders of the Apocalypse with citoles in the Lower Church of St. Francis at Assisi (1310–20), as well as a number of other sources of Italian provenance. Thumb-hole citoles, such as the British Museum example, are less frequently seen in Italian sources than free-neck citoles, but we do have isolated examples.[51] Wright remarked further that "the citole fell out of general use in the later fourteenth century, but was re-introduced in modified form from Italy in the sixteenth century under the name cetra."[52] In fact, there are enough citole sources from fifteenth-century Italy to establish that the instrument was still very much in use, although it was evolving into the sixteenth-century cittern. Citoles through the mid-fifteenth century, including the British Museum instrument, were of one-piece, carved construction. The later *intarsia cetulae* seem to have had a built-up construction—like some citterns in the sixteenth century—but perhaps what looks like this kind of construction in the marquetry panels has more to do with the characteristics of the medium (wood inlay) rather than with the instruments that were being depicted.

Pl. 25.5. Citole from a fresco (ca.1495) by Girolamo Benvenuto (Oratorio della Madonna della Neve, Torrita). Photo by Crawford Young.

Some citterns in the sixteenth century had chromatic frets while others had diatonic frets, and questions have been raised about the fret system of the citole in this regard. I have yet to see a convincing representation of a diatonic fret system on any plucked instrument before the sixteenth century, and while artists did not place frets with realistic precision upon the fingerboards of the instruments they painted, they did tend to space frets evenly, if sometimes widely spaced. It is this regularity which points to chromatic frets on pre-1500 instruments.[53]

If there are still unanswered questions about repertoire, ensemble use, and musical function of the pre-1400 lute, there are many more about the citole. Tinctoris described the form, tuning, and musical uses of the *cetula*, but his description remains in certain respects enigmatic. While the earlier French (and perhaps Northern in general) citoles had gut strings, Tinctoris said that the four-course Italian instrument had "brass or steel" strings (Baines translation) and wooden block frets, and it was "usually tuned *ad tonum et tonum: diatesseron: ac rursus tonum.*"[54] Baines, following Dart, interprets this to mean a tuning of *e' d' a b*, but it is unclear whether Tinctoris really meant such a "re-entrant" tuning, and further, what the history of such a tuning could be.[55] Whether re-entrant or not, Tinctoris's cetula tuning shows certain similarities with Boethius' four-string cithara. The strings of this symbolic instrument were given as root, fourth, fifth, and octave, that is, with a "tonus" between two of the four strings. The order of these strings seems to have been a subject of confusion to at least one late medieval theorist, as shown by the diagram of the Boethian cithara of Mercury in the Berkeley treatise of 1375; here the order of the strings is given as root, octave, fifth and fourth (i.e., re-entrant). It is possible to imagine that the medieval cetula/cetra tuning was derived from or influenced by Boethius' cithara. Tinctoris, however, associates the cetula not with learned musicians but with "rustics" who use the instrument to "accompany light songs and lead dance music." This somewhat Dionysian reference to performance practice retains an echo of Classical Antiquity. The citole's connection with dance music was strong; in addition to Tinctoris's comment, the Muse Terpsichore was sometimes depicted playing a citole, fourteenth-century illuminated manuscripts show marginal grotesques playing citoles while dancing, and there are also literary references to the instrument's dance connection, as in, for example, *Libro de buen amor.*

Early Medieval Lutes

Carolingian, pre-Romanesque, and Romanesque lute types can only be briefly mentioned within the context of this article, because they present greater problems of interpretation. Such instruments include both long- and short-necked lutes, and both A (pear-shaped) and B (waisted or straight-sided) types. From the ninth century come the Carolingian-school sources showing King David with his *cithara* for example, the Utrecht Psalter, Stuttgart Psalter, First Bible of Charles the Bald, and the Bible of Callisto. Some sources show a strong iconographical relationship with the Roman *kithara*, and others (in particular the Stuttgart Psalter) present straight-sided instruments which look like early citoles and are held in exactly the same playing position. The relationship of the medieval citole to the Roman cithara is unclear, yet some researchers have seen a direct line of evolution between the two.[56] The answer, if indeed available to us, lies in a thorough examination of the David iconography of this period.

Notes

[1]   O. Körte, *Laute und Lautenmusik bis zur Mitte des 16. Jahrhunderts* (Leipzig, 1901), p. 1.

[2]   "A serious terminological problem complicates the task of studying the principal plucked string instruments of the Middle Ages." See H. M. Brown in "Instruments [of the Middle Ages]" in H. M. Brown and S. Sadie, eds. *Performance Practice: Music Before 1600* (New York, 1989), p. 27.

[3]   All pre-1400 terms are listed in L. Wright, "The Medieval Gittern and Citole: A Case of Mistaken Identity," *Galpin Society Journal* 30 (1977), 8-42.

[4]   See Brown, "Instruments," p. 32, n.3.

[5]   See Wright.

[6]   See L. Lockwood, "Pietrobono and the Instrumental Tradition at Ferrara," *Rivista Italiana di musicologica* 10 (1975), 115-33.

[7]   For a complete picture of the problem of terminology, see (in addition to Wright): K. Geiringer, "Der Instrumentenname 'Quinterne' und die mittelalterlichen Bezeichnungen der Gitarre, Mandola und des Colascione," *Archiv für Musikwissenschaft* 6 (1924), 104; W. Stauder, "Zur Entwicklung der Cister," *Festschrift zum 80. Geburtstag Helmuth Osthoff* (Tutzing, 1979), pp. 223-255. Many of the points made in Lawrence Wright's much-heralded article of 1977 had already been made in Geiringer's article of 1924. See also C. Page, *Voices and Instruments of the Middle Ages: Instrumental Practice and Songs in France, 1100-1300* (Berkeley, 1986).

[8]   Wright, p. 11.

[9]   For one example (in the Book of Hours of Jeanne d'Evreux), see E. Winternitz, *Musical Instruments and Their Symbolism in Western Art* (New Haven and London, 1979), pl. 61b; for Tinctoris's comment see Anthony Baines, "Fifteenth Century Instruments in Tinctoris's *De Inventione et Usu Musicae*," *Galpin Society Journal* 3 (1950), 25.

[10]   Grocheo's treatise, *De musica*, has been translated by Ernst Rohloff as *Der Musiktraktat des Johannes de Grocheo* (Leipzig, 1943); and Albert Seay as *Johannes de Grocheo: Concerning Music* (Colorado Springs, 1974). See also Christopher Page, "Johannes de Grocheio on Secular Music: A Corrected Text and a New Translation," *Plainsong and Medieval Music* 2 (1993), 17-41.

[11]   Guillaume de Machaut, *Remede de Fortune*, lines 3964-66, 3983; see the edition by J. Wimsatt and W. Kibler, *Guillaume de Machaut: Le Jugement du roy de Behaigne and Remede de Fortune* (Athens, GA, 1988).

[12]   Wright, p. 10. On the question of names related to *viola*, see Pierre Bec, *Vièles or Violes?* (Paris, 1992).

[13]   A good starting point for a discussion of the early medieval lute is K. Geiringer, "Vorgeschichte und Geschichte der europäischen Laute bis zum Beginn der Neuzeit," *Zeitschrift für Musikwissenschaft* 10 (1927/28), 560-603.

[14]   G. Le Cerf, and E. R. Labande, *Les Traités d'Henri-Arnaut de Zwolle et de divers anonymes (MS B.N. Latin 7295)* (Paris, 1932), pp. 32-34.

[15]   There is a tuning diagram of the fingerboard of a six-course lute in the Pesaro manuscript, which is thought to date from the 1490s. The tuning diagram is in a later section of the

manuscript and is not earlier than ca.1545; see V. Ivanoff, *Das Pesaro Manuskript* (Tutzing, 1988), pp. 128-129.

[16] See C. Page, "The 15th-Century Lute: New and Neglected Sources," *Early Music* 9 (1981), 16. Here Ramos remarks that the tuning which he gives is the most common, but that others are used according to the wishes of the player.

[17] Tinctoris's Latin treatise was partly translated into English in Baines, "Fifteenth Century Instruments," and in German in K. Weinmann, *Johannes Tinctoris (1445–1511) und sein unbekannter Traktat 'De Inventione et Usu Musicae'* (repr. Tutzing, 1961). Note that Tinctoris's tuning description pertains directly to the six-course lute as having a third between the middle courses (third and fourth strings); on a five-course lute, the "middle courses" can be the third and fourth strings or the second and third, as there is no "middle" pair.

[18] See Page, "15th-Century Lute," pp. 13-14.

[19] See Page, "15th-Century Lute," p. 14, for reasons why this source is problematic.

[20] For a facsimile, see Don Harrán, "Intorno a un codice veneziano quattrocentesco," *Studi musicali* 8 (1979), 41-60. To my knowledge, it is nowhere stated in the Venetian manuscript that the fingerboard chart is of a lute *per se*. It is not out of the question that the scribe had not a lute but a bowed *viola* in mind, or perhaps the material was included as generic information for bowed and plucked instruments. Two features are strikingly similar to the Bologna fragment, that is, this diagram combines tablature and note-names in letter form, and the tablature referred to is the Neapolitan system with the numeral "1" (rather than "0") indicating an open string. Even more striking is the indication that the fifth string or course should be tuned to *gamma* ut (G), with the sixth string a fourth below at low D. Allowing for the fact that pitch indication is relative, it would still seem that the instrument depicted in this source is a very large one, the largest of any of our late fifteenth-century sources.

[21] See C. Meyer, "Eine Lauten-Unterweisung aus dem späten 15. Jahrhundert," *Musik in Bayern* 49 (1994), 25-33.

[22] Facsimile in D. Fallows, "15th Century Tablatures for Plucked Instruments: A Summary, A Revision and a Suggestion," in *Lute Society Journal* 19 (1977). Note that the top string (a¹) and the lowest string (E) are problematic: would a gut low E string sound well at a short (a¹) string length?

[23] See previous note.

[24] See Page, "15th-Century Lute," p. 14.

[25] "Lutes originally had just four courses of double strings tuned *c–f–a–d'* like a quintern. Later, one more course was added on top, giving *c–f–a–d'–g'*." See M. Praetorius, *Syntagma musicum II, De Organographia* (Wolfenbüttel, 1619; repr. Kassel, 1985), p. 49.

[26] See Page, *Voices and Instruments*, p. 133. A medieval Arabic lute tuning with consecutive fourths (for a four-course instrument) was given by Henry George Farmer as the "Old Arabic" tuning in H. G. Farmer, *Historical Facts for the Arabian Musical Influence* (London, 1930), esp. Chap. 24, "The Accordatura of the Lute."

[27] For more on this and other Arabic tunings, see Farmer.

[28] This quote is taken from Paulus Paulirinus, *Liber viginti artium*. See S. Howell, "Paulus Paulirinus of Prague on Musical Instruments," *Journal of the American Musical Instrument Society* 5-6 (1979-80), 16.

[29] From Gervasio, 1767: see James Tyler and Paul Sparks, *The Early Mandolin* (Oxford, 1989), p. 114.

[30] On the same subject, see below for a brief discussion of bray frets.

[31] See H. M. Brown in "Instruments [of the Renaissance]" in H. M. Brown and S. Sadie, eds. *Performance Practice: Music Before 1600* (New York, 1989), p. 175.

[32] C. Sachs, *Handbuch der Musikinstrumentenkunde* (Leipzig, 1920); K. Geiringer, *Die Flankenwirbelinstrumente in der bildenden Kunst des 14. bis 16. Jahrhunderts* (Diss. Vienna, 1923) = *Wiener Veröffentlichungen zur Musikwissenschaft* 17 (Tutzing, 1979), p. 44.

[33] Within the context of "buzzers," another intriguing reference must be mentioned, specifically the *Nägel* referred to in two sixteenth-century lute-related documents mentioned by Friedemann Hellwig. These "nails" were described in an inventory of Raimund Fugger's musical instrument collection as being made of ivory, whereas another reference from the mid-sixteenth century mentions a "silver lutenail." An alternative hypothetical reading of *Nägel* could be a type of finger-pick (or a set?), although there is a total lack of evidence for the use of finger picks in sixteenth-century lute practice. See Friedemann Hellwig, "Lute-Making in the Late 15th and 16th Century," in *The Lute Society Journal* 16 (1974), 36.

[34] See Federico Marincola, "The Instructions from Vicenzo Capirola's Lute Book: A New Translation," in *The Lute Society Journal* 23 (1983), 27; the suggestion of buzzing frets in Capirola was made by Ray Nurse and communicated to me by Herbert Myers.

[35] Thanks are hereby humbly acknowledged to Guy Biechelle and Lawrence Witten II. In 1978, Mr. Biechelle was instrumental in organizing the meeting between me and Mr. Witten, in whose private collection the above-mentioned lute was included.

[36] Or solo performance of polyphony? See R. Strohm, "'La harpe de melodie' oder Das Kunstwerk als Akt der Zueignung," in H. Danuser, *Das musikalische Kunstwerk: Festschrift Carl Dahlhaus zum 60. Geburtstag* (Laaber, 1988).

[37] For further information see H. M. Brown, "St. Augustine, Lady Music and the Gittern," *Musica Disciplina* 38 (1984).

[38] Archival documents providing information about such ensembles in German cities have been studied by Keith Polk; see his *German Instrumental Music of the Late Middle Ages: Players, Patrons and Performance Practice* (Cambridge, 1992).

[39] My thanks are due to Ralf Mattes, who brought my attention to the recent article by Meyer on the Kassel MS; Ralf also pointed out the keyboard-lute connection in this source.

[40] See Baines, p. 23.

[41] My deep thanks go to Wolfgang Wenke and the Wartburg Stiftung for allowing me to examine the instrument in detail.

[42] See Wright, p. 14.

[43] See Antoine Jean Le Macon, *Le Decameron de Boccace* (Lyon, 1551).

[44] See A.V.C. Schmidt, ed., *Piers Plowman* (London and New York, 1978), p. 154.

[45] An account of Pietrobono is given in Lockwood, pp. 115-33.

[46] For example, see references to the cithara in the writings of the Church Fathers in J. McKinnon, *Music in Early Christian Literature* (Cambridge, 1987).

[47] Baines, p. 25.

[48] Chaucer, *The Knight's Tale*, lines 1955-62.

[49] A convenient set of photos of the British Museum instrument is published in M. Remnant and R. Marks, "A Medieval 'Gittern'," in *Music and Civilisation,* British Museum Yearbook 4 (1980) Pls. 76–80. For a reproduction of the Monte Oliveto intarsia, see G. Brizzi, *Il coro intarsiato dell' Abbazia di Monte Oliveto Maggiore* (Milan, 1989), Pls. 10, 18.

[50] Brown, "Instruments [of the Middle Ages]," p. 27.

51   For one example see C. Young, "Zur Klassifikation und Ikonographischer Interpretation mittelalterlicher Zupfinstrumente," *Basler Jahrbuch für Historische Musikpraxis* 8 (1984), 100.

52   Wright, p. 32.

53   See Young, pp. 90-95, 103.

54   For information about strings, see Page, *Voices and Instruments,* App. 4, p. 242.

55   See Thurston Dart, "The Cittern and Its English Music," *Galpin Society Journal* 1 (1948), 48.

56   E. Winternitz, "The Survival of the Kithara and the Evolution of the English Cittern: A Study in Morphology," in *Musical Instruments and Their Symbolism in Western Art* (New Haven, 1979). For a contrasting view, see Stauder, pp. 223-255. More recent research includes M. Burzik, *Quellenstudien zu europäischen Zupfinstrumentenformen* (Kassel, 1995), which does little to contribute to our knowledge of early medieval plucked instruments; much more reliable on this subject is Catherine Homo-Lechner, "Les Cordophones dans l'Occident médiéval du VIe au XIIe siécle" (unpublished doctoral thesis, University of Paris–Sorbonne, 1991).

VIII. WINDS

26. Flutes

Herbert W. Myers

Q: What is the difference between a vielle and a rebec? A.: A vielle burns longer. Recycled viola joke, to be sure, but also a poignant reminder as to why there are so few extant medieval instruments for us to study: in eras before the late Renaissance, when wooden instruments became obsolete, they were immediately assigned a new rôle—as potential firewood. Woodwinds were particularly susceptible to such reclassification; strings, after all, are a little more adaptable to changing requirements. But ultimately the revolution in lutherie that led to the viol and violin families—a revolution that began in the late fifteenth century—rendered earlier forms of strings inadequate as well. Thus the majority of winds and strings that survive from before 1500 do so either by chance or because of some extra-musical attribute—decorative value or supposed association with a famous personage; we have no reason to think what has come down to us constitutes a representative sampling.[1]

As a result, those of us interested in medieval instruments and their performance are forced to explore two other avenues of research: iconography and folk instruments. Both have enormous potential, but both are subject to obvious limitations. In the first place, no medieval picture is a photograph; this is particularly important to bear in mind when we observe the apparent photographic realism of late medieval art.[2] But perhaps more crucial, pictures cannot begin to tell us what is hidden from view—often some of the acoustically most significant information, especially for winds. As to the traditions of folk music and instruments, these are often quite fluid in the Occident and subject to influences from "art" music, particularly in cosmopolitan areas; the more stable traditions of the Orient may or may not be relevant. "Knowledge" in this field thus remains a collection of educated guesses, many of them just waiting to be revised in light of further investigation and thought.

As reported by Anthony Baines,[3] the woodwinds most prized by the ancient Greeks and Romans were reed instruments—the *aulos* and *tibia*; flutes (using this term in its widest sense) they regarded as rustic. However, flutes were held in higher esteem by the European peoples further to the north. In the early Middle Ages the types available seem to have been limited to panpipes and small duct flutes (instruments with built-in windway, as found in the recorder); the cross flute, though known to the Etruscans and to primitive peoples the world over, appears to have been unknown in medieval Europe until the twelfth century. In the panpipes (or *syrinx*; *frestel* in Old French) a series of tubes (usually closed at the bottom) is arranged so that the player can selectively blow across their tops, much as one does to elicit a tone from a pop bottle. European panpipes are all of so-called "raft" form (as opposed to the "bundle" form sometimes found elsewhere), although the tubes might sometimes be disposed in an arc rather than a straight line in order to facilitate access. The tubes were commonly of cane or other quasi-cylindrical material produced by nature, although instruments were also made of metal, stone, ceramic, or wood. In this last case, a block of wood was provided with several blind holes of different depths drilled in a row along one edge; it sometimes appears in pictures decorated to resemble a small book. The number of pipes varied considerably, although seven—the standard in classic Greece—remained common. In an offshoot of the panpipes, preserved in a few terra-cotta examples from the lower Rhine, built-in ducts were provided that would have greatly simplified the blowing process[4]; at the same time these would have eliminated the possibility of altering the pitch by embouchure adjustment—a technique exploited to the full by some modern players of the panpipes (such as the famous Rumanian virtuoso Gheorghe Zamfir) to produce chromatic alterations. Whether this practice was employed by early players we cannot know, but we should not automatically assume, at least, that mechanical simplicity brings with it a simplicity of technique.

Numerous small duct flutes of bone survive, few of which can be precisely dated; some may be older or newer than the Middle Ages according to Crane, who lists those found up to 1972.[5] Few have their so-called "fipples"—the plugs (generally of wood) that close the top and help form the duct or windway. The number of fingerholes varies from one to seven, three to five being the most common; most examples can be played with one hand. As pointed out by several authors, the fact that so many of bone survive does not necessarily mean that was the most common material; cane and wood were probably more usual, but are subject to more rapid decay. Still, these bone examples taken as a whole are indicative of the type of instrument executed in the more ephemeral plant material. None, it should be said, is yet a recorder (with all that implies as to scale and range). We can only guess about the nature of the music played on such instruments, which is likely to have been highly idiomatic.

The twelfth and thirteenth centuries witnessed an expansion in the number and quality of European woodwinds, many of them imported from the Islamic world as a result of the Crusades. Innovations of this period included the pipe and tabor—the urtypical "one-man band" that remained popular throughout much of Europe through the Renaissance and one that can still be heard in some of its more remote areas to this day. In what might be called the "classic" form (the one usually described in textbooks) the pipe has three fingerholes, generally manipulated by the thumb and first two fingers of the left hand; the other two fingers are then free to support it. It is a duct flute with a narrow bore, meaning that it can easily be induced to overblow under increasing breath pressure to produce the octave, twelfth, fifteenth, seventeenth, and so forth—the "harmonic series." The fundamental is, in fact, never used, so that the largest interval to be filled in is a fifth; for this job the three fingerholes are entirely sufficient. Cross-fingerings and partial coverings can be employed throughout the range in order to produce semitones; on the smaller versions the little finger can reach down to shade the bell opening, giving a further small extension downwards. Although this three-hole pipe is clearly the instrument depicted in most sources from the fourteenth century onwards, earlier ones show pipes that are rather short and fat, or ones on which the finger placement is inconsistent with its rather low-lying fingerholes. Such depictions suggest something closer to the flutelets described above or to the modern *fluviol* used in Catalan sardana bands (but of course without the keywork found on the latter); on the *fluviol* fundamentals *are* used and the holes are covered by all five digits—thumb and little finger (its upper surface!) on the back of the instrument and the other fingers on its front.[6]

The tabor itself was generally a two-headed, rope-tensioned drum beaten by a stick held in the right (*i.e.*, dominant) hand. Although its proportions might vary, its depth was commonly about the same as its diameter. It was usually small enough to be suspended from the left wrist or arm, although other slinging systems were known as well. It is almost invariably depicted with a snare on the beaten head, and it probably had a snare on the other head, too (as suggested by those few depictions or carvings that afford us a view from the back).[7] In any case, it is important to realize that the predilection of Europeans for percussion with snares, jingles, or other noise-producing elements is nothing new, nor is their habit of using sticks or other beaters a development of the modern era. These facts have often been found frustrating or embarrassing by modern "early music" percussionists, some of whom prefer the primal affect evoked by snare-less drums and others the complex rhythms available using the hand and finger techniques typical of musical cultures further east. As indicated decades ago by Jeremy Montagu, both of these approaches would seem wrong for the mainstream of medieval European practice.[8] The tabor rhythms of modern folk practice tend to be simple patterns repeated over and over, just like the examples given by Arbeau in the late sixteenth century.[9]

An alternative to the tabor in some regions was the string drum (*timbourin à cordes*), still found in the south of France (where it is also known as the *tambourin de Béarn*) and in Basque areas. This is a long and narrow rectangular instrument with multiple gut strings, which are nowadays tuned to the tonic and dominant of the pipe's scale; it is suspended tabor-fashion from the left forearm and beaten with a stick to provide a rhythmic drone. Staples driven into the wood near one end of the strings and adjusted to buzz against them serve to prolong and amplify the tone (as do the "brays" of the Gothic harp).

The twelfth and thirteenth centuries also saw the adoption of improved forms of *flageolet*—the catch-all term often employed by organologists to refer to duct flutes of the penny whistle and recorder type. (As with "flute," the word "flageolet" has some specific meanings for later eras in addition to its generic technical meaning, but any potential confusion is usually cleared up by context.) The word *flageol* or some variant (*flaiol, flagel*) often shows up in French sources of this period, occasionally gaining a diminutive suffix from the thirteenth century on. *Flute* (*flaute; fluste*) often occurs in the same sources, sometimes with mysterious qualifiers (*flûte de Behaigne* or *de Brehaigne*, for instance) whose meaning is anyone's guess. In fact, tying what would appear from our vantage point as a fairly fluid terminology to specific types of flute seems an impossible task. The instruments themselves, in any case, would appear from pictures to be still quite limited in size by later standards, rarely reaching the length of an alto recorder; soprano recorder size is typical. The number of fingerholes seems still unstandardized. In a cylindrically bored flutelet, overblowing at the octave, six holes suffice to produce a complete and reasonably in-tune scale over the range of two octaves or so (as, for example, in the penny whistle), and among the various ethnic duct flutes thought to descend from medieval prototypes, six-holed examples abound.[10] The disadvantage to this system is that the overblowing process is completely dependent upon breath pressure; the low notes tend to be quite soft in relation to the high notes. An elegantly simple solution is found on the recorder: a hole situated on the back side of the instrument and controlled by the upper thumb may be made to act as a "speaker" hole, inducing overblowing without a change in air pressure. By regulating the exact size of the opening, the player can make the hole serve a large range of pitches. The thumb hole acts as a tone hole as well, absolving the six-finger note from having to overblow as an octave; adding a seventh fingerhole (to give an extra note at the bottom) completes the picture of the recorder. (This fingerhole, intended for the little finger of the lower hand, is offset from the straight line of the other holes in all but the smallest forms of the instrument. For one-piece types—the norm through the Renaissance—this usually meant duplicating the bottom hole in order to accommodate all players, regardless of which hand they held lowermost; the unused hole is then plugged with wax. The total number of holes is then nine, giving rise to the Renaissance French term *flûte à neuf trous*— "flute with nine holes.")

Just when the developments leading to the recorder took place is difficult to determine. Iconography is of little help here, since the most crucial element—the thumb hole—is usually hidden from view, and artists tended to be rather casual about such details as fingerholes anyway. Excavations have yielded a few actual instruments or fragments thereof, but not enough of them to give us a complete picture. Two of the finds have been known for some time; these are the famous recorder excavated from the moat of a fourteenth-century castle near Dordrecht, Holland in 1940 and a roughly contemporaneous fragment of what *may* be a recorder, found in a well in Würzburg, Germany in about 1952.[11] More recently (in 1987) a recorder was unearthed from the latrine of a medieval house in Göttingen, Germany; it also appears to be from the fourteenth century.[12] All of these are small—sopranos by modern reckoning. All have a basically cylindrical bore, narrow by later standards, although the Göttingen example has noticeable (and presumably intentional) narrowings near the second and seventh fingerholes and flares out somewhat at the end. The Dordrecht recorder has turned tenons at both ends, as if for ferrules (which are missing). The fact that the bottom note—on reproductions, at least—is a semitone below the six-finger note has suggested to some builders that more than a simple ferrule is missing, and different appendages have been tried in order to remedy this perceived problem.[13] However, the fact that the Göttingen example has the same semitone interval at the bottom suggests that it was a characteristic of the earliest forms of the recorder, and that there is thus nothing of acoustical relevance missing from the Dordrecht recorder after all. Certainly this tuning (with the seventh finger giving the leading tone to the six-finger "key-note") is quite normal for bagpipes, and it makes a great deal of sense for an instrument performing primarily monophonically.

Common in the iconography—perhaps even more common than single duct flutes—are multiple pipes (usually double, although occasionally triple; the former are presumably the *flajos doubliers* mentioned at the time). The pipes might be separate or bored from a single piece of wood, but diverged just enough so that the hands could be held at the same level. Sometimes one of the pipes appears to be unfingered, acting as a drone. Jeremy Montagu has warned against taking some of the later appearances of double pipes at face value, however, particularly the widely divergent duct flutes found in Italian art from the fourteenth century on; as he points out, such depictions are often misrepresentations of the Greek *aulos*, which was incorrectly thought to have been a flute rather than a reed instrument—just another example of the pitfalls of iconology.[14] But the earlier depictions were clearly representations of current practice; multiple pipes would have suited the needs of the medieval minstrel, whose function was still primarily that of a self-supporting soloist.

The development of the recorder as a consort instrument belongs to the later Middle Ages. Evidence pointing to the existence of a family of recorders (and thus, by extension, to the performance of polyphony on them) comes from fairly early in the fifteenth century: a set of four recorders (along with four shawms and four douçaines) were ordered by Duke Philip the Good of Burgundy in 1426 to be sent to the Marquis of Ferrara. A quartet of recorders performed at the Banquet of the Vow (a.k.a. the Feast of the Pheasant) given by Philip in 1454, and another such quartet (dressed as wolves and playing a chanson) performed at the marriage of his son Charles the Bold to Margaret of York in 1468.[15] The practice may well be older, however; at the marriage of Philip's grandfather Philip the Bold to Margaret of Bavaria at Cambrai in 1385, *molt brafs contres et flusteurs musicals* ("excellent singers and flute [i.e., recorder] players") joined to perform the mass. While we may be jumping to an unwarranted conclusion to assume, as did the late David Munrow, that instrumental doubling of vocal lines is implied here—*alternatim* practice seems more likely for this period—the context at least suggests the involvement of the instruments in the performance of sophisticated polyphony.[16]

Fifteenth-century representations of recorders show an increasing resemblance to the characteristic pattern of surviving Renaissance examples: smooth in outline, generally cylindrical or tapering slightly down to the bottom fingerholes, and then flaring somewhat to the end. (This is actually a fairly accurate description of what is going on inside as well; Renaissance winds are basically "honest" in this regard. See the chapter "Recorder" in the *Renaissance* guide in this series for more information about surviving recorders and modern reproductions of them.) Two sizes of recorder built a fifth apart would suffice for most written polyphony of the early fifteenth century; three sizes become necessary with the general adoption of the contratenor bassus, whose range is typically a fifth below that of the tenor. What may be the first picture to document the existence of three sizes of recorder comes from rather late in the game; it is the Flemish painting *Mary Queen of Heaven* by the Master of the St. Lucy Legend (ca.1485), now in the National Gallery of Art, Samuel H. Kress Collection, Washington, DC. Here three angels in the "inner heaven" appear to play soprano, alto, and tenor recorders.[17] (Illustrations of complete families of instruments are rare at any period, it should be noted; artists generally seem to have preferred the visual variety of mixtures of instruments regardless of current practice.) The first evidence of a bass recorder (with its characteristic key and protective "fontanelle") comes from the early sixteenth

century.[18] There seems to be some discontinuity between the small surviving (and illustrated) medieval recorders and those of the sixteenth century: the standard consort from Virdung onwards consisted of alto,[19] tenor, and bass instruments, and the soprano (first mentioned in the sixteenth century by Jerome Cardan, ca.1546) seems to have been a reinvention—and one not immediately accepted by all players even then.

Plate 26.1. Recorder trio (detail) from *Mary, Queen of Heaven* (ca.1485) by the Master of the St. Lucy Legend. National Gallery of Art, Washington, DC, Samuel H. Kress Collection, 1952.2.13.

The gemshorn—an ocarina-like duct flute made from an animal horn—seems, in spite of its current popularity among certain players, to have been of only peripheral importance in the Middle Ages. It is unlikely to have possessed the recorder-like fingering system given it by modern builders, and even less likely to have been built in consorts or families.

The cross flute seems to have remained less popular than the various forms of duct flute throughout most of the medieval period. It came to Germany from Byzantium sometime in the twelfth century, and its use remained somehow associated with Germany long after that. It was there often an aristocratic instrument, appearing alongside other Minnesinger instruments such as the fiddle and harp. From the thirteenth century comes evidence of its use (alongside the side drum) as a military instrument as well; we can think of this form as the fife. The flute became established west of the Rhine first in the fourteenth century; Machaut, for instance, distinguishes between *flaustes traversaines* and *flaustes dont droit joues quand tu flaustes*— "cross flutes" and "flutes you hold straight when you play."[20] It mysteriously drops out of sight during the fifteenth century, some of its last appearances before its eclipse being in the miniatures of the Limbourg brothers, who may have been following a formulaic artistic tradition rather than painting from life at that point.[21] Since no examples of medieval flutes or fifes survive, it is difficult to know what they were like physically beyond the fact that they would—like the Renaissance flutes and fifes that followed—have had cylindrical bores and six fingerholes. Medieval flutes usually look to be about the size of a Renaissance tenor or a little smaller; we can surmise that the main difference would have been in the intonation system—Pythagorean (with large major thirds and thus high leading tones) for the medieval instrument in contrast to the pure thirds and low leading tones characteristic of Renaissance examples. The fife would presumably have had a narrower bore than the flute, just as it did in the Renaissance; we can imagine that it possessed comparatively large fingerholes, imparting a bright timbre. The smaller holes of the flute, along with its fatter bore, would have mollified its tone somewhat; they also provide more effective cross-fingerings for *ficta* (which are unlikely to have been as necessary on the fife). Some idea of traditional fife music may be gleaned from examples written down in the Renaissance. Arbeau,[22] for instance, gives a couple of tunes for the fife (or, alternatively, the *arigot*, a form of *flageolet*), and these are echoed in style in "The flute and the droome" section of William Byrd's "The Battell."[23] These fife tunes consist primarily of conjunct melodic "cells"—turns, mordents, and the like—strung together and often repeated sequentially up and down the scale.

Concerning technique on all of these instruments, we are almost completely in the dark as to specifics. I have come to believe, however, that the basic style was articulated rather than slurred, since articulation was such a universal concern of Renaissance pedagogy; it did not grow up overnight. It would thus seem appropriate to apply the variety of Renaissance articulation practices to the music of the earlier period, at least as a point of departure. It would appear, in any case, that the slurred style now characteristic of the penny whistle in Irish music has been adopted from bagpipe playing, and would seem inappropriate as a basis for the majority of medieval European music.

Notes

[1] Much of what does exist is listed in Frederick Crane, *Extant Medieval Musical Instruments: A Provisional Catalogue by Types* (Iowa City, 1972). This resource is somewhat out of date but still invaluable.

[2] This caveat regarding iconography is particularly well demonstrated in Edwin Ripin, "The Norrlanda Organ and the Ghent Altarpiece," *Studia instrumentorum musicae popularis III* (Stockholm, 1974), pp. 193-96.

[3] *Woodwind Instruments and their History*, rev. ed. (New York, 1963), p. 209.

[4] Crane, p. 42.

[5] Crane, pp. 29-39.

[6] See Baines, pp. 226-28, and and Jeremy Montagu, "Was the Tabor Pipe Always as We Know It?," *Galpin Society Journal* 50 (1997), 16-30.

[7] Arbeau (in the late sixteenth century) mentions snares on both heads as characteristic of the tabor, as opposed to the military drum that had a snare on only one head. See Thoinot Arbeau (Jean Tabourot), *Orchésographie: Et Traicte en forme de dialogue* (Langres: Jehan des Preyz, 1589). Facs. ed. Geneva, 1972; *Orchesography*, trans. Mary Stewart Evans (Kamin Dance Publishers, 1948), republished with new introduction and notes by Julia Sutton (New York: Dover, 1967), p. 46.

[8] James Blades and Jeremy Montagu, *Early Percussion Instruments from the Middle Ages to the Baroque*, Early Music Series: 2 (London, 1976), especially pp. 69-71.

9   Arbeau, pp. 51-64. One caution: modern players are often misled by Arbeau's notation, since his note values (halfnote and two quarternotes in duple time; half and four quarters in triple) imply comparatively slow tempi nowadays. However, the dance steps take place on the bar-line level (wholenote in duple; dotted whole in triple), so that even at a stately pace for the dance the drum pattern moves quickly—more like "tum-t-t-tum-t-t-" than the "BOOOOM-boom-boom, BOOOOM-boom-boom-" often heard on recordings.

10 See Hermann Moeck, *Typen europäischer Blockflöten in Vorzeit, Geschichte und Volksüberlieferung* (Celle, 1967), pp. 29-32.

11 See Rainer Weber, "Recorder Finds from the Middle Ages, and Results of Their Reconstruction," *Galpin Society Journal* 29 (1976), pp. 35-41. Horace Fitzpatrick ("The Medieval Recorder," *Early Music* 3/4 [1975]), 361-364) claims that radiocarbon dating of items found with the Dordrecht recorder "proves" a date of ca.1250; other circumstantial evidence, however, suggests a later date (the castle itself was inhabited from 1335-1418).

12 See Dietrich Hakelberg, "Some Recent Archaeo-organological Finds in Germany," *Galpin Society Journal* 48 (1995), 3-12. Hakelberg expresses some reservations about the certainty of the assumption that the Würzburg fragment is part of a recorder, suggesting that it might instead be part of a reed instrument. See also Hans Reiners, "Reflections on a Reconstruction of the 14th-Century Göttingen Recorder," *Galpin Society Journal* 50 (1997), 31-42.

13 Horace Fitzpatrick (*loc. cit.*) has opted for a short foot joint providing a cylindrical extension, while Rainer Weber (*loc. cit.*) after trying that contrived an even shorter foot that makes a sudden constriction of the bore; the latter solution is based on certain antique and folk examples and is, according to Weber, the superior one for timbre and intonation.

14 Jeremy Montagu, *The World of Medieval & Renaissance Musical Instruments* (New York, 1976), pp. 42-45.

15 Jeanne Marix, *Histoire de la musique et des musiciens de la cour de Bourgogne sous le règne de Philippe le Bon (1420-1467)* (Strasbourg, 1939), pp. 105-106. The word *fleutes* (or *flustes*) employed in Burgundian records can be taken only to mean recorders or other duct flutes, given the lack of evidence for transverse flutes in fifteenth-century Europe.

16 See David Munrow, *Instruments of the Middle Ages and Renaissance* (London, 1976), p. 14.

17 See Mary Remnant, *Musical* Instruments: *An Illustrated History from Antiquity to the Present* (London, 1989), p. 117.

18 Sebastian Virdung, *Musica getutscht* (Basel, 1511).

19 Modern terminology, of course; for Virdung this was the *discant*.

20 Curt Sachs (*The History of Musical* Instruments [New York, 1940], p. 287) mentions the appearance of the term *flauste traversaine* in thirteenth-century France, but he fails to say where it occurs.

21 See Howard Mayer Brown, "Notes (and Transposing Notes) on the Transverse Flute in the Early Sixteenth Century," *Journal of the American Musical Instrument Society* 12 (1986), p. 6 (particularly fn. 5).

22 Arbeau, pp. 39-46.

23 William Byrd, *My Ladye Nevells Booke of Virginal Music*, Hilda Andrews, ed. (London, 1926); repr. with a new introduction by Blanche Winogren (New York, 1969), pp. 30-33.

27. Reeds & Brass

herbert W. Myers

The Middle Ages witnessed two pivotal developments in wind instruments—developments that continue to affect their destiny to the present day. The first, whose importance has long been recognized by instrument historians, is the adoption into Europe (apparently as a byproduct of the Crusades) of instruments from the East. The second, no less important, is the formation of instrumental "families" modeled after human voice ranges and intended to perform vocal-style polyphony. Although we usually think of the second of these developments as occurring in the closing years of the fifteenth century, there is evidence of the beginnings of the process as early as the middle of the fourteenth.

Early Middle Ages

But before instruments could be expected to mimic the organization of vocal polyphony, they had to be capable of imitating the other attributes of the human voice as it was employed in Western art music; at the very least, they had to be able to reproduce its range and scales, as well as its power to articulate or join notes at will. It is easy to forget just how limited in one or more of these respects were most of the wind instruments available in Europe in the early Middle Ages: hand-stopped or fingerhole horns, panpipes, small flageolets, and hornpipes with limited number of fingerholes—all of these would be hard put to cope with reproducing the simplest chant melody. This is not meant to denigrate what can be accomplished on such simple instruments; after all, complex art can result from extreme economy of means. But it *is* meant to remind us that the purpose of such instruments was not yet to imitate vocal music, at least not of the sort beginning to be notated at the time; we must look to relevant unnotated, local folk traditions (if and when these exist) for any inkling of what might have been performed on them. Above all, as performers we must be as aware of the limitations as the capabilities of instruments in their early stages of development: not every duct flute is yet a recorder; not every fingerhole horn is yet a cornett.

It may be noticed that already missing from this discussion are some of the more prominent sound-producing devices of the era—the various wood, wood and leather, metal, and elephant tusk horns (the last known as "olifants") employed primarily as signal instruments (see Pl. 29.2). Such horns are on the periphery of our usual definition of "music"; for those interested, their known particulars are well covered by Anthony Baines.[1] The various flute-related instruments are dealt with in the chapter "Flutes" in this volume. Eliminating these, all we really have left is a small selection indeed: the above-mentioned fingerhole and hand-stopped horns and a few cylindrically bored reed pipes. The first of these is a naturally occurring horn, usually bovine, with its short end cut off to produce an integral "mouthpiece." It is pierced with three or four large fingerholes and thus gives four or five strong and clear treble notes; partial coverings or "shadings" are available to give some notes in between. Occasionally we see horns pictured with the player clearly occluding the bell with one hand (hand-stopping)—another way (besides fingerholes) of changing their pitch. There is no reason the two techniques could not be combined, although there seems little direct evidence for such a mixture historically. The reed instruments would appear to be survivals of the Greek *aulos* (Roman *tibia*)—if not directly, at least of some common ancestor. The ancients knew both the double reed (made, in principle, like the modern one by folding a strip of cane lengthwise and separating the tip) as well as the single (made like a bagpipe drone reed by cutting a tongue in the side of a short tube of cane). The single reed was certainly known in early medieval Europe, but whether the double survived there is uncertain. The pipes themselves might be single or—more often—double, and they might be provided with a resonating bell of horn (producing the "hornpipe"). In certain areas (particularly Basque and Welsh) the top end might be fitted with a horn as well, which acts rather like the windcap of Renaissance winds in protecting the reed and preventing direct control of it.[2]

Contact with Islam

While instrument historians may wrangle over whether the instruments introduced into Europe beginning in the twelfth century were, in fact, new or represented re-introductions, as performers we merely have to recognize their novelty at the time.[3] On the woodwind front were the shawm and bagpipe; on the brass, the long trumpet (distinguished by its "pommels" or decorative bosses, characteristic of Indo-Persian trumpets but new to the West). Both the shawm and trumpet (along with the small kettledrums called "nakers") were elements of the ceremonial loud band of the Arab world, which was adopted in Europe by the thirteenth century. The function of the trumpet in European bands would presumably have remained the same, at least at first, as in the Moorish band; employed in pairs and often sounding but a single note roughly an octave (sometimes two) below the keynote of the shawms, the Saracen trumpets "burst in intermittently with hoarse interruptions through which the shawmists unconcernedly play on."[4] When European trumpeters might have begun experimenting with higher "harmonics" (or, more correctly, partials) is anyone's guess, but some evidence suggests it was fairly early on.[5] Equally unknowable is when the shawm began its transformation from the typical Arabic design (with a thumbhole and with its reed untouched by the lips) to the lip-controlled and usually thumbhole-less form typical in the West. We can only speculate that both the availability of a different reed material in the West and the Western proclivity for a more articulated musical style played parts in the story. In any case, the absence of a thumbhole and the use of lip control are probably related: through manipulation of the reed by the lips a conically bored instrument can be induced to overblow at the octave, thus getting by with a minimal number of fingerholes. Of extreme interest regarding the transition to lip control is one famous pictorial source: Escorial J.b.2 (one of the *Cantigas de Santa Maria* manuscripts, ca.1270). The shawm-playing musicians (f. 350) are depicted with what look surprisingly like modern embouchures, implying full control of the reed. Present still is the disc typical of the Arabic shawm, but its function here appears entirely ornamental; it is not being used to support the players' lips.[6] Sadly, however, such informative pictures are few and far between.

Polyphonic Shawm Band

It is well known that in the Renaissance the highest attainment of an instrument was to imitate the human voice, and that (as mentioned above) instruments were built in families after the model of vocal polyphony. It may appear somewhat ironic, then, that the first evidence of such expansion to create instrumental families is associated with the loud band, and specifically the shawm—not an instrument we now usually equate with the voice! In French sources from the mid-fourteenth century we read of a musical instrument called the *bombarde*, which turns out in effect (if not in name) to be a lower-pitched form of the *chalemie* or treble shawm. (The latter, it should be mentioned, appears already to have become a rather larger and lower-pitched instrument than its forebear, the Arabic shawm.) In fact, one fifteenth-century source refers to a *chalemie apelé bombarde* ("a shawm called bombard"), a phrase that pretty well sums up the equivocal nature of the shawm's status as a family through much of its life. While French writers generally continue to distinguish between *chalemie* and *bombarde* through the fifteenth century, in about 1500 they switch to the term *hautbois* (literally "high wood," "high" often meaning "loud" as well as "high in pitch") to include all shawms. This term is adopted into English as "hoboy," which then joins "shawm" itself as well as "waits (pipe)" as possible appellations for any member of the family. (The term "wait" apparently derives from the city watchmen, or "waits," whose primary instrument the shawm had become.[7]) German terminology, on the other hand, long continues to reflect the medieval French distinction between *chalemie* and *bombarde*: in the seventeenth century, Praetorius, while treating the shawms as a single family (now grown to six sizes), still takes pains to distinguish the keyless *Schalmeyen* from the keyed *Pommern*.[8] (*Pommer* is, of course, a corruption of *Bomhart*, itself a corruption of *bombarde*.)

Thus the distinguishing characteristic of a *bombarde* comes to be its key (or keys, on the larger forms that come later). Invented no later than the early fifteenth century, this device allows the lowest finger to cover its hole in spite of the greater spread between holes. The mechanism is then partly covered by a protective barrel or "fontanelle"; it is actually this fontanelle that constitutes the most obvious visual manifestation of the *bombarde*. We can be fairly certain that from the beginning the *bombarde* stood a fifth below the *chalemie*, although the earliest sources that spell this out come from the sixteenth century. However, the two instruments are considerably closer in length than the difference of a fifth would suggest, due to the proportionately longer "bell section" typical of the *chalemie*. Thus we are lucky to have the fontanelle as such a clear visual marker for the distinction between *chalemie* and *bombarde*, since much of what we can ascertain about the makeup of shawm bands comes from pictures. Nevertheless, the significance of the fontanelle seems to have been lost on some artists, for we occasionally see bands depicted in which all shawms have fontanelles (and others in which all lack them) when musical considerations would demand combinations of instruments of different registers. We must remind ourselves that before the invention of the camera, no picture is a photograph.

The fourteenth century saw a great change in the constitution of the loud band, the most obvious manifestation of which was its separation into two groups, the military or "fanfare" trumpets and nakers, on the one hand, and the more freely melodic instruments (shawms and bagpipes) on the other. Other percussion might, at this stage, still join with either group. Soon after the beginning of the fifteenth century the bagpipe had all but disappeared from the company of shawms; so too had percussion instruments, which are conspicuously absent from most fifteenth-century representations of shawm bands. The trumpet, instead, began to be included, becoming well established by 1430 or so. The form most often depicted is the folded trumpet developed in the late fourteenth century, built first in the shape of a flattened S and then (early in the fifteenth), of a flattened loop.[9] Whereas trumpets had appeared in the earlier loud band typically in pairs, the trumpet's presence in the fifteenth-century shawm band was as a single brass instrument among the reeds. From early in the fifteenth century we begin to find references to players specializing in different parts—contratenor, tenor, soprano; from these part names it is clear the organization of the shawm band's music was along the same lines as vocal polyphony. From the fourteenth century through much of the fifteenth, a three-part texture predominated in composed polyphony. Not surprisingly, shawm band iconography also shows a prevalence of trios—three shawms, or two plus trumpet—although exceptions abound. Payment records and other archival data indicate somewhat greater variation in numbers, but are of course less likely to specify the number of players involved in any one piece.[10]

The first surviving shawms come from the sixteenth and seventeenth centuries, leaving us guessing somewhat about their progenitors. Extant examples resemble those shown by Praetorius and conform, with only a few exceptions, to his pitch specifications. His *Discant Schalmey* (the *chalemie* or treble shawm) has d' as its bottom note and his *Altpommer* (the original bombarde or "tenor" shawm—often called "alto" nowadays) has g; his reference pitch standard (*Kammerton*) seems to have been about a semitone above modern. Sixteenth-century sources—specifically both the 1529 and 1545 versions of Martin Agricola's *Musica instrumentalis deudsch*—indicate nominal pitches for these same instruments a fifth lower, that is, g and c, the typical pitches of treble and tenor members of any woodwind family in the Renaissance. There is every reason to read these nominal pitches backwards into the previous period as well. This information implies that the shawm band sounded up a fifth or so from vocal pitch, just as recorders sound up an octave. As to the exact pitch of shawms of the time before examples exist, we have no direct evidence. Performing generally in an ensemble by itself, the shawm band would have had little cause to match the pitch standard of other instruments. At the same time, as pointed out by Keith Polk,[11] the well documented exchange of shawm players from city to city and even country to country points to some measure of pitch standardization among shawms already in the fifteenth century. There are no grounds to think the earlier standard would have differed greatly from that demonstrated by surviving examples.

As it is known from surviving Renaissance specimens, the shawm is a remarkably sophisticated instrument from an acoustical point of view. The treble (*chalemie*) in particular demonstrates qualities easily missed by a casual observer. Its fingerholes—the seven holes manipulated by the player—occupy roughly the upper half of the tube, the lower half containing only resonance holes. This means that the instrument is about twice as long as it needs to be to produce its lowest note. One might conclude that the lower half was there merely for looks, or at most for its effect on timbre, but experiments with surviving examples suggest that the size and position of the resonance holes (which are five in number) have been carefully chosen for their stabilizing effect. In the case of the five-finger note, the resonances have been cunningly adjusted to render it "bistable"—that is to say, stable at two different pitches, in this case a semitone apart. By this means, in addition to the expected pitch ($f\sharp$ on a treble in d'), the one a semitone below can be elicited securely. This is done mainly through relaxing the embouchure, aided by a bit of fingerhole shading; the technique works in the overblown octave as well.[12] This trick of design is all the more amazing when we consider that the analogous semitone on the Baroque oboe requires the use of a key. The musical significance of the achievement becomes perhaps more evident when we think of the treble shawm in its original nominal pitch of g rather than d'; the F/F$\sharp$ semitone then becomes B$\flat$/B, in which both members of the pair are essential as *musica vera*.

Pl. 27.1. Bombarde (left) and treble shawm (details) from *Mary, Queen of Heaven* **(ca.1485)** by the Master of the St. Lucy Legend. National Gallery of Art, Washington, DC, Samuel H. Kress Collection, 1952.2.13.

Exactly when such a sophisticated shawm design was developed is impossible to determine in the absence of examples from before the sixteenth century. To be sure, most (though by no means all) fifteenth-century representations attest to the long bell section (or high-placed fingerholes—the same thing) of the treble shawm as we know it; unfortunately, however, few demonstrate the attention to proportion and detail that we might like to find. One exception is the Flemish painting *Mary Queen of Heaven* by the Master of the St. Lucy Legend (ca.1485), now in the National Gallery of Art, Samuel H. Kress Collection, Washington, DC; here the rendition of the treble shawm might easily be mistaken for a photograph of a surviving example from a century later.[13] To determine that the highly developed design is at least plausible for the fifteenth century is about the best we can do; such knowledge certainly accords with Tinctoris's remark regarding the shawm of his day that, "provided its holes are correctly placed, any melody can be played on it and it is completely perfect."[14]

Pl. 27.2. Shawm pirouette and embouchure (detail) from *Mary, Queen of Heaven* (ca.1485) by the Master of the St. Lucy Legend. National Gallery of Art, Washington, DC, Samuel H. Kress Collection, 1952.2.13.

Another mystery concerns the origin and development of the shawm's pirouette—the vase-shaped piece of turnery that surrounds the upper part of its staple and the base of its reed. This appurtenance has often been cited by organologists as one of the defining features of the Western shawm, the standard theory being that it represents a direct development from the lip-supporting disc of the Eastern shawm. If the story were only that simple! To be sure, there is a superficial similarity of function between the Western pirouette and the Oriental shawm's disc: both present a flat surface against which the player can place his lips. But in the case of the Eastern shawm, the reed is placed well into the mouth cavity, where it vibrates untouched by the lips. In the Western shawm, by contrast, the pirouette is so arranged as to allow lip control of the reed. At least this is the nature of the pirouette as we know it from art works and treatises of the sixteenth and seventeenth centuries; the exact course of its development in earlier centuries is impossible to determine.[15] In any case, there is little evidence of a direct evolution from disc to pirouette. There is a long period between the introduction of the shawm into Europe and clear depictions of pirouettes. The top ends of shawms shown in fourteenth-century pictures appear either with a plain, almost cylindrical profile or with what looks to be an integral bulbous or bowl-shaped expansion; the latter often resembles a trumpet mouthpiece as depicted in the same sources. Funnel-shaped, apparently separable pirouettes begin making sporadic appearances in the first half of the fifteenth century, becoming almost ubiquitous by 1500.[16] Assuming (as we have been) that the reed of the western shawm was already lip-controlled before the advent of the pirouette, it would seem that the function of the latter was merely to replace the top of the instrument as a surface against which to place the lips. What, then, was the advantage conferred by the detachable pirouette over the integral arrangement? One plausible answer is that it allowed some measure of pitch adjustment, for not only would it permit the staple to be moved in and out, but longer or shorter ones could be substituted as well.

The musical implications of the pirouette remain somewhat controversial. Organologists have often viewed it as an impediment to embouchure control, but investigation of the modern descendants of the shawm still in use in Catalonia casts strong doubts upon this assessment; here full control of the reed is maintained, the pirouette providing support without getting in the way. The puffed-cheek embouchures depicted in many early artworks (see Pl. 28.4) have also been seen as indicative of a "flat out," unmodulated playing style, but again, experiment shows that control of the reed is still possible in spite of distended cheeks. Then too, there are some careful renditions of shawm players with surprisingly "modern" looking embouchures; one (see Pl. 27.2 above) even shows some exposed reed between lips and pirouette.

Appearing occasionally alongside *chalemie* and *bombarde* in fifteenth-century accounts is the term *contre* (or its equivalent) as an instrument name. It is definitely some sort of shawm, but what sort? One theory is that it was a large *bombarde* sounding a fifth lower than the normal one—essentially the instrument Praetorius calls the *Nicolo*, a *Tenorpommer* lacking extension keys below the seven-finger note (*c*). Such an instrument would certainly represent a logical lower extension of the shawm family, going down to a nominal low *F* at "shawm band" pitch and thus providing a bass or *contratenor bassus*. There are, however, several objections to this theory. One is chronological: when, for instance, in Florence in 1406 a German was hired to play *ceremella contra tenorum* (contratenor shawm) the typical *written* contratenor part was of the same range as the tenor; the *contratenor bassus* was still unknown. Another objection is iconographic: amid the rich store of depictions of shawm bands, there are virtually none that show anything resembling a *Nicolo*.[17] Instruments of the *Nicolo* variety seem to have been rare in any period. They are not mentioned in any sixteenth-century source; Agricola, who includes the *Schalmey* in his composite chart for *discantus* winds and the *Bomhart* in the chart for *tenor-altus*, significantly leaves out any mention of a corresponding shawm in the chart for *bassus*.

Perhaps a more promising theory is that the *contre* was of the same basic range as the normal *bombarde* but was given some alternative construction that better suited its rôle as a *contratenor altus*. One idea is that it had a different bell shape, imparting a different timbre. This is suggested by some early illustrations that show barrel-shaped or cylindrical elongations of the bell beyond the normal flare (see Pl. 28.4); however, these alternative bell shapes were fairly short lived, dying out by about 1420, while references to shawm-playing contratenor specialists continue through the century.[18] Another suggestion is that the *contre* might have been tuned differently or given some small extensions to range as might befit a part complementing the tenor. In this case, the distinguishing characteristics are likely to be rather subtle and unlikely to show up in pictures.

Also connected throughout the period to the contratenor function—and probably of greater significance than any contratenor *bombarde*—are the brass instruments that were regularly employed in the shawm band. Here we enter probably the most hotly contested area of shawm band research. The question is not whether the brass were so employed; both archival and iconographic sources are in complete agreement about this. The burning issue, however, is the nature of the instruments themselves. Beginning in the early years of this century, instrument historians started to recognize evidence of the development of a slide trumpet in the fifteenth century. Noticing that the trumpets intermixed with shawms were often held quite differently from the fanfare or herald trumpets of the same era (that is, slanting downwards, with one hand pressing the mouthpiece to the lips, rather than heroically upwards) Curt Sachs in particular advanced the theory that these were special trumpets equipped with a long, telescoping extension to the mouthpiece; this would have allowed the player to fill in some of the gaps in the harmonic series, rendering such trumpets more freely melodic. (This form of slide trumpet, consisting of a stationary, single slide and a moveable instrument may seem a cumbersome contraption, but in fact the idea works quite well; such an instrument was definitely in existence in the Baroque, being specified by J.S. Bach as the *tromba da tirarsi*.) Some found linguistic support for the slide trumpet, as for instance in the fifteenth-century French distinction between *trompette de ménestrels* ("minstrels' trumpet") and *trompette de guerre* ("war trumpet"), while others saw in the slide trumpet (or its successor, the trombone) an explanation for the parts labeled *trumpetum* or something similar. (Such parts are clearly not performable on a "natural" trumpet—one limited to the notes of the harmonic series—but would demand some sort of slide to make more notes possible.) Heinrich Besseler even went so far as to propose that the bass trombone (which would be necessary to play one such part at written pitch) had been invented by the 1430s![19] While most researchers realize that the iconographic record suggests a little more caution than was exercised by Besseler, they have generally accepted the idea that a trumpet with single slide preceded the trombone, with its more efficient double or "U" slide.

Until Peter Downey, that is. Downey[20] quite correctly pointed out that none of the written sources of the fifteenth century refers unequivocally to the (single) slide action in connection with the trumpet, nor does the way trumpets are held, as shown in art works, constitute proof of such an arrangement. He argued furthermore that not only was the *trumpetum* described by theorists as a part in the *style* of trumpets, not one *performed* on them, but that most of the extant examples are well nigh impossible to play on a slide trumpet, at least at vocal pitch. (They would in any case demand an instrument considerably larger than that normally depicted with shawms.) Downey's assertions elicited some strong responses defending the basic logic of the slide trumpet theory, at least as it applies to the shawm band; tenuous as it is, it still seems the best explanation for the known facts.[21] Downey's challenge has none the less brought many of the issues into sharper focus, particularly those concerning the chronology of the trombone's development. Although a handful of paintings from the second half of the fifteenth century show some trombone-like elements,[22] the first to have all of them in place—size, layout, stays, and a credible grip by the player—hails from just before 1490.[23] Despite what we might consider its obvious advantages, the new instrument did not take over immediately, for representations of the trumpet format prevail through the fifteenth century and are still to be met with well into the sixteenth.

With only pictures and practical experience to go on, the modern builder trying to reconstruct a slide trumpet has many details to work out: dimensions, thickness of material, whether to add stays or other stiffening devices (for which there is little fifteenth-century documentation), and so forth. One of the basic decisions concerns pitch. There is no one, simple answer to this question, in part because of one of the fundamental limitations of the single-slide mechanism as it relates to the arm of the player: since the reach of the arm remains relatively fixed, an increase in the size of the instrument finds a concomitant reduction in the interval by which it can be lowered by the slide. Thus all slide trumpets tend to have about the same range, even though the specific lacunae in their scales may differ. Instruments have been made in pitches over a range from C to G (corresponding to F to C, "shawm band" pitch). In deciding this issue one might bear in mind that iconography suggests a pitch somewhere near modern F, which would then be E according to Praetorius's reckoning and nominal A, "shawm band" pitch.

The repertory of the fifteenth-century shawm band consisted of polyphonic elaborations of monophonic tunes (popular and sacred melodies; basse dance tenors) as well as "composed" polyphony (chansons, motets, and—by the end of the century—instrumental fantasies). Thus the corresponding repertory of a modern shawm band is limited only by the imagination and creativity of its players, for the rules and techniques by which both the tenors were elaborated and the polyphony was adapted are well understood today. Iconography shows almost conclusively that the shawm band performed without written music, a fact which has fostered the notion, popular in certain circles, that the improvised performances of such a band could only have been crude or at best formulaic in style. Keith Polk has perhaps done more than anyone else to dispel this myth, showing not only why we should imagine such performances often rivaled in sophistication the best efforts of composers, but also how in practice refined counterpoint could be achieved.[24] He has underscored the point, too, that the lack of written music at the instant of performance is perhaps more of a testimony to the memories of the players than an indication of a crude product; at the same time, however, he has admitted there are some indications the quality of counterpoint practiced by the earliest bands was not as high as it ultimately became. But certainly by the end of the period many ensembles had access to the best compositional material available in Europe, as attested by surviving manuscripts either putatively or explicitly associated with wind bands.[25] To the modern player, perhaps the most fascinating of the latter is Rome, Biblioteca Casanatense, MS 2856, a collection assembled for the shawm band of Ercole I d'Este of Ferrara beginning in about 1480. Concordances with other sources show the process by which the part ranges in this manuscript were adjusted to fit the specific instruments of the band.[26]

Douçaine

This remains very much the "mystery instrument" of the Middle Ages and Renaissance. Beginning in the thirteenth century and lasting into the seventeenth there are references in several languages to wind instruments whose names derive from Latin *dulcis*, "sweet." These include *douçaine* (also spelled *douchaine*) in French, *dolzaina* in Italian, *dulceano* and *dulzayna* in Spanish, "doucet" and "dulceuse" in English, and finally even *Dulcian* in German. Given the radical changes in winds over such a long period, these names obviously cannot refer to one single object. The one thing most historians agree on is that these words refer to reed instruments, the only exception being "doucet," which may mean recorder. (In fact, only one of them is certain in meaning: *Dulcian* is equivalent to *fagotto* or curtal, an instrument known to have been invented in the sixteenth century. But even the beginning uses of this word are ambiguous, and it is unclear for some time if some simpler forebear is not intended.) Attempting to bring some order to this jumble of names, Barra Boydell noticed something of a historical division between what had heretofore been assumed to be coeval expressions. Whereas the French and Spanish names are found from the earliest period, reaching a peak in frequency in the fourteenth and fifteenth centuries and declining in use in the sixteenth, the Italian word *dolzaina* first appears in 1520 and recurs frequently thereafter in Italy and Germany. Put succinctly, *dolzaina* seems not simply to be the Italian word for douçaine as previously assumed, but perhaps a word denoting a new—though possibly related—instrument of the Renaissance.[27]

As to the medieval and early Renaissance douçaine, there is but one description—that by Tinctoris, ca.1487.[28] Writing in Latin, he says that the *dulcina* (so called because of the sweetness of its sound) is a kind of *tibia* (here a catchall term for reed instrument) with the fingering of a recorder (*i.e.*, seven fingerholes in front and one behind, in contrast with the shawm, which lacks a thumbhole); since not every melody can be played on it, it is considered to be imperfect. This is not a lot to go on, but it is suggestive of an instrument with narrow cylindrical bore; such an instrument would not only be quiet but also limited in range— "imperfect." (All this follows from acoustical considerations: a conical bore like that of a shawm tends to be loud, and it overblows at the octave, obviating the need for a thumbhole. A cylindrical bore, on the other hand, overblows at the twelfth if at all, leaving a gap in the scale; filling that gap requires closed-standing keys, first applied for that purpose, so far as we know, in the chalumeau or proto-clarinet near the beginning of the eighteenth century. Overblowing generally was not practiced on earlier cylindrical reeds, which were thus limited in range to the number of fingerholes plus one note—they needed every hole they could conveniently possess!) However, as pointed out by Anthony Baines, a conical bore is not absolutely ruled out by this description, and—just for spite—there exists a Spanish folk shawm called the *dulzaina* to keep us guessing.[29] All in all, though, the idea of the cylindrical bore seems to have the most going for it, particularly since it would offer the greatest contrast to the shawm itself.

The similarity of this concept of the douçaine to that of the crumhorn initially led some instrument historians to equate the two. However, not only is there no mention of a windcap in Tinctoris's description, but no evidence of windcaps in Europe during the heyday of the douçaine. (They first appear in the closing years of the fifteenth century.) It seems most probable that the douçaine, like the European shawm, had an exposed, lip-controlled reed. To what extent it otherwise resembled the shawm we can only conjecture. Baines long ago pointed the way to plausible solutions based on context. Citing the strong and consistent medieval division between *haut* (loud) and *bas* (soft) music, he wrote, "when a picture appears to show a shawm-like instrument intruding amongst strings, it must be some sort of douçaine; the literary evidence admits no alternative."[30] Fourteenth- and fifteenth-century art is in fact full of such intruders—candidates for the name "douçaine." While builders trying to recreate the instrument have generally made use of this kind of pictorial evidence, no one, to my knowledge, has yet made a systematic iconological study based on Baines' idea; such a study might be very revealing.

The idea of the douçaine as a "quiet shawm" suggested to Barra Boydell there might be some connection between it and the references to "still shawms" found in sixteenth-century English sources.[31] (A parallel term found in early fifteenth-century Italy is *piffari sordi*— "mute shawms;"[32] one can only wonder if it too might refer to *douçaines*.) Shortly after his study was published a report appeared describing instruments recovered with the remains of the *Mary Rose*, the vice-flagship of Henry VIII that sank in Portsmouth Harbor in 1545. One of these instruments resembles superficially a shawm; indeed it was so identified at first,[33] but turns out to be something rather different, namely, a developed form of the douçaine (as we have understood it from Tinctoris).[34] Its discovery at the very least confirms the existence of the basic instrument type—straight, uncapped, cylindrically bored reed—and verifies its presence in sixteenth-century England. The *Mary Rose* still shawm/douçaine is approximately of bass crumhorn pitch and has been provided with not only every tonehole it could *conveniently* possess (the eight mentioned by Tinctoris) but a couple in addition, giving it a range of an eleventh. The two extra holes have been assigned to the little fingers of each hand—an extra extension key (besides a normal *bombarde*-style key) for the right-hand little finger and a plain tonehole for the left. (This employment of the little finger of the upper hand seems unique in the history of Western woodwinds.)

Fifteenth-century douçaines seem to have been made in sets: a set of four of them (along with four shawms and four recorders) was ordered in 1426 by Duke Philip the Good of Burgundy to be sent to the Marquis of Ferrara.[35] Surely such quartets would have been made up of instruments of different sizes. Already in the fourteenth century Machaut (in *La prise d'Alexandre*, ca.1367) mentions *doussaines* and *demi-doussaines*, implying as much.[36] Ones a fifth apart (treble in *g* and tenor in *c*) would fit what we know about the development of Renaissance instrument families. However, many tenor and contratenor parts would demand models in *f* instead—if one expects to play such parts "at pitch," that is. Recently some builders have experimented with a fingering system for medieval douçaines based on the left-hand pattern of the *Mary Rose* instrument, that is, adding a tonehole "between the hands" (as it were) to be governed by the left little finger. Such a system is completely conjectural for the fifteenth century, of course, not even having the blessing of Tinctoris. It also takes some getting used to, but the expansion of range it affords is very welcome; the addition of just the one note to the ninth implied by Tinctoris increases the number of playable tenors and contratenors by a large percentage.

Cornett

It is perhaps appropriate that we close this discussion of medieval brass and woodwinds with the cornett, for as the embodiment of both the brass and woodwind principles it is the instrument that, of all the winds, came to typify the sixteenth century in the way that the shawm band had the fifteenth. The principle of the fingerhole horn, as we have seen, was known in the early Middle Ages. We find illustrations of comparatively short, wide-bore horns with a few fingerholes all the way through to the sixteenth century; under the name *Krum horn* one is shown (alongside a true cornett—and in addition to the crumhorns or *Krumhörner*!) by Virdung in 1511.[37] We also find references in France to the *coradoiz* or *cor à doigts*—literally "fingered horn"—from the thirteenth to fifteenth centuries. Beginning already in the eleventh century, however, there are pictures of somewhat longer and much more gently expanding horns, often straight, with enough fingerholes to occupy two hands; sometimes the bells take the shape of an animal or monster head.[38] It is hard not to see these as proto-cornetts, although we cannot really be sure of the tone-producing apparatus; they could even be reeds. In any case, we may not assume automatically that such instruments yet possessed all the musical qualities of the developed Renaissance cornett. Experiments with their folk survivals urge caution in this regard.[39]

The word *cornet*— "little horn"—is found in French from the thirteenth century onward, not always necessarily referring to a woodwind. (The *cornet sarrazinois* or *cor sarrazinois* was a short, straight metal trumpet, for instance.) "Cornet" in English (usually spelled with one t at the time, since there was then no need to distinguish it from the nineteenth-century variety) dates from about 1400. In this case, continuity of use through the Renaissance suggests (but does not confirm) continuity of meaning. Machaut's *grant cornet d'Alemaigne* (*Remède de Fortune*, ca.1342) may be a cornett in the later sense, as may be the *cornet d'Allemagne* that was played "most strangely" at the Banquet of the Vow given by Philip the Good of Burgundy in 1454. But, more to the point, the latter appearance clearly constituted a solo performance; the cornettist joined with neither the loud minstrels nor with the choir. Thus two of its most characteristic rôles in Renaissance music—as a member of the shawm band and as a support to voices—seem still a few decades away.[40]

Notes

1   Anthony Baines, *Brass Instruments: Their History and Development* (New York, 1976), Chapter 3 "The Middle Ages."

2   See Anthony Baines, *Woodwind Instruments and their History*, rev. ed. (New York, 1963), Chapter 8 "Early Reed Instruments and Double-piping."

3   For instance, in a recent book review Frederick Crane questions the "common notion that the shawm was an import from Asia," pointing to shawm-shaped reed instruments known in Europe from antiquity onward (*JAMIS* 22 [1996], p. 135). However, it is not enough to have the superficial *look* of a shawm, as for instance the instruments listed as "shawms" in his book, *Extant Medieval Musical Instruments: A Provisional Catalogue by Types* (Iowa City, 1972), p. 45; in order to *behave* as a shawm, an instrument must possess a conical bore (which these examples do not).

4   Baines, *Woodwind Instruments*, pp. 230-33.

5   Baines, *Brass Instruments*, p. 83.

6   For a reproduction see Jeremy Montagu, *The World of Medieval & Renaissance Musical Instruments* (New York, 1976), p. 40.

7   The etymology tendered by Montagu (*op. cit.*, p. 40)—from *gaida*, an Arabic word for the shawm—seems less probable.

8   *Syntagma musicum* II, 1618, 36-37. Such differences in nomenclature from country to country as well as changes from era to era make it difficult to settle on a single, consistent English terminology for shawms. For instance, the original *bombarde* of the late medieval period (the one Praetorius calls *Altpommer*) was known in England, up until the end of its use, as the "tenor"—a designation reflecting its original rôle; Praetorius's *Tenor* (the next size down, which he also calls *Bassett*) seems to have been unknown in England. Thus the modern term "alto shawm," adapted from his nomenclature and admittedly very handy when we are dealing with the expanded shawm family of his era, did not exist historically in English. We often need to adopt different approaches for different eras.

9   On the changes in the trumpet at this period, see Ross W. Duffin, "Backward Bells and Barrel Bells: Some Notes on the Early History of Loud Instruments," *Historic Brass Society Journal* 9 (1997), 114-17.

10 For a more detailed examination of the composition of the shawm band (especially in Germany, but with relevance to the rest of Europe) from the fourteenth to early sixteenth centuries, see Keith Polk, *German Instrumental Music of the Late Middle Ages* (Cambridge, 1992), pp. 56-70.

11 *German Instrumental Music*, p. 225.

12 For an astute acoustical explanation of this phenomenon see David Hogan Smith, *Reed Design for Early Woodwinds* (Bloomington, 1992), pp. 29-35.

13 In spite of the apparent photographic realism, however, the instrument still differs in its proportions from the "standard" museum example, whose uppermost resonance hole is situated almost exactly at the midpoint of its body; in the painting, the hole lies noticeably lower than that. There is, on the other hand, at least one museum specimen proportioned similarly to the treble in the painting; this is an anonymous seventeenth-century instrument, possibly Catalan, in the Museo Municipál de Música, Barcelona, no. 608 (pictured in Anthony Baines, *European and American Musical Instruments* [London, 1966], no. 526; compare no. 525, which has the normal layout). I am personally

unacquainted with the playing characteristics of the Barcelona treble. The bombard shown in Pl. 27.1 differs slightly from most preserved examples, since its tuning/resonance hole is single and rather high up the bell, whereas in most originals the holes are double (placed symmetrically on either side) and somewhat further down.

[14] Johannes Tinctoris, *De inventione et usu musicae*, Naples, ca.1487, trans. Anthony Baines, "Fifteenth-Century Instruments in Tinctoris's *De Inventione et Usu Musicae*," *Galpin Society Journal* 3 (1950), 20-21—with slight amendments.

[15] See Herbert W. Myers, *The Practical Acoustics of Early Woodwinds*, D. M. A. Final Project (Stanford University, 1980), pp. 104-114 for a discussion of the available historical information regarding shawm reeds and pirouettes from the late fifteenth century to the late seventeenth.

[16] On the other hand, a definition—admittedly somewhat vague—supplied by Konrad of Megenberg may imply the existence of a separable pirouette by the mid-fourteenth century; see Christopher Page, "German Musicians and Their Instruments: a 14th-century account by Konrad of Megenberg," *Early Music* 10 (April, 1982), 192-200. This information may imply there was some lag between reality and its iconographic representation.

[17] The only illustration I know of that might qualify as an exception is of a mounted shawm band, ca.1420-30, which includes shawms of three different lengths as well as a trumpet; however, the longest of the three is still significantly shorter than the two extant examples of the *Niçolo* (both in Prague, and both about 100cm long—long enough to require a bent bocal). See Edmund A. Bowles, *Musikleben im 15. Jahrhundert (Musikgeschichte in Bildern III)* (Leipzig, 1977), ill. 62, p. 77.

[18] See the discussion of barrel bell instruments in Duffin, "Backward Bells," 117-25.

[19] Heinrich Besseler, "Die Entstehung der Posaune," *Acta Musicologica* 22 (1950), 8-35.

[20] Peter Downey, "The Renaissance Slide Trumpet: Fact or Fiction," *Early Music* 12 (1984), 26-33.

[21] See in particular the trio of responses to Downey published in *Early Music* 17 (1989): Herbert W. Myers, "Slide Trumpet Madness: Fact or Fiction?," 382-89; Keith Polk, "The Trombone, the Slide Trumpet and the Ensemble Tradition of the Early Renaissance," 389-96; and Ross Duffin, "The *trompette des menestrels* in the 15th-Century *alta capella*," 397-402.

[22] The so-called "Adimari Wedding Cassone" panel, often cited as an example from the early fifteenth century (with datings from ca.1420 to ca.1440), has recently been shown to emanate more plausibly from about a generation later; see Timothy McGee, "Misleading Iconography: The Case of the 'Adimari Wedding Cassone'," *Imago Musicae* 9-12 (1992-95), pp. 139-57. While McGee's reasoning is sound concerning the origin and purpose of the panel (including the points that it depicts no specific event, let alone the Adimari wedding of 1420, and that it was unlikely ever to have been part of a wedding chest or *cassone*), his suggestion that restorations over the centuries have fundamentally altered the outlines of the instruments is based on some demonstrably false premises. In particular, the idea that the current colors of the instruments (gold for the slide trumpet/trombone; light tan for the shawms) are "wrong" for the period is belied by a multitude of other iconographic evidence. It seems, in any case, there is no direct physical evidence from the painting itself that the instrument shapes have been significantly modified since the fifteenth century.

[23] This is a detail of the fresco *The Assumption of the Virgin* by Filippino Lippi in the church of Santa Maria sopra Minerva, Rome; it is reproduced in the article "Trombone" by Anthony Baines, *New Grove.*

[24] Polk, *German Instrumental Music*, Chapter 7, 163-213. See also Ross W. Duffin, "Ensemble Improvisation in the 15th-Century Mensural Dance Repertoire," paper read at the conference, "Performance Practice and Repertory of Loud Minstrels in the 15th Century," at Alden Biesen, Belgium, June, 1995.

[25] For a discussion of the written sources of instrumental repertory, especially German, see Polk, *German Instrumental Music*, Chapter 6, pp. 132-62.

[26] For a short discussion—including a few tantalizing examples—see Lewis Lockwood, *Music in Renaissance Ferrara* (Cambridge, MA, 1984), pp. 268-72. The complete contents of the manuscript are transcribed in Arthur S. Wolff, "The Chansonnier Biblioteca Casanatense 2856: Its History, Purpose, and Music" (Ph.D. diss., North Texas State University, 1970).

[27] See Barra Boydell, *The Crumhorn and Other Renaissance Windcap Instruments* (Buren, 1982), pp. 384-418.

[28] Baines, "Fifteenth-Century Instruments," *loc. cit.*

[29] See Anthony Baines, *Woodwind Instruments* , pp. 234-35.

[30] Baines, *Woodwind Instruments*, p. 235.

[31] Boydell, *The Crumhorn*, pp. 403-04.

[32] Simone Prudenzani, *Il Saporetto*, a *roman* of 1412, sonnet 33.

[33] See Frances Palmer, "Musical Instruments from the *Mary Rose*," *Early Music* 11 (1983), 53-59.

[34] See Herbert W. Myers, "The *Mary Rose* 'Shawm'," *Early Music* 11 (1983), 358-60.

[35] Boydell, *The Crumhorn*, p. 386.

[36] Boydell, *The Crumhorn*, p. 385.

[37] Sebastian Virdung, *Musica getutscht und ausgezogen* (Basel, 1511), fol. B iv r.

[38] For examples see Dietrich Hakelberg, "A Medieval Wind Instrument from Schlettwein, Thuringia," *Historic Brass Society Journal* 7 (1995), 185-96.

[39] See Raymond Parks, "The *Tuohitorvi*: Cornett Survival or Re-Creation," *Galpin Society Journal* 48 (1995), 188-93.

[40] Concerning the rise of the cornett in German ensembles, beginning in the 1470s, see Polk, *German Instrumental Music*, pp. 72-73.

28. Bagpipe
Adam K. Gilbert

"superexcellens omnia instrumenta"

BEFORE 1300

The bagpipe played an integral role in musical life throughout the Middle Ages and inspired a rich tradition of symbolism. Despite the lack of surviving instruments, a substantial body of literature, iconography and archival records allows a glimpse at the bagpipe's physical characteristics, its popularity, and its place in society. Today, a variety of stylistic approaches and techniques waits to be explored, and the potential repertory is limited only by a nine-note ambitus and the imagination of the performer.

By the fall of the Roman Empire, the idea of attaching a bag to a reed-pipe was nothing new. Applying pressure to a goat, sheep or dog skin—or a bladder—spared the player the necessity of circular breathing to create a constant air-stream. Aristophanes' pipers who "blow the butt of a dog" might well have been prototypes of bestial illuminations (see Pl. 28.1), and some ancient stones may suggest the existence of some kind of bagpipe. As early as the first century Dio Chrystostom and Suetonius mention the emperor Nero "playing both pipe with mouth and bag under the arm."[1]

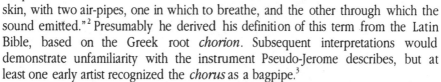

Pl. 28.1. Marginal figure with bestial bagpipe.
French MS (1325-28), The Hours of Jeanne d'Evreux, by Jean Pucelle. Metropolitan Museum of Art, the Cloisters Collection, 1954 (54.1.2 f.35r).

Although the Biblical *sumponiah* (Daniel 3:5) was probably not a bagpipe, the first medieval references to the instrument originate in discussions of Hebrew music. In his famous ninth-century letter to Dardanus, Pseudo-Jerome describes: "In the temple of ancient times the chorus was made of skin, with two air-pipes, one in which to breathe, and the other through which the sound emitted."[2] Presumably he derived his definition of this term from the Latin Bible, based on the Greek root *chorion*. Subsequent interpretations would demonstrate unfamiliarity with the instrument Pseudo-Jerome describes, but at least one early artist recognized the *chorus* as a bagpipe.[3]

Reginald of Prüm includes the *musa* in his instrumentarium and regards it as the inspiration for the word *musa*. Although it is impossible to be sure what instrument Reginald is describing, the name *musa* would become inseparably attached to the bagpipe:

> Music is named after the muse, which is an instrument preferred by the ancients above all other musical instruments, because by its nature it contains all the

399

perfections. It can be demonstrated above to contain the consonances and tones, and below the two semitones, major and minor.[4]

There is little doubt, however, to which instrument the twelfth-century theorist John of Cotton refers. In a passage that is very likely a commentary on Reginald, he offers the bagpipe, *superexcellens omnia instrumenta*, its highest praise:

> It is called music, as some would have it, from *musa* [bagpipe], which is a certain musical instrument proper and pleasant enough in sound. But let us consider by what reasoning and what authority music derives its name from *musa*. *Musa*, as we have said, is a certain instrument far surpassing all other musical instruments, inasmuch as it contains in itself the powers and methods of them all. For it is blown into by human breath like a pipe, it is regulated by the hand like the fiddle, and it is animated by a bellows like organs. Hence *musa* derives from the Greek. μεση (*mese*), that is, "central," for just as divers paths converge at some central point, so too do manifold instruments meet together in the *musa*. Therefore, the name "music" was not unfittingly taken from its main exponent.[5]

Eleventh-century Arabic sources define the *mizmar al jirab* as a pipe with a bag, and the twelfth-century Jewish commentator Saadyah maintains that "the *sumponiah* was the instrument of shepherds activated by a bag.[6] The bagpipe also begins to appear in instrument lists under variations of *muse*, like *cornemuse* and *musette*. Some names—like *chevrette*, *bock* or *gaita* (Arab. "*gdi*") refer to the goat skin from which the bag was made. The term *sampogna* was probably a corruption of the Greek *symphonia*.[7] In a late source, the theorist Gafurius invokes the piercing sound of the bagpipe in the etymology for one of its names: "They call a bagpipe a *piva* from its shrill sounds which seem to cry "pi vi."[8] While various early sources certainly establish the bagpipe's existence, they offer little evidence of one of its most recognizable features—the drone. However, the ubiquitous appearance of bag-less double pipes and what appear to double-bore chanters suggests that the drone principle was not foreign to the instrument.

Pl. 28.2. Marginal figure with bagpipe. French MS (1325-28), The Hours of Jeanne d'Evreux, by Jean Pucelle. Metropolitan Museum of Art, the Cloisters Collection, 1954 (54.1.2 f.49r).

AFTER 1300

It is not until the second half of the thirteenth century when Adam de la Halle's Robin ushers in his "*muse au grant bourdon*" that bagpipes with drones on separate stocks suddenly burst upon the scene.[9] A lower drone pitch may have made the separation of the two pipes necessary.[10] Although the drone-less bagpipe would survive well past the Middle Ages, the drone would become a prominent feature of the bagpipe, which would remain largely unchanged throughout the fifteenth century.

The Instrument

A typical bagpipe consists of a bag made from a whole sheepskin (or two pieces of leather sewn together) and sealed with a mixture containing honey or brandy. A blowpipe equipped with a leather flap closes against the pressure of a full bag, thus preventing air from escaping. Wooden stocks placed in the bagpipe both hold the pipes and protect the reeds. Until the end of the fifteenth century, the sounding portion of the bagpipe commonly consisted of a conical-bore chanter with a double reed, and a cylindrical-bore drone of about twice the length with a single free-beating reed.[11] However, we cannot rule out the existence of cylindrical chanters, and acoustical differences between the two bore shapes are significant.[12] Because the cylindrical bore produces only odd-numbered overtones, it over-blows at the twelfth. The conical bore over-blows at the octave, creating a richer, more raucous sound.[13] Because the cylindrical bore produces a lower pitch than its conical counterpart, the medieval drone was probably tuned two octaves below the second note of the chanter, a configuration common among modern Western European bagpipes.[14]

Tuning

There is little reason to doubt that the medieval chanter typically had—like its cousins the shawms—seven finger-holes.[15] Thus, the chanter probably played an octave, with either a semi-tone or whole-tone below the drone pitch. The possibility should not be ruled out of a drone tuned to either the fourth or fifth note of the chanter, as found in many Eastern European bagpipes. The existence of the thumb-hole remains open to conjecture, yet probably bagpipes both with and without thumb-holes co-existed. Praetorius mentions: "Shepherds pipes are out of tune on the notes controlled by the upper holes; the reason for this, in my opinion, is that they have no thumb-hole at the rear. Other bagpipes...have this thumb-hole, which considerably helps control of tuning."[16] His description also points to the "closed" fingering, in which the upper four notes of the chanter are tuned by covering some or all of the right hand fingers.

The fourth note of the chanter warrants special mention. On many modern bagpipes, this sounds somewhere between a major and minor third above the drone, earning it the term "neutral third." This feature is probably a result of the equidistant placement of finger holes along the bore, rather than on any specific "eastern" influence. It is likely that many medieval pipers performed in an *ad hoc* temperament and that neutral thirds were commonly heard.[17]

Graces

One of the paradoxes of "this most variable of wind instruments" is that differences in size, shape, and inner mechanism pale in comparison to the unity of principle that rules the bagpipe. Endless tone, lack of dynamics, and the inability to use lingual articulation set the instrument apart from other woodwinds. Finger articulations ("graces") are thus necessary when playing a repeated note or marking a stress. Bagpipers have developed a repertory of these graces for expressive purposes, ranging from sparingly to highly ornamental, and from strictly prescribed to intensely personal. The modern player cannot hope to duplicate the choices made by his medieval counterpart, but he can avail himself of the same repertory of devices.

Although the effect of lifting a particular finger varies among different instruments, graces can be divided into a few basic types. First, lifting a single finger high up on the chanter creates a clicking sound (rather than an identifiable pitch) to separate the main melody notes. In one folk style, the third finger of the left hand is lifted between notes played by the right-hand, while the left thumb articulates notes played by the left hand. One can explore a range of possible graces by playing a single note on the chanter, and quickly lifting other fingers individually or in combination. Secondly, quickly dropping fingers also produces a grace. Common to Eastern European traditions is the playing of a grace-note either at drone pitch or its dominant, creating an illusion of silence between the main melody notes. This type of grace produces quite an effective staccato when the main note is played very shortly. Finger vibrato is another common folk technique, and probably existed long before it was called *flattement* in the seventeenth century. "Trilling" a finger lower than the main note creates a pitch that is slightly lower—or in some cases higher—than the main note.[18] Finally, graces can be played as identifiable pitches as well, by lifting more than one finger simultaneously, making possible a kind of counterpoint. From a combination of these devices—finger graces, vibrato, turns and trills—the medieval player had an infinite range of expressive possibilities in hand. It is in the application of these graces that the medieval bagpipe lies, and its technical language awaits to be fully explored.

Ex. 28.1 Winter wie ist nu dein kraft.

Pastoral Symbolism

As colleagues in the *pui d'Arras*, Jean Erart and Adam de la Halle shared a fascination with the bagpipe, giving it center stage with Robin and Marion in numerous *pastourelles*. But for the trouvères the *muse* symbolized more than mere rusticity. Its size (*au grant forel* and *au grand chalemelle*), animal nature, and "staying power" are enlisted as sexual symbolism. In Jean's *Au tens pascour*, a competition for the affection of a shepherdess ends when a fight ensues and the piper's bag is pierced. The instrument's name is also the subject of clever word play. In the refrain of another of Jean's *pastourelles*, Robin is too busy "playing his muse" to notice that Marion is cuckolding him. Years later, in Elizabethan England, the expression "Robin turelure" would remain a synonym for cuckold.[19]

Pl. 28.3. Shepherd with bagpipe.
Detail from Annunciation to the
Shepherds. Book of Hours from
Northern France or Flanders (ca.1445).
The Pierpont Morgan Library, New
York. M287, f.64v.

Trouvère symbolism would be also echoed in recognition of the bagpipe's use as an instrument of war. In a tale from *Les Cent Nouvelles Nouvelles*, a half-wit Burgundian soldier saves the day and his neck when he begs to play the bagpipes on the gallows, thus alerting his comrades sleeping in the woods. His choice of refrain, "Tu demoures trop, Robinet!" hearkens almost verbatim back to an early-thirteenth-century *pastourelle* by Jean Bodel, where it is heard on the lips of a wavering Marion.[20]

Just as the trouvère focus on the bagpipe reflected a growing interest in realistic representation, so did the emergence in painting and illumination of shepherds with bagpipes in hand. Lutes and vielles gradually gave way to instruments like the bagpipe in Christian pastoral iconography. Nativity scenes from fourteenth-century Italy commonly show a shepherd playing a bagpipe, or holding it silently in his hands while gazing in awe at an angel (see Pl. 28.3). The nature of the symbolism is evident: the bagpipes "are played by shepherds as distinguishing attributes and symbols of the participation of mankind in the celebration of the coming to earth of God in human form."[21] The arrested playing may not only represent wonder at the appearance of the angels, but the cessation of worldly things for the coming of the divine. The bagpipe is also held by shepherds in the Annunciation of Joachim, and in the hands of angels in the Coronation of the Virgin. Although bagpipes do not appear amidst representations of the Apocalypse, the instrument is no stranger to the hands of Death. Antecedents of the perverse bagpipes so typical of Hieronymus Bosch's paintings may be seen in the grotesqueries of northern medieval marginalia.[22]

Sound

The trouvère repertory offers our earliest hints at the sound of the bagpipe, or at least how it was perceived. The onomatopoeic refrains of Jean Erart's *pastourelles* and Adam de la Halle's *Li Gieu de Robin et Marion* (Ex. 28.2a-c)[23] are just a few examples from a rich tradition. The lilting *leure leure*—invariably represented in triple time—evoked the sound of the bagpipe well past the Middle Ages, and even inspired some names for the instrument.[24]

Ex. 28.2a. *Au tens pascour.*

Ex. 28.2b. *Trairi.*

Ex. 28.2c. *Hè! Robechon.*

When considering the "mimesis" of the Ivrea Codex,[25] it does not take a great leap of imagination to hear the echo of an ancient pipe in a fragment of Antonio Zachara da Teramo's *Amor de tosa* (Ex. 28.3). This mimicry may also suggest relationships between melody and drone, common figurations of notes thought to be most consonant or pleasing, and even a starting point for imagining possible finger articulations.

Ex. 28.3. *Amor ne tosa* by Antonio Zachara da Teramo.[26]

la   sam - po - gnia;   be,   be - lu, lu,   lu, lu,   lu,

lu, lu, lu, lu, lu, lu,   lu, lu, lu, lu, lu, lu,   lu, lu, lu, lu, lu, lu,   lu.

Syngynge, Pypynge, Gyngelynge, Berkynge

Shepherds were not the only players of bagpipes. The troubadour Bleheris was noted as "a master of all instruments and skilled in song, and familiar with many *lais* and tunes, able to play viele and psaltery, harp and bagpipe." Ability on the pipes was considered a must for the professional performer: "Jongleur, you should be able to handle nine instruments...bagpipes, pipe,...you will be equipped to deal with every eventuality."[27] The bagpipe also served as travel companion to pilgrims, in fact and fiction. In addition to having a heavy hand on the scale, Chaucer's Miller was something of a performer himself:

> He was a Iangler and a Golyardes
> And that was mooste of synne and harlottryes
> Wel koude he stelen corn/and tollen thryes
> And yet he hadde/ a thombe of gold pardee
> A whit coote/and a blew hood wered he
> A baggepipe, wel koude he/ blowe and sowne
> And the withal he broghte us out of towne[28]

The Testimony of William Thorpe (1407) graphically confirms that the Miller represented more than a mere literary conceit, and illustrates the derogatory association between pipe and jongleur.

> And also summe of these pilgrimes wolen have with hem baggepipes, so that in each town thei comen thorough what with noyse of her syngynge and with the soun of her pypynge and with the gyngelynge of her cantirbirie bellis and with the berkynge out of dogges aftir hem, these maken more noyse than if the king came there awaye with his clarioneris and manye other mynstrels. And if these men and wymen ben a monethe oute in her pilgrymage, manye of hem an half yeere after schulen be greete jangelers, tale-tellers and lyeris.[29]

No less than the Archbishop of Canterbury comes to the rescue of the maligned instrument. After listing the many sufferings of the pilgrim, he defends the use of the "baggepipe for to dryve away with sich myrthe the hurt of his sore. For with siche solace the traveile and werinesse of pylgrymes is lighlti and myrili brought forth." Finally he invokes a biblical defense (reminiscent of Pseudo-Jerome): "for Davith in his last psalme techith man to use dyverse instrumentes for to praise with God."[30]

Although one may doubt that the Miller was playing devotional music on his pipes, medieval pilgrimage music offers a wealth of potential bagpipe tunes, from the *Cantigas de Santa Maria* to the songs of the *Libre Vermell*. The melody of *Da que Deus* (Ex. 28.4a) typifies much of the *Cantigas* repertory, with a dual tonality reminiscent of later Gaelic folk music. *Stella splendens* (Ex. 28.4b) may represent the kind of simple polyphony that is not disturbed by a drone, and fits well within the range of two equal bagpipes. Might the famous musician duos of the *Cantigas* illuminations have performed *Da que Deus* polyphonically in similar fashion?

Ex. 28.4a. *Da que Deus.*

Ex. 28.4b. *Stella splendens.*

Dance

Its capability for continuous and audible playing made the bagpipe—like the pipe and tabor—ideally suited to accompany the dance. Boccaccio's account of Tindaro (the Miller's Italian cousin) finds its reflection in more than one fourteenth-century Italian painting:

> But the king, being in a good humor, called for Tindaro, and commanded him to go and fetch his bagpipe, to play for many dances, and so they spent the better part of the night before each went to sleep.[31]

Although a real-life Tindaro had ample precedent for playing any tune as a dance, modern pipers have embraced the *Istanpitta Ghaetta* as a mainstay of modern medieval repertory. Ignoring suggestions that the title honors a forgotten person or an Italian city, they prefer to imagine that it indicates an idiomatic representation of the bagpipe. Unlike many surviving medieval dances, it remains almost entirely within the limited range of the bagpipe. Chromatic emphasis of the fifth and first tones offer piquant commentary against a drone, and *f♯* below the drone pitch seems quite plausible when one considers surviving medieval recorders, in which the lowest note is a semi-tone.[32]

Ex. 28.5. *Istanpitta Ghaetta.*

The Bagpipe in the *Alta Capella*

Between about 1360 and 1390, and even into the first quarter of the fifteenth century, the bagpipe performed with shawms as a member of the *alta capella*.[33] Decisions about its participation in one of the most important ensembles of the Middle Ages have yet to be fully explored in performance. Did the ensembles perform polyphony? What was the pitch relationship between bagpipe and shawms? Which voice did the bagpipe play? These questions warrant further study, but a few possibilities may be briefly considered.

Pl. 28.4. Bagpipe with shawm and barrel-bell shawm. Detail from MS of *Le Roman de la Rose*, French, late fourteenth century, Oxford, Bodleian Library, MS e Mus.65, fol.3v.

The frequent appearance of shawm and bagpipe in duo may suggest that the two doubled a melody at the octave or unison, much like their later folk counterparts. With the addition of a lower pitched bombard, the combination of differently pitched instruments suggests the performance of some kind of polyphony.[34] Although it would seem ideally suited for sustaining the notes of a *basse danse* tenor, most chanters were almost certainly pitched too high. It is tempting to imagine an ensemble with a shawm and bombard tuned a fifth apart (in *g* and *d'*) with a bagpipe at the same pitch as the treble shawm, or even more likely a fifth higher. This configuration would agree with what we know of later shawms, and the bagpipe would be approximately the same pitch as that mentioned by Praetorius and found on modern Highland pipes. The bagpipe would thus be suitable for the performance of a high melody or an altus part of equal range with the treble shawm.[35] The degree to which a drone would disturb polyphony is open to conjecture, but drone-less pipes do appear in illustrations, and drones can be easily stopped with a quick flick of the finger on over the bell or by the use of a plug.

Of the surviving basse danse repertory, the bagpipe may claim a tenuous connection to the tenor *Quene note,*[36] (Ex. 28.6) which survives along with a polyphonic setting. Though a single dictionary reference connects the derivation of the word *quene* to the bagpipe,[37] the setting fits credibly within the confines of a bagpipe and shawm duo.

Ex. 28.6. *Quene note.*

Farewell to the Medieval Bagpipe

By the early fifteenth century the bagpipe had largely disappeared from the *alta capella.* One late record (1415) shows a piper among the shawms, but paid a lower fee.[38] Range, tuning limitations, and perhaps even the different articulation of the shawm and bagpipe, no doubt played a part in the inability of the bagpipe to keep up with the evolution of the *alta capella.* Although the bagpipe experienced a brief vogue in court circles during the latter part of the fifteenth century, its days performing as a member of the polyphonic ensemble were numbered.[39] The arrival of the "Renaissance" bagpipe might best be marked by the adoption of a second drone and a longer, narrower chanter during the early sixteenth century. The bagpipe would continue to enjoy a vibrant life as a folk instrument until its near demise in the twentieth century. Perhaps Jacopo Sannazaro offers the most appropriate farewell to the "medieval" bagpipe:

Behold how here your travails are completed, O rustic and rural sampogna...It is not for you to go seeking the lofty palaces of princes, nor the proud piazzas of the populous cities, in order to have the resounding applause, the shadowy favors, or the windy glories, most vain deceits, false allurements, stupid and obvious flatteries of the faithless crowd. Your humble sound would ill be heard amid that of the fearsome cornets or the royal trumpets. Let it suffice you here among these mountains to be given breath by the mouth of some shepherd...[40]

Pl.28.5. Marginal figure with bagpipe. French MS (1325-28), The Hours of Jeanne d'Evreux, by Jean Pucelle. Metropolitan Museum of Art, the Cloisters Collection, 1954 (54.1.2 f.143r).

Notes

---

[1] Curt Sachs, *The History of Musical Instruments* (New York, 1940), p. 141; and Anthony Baines, *Bagpipes* (Oxford, 1960), pp. 63-67.

[2] "Synagogae antiquis temporibus fuit *chorus* quoque simplex pellis cum duabus cicutis aereis, et per primam inspiratur per secundum emittit." See Elena Ferrari Barassi, *Strumenti Musicali E Testimonianze Teoriche Nel Medio Evo* (Cremona, 1979), p. 59.

[3] Mantua, B. Civica PS C III 20. Psalter, fol. 1v: David and four musicians, first half of the twelfth century. Other depictions show a circle with two rods attached of uncertain identity. See Tilman Seebass, *Musikdarstellung und Psalterillustration im früheren Mittelalter: Studien Ausgehend von einer Okonologie der Handschrift Paris Bibliothèque Nationale Fonds Latin 1118* (Berne, 1973), Vol. 1, pl. 141, and Vol. 2, plates 106, 112, 116, 118, 119. Curt Sachs, *The History of Musical Instruments*, p. 63. The venerable tradition of misinterpretation extends to Praetorius's fanciful "Instruments of Jerome." Michael Praetorius, *Syntagma Musicum* II: *De Organographia*, ed. and tr., David Z. Crookes, (Oxford, 1986), Plate 32. For another interpretation of the term *chorus* see Peter Williams, *The Organ in Western Culture 750-1250* (Cambridge, 1993), p. 284.

[4] "Musica dicitur a musis, quod instrumentum omnibus musicis instrumentis veteres prefereendum dignum duxerent; sive quod primum, ut aiunt, a natura inventum est, sive potius quod in ipso omnis musica perfectio continetur. Nam in superioribus foraminibus omnes consonantiae et toni demonstrari possunt; in duobus inferioribus duo semitonia, maius ac minus." See Elena Ferrari Barassi, *Strumenti Musicali*, p. 59; and Sister Mary Protase Larue, "The 'De Harmonica Institutione' and 'Tonarius' of Regino of Prüm" (Ph.D. Diss., Catholic University, 1965), pp. 44, 45. But he may here be referring to the pipes of the muses. Peter Williams, *The Organ in Western Culture*, p. 193.

[5] "Dicitur autem musica, ut quidam volunt, a musa, quae est instrumentum quoddam musicae decenter satis et iocunde clangens. Sed videamus, qua ratione, qua auctoritate a musa traxerit nomen musica. Musa, ut diximus instrumentum quoddam est omnia musicae superexcellens instrumenta, quippe quae omnium vimatque modum in se continet: humano siquidem inflatur spiritu ut tuba, manu temperatur ut phiala, folle excitatur ut organa. Unde eta Graeco quod est MCHA mesa, id est media, musica dicitur, eo quod sicut in aliquoe medio diversa coeunt spatia, ita et in musa multimoda conveniunt instrumenta. Non ergo incongrue a principali parte sua musica nomen

sortita est." See Johannis Affligemensis, *De Musica cum Tonario*, ed. Smits van Waesberghe (Rome, 1950), p. 54; translated by Warren Babb in *Hucbald, Guido, and John on Music*, Ed. Claude V. Palisca (New Haven and London, 1978), pp. 100, 105.

[6] Baines, *Bagpipes*, p. 67. Alfred Sendrey, *Music in Ancient Israel* (New York, 1969), p. 330. Avraham Portaleone, *Shilte ha-Gibborim*, Mantua, 1612, translated in "The Music Chapters of 'Shiltey haGiborim'," Critical Edition by Daniel Sandler (Ph.D., diss., Tel Aviv University, 1980), p. 91.

[7] Hubert Boone, *La Cornemuse* (Brussels, 1983), p. 11.

[8] Irwin Young, *The Practica Musica of Franchinus Gafurius* (Madison, 1969), p. 162.

[9] Adam de la Halle, *Li Gieus de Robin et Marion*, in *Œuvres Complètes*, ed. E. de Coussemaker (Paris, 1872; repr. Ridgewood, 1965), line 232.

[10] Curt Sachs, *The History of Musical Instruments*, p. 283.

[11] Baines, "Bagpipe," *New Grove Dictionary of Musical Instruments* (London, 1984), vol. 1, p. 99.

[12] For at least one cylindrical bore chanter in a fourteenth-century painting by Giottino, see Peter Gülke, *Mönche, Bürger, Minnesänger* (Vienna, 1975; repr. Laaber, 1998), p. 242.

[13] Arthur Benade, *Fundamentals of Musical Acoustics* (New York, 1990), p. 430ff. Curt Sachs, *The History of Musical Instruments*, p. 283, and Baines, *Bagpipes*, p. 19.

[14] Some of the best modern makers of bagpipes, offering a variety of styles, include Paul Beekhuisen of The Hague, Julian Goodacre of Peebles, UK, Fritz Heller of Haarlem, Joel Robinson of New York, and Bodo Schulz of Hachemühle, Germany.

[15] "What you learn on recorders you have subsequently all the easier to learn on all other pierced pipes," Sebastien Virdung, *Musica Getutscht* (Basel, 1511); and "Furthermore, cornetts, crumhorns and recorders all follow one practice in fingering. Bagpipes also belong with these..." Martin Agricola, *Musica instrumentalis deudsch* (Wittenberg, 1529, 1545), tr., William E. Hettrick, *The 'Musica instrumentalis deudsch' of Martin Agricola* (Cambridge, 1994), p. 96. See also Kenton Terry Meyer, *The Crumhorn: Its History, Design, Repertory and Technique* (Ann Arbor, 1983), pp. 95-96.

[16] Michael Praetorius, *Syntagma Musicum, De organographia*, Chapter 19 and Plates 5, 11, 13.

[17] Theodor Podnos, *Bagpipes and Tunings* (Detroit, 1974), and Baines, *Bagpipes*, p. 24.

[18] See Jerome of Moravia on ornaments in Carol McClintock, ed., *Readings in the History of Music in Performance* (Bloomington, 1979), pp. 3-7, and Timothy J. McGee, *Medieval Instrumental Dances* (Bloomington, 1989), pp. 27-37.

[19] Howard Mayer Brown, *Music in the French Secular Theater, 1400-1550* (Cambridge, MA, 1963), p. 277; and Catherine Homo-Lechner, "De l'usage de la cornemuse dans les banquets: quelques exemples du XIVe au XVIe siècle," *Imago Musicae* 4 (1987), 111.

[20] *Les Cent Nouvelles Nouvelles*, ed. Franklin Sweetser (Paris, 1966), Nouvelle LXXV, p. 452: and William D. Paden, *The Medieval Pastourelle*, Garland Library of Medieval Literature (New York, 1987), Vol.1, p. 72.

[21] Nico Staiti, "Satyrs and Shepherds: Musical Instruments within Mythological and Sylvan Scenes in Italian Art," *Imago Musicae* 7 (1990), 81-82. Pier Maurizio Della Porta and Ezio Genovesi, "The Figure of the Shepherd-Musician from the Late Middle Ages to the Renaissance: Some Iconographical Examples from Central Italy," *Imago Musicae* 7 (1990), 26. Howard Mayer Brown, "Catalogus, A Corpus of Trecento Pictures with

Musical Subject Matter" *Imago Musicae* 1 (1984), 189-244. [Also 2 (1985), 179-282; 3 (1986), 103-187; 5 (1988), 167-242.]

22 Reinhold Hammerstein, *Diabolus in Musica: Studien zur Ikonographie der Musik im Mittelalter* (Bern and Munich, 1974), plates 8, 18, 93, 110, 139; and Genette Foster, "The Iconology of Musical Instruments and Musical Performance in Thirteenth-Century French Manuscript Illuminations" (Ph.D. diss., City University of New York, 1977), and Charles J. P. Cave, *Roof Bosses in Medieval Churches* (Cambridge, 1948).

23 Jean Erart, *The Songs of Jean Erart*, ed. Terence Newcombe (Rome, 1975), p. 9. *Li Gieus de Robin et Marion*, in Adam de la Halle, *Œuvres Complètes*, ed. E. de Coussemaker (Paris, 1872; repr. Ridgewood, 1965), pp. 356, 358.

24 The sound may have inspired the name of the extinct French *loure*. On the sound of shepherds at Christmas, see Baines, *Bagpipes*, p. 99.

25 Margaret Paine Hasselman and David McGown, "Mimesis and Woodwind Articulation in the Fourteenth Century," In *Studies in the Performance of Late Medieval Music*, ed. Stanley Boorman (Cambridge, 1983), p. 105.

26 Antonio Zachara da Teramo, *De amor tosa* in *Early Fifteenth Century Music* 6, Corpus Mensurabilis Musicae 11, ed. Gilbert Reaney (Rome, 1977), p. 19.

27 Susan Palmer, *The Hurdy-Gurdy* (Newton Abbot, 1980).

28 Geoffrey Chaucer, *The Canterbury Tales*, lines 560-566.

29 Ann Hudson, *Two Wycliffite Texts*, Early English Text Society (Oxford, 1993), pp. 64-66 (lines 1320-1389); and Douglas Gray, ed., *The Oxford Book of Late Medieval Verse and Prose* (Oxford, 1985), pp. 15-16.

30 Ibid.

31 "Ma il re, che in buona tempera era, fatto chiamar Tindaro, gli comandò che fuori traesse la sua cornamusa, al suono della quale esso fece fare molte danze; ma essendo già molta parte di notte passata, a ciascun disse ch'andasse a dormire." Boccaccio, *Il Decamerone*, Tutte le opere 4, ed. Vittore Branca (Milan, 1976), Conclusion, Day VI, p. 582.

32 Herbert Myers, see chapter 26 above, pp. 379-80.

33 Keith Polk, *German Instrumental Music of the Late Middle Ages*, pp. 55, 61; and Edmund A. Bowles, "Instrumente des 15. Jahrhunderts und Ikonographie," *Basler Jahrbuch für historische Musikpraxis* 8 (1984), p. 32. See also Patrick Tröster, "Außermusikalische Aspekte des Alta-Ensembles auf Bildwerken des 15. Jahrhunderts," In *Musikalische Ikonographie*, ed. Harald Heckmann, Monika Holl, and Hans Joachim Marx, Hamburger Jahrbuch für Musikwissenschaft 12 (1994), p. 273.

34 Edmind A. Bowles, "Instrumente des 15. Jahrhunderts und Ikonographie," *Basler Jahrbuch für historische Musikpraxis* 8 (1984), 24-25 (Plates 7 and 8), and p. 32.

35 Polk, *German Instrumental Music*, p. 60.

36 Ms. Digby 167, fol. 31v. Facsimile in John Stainer, ed., *Early Bodleian Music*, Volume 1, (London, 1901; repr. Farnborough, 1967), Plate 98.

37 See Hubert Boone, *La Cornemuse*, p. 22.

38 Polk, *German Instrumental Music*, p. 55.

39 Ibid.

40 Jacopo Sannazaro, *Arcadia*, 1504; tr. in Ralph Nash, *Arcadia and Piscatorial Eclogues* (Detroit, 1966), p. 151.

IX. KEYBOARD & RELATED TYPES

29. Organ
Kimberly Marshall

BEFORE 1300

Since its invention in the third century BCE, the organ has been prized for its multifarious sounds and technical complexity. The Greek Athenaeus and his guests were "fascinated by the harmony [of the hydraulic organ], ...a wondrous symphony which caused us to look round in rapture."[1] Vitruvius found it to be "constructed in a most curious and ingenious fashion."[2] An organist was crowned victor of the music festival at Delphi ca.90 BCE, and the Emperor Nero seems to have been more interested in new organ designs than in restraining barbarian revolts.[3] In addition to these anecdotes and colorful descriptions, surviving treatises by Hero of Alexandria and Vitruvius give precise information about the construction of the instrument. These sources help us to formulate an impression of the music created by early organs in the absence of surviving contemporary music.[4]

In the Middle Ages, we must wait until the eleventh century for similarly detailed accounts of the instrument after its reappearance in the West in the year 757. The organ was part of a diplomatic tribute to King Pepin the Short from the Byzantine Emperor Constantine V.[5] The complex instrument seems to have enchanted the Franks: several of Pepin's chroniclers make special mention of the organ, which they considered the first to exist in their kingdom. A later account by Notker the Stammerer that probably refers to the same organ relates that it was of particular interest to the King's workmen, who examined it virtually in secret. They sought to copy the impressive *organum*, which "with vessels cast in bronze and bellows of bullhide blowing magnificently through the bronze pipes, matched the very roar of the crash of thunder, the chattering of the lyre, or the sweetness of bells."[6] Already in this early report the organ is characterized by its power and the variety of its timbres.

It is hardly surprising that Western rulers wished to duplicate the technological prowess exhibited by the Byzantines in their construction of organs. In the year 826, Charlemagne's son, Louis the Pious, commissioned a Venetian priest named Georgius to build an organ for the palace at Aix. It is not known where Georgius learned the craft of organbuilding; Venice was a dependency of Constantinople in the ninth century, so he may have had occasion to experience the Byzantine style firsthand in that city.[7] Both Einhard and the Annals of Fulda report that Georgius constructed a hydraulis, which might indicate that he built a water-organ rather than the bellows organ of the Byzantines.[8] His knowledge of organbuilding could have stemmed directly from a Greek scientific treatise, such as Hero of Alexandria's *Pneumatics*. The exact conditions of the commission are obscure: it appears that one Count Baldric brought Georgius before the Emperor where he proclaimed his organbuilding abilities. Louis sent him to Aachen and commanded that he be given everything necessary to construct the instrument. Georgius's organ was a source of great prestige for the Frankish court, as documented in the laudatory poems of Ermold le Noir and Walahfrid Strabo. Ermold goes so far as to equate organ-building with military superiority:

> Even the organ, never yet seen in France,
> Which was the overweening pride of Greece
> And which, in Constantinople, was the sole reason
> For them to feel superior to Thee—even that is now
> In the palace at Aix.
> This may well be a warning to them, that they
> Must submit to the Frankish yoke,
> Now that their chief claim to glory is no more.[9]

This reference to the glory wrested from Byzantium may help to elucidate the role of the organ after its reintroduction to the West. The impressive sound of the instrument lent splendor to ceremonial occasions, and its use may have been similar in both Eastern and Western empires. At the Byzantine court in the late eighth and ninth centuries, the *organon* was used for processional receptions by signalling the end of parts of the ceremony, punctuating the people's greetings and acclamations, and providing festive sound during the emperor's movements.[10] It was accordingly moved from place to place and used to guide people through the service. Western emperors emulated the pomp of these imperial acclamations; the fusion of sacred and secular elements in the ceremony symbolized the dual leadership role of the Holy Roman Emperor. The organ contributed greatly to the splendid ambiance of royal receptions. When ambassadors were received in the royal chapel, portable instruments would have been positioned near the king to participate in his *acclamationes*.[11] The organ seems to have been used alone, as a signalling instrument to direct the ritual proceedings. Its early use in such sacred-secular ceremony may have been a crucial factor in its subsequent adoption as the instrument of the church, perhaps more so than the often reported link between the clergy and organbuilding attributed to Georgius and his students.

Because of its ceremonial prestige and display of erudition, the organ was fostered by the Benedictines in their monastic centers. In 873, Pope John VIII wrote to request that the bishop of Freising send him a very good organ (*optimum organum*) to teach the discipline of music (*ad instructionem musice discipline*). Even if *organum* here refers to a book for teaching instead of the musical instrument itself, the Pope's entreaty demonstrates the Benedictines' renown for cultivating the art of music. The Cluniac reform of the Benedictine order at the end of the tenth century promoted polyphony, musical notation, and presumably organbuilding, as part of an international movement to enhance liturgical ceremony. From this time organs were given as gifts to monastic institutions by founders and benefactors. In 992 St. Oswald gave a monastery thirty pounds to make copper organ pipes, and some time earlier St. Dunstan provided an organ for the monastery at Malmesbury, England.[12] Pipe proportions were studied at the Abbey of Fleury and large organs were installed at Halberstadt and Winchester. Monastic scribes documented the acquisition of instruments and copied treatises relating to aspects of construction.

Most of the surviving written sources concerning organ pipes were copied by Benedictine scribes,[13] but one must not be misled into considering these texts as guides to practical organbuilding. Rather, the mensuration treatises attempted to codify received knowledge of musical number-theory for wind instruments, in the same way that *mensura monochordi* and *mensura cymbalorum* noted the measurements for stringed and percussion instruments.[14] They are therefore of little use in understanding the practical side of medieval organbuilding.

Similarly, accurate details of organ construction and musical use may be obfuscated by exaggerated accounts of the instrument's overwhelming sound and impressive size. In his metrical prologue to a poetic life of St. Swithun, composed between 984 and 1005, the monk Wulfstan makes reference to a large organ at the Old Minster in Winchester.[15] According to Wulfstan's account, the organ contained 400 pipes and required 70 strong men to operate its 26 bellows. Forty sliders, each perforated with 10 holes, were drawn and returned by two monks "of harmonious spirit." The hyperbolic tendency of Wulfstan's style, the technical problem of building a ten-rank mixture based on a five-octave diatonic scale, and the difficulty of placing such an instrument in the Old Minster severely undermine the organological accuracy of this description.[16]

The earliest surviving pictorial evidence for the Western organ is an illustration of Psalm 150 in the Utrecht Psalter, a source whose iconographical details may rely on earlier models.[17] Surprisingly, the drawing shows a hydraulic organ, with wind provided by piston pumps rather than the bellows organs of the Byzantines. Like the description of the Winchester organ, there are two organists, each with his own set of pipes. The playing technique and keyboard are difficult to discern. One of the organists plays with his left hand only, using the other hand to admonish the wind pumpers; the other organist seems to have three hands, two playing the organ and a third used to hide his face. Dark lines in front of the pipes may indicate a keyboard, although the organists' fingers must pass between the pipes to reach the keys. Although similar representations are found in the *Canterbury Psalter*, it was copied from the *Utrecht Psalter* which was brought to Canterbury around 1000.[18] Again, little practical information about the use and construction of the organ is contained in these sources.

Two eleventh-century treatises provide more detailed information about the organ. The first, entitled *De Diversis Artibus*, was complied in the period 1110-40 by the monk Theophilus, who is presumed to have lived in Germany or eastern France; the second of these treatises is a compilation of the tenth and eleventh centuries formerly called the Bern Anonymous and believed to have originated at the Abbey of Fleury, which was an important center for organbuilding.[19] The two works give a rather homogenous view of the organ, exhibiting many similarities in the manner of fabricating pipes, windchests, sliders, and the air-collector or *conflatorio.* According to both treatises, the pipes are made of copper that is beaten very thin and rolled around an iron mandrel before its long edges are soldered together. The diameters are identical for pipes of the same rank, which suggests a restricted compass. This is borne out by the fifteen-note range specified by the Bern Anonymous: A.B.C.D.E.F.G.A.B.C.D.E.F.G.H.[20]

Both treatises discuss the air collector, a reservoir of copper or wood that transmits wind from several blacksmith's bellows to the windchest. This type of winding system is pictured in the following twelfth- and early thirteenth-century iconographical sources: the *Harding Bible* (Dijon, Bibliothèque Municipale MS 14 vol. 3, f. 13v: dated 1109); the *Cambridge Psalter* (Cambridge, St. John's College, MS B 18(40), f. 1r: early twelfth century); and the *St. Elizabeth Psalter* (Cividale dei Friuli, Museo Archeologico Nazionale, f.295r: early thirteenth century).[21] Theophilus alone gives directions for the installation of the organ; he recommends placing it in the wall of a monastery church. The bellows and organist are located in an archway cut into the wall, and only the windchest and pipes are visible to those in the nave of the church. The organ is covered with a thick curtain when it is not in use. A pulley system enables the curtain to be lifted by a rope when the organ is played.

Like the air collector, Theophilus's windchests can be made of either copper or wood, while the Bern Anonymous seems to indicate a wooden chest covered with copper. Another copper sheet inside the chest and opposite the opening of the air-duct distributes the wind evenly. Both authors describe several ranks of pipes for each note without any mechanism for separating individual ranks.[22] The Bern Anonymous reports that each note has two pipes, one for the note and another at its lower octave. Theophilus provides for several pipes per note but does not specify the pitches. A contemporary manuscript in the Sélestat Library (MS lat. 17, f. 37) describes a wind chest for a seven-note compass with three ranks, the outer ranks at unison pitch and the middle one speaking an octave higher.[23] Again, there is no mention of a mechanism to separate the individual ranks.

The first documented use of fifth-sounding ranks in the organ may be found in a Hebrew translation of an eleventh-century Latin *mensura* treatise now in the Bibliothèque Nationale (MS Héb. 1037, f.27r). The author of this manuscript recommends that each manual note of the organ be reinforced with pipes at the fifth and octave above; large instruments should also include doublings at the interval of a fourth. Although the treatise is not explicitly describing an organ mixture, it does suggest the practice of accumulating smaller pipes at octave and fifth ranks.[24]

The eleventh-century organ manual was composed of wooden sliders with perforations corresponding to the number of pipe ranks. These were fitted into channels in the chests; each slider handle was marked with the letter of its position in the scale. The Anonymous of Bern provides for keys that are attached to the sliders: when the key is depressed, the slider is pushed forward to align holes with the pipe feet, allowing the passage of wind to the pipes. The author even includes the detail of a semicircular horn spring to bring the key back to its original position when released by the organist.[25] Theophilus does not include a key system to activate the sliders; rather, the organist pulls a slider out to open the passage of air to pipes and pushes it back to block the same passage of air.[26] To play a continuous monophonic musical line, this mechanism requires both hands, although drones can be used creatively and the sliders can be made light enough to execute rather ornate melodies, as demonstrated by the modern reconstruction in Royaumont Abbey near Paris. (See Plate 29.1.)

Pl. 29.1. Modern reconstruction by Antoine Massoni (1993) of a Romanesque organ as described in the treatise of Theophilus (eleventh century), Old Refectory of Royaumont Abbey.
Photo courtesy of Guy Vivien.

Although Theophilus's slider system is less sophisticated than the one described by the Bern Anonymous, it is documented in several iconographical sources from the eleventh and early twelfth centuries: the *Pommersfelden Psalter* (Pommersfelden, Gräfliche Schönbornsche Bibliothek Cod. 2777, f. 1r: ca.1070); and the *Harding Bible* and the *Cambridge Psalter* mentioned above.[27] All of these illuminations were produced on the Continent, but there is evidence to suggest that a similar instrumental alphabet was in use in Canterbury, England, around 1100.[28] This gives greater significance to the sources because it demonstrates that they were depicting an arrangement of keys or sliders that was then common on both sides of the Channel.

The tenth-century trend of endowing religious institutions with organs continued in the eleventh and twelfth centuries, especially in northern Europe, where organs were constructed in Augsburg, Fleury, Canterbury, Utrecht, and Constance. The association between organ and church is reiterated by literary references to the instrument in Wace's *Roman de Brut* and Chrétien de Troyes's *Lancelot*; both authors mention the organ's sound in the context of a church service, the latter specifying the annual feasts of Pentecost and Christmas.[29] We know very little about the precise use of the organ in these services. It may have retained the signalling function noted in the Byzantine rite, serving to punctuate the liturgy at strategic points.[30] According to Guido of Arezzo, the organ was used for "hymns, antiphons, and other offices as well."[31] In the thirteenth century, Gilles de Zamore reports that the Church uses only the organ for its various chants, sequences, and hymns.[32] Unfortunately, he does not explain whether the organ merely introduced the chant, accompanied it, or played in alternation with it; these three possibilities for the organ's participation might similarly have been used centuries earlier for the cries of *trishagios* (Thrice Holy!) sung by the people to the

Byzantine emperor.[33] Although the status of the organ as "instrument of the Church" was assured by 1300,[34] everyone did not agree about its ability to impart grandeur to the service. In 1166, St. Aelred, Abbot of Rievaulx, condemns the use of organs and bells in church, making it less a "place of worship" than a "theater."[35]

In twelfth-century literature the organ is part of secular musical ensembles, playing with strings, fiddles, and pipes in Heinrich von Veldecke's description of a festival in Mainz in 1184, while in the poem *Leiden und Lebens Jesu, vom Antichrist und vom jüngsten Gericht*, the organ accompanies singing and dancing along with harps, *gigen*, and lyres.[36] Since there is no evidence to suggest that the larger "church" organ played in such contexts, these references may be the earliest documentation for a small portable form of the organ that was to become increasingly frequent in the performance of secular music. Portative organs were small instruments that could be carried and manipulated by one person; these were later distinguished from "positives," moveable organs that were played in a stationary position, requiring both an organist and someone to pump the bellows.

The invention of the portative organ required the development of a more efficient key action than was possible with pierced sliders. The manner of playing a portative, with one hand pumping the bellows while the other hand plays the keyboard, does not permit the use of two hands to pull out and push in sliders; instead, a pin action, where the depressed key pushes a pallet open directly, is the most effective type of action for the portative. The portative's pipes are smaller than those on stationary instruments (probably an octave or two higher), so the keys opening the pallets underneath them are smaller, adjacent and, most importantly, played with individual fingers.

Thirteenth-century iconographical sources for the organ confirm the presence of keys. Although the old hand sliders are still portrayed in the early part of the century, such as in the *St. Elizabeth Psalter* mentioned above,[37] sources after 1250 show a key mechanism that is clearly played by individual fingers. The *Rutland Psalter* (London, British Library, Add. MS 62925, f.97v) contains a luxurious miniature of King David playing a positive.[38] Although the keys appear large in comparison with the hands, it is clear from the hand positions that individual fingers are used to depress the keys.

This innovation in key action may have been the catalyst for the invention of the portative organ, which harkens back to the small organs of Antiquity.[39] Portatives are first documented in pictures during the thirteenth century. Corroborating the literary references cited above, the portative is usually depicted as one of several musical instruments; it occurs most frequently in Psalters (Psalms 1, 80, 97) and Apocalypses, as well as in illustrations of secular texts, manuscript marginalia, and stained-glass windows. The portatives in these depictions are either carried by the organist or held on the knee; they usually have one or two rows of about eight pipes, often with one or several long bourdons at one end of the instrument. When keys are shown, they constitute one row under the pipes and are clearly played by the fingers of the organist, rather than by the entire hand, as is the case with sliders. This implies that a pin action was already in use for the portative, although there is no mention of this mechanism in treatises before Arnaut de Zwolle describes it around 1440.[40]

It is difficult to know what music these small organs played, but the usual depiction of the portative in ensembles and the presence of what appear to be drone pipes suggests three possibilities: monophonic lines in conjunction with other instruments, melodies over a drone, and simple accompaniments, with or without drones, to singing. Speculations that "many a troubadour must have sung his songs to that frail accompaniment" cannot be substantiated.[41] The portative would be less practical for song accompaniments than stringed instruments because the wind breaks occurring during the refilling of the bellows could create gaps in the texture unless another instrument were also playing.[42] Given its limited range and timbre, the thirteenth-century portative was hardly more musically sophisticated than a recorder. What additional use might justify the technical complexity, added expense, and maintenance problems of the portative? Two important musical advantages would be the potential for a larger and steadier wind supply, and the liberation of the player's mouth for simultaneous singing. Unfortunately, such hypotheses for the portative's musical *raison d'être* are difficult to investigate. There are no surviving portatives to instruct us about early winding systems, and singing is rarely discernable in iconographical depictions. Moreover, literary accounts strongly suggest that the fiddle (viella) was the preferred instrument for vocal accompaniment.[43]

The medieval portative may have been intended to reflect the pomp and splendor of its Byzantine ancestor, which was also a moveable instrument used in processions. Its carefully measured pipes represented the Pythagorean principles of interval and proportion that were so fundamental to medieval musical theory. These symbolic associations may have dictated the portative's use and depiction more than the actual musical capabilities of the instrument.

The range of portative keyboards does not appear to have exceeded an octave of seven or eight notes in the thirteenth century. The compass of stationary organs, however, increased from the one- and two-octave alphabets reported in eleventh-century sources. Anonymous IV reports that a triple octave range existed on "organs and other instruments," and an early thirteenth-century manuscript in the Bibliothèque Nationale gives instructions for making an organ with more than three octaves.[44] But builders were cautioned against extending the range too far, since notes at the extremes might be distorted or sound thin and shrill.

When combined with the use of keys played by individual fingers, the increased range of the organ undoubtedly led to new possibilities for music-making. These developments enabled one organist to execute two and three parts simultaneously, provided they did not exceed the diatonic compass and the reach of the hands. The move towards plurilinear textures seems to have happened progressively rather than suddenly, and organplaying probably did not exceed the bounds of improvised or memorized practice until the fourteenth century, when the first surviving compositions for keyboard, requiring a fully chromatic compass, were written.

AFTER 1300

After its reintroduction to the West in the eighth century, the organ became increasingly prevalent in Europe. Psalm commentators, such as St. Augustine on Psalm 150, were interpreted to advocate the use of the organ, and organs were often given to or built for religious institutions by their benefactors so that they gradually became a "familiar part of church-furnishings."[45] These and other factors led to the organ's adoption as the instrument of the Church, where it seems to have been played alone on certain feast days at specified points in the service. There is also evidence that organ range was extended to more than three diatonic octaves on some instruments during the thirteenth century.

Perhaps the most significant development before 1300 was the invention of a small, portable organ that could be operated by one person pumping the bellows with one hand and playing the keyboard with the other. Fourteenth-century manuscripts contain illustrations of such instruments in similar as well as new contexts.[46] Angels playing portatives are also depicted in paintings, wooden altarpieces and choir stalls, and stained glass. Stone sculptures of the instrument survive in the portals of churches as distant as Uppsala Cathedral, Freiburg Münster, Saint-Ouen in Rouen, and the Cathedral of Saint-Maurice in Vienna.[47] The portative becomes an integral part of the instrumentarium used to decorate European churches, and it is often depicted in both large- and small-format Coronation of the Virgin scenes. Such representations do not necessarily indicate performance conventions, but may be intended merely as decorative or symbolic motifs that continued to be used during later centuries. The portative is an iconographical attribute in depictions of King David, Saint Cecilia, and allegorical figures representing the sixth liberal art "Musica." Like the psaltery and cymbala, it symbolizes the science of proportions because the relationship between pipe lengths demonstrates a practical application of Pythagorean monochord theory. Composers are also represented with the instrument: Landini plays a portative in the portrait on his tombstone; in a manuscript of Martin le Franc's *Le Champion des Dames*, Du Fay is depicted with a small organ.[48]

An important innovation during the fourteenth century was the expansion of organ range to include pitches outside of the diatonic alphabet. Jacobus of Liège, writing ca.1330, specified that in certain instruments, including the organ, almost everywhere the tone is divided into two unequal semitones.[49] The appearance of a second row of keys on organ depictions beginning in the fourteenth century is undoubtedly related to the inclusion of these new pitches.[50] A late fourteenth-century miniature illustrating Deguileville's *Pèlerinage de la Vie Humaine* (see Plate 29.2) shows two differentiated rows of keys, whose shapes and placement are not dissimilar to the earliest surviving keyboard.[51] Later depictions of this same scene show two identical rows of keys, so it is possible that the original model was simplified in this manner to include the new keys for chromatic notes that were found with increasing frequency on late-medieval organs.

Pl. 29.2. Miniature illumination illustrating Guillaume de Deguileville's *Pèlerinage de la Vie Humaine*, showing a key disposition that seems to reflect the placement of chromatic keys on the Norrlanda keyboard. Aix-en-Provence, Bibliothèque Méjanes, MS 100, p. 183.

The oldest surviving organ, built for a church in Norrlanda, Gotland, ca.1400, has a completely chromatic manual compass from *c - a!*[52] (See Plate 29.3.) The keys for diatonic notes, including B♭, are on one level, with keys for C♯, D♯, F♯, and G♯ arranged in pairs on a higher level. The two *Diskant* keyboards of the fourteenth-century organ in Halberstadt Cathedral were similarly organized, but with B♭ among the upper row of keys for chromatic notes.[53] The compass for these manuals was 22 keys from *b* to *g"a"*, i.e., without *g♯"*. (In his depiction, Praetorius shows only the first 14 notes of this range.) A third manual, called *Bassklavier* by Praetorius, consisted of twelve protruding levers from *b-a"b"* that played the twelve lowest pipes; the 12 pedals of the pedalboard duplicated this compass, perhaps by pulling down the keys of the *Bassklavier*, and added a 16-24-rank Basshintersatz.[54] The two *Diskant* keyboards permitted the separation of timbres without a stop mechanism: one of these keyboards played the full chorus of case-principals with the 23-56-rank Hintersatz, while the other played the case-principals only.

Pl. 29.3. The earliest surviving organ keyboard, with B♭ among the diatonic keys and the chromatic keys C♯, D♯, F♯, and G♯ located on a higher level above them. Keyboard of the organ formerly in Norrlanda Church, Gotland (now in the National History Museum, Stockholm), late fourteenth century.

Photo courtesy of Göran Tegnér, National History Museum, Stockholm.

The presence of two manuals on a fourteenth-century organ may be suggested in a contract dated 1386 between the chapter of Rouen Cathedral and the organbuilder Godefroy de Furnes.[55] After being asked to reinforce 16 notes in the treble, de Furnes could not find sufficient room on the main windchest and was forced to build another chest for the extra pipes. These may have been controlled by a special keyboard, because it was possible to play these "reinforcing" pipes alone, or the main part of the organ without them, or the two together. It is unlikely that chest divisions or slider mechanisms were used for the separation here indicated, since there is no evidence for them on fourteenth-century Blockwerks.

Swedish organ fragments include five windchests from the late fourteenth and early fifteenth centuries: Norrlanda, Sundre, Anga, Etelhem (Gotland); and Knutby (Uppland). All of these provide for several ranks of pipes per note without any means of separating them.[56] There is documentation for contemporary Blockwerks in Praetorius's *Syntagma musicum* and Arnaut de Zwolle's treatise.[57] Praetorius's description of the Halberstadt Blockwerk (1357-61) contrasts the deep rumbling sound of the Praestants and the powerful shrillness of the Mixture. This account was written over two hundred years after the initial construction of the instrument, however, so its fidelity in reflecting the organ's original sound could be questioned. The largest Blockwerk included in Arnaut's treatise has the range B'-$a'b'$, with ten ranks in the bass and 26 in the treble. Two smaller examples have compasses of B'-f'', with 6-21 and 6-15 ranks respectively. The latter has been identified as that of the organ at Salins, which had a cumulative Blockwerk with ranks duplicating in the treble but not breaking back. Arnaut's treatise also describes a Blockwerk built much earlier, that of the old organ in Notre-Dame, Dijon (ca.1350). The Fourniture is specifically mentioned, perhaps because it could be played from a separate manual. The compass from B to a'' was fully chromatic, as at Halberstadt.

The prevalence of fully chromatic keyboards before 1350 is corroborated by the earliest surviving source of keyboard music, the *Robertsbridge Codex*.[58] These two folios of music contain four complete and two incomplete pieces, requiring a fully chromatic compass from c-e'' that exceeds by one fifth the manual range of the Norrlanda organ, but lies well within the range of the Notre-Dame, Dijon organ.

The growing compass and proliferation of organs during the fourteenth century led to larger instruments and the need for a new category of classification. The term "positive" designates an organ that rests upon, but is not permanently attached to, a surface such as a table or floor, and whose keyboard is played with both of the organist's hands while another person pumps the bellows. Strictly speaking, the earliest Western pneumatic organs—depicted in sources such as the *Harding Bible*, dated 1109, and the *Pommersfelden Psalter*, ca.1070—are positives, since they are stationary and require someone to pump the bellows while the organist plays. But the term "positive" was not needed before the fifteenth century, when it became necessary to distinguish moveable organs that were played in a stationary position by an organist with both hands, from portatives, smaller instruments that were carried and manipulated by one person, and from the larger organs that were being permanently installed in church galleries.

A small Blockwerk is denoted as "tergali positivo" in Arnaut de Zwolle's treatise (ca.1440);[59] both Virdung (1511) and Praetorius (1619) depict the positive as a table organ with two bellows.[60] These large instruments provided the possibility of including lower pitches than the portative, while still being small enough to move easily. Thus the adjective "portable," which in most Romance languages is identical with the term for a portative organ, was sometimes applied to positives. The court archives of Philip the Bold record the acquisition of a portable organ for the Duke in 1388. This instrument was purchased from a Parisian scribe and dispatched one hundred and fifty miles from Paris to Villaines in Burgundy under a sheet of oilcloth, carried by two valets.[61] Given the need for two people to carry the organ, this might have been too large to be a portative in the strict sense of the term, an instrument to be carried by the organist while playing it. The same is true for another Burgundian "portatif," bought in 1393 by the dean of the Cathedral of Notre Dame in Paris, and placed in the chapel of the hôtel d'Artois "to play before him [the duke] on solemn feast days."[62]

This citation implies that small organs were sometimes used for liturgical music, although it is unlikely that such organs were true portatives because these would be very restricted in the execution of polyphony. Miniature illuminations from the fifteenth century reflect the expanding keyboard compass.[63] The famous portrait of Du Fay from a manuscript of Martin le Franc's *Champion des dames* in the Bibliothèque Nationale, mentioned above, shows a large portative with what appear to be buttons for chromatic notes, and a miniature decorating a manuscript copy of Gossuin de Metz's *L'Image du Monde* in the British Library also depicts a large portative with a special key which may indicate the inclusion of a new chromatic pitch.[64] The extended compasses of these organs suggest that larger instruments were replacing the earlier portatives during the fifteenth century.

Small organs were very much in demand for the performance of secular music. In a series of frequently-cited letters written in 1388, King John I of Aragón attempted to procure the services of a Flemish minstrel named "Johan dels orguens" for his own court.[65] The letters report that Johan played the "exaquir o los petits orguens," the latter possibly being a reference to the portative. In addition to providing his own instruments, Johan is requested to bring "the book in which he has notated the 'estampides' and other works that he knows how to play on the chekker and organ."

The three estampies and two motet intabulations in the Robertsbridge Codex[66] coincide with the type of keyboard repertoire reported in this letter and other literary sources. Similarly, the Codex Faenza contains two-part song and dance intabulations in addition to Mass movements.[67] These heterogenous collections of sacred and secular music may reflect the sort of compilations made by fourteenth-century organists like Johan. Although it is presumed that the music in both codices was intended for performance by one organist playing with both hands, it is possible that either the decorative upper voice or the lower voice in longer note values was realized on a small portable organ with another instrument furnishing the other part.[68] These sources, exceptional in that they contain written evidence of what was almost exclusively improvised music, might provide clues for the style of the portative repertory.

Arnaut de Zwolle's fifteenth-century treatise includes diagrams of two portative windchests: one has the usual arrangement of two rows of pipes decreasing in length from left to right, while the other shows two rows of pipes arranged in the shape of a bishop's mitre, with the longest pipes in the center. Both portatives are fully chromatic from B, with 31 (*B-f'*) and 34 notes (*B-g'a'*) respectively.[69] These compasses are sufficient for almost all surviving fifteenth-century keyboard music, excluding eleven pieces in the Buxheim Organ Book which require low *Bb*, *A*, and *G*.[70] It is surprising that the "portatives" described by Arnaut have at least the same keyboard compass, *B-f'*, as the large organ depicted on f. 131r of his treatise. The main difference between the large and small organs described seems to be their fundamental octave pitch rather than the range of pitches available. As in the earlier Burgundian examples, the portatives in Arnaut's treatise were probably played in a stationary position because of the weight implied by their relatively large compasses. But they were apparently played like portatives since Arnaut describes a divided bellows that enabled the organist to provide continuous winding to the instrument with one hand. The upper part of the bellows sent air to the windchest as it received wind through a valve from the lower part; this prevented the breaks in winding created when a single bellows refilled.[71]

A similar result was obtained using a double bellows system, where one bellows served as a wind reservoir while the other filled with air. Iconographical evidence for this is found in a painting in London's National Gallery, "Coronation of the Virgin, with Adoring Angels," attributed to Jacopo di Cione and workshop (ca.1370). It is also depicted in a sculpture of an angel organist by Giovanni Tedesco (1386) in Florence's Museo dell'Opera del Duomo.[72] (See Pl. 29.4.) Both representations show two bellows, one behind and another beneath the case of a portative; while the lower bellows filled, the other, serving as a reservoir, emptied into the windchest. These methods for providing continuous wind made the portative capable of executing long melodic lines without awkward interruptions. The constant wind supply would also benefit drone pipes, although the iconography suggests that the presence of bourdons became less frequent on organs during the course of the fourteenth century.[73]

Pl. 29.4. Bellows/reservoir system on a portative organ. While the bellows underneath the instrument fills with wind, the reservoir, controlled by the organist's thumb, feeds the windchest. Sculpture of angel organist by Giovanni Tedesco, formerly on the façade of Santa Maria del Fiore, Florence (now in the Museo dell'Opera del Duomo), 1386.

By the time of Arnaut's treatise ca.1440, the two rows of keys shown in fourteenth-century keyboards had been consolidated into one, with shorter keys for chromatic notes interspersed between the diatonic keys. Of particular interest in this regard is the positive organ painted in the Ghent Altarpiece by Jan and Hugo van Eyck. Ripin has shown that the keyboard of this instrument originally resembled that of the surviving Norrlanda organ (ca.1400), with two separate rows of identically formed keys. When the altarpiece was repainted in 1432, the keyboard was "modernized" and block-form chromatic keys were inserted among the diatonic keys. The compass was also changed from a diatonic lower octave starting on *G* to a fully chromatic keyboard beginning on *B*.[74] This painting is exceptional because of its detail; it is rarely possible to determine exact pitches in pictorial representations of the organ keyboard. Nevertheless, the generally increasing numbers of keys and pipes depicted in the iconography reflect the organ's enlarged compass during the course of the fourteenth and fifteenth centuries.

Individually separable registers were present on organs by the early fifteenth century. A large positive at the Aragonese royal chapel is reported to have "cinch tirants" in 1420, and Arnaut de Zwolle also describes "quinque registra" (divided or double principal, two quints, and an octave) on the "misse Domini" organ, which seems to have been a small positive at the Dijon court chapel.[75] Unfortunately, no further details are given concerning this organ, yet the possibility of isolating individual registers implies the presence of either slider- or spring-chests.

As might be expected, iconographical sources depict the appearance of separable registers many years after they were first implemented in organbuilding. The latch-key below and to the left of the organ keyboard in the Ghent Altarpiece has been interpreted as a device to admit wind to a separate row of pipes or to a drone, but it was most likely an evacuant to empty the windchest after playing, such as that present on the Norrlanda organ.[76] Later representations clearly show sliders for separable registers on small organs. Israhel van Meckenem's engraving of a bourgeois organ-player and his wife, ca.1500, depicts a positive with four registers, and a similar function can be attributed to the sliders that appear on positive organs in sixteenth-century paintings and tapestries.[77]

Like the separate registers of small organs, ranks of pipes from large Blockwerks could be isolated by means of a ventil system which admitted wind into different sections of the windchest, making it possible to play the principals independently of the upper work and vice versa. The earliest surviving documents for this type of construction concern Dutch organs: the 1447 contract for the organ at Zwolle specifies that the Positive will have "double principal and three sounds," while the 1458 contract for the organ at Delft's Oude Kerk provides for a register to shut off the mixture.[78] The "three sounds" referred to at Zwolle may have been principal alone, mixture alone (probably coupled to the main Blockwerk in this case), and the two together. A double-chest system enabled the organist to select the desired timbre, shutting off wind from either chest by means of a Sperrventil.[79] This innovation in chest design made it possible to separate principals from mixtures without an additional keyboard like the second *Diskant* keyboard at Halberstadt.

Just as the addition of treble pipes at Rouen in 1386 may have necessitated a second keyboard, so Arnaut describes a special keyboard for the ten lowest ("tenor") pipes on the Cordeliers organ.[80] This reference is noteworthy because the author specifies that these keys could be played separately or coupled to the main manual to produce four different effects, including doubling all of the pitches an octave lower.[81]

Such an intricate keyboard system fulfills the same function as a complex chest design, where instead of multiple keyboards, a stop mechanism controls the passage of wind to certain groups of pipes. Arnaut's treatise does not indicate the use of divided windchests. But one of the four Blockwerk choruses described (probably that of the 1447 organ in Notre-Dame, Dijon) is outlined by the scribe in three unnamed parts, corresponding to Principal, Cymbale, and Fourniture.[82] This tripartite division suggests that it was possible to play each set of pipes separately by means of a mechanical device or additional keyboards. Of special interest is the composition of the three-rank Cymbale, which contains a Tierce rank, the earliest known reference to a *Terzzimbel.*

The three-part chorus division of Principal, Fourniture, and Cymbale described by Arnaut was in common use during the fifteenth century. It is documented for the Rückpositiv built by Hendrik van den Houwe at St. John's, Malines (1498), and on the instruments in St. Sebald, Nuremberg (H. Traxdorf, 1439-41), St. Florian, Koblenz (1467), St. George, Hagenau (1491), and St. Quintinus, Louvain (1522).[83]

The presence of reed pipes on large organs is scantily documented before the sixteenth century. The earliest written source for reed pipes is Arnaut's mention of "l'anche de F" on the organ of the Dei Custodientes church, but this occurs on an incomplete page of the treatise and little can be deduced from such an isolated reference. Surviving fifteenth-century specifications indicate that contrasting sounds were produced by admitting wind to different groups of flue pipes only.

Sometimes new pipe divisions with separable sounds were appended to preexisting Blockwerks to obtain a greater diversity of timbre. This occurred on the organ formerly in St. Nicholaas, Utrecht (now in the Middleburg Koorkerk), where in 1580 a Chair organ (the Rückpositive division located behind the organist's "chair") was appended to the 1479-80 Blockwerk by Pieter Gerritsz.[84] When the technology of separable registers was applied to larger organs, spring-chests and slider-chests replaced the old Blockwerks. This happened very early in Bordeaux, Lombardy, and Tuscany: the one-manual organ of San Petronio, Bologna, had nine single-rank stops and a 50-note compass in 1474-83.[85] Refinements in chest design and the expansion of the keyboard compass yielded an increased variety of sounds without the multiple keyboards typical of contemporary northern organs. By the end of the fifteenth century, the technology of separable registers was also exploited by northern organbuilders on two- and three-manual instruments. Innovative and unusual sounds mimicking other instruments were especially prized. This desire for diverse timbres seems to have led some organbuilders astray, for in 1511, Arnolt Schlick warns against building organs with too many registers and with multiple Positiv divisions, which he considers to be "much broth and little fish."[86]

Notes

[1] Jean Perrot, *L'Orgue: de ses origines hellénistiques à la fin du XIIIe siècle* (Paris, 1965; Eng. trans. Norma Deane, *The Organ,....* London, 1971), p. 6.

[2] English trans. in Frank Granger, ed. *Vitruvius on Architecture* (Loeb Classical Library) 2 vols. (London, 1931 and 1934). The text concerning the hydraulic organ is found in Perrot (1971), pp. 296-7 and is discussed in Peter Williams, *The Organ in Western Culture 750-1250* (Cambridge, 1993), pp. 235-40.

[3] Perrot (1971), pp. 44, 48-49.

[4] Hero of Alexandria's *Pneumatics* and Vitruvius's *De architectura* were both written during the first century CE and are discussed at length by Perrot (1971) and Williams (1993).

[5] Perrot (1971), pp. 205-10; Williams (1993), pp. 137-42.

[6] Williams (1993), p. 143.

[7] Caffi postulates that the Venetian priest Georgio built the organ of Grado (Venetian lagoon) in the ninth century. This "most excellent and marvelous" instrument was destroyed in the pillage of the Patriarch of Aquileia in 1022. F. Caffi, *Storia della Musica sacra nella già Cappella ducale di S. Marco in Venezia* (Venice, 1854/R Milan, 1931), Vol. II, pp. 9-11.

[8] Williams (1993), pp. 144-5.

[9] Perrot (1971), p. 213.

[10] Peter Williams, "How did the Organ Become a Church Instrument? Some Preliminary Questions," *Organ Yearbook* 17 (1986), 11. See also Williams (1993), pp. 71-72; 146-49.

[11] Williams (1986), p. 12.

[12] Perrot (1971), p. 223; Williams (1993), pp. 199-200.

[13] K. J. Sachs, *Mensura fistularum: die Mensurierung der Orgelpfeifen im Mittelalter* (Stuttgart, 1970), pp. 19-41.

[14] K. J. Sachs, "Remarks on the Relationship between Pipe-Measurements and Organ-Building in the Middle Ages," *Organ Yearbook* 4 (1973), 92-93.

[15] For a critical edition of the text, see Alistair Campbell, ed. *Frithegodi Monachi Breviloquium Vitae Wilfredi et Wulfstani Cantoris Narratio Metrica de Sancto Swithuno* (Verona, 1950).

[16] James W. McKinnon, "The Tenth Century Organ at Winchester," *Organ Yearbook* 5 (1974), 4-19.

[17] Utrecht, Universiteitsbibliotheek, MS 32. The source is described in Williams (1993), pp. 150-63 and Perrot (1971), pp. 278-9; the miniature showing the hydraulic organ is reproduced on p. 156 and in Plate XXIV respectively. For earlier views on the iconography, see E. T. De Wald, *The Illustrations of the Utrecht Psalter* (Princeton, London and Leipzig, 1933) and G. R. Benson and D. T. Tselos, "New Light on the Origin of the Utrecht Psalter," *The Art Bulletin* 13 (1951), 13-79. Dufrenne argues that a fourth- or fifth-century Christian psalter might have served for some details as a model for the artist of the Utrecht Psalter. See S. Dufrenne, *Les illustrations du Psautier d'Utrecht: sources et apport carolingien* (Paris, 1978), pp. 175, 218-19.

[18] Cambridge, Trinity College, R.17.1 (MS M987). See Montague Rhodes James, *The Canterbury Psalter* (London, 1935), pp. 3-4, and Perrot (1971), p. 279. Williams (1993) discusses the changes made to the Utrecht Psalter organ model by the Canterbury artist, pp. 163-4.

[19] Williams (1993), pp. 253-67 and 277-83. The writings of both authors are cited, translated, and interpreted in Perrot (1971): Theophilus, pp. 297-302, trans. pp. 238-42; Bern Anonymous, pp. 302-04, trans. pp. 242-43.

[20] Perrot (1971), p. 303 and p. 243.

[21] The first two of these illuminations are reproduced in Williams (1993), pp. 174-75, 179; all are found in Perrot (1971), Plates XXV and XXVII.

[22] A mechanism for separating individual ranks of pipes or for changing pitches/tunings was described in Vitruvius's *De Architectura* in the first century CE. See Williams (1993), pp. 238-39 and Perrot (1971), pp. 37 and 40-41.

[23] Perrot (1971), p. 262.

[24] H. Avenary-Loewenstein, "The Mixture Principle in the Mediaeval Organ: An Early Evidence," *Musica Disciplina* 4 (1950), 51-57; see also Williams (1993), pp. 289-90.

[25] Perrot (1971), p. 303 and pp. 242-3. The presence of horn springs to return the keys of an organ to their original positions after being depressed is documented in the first century CE by Hero of Alexandria in his *Pneumatics*. See Perrot (1971), pp. 32-33 and Plate XXIII.

[26] This is clear from Theophilus's description of the windchest. See Perrot (1971), p. 300; diagram on p. 241.

[27] These illuminations are reproduced in Perrot (1971), Plate XXV.

[28] Christopher Page, "The Earliest English Keyboard: New Evidence from Boethius' *De Musica*," *Early Music* 7 (1979), 308-13.

[29] Perrot (1971), p. 268.

[30] Williams (1986), p. 10, suggests that organs were not very different from bells in the contexts implied for their participation in medieval liturgy.

[31] Edmund A. Bowles, "Were Musical Instruments Used in the Liturgical Service during the Middle Ages?" *Galpin Society Journal* 10 (1957), 50.

[32] Gerbert, *Scriptores*, II, p. 388; also Bowles (1957), p. 49.

[33] Williams (1986), pp. 11-12.

[34] The *Livre des Propriétés et des Choses*, a widely disseminated French translation of a Latin text dating from the first half of the thirteenth century, reports that the organ is the instrument commonly used in church and not any others. Cited in Perrot (1971), p. 269. In 1287, the Council of Milan decreed that only the organ was to be used inside the church. Bowles (1957), p. 49.

[35] An English translation of the Latin text may be found in Perrot (1971), p. 221.

[36] E. Buhle, *Die musikalischen Instrumente in den Miniaturen des frühen Mittelalters*, Vol. I: *Die Blasinstrumente* (Leipzig, 1903), p. 62, cited in Hickmann, *Das Portativ* (Kassel, 1936/R 1972), p. 16. See also Perrot (1971), p. 268.

[37] Examples in addition to those mentioned above are found in Munich, Universitätsbibliothek, MS 24 quarto, f.2r; Paris, Bibliothèque Nationale, MS lat. 11560, f.36r; and Oxford, Corpus Christi College, MS 17, f.99r.

[38] Complete facsimile in Eric George Millar, ed., *The Rutland Psalter: A Manuscript in the Library of Belvoir Castle* (Oxford, 1937). The manuscript was acquired by the British Library several years ago and is now Add. MS 62925; the miniature in question is found on f.97v.

[39] Hero of Alexandria describes the use of keys to move sliders; Perrot (1971), p. 32 and Plate XXIII. Hickmann (1972) suggests a bridge between the ancient "portatives" and medieval ones, p.15, note 55.

[40] G. Le Cerf and E.-R. Labande, eds. *Les traités d'Henri-Arnault de Zwolle et de divers anonymes* (Paris, 1932, R/Kassel, 1972), pp. 23-26 and ff. 130r-130v.

[41] Perrot (1971), p. 272. This is a romanticized view that one finds in some secondary literature. Lavoix even goes so far as to suggest that the portative organ was for

medieval musicians what the piano is for us today. See Henry Lavoix fils, *La musique au siècle de Saint Louis* in *Receuil de Motets Français* (Paris, 1883), p. 335.

[42] There is late fourteenth- and fifteenth-century documentation for bellows/reservoir and divided-bellows systems on portative organs, showing that later efforts were made to provide continuous winding on these small instruments. See p. 421 below and my article "Innovations in Organbuilding: 1250-1500," in *Music in Performance and Society: Essays in Honor of Roland Jackson*, Malcolm Cole and John Koegel, eds. (Warren, MI, 1997), pp. 97-98.

[43] Christopher Page, *Voices and Instruments of the Middle Ages*. (Berkeley, Los Angeles, 1987), p. 111.

[44] Paris, Bibliothèque Nationale MS lat. 8121 A. Both sources are cited in Perrot (1971), p. 261.

[45] Peter Williams, *The Organ in Western Culture 750-1250* (Cambridge, 1993), p. 103. This book presents a thorough discussion of the issues surrounding the Church's adoption of the organ.

[46] For a study of fourteenth- and fifteenth-century miniatures, see my *Iconographical Evidence for the Late-Medieval Organ in French, Flemish and English Manuscripts*, 2 vols. (New York, 1989).

[47] Photographs of the Freiburg and Vienna sculptures can be found in Hans Hickmann, *Das Portativ* (Kassel, 1936/R 1972), Figs. 17, 19.

[48] Landini's tombstone is reproduced in Georg Kinsky, *A History of Music in Pictures* (Leipzig, 1929), p. 49, and the miniature on fol. 109v of Paris, Bibliothèque Nationale, MS fr. 12476 is reproduced in many places, including the article on Du Fay in the *New Grove Dictionary of Music and Musicians*, Stanley Sadie, ed. (London, 1980).

[49] R. Bragard, ed. Jacobus of Liège, *Speculum musicae. Corpus scriptorum de musica* (Rome, 1955-73). VI, pp. 146 and 187.

[50] A marginal miniature executed between 1300 and 1325 (Manchester, John Rylands Library, French MS 1, f. 82r), shows a portative with keys on two levels; the keys on the upper row probably correspond to notes outside the diatonic alphabet. For a reproduction, see Marshall (1989), Vol. 2, Plate 61.

[51] For a study of the organ illustrations in copies of this text, see Marshall (1989), Vol. 1, pp. 27-39.

[52] This instrument is now on display in the National Historical Museum in Stockholm, Inv. No. 12910.

[53] Michael Praetorius, *Syntagma musicum* II: *De Organographia* (Wolfenbüttel, 1619; facsimile *Documenta Musicologica*. ed. Wilibald Gurlitt. Kassel, 1958), Plate XXV and pp. 98-101.

[54] There are several important discrepancies between Praetorius's description of the keyboards on pp. 98-99 and the illustration provided in Plate XXV of *Syntagma Musicum*. The most plausible reconciliation of these differences is found in Karl Bormann, *Die gotische Orgel zu Halberstadt* (Berlin, 1966), pp. 42-43.

[55] Norbert Dufourcq, *Documents inédits relatifs à l'orgue français*. (Paris, 1934 and 1935); repr. in Norbert Dufourcq, *Le Livre de l'Orgue Français*, I (Paris, 1982), Document 10, p. 26.

[56] Mads Kjersgaard, "Technische Aspekte des mittelalterlichen Orgelbaus in Schweden," *ISO Information*, No. 27 (1987), 5-18. In his description of the late fourteenth-century swallow's nest organ previously in the Stadtkirche, Bartenstein, Werner Renkewitz reports that two registers could be added and taken away from the permanent Octaves

8 and 4: Principal 16 (facade) and Hintersatz VI-XVIII. These registers were controlled by a slider mechanism (Muschelschleifen), but it is not clear that this was present in the original design of the organ. Quite probably the slider mechanism was added later, since many Blockwerks were so altered during the second half of the fifteenth century. For the description of the Bartenstein instrument, see Werner Renkowitz and Jan Janca, *Geschichte der Orgelbaukunst in Ost- und Westpreußen von 1333 bis 1944*, Vol. 1 (Würzburg, 1984), pp. 5-7.

[57] Praetorius (1619), pp. 98-101; Georges Le Cerf and E.-R. Labande, eds., *Les traités d'Henri-Arnault de Zwolle et de divers anonymes*. (Paris, 1932, R/Kassel, 1972), pp. 28, 54-6 and ff. 131v, 132v-134r.

[58] This manuscript is owned by the British Library, Add. MS 28550; the keyboard music appears on ff. 43-4. A modern edition of the Robertsbridge Codex is found in Willi Apel, ed. *Keyboard Music of the Fourteenth and Fifteenth Centuries*, Corpus of Early Keyboard Music 1 (American Institute of Musicology, 1963). Although Apel dates the manuscript ca.1325, notational peculiarities, in particular the use of the minim, suggest a somewhat later date.

[59] This instrument had a three-octave compass of F*G-f*' at 4' pitch; it contained 195 pipes, reinforced with octave ranks only (4 in the bass to 7 in the treble). This "positive" is a small-scale version of the Blockwerks found in large churches, where numerous ranks doubling the octave and fifth reinforced the sound in a large acoustic. Le Cerf and Labande (1972), pp. 39-40 and ff. 123v-124r.

[60] Sebastian Virdung, *Musica getutscht* (Basel, 1511), sig. Cv, facs. by Klaus Wolfgang Niemöller, Documenta musicologica 1/31. (Kassel, 1970); Eng. trans. by Beth Bullard, *Musica getutscht: A Treatise on Musical Instruments (1511) by Sebastian Virdung* (Cambridge, 1993), p. 109; Praetorius (1619), Plate IV. Virdung also includes a woodcut of a portative organ with only one bellows and a keyboard range similar to that of the positive, with correspondingly few pipes arranged in a circular fashion, the longest pipes in the middle.

[61] Craig Wright, "The Organists of the Court," *Music at the Court of Burgundy: 1364-1419* (Henryville, PA, 1979), p. 112.

[62] Ibid., pp. 112-13.

[63] Oxford, Bodleian Library, MS Douce 267, ff. 7r and 7v, depicts large free-standing organs that are played like portatives by angel organists. See Marshall (1989), Vol. 2, Plates 43-44.

[64] Paris, Bibliothèque Nationale, MS fr. 12476, f. 109v; British Library, MS Harley 334, f. 25v. For iconographical data about these depictions, see Marshall (1989), Vol. 1, pp. 373, 251.

[65] These documents have been cited by several modern authors, the earliest of which known to me is Edmond vander Straeten, *La Musique aux Pays-Bas*. (Brussels, 1867-88 R/New York, 1969), VII, pp. 64-67. For more details about these letters, see my article "The Organ in 14th-Century Spain," *Early Music* 20 (1992), 549-57.

[66] A modern edition of this music is found in Willi Apel, ed. *Keyboard Music of the Fourteenth and Fifteenth Centuries*, Corpus of Early Keyboard Music 1 (American Institute of Musicology, 1963).

[67] A transcription of the *Codex Faenza* has been published by Dragan Plamenac in *Keyboard music of the Late Middle Ages in Codex Faenza 117. Corpus Mensurabilis Musicae*, 57. (New York, 1972).

68 Paintings by Hans Memling, "The Mystic Marriage of St. Catherine" (1479) and "The Musicians' Angels" (1480), show portatives with compasses of about two-and-a-half octaves. Such instruments, which because of their large sizes might more appropriately be considered portative/positive hybrids, would be capable of executing the ornate treble parts of all preserved fourteenth- and fifteenth-century keyboard music, although transpositions might be necessary. On the use of the lute and harp in the performance of this early "keyboard" repertory, see Timothy J. McGee, "Instruments and the Faenza Codex," *Early Music* 14/4 (1986), 480-90.

69 Le Cerf and Labande (1972), f. 130v.

70 B. A. Wallner, *Das Buxheimer Orgelbuch*, Das Erbe deutscher Musik, 37-39 (Kassel, 1958-59). Two pieces require low G: nos. 162, 231; two require low A: nos. 5, 164; and seven pieces require the low Bb: nos. 232, 233, 234, 238, 246, 249, 252. My argument here is based exclusively on range; there are many places where it would be very difficult to perform the music on one keyboard because of awkward crossings.

71 Le Cerf and Labande (1972), f. 130r.

72 The statue was later removed from the cathedral and is now protected from further erosion in Florence's Museo dell'Opera del Duomo. For information about Jacopo de Cione and the attribution of the altarpiece, see Martin Davies, revised Dillian Gordon, *The Early Italian Schools before 1400* (London), pp. 45 and 52-54. The provenance of the Tedesco statue is related in Luisa Becherucci and Guilia Brunetti, *Il Museo dell'Opera del Duomo a Firenze*, Vol. I, pp. 248-49. For further discussion, see Geoffrey Bridges, "Medieval Portatives: Some Technical Comments," *Galpin Society Journal* 44 (1991), 103-16. A detail of the Jacopo da Cione triptych, "The Coronation of the Virgin, with Adoring Saints" (ca.1370) is reproduced there as Plate XVII.

73 Kimberly Marshall, "Bourdon Pipes on Late-Medieval Organs," *Organ Yearbook* 18 (1987), 19.

74 Edwin M. Ripin, "The Norrlanda Organ and the Ghent Altarpiece," *Emsheimer Festschrift. Studia instrumentorum musicae popularis*, ed. Gustaf Hilleström (Stockholm, 1974). III, pp. 193-96 and 286-88.

75 Le Cerf and Labande (1972), pp. 30-31.

76 Ripin (1974), p. 193; see also Peter Williams, *A New History of the Organ* (Bloomington and London, 1980), pp. 56-57.

77 The Meckenem engraving is reproduced in Edmund A. Bowles, *La pratique musicale au Moyen Age* (Minkoff and Lattès, 1983), p. 129. See also the organs shown in fifteenth-century depictions of Saint Cecilia reproduced in Bowles (1983), p. 134, and in Hickmann (1972), Fig. 42.

78 M. A. Vente, *Bouwstoffen tot de Geschiedenis van het Nederlandse Orgel in de 16de Eeuw* (Amsterdam, 1942), pp. 179 and 114.

79 M. A. Vente, *Die brabanter Orgel* (Amsterdam, 1958), p. 15.

80 Le Cerf and Labande (1972), p. 30.

81 For a detailed discussion of these different effects and the problems raised by Arnaut's explanation, see Kimberly Marshall (1987), pp. 24-27.

82 The composition of this Blockwerk is given in full in Williams (1980), p. 61.

83 Williams (1980), p. 64.

84 For a photograph of this famous instrument, see Williams (1980), Illustration 7.

85 Williams (1980), p. 64.

86 Arnolt Schlick, *Spiegel der Orgelmacher und Organisten* (Mainz, 1511), trans. Elizabeth Berry Barber (Netherlands, 1980), pp. 59 and 67.

30. String Keyboards

herbert W. Myers

Of the instruments that are the focus of this chapter, the majority—clavichord, harpsichord, clavicytherium, and virginal—are known to the modern world in their fully developed forms as found in the Renaissance and Baroque. Only one—the *dulce melos*, with its primitive hammer action—is known only through verbal and graphic description, having died out some time in the fifteenth century. Nevertheless, all have yet to find their place in modern performance of late medieval and early Renaissance music. It is hoped that the present discussion may inspire interest in the reconstruction and use of the early forms of these instruments, which have not yet caught the imagination of either builders or players.

The lever-action keyboard principle was known to the organ builders of late antiquity, but it seems to have been subsequently lost and then either reinvented or rediscovered (from ancient writings) in the Middle Ages. It appears first to have been applied to stringed instruments in the fourteenth century, as indicated by written sources; the first iconographic evidence comes from the fifteenth.[1] Extant examples of the major types of string keyboard date from the early sixteenth century at the earliest, the sole fifteenth-century survivor being a clavicytherium or upright harpsichord—a comparatively late and rare form—probably built about 1480. Details of early development are thus somewhat unclear; terminology, too, remains a matter of some controversy. Depictions are rarely labeled before the advent of didactic treatises in the sixteenth century. Even when we can tie a particular word to a specific form of instrument, we can rarely be sure the connection is exclusive. An instrument could often have more than one name, even at the same place and time; conversely, a name might be applied casually and generically to refer to different related forms. For instance, the word *clavicordium* or one of its cognates usually specified the instrument we now distinguish as a clavichord (rectangular instrument with strings struck by blades or "tangents" driven into the key tails) although other names were used also. However, in Spain and Portugal, *clavicordio* was used from early on to refer to string keyboards in general (not an illogical extension, given the simple etymology— "key" plus "string") and it may occasionally have been used in this sense elsewhere as well. *Clavicimbalum* and its variants usually meant harpsichord as we would now define it—that is, a horizontal, wing-shaped instrument with plucking action—but it was used by Sebastian Virdung in the early sixteenth century to mean instead a rectangular instrument, similar to his virginal.[2] Thus we need to be cautious in reading modern accounts, particularly ones that are too categorical in their statements about either developmental history or nomenclature. There is often more than one plausible interpretation of the evidence.

Probably the most controversial terminological puzzle is presented by the word "chekker" and its cognates (*eschiquier, exaquier, Schachtbrett,* etc.). Various identifications have been proposed, based on various notions—some quite fanciful—of etymology: a form of *dulce melos* (from the stop or "check" that is essential to its action); keyboards in general (from the resemblance of a keyboard to a chess- or checkerboard); or a proto-virginal (from the resemblance of hypothetical lathe-turned bridges to chessmen).[3] The late Edwin Ripin believed, after assembling all the chekker-related references he could find in the early literature, that he had found the missing connection, and that "chekker" simply meant "clavichord." The etymology, if not directly from the resemblance of the whole instrument to a chessboard, is evidently from its similarity to the rectangular counting-board called the *exchequier* (whose own name seems in turn to derive from the imagery of the gaming board).[4] Christopher Page has countered with evidence that early definitions are not as hermetic as we would like, and that "chekker" may after all be generic.[5] Still, as pointed out by Denzil Wraight, from chronological considerations alone Ripin's thesis seems the most plausible, since both evidence of the clavichord and occurrences of the word *exaquier* in a musical context predate by almost a century the evidence of other rectangular forms of string keyboard.[6] The most recent entrant into the controversy is David Kinsela, who proposes that the word "chekker" referred to a putative early form of clavichord with strings running parallel to the keys (i.e., perpendicular to the keyboard); with strings all of the same length, the shape would have been basically square (and thus even more checkerboard-like than its more efficient successor, the rectangular clavichord with strings running across the keys).[7]

Of all the early documents relating to these instruments, one stands out for its remarkable descriptive thoroughness—quite atypical for the period. This is the manuscript treatise produced in about 1440 by Henri Arnaut de Zwolle and now preserved in the Bibliothèque Nationale, Paris.[8] Arnaut was physician, astrologer, astronomer, and horologist to Duke Philip the Good of Burgundy, and his interest in clockworks and other gadgetry is quite evident in the choice of instruments he describes: most are keyboards (organ, clavichord, harpsichord, and *dulce melos*) with actions of varying mechanical complexity. (Besides these, only the lute seems to have commanded much of his attention, probably because of the mechanical problem of constructing a mold for its shell; the harp gets a passing mention, but only as an additional candidate for the use of the protractor-like device he recommends for laying out the strings of a harpsichord.) Although Arnaut can be frustratingly vague about certain crucial aspects—he deals in proportions, for instance, rather than absolute measurements, making it impossible to pin down string lengths and thus absolute pitches—we are indebted to him for the only window we will ever get into details of early development of these instruments in the absence of actual specimens.

All of Arnaut's keyboards have as their bottom note a nominal *B* (that is, the note just below tenor *c*), although their upward limit varies. His church organ extends to *f″* (one note above the gamut), as does one form of *portivus* (literally "portative," but of a size we would now usually call a small positive). This range, *B* to *f″*, was common for keyboards long into the second half of the century, as witnessed by the opening chart (explaining musical notation) of the Buxheim Organ Book, assembled ca.1470. Arnaut's other *portivus*—that having its pipes disposed symmetrically "in the shape of a bishop's miter"—extends up to *a″*, as do his harpsichord and both forms of *dulce melos*.[9] The largest range of all is that of his clavichord: a full three octaves, from B to *b″*. This range, as shown by Edwin Ripin, is close to the practical limit implied by one of the basic features of Arnaut's clavichord design: all of the strings are of the same length and pitch.[10] (The theoretical advantage of this system is that one can tune the instrument simply by removing temporarily the cloth damping or "listing" and putting all strings in unison.) Such an instrument is, both mechanically and historically, a collection of keyed monochords; in fact, *monochordium* (or, in corrupted form, *manichordium*) was one of the first words used for the clavichord and long remained one of its alternative names. (Since the monochord—in the original sense—also survived and was used sometimes as an instrument of performance, not just as a didactic tool, we cannot always know which instrument is meant in early accounts. To add to the confusion, the tromba marina was sometimes called a monochord as well.)

Arnaut's clavichord is quite small—probably no greater than thirty-three inches (ca.84cm) in length and eight-and-a-half inches (ca.22cm) from front to back, excluding the projecting keyboard.[11] Its small size is in accord with iconographic evidence from the period. Efficient use is made of this small space, the three octaves of notes being elicited from but ten pairs of strings. This is done by so-called "fretting": assigning more than one note (usually three or four) to each string. Since only one note per string pair can sound at a time, the fretting scheme is worked out so that no consonant interval normally found in music will fall on any one string pair. Due to the proportional nature of musical intervals (that is to say, because any particular musical interval represents a physically larger distance in the bass than in the treble) the key tails of Arnaut's clavichord are very much "cranked" or "doglegged": they are splayed out in the bass and crammed together in the treble—nearly to the limit of feasibility, according to Ripin. As he explains, a significant increase in range can only be bought by giving up having all the strings in unison, and this is precisely what was done (along with adding unfretted bass courses) in the next stage of the clavichord's development. This stage is documented by the carefully rendered intarsia of a clavichord found in the Studiolo of Duke Federico da Montefeltro, Urbino, which was executed sometime between 1487 and 1490.[12] Nevertheless, the unison-strung clavichord persisted as a common type into the sixteenth century as witnessed by Virdung, who gives it a range of three octaves and a tone (F to *g″*, omitting F♯—thirty-eight keys, an increase of only one over Arnaut's instrument).

The clavichord would from the beginning have been capable of the expressive effects for which it became famous in later centuries. Because of its low volume, however, it is difficult to imagine its ever having enjoyed much of a social life—at least before the eighteenth century, when a few examples were produced that were loud enough to serve as (still quite quiet) accompaniment instruments. Its main function would have been as a solo instrument (for an audience of *very* limited size) and as a practice instrument for organists; already in the fifteenth century it was sometimes fitted with "pulldowns" attached to a pedal board as found on church organs.[13]

Pl. 30.1. Detail of harpsichord from Virgin and Child by Jean Fouquet (ca.1420–ca.1480) The Pierpont Morgan Library MS M.834, fol. 25.

More effective in both ensemble and solo rôles would have been the harpsichord, for its plucking action is inherently louder—though less subtle—than the tangent action of the clavichord. The harpsichord (*clavisimbalum*) described by Arnaut is again quite diminutive by later standards—probably no longer than three feet (ca.91cm), depending, once again, upon one's estimate of keyboard width. It exhibits several characteristics we now associate with string keyboards of the northern (and particularly the Flemish) school as contrasted with those of the Italian school. The most obvious is its so-called "thick-cased" construction, as opposed to the thin-cased construction of most surviving Italian instruments. (At least we *assume* it is thick-cased, based upon Arnaut's other instruments and upon the preponderance of clear iconographic evidence from the period. He does not actually include the harpsichord case walls in his diagram nor mention their thickness.) Another northern characteristic is the strongly tapered bridge, thicker and taller in the bass than the treble; yet another is the rectangular wrestplank. (Italian bridges are usually equal, or nearly so, in cross-section from end to end; Italian wrestplanks, on the other hand, often taper from bass to treble.) Less obvious is the fact that Arnaut's instrument is constructed using proportions "from the outside in." This has been found to be a feature of later Flemish harpsichords, while Italian instruments seem to be designed from the musical proportions of the strings outward.[14]

What is odd about all this is that the extant northern examples from before 1550 or so actually resemble Italian instruments more than they do later northern ones, calling into question any direct connection between Arnaut's design and those developed after 1550. In any case, his design shows features not found on the instruments of any later school: both bridge and bentside are described as arcs of a circle (even though a circular arc is a poor approximation of a harmonic curve—one in which the string lengths halve at the octave); the bridge is capped with a wire, while a wire (rather than a wooden batten) serves as a nut on the wrestplank; and the case sides extend below the bottom board, in order to allow the keyboard to be placed beneath it. Arnaut also suggests an unusual form of double stringing, in which the additional strings are mounted *above* the first set, rather than alongside them as became normal later; each plectrum then plucks two strings, so there is no need for a second set of plectra. In the double-strung version the strings are to be supported by metal pins, each with two notches in the side, which then obviate the need for wires capping the bridge and forming the nut.

Probably the most remarkable aspect of Arnaut's *clavisimbalum*, however, is the set of four possible systems for exciting the strings. Three are plucking mechanisms, while the fourth is the hammer action associated with the *dulce melos*. All involve lever motion; none is what we would now recognize as a "jack"—a small stick of wood arranged to slide up and down in a rack ("register" or "jackslide"). Those of the first type (which he says is best) are pivoted on a wire at the back of the wrestplank and guided by slots in the latter; they are lifted from below by pushrods set in the tails of the keys and passing through holes in the bottom board. In the second and third systems the levers are pivoted on individual posts; here the keys themselves have to be pivoted from the rear (as in organs) so that they can operate pulldown chains (second system) or pushrods from above (third system—in which case the keyboard has to be situated above the action). In the first and third systems the plectrum is mounted in a pivoted tongue very much like that in a standard harpsichord jack, although there is no mention of a spring for it—it may be meant to return by gravity. The purpose of such a tongue, of course, is to allow the plectrum to pass the string without plucking on the return stroke; this "escapement" is effected in the second system by an additional lever and chain that are supposed to deflect the plectrum after it has done its job. (How this works is not quite clear.) In none of these systems is there a hint of a damping mechanism, so that the concept of articulation that we take for granted in harpsichord performance would seem to be meaningless here.

In contemplating the maze of interlocking levers implied by Arnaut's designs we cannot help admiring the elegant simplicity of the standard jack mechanism, which, once invented, survived with only minor regional variations until the demise of the harpsichord itself. We can see, too, just how crucial the invention of the jack was to the subsequent development of plucked string keyboards: the creation of virginals and spinets, as well as more elaborate harpsichords. The levers of Arnaut's plucking systems take up a fair amount of space, and they have to run parallel to the strings; they do not lend themselves readily to a transverse orientation with respect to the keys (as would be necessary in a virginal, for instance). To be sure, he twice mentions building clavichords with the plucking action (and thus the sound) of a harpsichord, and in the second instance even shows a mechanism resembling a jack in some ways; this information has often been interpreted as the first evidence of the concept, if not the name, of the virginal.[15] However, in both cases the plucking mechanism is apparently fastened rigidly in the tail of the key and guided by it—a fairly rickety system, prone to inaccuracy; there is no mention of a rack. It is not certain whether this is for him a real or merely hypothetical instrument; in any case, it would seem that a really viable version had yet to be worked out at the time of his writing.

Finally, there is the *dulce melos*. Arnaut tells us there are three kinds, the first "played by hicks with sticks" (rough translation!) and the other two fitted with keyboards and resembling the clavichord. (This statement makes it clear that "*dulce melos*" is merely the Latin for "dulcimer"; nevertheless, it has become customary in the literature to distinguish Arnaut's keyed version by the Latin term. His own cultural bias against the simple form of the instrument is obvious. Paulus Paulirinus, who has nothing but the most positive things to say about the hammered dulcimer, seems to have been unacquainted with the keyed variety; this makes one wonder if the latter was known outside Arnaut's rarefied Burgundian court circle.[16]) Arnaut gives plan drawings of both keyed versions, which are similar in principle. As in many hand-hammered dulcimers, the strings of the *dulce melos* pass over multiple bridges; in it they are so arranged that they divide the strings into three vibrating sections, whose lengths stand in the ratio of 4:2:1. The middle section thus gives the octave (and the shortest section, the double octave) of the longest. With each pair of strings producing three notes, twelve pairs are capable of producing thirty-six—just one semitone shy of three octaves. In practice, however, the top $bb\,''$ is ignored by the keywork; keyboards generally do not terminate in accidentals. In the first of the two models drawn by Arnaut, the bridges are all parallel, meaning that all the strings in any one section are of the same length. As a result, only the highest in pitch—the B♭s—can be near their optimal tension for timbre and pitch stability; all the rest will be under-tensioned, getting progressively worse as they go downward. Indeed, in reconstructions of the *dulce melos* there is a noticeable discontinuity in timbre at the two transitions between the low- and high-tensioned strings ($bb\,$-b and $bb\,'$-b'). As a solution, Arnaut presents a second model, this time with slanted bridges so as to shorten the higher-tuned strings of each section. It is once again unclear from his wording if this improved model ever made it out of the conceptual stage into the real world; in any case, the slanted bridges are a mixed blessing, since they increase the cranking of the keys—already rather severe in the parallel-bridged version. Possibly the best solution would be to follow another of Arnaut's suggestions, building a harpsichord using the *dulce melos* action—in effect, a fifteenth-century piano!

The basic layout of both forms of *dulce melos* is clear enough so that there is little room for misinterpretation. The function of the hammer mechanism, however, is a little less clear and has often been misunderstood by modern scholars. That it is a percussion mechanism distinct from that of the clavichord (whose tangent remains in contact with the string while it is sounding) is hardly in doubt: Arnaut says it consists of a weighted "piece" (of wood, evidently) glued to the end of the key and provided with a (metal) staple like that serving as a tangent in the clavichord; when the key hits a stop, the piece of wood continues moving, hitting the string and then falling back even if the key is still depressed. What makes for all the confusion is that Arnaut's diagram of this mechanism shows the piece of wood standing on end on the key tail and looking rather like a jack, giving rise to the mistaken notion that Arnaut was describing something akin to the action of an eighteenth-century *Tangentenflügel* (in which jack-like "tangents," riding freely in a rack, are thrown upwards to hit the strings). If this were true, the statement that the piece of wood is glued to the key would of course make no sense, and at least one writer has thus offered an awkward reinterpretation of Arnaut's Latin in order to try to make it make sense.[17] The solution (as offered by the French translators of Arnaut[18]) is that the piece of wood is, in fact, glued to the key tail, but by means of a leather hinge that allows both the requisite freedom of motion *and* attachment to the key. The beauty of this solution is that it does not require the invention of a jackslide, for which there is no other evidence from the period. Furthermore, it works; reconstructions (by Clyde Parmelee, Jr. of Menlo Park, California) of Arnaut's *dulce melos* using leather-hinged hammers operate efficiently and have stood the test of time.[19]

Fig. 30.1. *Dulce melos* action.

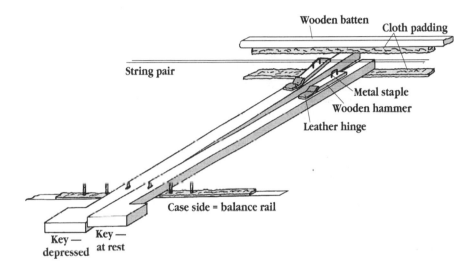

Arnaut's information represents a small island of comparative certainty in an ocean of doubt about instruments of the late Middle Ages; for once we are blessed with reconstructable instruments that can be plausibly (if not exclusively) connected with a significant surviving repertory—the manuscript keyboard collections from Robertsbridge to Buxheim.[20] For Arnaut's instruments we even know the tuning system, since it is specified in a diagram pertaining both to the clavichord layout and to the pipes of the *portivus*.[21] In fact, the most important detail we are lacking would seem to be the pitch level—more significant, obviously, for the question of ensemble participation than solo performance.[22] Several of the design characteristics that we would regard as primitive— occasionally overly complicated actions, lack of damping, keyboard balance points all in a straight line[23]—have their own messages to impart regarding technique; the short, stubby keys in particular make a strong case for the use of early fingerings, since the player immediately perceives the thumb as a detriment rather than a boon. We can thus regard Arnaut's instruments in and of themselves as important documents of performance practice just waiting to be translated by modern builders and read by modern performers.

Notes

[1] A large portion of the relevant iconography is listed and reproduced in Edmund A. Bowles, "A Checklist of Fifteenth-Century Representations of Stringed Keyboard Instruments," *Keyboard Instruments: Studies in Keyboard Organology 1500-1800*, Edwin M. Ripin, ed. (New York, 1977), pp. 11-17; pls. 15-31a. (This is a revised edition of *Keyboard Instruments: Studies in Keyboard Organology,* Edinburgh University Press, 1971; most of the revisions consist of additions to Bowles's checklist.) See also Christopher Page and Lewis Jones, "Four More 15th-Century Representations of Stringed Keyboard Instruments," *Galpin Society Journal* 31 (1978), 151-55; pls. XI-XII; and Jeremy Montagu, *The World of Medieval and Renaissance Instruments* (New York, 1976).

[2] See Sebastian Virdung, *Musica getutscht* (Basel, 1511), fol. Bi^V.

[3] For this last theory see Wilson Barry, "Henri Arnaut de Zwolle's *Clavicordium* and the Origin of the Chekker," *Journal of the American Musical Instrument Society* 11 (1985), 5-13. Such turned bridges are indeed found on later hammered dulcimers, but their existence in fourteenth- and fifteenth-century keyboard instruments is not supported by any direct evidence.

[4] See Edwin Ripin, "Towards the Identification of the Chekker," *Galpin Society Journal* 28 (1975), 11-25.

[5] Christopher Page, "The Myth of the Chekker," *Early Music* 7 (1979), 482-89.

[6] Denzil Wraight, "Chekker," *The New Grove Musical Instrument Series: Early Keyboard Instruments* (New York, 1989), pp. 173-75.

[7] David Kinsela, "The Capture of the Chekker," *Galpin Society Journal* 51 (1998), 64-85.

[8] Bound together with other treatises as MS lat.7295. A facsimile, transcription, and translation (into French) of the musical portions is to be found in G. Le Cerf and E.-R. Labande, *Instruments de musique du XVe siècle: les traités d'Henri-Arnaut de Zwolle et de divers anonymes* (Paris, 1932); this work was reprinted with an afterword by François Lesure (Kassel, 1972).

[9] The *B-f''* range has the visual advantage of a symmetrical keyboard. Arnaut's reason for including more pipes in the "bishop's miter" version of *portivus* also has to do with symmetry, in this case that of the pipes rather than the keyboard. In order to have the tallest pipe in the middle, there must be an odd number of pairs of pipes—in this case seventeen, making thirty-four pipes in all, or a range of *B* to *a''* (omitting *g♯''*). The other *portivus* (that with its pipes in logical "musical" order) has sixteen pairs, or thirty-two potential pitches; the keyboard range of *B* to *f''* includes only thirty-one, so that the top *f♯''* pipe shown by Arnaut is, in effect, a dummy.

[10] See Edwin Ripin, "The Early Clavichord," *Musical Quarterly* 53 (1967), 518-38.

[11] These dimensions—given by Ripin, "Clavichord," p. 520—are based on a fairly generous estimate of the octave span (seven inches, or 17.8cm—a little more than a half inch larger than the span of a modern piano keyboard). Wilson Barry (*op. cit.*, p. 7) proposes very similar measurements, based apparently upon different criteria, however; he claims there are reasons to believe Arnaut "used a medieval Roman *pes* amounting to about 296mm" and that Arnaut's clavichord drawing was to the scale of 1:4. (He promises to divulge the reasons for these assertions in his—apparently still—forthcoming book *Henri Arnaut de Zwolle on Small Keyboard Instruments*.) It

seems odd, however, that if Arnaut had absolute dimensions in mind, he makes no mention of them.

[12] The amazing photographic realism of this intarsia flies in the face of the established wisdom that such realism is usually more apparent than actual in the artworks of the fifteenth century. See Ripin, "Clavichord," p. 528, for a plan drawing realized from the Urbino intarsia.

[13] See Jacques Handschin, "Das Pedalklavier," *Zeitschrift für Musikwissenschaft* 17 (1935), 418-25.

[14] See Ferd J. de Hen, "Problemen rond het Cembalo of Steertstuk in de Nederlanden," *Handlingen van het XXVIe Vlaams Filologencongres* (Ghent, 1967), 563-67.

[15] First mentioned by name by Paulus Paulirinus of Prague, ca.1460; see Standley Howell, "Paulus Paulirinus of Prague on Musical Instruments," *Journal of the American Musical Instrument Society* 5-6 (1979-80), 9-36.

[16] Howell, *op. cit.*, 15-16.

[17] See Cecil Clutton, "Arnault's MS," *Galpin Society Journal* 5 (1952), 3-8 [specifically 5-6]. Clutton seems to have been misled here by Canon Francis W. Galpin, whose interpretation of Arnaut's dulce melos action as similar to that of a *Tangentenflügel* was still in circulation as late as *Grove* 5 (in the article "Chekker").

[18] Le Cerf and Labande, *op. cit.*, p. 5.

[19] Parmelee, who is no longer active as an instrument builder, made a small batch of these reconstructions about 1970, utilizing the then fairly recent research (Ripin, "Clavichord") about contemporaneous clavichords for details of design not specified by Arnaut. For instance, it seems certain that Arnaut had in mind a keyboard situated above the soundboard, just as in the early clavichord. The action thus occupied the space between the soundboard and the strings, which would have been supported by high bridges like that shown in the Urbino intarsia of a clavichord (see fn. 11 above). It should be mentioned that the present article owes an immeasurable debt to Parmelee's research, experimentation, and creative insight.

[20] See the chapter "Repertory," *New Grove: Early Keyboard Instruments*, pp. 199-203.

[21] Arnaut's system of tuning is a transposition of Pythagorean, which results in four almost pure major thirds: B-D♯, D-F♯, E-G♯, and A-C♯. (As pointed out by Ross W. Duffin, "Tuning and Temperament," *A Performer's Guide to Renaissance Music*, p. 240, these are often useful consonances at approaches to cadences in music of the period.) This system is produced by tuning in pure fifths the series B-F♯-C♯-G♯-D♯-A♯-E♯-B♯-F×-C×-G×-D× and then retuning B as a pure fifth to D×. (The notes from A♯ on are, of course, used as their apparent enharmonic equivalents: B♭-F-C-G-D-A-E.)

[22] Arnaut is strangely silent about the stringing material; the choice would be between brass and iron, which differ by about a major third in their breaking pitch for any one string length. One thing is clear: none of the string keyboards is at anywhere near eight-foot pitch; they would seem to range in pitch from about a fifth to a seventh above modern, depending upon exact dimensions and stringing.

[23] In later, more developed keyboards the balance points are staggered, in order to even out the touch between the (longer) naturals and (shorter) accidentals; in Arnaut's instruments the latter are noticeably harder to push down.

31. Psaltery & Dulcimer

Herbert W. Myers

These instruments are related to the harp in that they share the principle of one note per string, all strings being normally sounded 'open'. They are classed organologically as board zithers, in which the sound-radiating plate runs under the plane of the strings; the strings of the psaltery are plucked, while those of the dulcimer are struck. (Note that we are using these instrument names in their common *modern* senses. They—and the harp as well—were not always called by these names, nor were the names always applied as we now use them. The history of the terminology is exceedingly complex for these instruments, and one should consult individual entries in the *New Grove Dictionary of Musical Instruments* for attempts to unravel it.) In most Western versions of board zithers the soundboard forms the top of a resonating box (that is, there is a bottom plank running parallel to the soundboard, separated from it by the sides), although one cannot always be sure from iconography alone. There may be one or more soundholes, usually in the soundboard itself, whose function is ultimately more decorative than acoustical.

Psalteries came in a wide variety of shapes and sizes, from square or rectangular to triangular or trapezoidal. (Hardest to categorize is that called the *ala bohemica* or "Bohemian wing," which combines a roughly circular form on one end with a rectangle or trapezoid on the other; its use, as implied by its name, was primarily confined to Eastern Europe.) Triangular or trapezoidal forms, of course, better accommodate the need of the strings to diminish in length from bass to treble; one should be allowed some incredulity regarding those depictions in which all the strings are of the same length—they may be the product of an idealizing habit of mind more often than a reflection of actual practice. The shape that seems to have won out in the end over most of the others is that called the "pig's snout," a modified trapezoid in which the two angled sides (forming or closely paralleling bridges) are given an inward curve (see Pl. 29.2); by this means the strings can come close to halving in length at the octave for much of the range—something impossible to achieve with straight bridges.

Psalteries were held in a wide variety of ways, some of which were less efficient than others in allowing a two-handed playing style. Even so, illustrations abound showing a plectrum in each hand of the player.

Psalteries were sometimes single-strung, like the harp, but were quite commonly provided with multiple strings per note; one often sees the resulting grouping of strings into "courses." Metal stringing is mentioned from early on, and this, coupled with the use of the plectrum, suggests a very different tonal concept from that of the gut-strung, finger-plucked harp. For much of its life the psaltery rivaled the harp in size and string length, but seems not to have participated in the same enlargement in the fifteenth century that produced true tenor and bass pitches from the lower strings of the harp; the psaltery would seem to have remained a soprano (or, at the lowest, alto) instrument until the end. Its doom as a serious instrument in the Renaissnce seems to have been spelled by its basic diatonic nature, increasingly found inadequate in a chromatic musical world. For the harp this represented a temporary setback; it was ultimately able to develop chromatic forms, but these seem to have been more difficult to achieve in the case of the psaltery.

Pl. 31.1. Dulcimer (detail) from *Mary, Queen of Heaven* (ca.1485) by the Master of the St. Lucy Legend. National Gallery of Art, Washington, DC, Samuel H. Kress Collection, 1952.2.13.

Like the psaltery, the dulcimer would appear to have been primarily a diatonic instrument of treble register in the Middle Ages. It seems to have been rather less common than the psaltery for most of the period, reaching an apogee of popularity in the fifteenth century. (It experienced its next in the early eighteenth.) It was even more likely than the psaltery to have its stringing duplicated (or even triplicated or quadruplicated)—possibly, as some have suggested, in order to improve the chances of the strings being hit by the player, but more likely because hammering is a less efficient way of exciting a string than plucking. (A lot of energy is absorbed in the hammer's bounce; multiple stringing gives back some of the lost volume.) Characteristic of the dulcimer are bridges in the middle of the soundboard that divide the string into proportionate parts (commonly a fourth or fifth apart in pitch) and raise certain sets of strings above the others so that the hammer can get at them more easily. There seem to have been many different bridging and tuning systems for dulcimers, if we are to believe pictures.

Finally, there is the hybrid instrument known variously as the "harp-psaltery" or the "psaltery-harp." Here the strings are attached to a harp-like body at the bottom and a neck-like bar carrying tuning pins at the top, but the two are held apart by a board running behind the strings, parallel to their plane. It is thus acoustically very much a harp, but it has the psaltery's disadvantage that the strings are approachable from only one side. Nevertheless, it experienced considerable popularity in the Middle Ages, often being found in art works through the fourteenth century.

X. Percussion

32. Percussion

Peter Maund

Percussion was a vital part of medieval music-making: illustrations, sculptures, literary descriptions, and archival records indicate that numerous instruments were commonly used in medieval Europe.[1] The use of percussion in today's medieval music ensemble however, can be problematic. Percussion parts were not notated in the Middle Ages, nor are there detailed descriptions of the drummer's role in the ensemble.[2] Although we have knowledge of the instruments, we do not know what percussionists actually played on them.

We therefore supplement the evidence from the Middle Ages with information from other ancient and contemporary musical traditions, drawing upon sources in ethnomusicology, anthropology, and archaeology. All of these resources should be considered to determine which instruments were used and how they might have been associated with a particular repertory at a particular time and place.

IDIOPHONES

Bells, cymbals, and clappers made of metal, wood, and bone are among the earliest known percussion instruments. In addition to their use as noise-makers and signaling devices, they have long been associated with both sacred rituals and secular festivities.[3]

Bells / Chimes

In medieval Europe, small bells used as noise-makers and amulets, or pellet bells, were attached to animals or clothing. They were also attached to the costumes of entertainers and dancers, such as Morris dancers. Forged iron hand bells were used primarily as signaling devices in religious contexts.

By the end of the sixth century larger cast iron bells were installed in church towers for regulating religious life.[4] By the tenth century sets of 4 to 12 small bells were suspended on a frame, enabling a player to produce melodies.[5]

Sets of bells, known as chime sets or *cymbala*, are almost invariably seen with depictions of King David. They are seen played by one or more players, usually using hammers. Sometimes the bells are played with ropes attached to the clappers.

Depictions of *cymbala* seem to be primarily symbolic, which makes their actual use in ensembles difficult to determine. Moreover, the literature of the period uses conflicting terminology when referring to small bells and cymbals.[6]

Medieval theorists used the weights and tunings of chime sets to describe pitch relationships. Chime sets served a didactic function in medieval Europe,[7] and by the eleventh or twelfth century they were also used to play a melodic role in ensembles.[8]

Cymbals / Clappers

Metal clappers appear to have been associated with ritual and dancing in Mesopotamia as early as 3000 BCE. Depictions exist from first century BCE. Babylonia and Assyria, and there is evidence of their use in ancient Egypt, Greece, and Rome. Cymbals were used in rituals associated with the goddess Cybele. There are numerous Biblical references, some supporting the use of cymbals in worship.[9] In medieval Europe cymbals were used in both sacred and secular contexts. Small cymbals attached to tongs are depicted in the Stuttgart Psalter (ca.830) and the Utrecht Psalter (ca.825). The association of cymbals with secular music is seen in Byzantine manuscripts from the ninth and tenth centuries.[10] There is no evidence of the use of finger cymbals in medieval Europe.

Cymbals appear to be six to twelve inches in diameter; they are frequently seen played by women and angels. There were two distinct types of instruments:
1) Hemispherical or cup-shaped cymbals, usually seen played horizontally.
2) Flat plates with a large raised center dome. Similar in appearance to today's Chinese and Southeast Asian cymbals, but without the upturned edge usually seen on those instruments.

Cymbals were held and played in both horizontal and vertical positions. Both styles are illustrated in the *Cantigas de Santa Maria* manuscript (ca.1270) as well as in wall paintings in Westminster Abbey (ca.1400). Some cymbals could have been tuned to definite pitches, and for that reason might have been connected with a cord, as illustrated in the *Cantigas* manuscript.[11] In addition to their possible use as a pitched instrument, cymbals can be used to mark the tempo or articulate phrases or sections of a piece.

Triangles were also used for marking the tempo and articulating phrases. They are usually seen with rings suspended from the lower bar, which would continue to rattle after the instrument was struck. The instrument is also seen shaped as a trapezoid, both with and without the rings.

MEMBRANOPHONES

Cylindrical and barrel drums

There are Babylonian depictions from as early as 2000 BCE of small double-headed cylindrical drums, suspended at the waist and played with both hands. Other types of single- and double-headed drums, some similar in appearance to drums found in India, are seen in Babylonian and Assyrian sculptures and bas reliefs.

An hourglass drum, played with the hands and suspended in front of the player is found in the Utrecht Psalter, ca.825.[12] A single-headed goblet drum, similar to the modern Arabic *darabuka* is pictured in the *Cantigas* manuscript, being played by a woman who holds it on her right shoulder.

The most common cylindrical drum in medieval Europe was the tabor. It came in a variety of shapes and sizes, but it is usually depicted with two cord-tensioned heads with a snare (gut string) on the struck head. It is played with one stick or, more rarely, two. Most often the tabor player also plays a small pipe, which can be used as a second stick.

The pipe and tabor was the basic medieval dance band from thirteenth century to the Renaissance.[13] Larger tabors, usually played with two sticks, were used in military music from the thirteenth century onwards.[14]

Kettledrums

There is evidence of kettledrums in Babylonia from as early as 1100 BCE, and their use can be traced throughout the Near East. The Arabic *naqqara*, a pair of small kettledrums made of metal, wood, or clay, were the prototype for the medieval European nakers. It is not clear if the *naqqara* were introduced by the Moors in Spain, possibly as early as the ninth century, or if they were introduced at the time of the Crusades. In any case, they were certainly used in France by the thirteenth century and in England by the fourteenth century.[15]

Nakers are most often depicted in pairs, usually suspended in front of a musician playing them with two sticks. They are occasionally seen strapped to the back of another musician or set on the ground before a seated player. Head sizes were approximately 6 inches in diameter up to 12 inches or so; one or both heads may have a snare. The bowls appear to be the same size, which, given equal tensioning, would result in similar tones or pitches on both drums.

Nakers were traditionally paired with brass instruments in military music as well as for signaling messages during battle. In medieval Europe, nakers were also used for secular and sacred processional music, dance music, and vocal music.

Frame drums

Frame drums are defined as having a diameter as great or greater than the depth of the shell. They may have one or two heads; their shell may be round or rectangular. Some instruments have small cymbals (jingles) and/or pellet bells inserted in the shell. Snares are sometimes used on one or both heads. Frame drums appear in depictions of ritual dances as early as the neo-Sumerian period (twenty-second to the nineteenth century BCE). Their sizes range from large instruments played by two people to small hand-held drums played by dancers.

Frame drums often appear in scenes of revelry and dancing, usually played by women musicians. Ter Ellingson notes that these associations have been retained throughout the frame drum's history and geographical range. He argues that the cultic associations of the small frame drum with dance and sexual license helped shape Judaeo-Christian attitudes to drums through the Middle Ages and up to the present day.[16]

Frame drums were used throughout medieval Europe to accompany sacred and secular vocal and instrumental music, as well as to accompany dancers. The most commonly used frame drum from the eleventh century onwards was the tambourine, also known as the timbre, timpanu, and timbrel. It is often seen in Bibles and Psalters representing the Latin *tympanum* as, for example, Psalm 150 in the Stuttgart Psalter, ca.830.[17]

The medieval tambourine is usually depicted with four or five pairs of jingles set in the frame. It often has pellet bells in place of, or in addition to, the jingles; occasionally it has a snare across the head. Tambourines are usually seen held upright in front of the player, in a playing position similar to that used by today's Middle Eastern musicians. In fact, modern tambourines from the Middle East (e.g., the Egyptian *riqq*), look similar to their medieval European counterparts.

For both historical and practical reasons, the tambourine is probably the most versatile and important percussion instrument in today's early music ensemble. It was found all over Europe and associated with many repertories throughout the Middle Ages and Renaissance. The instrument itself offers a wide variety of tonal possibilities for both the novice and experienced player: one can play it like a drum, using different fingers and striking different parts of the head; shake it like a rattle; play only on the jingles making dry or ringing sounds; or combine all the above.

The physical similarity of medieval percussion instruments to their modern Middle Eastern counterparts has suggested to some players similarities in playing technique. This theory is supported by a remarkable continuity of several elements in Arabic music from the tenth century to today.[18]

However, due to the lack of historical evidence, we cannot assume that playing techniques were adopted in Europe along with the instrument. More often than not, a process of adaptation or transformation accompanies an instrument as it is brought from one musical tradition to another.[19]

Rather than apply specific theories or practices from one musical tradition to another, we should apply a shared conceptual system of music. We can, for example, learn technical expertise from hand drummers in other musical traditions, as well as techniques of improvisation and interaction in performance. No doubt medieval musicians played with the same imagination and virtuosity we hear today in other monophonic musical traditions.

Unlike classical Arabic music, European medieval music did not use percussion to articulate rhythmic modes, nor were there standard beats or patterns associated with a particular repertory. In fact, most of the medieval repertory can be performed without any percussion at all: if percussion is used, it should be integrated into the concept of the piece.

The percussionist's primary role in the medieval music ensemble is to provide rhythmic support. Beyond that, the player should articulate the phrases and overall design of the piece while providing a variety of colors, textures, and dynamics.

Usually, the percussion part should be kept relatively simple, but never lifeless. For example, the ubiquitous tabor rhythm of "long – short-short long – short-short" should never be stiff and mechanical. Depending on the piece and the phrasing, the player might vary the dynamics and the intensity of the strokes. Other possibilities include striking different areas on the head, using "dead strokes" (i.e., keeping the stick on the head at the end of the stroke), or even tapping on the rim or shell of the drum.[20] When accompanying a singer, the text content as well as the colors and placement of vowels and consonants can suggest specific strokes and patterns.

The complexity of the percussion part will depend on the particular rendition of the piece: its purpose or function; its character and intended effect. One must consider the other instruments and singers in the ensemble and the acoustics of the performance space. Even the order of the piece in the program and the weather can influence one's choice of instrument and the part one plays.[21] There is not necessarily one right instrument or accompaniment, even from performance to performance.

The medieval percussionist must ultimately rely on his or her informed intuition to re-create each piece in performance. This interactive and unique process is the greatest challenge—and joy—in playing medieval percussion.

Sources of Instruments

Tambourines, frame drums, *darabukas*, clay nakers, bells, and cymbals can sometimes be found in import stores or "ethnic arts" stores. Due to the current demand for "world beat" and "ethnic percussion" several makers around the country are offering excellent instruments, and many have websites and online catalogs.[22] Reproductions of some medieval percussion instruments are made by two members of Early Music America: Ben Harms in New York and Lyn Elder in California.

Notes

[1] We must however, proceed cautiously: these various sources pose just as many questions as they offer answers. Medieval artists were not necessarily concerned with a realistic portrayal of instruments or performance contexts. For further discussion on working with iconography, see for example Emanuel Winternitz, "The Iconology of Music: Potentials and Pitfalls," in Brook, Downes, Solkema, eds., *Perspectives in Musicology* (New York, 1972); James McKinnon, "Iconography," in Holoman, Kern and Claude Palisca, eds., *Musicology in the 1980s* (New York, 1982), pp. 79-93; and Brown "Iconography of Music," in Stanley Sadie, ed. *The New Grove Dictionary of Music and Musicians* (London, 1980); and Brown, "Introduction" and "Instruments" in *Performance Practice: Music Before 1600* (New York, 1989). See also James Blades and Jeremy Montagu, *Early Percussion Instruments from the Middle Ages to the Baroque*, Early Music Series 2 (Oxford, 1976).

[2] See Jeremy Montagu, "Early Percussion Techniques," *Early Music* 2 (1974), 20-24.

[3] A connection between percussion instruments and transitional states has been discussed by anthropologists, ethnomusicologists, psychologists, and more recently, by "New Age" practitioners and rock musicians. See Rodney Needham, "Percussion and Transition," *Man* 2 (1967), 606-14; Anthony Jackson, "Sound and Ritual," *Man* 3 (1968), 293-99; and Bruce M. Knauft, "On Percussion and Metaphor," *Current Anthropology* 20 (1979), 189-91.

[4] Percival Price, "Bell," in Stanley Sadie, ed. *New Grove* (London, 1980), vol. 2, p. 433.

[5]   James Blades, *Percussion Instruments and Their History* (New York, 1970), p. 198; Price "Chimes," in Stanley Sadie, ed. *The New Grove Dictionary of Music and Musicians* (London, 1980), vol. 4, p. 242.

[6]   Blades, *Percussion...History*, p. 200.

[7]   Brown, "Instruments," p. 31.

[8]   Blades, *Percussion...History*, p. 200, Jeremy Montagu, *The World of Medieval and Renaissance Musical Instruments* (Woodstock, NY, 1976), p. 16, Price, "Chimes," 242.

[9]   Blades, *Percussion...History*, pp. 165-174; Ter Ellingson, "Drums," in Milcea Eliade, ed., *Encyclopedia of Religion* (New York, 1987), vol. 4, p. 499.

[10]   Joachim Braun, "Musical Instruments in Byzantine Illuminated Manuscripts," *Early Music* 8 (1980), 312-27.

[11]   See Montagu, *The World*, p. 49.

[12]   Pictured in Montagu, *The World*, pp. 15-16.

[13]   See for example the numerous depictions in Bowles, *Musikleben im 15. Jahrhundert* (Leipzig, 1977); and *La Pratique Musicale au Moyen Age / Musical Performance in the Late Middle Ages* (Genève, 1983). For further discussion, see Chapter 26, above.

[14]   Blades *Percussion...History*, pp. 208-10.

[15]   See Blades *Percussion...History*, pp. 223-24.

[16]   Ellingson, 499.

[17]   Reproduced in Montagu, *The World*, p. 46.

[18]   See George Sawa, "The Survival of Some Aspects of Medieval Arabic Performance Practice," *Ethnomusicology* 25 (1981), 173-186. Other striking examples of continuity from the middle ages to contemporary practice are found in Spanish folk music. On this subject, see Israel J. Katz, "The Traditional Folk Music of Spain: Explorations and Perspectives," *Yearbook of the International Folk Music Council.* 6 (1974), 64-85. Such continuity can also be seen in the Andalusian *muwassaha* and *zajal.* On this subject, see Benjamin Liu, and James T. Monroe. *Ten Hispano-Arabic Strophic Songs in the Modern Oral Tradition*, University of California Publications in Modern Philology 125 (Berkeley, 1989).

[19]   Rarely is an instrument or genre absorbed without some modifications. For a theoretical overview, see, for example E. Stockman, "Diffusion of Musical Instruments," *Yearbook of the International Folk Music Society* 3 (1971), 128-37. For a study of the diffusion of one instrument, see Theodore Grame and Genichi Tsuge, "The Horse and the Fiddle: Steed Symbolism on Eurasian Stringed Instruments," *Musical Quarterly* 58 (1972), 57-66. On the cross-fertilization between medieval Romance and Arabic music and poetry, see Liu and Monroe.

[20]   Isidore of Seville, writing ca.622-33, notes the how a drum was struck "in one place and another with small sticks, and there results a most delightful sound from the concord of low and high." See Oliver Strunk, *Source Readings in Music History: Antiquity and the Middle Ages* (New York, 1965), p. 99.

[21]   In humid or wet weather, drum heads absorb the moisture in the air and slacken. The heads must be kept warm and dry. The first thing I do upon arriving at a rehearsal or concert is find an electrical outlet to plug in my heating pad.

[22]   Information for those wishing to make their own instruments can be found in Jeremy Montagu, *Making Early Percussion Instruments*, Early Music Series 3 (Oxford, 1976).

XI. Instrumental Usage

33. Untexted Repertoire
Timothy J. McGee

Medieval music that was probably intended for instrumental performance consists of a relatively small number of compositions, most of which are dances. There is no doubt that instruments were constantly played throughout the period; it is just that very little music intended for them was actually written down. The instrumentalists' repertory apparently consisted primarily of improvisation and melodies that circulated only aurally for which we have no information at all, ornamented versions of the monophonic vocal repertory, and dances. If at first this would seem surprising, it becomes more understandable if we view the social setting and the position of instrumentalists within the society of the Middle Ages.

Instruments were played by people of all social levels, and it seems clear that there was little social distinction about the company in which the instruments were used. From iconography and literary accounts we know that most, but not all, instruments were played for all classes. What does seem to have been a point of distinction was *who* played certain instruments; many were played only by the servant class. It is probable that the repertory may also have had class distinctions, e.g. a bagpiper may have played a different sort of dance when playing at a peasant gathering than in courtly circles. This would be consistent with what is known about other social differences in the classes, but since nothing at all is known about the music of the lower classes, it must remain on the level of conjecture.

Some instruments were reserved for particular functions, foremost among which were the trumpets. In all large European communities before ca.1350, trumpeters served as watchmen on the towers of the city walls. During the late Middle Ages, they also served with the military and within the cities as employees of the civic government and some of the wealthier citizens. In both of these capacities their duties were to play fanfares and heraldic-type sounds. With the military they signalled the troops during maneuvers and in battle; in the cities they served as symbols of the royalty and ruling classes, preceding the rulers and heralding their movements through the city and accompanying them on official journeys to foreign places.

There is no surviving direct evidence of what the trumpeters played on any of these occasions, but a small amount of oblique evidence can be put together to give at least a suggestion. First is the occasional passage or part in fourteenth- and fifteenth-century music marked "*ad modum tubae*" or something similar. These were most likely parts intended for singers, but written to resemble the kinds of things trumpets played.[1] The other help is surviving trumpet sources from slightly later, namely, military trumpet calls from fifteenth- and sixteenth-century Germany, and the 1614 trumpet instruction manual by Cesare Bendinelli.[2] Both of these tend to support what one might assume these instruments would play—fanfare figures full of repeated rhythms, and occasionally passages in imitative style for ensembles of trumpets. Given no more evidence to deal with in this matter, it is suggested that performers wishing to add trumpets for festive sounds, simply have the trumpet players work on full passages such as those found in the sources cited, and then request that they improvise similar passages. For military use and on some festive occasions there is a record of large drums and cymbals being added to the trumpets. Again, no repertory is known.

The only other fixed group that had any stability in the Middle Ages was the other loud ensemble, the shawm band, known variously as the civic pifferi, town Waits, Wachters, and Stad pijpers. Between 1350 and 1400 these groups usually consisted of two or three shawm players, and in the fifteenth century a brass instrument was added—probably slide trumpet before ca.1460 and a trombone afterwards. Two treble shawms were in use from the early fourteenth century, and by the mid-fourteenth century a tenor instrument (bombard) was introduced.[3] Although the ensembles originated as signalmen (tower lookouts, fire alarm), during the fourteenth century they took on a more musical function, performing at civic and private celebrations such as public dances, wedding receptions, and political installations. Repertory that is known to have been played by this ensemble was polyphonic elaborations over *basse danse/bassadanza* tenors for dancing, and the polyphonic vocal repertory, a repertory they shared with the *bas* ensembles discussed below.[4] The shawm band, therefore, can select from any of the fifteenth-century polyphonic vocal music, although the earliest documentary evidence that they played composed polyphony dates from 1468.

Late in the fifteenth century in the Low Countries the civic pifferi were regularly directed to perform motets in public, bringing into the possible instrumental repertory any of the sacred collections from that time. One additional manuscript, Rome, Bibl. Casanatense 2856, containing only untexted polyphony, has been thought to be instrumental repertory for the shawm band: it may be the manuscript referred to as *a la pifferesca* in the Ferrara accounts because the ranges of the vocal parts seem to have been altered to fit the instruments. On the other hand, even if this is the MS referred to, the inscription may mean "in the style of the pifferi"—vocal music without text—rather than "written for the pifferi."[5] In any case, since it is clear that by the end of the fifteenth century instrumentalists freely chose to play vocal polyphony, all of the surviving music from this period is open to performance by all instrumental ensembles (excluding, of course, trumpets). The only restrictions would be to choose instruments that were in use during that period.[6]

Polyphonic elaboration over dance tenors requires one instrument to play the tenor notes and at least one other to play spontaneous elaborations above it. If three musicians are to perform, the third player should play notes harmonically compatible with the tenor; before ca.1450 this harmonic part should be placed above the cantus firmus tenor, after 1450 it should be below.[7] Although no instructions for improvisation are known to exist, a few examples of elaborations over dance tenors have survived,[8] and elaborations over cadence patterns and sustained tenors intended for instruments can be used as models.[9]

Most of the other instruments fall under the heading of *bas* instruments, and from pictorial and literary evidence it is clear that although they were mixed together in performance, there were no set ensembles. Unfortunately we do not know what formed the bulk of their repertory before the end of the fifteenth century. Although it had been thought for a long time that *bas* instruments played the textless lines that are found with the texted songs, and all music without text, that has recently been seriously questioned.[10] It is more likely that prior to the mid- to late-fifteenth century, instruments only rarely performed written polyphony—either with voices or in instrumental ensembles. The usual repertory for instruments at that time—both solo and in mixed ensembles—was probably monophony, most of it improvised, but also including that written for voices and the untexted dance music. The total surviving medieval dance repertory is quite small; it includes perhaps 46 compositions written before 1430 (a few of them polyphonic), ranging from the thirteenth to the fifteenth century, and including repertory from France, Italy, England, and Czechoslovakia.[11] This is somewhat enlarged during the fifteenth century by the *basse danse* and *bassadanza* repertory, intabulations, and a few other compositions that may be composed instrumental music (see below). Beyond that small repertory and the polyphonic vocal repertory after the mid-fifteenth century, what instrumentalists played apparently was rarely written down and is now completely lost to us.

Nearly all instruments known to have been in use during the late Middle Ages are named or depicted in association with dance music. The only known use of percussion in association with dance, however, is tambourines accompanying vocal performances of dances where no other instruments are present, and the tabor with pipe; there is no historical justification for percussion in conjunction with any other melody instruments. Otherwise, it would seem that the only restrictions in choice of instrument would be the obvious ones of range and technical demands; even then, small adjustments or octave transpositions of certain notes would make many of the pieces available to most instruments. The instruments most frequently mentioned and pictured in conjunction with dance are vielle, lute, harp, shawm, bagpipe. For the two-part dances, the most common medieval duet instruments seem to have been lute, citole, harp, and vielle, in any combination. Shawm and bagpipe are also mentioned and depicted, although considering the drone problem this may have been only in conjunction with performances of monophonic music.[12]

The monophonic instrumental dance performance tradition would seem to have included both solo and ensemble playing, and both loud and soft instruments (although never mixed). In ensembles the instruments can play either simultaneously or sequentially, or a combination of both. Addition of drones was apparently part of the tradition, as was simultaneous but independent ornamentation of the line (which will produce a form of heterophony). In the longer dances (such as the Italian istanpittas and some of the saltarellos) performers may wish to change instrumentation by section in order to emphasize the formal structure; for example by changing, adding, or deleting instruments in the refrain sections or on repeats. This type of performance detail is mere conjecture based on the observable medieval interest in bringing out the formal structure in many compositions (such as in motets), and need not be done; performance of the lengthy dances as solo or with an unchanging set of instruments is also acceptable.

The small polyphonic repertory known to be for instrumental performance before 1500 consists of two large collections: the Faenza Codex from ca.1430, and the Buxheimer manuscript from ca.1470, and a few smaller MSS.[13] The actual instrumental intention of the Faenza codex is in some dispute. Since its rediscovery in 1939, it had been thought of as keyboard repertory, but that has been questioned recently and a proposal put forth that it could have been intended for duets by two lutes or lute and harp. To complicate the issue it has been shown recently that in some northern Italian courts the performers of this repertory would have been the same people no matter what the instrumentation, bringing up the possibility that the Faenza Codex is a "performers' manuscript," to be used in a variety of instrumental combinations depending on need, availability, etc.[14] The Faenza repertory includes French and Italian secular songs, at least three dances, a hymn, two Bendicamus Domino settings, instrumental *alternatim* verses for 3 Kyries and 2 Glorias, and several pieces whose types are not known. If these pieces are to be performed on a keyboard instrument, either a two-manual or pedal instrument should be chosen (although none is known from that period) in order to avoid the fingering problem that occurs when the two parts play in the same range. For duets, the ideal choices are lute, harp, and vielle (for the bottom line) and lute, citole, and vielle (for the top line).

The Buxheimer manuscript also has been considered to be exclusively a keyboard manuscript owing to the inclusion of Conrad Paumann's organ treatise, but recently it has been noticed that there is evidence that some of the compositions could also have been intended for lute or citole. The repertory here consists of over 250 pieces, including intabulations of French, German, and Italian sacred and secular works, *alternatim* verses for Kyries, preludes, cadence formulas, and a number of unidentified pieces, some of which could be dances. Many of the works are in three parts, and the most obvious performance choice would be pedal organ—especially so because of the presence of the organ treatise and the knowledge that Conrad Paumann was an organist. But Paumann was also a lutenist, and duets were some of the most frequently described and depicted ensembles in the fifteenth century. A number of the pieces in this source are in two parts, suggesting duets such as 2 lutes, lute-harp, lute-vielle, as possibilities, including one piece marked in the source "*in Cytaris vel etiam in organis*," indicating that this, and perhaps other works, would also be suitable for citole.[15]

The Robertsbridge Codex, from ca.1370, includes two-part intabulations of six works: two dances, two motets also found in the *Roman de Fauvel* and possibly by Philippe di Vitry, a hymn, and an unidentified fragment.[16] All works could be performed on keyboard, but may just as well have been intended for duets by the same instruments named above.

A set of five textless 3-part compositions from late thirteenth-century France, labeled "*in saeculum viellatoris*," have often been thought to have been for performance on vielle.[17] On the other hand, another composition in the same MS is labeled "*in saeculum d'Amiens*," suggesting that the name on the other five compositions may refer to something other than mode of performance. In any case, if these are instrumental works, they are the only surviving polyphonic instrumental compositions from before 1300.[18]

The remainder of material possibly intended for instrumental performance consists of preludes and cadential decorations (*fundamenta*), possibly for lute as well as keyboard,[19] and seven textless compositions in three parts, probably by English composers from the mid-fifteenth century.[20]

This does not add up to a large written repertory for instrumentalists, but if tenor elaborations and highly ornamented versions of the vocal repertory are taken seriously, there is plenty to occupy the time and tax the technique of even the finest performers.

Notes

[1] As for example, the lower two parts in Guillaume Du Fay's *Gloria ad modum tubae*, published in *Opera Omnia*, vol. 4 (Rome, 1965), pp. 79-80.

[2] Published in *Das Erbe deutscher Musik*, vol. 7, Kassel: Bärenreiter, 1936; Cesare Bendinelli, *Tutta l'arte della trombetta*, 1614, facs. (Kassel, 1975). Translation and commentary by Edward H. Tarr (but no music) in Cesare Bendinelli, *The Entire Art of Trumpet Playing 1614* (Nashville, 1975).

[3] For further discussion, see chapter 27.

[4] Modern editions of the basse danse/bassadanza repertory can be found in Frederick Crane, *Materials for the Study of the Fifteenth Century Basse Dance* (Brooklyn, 1968); H. Jackman, ed., *Fifteenth Century Basse Dances*, The Wellesley Edition, Vol. 6; Otto Kinkeldey, "Dance Tunes of the Fifteenth Century," in *Instrumental Music*, ed. David Hughes (Cambridge, MA, 1959, repr. New York: Da Capo, 1972); and Timothy J. McGee, *Medieval Instrumental Dances*, Bloomington, 1989).

[5] A complete transcription of this manuscript is found in Arthur S. Wolff, "The Chansonnier Biblioteca Casanatense 2856: Its History, Purpose, and Music" (Ph.D. diss., North Texas State University, 1970).

[6] For a chart of instruments, their uses and combinations, see Timothy J. McGee, *Medieval and Renaissance Music; A Performer's Guide* (Toronto, 1985), Ch. 4, esp. pp. 62-77.

[7] Rules for inventing the counterpoint and the elaborations, as well as instructions for developing the techniques, are given in McGee, *Medieval and Renaissance Music*, Ch. 8.

[8] See Archibald T. Davison and Willi Apel, *Historical Anthology of Music* (Cambridge, MA, 1949), no. 102a; Manfred F. Bukofzer, *Studies in Medieval and Renaissance Music*, New York, pp. 199-200; and Crane, *Materials for the Study of the Fifteenth Century Basse Dance*, pp. 62-66.

[9] Models can be found in the Faenza Codex and the Buxheimer MS; see below.

[10] See, for example, Christopher Page, *The Owl and the Nightingale: Musical Life and Ideas in France 1100-1300* (London, 1989); David Fallows, "Secular Polyphony in the 15th Century," *Performance Practice: Music Before 1600*, ed. Howard Mayer Brown and Stanley Sadie, The Norton/Grove Handbooks in Music (New York, 1989), pp. 201-21; and Timothy J. McGee, "Singing without Text," *Performance Practice Review* 6 (1993), 1-32.

[11] Modern edition in McGee, *Medieval Instrumental Dances*. Only half are certainly dances, the remainder are unidentified and are classified as dances only by their association with other dances or their resemblance to dances.

[12] See chapter 28.

[13] Modern editions are Dragan Plamenac, *Keyboard Music of the Late Middle Ages in Codex Faenza 117* (American Institute of Musicology, 1972); Bertha Wallner, ed., *Das Erbe deutscher Musik*, vols. 37-39; Willi Apel, ed., *Corpus of Early Keyboard Music* 1 (Rome, 1963).

[14] Keith Polk, "Fiddle and Viol: German String Traditions in the Fifteenth Century," *Journal of the American Musicological Society* 62 (1989), 520. This possibility would help to answer the question of why the manuscript contains both elaboration of secular songs, and alternatim verses for Kyries and Glorias.

[15] On the view that cytaris in this context probably refers to the lute, see Keith Polk, "Voices and instruments: soloists and ensembles in the 15th century," *Early Music* 18 (1989), 179-98, and *German instrumental music of the late middle ages* (Cambridge, 1992), 137.

[16] Modern edition in Corpus of Early Keyboard Music, vol. 1. Two dances and fragment in McGee, *Medieval Instrumental Dances*.

[17] Modern edition in Pierre Aubry, *Cent motets du XIIIe siècle* (Paris, 1907).

[18] For a suggestion that they were intended for vocal performance, see Peter Jeffery, "A Four-Part In Seculum Hocket and a Mensural Sequence in an Unknown Fragment," *Journal of the American Musicological Society* 37 (1984), 16-19.

[19] All transcribed in Corpus of Early Keyboard Music, vol. 1.

[20] All of these compositions are found in the Trent manuscripts: six in MS 87 and one in MS 89. Discussion in Charles Hamm, "A Group of Anonymous English Pieces in Trent 87," *Music and Letters* 41 (1960), 211-15; transcriptions in Benvenuto Disertori, "Un primitivo esempio di variazione nei codici musicali tridentini," *Studi trentini di scienze storiche* 35 (1956), 1-7; Disertori, "Tyling musico inglese nei codici tridentini," ibid. 36 (1957), 10-13; and Disertori, "L'unica composizione sicuramente strumentale nei codici tridentini," *Collectanea historiae musicae* 2 (1957), 135-45.

34. Improvisation & Accompaniment before 1300

Margriet Tindemans

The medieval instrumentalist was very much part of an oral tradition. Even if one was musically educated and could read and write music, knew about the basics of music theory (solmization, hexachords, *musica ficta*) as was the case with the Parisian clerics and university students of the thirteenth century who developed an interest in playing string instruments, one would learn new repertory by memory; one would learn technical skills by apprenticing oneself to a master, or by going to one of the minstrel schools. At the beginning of the fourteenth century there were famous schools for players of the fiddle at least in Mechelen, Ieper, and Deventer in the Low Countries. Very little of the learning process or of the actuality of performance was ever written down, leaving twentieth-century musicians the task of trying to reconstruct and re-invent a tradition. The areas of ornamentation, accompaniment and improvisation are very closely related, and they are hard to separate from each other. There are many overlapping considerations and ideas, so the reader is encouraged therefore to consider the exercises and guidelines in the following paragraphs as interdependent. For the sake of clarity I have tried to organize them in separate areas of concentration.

IMPROVISATION

A core part of a minstrel's trade besides learning by memory a vast repertory of existing songs and melodies would have been to make up new melodies, preludes and postludes in various modes, set poetic texts to music, make up motets and other polyphonic forms and provide dance music. Certainly the better minstrels would have been expected to have a working knowledge of the rules of discant and to be able to improvise simple counterpoint. While the sacred repertory provides some sources concerning the actual learning process of discant and counterpoint (the Vatican manuscript) I know of no such examples for the secular instrumentalist. Because of the paucity of source material on improvisation it is important to look at related arts such as poetry for inspiration and help, and for a way to gain some insight into the creative mind of the medieval musician.

The following are some exercises and guidelines that I have developed over years of performing and teaching:

General rules

1. Keep it simple.
2. Be deliberate: make choices before you play.

3. Do not try to be overly creative: improvising is a trade that can be learned by setting up rules for yourself and simply sticking by them at first. The perfect melody will come when you least expect it.

4. Practice: since most musical training nowadays concerns itself primarily with written music and instruction, it may take a little while to learn to keep track of what you are playing in your head instead of on paper, and to make up new things while you are playing.

Exercises

1. Learn your modes. (Refer to Chapter 36 for further explanations on modes.) Be very aware of the species of fifth and the species of fourth in each mode.

2. Familiarize yourself with as many vocal models as you can find, especially monophonic songs of all kinds. In the chapter on medieval fiddle you will find a more detailed listing of various repertories and styles.

3. Learn about different forms: for example sequence, estampie, lai, rondellus, pastourelle, courtly love song. For more information, refer to the appropriate chapters above.

4. Look at and try to learn different languages. Even if you do not speak or understand them much information can be gathered from the sounds. How do they sound different one from the other, and how could you imitate these differences on your instrument?

5. Look at texts; learn about poetic and other forms; learn about poetic devices such as rhyme, form, alliteration etc.

6. Playing an instrument was considered a science as well as a craft: to be versatile you have to do it enough. Make up short patterns and repeat them on each degree of the mode you have chosen. Then repeat the same pattern backwards, in mirror (inversion), in mirror and backwards at the same time, again on each degree.

Ex. 34.1.

7. Choose a mode and consider its different "registers": some melodies stay around the *finalis* (F), others explore the species of fifth or fourth, others stay around the dominant *cofinalis* (D), some combine the species of fifth and the species of fourth, some end on the *finalis*, some on the *cofinalis*, some on the *subfinalis* (SF), some on other degrees.

Ex. 34.2.

8. Choose a pattern for a simple song, for example, a four-line verse, using the above "registers" to define each line; for example, you can decide that

>   line 1 stays around the *finalis*
>   line 2 explores the species of fifth
>   line 3 stays around the dominant
> *and*   line 4 comes back to the *finalis*

Ex. 34.3.

or   line 1 explores the species of fifth, but ends on a note that is not
the finalis
line 2 is a repeat of 1, but it ends on the finalis
line 3 explores the species of fourth above or below the fifth
line 4 comes back to the finalis

Ex. 34.4.

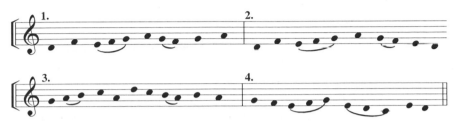

The possible combinations are endless; you will notice that by deciding on a pattern before you start you make it easier for yourself to come up with something because you have limited your choices.

9.   Choose a poem as an example, consider its rhyme scheme and make up your own "instrumental" rhyme; for example: if the poem's rhyme scheme is a b b a c d you could translate this into

Ex. 34.5.

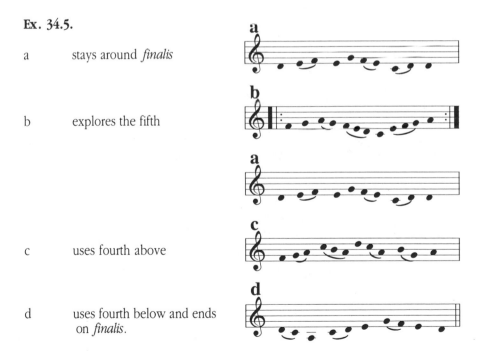

a   stays around *finalis*

b   explores the fifth

c   uses fourth above

d   uses fourth below and ends
on *finalis*.

457

10. Find a medieval Latin poem and make up a melody for it using some of the above ideas. Make up a different melody every day. Change the rules.

11. Sometimes decide to make all your phrases the same length; other times you may make them of different lengths.

12. In the exercises until now you will have used a free rhythm, all notes being of unequal, non-proportionate length. Now decide on a rhythmic pattern (you may use rhythmic modes or verse meters as examples) and return to exercises 8, 9, 10, and 11.

13. Decide on a mode: with a stop watch time yourself and force yourself to play for 30 seconds; one minute; two minutes; etc., first in a free flowing rhythm, then with a rhythmic pattern in mind.

14. Decide on a form (see exercises 8, 9, 10, 11) and make yourself play for one minute, two minutes, etc. in this form, in a specific mode and using a specific rhythmic pattern.

15. Find a trouvère song you like. Memorize it. Then make it into an estampie.

The estampie is a dance form, in which each phrase repeats first with an open ending (*ouvert*) then with a closed ending (*clos*). The endings can be quite long.

A	open
A	closed
B	open
B	closed
C	open
C	closed, etc.

To make an estampie out of a trouvère song you must first find a phrase or a part thereof that can serve as your *clos*: it needs to end on the *finalis*. Decide how you can change the ending to make an *ouvert* out of it: you need to change the ending to a note different from the *finalis*. (Sometimes the trouvère will provide you with both.) Since the Estampie is a dance , you will want to play it in a dance rhythm. Arrange all unused material into *puncta*. Make up more *puncta* if you wish.

Ex. 34.6a. *Quant voi renverdir* **by Gace Brulé (Paris, BN, f. fr. 846, fol. 123v.).**

Ex. 34.6b. *Quant voi renverdir* **as an Estampie.**

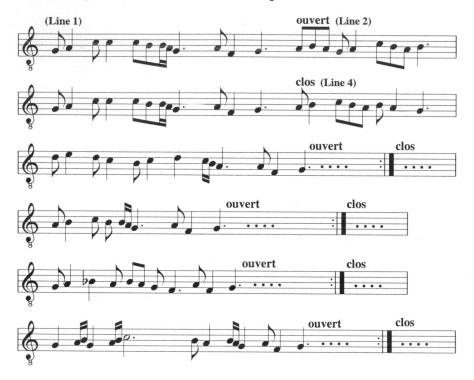

16. Decide on a mode and a rhythmic pattern and make up your own estampie.

17. Using the same trouvère song you had in No. 15 or choosing another one, make up a different refrain form: this can be a rondellus:

a A ba BA or similar form with one short and one long refrain.

Ex. 34.7. *Quant voi renverdir* **as a Rondellus.**

or a rondeau: ABaAabAB

or another from using one or more recurring refrain(s). Since in this case the **B** phrase has to end on the *finalis* you might want to choose different phrases for your **A**'s and **B**'s, or change the endings of the ones you were using in 17.

Ex. 34.8. *Quant voi renverdir* **as a Rondeau.**

Capitals stand for phrases with the same text and melody; lower case letters for the same melody but changing texts.

You may choose to use the same phrase for **a** and **A**, for **b** and **B**, or you may choose to make your own musical scheme: you might decide to use the same melodic or rhythmic pattern for **a** and **A**, but change all the lower case ones in such a way that they stay recognizable as being related to **A**, but not exactly the same.

Ex. 34.9. *Quant voi renverdir* **as a varied Rondeau.**

18. Find a lai to use as an example and then try to make up your own: lai melodies are very formulaic and gestural; they are organized in clear sections. Many repeats are possible (irregular numbers) Some sections might reappear later in the piece. This is a fun project to do with friends and colleagues: everybody can make up their own section. There is no limit to the number of sections.

19. Find a chant melody you like, learn it by memory in equal note values. Now impose very simple rhythmic patterns on it. Keep it simple! You now have a motet tenor.

Ex. 34.10. Chant melody from Easter Gradual, *Haec dies,* used as a patterned tenor (two versions: mode 5 and mode 3).

* Melody repeats

20. Return to the chant melody in equal note values; play a counterpart (discant) using only consonances: unison, fourth, fifth, and octave. You may use parallel intervals but no more then two in a row.

Ex. 34.11. Chant melody as a basis for discant.

21. Using the same melody with the rhythmic variant you have chosen in 19 as your tenor, make your discant over the first and the last note of each rhythmic pattern only.

Ex. 34.12. Mode 3 tenor melody (from Ex. 34.10) with discant on first and last of each group of notes.

22. Connect the discant notes you came up with in 21. You may now use dissonances to get from one consonance to the next one. You now have a duplum (motetus) part.

Ex. 34.13. Florid version of discant from Ex. 34.12.

23. Return to your original chant melody in equal note values (or choose a different one). Decide which is the central fifth in this melody. Play your discant using this central fifth; within this fifth you will mirror each note:

Ex. 34.14. Discant centered on F-C fifth.

Decide what you will do with the notes that fall outside the range of the fifth; you must have a consonance on these notes. Over the note below the lowest note of the fifth you can often use the octave. You must start and end on a unison, octave, or fifth. Adjust if necessary.

24. Try the same procedure, but choose a different fifth as your central one: compare the two options. Remember that you must start and end on unison, octave, or fifth. If this results in many thirds in a row, this might not be the best fifth to choose unless you are doing an English piece: whereas the third was not allowed as a consonance in continental Europe, England favored it.

Ex. 34.15a. Discant centered on G-D fifth.

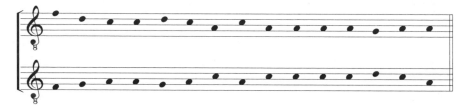

Ex. 34.15b. Discant centered on D-A fifth.

Ex. 34.15c. Discant centered on A-E fifth.

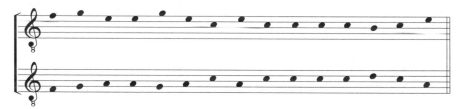

25. Return to the rhythmic version of your melody, your Tenor (or make up a new one). Make up a *duplum* (*motetus*) part using your preferred central fifth. If possible, the first and last note of your rhythmic patterns should be consonances, so adjust accordingly.

Ex. 34.16. Florid discant on the Mode 3 tenor melody.

26. Learn to hocket: you will need to do this with at least one other player. Play your chant melody with various rhythmic patterns, alternating notes.

Ex. 34.17. Chant melody divided for two instruments.

27. Make up a rhythmic pattern with many rests; the second player repeats the last note of the first player in the rest.

Ex. 34.18. Chant melody patterned and divided.

28. You may now incorporate the hocket technique in your *duplum*.

Ex. 34.19. Discant style with hocket.

ACCOMPANIMENT

The accompaniment of medieval song is a complicated and exciting process. While many sources talk about instruments accompanying singers, very few of them actually tell us what they played. If they do, it is often in ambiguous terms that are hard to interpret after eight centuries. In his "*Sermones*," the twelfth-century German writer Sextus Amarcius describes performances of narrative songs where the musicians "repeatedly adjust the melodious strings in fifths" which Christopher Page reads as referring to an accompaniment in parallel fifths.[1] Other sources talk about "*chanter*" and "*organer*" in a way that does not make it clear whether "*organer*" means playing the organ, or playing in organum style, i.e. in parallel intervals.

Troubadour and trouvère texts talk about accompaniment by fiddle or harp. The opening page of the Chansonnier de l'Arsenal has an illumination of the King and the Queen together with a solo fiddler.

Before we can answer the question of when instruments accompanied song, a distinction must be made between the various genres and their social context. Instruments were played throughout all layers of society, but documentation of instruments in the lower classes is virtually non-existent. More information is available about musical practices at the courts, among the clergy, and at the monasteries and churches.

Loosely based on the descriptions of genres by Johannes de Grocheio (described in the chapter 21a above) we can make some distinctions, always keeping in mind that the dividing line between one genre and the next is often not so clearly drawn as we might wish it for our understanding.

Sacred music: liturgical and non-liturgical

The involvement of instruments other than the organ in liturgical music is disputed. We are on firmer ground in non-liturgical music, where instruments are thought to have accompanied monophonic *conducti*, sequences and hymns. They might have played in parallel intervals as accompaniment to chant. It is less clear whether they performed in polyphonic compositions. It would seem that the popularity of the fiddle among Parisian clercs of the thirteenth century, who certainly would be well trained in polyphony, would not preclude the use of instruments in such settings.

Furthermore there is the genre of the *chants pieux*, religious songs, often closely related if not in fact contrafacta of secular songs: miracle stories such as the *Miracles de Nostre Dame* by Gautier de Coinci and the vast repertoire of *Cantigas de Santa Maria*, compiled by Alfonso el Sabio. The many illustrations of instruments in this collection make instrumental involvement in these pieces highly likely. Gautier de Coinci recounts the story of the fiddler at Rocamadour, who played so well before the Virgin that she has a candle descend onto his instrument: "he takes his vielle and raises his head up to the Virgin; he sings and plays his vielle so well that you could not wish to hear a sequence or kyrie better played...he again begins his song and his melody, his mouth sings and his heart is happy." There are also the biblical *lais* and sequences, such as the *Lai of the Flood* from the Dublin Troper and the *Samson Lai* from the Harley manuscript (London, BL Harley MS 978), and from Italy the collections of *Laude*.

Secular repertoire

The secular repertoire of clercs and university students offers a wealth of material: political, satirical and moralistic texts set as sequence, Latin *cantus* (closely related to the trouvère repertoire), polyphonic conductus and motet, *rondellus* (Latin *rondeau* form). It is found in many collections such as the Florence and Wolfenbüttel manuscripts, and the Carmina Burana.

The secular court repertoire includes:

- sung epic poetry such as the *chanson de geste*, often self-accompanied with harp or fiddle
- courtly love songs as practiced by troubadours, trouvères, and Minnesänger
- "lighter" songs such as *pastourelles, caroles, rondeaux* and other dance-songs
- *lais* and *descorts*
- the motet repertoire, which seems like a combination of all of the above: tenors often based on chant, courtly love texts, sacred texts and dance songs.

Ideas and suggestions for accompaniment models

1. drone, on *finalis* or *cofinalis* or both, continuous or interrupted, with or without rhythmic impulses

2. "changing drone" or moving tonal center; often going back and forth between *finalis* and *subfinalis* works well, but other combinations are possible too.

3. double the voice: this will work better in less complicated pieces and might not be the best solution for an elaborate troubadour song

4. outline or shadow the vocal line: choose important notes and /or words

5. double the vocal part in a more ornamented way: again this is not a good technique when the vocal part is highly ornate already, but can work nicely in simpler songs

6. alternate with the voice: extend or bridge vocal phrases or comment on them

7. provide prologue or prelude: *Tristan en prose* mentions preludes on the harp; *Le Somme de Roi* (1279) by Laurent mentions a fiddle prelude

8. provide postlude or epilogue: Johannes de Grocheio says when fiddlers performed a *cantilena* they end with an improvised tag, which they call *modus*

9. provide interludes between verses or sections

For polyphony

10. provide a tenor-like part

11. play a counterpart, note against note

12. play a counterpart, but only against the main words or notes

13. play a part that is more active than the vocal part

14. combinations of all of the above

Which of the above models work best with a given song is determined by many factors: What do we know about the availability or admissibility of instruments in the context of the given song? How important is it that the text be understood? Obviously, when you are telling a story you want people to hear what you are saying, and instruments will want to stay out of the way. In dance songs the text might not be as important as the rhythmic impulses and the melody: this leaves more room for instrumental activity. Twentieth-century performers have to address the problem that few modern audiences can understand medieval languages, even if the performance is perfect. On the other hand it might not be necessary to assume the audience is going to fall asleep if a new instrumentation is not used for each verse of a strophic song. Both audience and the power of medieval melodies and languages deserve more credit.

The more important the text is, the less instruments should be used, and the less the instrumentalists should play: a "high-style" troubadour or trouvère song should be accompanied very sparsely, by only one or two instruments, whereas dance-songs can be played by instrumental "bands" playing a rather active role. The use of percussion should be regarded with extreme caution: there is an obvious role for percussion in dances, much less so in any repertoire where text is important. It can be used for special effects, but sparingly.

Because of the lack of medieval source material it can be very inspiring to look at musical traditions of other cultures, European and non-European, folk and art traditions. While learning from the different playing techniques and models these traditions might offer, it is necessary to remember that not all of their instruments and techniques can be transferred to medieval music. Oral traditions do change over time and what at one point in time might have been a direct link between one culture and another might not be one any more in the twentieth century. Just because instruments may look somewhat similar to pictures in medieval manuscripts, more research is necessary before one can use them convincingly in medieval music.

With many thanks to Shira Kammen and Robert Mealy for sharing their ideas and for their help in writing this article.

Notes

[1]   Christopher Page, *Voices and Instruments of the Middle Ages* (Berkeley, 1986), pp. 120-21.

35. Ornamentation & Improvisation after 1300

Ralf Mattes

Introduction

While new forms of notation and a growing interest in secular music, as well as a greater number of surviving manuscripts, make the vocal music of this period more accessible to the modern singer, instrumentalists face an almost complete lack of sources. By their very nature, improvisation and ornamentation remove themselves from musicological research that is traditionally based so much on written material, both theoretical and practical. Due to this lack of information, most modern musicians do not incorporate a substantial amount of improvisation or ornamentation into their performances, and the little that can be heard is often based as much on modern performance traditions as on historical sources.[1]

It has often been claimed that medieval instrumentalists usually improvised the music they played, but a non-written practice is not necessarily an improvised one.[2] Existing descriptions of improvised performance may not be reliable sources of contemporary "everyday" practice because they typically describe musicians of extraordinary skill. Already the earliest surviving sources of organ music show a grade of standardization in notation and manuscript layout that can only be explained by an existing tradition. Therefore, we have to infer the existence of notated instrumental music already in the fourteenth century.[3]

To further investigate traces of ornamentation and improvisatory practice we first have to define criteria by which we can decide whether a piece may be instrumental. Unfortunately, most attempts to give an all-purpose definition of "instrumental" fall short when seen against the background of sources we have. The study of clearly vocal repertoire has shown that criteria such as big melodic leaps or textless transmission—once considered clear signs of instrumental practice—can also be found in vocal compositions and therefore cannot be considered idiomatic of instrumental music. Perhaps the strongest clue to the instrumental nature of an existing work in a manuscript is its form: Most vocal compositions from the late Middle Ages reflect in their musical setting the fixed form of their text (*ballade, rondeau, virelai,* etc.). Music that does not fit into one of these is a promising candidate for being instrumental. Certain forms, like the estampie or its Italian counterpart, the *istanpitta,* are associated with instrumental dance music even by theorists,[4] and indeed, we do have two manuscripts that contain examples of these types of music (but we should keep in mind that the *estampie* also was a poetical form).

One obvious difference between vocal and instrumental music is the lack of text in the latter. Because text plays such an important role in medieval music, its absence must have induced a change in musical grammar. The medieval instrumentalist very likely had to find a melodic or contrapuntal substitute for the missing linear direction usually given by the text. (Here again we encounter a change in aesthetics that separates the modern-day performer from his medieval colleague. The almost literal instrumental performance of vocal music often heard in modern concerts or recordings quietly ignores the fact that the central part of the work is missing. In medieval vocal works the purpose of the music is to provide a "reading"—one possible interpretation—of the text.)

Improvised music has been described as a "...creation of a musical work, or the final form of a musical work, as it is performed."[5] This implies that the music is not performed from musical notation (a concept alien to medieval performers) and shows a certain amount of variety between performances of the same piece. The created work "... may involve the work's immediate composition or the elaboration or adjustment of an existing framework, or anything in between."[6]

Already this definition shows that we can not draw a clear line between the performance of composed versus improvised music.[7] From modern-day improvised music we can conclude that performers try to remember especially successful manifestations of their improvisations to use them in later performances. Often—especially in the fifteenth century—the difference between improvisation and composition might have been one of the process of creation (at one time versus over a period of time) rather than one of style. Even then, composers tended to revise their works at a later date.

But the way of creation might have left certain traces that help us to identify possible models of improvisation within the surviving corpus of medieval music. Playing in an ensemble, the improviser of polyphonic music had to ensure that his improvised part did not produce unwanted dissonances with the given tenor (the framework) on which he was improvising. He therefore very likely observed some rules to control the created sonority. Since improvisation was used in vocal music to create simple polyphonic settings of a given chant, we do have a certain amount of theoretical information on techniques to regulate the sonority of polyphonic vocal improvisation[8]

ORNAMENTATION

It is difficult to separate ornamentation from improvisation, because a substantial part of the instrumentalist's repertoire (as we see it from the surviving sources) was based on the elaboration of given material. However, these two terms should not be confused: while "improvisation" refers to the fundamental process of creating music, "ornamentation" indicates a musical function. Often, excessive ornamentation can be used as a starting point for improvisation, but we also find instrumental music in which the improvised line has no or only a remote resemblance to its vocal model. Our two main sources for fifteenth-century keyboard music, *Codex Faenza*[9] and the *Buxheimer Orgelbuch*,[10] might well serve to illustrate the continuum existing between mere ornamentation of the original setting and free improvisation on a given tenor.

In our search for traces of improvisation in instrumental music we have to be careful not to reverse this chain of thoughts and claim improvised origin for music that is "just" highly ornamented. Therefore, the fast and elaborate pieces of Buxheim and Faenza might have been improvised—and there are certain arguments which we will discuss later in this chapter, speaking for this thesis—but it is just as likely that this reflected a particular style of composition.[11] As a result I will often use the term "elaboration," describing both the function and the process of creation of music based on given material.[12]

Sources of Ornamentation Signs

While manuscripts of instrumental music from the sixteenth and following centuries often are speckled with ornamentation signs, the surviving sources before 1500 almost entirely lack those abbreviations for the use of ornaments (this phenomenon is of course also true for the vocal music of the time).

Only one clear ornamentation sign can be found in manuscripts from the German speaking countries that are notated in the so-called "older German" organ tablature. In this type of notation the upper voice is notated very similar to the mensural music of that time (the main difference being the lack of ligatures) while the lower voices are written as letters, using the symbols C-c with the addition of dashes above the letter to indicate higher octave or the attachment of a "hook" to show *musica ficta*.[13] Within this notational system we can find an ornamentation sign, written as a downward *cauda* attached to a note in the upper voice (this *cauda* should not be confused with a similar sign that indicates *musica ficta* in the upper voice). Unfortunately, none of these early organ manuscripts names this ornament or gives us information on its performance. The sixteenth century organist Hans Buchner is the first to describe it as an ornament of the main note with its upper neighbor and names it *murdent*. This naming is assured by the fragment of a lute manuscript now in the Murhardsche Bibliothek in Kassel.[14] This manuscript, very likely from the end of the fifteenth or beginning of the sixteenth century, describes a unique way of notating music for the lute by using a system similar to that of the German organ manuscripts. The single sheet of paper shows several diagrams explaining the notational symbols including the downward *cauda* which is called *murdent*.

Simple ornamentation of a given line

One of the earliest sources for instrumental music is the manuscript fragment added to a registry from the Robertsbridge Abbey.[15] Two of the pieces in this manuscript have been identified as arrangements of motets also found in the Paris manuscript of the *Roman de Fauvel*.[16]

Ex. 35.1. *Adesto*, in parallel edition from London BL Add. 28550, and Paris, Bibliothèque Nationale, fonds français 146.

Comparing the Robertsbridge intabulation (upper staff pair) with the vocal model from the *Roman de Fauvel* (lower)[17] we can easily extract the techniques the intabulator used. While the tenor of the motet is used with almost no alterations, the motetus is sometimes left out or altered. The duplum, the top voice of the composition, is the one with the biggest changes, a fact that we will find confirmed in almost all surviving instrumental arrangements. This short passage demonstrates the basic process of elaboration:

- by breaking down longer note values into smaller ones: mm. 61, 63 and 67
- by changing the rhythm of notes:[18] mm. 62 and 66
- by embellishing shorter notes with trill-like figures: last *g'* in m. 62
- by embellishing stepwise movement with the anticipation of the next note (this is one of the most idiomatic melodic figures that can be found in many instrumental arrangements).

We also find that the top voice sometimes uses material from the other voices, as seen in m. 65—a technique that can be found in many other intabulations. This incorporation of notes or melodic fragments make it evident that these arrangements do not try to recreate the linear polyphony of the original, but rather try to recreate an impression of the original's sonority. Examining the intabulation of *Adesto* we find an astonishingly small number of melodic and rhythmic patterns, out of which the top voice is "composed."

The usage of patterns, as seen in the previous example, is one way for an improviser to control the melodic and rhythmic material to be used in a piece. These patterns reduce the theoretically infinite possible continuations at any point of the improvisation to a more manageable number.[19] It is important to point out that the study of these formulae is fundamental to the understanding of a particular style of improvisation.[20] The size of this chapter defeats an extended study of all these different styles, but we will later return to pattern-based improvisation as described in some fifteenth-century sources.[21]

The *Buxheimer Orgelbuch*, our main source of fifteenth-century organ music, contains several intabulations of vocal pieces, some of them being almost literal, ornamented copies of the original, others only sharing the tenor and main cadence places. While these different versions show to us the multitude of possible styles an instrumentalist of the fifteenth century had at hand, the top lines of these variants are melodically too distant from each other to examine the possible melodic variation within the performance of one piece. Fortunately, an organ tablature fragment now in Munich[22] includes the beginning of an unnamed piece that is very closely related to the piece *En avois* from the organ part of the *Lochamer Liederbuch*[23] (Ex. 35.2).

Here we have the rare chance to study two surviving variants of the same voice that are close enough to examine melodic variance. As in Ex. 35.1, we can try to list the variations between the Munich and Lochamer versions:

- embellishment of longer note values: mm. 1, 16 and, 19.

- rhythmic displacement: mm. 2 and 13-14.

- substitution of a note by a shorter note and a rest: mm. 5, 9 and 10. (This is found very often in the German organ repertoire. It is not entirely clear, whether this rhythmic pattern is to be considered as a rhythmic ornament or as a reflection on contemporary articulation practice.)

- transposition of melodic phrases: end of m. 12

- substitution of one consonance with another of the same quality: m. 4

Ex. 35.2. *En avois* in parallel edition from Munich, Bayerische Staatsbibliothek, Ms. Clm 29 775/6 (incomplete) and the Lochamer Liederbuch (Berlin, Deutsche Staatsbibliothek, Mus. ms. 40613).

Besides these models of ornamentation we also find some harder to categorize alterations that result in the change of entire melodic phrases. On closer examination we see that these variations occur at or close to cadences. Studying the surviving repertoire we will find that there is a limited number of cadence patterns that can be freely exchanged. Many of these cadential patterns are bound to certain melodic phrases in the tenor voice that are changed accordingly.[24]

IMPROVISATION

As pointed out earlier in this chapter, improvisation describes the process used to create a work of music. Having only sparse information on the actual process of composition in medieval music, the art of improvisation seems to be lost forever. Belonging to the field of *musica practica* and—in the case of instrumental music—being used mainly by *menestrels*, the description of improvisation never gained the attention of medieval theorists. Without this theoretical material, our knowledge of medieval improvisation rests solely on descriptions of the performance of improvisers[25] and the conclusions we can draw from a small number of notated pieces that seem to show reflections of an improvisatory repertoire. (Since medieval music was almost never played from manuscripts, iconography is of little help; we cannot decide whether the depicted performance was improvised or not.) During the following attempts to analyze some of the few surviving instrumental pieces, we have to be aware of the paradox of this procedure: to fully understand the grammar of medieval extemporization we would have to study a great number of average performances, but we only have few surviving fragments of probably extraordinary music—otherwise it would be hard to understand the fact that they were written down. Furthermore, all of the surviving monophonic music is found in the form of addenda to existing (probably older) manuscripts. During the act of writing down the improvisation, not only did one version out of many possible versions get fixed, but the scribe might have adapted and changed some of the more uncommon features of the performance to conform with the grammar of written music.

Improvising Monophonic Music

We are faced with severe methodological problems in the study of improvised monody. The study of both ornamentation and improvisation involve the extrapolation of information from given sources, but unlike our investigation on ornamentation, we have no external "model" (i.e. a previously given model, on which the performance is based) with which to compare the improvisation.

The *estampie* and *danse royal* added to the *manuscript du roi*[26] are our main source of French monophonic dance music of the early fourteenth century. We will use these pieces to show certain important aspects of monophonic instrumental composition, even though there is no evidence that they reflect contemporary improvisational practice.

Ex. 35.3. *La Quarte Estampie Royal,* Paris, BN MS fr. 844, fol. 104.

The Use of Modality

In this analysis we will focus on the modal aspects of the piece.[27] The first *punctum* starts with the fifth *d-a*, a strong signal to the listener that he has to expect a piece in the first mode, an expectation that is confirmed by the *ouvert* on a. Therefore the final cadence on *f* is rather unexpected, creating an effect of astonishment. This forces the listener to reinterpret the just heard material, taking F as the *finalis* of the mode.

The second *punctum* establishes this F-tonality by elaborating the fifth *c'-f*. After this dramatic, condensed outset, the following *puncta* augment the range of the piece and focus on less strong notes of the mode. More and more, the piece drifts away from the mode's typical melodic formulae and finally ends with a *punctum* that—excluding the *ouvert/clos* section—stepwise covers the range of a ninth(!), starting on the high *e'*, a note absolutely alien to the F-mode. To a lesser degree this modal exploration and play with the listeners expectation can be found in all dances contained in this manuscript.

From the analysis above it seems clear that the use of a drone for this kind of repertory is at least problematic. Adding a bordun note will fix the tonality and prevent the modal/tonal ambiguity that is a central aspect of the composition.[28] There is iconographic evidence for the use of drones (vielle with drone-strings or organetti with a group of especially long pipes), but for hardly any of the surviving music from the fourteenth or fifteenth centuries do drones seem appropriate. It should be mentioned in this context that there is music with written out drones from sixteenth-century prints for lute.[29] But the melodic style of the upper voice in these compositions is very different from the refined modal melodies of the *estampie* or *istampitte*. One other source of music might give us information on the type of music played with drones, the so-called *redeuntes* from the pedagogical works of the German organist Conrad Paumann.[30] In these works—once probably played to the sound of the church bells—one or more voices play florid passages against a pedal tone in the lower voice. In his treatise Paumann gives models for an organist's improvisations in the form of examples of *redeuntes* for all six notes of the hexachord.

Polyphonic Improvisation

While in monophonic improvisation the main focus seems to lie on melodic development,[31] polyphonic playing introduces the question of simultaneous sounding notes. Looking at the surviving corpus of organ music from the fifteenth century we find a gradual shift from the simple technique of using octaves and fifth (therefore creating nothing but a florid version of the tenor) towards the more refined counterpoint found in contemporary vocal music.[32] Fortunately, we do have pedagogical writings that tell us how a medieval organ player learned and taught this kind of extemporization. Paumann's *fundamentum*, surviving in two versions, originates in a tradition of didactic organ treatises that can be found in manuscripts such as Munich, Bayerische Staatsbibliothek, ms. Clm 775 or ms. Cgm. 811.[33] These sources show us that medieval music teaching was mostly teaching by example. The student would memorize a great variety of patterns that later could be used to elaborate a given tenor. Here, the modern performer has a unique chance to follow his medieval precursor by studying and memorizing the patterns and models given in these manuscripts. Many of these formulae can be used equally well on instruments other than the organ.

The last instrumental repertory covered in this chapter will be the polyphonic versions of Burgundian *basse danse* that can be found in manuscripts from the end of the fifteenth century. We know that instrumentalist improvised *basse danse* over a preexisting *tenorr,* some of which can still be found in the few surviving dance manuscripts.[34] Most of the surviving settings of *basse danse* are based on the tenor *La Spagna.*[35] While some of these settings are clearly composed, others might reflect the techniques used by the players of the *alta capella* during their performance. Again, we find patterns and sequences that regulate the polyphonic structure of the piece and serve as an aid for the musicians to coordinate their improvisations.[36] Many of these patterns can be found in the early lute fantasias of Francesco da Milano or Marco d'Aquila, showing us that the instrumental music of the early sixteenth century is well based in the traditions of fifteenth-century instrumentalist improvisations.

Conclusion

Due to the limited extent of this introductory chapter, many aspects of late medieval instrumental improvisation could only be mentioned. Further important points omitted entirely include the rhythmic and melodic language of the complex *istanpitte* in the London manuscript, the fifteenth-century Italian dance repertory,[37] and instrumental preludes for voice. However, I hope that the information provided here will serve as a starting point for the modern performer's own investigation. Improvisation can only be learned by doing, so today's musicians will have to work closely with the little surviving material of the past, memorizing it and trying to produce their own versions of a tenor line or a polyphonic chanson (first written, then only *alla mente*), keeping in mind that medieval models might only show a small part of the variety of medieval instrumental music. Finding the balance between personal imagination and given styles must be the goal of any serious performer of this music today.[38]

Notes

1   Or it is based on the improvisation techniques of non-western cultures such as the music of northern Africa or Asia Minor that some ensembles—influenced by the theory of Arabian origin on some of the western secular medieval music—studied.

2   This can be seen in many non-western musical cultures. The gamelan music of Bali for example is transmitted completely orally but shows no signs of improvisation.

3   We have to assume that most of the manuscripts with instrumental music from the fourteenth and fifteenth centuries have been lost and that the few surviving ones did so

not necessarily because of their musical qualities. This makes it almost impossible to make any statements about the general style of the music.

[4] Johannes de Grocheio, *Ars musice*. Modern edition in E. Roloff, *Die Quellen-handschriften zum Musiktraktat des Johannes de Grocheio* (Leipzig, 1972).

[5] Imogene Horsley, from article "Improvisation," *The New Grove Dictionary of Music and Musicians* 9, ed. Stanley Sadie (London, 1980), p. 31.

[6] Ibid.

[7] See "Embellishment and Urtext in the Fifteenth-Century Song Repertories," David Fallows, *BJbHM* 1990, for variants in written fifteenth-century polyphony.

[8] For example, Guillelmus Monachus, *De preceptis artis musicae*, edited in A. Seay, *Guilielmi Monachi: De preceptis musicae*, CSM 11 (1965). See also Markus Jans, "Alle gegen Eine, Satzmodelle in Note-gegen Note-Sätzen des 16. und 17. Jahrhunderts," *BJbHM* 1986 for an overview of improvised note-against-note settings.

[9] See facsimile edition in Armen Carapeytan ed., *The Codex Faenza, Biblioteca Comunale*, 117 (Fa), MSD 10 (Rome, 1961). Modern edition in A. Carapeytan, ed., *Keyboard Music of theLlate Middle Ages in Codex Faenza 117* CMM 57 (Rome, 1972).

[10] Munich, Bayerische Staatsbibliothek, Mus. ms. 3725 (olim Cim. 352 b). Facsimile edition in Bertha Antonia Wallner, ed., *Das Buxheimer Orgelbuch* (Kassel, 1955). Modern edition in B. A. Wallner, *Das Buxheimer Orgelbuch*, Das Erbe Deutscher Musik 37–39 (Kassel, 1958–59).

[11] Some of the manuscripts transmitting Italian trecento music show a similar tendency towards highly melismatic writing.

[12] Our surviving sources suggest that most of the polyphonic instrumental music used existing material.

[13] On the notation of organ music, see Willi Apel, *The Notation of Polyphonic Music 900-1600*, 5th ed. (Cambridge, MA, 1961).

[14] Kassel, Murhardsche Bibliothek, 2° Ms. math. 31.

[15] Now London, British Museum, Mus. add. 28550. Edited in Willi Apel, *Keyboard Music of the Fourteenth and Fifteenth Centuries*, Corpus of Early Keyboard Music 1 (Rome, 1963), pp. 1-9.

[16] Even so, the peculiarities of the notation as well as the inclusion of two pieces in the form of an estampie make the fragments use as instrumental music very likely. Both motet intabulations—as well as the fragment *Flos vernalis*—do have text written next to the music.

[17] Here and in the following discussion I refer to Apel's edition of the fragment and its vocal model. See *Corpus of Early Keyboard Music* 1, pp. 3–6.

[18] The notation of the motets in the *Roman de Fauvel* has a certain level of rhythmic ambiguity, so we cannot rule out the possibility that the vocal model used the same rhythm.

[19] It is clear to the author, that much of what is said about the basic techniques of instrumental improvisation also applies to vocal music.

[20] To a player of medieval music this not only means theoretical studies, but also practical experiments using the patterns found in compositions.

[21] For an overview of these melodic patterns, see Howard Mayer Brown, "Improvised Ornamentation in the Fifteenth-Century Chanson," *Quadrivium* 12 (1971), 238–58.

[22] Munich, Bayerische Staatsbibliothek, Ms. Clm 29 775/6.

[23] Berlin, Deutsche Staatsbibliothek, Mus. ms. 40613. For an edition of the organ part, see Willi Apel, *Keyboard Music*.

[24] For an edition of the Lochamer version of the tenor voice, see Apel, *Keyboard Music of the Fourteenth and Fifteenth Centuries*, p. 41.

[25] But see the comments on literary descriptions of musical performances above.

[26] F-Pn fr. 844, fol. 176v–177v. Facsimile in Pierre Aubry, *Estampies et danses royales* (Paris 1907), and in *Le Manuscrit du roi, fonds francais no. 844 de la Bibliotheque nationale*, ed. Jean Beck and Louise Beck (New York, 1970).

[27] The notation of the pieces in the manuscript shows a certain rhythmic ambiguity that is of little importance for the discussion of the modal aspects.

[28] It is an open question whether a medieval performer was able to improvise pieces of such modal complexity. The mastery of the dances in the *Manuscript du roi* might well be the reason why they have been written down. Furthermore—as Martin Kirnbauer from the Basel Musicological Seminar pointed out to me—there seems to be a correction in the last *danse real*, so at least in this piece there was a certain amount of editing.

[29] For example, Joan Ambrosio Dalza, *Intabolatura de lauto libro quarto* (Venice, 1508).

[30] Conrad Paumann, *Fundamentum organisandi Magistri Conradi Paumanns Ceci de Nürenberga Anno 1452*, Berlin, Staatsbibliothek Ms. 40613, edited in Willi Apel, *Keyboard Music of the Fourteenth and Fifteenth Centuries*. See also Bertha Antonia Wallner, ed., *Das Buxheimer Orgelbuch*.

[31] While the dance music in the *manuscript du roi* is rather straightforward in its use of modal rhythm, there are some interesting aspects in the *istampitte* found in London, British Museum, Add. 29987. Facsimile edition in Gilbert Reaney, *The Manuscript London, British Museum, Add. 29987*, Musicological Studies and Documents 13, 1965.

[32] For an example of the first, see the *Kyrie* from Vienna, Nationalbibliothek Cod. 3617, edited in Willi Apel, *Keyboard Music,* for the later style, look at any of Paumann's works in Buxheim or the organ part of the Lochamer Liederbuch.

[33] A facsimile and edition of manuscript Clm 775 can be found in Theodor Göllner, *Formen früher Mehrstimmigkeit in deutschen Handschriften des späten Mittelalters* (Tutzing, 1961).

[34] For an edition of material related to the *basse danse*, see Frederick Crane, *Materials for the Study of the Fifteenth Century Basse Danse* (Brooklyn, 1968).

[35] See Otto Gombosi, *Compositione di Meser Vincenso Capirola,* The cantus Firmus Dances (Neuilly-sur-Seine, 1955).

[36] As an introduction to polyphonic ensemble improvisation, see Lewis Reece Baratz, "Improvising on the Spagna Tune," *American Recorder* (1988), and "Fifteenth-Century Improvisation, Take Two: Building a Vocabulary of Embellishments," *American Recorder* (1990).

[37] On this repertoire, see Ross W. Duffin, "Ensemble Improvisation in the 15th-Century Mensural Dance Repertoire," paper read at the conference, "Performance Practice and Repertory of Loud Minstrels in the 15th Century," at Alden Biesen, Belgium, June, 1995.

[38] Many ideas expressed in this chapter have been shaped by Ken Zuckerman's teaching at the Schola Cantorum Basiliensis as well as many discussions with Crawford Young and Jennifer Spielman.

XII. ESSENTIAL THEORY FOR PERFORMERS

36. Gamut, Solmization, & Modes

William P. Mahrt

GAMUT

The gamut is the *system* of medieval music, that is, the total range of defined notes (see Fig. 36.1). It can be described theoretically as a series of alternating conjunct and disjunct first-species tetrachords (tone-semitone-tone). These tetrachords can be expanded to hexachords by the addition of a whole step on each extreme (tone-tone-semitone-tone-tone), to which the syllables ut-re-mi-fa-sol-la are applied. The individual pitches of the gamut are designated by a series of seven letters with lower and higher octaves distinguished by capital, small, and double small letters: *A-G, a-g,* and *aa-ee;*[1] the lowest note receives the Greek letter, *Γ* (gamma), which, together with its solmization syllable, ut, gives the name to the whole system, *gamut.* These letters are the basis of the clefs, most usually *F* and *c,* but later also *g, dd,* and *Γ* itself. While the pitches of the gamut are clearly defined in relation to each other, they do not imply absolute pitch. The gamut is, rather, a closed speculative system of fixed relationships of pitches, but not of fixed pitches. Performers thus always need to keep in mind that all medieval notation is potentially "transposable" from the point of view of modern absolute pitch.[2]

The three hexachords are *natural* on *C, soft* on *F,* and *hard* on *G* (the latter two named for the soft, or round, *b,* and hard, or square, *♮,* which they contain); each has the identical pattern of whole and half steps, but is distinguished by the letter names of the pitches it includes. The crux of the hexachord is its half step, mi-fa. This occurs on *E–F* of the natural hexachord, and on *♮–c* of the hard, which locations are represented by the *F* and *c* clefs. The use of the *♭* as a signature specifies the soft hexachord, whose mi-fa is then *a–b.* The seven hexachords comprised by the gamut constitute *musica recta,* the range of established pitches; these include the two B♭s, *b* and *bb,* but not the flat on the lowest *B* of the gamut.[3] *Musica ficta,* on the other hand, is a range of additional pitches, available by imagining hexachords at other places. It includes not only the diatonic tones below *Γ* and above *ee,* but also the chromatic tones placed between the *musica recta* pitches of the gamut. These places are called *conjuncta,* and they are the location of the mi-fa of the imagined hexachords. Such *ficta* hexachords are indicated by the placement of a *♭* or *♯* on the *conjuncta;* this names the place fa or mi and implies the whole hexachord at that position (see *conjuncta* in Fig. 36.1).[4]

Fig. 36.1

A. Tetrachord

B. Hexachord

C. Gamut with hexachords and tetrachords

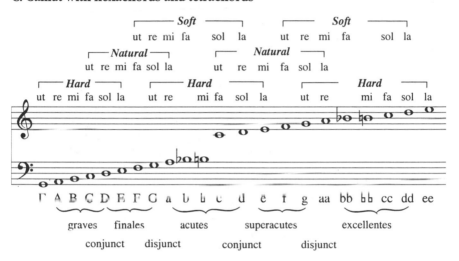

D. The most common *conjuncta*

SOLMIZATION

While the tetrachord is mainly a means of theoretical definition, the hexachord has a substantial pedagogical dimension.[5] It is pedagogically effective because its tones are expressed in discreet syllables, ut-re-mi-fa-sol-la, and because the expansion of the tetrachord to six notes, symmetrically arranged around the half-step, allows the singer a modicum of flexibility in not having to change hexachords too frequently.

Solmization is the process of naming the syllables in singing, as an aid to defining the pitches. Thus the melody *D-C-D-E-F-G-F-E-D-D-C*[6] is sung re-ut-re-mi-fa-sol-fa-mi-re-re-ut. When the melody exceeds the range of a single hexachord, the singer mutates, shifting to the adjacent hexachord by pronouncing the syllables of both the old and new hexachords on a pivotal pitch. Thus the melody *D-a-b-G-a-b-d-c-b-a-G-*

d^7 is sung re-*lare*-mi-ut-re-mi-sol-fa-mi-re-ut-re, with the mutation on the second pitch. Mutation is described as difficult by some writers, but it is a fundamentally simple process. I find that when it is apparent that a new hexachord will be needed, the notes ahead are best anticipated by mutating as early as possible, but others recommend mutating as late as possible.[8] The pronunciation of both syllables on the same pitch clarifies the relation of the two hexachords, but with a little experience it may be dropped, pronouncing only one syllable at the point of mutation. Mutation is generally not made from the soft to the hard hexachord or vice versa; this means that with no signature, the hard hexachord alternates with the natural, or, with a B♭ signature, the soft alternates with the natural; a shift between soft and hard hexachords is warranted only when there is a shift between B♮ and B♭.[9]

Solmization serves to distinguish clearly the functions and distinct character of pitches relative to each other. Thus *mi* instantly articulates the fact that it has a half step above, a whole below, etc.; saying "mi," immediately makes clear the relation of this pitch to the five others within the hexachord. Solmization has some other practical advantages: it uses all the five continental vowels, a, e, i, o, and u, and each syllable is articulated by a different consonant. Moreover, the most difficult interval, the half step, is aided by having its lower pitch set to the brightest vowel, which counteracts the tendency of singers to sing the lower note of the half step flat. Solmization thus instructs in singing as well as in reading. It even aids rhythm, since its consonants ensure a level of articulation while maintaining a variety of sounds.

Solmization also points up the affinity of tones at different points in the scale whose relation to the notes around them is identical. Thus, in the melody *a-b-a-G-a-D/F-G-a-b-a-G-F-E-D-C-D-D*[10] (mi-fa-mi-re-mi-re/fa-re-mi-fa-mi-re-fa-mi-re-ut-re-re), although the fifth *D–a* is the evident structural interval, a secondary symmetry between *d* and *G* is pointed up by their both being *re,* and in the descent *b-a-G-F-E-D,* fa-mi-re-fa-mi-re points to a symmetry that is almost motivic.

The placement of the syllables on the joints of the hand is yet another pedagogical device using hexachords (see Fig. 36.2).[11] It is remarkably simple but thoroughly effective. In a matter of a few minutes, a choir (or class) can be taught to sing from the hand by imitation. By singing the syllables with the choir, the leader easily settles any question of mutation. Moreover, the singers can have a tactile experience of the solmization by pointing to their own hands at the same time; some of them will immediately do this without being told. The pointing can even be done with only one hand: touch the joints of the thumb with the index finger; touch the joints of the fingers with the thumb. My strong recommendation to those who wish to teach solmization is to practice it well first, then have the singers do it by imitation, resorting to explanations of theory only after they have had some experience of its practice.[12]

Fig. 36.2. The Guidonian hand.

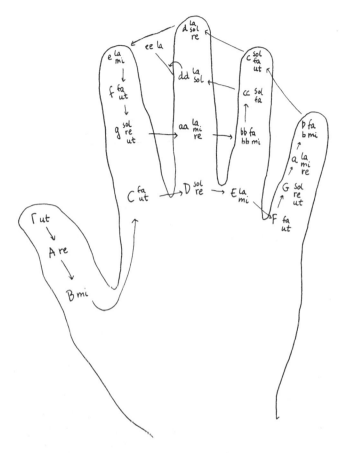

Hexachords in themselves do not designate modes—*ut* is in no way analogous to tonic. Rather they designate the pitches of the system upon which the modes are variously placed. Their syllables are used to identify the pitches and intervals of modal theory. The first-species tetrachord, D-E-F-G (re-mi-fa-sol), comprises the four principal modal finals, apparently the reason this tetrachord was the basis of the system. Solmization syllables thus characterize the functional differences of pitches as finals; thus *mi* (with a half-step above it) is a very different final from *re* or *fa*.

MODES

Earliest stage

A theory of mode was taught from the Carolingian era on, and medieval musicians were well aware of its parameters; many of the most fundamental aspects of the theory remained constant.[13] Nevertheless, during the period other aspects of both theory and practice shifted significantly, and so it is appropriate to speak, for example, of the modality of the ninth-century, or of any other century. Throughout the whole period, however, mode was much less and much more than just a scale: it was a complex system of pitch relationships and functions, whose basics were constant but whose specifics, both theoretical and practical, changed over time.

The most decisive criterion of mode is the final, the tone upon which the piece ends (see Fig. 36.3). The four finals, *D, E, F,* and *G* are the basis of the modal categories, and they are designated by the Greek ordinal numbers (in Latin form) *protus, deuterus, tritus,* and *tetrardus.* They can also be designated by the Greek place names, Dorian *(D)*, Phrygian *(E)*, Lydian *(F)*, and Mixolydian *(G)*. By the practice of solmization, they can be identified as *re, mi, fa,* and *sol* or *ut.* These finals are distinguished by the characteristic intervals closest to them; thus, F differs from G more by having a half step below it, than by the tritone above it.[14] Moreover, since Bb (on *b* and *bb*) is *musica recta,* a fundamental part of the gamut, it is easily admissible in some modes;[15] thus a mode on *a* has an identical constitution of half and whole steps as that on *D* with *b*(Bb), and these are both classed as protus. Protus, then may be placed on *D* or *a*, deuterus, on *E* or *b*, tritus, on *F* or *c*, tetrardus falls generally only on *G.* Thus, well into the sixteenth century, a mode on *C* is viewed as analogous to that on *F*, and called Lydian.

While these alternative finals (sometimes called cofinals, affinities, transpositions) were viewed as more similar to their comparable regular finals than different, there were some important differences as well, especially for the final on *a*. The possibliity of both *b* and *b* immediately above *a* makes for an ambiguity close to the final; such ambiguities can be merely passing,[16] or can contribute to a change of mode, from protus on *a* to deuterus on *a*.[17] Likewise, the final on *a* has a major third below it *(F)*, which is a perfect fifth below the mode-two reciting note *(c)*. This low *F* forms an important internal cadential point, often approached through the *b*.[18]

The next most important criterion is ambitus; on each final, the range of the chant may be either generally above the final—authentic—or generally around the final—plagal. When the Greek place names are used, the basic name designates the authentic, while the prefix hypo- indicates the plagal; thus, protus authenticus is Dorian, protus plagalis, Hypodorian. These eight modes are also designated by Arabic numbers, authentic then plagal on each final being numbered in order—mode 1: Dorian, 2: Hypodorian, 3: Phrygian, and so forth, and this eight-mode enumeration is probably the most common designation of the modes.

A principal impetus for the original classification of chant antiphons by mode was to specify the melody for the accompanying psalmody. This entailed a proper reciting note[19] for each of the eight modes, and the variation in the positions of these reciting notes relative to their finals accounts for some of the most interesting differences between modes. The position of the reciting note can be remembered this way: for the authentic modes, it is the fifth above the final, unless that note is B, in which case it is moved up to C (i.e., mode 3); for the plagal modes, it is a third below that of the associated authentic mode (including A for mode 4), unless that note is B, in which case it is moved up to C (i.e., mode 8). Not only are they the location of recitation in the psalmody, but they very often form a significant pitch focus above the final in antiphons and responsories, often bearing reiterated notes.

Fig. 36.3. The modes.

A significant aspect of the medieval tone-system, though one which received no explicit theoretical recognition in the Middle Ages, is the "chain of thirds."[20] A phenomenon first described by ethnomusicologists, it is a series of strong notes generally at intervals of thirds. Thus, observable strong notes in most Gregorian chants are *A, C, D, F, a, c, e*. Weak notes are, particularly *b*, then *e; G* and *d* are of intermediate strength. The strong notes are the location of most of the reciting notes. Moreover, they usually form a clear pitch framework upon which the whole chant melody is based. Similarly, the octave above the final is rarely an important note in the earliest chant repertory; thus in mode 1, the main notes are *D-F-a-c-e,* with *d* being subordinate.[21] It may be observed that the central pitches of this chain plus intermediate note *G* constitute a pentatonic scale, common to many music cultures.

Certain melodic figures are characteristic of each mode. The simplest of these are the psalm-tone intonations. For each mode, the conjunction of the reciting note with other strong notes seems to be the basis of a simple rising figure used to begin the psalm tone. More ample beginning figures are characteristic of each mode as well. These can be seen as the melodic connection of final and reciting note through the chain of thirds, often subsuming the simpler psalm-tone intonation. Thus a characteristic figure of mode one is *D-F-D-C-F-G-a;* beginning on the final, it touches the strong notes a step below and a third above and finally rises through the intermediate note *G* to the reciting note *a,* subsuming the psalm-tone intonation *F-G-a.* Such characteristic melodic figures differentiate one mode from the others, and derive from the differences in intervals between final and reciting note and their place in the chain of thirds. Related to these intonations are the psalm-tone *differentiae,*[22] variable endings for psalm tones which make for a smooth transition to the intonation at the repeat of the antiphon.

Another category of treatment of mode is that of a change of scale or final within a piece, that is, *modus commixtus,* or commixture. Medieval theorists paid particular attention to a body of exceptional pieces which seem to begin in one mode, move through another, and end in yet a third.[23] These exceptional and very interesting pieces shed light on the melodic process of chant, since they represent an extreme form of a process found in most melodies—the departure from and return to a principal reference pitch or pitches. It is this departure and return that gives even the simplest melody its dynamic complexity and interest and makes the modality of each piece be something much more than the realization of a flat matrix of pitches.

This principle of departure and return can be illustrated by a simple antiphon (see Ex. 36.1).

Ex. 36.1. Psalm antiphon *Justus ut palma.*[24]

Justus ut palma flo-re-bit: sicut cedrus Li-bani multipli-cabi-tur.

The antiphon begins on its final *D* but quickly moves to outline a pair of thirds, *C-E-G;* on "sicut cedrus Libani" it shifts to the third *F-a,* and then on "multiplicabitur" it passes through the next third down, *E-G* to the final *D.* At midpoint one could imagine the piece cadencing on *C* or *F,* and it is only on the arrival of the *D* final that the listener is reminded that the piece began on *D.* This ties the piece together, and the pleasure in hearing the ambiguity resolved is a fundamental part of the harmonic effect of the piece.

Pieces whose modes can be called commixture are thus but an extreme case of this principle of departure and return, sometimes not returning to the original point of departure, but rather creating a focus on a related final; the movement through two or three implicit finals makes for an extraordinarily persuasive piece.

Ex. 36.2. Introit *Deus in adjutorium meum intende.*[25]

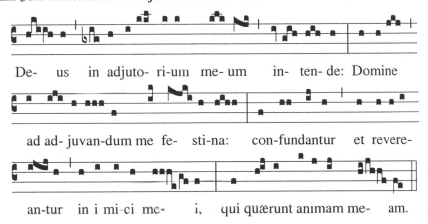

De- us in adjuto- ri-um me- um   in- ten- de: Domine

ad ad- juvan-dum me fe- sti-na: con-fundantur   et revere-

an-tur in i mi-ci me-   i,   qui quærunt animam me-   am.

For example, the introit *Deus in adjutorium meum intende* (see Ex. 36.2) begins in mode 0 on *c*; it has the whole step below the final on *b* (B♭), and a reciting tone a fourth above the final on *f* (characterized by reiterated syllable on that tone). The first shift is away from the *f* reciting note; on "Domine ad adjuvandum" *e* is more prominent and leads directly to *d*, and for the rest of the phrase the emphasis shifts between *d* and *c*. At "confundantur . . ." the *c* has become more prominent; at the conclusion of that phrase *b* (B♭) is introduced, and the shift of focus is very apparent; it is only completed with the ultimate descent to *G*, which now has to be heard as the final; because of the prominence of *c*, the piece now sounds like mode 8 on *G*. Yet, in retrospect, because of the higher range of the whole piece, and perhaps because of the passing emphasis upon *d*, the medieval classification of the whole piece was mode 7. The course of the piece thus entails emphasis upon a succession of stepwise descending pitches which, in turn, reflects a succession of modal references. With such a striking descent, this chant belongs to that group of pieces whose texts speak of the descent of divine aid from on high and whose melodies represent an exceptional descending contour.[26]

Later stages

A second stage in the historical development of modal theory and practice is the definition of the interval species. The modes can be distinguished by considering the fifth above the final and by noting the position of the half step among the intervening notes. Among the notes that fill in a perfect fifth, there are four possible places for the half step, and thus four species of fifth. These four species fall naturally on the four finals of the modes (see Fig. 36.4). Likewise there are three species of fourth, depending upon the place of the half step. Through them ambitus can be differentiated by the placement of the species of fourth conjunctly with the fifth, either above for the authentic modes, or below for the plagal modes. This conception of mode solved a specific theoretical problem: how can the scale-wise construction of modes best be represented to show the identity of authentic and plagal on the same final, when they do not share the same octave species? What they do share exactly is the same fifth, and the same fourth, and the placement of this fourth above or below the fifth differentiates between authentic and plagal. The interval species can be identified by the solmization syllables:

Fig. 36.4. Later developments of the modes.

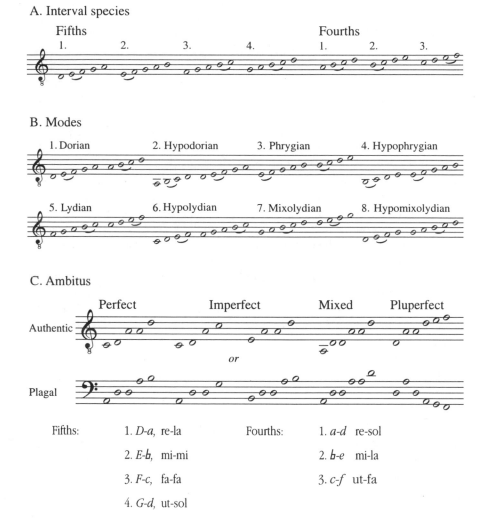

A. Interval species

B. Modes

C. Ambitus

Fifths:	1. *D-a,* re-la	Fourths:	1. *a-d* re-sol
	2. *E-b,* mi-mi		2. *b-e* mi-la
	3. *F-c,* fa-fa		3. *c-f* ut-fa
	4. *G-d,* ut-sol		

The interval species may have been purely theoretical at first, but they had significant ramifications for composition, since melodies composed at later stages of history often show the fifth and fourth as a framework, either in the complete filling out of an octave ambitus, or in the distinct melodic development of fifth and fourth. Comparison of earlier and later antiphons in the same mode illustrates this difference: the mode-1 antiphons *Majorem caritatem, Vos amici mei estis, Beati pacifici,* and *In patientia*[27] represent the earlier style in which the upper octave is not touched; *Sacerdos in aeternum* and *Gloria tibi Trinitas*[28] on the other hand, both pointedly fill out the upper fourth of mode 1 in one of their phrases.

The development of the interval species brings a clearer definition of the difference between authentic and plagal ambitus, and their use within a single composition. Longer pieces, such as sequences, need some sense of formal distinction between the parts of the piece, and this is often achieved by shifting between the two ambitus on the common final in the course of the piece. For example, in the sequence *Victimae paschali laudes,*[29] each successive phrase has a different description in the use of the fifth and fourth as the framework of the melody:

> Phrase 1: the basic fifth *D-a* with a single note below, using only notes common
>   to both plagal and authentic ambitus.
> Phrase 2: the fourth above added, filling out the complete authentic range.
> Phrase 3: the fourth below added to the fifth, filling out the plagal range.
> Phrase 4: a return to the fourth above and the complete authentic range.

NB: each new phrase begins with the fourth proper to its particular ambitus, pointing up the distinction of ambitus between phrases contributed by the placement of the species of fourth.

This is called a mixed mode—mixing the authentic and plagal belonging to a common final.

Ambitus plays an important part in distinguishing the parts of the *formes fixes.* In the religious villancicos of the *Cantigas de Santa Maria*[30] as well as in the miniature dance songs of the trouvères,[31] the A and B sections are set off by contour and ambitus, often particularly emphasizing the difference at the inital point of the B section.

By the fourteenth century, ambitus had become the subject of finely drawn distinctions. Marchetto defined ambitus as imperfect, perfect, or pluperfect (see Fig. 36.4.C): perfect—filling out the octave range plus one note (below the authentic, above the plagal octaves); imperfect—not filling out the perfect range; and pluperfect—exceeding it.[32] These distinctions seem to be highly scholastic and are often overlooked in the study of mode. Yet the distinction between imperfect and perfect ambitus is an important difference in both monophonic and polyphonic music. Guillaume de Machaut makes subtle and effective use of such differences in his monophonic chansons. In the virelai *Foy porter,*[33] for example, the A section consists of a rhetorical *climax,*—the placing of similar elements in ascending order—touching briefly upon the seventh note above the final, but never reaching the octave, thus, imperfect in ascent. The B section begins with the octave, descending to the second note above the final, thus reversing the contour, making effective use of a complementary ambitus imperfect in ascent, made perfect only at the second ending of the B section. These points are correlated with important semantic points in the text to create a superb marrying of text and music.[34]

Modes in polyphony

Mode may also pertain to polyphonic music, since it is the contrapuntal conjunction of melodic parts; it may even have played a formative part in their conception. To be sure, the voice-parts of a polyphonic piece must be constructed differently from independent melodies, since these parts must respond to each other and make a harmonious whole. Nevertheless, even in pieces which are not based on pre-existent chant melodies, one can observe melodic organization of individual voices that can be called modal. It is especially ambitus and the species of fifths and fourths that become prominent in polyphonic writing; reciting note and melodic intonation formulae sometimes also come into play. It is another question whether mode is significant for the polyphonic complex as a whole. It is true that theorists treat mode and counterpoint in very separate parts of their treatises or even in separate, unrelated treatises. Yet the Berkeley treatise states that mode is important for polyphony, albeit without specifying how.[35] It remained for Tinctoris to specify some of the principles of polyphonic modality: the mode of the piece resides principally in the tenor; the other parts may be in the same mode or associated modes, or even in contrasting ones.[36] While this may be a kind of Renaissance scholasticism, it reflects phenomena that can be observed in the repertories, especially those of the fourteenth century. Between the two-part structural voices (tenor and discant) of a polyphonic piece there existed in the works of several Italian and some French composers of the fourteenth century a normative relationship—if the tenor is plagal, the discant is authentic, and vice versa.[37] This allows for harmonic intervals from the unison to the twelfth and for the characteristic cadential progression of the sixth to the octave, and might therefore be principally for contrapuntal reasons. But the fact that the ambitus of each part is so frequently clearly comprised of fifths and fourths and outlines the octave suggests that cartain aspects of mode are important to these polyphonic pieces.[38]

By the time of Guillaume Dufay, and particularly in his chansons, there is a more highly self-conscious treatment of mode, especially in the interval species.[39] The chanson, with its clearly distinct lines of poetry was an ideal place for this development: each line of poetry receives a melodic and contrapuntal treatment which subtly distinguishes that line from the others. Each phrase clearly outlines interval species and contributes to a pattern of overall variety. Thus, the successive lines of the chanson *Adieu m'amour*[40] are:

Discant:	1. Hypolydian imperfect	2. commixture (Dorian)	3. Hypolydian perfect
Tenor:	1: Hypolydian perfect	2. commixture (Dorian)	3. Hypolydian perfect

4. Hypolydian imperfect	5. Hypolydian perfect
4. mixture Lydian perfect	5. Hypolydian perfect

The same paradigm serves the chansons of Ockeghem and Busnois, but each has his own personal style of employing it.

What does mode have to do with performance? The beauty of monophonic music resides in part in the harmonious relationship of the notes of the melody, a hierarchical relation in which each note has its own particular function, articulated by syllables and ordered in one mode or another. This can be expressed in the treatment of the individual notes, giving each note more or less weight and motion depending upon its function and position in the overall melodic contour. An incomplete ambitus can be left as such, the completion of a perfect ambitus can be a point of arrival, the extension upward into a pluperfect ambitus calls for an intense and exceptional kind of expression. An effective speaker intuitively emphasizes the important words in a sentence, but the study of grammar and rhetoric can clarify how and why those words are important. Likewise, the study of solmization and modes can clarify which notes are important and why; the singer need not always think of each note and its relative weight, but at least, reflection on these phenomena can establish and strengthen an intuitive sense of nuance which will be the basis for expressive singing of the melody. The same is true of the parts of a polyphonic piece; even though a part plays a role in counterpoint, it is still melodic, comprehension of its modal constitution aids the projection of its structure as an integral part of the expression.

Notes

[1] Letters in italics represent the specific locations on the gamut throughout this chapter; letters in Roman capitals represent the pitch class in general.

[2] Concerning transposition, see the argument from the ranges of modes in chapter 1 on Gregorian chant, above. For a theory of a transposition of the gamut itself, see Andrew Hughes, *Manuscript Accidentals: Ficta in Focus, 1350–1450*, Musicological Studies and Documents 27 (American Institute of Musicology, 1972).

[3] This is because there is no hexachord on F below Γ; see Margaret Bent, "Musica Recta and Musica Ficta," *Musica Disciplina*, 26 (1972), 81.

[4] Oliver Ellsworth, ed. & trans., *The Berkeley Manuscript: University of California Music Library Ms. 744 (olim Phillips 4450)*, Greek and Latin Music Theory (Lincoln, 1984), pp. 1–2, 50–67, 94–97; and Karol Berger, *Musica Ficta: Theories of Accidental Inflections in Vocal Polyphony from Marchetto da Padova to Gioseffo Zarlino* (Cambridge, 1987), pp. 48–55.

[5] For the theoretical dimension of the hexachord, see Richard Crocker, "Hermann's Major Sixth," *Journal of the American Musicological Society*, 25 (1972), 19–37.

[6] The antiphon *Justus ut palma*, see Ex. 36.1.

[7] *Ave maris stella*, the hymn for Vespers of Feasts of the Blessed Virgin Mary, *Liber Usualis* (Tournai, 1963), p. 1257.

[8] See Andrew Hughes, "Solmization, I. European Medieval and Renaissance Systems," *The New Grove Dictionary of Music and Musicians*, ed. Stanley Sadie (New York, 1980), vol. 17, p. 460.

9   For illustrations of mutation see Rob C. Wegman, "Musica ficta," in *Companion to Medieval and Renaissance Music,* ed. Tessa W. Knighton and David Fallows (London, 1992), pp. 265-74.

10   *Kyrie Orbis factor, Liber,* p. 6.

11   It should be noted that the position of *ee* la is the first joint on the *back* of the middle finger, not off the hand, as is sometimes mistaken from illustrations of the hand; see Karol Berger, "The Hand and the Art of Memory," *Musica Disciplina* 35 (1982), 94.

12   For some challenging exercises in solmization from the period, see Ellsworth, *The Berkeley Manuscript,* pp. 89–97.

13   See Harold S. Powers, "Mode," *New Grove* 12, pp. 376–450; Frederick Sturges Andrews, "Mediaeval Modal Theory" (Ph.D. diss., Cornell Univ., [1935]); and David Hiley, *Western Plainchant: A Handbook* (Oxford, 1993), pp. 442–77.

14   This is the principle called "the modal nucleus" in Andrews, *Medieval Modal Theory,* pp. 111–22.

15   B♭ (on *b*) is freely admitted in those modes where the reciting tone is *a*; this pitch normally has whole tones on either side of it unless a *b* is introduced above it; this *b* is found in modes 1, 4, and 6, where it clarifies the reciting tone *a* by placing a half step above it, and in mode 5, where it ameliorates the tritone with the final; it is less frequently found in mode 3, where the *b* a perfect fifth above the final seems to be more important, and it is generally not found in modes 7 and 8, where it would contradict the major third above the final.

16   See the graduals of the melody type *Justus ut palma,* particularly *Haec dies, Liber,* pp. 778–79.

17   See the large group of antiphons of the type *Apud Dominum misericordiam, Liber,* p. 412 *et passim.*

18   See the gradual *Justus ut palma,* on the word "cedrus"; *Liber,* p. 1201; this is a note that the final on *D* cannot provide, since there is no B♭ in the lowest octave of the gamut.

19   Also called *repercussa, tenor, tuba,* or dominant; I avoid the term dominant as too easily confused with the fifth degree, witness the erroneous statement, "The main note of the recitation . . . is always the fifth degree of the mode," in Willi Apel, *Harvard Dictionary of Music,* 2nd ed. (Cambridge, MA, 1969), s.v. "Psalm tone."

20   See Curt Sachs, *The Wellsprings of Music,* ed. Jaap Kunst (New York, 1965), pp. 143–52.

21   For an example of a piece that uses a clear series of thirds, see the introit *Suscepimus Deus, Liber,* p. 1361; for a piece based upon an alternative set of thirds, see *Qui timet Dominum,* the antiphon to Ps. 111 for Sunday Vespers, *Liber,* p. 254.

22   Or *saeculorum amen,* so called because they are often notated over the vowels of these final words of the doxology (euouae), which normally concludes the performance of every psalm; see *Liber,* pp. 112–17.

23   A number of these pieces are listed in the "Annotated Catalogue of Chants," in Christopher Page, ed. and tr., *The Summa musice. A Thirteenth-Century Manual for Singers,* Cambridge Musical Texts and Monographs (Cambridge, 1991), pp. 245–70; the chants with commixture are those showing more than one mode in the listing of modal categories.

24   *Justus ut palma florebit,* antiphon to Ps. 91 of Matins for the Common of a Single Martyr from the Italian tradition (Lucca Codex), in Peter Wagner, *Gregorianische Formenlehre: Eine choralische Stilkunde,* 3rd ed., Part Three of *Einführung in die gregorianischen Melodien: Ein Handbuch der Choralwissenschaft* (Leipzig, 1921; reprint, Hildesheim, 1970), p. 11.

[25] The introit for the Twelfth Sunday after Pentecost, *Liber,* pp. 1027–28; see Andrews, *Mediaeval Modal Theory,* pp. 128–29.

[26] See William Peter Mahrt, "Word-Painting and Formulaic Chant," in *Cum angelis canere: Essays on Sacred Music and Pastoral Liturgy in Honour of Richard J. Schuler,* ed. Robert A. Skeris (St. Paul, 1990 [1992]), pp. 113–44.

[27] For the First Vespers in the Common of Apostles and Evangelists, *Liber,* pp. 1111–12.

[28] For Second Vespers of Corpus Christi, *Liber,* p. 956, and Second Vespers of Trinity Sunday, *Liber,* p. 914; both these offices, in addition, show another systematic approach to mode: they are so-called "numerical offices," in which the antiphons are composed in numerical order of mode; each of these is the first antiphon of Vespers (to Ps. 109).

[29] *Liber,* p. 780.

[30] See Gerardo Victor Huseby, "The *Cantigas de Santa Maria* and the Medieval Theory of Mode" (Ph.D. diss., Stanford University, 1982).

[31] See, for example, Archibald T. Davison and Willi Apel, *Historical Anthology of Music,* vol. 1: *Oriental, Medieval and Renaissance Music,* rev. ed. (Cambridge, MA, 1959), pp. 16–17; for a discussion of modes in the music of the Troubadours and Trouvères, see Theodore Karp, "Troubadours, trouvères 3, 2: Modality," *New Grove* 19, pp. 199–201.

[32] The pluperfect ambitus exceeds the normal range in the opposite direction from the mixed, in other words, beyond the species of fourth.

[33] Guillaume de Machaut, *Works,* vol. 2, Polyphonic Music of the Fourteenth Century, vol. 3 (Monaco, 1956), p. 181; see Phyllis Rugg Brown and William Peter Mahrt, "The Interplay of Language and Music in Machaut's Virelai 'Foy Porter'," in *Tradition and Ecstasy—The Agony of the Fourteenth Century* (New York, 1996), pp. 235-50.

[34] For a system of analysis of fourteenth-century music not dependent upon strictly modal categories see Peter M. Lefferts, "Signature-Systems and Tonal Types in the Fourteenth-Century French Chanson," *Plainsong and Medieval Music* 4 (1985), 117–47; Yolanda Plumley, *The Grammar of 14th Century Melody: Tonal Organization and Compositional Process in the Chansons of Guillaume de Machaut and the Ars Subtilior* (New York, 1996); for an argument against modal analysis, see Kevin N. Moll, "Structural Determinants in Polyphony for the Mass Ordinary from French and Related Sources (ca. 1320-1410)" (Ph.D. diss., Stanford University, 1994), pp. 112–14.

[35] Ellsworth, *Berkeley Manuscript,* pp. 2–4, 75.

[36] Johannes Tinctoris, *Liber de natura et proprietate tonorum,* chapters 18 and 24, in *Opera Theoretica,* ed. Albert Seay, Corpus Scriptorum de Musica 22 (American Institute of Musicology, 1975), vol. 1, pp. 81, 85–86

[37] See George Louis Nemeth, "The Secular Music of Johannes Ciconia (ca.1335–1411)" (Ph.D. diss., Stanford University, 1977), pp. 112–14.

[38] This is thus the beginning of what becomes codified in the Renaissance, the alternation of authentic and plagal ambitus between voices, i.e., if soprano and tenor are plagal, alto and bass are authentic, and vice versa.

[39] See William Peter Mahrt, "Guillaume Dufay's Chansons in the Phrygian Mode," *Studies in Music from the University of Western Ontario* 5 (1980), 81–98.

[40] Guillaume Dufay, *Cantiones,* ed. Heinrich Besseler, rev. David Fallows, *Opera Omnia,* vol. 6 (Stuttgart, 1996), p. 91.

37. Musica Ficta
Lucy E. Cross

Twentieth-century performers do not usually trouble to distinguish between the medieval and the modern meanings of the term "*musica ficta*." As we become more comfortable with supplying and performing the accidentals that are required, but not notated, in medieval and Renaissance music, we come to refer to them ever more carelessly as "ficta." But strictly speaking, not every chromatic alteration or accidental sign is properly "ficta." Nor, on the other hand, is "ficta" confined to the accidentals that appear above the staff in modern editions. To the medieval musician, "*musica ficta*" meant a collection of pitches available in musical performance that were not part of the normal gamut: specifically, the semitones not provided in the normal three transpositions of the Guidonian hexachord.

Notes that were "*extra manum*," or "outside the [Guidonian] Hand," were used in polyphony when contrapuntal movement, if confined to the pitches of the normal scale, would produce vertical intervals that were undesirable.[1] A change in inflection "for the sake of necessity" (*causa necessitatis*) corrected diminished or augmented fifths and octaves between voices; an alteration "for the sake of beauty" (*causa pulchritudinis*) enhanced the contrapuntal momentum as thirds moved to fifths or unisons, or sixths moved to octaves. When changes for either cause were called for (and the technical requirements of this kind of "beauty" were no less imperative than those of necessity), they may or may not have been notated, for it was generally felt to be redundant, even wasteful, to write something that was universally understood.

Extrasystematic notes—notes outside the gamut—were considered "fiction" or "false" (they were originally termed "*musica falsa*") not because they were sometimes used without being signed, nor because their existence was imaginary, but rather because they were reached by imagined transpositions of regular hexachords, each made up of the solmization syllables "ut re mi fa sol la."[2] Theoretically, a note given a sharp (♯) or square b (♮) would be a new "mi"; one given a flat (♭) would be a "fa." In practice, musicians would often have occasion to alter a single pitch without executing the actual hexachord transposition that theory required. Some writers took the "falseness" in such a case to be in the solmization, since the semitone then occurred between syllables other than mi and fa (as when g-♯-g was sung sol-fa-sol).[3]

B♭, because it was found on the Guidonian Hand as part of the regular hexachord beginning on F, was never "fictive" or "false," although, like other "accidentals," it might not be specifically notated. Nor would medieval musicians have imagined that the two "*causae*" (*necessitatis* and *pulchritudinis*) were the "rules of *musica ficta*," since these rules applied as well to pitch alteration within the system, from B to B♭ and vice-versa. *Ficta* were simply the extrasystematic notes that the rules of alteration in counterpoint might make necessary.

Because accidentals in the Middle Ages and Renaissance, both within and outside the system, were incompletely and inconsistently notated, "*musica ficta*" has come to represent a complex of unforgiving problems that demand solutions in editions or performances of music from those periods. For us, the term means "application of sharps and flats," and most of our discussions of it center upon the situations in which we do or do not change inflections.[4] Medieval musicians would not have understood our terminology or our problems at all, although it does appear that performers of the Renaissance, while not sharing exactly the same difficulties, would have sympathized.

The modern performer's or editor's task is complicated by three factors. First, we are attempting to deal with four centuries of music armed with only two or three guidelines formulated in the mid-fourteenth century. Because the application of unwritten accidentals depended wholly upon contrapuntal progressions, when styles of counterpoint changed (with imitative writing, thickened textures, bass-dominated consonances, suspensions, and so on), new problems of inflection arose and new solutions had to be found. At the same time, the medieval guidelines were handed on and taught essentially unchanged until the advent of functional key-based harmony.

Second, to make matters worse, in an effort to fill the gaps in our understanding, modern scholars have repeatedly resorted to medieval rules on plainchant, even though those rules do not apply to polyphonic settings. "Una nota supra la semper est canendum fa" is one of them, as is the prohibition of the tritone[5] and the invariable reading of B♭ in the F-modes.[6] Applications of these rules have sometimes resulted in the tendency of flats to reproduce themselves *ad infinitum* at the fourth.

Last, and worst, accidentals in manuscript sources are unreliable. They may appear under, over, inches before or after the notes to which they should belong, or not at all; they are entirely incompatible with ligatures.[7] Contrary to expectation, scribes were not ordinarily musicians; indeed, the more they exercised musical judgement, the more likely they were to edit the music to suit themselves. They misread sharp-shapes, copied them as flats, and moved them about the staff to places that looked more likely. They put temporary accidentals into the signatures, and reproduced those signatures where they did not belong. The most venerable of scribal traditions was a reluctance to waste ink on signs that might appear redundant or obvious, and thus offend the sensibilities of trained musicians.

Owing to this confused state of affairs, musicological or "source-critical" editions upon which we depend are frequently less than satisfactory to performers for the very reason that their main purpose is to reproduce the hard documentary evidence. Some scholarly editors, recognizing the problems, have attempted to overlay their readings from manuscript or print with all the accidentals required by "performance practice" as they understand it.[8] Faced with a multitude of modern editorial styles, many musicians might prefer to consult or even read from the original notation.

Every performer at one time or another will be called upon to revise an edition at hand, old or modern, and this will require a great deal of experience, musicianship, sensibility, and nerve. I do not subscribe, however, to the currently widespread opinion that the choice of accidentals is meant to be up to the editor or player. "*Causa pulchritudinis*" does *not* mean "because it sounds beautiful to me." Serious decision-making responsibility begins when the rules, signatures, manuscript versions, or other guides appear to conflict: we must choose which to follow, and with what kind of consistency. The goal is of course to get as close as possible to what the composer intended.

The Rules

The rules or guidelines for chromatic alteration in counterpoint were fairly well established by the mid-fourteenth century. The following five points include them along with some other considerations that twentieth-century performers must bear in mind:

POINT 1: Whenever thirds or sixths progress to fifths or octaves, "for the sake of beauty" ("CAUSA PULCHRITUDINIS") they must be major; whenever thirds progress to unisons or lower fifths, "for the sake of beauty" they must be minor. Alteration from one type of interval to another may be accomplished with either a flat or a sharp.

For the following examples I have dispensed with conventional clefs, since any of the configurations may appear regularly in any of the three transpositions of the hexachord. Thus, the flat sign indicates the position of the "fa" note—C, F, or B♭—in one of the normal hexachords. In many positions, actual alteration of the other notes by an accidental sign is not necessary.

Ex. 37.1. Progressions to re, mi, and fa (or ut) in the Tenor.

To octaves or unisons:

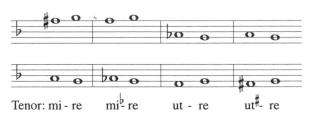

Tenor: mi - re   mi♭- re   ut - re   ut♯- re

Tenor: fa - mi   fa - mi   re - mi

Tenor: sol - fa (re-ut)   mi - fa

To fifths:[9]

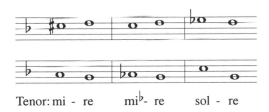

Tenor: mi - re   mi♭- re   sol - re

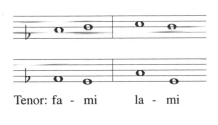

Tenor: fa - mi   la - mi

Tenor: sol - fa (re-ut)   fa - ut

When these guidelines are applied to three-voice counterpoint (which is in essence the conflation of two counterpoints upon one tenor), the frequent result, M6/M3 leading to P8/P5, is what we familiarly call "double-leading-tone"

499

movement. (This is a modern term; the word "cadence" for such a progression is too restrictive to be appropriate.) It does not occur when the the lowest voice progresses down a half-step, fa-mi, since the upper voices move by whole-step).

Ex. 37.2. "Double-leading-tone" progressions.

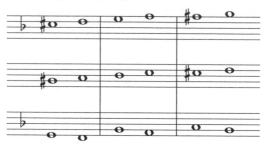

Tenor: mi - re   sol - fa (re-ut)   la - sol(re-ut)

Unusual chromatic progressions are caused not by unconventional placement of accidentals, but by unusual voice-leading. The Agnus Dei of Machaut's Mass is a case in point. The Contratenor outlines the augmented triad, which would never be found in a plainchant melody. In polyphony, however, it sounds unstartlingly smooth.[10]

Ex. 37.3. Guillaume de Machaut, Agnus Dei, *Messe de Nostre Dame.*

POINT 2: Whenever there is a unison, fifth, or octave (or multiple thereof) THAT IS NOT INVOLVED IN AN IMPERFECT-TO-PERFECT PROGRESSION, that interval must be perfect "for the sake of necessity" ("CAUSA NECESSITATIS"). If one voice comes to rest on B♭, for example, and there is a fifth below it in another voice, that fifth must be E♭.

In the vertical dimension, augmented unisons, augmented or diminished octaves, and diminished fifths must be corrected, but NOT TRITONES—augmented fourths (three whole tones). The "correction" of a vertical tritone to a fourth does not make a better consonance in fourteenth-century theoretical terms, and wherever it is done, the true reason for it is the correction of a complementary diminished fifth. A fourth by itself is just as dissonant as a tritone, but lacks the tritone's contrapuntal force. Thus, the tritone noted in Ex. 37.4 should not be "corrected."

Ex. 37.4. Machaut, Rondeau *Ce qui soustient moy.*

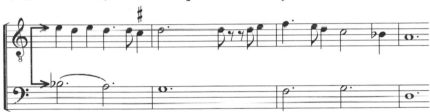

Guidelines for the correction of melodic tritones in plainchant are valid, but such rules should not be applied to polyphonic music, except where the vocal line is derived from, or imitative of, plainsong. Even so, plainsong-derived melodies in counterpoint are frequently subject to alteration as well.[11] Some fourteenth- and fifteenth-century theorists—and not a few modern writers—confuse the issue by calling diminished fifths "tritones."

POINT 3: Where the two rules would seem to call for contradictory solutions, contrapuntal momentum or tension favors the rule of PULCHRITUDINIS over NECESSITATIS; in such situations extrahexachordal and chromatic intervals, even augmented fifths, are usual.

Ex. 37.5. Machaut, Ballade *Amours me fait.*

Ex. 37.6. Giovanni da Cascia, Madrigal *Sedendo all' ombra.*

Ex. 37.7. Giovanni, Madrigal *Nascoso el bel viso.*

A progression that calls for alteration of thirds or sixths does not necessarily have to be resolved to a perfect consonance. "Deceptive" or avoided resolutions are characteristic particularly of Jacopo and Machaut.

In a case like the following Machaut example (Ex. 37.8), the pitch alteration is not itself "unconventional," although the progression that follows it certainly is.[12]

Ex. 37.8. Machaut, Sanctus, from *Messe de Nostre Dame*.

By Du Fay's time, and even by the time of Machaut's imitators in the late fourteenth century, the most aberrant chromaticisms (caused not by the unconventional application of sharps and flats, but by unconventional voice-leading) have begun to disappear. The famous *Fumeux fume* of Solage, for instance, though it includes an extraordinary number of signed and unsigned inflections, is conservative in the number of times the progressions suggested by those accidentals are avoided.

POINT 4: A single accidental, be it in a signature or within a musical text, affects the inflection of only one degree.

Since a ♭ implies nothing but fa, and a square b (♮) or ♯ nothing but mi, one accidental can transpose only one hexachord, not a whole octave, and not the entire Guidonian Hand. That single accidental may of course cause a coordinated inflection of a note a perfect fifth below in another voice, if there is a pause or hold on it.

In three-voice settings in the F-modes, B♮ is the predominant inflection of the fourth degree in the Contratenor, since that voice most frequently comes to rest on C when the Tenor moves from G to F.

Even when they appear in unusual places, accidentals may not always indicate fictive transposition of hexachords, i.e., *coniunctae*. Some accidentals demonstrably apply only to individual pitches, and do not involve whole hexachords. In these cases, the accidentals indicate false solmization rather than false mutation.

POINT 5: The guidelines may be followed with confidence, even when the notation contradicts them.

We must remember that when theorists first wrote of *causa necessitatis* and *causa pulchritudinis*, they were describing the music as it was composed, not making prescriptions for notating it or reading it off the page. Now we use these "rules" as aids to interpretation, which they were never meant to be. If we bear in mind that they describe the counterpoint and no more, we can usually determine, regardless of markings in the musical sources, whether any given interval is chromatically altered or not, even to the point of contradicting the given signatures.

In the overwhelming majority of cases, accidentals provided by the scribes are also dictated by contrapuntal movement. But where they are not, I do not see any compelling reason to attend to them.

Beyond these five basic points, I would like to review a few facts and questions that arise from them.

EXTRAHEXACHORDAL INTERVALS ARE PART OF THE VOCABULARY OF POLYPHONY.

In music up to about 1440, including early Du Fay, the consistent application of *causa pulchritudinis* results in diminished and augmented intervals in both the vertical and horizontal dimensions. Not to heed and appreciate this "chromaticism" is to neglect the subtle flavors and colors that distinguish styles—in many instances, it is to miss the musical point.

THE CADENCE IS NOT TECHNICALLY A FACTOR AFFECTING ALTERATION.

According to the strictest construction of fourteenth- and fifteenth-century guidelines, chromatic alteration is dependent neither upon approaching "cadences," nor upon any purely melodic conformations, but only upon intervals in counterpoint.[13] Because a cadence is most often a stepwise "fall" in the Tenor part, and the other parts approach perfect consonances in contrary motion, the conditions requiring alteration are of course almost always present.

By Josquin's time, thicker vocal textures, along with a growing focus upon modality and modulation, may have led, or forced, composers to treat the sixth-to-octave progression differently in the middle of a phrase, while following the usual process at a cadence. The first writer to associate "cadence" with pitch alteration was Zarlino in 1558: he said simply that everybody, even fools and rustics, raised the leading tone to the final of a mode. But he did not imply that there was any rule to cover it, just that Nature led them to do so.[14]

SIGNATURES NEED NEVER BE THOUGHT "PARTIAL" OR "CONFLICTING."

The controversy over "partial" or "conflicting" signatures (i.e., differences among the written signatures of different parts in a single piece) is something of a wild goose chase. Since it was by no means necessary to notate an accidental that was clearly intended, discrepancies among signatures cannot be in conflict. A flat in the signature makes an essential difference, as definer of the mode, only if the final is G or A, and only if it is in the cantus or tenor part. Otherwise, a signature flat (or its absence) does not carry much more authority than a flat before a note (or its absence), and may be dismissed as easily. Scribes appear frequently to have adopted the inflections of the first phrase of a piece of music into signatures for the whole, regardless of their pertinence.[15]

HOW LONG DOES AN ACCIDENTAL APPLY?

In the absence of modern bar-lines, which carry the power of cancellation of accidentals, how are we to know how long a sharp or flat should continue to apply? Where the alteration is *causa pulchritudinis*, the resolution of the contrapuntal progression is clearly the terminus, but in cases of *necessitatis*, an accidental may imply a change of mode, from which there may be no return.

A provisional approach to the problem taken by several modern musicians is to retain the accidental until the range of the melody exceeds that of the transposed hexachord (*coniuncta*) necessary to it. This practice is based upon Tinctoris (1476): "If [a flat] is placed at the beginning of a line, the whole *cantus* will be sung with *b mollis*. If, however, it is placed in any other location, the *cantus* will be sung with *b mollis* for as long as the *deductio* (hexachord) in which it is prefaced lasts."[16] It is not at all clear, however, to what extent this Renaissance approach is valid in medieval music.

Exceedingly difficult situations arise when elaborate figurations or divisions (particularly like those of the trecento) obscure the point at which a given pitch is felt to begin participating in a progression, when we must decide how much *before* the appearance of the sharp or flat in the manuscript, or *before* its obvious requirement in the counterpoint, it should apply.

NOT EVERY PROBLEM HAS A VERIFIABLE, WATER-TIGHT SOLUTION.

As the Renaissance approaches, the new compositional technique of vocal imitation begins to pose another vexing question: are points of imitation always to be intervallically congruent at the fifth? at the fourth? at the second? Even some caccias of the trecento, in strict canonic imitation at the unison, appear to violate the rules unless the two voices are read differently (the intrepid reader is referred to Jacopo da Bologna's *Giunge'l bel tempo*).

In conclusion, I examine two problematic examples from Jacopo da Bologna's *Aquil' altera*, not so much to give a definitive reading, but to show the typical train of thought one might ride to a working solution.

The sixth *e-c'* progressing to the octave *d-d'* in Ex. 37.9 must, *causa pulchritudinis*, be major, i.e., *e-c♯'*.[17] But the second Cantus at that moment sounds a *g*, which makes an undesirable diminished fifth with the *c♯*. The *g* does not proceed upward to a perfect consonance with the tenor—indeed it is the highest note of the line and proceeds downward—so there is no reason to raise it to *g♯*. If we do accept *c♯* against *g♮* (contrary to *necessitatis*, but favored because of the contrapuntal momentum), we must then consider all the *c*'s in the preceding phrase and ask at which point in the phrase *c* begins to be active in the process of moving to *d*, thus whether the alteration to *c♯* should be made earlier, and how much earlier. *Causae pulchritudinis* (with the second Cantus) argue for alteration of c at the eighth minim (sixteenth note) of the upper voice, but it will sound a tritone against the G in the tenor, as will the first minim of the measure.

Ex. 37.9. Jacopo da Bologna, *Aquil' altera*, m. 12.

In the Ritornello of the same piece, the performer encounters the daunting tangle shown in Ex. 37.10. Considering the counterpoint in m. 37 (a progression to *d-a-[d']* from *e-g#-c#*) as well as the sources (all four sources give *c#* for the Cantus, two also give a sharp for the *g* of the second voice), these "leading tones" must be raised. One source provides a sharp for the earlier *c* in the upper voice, but none provides one for the simultaneous *g* in the second. If that *g* were to be raised, the question would arise whether or not to raise the following *f* as well, in order to avoid a melodic augmented second. Yet that *f* may not be raised without violating the perfection of its octave relationship with the lowest voice. If, again, the *f* is *not* raised, a melodic augmented second will sound with the following *g#* (there is no rule to forbid this). There might also be some question whether, if the earlier *g#* in m. 36 is raised, the *c* preceding it (despite the intermission of a rest) should be raised also, because of its fifth-relationship to *g#*, and its cross-relation to the upcoming *c#* in the upper voice. Thus it appears that, although given by the editor as authentic, the *c#* in m. 36 is a scribal error; indeed, on the most detailed level, *causa pulchritudinis* cannot apply here since the tenor does not move down to *d*.

Ex. 37.10. Jacopo da Bologna, *Aquil' altera*, mm. 36-37.

There is no cut to this Gordian knot that does not produce some kind of extrahexachordal "chromaticism." Nor, unhappily, any way to know indeed what Jacopo intended. You are on your own.

Notes

[1] For one fifteenth-century definition of *ficta* as pitches outside the Hand, see Johannes Tinctoris, *Diffinitorum*, Cap. vi, s.v. "Ficta musica." The Carl Parrish translation and edition, *Dictionary of Musical Terms* (Glencoe, Illinois, 1963), 32-33, misinterprets the Latin abbreviation for "praeter" as that for "propter," thus rendering "because of" where it should read "outside of." The following list contains some of the more important studies on the subject of *musica ficta* in our era: Edward E. Lowinsky, foreword to *Musica Nova accommodata per Cantar et Sonar Organi*, edited by H. Colin Slim, Monuments of Renaissance Music I (Chicago and London, 1964), viii-ix; also his "Adrian Willaert's Chromatic 'Duo' Re-examined," *Tijdschrift voor Muziekwetenschap* 18 (1959), 1-36, and "Echoes of Adrian Willaert's Chromatic Duo in 16th-and 17th-century Compositions" in *Studies in Music History: Essays for Oliver Strunk*, edited by Harold Powers (Princeton, 1968), 183-238. Lowinsky also did important groundwork on conflicting or partial signatures beginning with "The Function of Conflicting Signatures in Early Polyphonic Music," *Musical Quarterly* 31 (1945), 227-60. Richard Hoppin aired a differing view in "Partial Signatures and Musica Ficta in Some Early Fifteenth-Century Sources," *JAMS* 6 (1953), 197-215, and the correspondence continued with Lowinsky's "Conflicting Views on Conflicting Signatures," *JAMS* VII (1954), 181-204, and Hoppin's "Conflicting Signatures Reviewed," *JAMS* 9 (1956), 97-117. See also Lewis Lockwood, "A Sample Problem of *Musica Ficta*: Willaert's *Pater Noster*" in the Strunk *Studies in Music History*, 161-82; Margaret Bent, "Musica Recta and Musica Ficta," *Musica Disciplina* 26 (1972), 73-100, also "Musica Ficta," *The New Grove Dictionary of Music and Musicians*, edited by Stanley Sadie (London, 1980), also "Diatonic *ficta*," *Early Music History* 4 (1984), 1-48; also with Andrew Hughes, Introduction to *The Old Hall Manuscript*, CMM 46 (1969-73), pp. xviii-xxiii; Andrew Hughes, "Ugolino: The Monochord and Musica Ficta," *Musica Disciplina* 23 (1969), 21-39; Albert Seay, "The 15th-Century *Conjuncta*: A Preliminary Study," in *Aspects of Medieval and Renaissance Music: A Birthday Offering to Gustave Reese*, edited by Jan LaRue (New York, 1966), pp. 723-37, also "The Beginnings of the *coniuncta* and Lorenzo Masini's 'L'Antefana'," *L'ars nova italiana del Trecento: Secondo Convegno Internazionale, 17-22 luglio 1969* (Certaldo, 1970), 51-65; Karol Berger, *Musica ficta: Theories of Accidental Inflections in Vocal Polyphony from Marchetto da Padova to Gioseffo Zarlino* (Cambridge, 1987); and Robert Toft, *Aural Images of Lost Traditions: Sharps and Flats in the Sixteenth Century* (Toronto and Buffalo, ca. 1992). Peter Urquhart has taken a refreshingly flexible approach to the subject of ficta in the Renaissance in "Cross-Relations by Franco-Flemish Composers after Josquin," *Tijdschrift van de Vereniging voor Nederlandse Muziekgeschiedenis* 43 (1993), 3, and in subsequent writings; Sarah Fuller has written on the intimately related field of 14th-century counterpoint in "Tendencies and Resolutions: The Directed Progression in Ars nova Music," *Journal of Music Theory* 36 (1992), 229-58, and in "Guillaume de Machaut: *De toutes flours*," in *Music Before 1600*, ed. Mark Everist, Models of Musical Analysis (Cambridge, MA, 1992), pp. 41-65. Although the approach of Thomas Brothers in *Chromatic Beauty in the Late Medieval Chanson: An Interpretation of Manuscript*

Accidentals (Cambridge, 1997) is diametrically opposed to my own in that he puts all of his faith in scribal accuracy and fails to recognize the term *"pulchritudinis"* as a technical one, his book is particularly valuable for its musical insights and for critiques of other 20th-century scholars' work; it is excerpted in "Musica ficta and harmony in Machaut's songs," *Journal of Musicology* 15 (1997), 501-28, but the article is hard to grasp outside the context of the whole book. The reader is also referred to my Ph.D. dissertation, "Chromatic Alteration and Extrahexachordal Intervals in Fourteenth-Century Polyphonic Repertoires," (Columbia University, 1990), for further references and expansion upon many of the subjects touched upon here.

[2] The theory of these transposed hexachords is called *"coniuncta"* theory, beginning with the Berkeley Anonymous in 1375. See also Gaston G. Allaire, *The Theory of Hexachords, Solmization and the Modal System: A Practical Application*, Musicological Studies and Documents 24 (Rome, 1972).

[3] Franchinus Gaffurius describes the practice clearly in *Practica Musica*, translation and transcription by Clement A. Miller, MSD 20 (1968), p. 142.

[4] Allaire, 33: "The *coniunctae* are nothing but our flats and sharps." *Coniunctae* actually are *extra manum* transpositions of the diatonic hexachord, one theoretical means (though not the only one) for introducing new accidentals. Allaire's work does not deal simply with Renaissance theory, but specifically addresses modern performance problems. Karol Berger's stated object in *Musica ficta* is the same: see p. xi: "The main purpose of the present book is to offer assistance by clarifying the meaning and use of the conventions governing the practice of implied accidentals in vocal polyphony."

[5] Imagine, for example, Matteo da Perugia's *Pres du soloil* or Machaut's *Amours me fait desirer* without the tritone!

[6] "Una nota . . ." is quoted as "the old rule," without attribution, by August Wilhelm Ambros in *Geschichte der Musik* (1868), repr. Hildesheim, 1968), vol. II, p. 199, and elsewhere. It did not appear in theoretical writing, according to Andrew Hughes in the *New Grove*, until the early seventeenth century.

[7] In Apel's 1950 edition of *Calextone qui fut*, the jarringly incorrect c♯ against a♭ (corrected in the 1970 edition) is a result of his having read a sharp before a ligature for its first note instead of its last. Referring the question to the contrapuntal guidelines would easily have avoided the mistake.

[8] Arthur Mendel argues in "The Purposes and Desirable Characteristics of Text-Critical Editions," E. Olleson, editor, *Modern Musical Scholarship* (Sticksfield, 1980), pp. 14-27, that since implied accidentals were a matter of performance practice, they should not be included in modern critical editions. Berger disagrees: "spelling out the inflections implied in the sources is the inescapable responsibility of the editor." See *Musica ficta*, pp. 170-71. It used to be a reliable assumption that an editor would place within the staff only those accidentals found in at least one original source, and all editorial suggestions for inflection would be found above the affected notes. This may not be the case; you should read all introductory commentaries carefully.

[9] The guideline for the progression in which the Tenor descends by a fourth is given by Petrus dictus Palma ociosa (1336), Jehan de Murs (c. 1317), and Prosdocimus (1412). Although the progression itself is not rare in music of the fourteenth century, in most examples the minor third is already present.

[10] Although Machaut manuscript G gives this reading, it is not found in any modern edition. Additional evidence that it is good appears in the confused signatures of the Contratenor in other sources: square b appears on b in source A; a flat appears on c in

source E. I surmise that in the original the sign was a square b on c, conforming to the rules of alteration *causa pulchritudinis.*

[11] In the *Lucidarium* (8.1.6-7), Marchetto says, "The first two signs, ♮ and ♭, are, or may be, in any song, plain or measured, but the third sign [♯] is used only in measured song, or in plainsong that is either sung chromatically or else laid out in measure, such as the tenors of motets or other measured music." The Kyrie *Cunctipotens genitor* melody altered by Machaut in the *Messe de Nostre Dame* is just such a case. See also Jan W. Herlinger, *The Lucidarium of Marchetto of Padua: A Critical Edition, Translation, and Commentary* (Chicago, 1985), pp. 274-75.

[12] Karol Berger, in *Musica ficta*, pp. 174-88, identifies two types of source accidentals, those that are "unconventional and authorial," and others that are "conventional and non-authorial." The "conventional" accidentals are those that are understood to apply through *causa pulchritudinis* and *causa necessitatis.* "Unconventional" accidentals, along with signatures, fall into a class that "absolutely had to be written, because they were not implied by the musical context at all." In other words, these are the inflections that define the interval species, or "mode," if you will. Berger believes that manuscript variants can help to distinguish between one type and another.The distinction between signs that define species or mode and signs that are provided by the contrapuntal rules is a valid one (in fact, confusion of *causa necessitatis* flats with the first type has given rise to many errors). But unfortunately, to say that "mode-defining" accidentals absolutely must be notated is not to say that they are. The condition of the sources, due to scribal intervention, does not permit Berger to draw the conclusions he would like to draw. His reading of the accidentals in Du Fay's *Navré je sui*, and his conclusion that certain ones are "unconventional and authorial," is based upon two different sources (GB: Ob 213, "Canonici MS," and F: Pn 6771, "Reina Codex"), while he completely ignores a third source (St. Emmeram) that transmits none of the inflections, not even the signatures.

[13] Two apparent exceptions to this are 1) the descriptions by Jehan de Murs and others of alteration before pauses in chant, and 2) the melodic rule of *causa tritoni* in the fifteenth-century Seville treatise. See Margaret Bent in "Musica Recta and Musica Ficta." *Causa tritoni* is in fact the rule for B♭ in the F modes, which applies generally to plainchant.

[14] Gioseffo Zarlino, *The Art of Counterpoint*, Part Three of *Le Istitutioni Harmoniche*, 1558, translated by Guy A. Marco and Claude V. Palisca (New Haven, 1976), p. 83. Zarlino goes on to say that Gaffurius, too, had associated the sixth-to-octave progression with "cadenza," but he misrepresents the earlier theorist's discussion on this and several other counts: see Gaffurius, *Practica Musica*, p. 145.

[15] Lorenzo's Madrigal *Ita se n'era a star* in Pirrotta, Corpus Mensurabilis Musicae 8/4, 1-2, is an outstanding example.

[16] "Quodsi [signum b mollis] in exordio linearum ponatur, totus cantus per b molle cantabitur. Si vero in quavis alia parte positum sit, quam diu deductio cui praeponetur durabit, tam diu cantus b mollaris erit." Tinctoris (1476) NPT 8, p. 74. The statements of both Lanfranco (1533) and Gerle (1546), however, indicate that flats apply only to those notes they immediately precede. See Toft, pp. 14-15.

[17] Of the four sources for the vocal version of this piece, only one provides a written sharp, and there only on the last of the c's. No other accidentals are indicated.

38. Proportion

Alexander Blachly

Around 1473, Johannes Tinctoris succinctly articulated the long-understood concept of proportion as an arithmetic ratio between two quantities (or what we, more simply still, would call a fraction).[1] The ancient Greeks had many centuries before recognized the ratios between musical pitches to be proportions of this type. To Boethius the Middle Ages owed the notion that Pythagoras was the discoverer of these ratios (which correctly pertain to the sounding lengths of a string or pipe, though according to Boethius, and many others before and after him, Pythagoras derived the ratios from the weights of hammers struck on an anvil).[2] Boethius, living in the sixth century A.D., may have learned about Pythagoras from Nichomachus, who lived in the second century A.D. Both writers knew that the Greeks understood the octave to represent a ratio of 2:1, the fifth a ratio of 3:2, and the the fourth a ratio of 4:3. Other intervals could be derived from these three by a process of addition and subtraction.[3]

The idea of extending arithmetic proportions to the domain of the durations of notes was new in the late Middle Ages. By the introduction of this idea, evidently in the twelfth century, the very language of musical utterance was transformed. This essay will focus on the evolution of increasingly complex durational proportions in the later Middle Ages and will propose some techniques for performing them. Following the model of Nichomachus, Boethius, and the more recent Prosdocimus de Beldemandis,[4] Tinctoris divided proportions into the categories of equal and unequal. The former consisted of any ratio of the type x=x; thus any note of a given denomination would equal a similar note of the same denomination in a proportion of equality. The note values available in the earliest measured system, that of modal notation ca.1200, consisted initially just of longs and breves, with a long equaling two breves (in a *proportio dupla*, 2:1). To say this another way, the earliest measured notation limited proportions of inequality to the *genus multiplex* (*i.e.*, of the type y=nx). As late as the mid-thirteenth century, theorists considered a long worth three breves to be *ultra mensuram* (beyond measure), although soon the 3:1 durational relationship, or *proportio tripla*, came to be fully accepted. Indeed, Franco of Cologne, in the *Ars cantus mensurabilis* of ca. 1280, called the long worth three breves "perfect," as opposed to the "imperfect" long worth two breves.

In the mensural notation of the later thirteenth century, and continuing until roughly the end of the sixteenth, *proportio equalitatis* stood as the primary durational proportion a musician would anticipate between any two notes of the same name within a single piece—say, a breve in one voice and a breve elsewhere in the same voice or in another voice. Already in the thirteenth century, however, the rules of imperfection and alteration, codified by Franco, had begun undermining this expectation by producing inequalities between notes of the same name and shape.

Imperfection allowed a perfect value (such as a long), which was normally worth three notes of the next smaller denomination (breve), to lose a third of its value when preceded or followed by the smaller note. An imperfected long and the breve that imperfected it would then together comprise the value of a perfect long, with the imperfected note related to a perfect one of the same denomination in a 2:3 proportion of inequality (*i.e.*, a *proportio sesquialtera*):

Fig. 38.1.

The inviolate rule of *similis ante similem perfecta* required a (normally perfect) note of a given name preceding another note of the same name to be perfect. In the following example, the first note, a long, must be perfect because it precedes another long.

Fig. 38.2.

The rule of *similis ante similem*, while codifying and bringing certainty to one type of situation, created difficulties elsewhere. It made, for instance, the writing of the rhythm of Figure 38.3 a counterintuitive procedure:

Fig. 38.3.

Because of *similis ante similem*, the writing of this rhythm as one might be inclined to do on the model of modern notation resulted in a syncopation:

Fig. 38.4.

So strong was *similis ante similem* that even a dot of division placed between the two adjacent longs in Figure 38.4 would not have been able to override it to achieve the rhythm of Figure 38.3. Instead, musicians relied on the practice of "alteration," first described by Franco. This odd practice, which exemplifies a characteristically medieval solution to the problem it was created to solve, increased the duration of an altered note to twice its normal value. Restricted in its application to filling the rhythmic gap created by the rule of *similis ante similem*, alteration increased the duration of an altered note in a 2:1 proportion of inequality (*i.e.*, a *proportio dupla* of the *genus multiplex*) with respect to an unaltered one:

Fig. 38.5. ▟ ▪ ▪ ▟ = ♩. | ♪♪ | ♩.

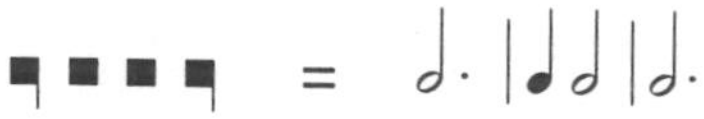

From Examples 38.1-38.5 it can be seen that mensural notation (the system in use from the late thirteenth to the sixteenth centuries) differed from modern notation in its reliance on *context* to define certain durations. Franco's greatest achievement may have been to reduce the context-dependent options of modal notation from the large number encountered earlier in the thirteenth century. He favored absolute meanings, where a particular note shape always signified a long, another always signified a breve. As Margaret Bent has characterized Franco's achievement, "[his] system required that note symbols should be capable of indicating the rhythmic modes rather than being determined by them."[5] Even so, mensural notation, in the fourteenth century and beyond, left the durational meaning of a given note to be determined, in a significant number of cases, by its context. More importantly for the present study, mensural notation by its very nature embodied proportions of equality and inequality in the relationships of notes to one another. Although we do not normally regard a relationship such as ▟ = ▪ ▪ ▪ (equivalent to the modern ♩. = ♪♪♪) as a "proportion" in the same sense that we would consider the complicated durational relationships found in the music of the late fourteenth and early fifteenth centuries, it is helpful in understanding these latter to realize that they derive logically, if not necessarily inevitably, from the simple proportions that form the basis of all measured music.

The anonymous motet *Garrit gallus/In nova fert/[Neuma]* in the Roman de Fauvel[6] presents the earliest known example in which red ink is used to indicate imperfect longs and breves (the notes shown here as hollow representing solid red):

Fig. 38.6. Tenor rhythm of *Garrit gallus*.

▟ ▪ ▪ ▪ ▢ ▢ ▢ | ▢ ▢ ▢ ▪ ▪ ▪ ▟ | ▟ ▪ ▪ ▪ ▢ ▢ ▢ | ▢ ▢ ▢ ▪ ▪ ▟

The principle of imperfection, limited in the thirteenth century to single notes imperfected by smaller notes that completed the longer note's perfection, is now applied—by means of red ink—to any number of longs and breves in succession; soon it would be applied to perfect notes of any size. We observe that the composer of *Garrit gallus* has achieved the proportion of *sesquialtera* (3:2) at the level of the long, where three imperfect (red) longs equal two perfect (black) longs (with all red breves sharing the value of unaltered black breves). The purpose of coloration here is not to emphasize the rhythmic friction of red and black notes sounding simultaneously in different voices, as would become common later in the century, but rather to change the large-scale metrical feeling of the motet as part of a repeating palindromic pattern:[7]

Ex. 38.1. Opening of *Garrit gallus.*

Machaut also writes colored tenor notes (mostly longs and breves) in his motet *Felix virgo/Inviolata/Ad te suspiramus/[Contratenor]*, but provides an explanatory rubric: "Nigre sunt perfecte et Rubee imperfecte" (the black [notes] are perfect and the red ones imperfect).[8] Philippe de Vitry had used coloration in his motet *Tuba sacre/In arboris/Virgo sum* with reversed meaning (also explained by rubric): "Nigre notule sunt imperfecte et rube sunt perfecte."[9] The effect specified by Machaut's rubric (colored ink indicates imperfection) came to be the standard use for coloration in the second half of the fourteenth until the seventeenth centuries.

The transformation, by means of red ink, of perfect into imperfect notes helps set the stage for the proportional complexities of French music in the later fourteenth and early fifteenth centuries. The changes noted already, which involve mostly longs and breves, do not normally present difficulties in performance. It is now thought that the earliest music to do so—both because the proportional relationships relate to smaller notes and because the proportions involved belong to a more complicated species of *proportio inequalitatis*, namely, to the *genus superparticularis* proportion of *sesquitertia*—comes from Italy. (However, because the dating of individual pieces from the early fourteenth century remains so uncertain in the majority of cases, we cannot yet determine whether proportional relationships involving small notes in French music indicate a borrowing of Italian effects or whether both repertories developed such effects independently.)

Example 38.2 shows the opening of Giovanni da Firenze's madrigal *La bella stella*, which opens in *octonaria* in both voices (four eighths per half note; see below, Figure 38.1), indicated in the sources with the letter ".o." written above the staff, just as in the transcription.)

Ex. 38.2. Opening of Giovanni da Firenze's *La bella stella.*

At m.13 the upper voice changes to *senaria imperfecta* (also known as *senaria gallica*, indicated by ".sg." written above the staff). Since the lower voice continues in *octonaria*, three minims (eighth notes) of the newly introduced *senaria imperfecta* must equal four minims of *octonaria*—a *sesquitertia* proportion.

Before we examine French works that exhibit *sesquitertia*, it may be useful to consider the rhythmic context into which such proportions were first introduced.

Notational developments in the fourteenth century display the fruitful result of combining logical rigor with imaginative analogies. For example, the notion of alteration, originally devised as a way of writing an imperfect note before a perfect one of the same denomination (and thereby circumventing the Franconian axiom of *similis ante similem*), was extended in the fourteenth century to include notes separated by one or more perfections:[10]

Fig. 38.7.

Similarly, the Franconian dot of division, used to prevent imperfection, as here:

Fig. 38.8.

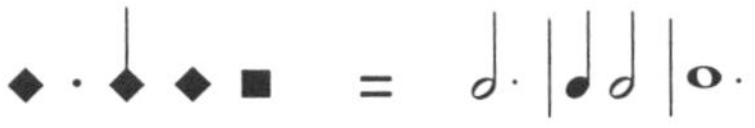

or to ensure it, as here:

Fig. 38.9.

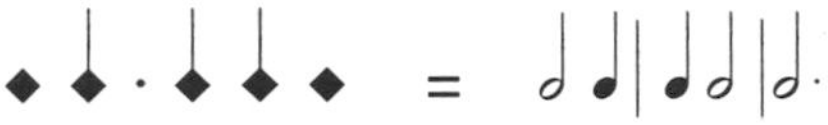

soon seems to have been regarded not so much as a dot dividing one perfection from another as a dot of *prevention*—that is, as a device for preventing a normal relationship. No longer limited to separating perfections from one another, the dot, or many dots, could now occur at any point *within a perfection*, often with long term consequences:[11]

Fig. 38.10.

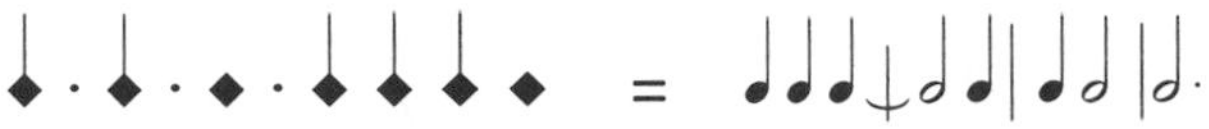

To understand this example, we must think methodically. The first dot serves to prevent alteration of the second minim. The next dot isolates the following semibreve in the manner of a dot of division, preventing its imperfection by the aforesaid second minim and allowing it to begin before the *mensura*.[12] The dot following the semibreve prevents its imperfection by the following minim, thereby ensuring its perfection. This following minim is, consequently, free to "complete" the semibreve begun by the first two minims. Next come two minims and a semibreve. The second of these minims must be altered so as to allow the final semibreve to begin on the *mensura*. (Dots before and after the final minim would have prevented this alteration and allowed the semibreve to begin a minim before the *mensura*, as does the first semibreve in the example.)

The foregoing suggests that the unexpected rhythms that result from adding dots in unusual places within otherwise conventional patterns of notes must have stimulated composers' imaginations. The rhythm of Figure 38.10, of course, is not a proportion but rather a syncopation. Yet the musical style that exploited the one also provided a hospitable climate for the cultivation of the other. To see how this is true we need only examine the opening of Mattheus de Perusio's ballade *Le grant desir*,[13] where the first 13 measures of the upper voice, laden with syncopation, finally break into *sesquitertia* at measure 14:

Ex. 38.3. Opening of Mattheus de Perusio's *Le grant desir.*

This brings us to the question of how in the Middle Ages such a *sesquitertia* was executed by singers in performance. Despite a dearth of direct evidence, but we may draw some far-reaching conclusions by considering, first, how performers beat time. Descriptions by such theorists as Anselmus of Parma (ca.1434)[14] and pictorial evidence, such as that provided by Luca della Robbia's *Cantoria* (ca.1434), teach that the beat was transmitted by tapping, usually by one singer tapping another's shoulder or arm. Although this constituted a literal "touching," the beat was not called a *tactus* ("touch") but a *mensura*. It was a single-event tapping corresponding to a single note, "the note that receives the beat," as Tinctoris phrases it. The term *tactus*, appearing first in Adam von Fulda's *De musica* of 1490 with the same meaning as *mensura*, was taken up by sixteenth-century writers to refer to a two-fold beat consisting of an *elevatio* and a *positio*. It is a curiosity of history that the sixteenth-century beat, marked in the air by a finger, a hand, or a baton, should have been called a "touch", while the fifteenth-century beat, executed by one singer actually touching another, should have been given the more netural term of *mensura* ("measure").

Because the *mensura* lacked the internal subdivision intrinsic to the sixteenth-century *tactus*, it could be subdivided into any number of smaller units as required, without the danger that these might themselves conflict with the sub-beats of *elevatio* and *positio*. Indeed, the single-touch *mensura*, by its very nature, most likely encouraged the development of small-note proportions in the late fourteenth and early fifteenth centuries. An examination of Example 38.3 will show why this may have been so.

We can deduce the note receiving the *mensura* in Example 38.3 by a process of elimination. In the course of experimenting, we will discover that putting the beat on the minim (quarter note) or smaller value will not help to find the correct speed of the sesquitertia notes in m.14, because the different speeds of quarter notes will have no common point of reference. The placing of the beat on the perfect semibreve (dotted half note), however, as recommended for ₵ by various writers in the fifteenth century, demonstrates that the problem of m.14 can be reduced simply to subdivision—more specifically, to the subdivision of a constant, *i.e.*, subdividing the *mensura* on the perfect semibreve. And it is this constant that not only provides the necessary point of reference for calculating the smaller subdivisions but also makes such calculations relatively easy. (Were this constant itself to be subdivided into an *elevatio* and *positio* in the manner of the sixteenth-century *tactus*, the *elevatio* and *positio* would necessarily conflict with one speed of quarter note or the other. In this respect, particularly, the sixteenth-century style of beating time proves alien to the needs of fourteenth- and fifteenth-century music.)

Another instance of *sesquitertia* at the minim level occurs in mm.12-13 of the top voice of Baude Cordier's famous song notated in the shape of a heart, *Belle, bonne, sage*.

Ex. 38.4. Opening of Baude Cordier's *Belle, bonne, sage.*

As in Example 38.3, the placing of the beat on the minim of **C** (or the semibreve of **Ø**) will not facilitate the task of calculating the speed of the notes in the top voice at mm. 12-13; for in either case the change from:

$$\mathbf{C} \downarrow\downarrow\downarrow \ \downarrow\downarrow\downarrow \ \left(= \mathbf{Ø} \blacklozenge\blacklozenge\blacklozenge \ \ \blacklozenge\blacklozenge\blacklozenge \right)$$

i.e., black solid minims (or semibreves), to: $\lozenge \ \lozenge \ \lozenge \ \lozenge \ \lozenge$

(*i.e.*, black void minims and semibreves, where C ♩ ♩ ♩ = ♢ ♢ ♢ ♢), must be accomplished without the benefit of retaining in current memory the value both groups of notes have in common, namely, C ♦ = ▫ .

Practical experience soon teaches anyone attempting to perform *sesquialtera* or *sesquitertia* proportions, in modern as in medieval music, that maintaining mental focus on the larger value that stays constant provides an internal mental check on accuracy and also allows the performer to capture the "gesture" of both the duple and triple sub-division. While the small values in the cross-rhythms in mm.12-13 of *Belle, bonne, sage* (top voice and contra) are extremely difficult to perform *correctly* in relation *to each other*, they are surprisingly easy to perform with confidence and expression if calculated with reference to a larger duration that is common to both, *i.e.*, to a beat lasting one measure of the transcription. For this reason, the performer of one of the lines may wish partially to block from awareness the sound of the other line, so as to concentrate instead on the unchanging *mensura*. The lesson to be learned from this, which can be verified over and over in passages from fourteenth- to sixteenth-century musical works, is that the practical means of calculating proportions may nearly always be reduced to the calculating of *subdivisions* of a constant unit.

With *sesquialtera* (3:2), the corollary notion of *hemiola* also comes into play. Hemiola requires the mental regrouping of subdivided notes. For example, the performance of mm. 8-11 of the contratenor of *Belle, bonne, sage* requires the mental *grouping* of half-notes into undotted whole notes, the larger meter of which cuts across the continuing measure-long beat. To put this another way, hemiola represents the replacing of two triply-divided notes by three duply-divided ones:

Fig. 38.11. (o· o· = o o o)

Hemiola may rightly claim the honor of being the most prevalent form of proportion in the later fourteenth and early fifteenth centuries. In some works by Du Fay, it wholly dominates the texture, even when sparkling harmonies that fluctuate between "major" and "minor" also vie for the listener's attention, as in Example 38.5. (Hemiola is shown here by means of square brackets surrounding the notes written in red ink, as in the transcription of *Belle, bonne, sage*.)

Ex. 38.5. Opening of a Gloria by Du Fay.

In this example, the *mensura* falls on the perfect semibreve (dotted quarter), and the notes in hemiola cut across this beat.

Sesquitertia, on the other hand, normally requires simultaneously contrasted subdivisions in different voices but does not require for groupings of the resulting notes to conflict with the *mensura*. In both types of proportion the performer must focus on the large note that serves as the point of reference. In *Belle, bonne, sage,* this is the value equal to one measure of the transcription. Indeed, if one taps one's own arm or shoulder, fifteenth-century style, once per measure, the practical advantages of this method for performing *Belle, bonne, sage* become evident. The tapping corresponds to the dotted whole note and remains constant throughout the entire piece. One may then sing the rhythms of each of the voices as various subdivisions of the continuing *mensura*. With sufficient practice, a performer develops a highly reliable inner clock that ticks in reference to the large notes of a piece that do not change except with respect to their subdivisions. The subdivisions are free to change rapidly back and forth as required.

For a famous passage involving a more complicated proportion, we may look next at the "Qui cum patre et filio" of the Credo of Du Fay's *Missa Sancti Anthonii de Padua* (Example 38.6). What excited the interest of a long succession of theorists, beginning with Tinctoris in the *Proportionale musices*, was the sign **O3** Du Fay introduced into the superius to indicate that three perfect breves in that voice should equal two imperfect breves in the contratenor.

For the theorists it was Du Fay's sign (to which most of them objected strenuously) that generated interest, but we direct our attention to the formidable problems the passage poses with respect to execution. Because of its difficulty, Du Fay's "Qui cum patre," once figured out, should serve as a good model for dealing with similar situations. Viewed literally, the *sesquialtera* relationship of three perfect breves to two imperfect breves is also a "duple *sesquiquarta*" relationship of 9 to 4 at the semibreve level (Tinctoris's way of characterizing it). It is much easier, however, to execute a *sesquialtera* than a duple *sesquiquarta*. From the perspective of performance, a kind of "Occam's razor of performance"—to give a name to an *ad hoc* approach—suggests that performers should embrace the easiest method to assure the correct result. This would be the *mensura* that produces the fewest conflicts with the other voice. Shifting the *mensura* from the breve of ₵ in the measures preceding the proportion to the perfect breve of **O3** in the superius at "Qui cum patre" (a *sesquialtera* relationship, with three beats on perfect breves of **O3** equaling two beats on imperfect breves in ₵) results in 21 cases where the contratenor sings two breves against three upper-voice *mensurae* (a relatively easy easy problem to handle, being nothing more than hemiola in reverse) and 7 additional cases where these breves need to be subdivided into semibreves (a *sesquitertia* relationship if calculated against upper-voice *mensurae*). To retain a *mensura* on contratenor breves throughout the "Qui cum patre," on the other hand, results in the "tuneful" voice (the superius) being at odds with the beat for the entire passage—results, that is to say, in an "untuneful" performance because of the virtually unceasing conflicts. Unlike most examples of *sesquitertia* from the fourteenth century, where the proportion may be understood as the subdivision of a constant and continuing beat, Du Fay's "Qui cum patre," even in the "easier" mode of performance that has the *mensura* beat in superius breves, requires the subdivision of notes that are already in metrical conflict with this *mensura* (namely, breves of ₵ in the contratenor). The difficulty arises from having the *mensura* at one further remove from the notes in proportion than we typically find in fourteenth-century music.

Ex. 38.6. "Qui cum patre" of Du Fay's *Missa Sancti Anthonii de Padua*.

The second Agnus of Josquin's *Missa L'homme armé super voces musicales*, a three-voice mensuration canon that won the admiration of theorists throughout the sixteenth century, may appear to require a similar approach:

Ex. 38.7. Agnus II from Josquin's *Missa L'homme armé super voces musicales.*

Here, however, "Occam's razor" shows that the easiest method for obtaining a correct performance involves keeping the *mensura* on the semibreve of the voice in 𝄵, namely, the lowest voice. In this piece the top voice can be measured throughout in "triplet" subdivisions of such a *mensura*, whereby the performer of the top voice conceptualizes each semibreve beat of the bottom voice as triply divided (in opposition to the duple divisions of the *mensura* conceptualized by the performer of the bottom voice). For the most part, the top voice will then express hemiola cross-rhythms with the bottom voice, except where the rhythms may be understood as two groups of three quarter notes, as in measures 2, 4, 12, 14, and 16. Thus, just as singers had to decipher the relationships between opposed mensurations in different voices by a process of trial and error—a method they must also have used to determine the best *musica ficta* for any given passage—so also must they have experimented to discover the "easiest" *mensura* in pieces such as Example 38.7.

Ex. 38.8. Opening of *Secunda pars* of Busnoys's *Regina celi I*.

The complication in Example 38.8 is more like that of Du Fay's "Qui cum patre," where a *sesquitertia* proportion (indicated by the proportion sign Ɔ) in the superius of Busnoys's *Regina celi I* near the opening of the *secunda pars* requires a shift of *mensura* for both voices. (At mm. 78-81 the lower voice is barred in 3/2 for convenience, but the duration of the half note does not change.)

In this case, the semibreves of the altus remain constant throughout the passsage. The requirement of four semibreves of the superius to equal three of the altus semibreves, however, defies execution unless a common denominator can be found. The fourteenth-century model of *sesquitertia* (as in Example 38.3 above) suggests the need for a large *mensura* equaling three altus semibreves and four superius semibreves. With only moderate difficulty, such a *mensura* can be achieved, so long as the tempo of the altus semibreves beginning at **C2** (m.65) is sufficiently fast. (The passage, however, does seem to demand a conductor.) A three-semibreve mensura at m.78 can now replace the two-semibreve mensura of mm. 65-77 (measures 78 through 81 each now becoming one-third longer in duration than the measures that preceded them). With practice, the conductor will develop a body sense of the speed of the *mensura*-beating arm as the *mensura* changes from a two-semibreve beat to a three-semibreve one and back again, and each of the two voices can subdivide the large *mensura* fourteenth-century style for the four longer measures. From m.82 on, both voices accord with the two-semibreve *mensura* that preceded m.78. (It merits our attention and contemplation to note that Brussels 5557, the sole source for this work, supplies, in what looks like a footnote at the bottom of the page, an alternate notation of the superius notes of mm. 78-81 devoid of proportions. This easier, or "ossia," version, which is written on the tenor staff in Example 38.8 beginning at m.78, perhaps betrays an acknowledgement on the part of Busnoys or of the scribe of Brussels 5557 that a slow *sesquitertia* like the one in this example, introduced in a passage in duple meter, exceeds the limits of what many performers of the time could cope with—surely a reassuring thought to present-day performers as they struggle to master such passages. [15]

Turning our attention once again to the fourteenth century, we find, upon consideration of the problem, that the highly syncopated melodic style of post-Machaut/pre-Du Fay music requires a continuing awareness of the *mensura* not unlike that required for the execution of *sesquialtera* and *sesquitertia* proportions. Often the tenor, typically moving in large, unsyncopated notes, provides in sound just such a regularly recurring point of reference. As we have seen above in the discussion of Figure 38.10, the correct interpretation of the actual duration of notes in syncopated lines depends upon knowing their placement within a perfection, that is, where they fall relative to the evenly recurring large beat. Thus, we may state as a general rule that the performance of both syncopations and proportions requires reference to the anchor provided by a *mensura*. The syncopations are dependent on placement within a perfection for the determination of durations, and any attempt to perform proportions without a large-note point of reference will result in guesswork and inaccuracy, as performers of this repertory know from experience.

We may well wonder how such an awareness of the utility of the large-note *mensura* first arose. In this connection, it is surely significant that the Italian notational system of the trecento has built into it just the sort of large-note constant relative to small-note proportions we have been speaking of. Marchetus of Padua's *Pomerium* (ca.1318), the earliest and most comprehensive treatise on Italian Ars nova notation, provides the best guide for understanding the Italian system generally.[16]

Fig. 38.2. Marchetus's four *divisiones.*

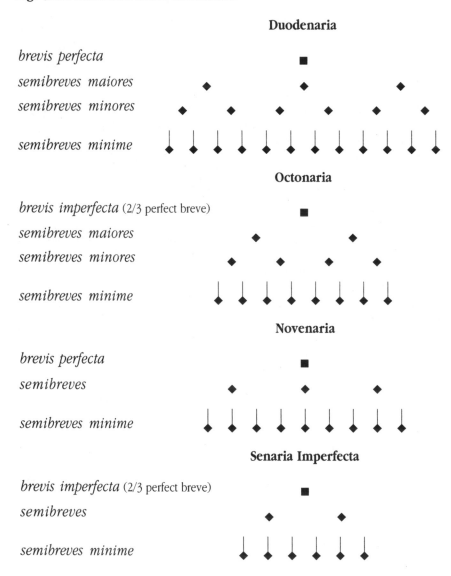

Here we learn that the perfect breve serves as the conceptual point of reference for the four primary *divisiones* of *duodenaria, octonaria, novenaria,* and *senaria imperfecta.* Below the breve, the next level of division consists of semibreves (major semibreves in the case of *duodenaria* and *octonaria*). These equal one another in all four *divisiones.* Below these we find minor semibreves in *duodenaria* and *octonaria* and minims (*semibreves minime*) in *novenaria* and *senaria imperfecta.* Still another division in *duodenaria* and *octonaria* produces four minims (*semibreves minime*) per major semibreve. (*Novenaria* and *senaria perfecta* each have three minims per semibreve.) For our purposes, it is sufficient to observe that the minims of *duodenaria* and *octonaria* relate to the minims of *novenaria* and *senaria imperfecta* in a *proportio sesquitertia.* That is, four minims of *duodenaria* equal three minims of *novenaria,* as shown in Figure 38.2.

Marchetus does not explain two *divisiones* found in the earliest musical sources, *senaria perfecta* and *quaternaria.* *Quaternaria* Marchetus does not mention at all. He does mention *senaria perfecta* but dismisses it as an independent *divisio,* arguing that it already occurs in *duodenaria* (*i.e.,* that the six *semibreves minores* of *duodenaria* constitute the true *senaria perfecta,* which therefore cannot contain any *semibreves minime*).We would thus understand the total absence of minims as the identifying feature of any piece written in Marchetus's *senaria perfecta.* But there are no such pieces; in all the surviving sources, works written in *senaria perfecta* invariably have minims.

Why might Marchetus have wished to conceal two *divisiones,* and how may we hope to understand their proper relationship to the other four? Let us consider the theorist's desire for consistency. He seems to have wanted all *divisiones* to derive logically from a single point of reference, the perfect breve. If, in reality, *senaria perfecta* shared a minim of equal value with *senaria imperfecta,* comparable to the minim shared by the French *prolacions* O and C well into the fifteenth century, there was no way to fit *senaria perfecta* into the two branches of division shown above, since a) its semibreve was shorter in duration than the first-tier semibreves of *duodenaria, octonaria, novenaria,* and *senaria imperfecta* and b) even more problematically, the perfect breve of *senaria perfecta* equaled the imperfect breve of *senaria imperfecta.* A similar problem attends a *quaternaria* in which the minim is as fast, or even approximately as fast, as a minim in *duodenaria.*

Since pieces exist in which the minims and breves of *senaria imperfecta* match in value the minims and breves of *senaria perfecta,* and since *quaternaria* is found in the earliest layers of the earliest of the Italian musical sources, Vatican City, Biblioteca Apostolica Vaticana, MS 215 ("Rossi"), dating from ca.1360,[17] we may begin to suspect that Marchetus's omissions obscure the true state of Italian practice in the earliest phase of trecento polyphony. Nevertheless, what we do have from Marchetus is invaluable: a set of relationships in which minims of *duodenaria* and *octonaria* relate to those of *novenaria* and *senaria imperfecta* in a *sesquitertia* proportion, a proportion easily calculated by reference to the first-division semibreve all four *divisiones* have in common. Only *quaternaria* remains to be accounted for. The simplest explanation may well be the correct one: *quaternaria* simply represents an alternative *divisio* in which to notate music that could also be written in *duodenaria* or *octonaria*, *i.e.*, a *divisio* with a minim equal in speed to that of the latter two.[18] Prosdocimus de Beldemandis, in his *Tractatus practice cantus mensurabilis ad modum Ytalicorum* (1412), confirms that minims of *duodenaria* and *octonaria* relate to those of *novenaria* and *senaria perfecta* in a *sesquitertia* proportion in the earliest phase of the repertory.[19]

Trecento composers, however, often introduce proportions not by way of changes of *divisio* or *prolacio* but by special note shapes. Especially popular in Italy are notes with curved flags, ↓ or ↾, notes with stems extending both upward and downward (a shape known as the *dragma*), and dragmas with flags either above or below or both (see above, Example 38.3). As the fourteenth century progresses, and French elements get mixed in with Italian, we find that coloration may be introduced in any of the note shapes discussed so far. Moreover, there soon comes to be more than one form of coloration. By the end of the century both Italian and French sources show the following color possibilities for all note shapes: solid black, solid red, void black, void red. In the Old Hall Manuscript,[20] still another color is added: blue notation. At this point, any sense of consistent system has long broken down. Composers combined the various elements in various ways, which have to be decoded on the basis of experimentation. Normally, an experienced performer or editor will quickly determine what the contrapuntal context requires. But occasionally a piece reaches such a level of complexity, with coloration of coloration piled on proportions prescribed either by verbal canon or by numbers preceding groups of notes, that sorting out the composer's intentions becomes literally a decipherment. Among composers most prone to such practices, Leonel Power, in his works in the Old Hall Manuscript, wins the prize. For the modern performer, however, the decipherment has normally already been accomplished by the editor of the music singers have in hand. The Himalayan heights of proportional difficulty today's performer most often confronts apply to execution.

Confusing the trecento situation further is, first, a loss of interest on the part of the second phase of trecento composers in the built-in sesquitertia relationships between minims of *duodenaria* and *octonaria*, on the one hand, and those of *senaria imperfecta* and *novenaria*, on the other. The composers of the second stage of trecento composition, pre-eminently Landini and Lorenzo, instead adopted the French style of a single minim for all *divisiones*. (With Prosdocimus, Ciconia, and other composers of the third phase of trecento composition, however, an interest in sesquitertial relationships reappeared in Italian music around 1400.) Second, scribes from the 1380s on began to rewrite earlier music in the so-called "longa" notation in which the "modern" *quarternaria* replaces the "obsolete" *divisiones* of *duodenaria* and *octonaria*.[21] Once a performer or editor has recognized a scribe's use of "longa" notation, the mental reconstruction of the original necessary for determining proportional relationships normally poses no great difficulties.

As an appendix to this brief survey, we note the confusion that entered into musical practice in the early fifteenth century in both France and Italy when composers and scribes began indicating proportions by means of mensuration signs. Where formerly all French *prolacions*, at least in theory, had shared a minim of common value, composers such as Mattheus de Perusio began to use the sign ¢

to indicate the equivalence of a ternary semibreve in one voice to a binary semibreve in the the others.[22] In other works by the same composer, however, the sign Ȼ could be introduced in a single voice with a minim equal to the minim of a binary semibreve elsewhere.[23] Again, it required, and continues to require, trial and error to determine how such pieces are meant to work. The constraints of musical counterpoint normally allow only one solution.

Sometime in the early fifteenth century, first visible to us in the two best-known works of Baude Cordier, his heart-song (*Belle, bonne, sage*)[24] and circle canon (*Tout par compas*), composers began to use cut signatures. Though prominent in the three great Italian musical anthologies from the 1420s and '30s,[25] cut signatures do not receive attention from music theorists until several decades later. Then, as Tinctoris helpfully implies on various occasions in his *Proportionale* and *Liber de arte contrapuncti* (1477), we learn that such signatures normally lie outside the domain of arithmetic proportions altogether, although the exceptional case of the simultaneous operation of a cut signature in one voice against an uncut signature in another does normally signal a proportional relationship of 2:1. Elsewhere the present author has argued that in "successive" cut signatures, as when a passage with all voices in Ȼ follows a passage in O, the composer almost never intends an arithmetic ratio but merely an acceleration of tempo—an effect known to musicians today as *più mosso* and referred to by Tinctoris as an *acceleratio mensure* (acceleration of the beat).[26] The misunderstanding in this case, which remains widespread, arises from the anachronistic application of sixteenth-century *tactus* theory to fifteenth-century music intended to be gauged with reference to a single-motion *mensura*, a basically unworkable practice that vexed several sixteenth-century theorists and has confused many twentieth-century editors and performers. As in other repertories, we are learning that the best way to understand specific problems in musical performance is by trying to approach the music from the perspective that guided composers and performers of the time. We must constantly be vigilant for anachronistic presuppositions. With respect to fifteenth-century pieces with successive cut signatures, anachronistic presuppostions have sometimes led to extreme, exaggerated performances that can only be characterized as being at odds with the prevailing aesthetic values to be perceived in the products of the painters, architects, and sculptors who lived when the composers in question were active.

At the same time, we must be practical and willing to experiment. The present author has shown that cases exist where performers could not have sung a piece purely on the basis of the verbal instructions provided by the composer.[27] Thus, performers must have used the "Occam's razor" method suggested earlier; otherwise, the mental calculations required would be so far removed from—and in contradiction of—the sensory information of the moment that only an indifferent machine could accomplish the task. Clearly, the performance of proportions in the fourteenth and fifteenth centuries cannot have required superhuman abilities. It follows that modern performers, like their medieval counterparts, will want to discover the most practical and convenient methods for calculating and executing the proportions they have identifed through analysis of the notation. The present author believes that trial-and-error experiments represent both the historical and the most utilitarian model.

Notes

1 In the *Proportionale musices.* For a modern edition see Albert Seay, ed., *Johannes Tinctoris, Opera theoretica,* Corpus scriptorum de musica 22 (Neuhausen-Stuttgart, 1975-78). For further discussion of the *Proportionale,* see Alexander Blachly, "Mensuration and Tempo in 15th-Century Music: Cut Signatures in Theory and Practice" (Ph.D. diss., Columbia University, 1995), Chapter 3.

2 The definitive translation in English is by Calvin M. Bower, *Fundamentals of Music: Anicius Manlius Severinus Boethius* (New Haven & London, 1989), based on *Anicii Manlii Torquati Severini Boetii De institutione arithmetica libri duo, De institutione musica libri quinque, accedit Geometria quae fertur Boetii,* ed. Gottfried Friedlein (Leipzig, 1867).

3 Subtracting a fourth from a fifth gave the whole tone: 3:2 - 4:3 (3/2 x 3/4 = 9/8), as did ascending two fifths and descending an octave: (3:2 + 3:2) x 1:2 ([3/2 x 3/2] x 1/2 = 9:8). The addition of two whole steps gave the major third: 9:8 + 9:8 (9/8 x 9/8 = 81/64), as did ascending four fifths and descending two octaves: (3:2 + 3:2 + 3:2 + 3:2) x 1:4 ([3/2 x 3/2 x 3/2 x 3/2] x 1/4 = 81/64). By the process of "continuous subtraction" the Greeks determined the "small intervals" of *semitone, apotome,* and *comma.* For a detailed discussion of the transmission of Pythagorean ideas into the musical theory of the Middle Ages, see Charles André Barbera, "The Persistence of Pythagorean Mathematics in Ancient Musical Thought" (Ph.D. diss., University of North Carolina at Chapel Hill, 1980).

4 In 1409 Prosdocimus explained the principles of proportion in his *Brevis summula proporcionum quantum ad musicam pertinet* (Coussemaker, *Scriptores,* III, 258-61).

5 Margaret Bent, "Notation, §III.3: Western, c1260-1500," *New Grove Dictionary of Music and Musicians,* Vol. 13, 362b.

6 Paris, Bibliothèque Nationale, MS fonds français 146, copied, according to the *explicit* in the hand of the main scribe, in 1316. For a recent complete facsimile edition, see Edward H. Roesner, François Avril, and Nancy Freeman Regalado, eds., *Le Roman de Fauvel in the Edition of Mesire Chaillou de Pesstain* (New York: Broude Brothers, 1990). *Garrit gallus* has been attributed by some modern writers to Philippe de Vitry.

7 Note that alteration, which occurs in the tenor in black notation at mm. 4-6 and 17-19, does not occur in red notation at mm. 7-8. Red notation, by making all notes imperfect, eliminates the need for alteration by making the long imperfect. The alteration of the second black breve in mm. 18-19, on the other hand, is correct and necessary because a) longs are perfect in black notation and b) the second breve is followed by a long in m. 20. It is not clear why the composer requires alteration in mm. 4-6. According to the rules of mensural notation, a breve can only be altered when followed by a long.

8 See Carl Parrish, *The Notation of Medieval Music* (New York, 1957; repr. 1978), Plate LIII, a facsimile of Paris, Bibliothèque Nationale, MS fonds français 22.546, fol. 125, and pp. 159f.

9   See Leo Schrade, ed., *Polyphonic Music of the Fourteenth Century*, Vol. I ("The *Roman de Fauvel*; the Works of Philippe de Vitry; the French Cycles of the *Ordinarium Missae*") (Monaco, 1961), pp. 88-90, and *Commentary to Volume I*, p. 109. The piece survives in Ivrea, Biblioteca capitolare, [without shelf-mark], fol. 15'-16.

10 The change here in the rate of reduction from original notation to modern notation among the thirteenth-century, fourteenth-century, and fifteenth-century examples has no intrinsic significance but simply represents the author's preferences for the transcription of the various repertories.

11 This and Figure 38.7, cited by Johannes Wolf in his *Geschichte der Mensural-Notation* (Leipzig, 1904), p. 137, come from Johannes Vetulus de Anagnia's *Liber de musica* of ca.1360-80.

12 The *mensura* was the medieval term for beat, applied to the perfect semibreve in Figure 38.10, which presupposes the mensuration [Ɔ] (*tempus imperfectum cum prolatione maiore*).

13 Modern edition in Willi Apel, ed., *French Secular Music of the Late Fourteenth Century* (Cambridge, MA, 1950), 3*-5*. Mattheus was active in the early fifteenth century.

14 Modern edition in Giuseppe Massera, ed., *Georgii Anselmi Parmensis 'De musica'* (Florence, 1961).

15 Richard Taruskin makes essentially the same point in his edition of Busnoys's Latin-texted works in Masters and Monuments of the Renaissance, 5 (New York, 1990), Part II, p. 173, note.

16 For a fuller discussion, see Chapter 15, "Italian Ars nova."

17 Michael P. Long points out this fact in "Musical Tastes in Fourteenth-Century Italy: Notational Styles, Scholarly Traditions and Historical Circumstances" (Ph.D. dissertation, Princeton University, 1979), pp. 76-87.

18 See the discussion in Chapter 39 of *longa* notation, which supports this hypothesis.

19 "...inveniemus octonariam mensuram ad senariam reduci, et duodenariam ad novenariam, que ambe mensure majores, ad ambas mensuras minores, in sexquitertia proportione se habet" (...we will find the *octonaria* mensuration reduced to the *senaria*, and the *duodenaria* to the *novenaria*. For it can be seen that the two larger measures are in *proportio sesquitertia* to the two smaller). *CS* III, 234b-235a. At the same time, he tries (without success) to establish a meaningful distinction between *quaternaria*, on the one hand, and *duodenaria* or *octonaria*, on the other.

20 British Library, MS Additional 57950.

21 For an explanation of this practice, see Chapter 15; see also Alexander Blachly, "Mensuration and Tempo in 15th-Century Music: Cut Signatures in Theory and Practice" (Ph.D. dissertation, Columbia University, 1995), pp. 104-07.

22 See, for example, this composer's *Le greygnour bien* (facsimile and transcription in Apel, *French Secular Music*, Plate I and pp. 1*-3*.

23 See Mattheus's virelai *Dame que j'aym* (transcription in Apel, *French Secular Music,* 9*-10*).

24 See above, Example 38.4.

[25] Bologna, Biblioteca Universitaria, MS 2216 (*BU*), Bologna, Civico Museo Bibliografico Musicale, MS Q 15 (*olim 37*) (*BL*), and Oxford, Bodleian Library, MS Canonici misc. 213 (*Ox*).

[26] Blachly, "Mensuration and Tempo," Chapter 3, esp. pp. 168, 170, and 180-83; also by the same author, "Reading Tinctoris for Guidance on Tempo," in Paula Higgins, ed., *Antoine Busnoys: Method, Meaning, and Context in Late Medieval Music* (London & New York, 1996). Rob C. Wegman, in *Born for the Muses: The Life and Masses of Jacob Obrecht* (Oxford, 1994), pp. 375-83, makes a similar argument for the non-proportional interpretation of cut signatures in what he calls the O ₵ period, roughly 1430-1500.

[27] See "Mensuration and Tempo," p. 389f., where the notation of Damett's *Salvatoris mater* in the Old Hall Manuscript reveals that the singer(s) of the tenor must have calculated values not by reference to the unchanging constant implicit in the verbal instructions but by reference to the sounding values of the upper voices in proportions not named in the verbal canon but arrived at by experimentation in rehearsal.

39. Notation & Editions
William P. Mahrt

The notation of medieval music includes information not easily retained in modern transcription. Original ligatures, clefs, signatures, text placement, and even page layout may contain clues to important aspects of performance. A good edition should thus permit the reader to reconstruct every significant element of the notation. But this information is useful only to the extent that the reader understands its meaning in medieval notation, and so the study of the literature on notation is indispensable to the serious performance of medieval music.[1]

Notation can be used in a more fundamental way, however: the works can be performed from the original notation itself. While the fashion for performing from old notation may at first have been for vague or even naive reasons, there is a methodical reason to perform early music from its own notational sources. Observing historical processes of performance can reveal unanticipated aspects of the works and their interpretation. This can be seen in the case of singing Gregorian chant from a choir book:

> I acquired a large folio-size choir book, and my liturgical chant choir began to sing from it. I was confident that there would be some advantages, but had only a rough idea of what they would be. It was much more practical than I had thought: with the book at eye level, the singers stood up straight and sang out well. The individual chant books had been heavy and tended to weigh down the arms; the singers slouched and sang into the books. Singing from the large book, on the other hand, made it easy to sing with good posture and to project the voice; the sound of the choir improved remarkably. The singers saw my conducting easily, because it was close to the music. The improvement in the sense of ensemble and even the spirit of collaboration that came from singing from a common source was quite noticeable. Even the sense of participation in the liturgy was improved, since the singers' attention was focused by a communal object rather than an individual one.

Musicians who regularly sing from old notation have similar stories. In the case of polyphonic music, awareness of ensemble and counterpoint is heightened by necessity—without the score to see, the singer must rely directly upon hearing the other parts; ensemble rhythm and tuning are thus made more conscious. The difficulties of the process enforce a discipline which aids in learning the work thoroughly. Needless to say, the mastery of old notation is not an end in itself, but a foundation upon which to build an interpretation. The essay which follows addresses some principles of performance from original notation for various medieval repertories and then surveys the kinds of editions available.

Liturgical Chant

Reading from old notation is the modern way to sing chant. Square notation, stemming from the Gothic period (as early as the twelfth century), is the notation of preference for most who sing chant regularly. It binds the pitches of a syllable in a single neume or neume group, representing the integrity of the syllable in singing. Transcriptions—either those found in chant books in "modern notation" (eighth and quarter notes of the conventional sort) or modern scholarly notation (stemless note heads bound by phrase markings)—give the prevailing impression of a series of single pitches weakly related, and performers generally respond honestly to such notation by singing a succession of single pitches barely joined by anything stronger than a sense of logical succession. By contrast, the identity of the syllable is a prominent visual feature of square notation, and the notes which fall upon a syllable can more easily be grouped into single rhythmic gestures, thus enhancing the sense of shape and motion; square notation, is also much more compact, and makes it easier to view the overall contour of a phrase and respond to it in singing. It is an excellent exercise to learn to write square notation: its rules can be derived by imitation of written examples, it can be written fluently with a broad-nibbed pen, and the knowledge obtained by writing is valuable in reading not only chant but also the ligatures of mensural notation.

But why be satisfied with the notation of the twelfth century for pieces which began to be notated in the ninth? Singing from the Carolingian staffless notation (especially the notation of St. Gall, but also that of Metz, both given in the *Graduale triplex*)[2] is admittedly more challenging. It requires more of the melody to be retained by memory, but that is just the point. The singer assimilates the basic melodic formulae as entities, and sings them as such, dealing with the music on a level higher than that of the succession of individual pitches or neumes. The relation of text to music comes more into focus, since differences in the application of the formulae derive largely from differences in the texts. Moreover, singing from staffless neumes provides an experience of something fundamental to medieval music making—that of singing from memory itself. The Middle Ages placed relatively less importance upon sight reading and more on singing from memory. This is a fundamentally different experience: while sight reading converts visual signs to musical sounds, singing from memory draws from one's inner store of melody, and the experience of the music is more intimate and direct, an experience we still call "singing by heart."[3]

Singing from staffless neumes, likewise, opens up other possibilities of interpretation. The Romanian letters and the horizontal bars (*episemata*) added to the neumes prescribe rhythmic subtleties that were evidently lost—at least to the writing—in a fairly short time; they can contribute variety and nuance to the performance. (These are only very imperfectly reflected in the rhythmic signs of the Solesmes publications.) Moreover, there is a greater subtlety in the flexible, cursive shape of the notation itself. The fact that it can be used to write chant down in dictation at performance tempo suggests just how cursive a notation it is. This may also suggest a quicker tempo than does the square notation, but even the curving shape of the neumes themselves conveys more strongly than square notation the *ductus* of the melody, the *motus cantus*. When I perform from square notation, if the singing sometimes becomes too square and the pitches get rather equal weight, then I write the melody out in St. Gall notation and have the singers read from it; this immediately produces a more flexible performance and clarifies the graceful contours of the melody which the neumes reflect.

From a historical point of view, however, the differences between the Carolingian and the Gothic notation are even much greater. The staffless neumes together with their rhythmic signs, point to a remarkable difference in the style of performance that must have existed between the tenth century, when the rhythms were probably highly inflected and note durations differed considerably, and the thirteenth century, when the name *cantus planus*, plainsong, suggests that the notes were treated more or less equally. This difference can be the subject of fruitful experimentation and even beautiful, subtle performance.[4]

Courtly Lyrics

Singers accustomed only to transcriptions in fixed note-values can make important musical discoveries by reading the original notation of courtly lyrics, particularly those of the troubadours. These melodies may not have been conceived in any notation at all; they were first notated by scribes familiar with plainsong, but adapting chant notation to a very different repertory.[5] Thus, even though plainsong might warrant a comparable rhythmic style from piece to piece, no such criterion need pertain to lyrics; nor does the fact that the melodies were notated in "plainsong notation" mean that they were all performed with a declamation that simply reflected the rhythm of the poetry. Rather, each piece may be judged individually and receive its own characteristic style of performance. If one considers any body of lyric poetry set to music in specific rhythmic notation (e.g., Lieder, popular song), it is clear from the notation that there are remarkable differences from piece to piece, some having precise and emphatic rhythms, others being much more "lyrical," some realizing much of the rhythm of the text, others being neutral to it or even contradicting it for a specific effect.[6]

Pitch-only notation thus suggests a method: first, consider the text as poetry; then analyze the text and melody for indications of possible rhythmic groupings and emphasis; finally, seek a convincing performance consistent with the affect and genre of the text, in some cases more metrical, in some more declamatory, in some cases more lyrical, in some, more incisive.[7] The highly personal nature of this poetry, with the poets being known and their personalities even being an object of attention, suggests that a substantially greater element of subjectivity may enter into the performance than for chant. This subjectivity should naturally give rise to an aura of spontaneity and expressive singing, though too cultivated a "spontaneity" can easily seem arbitrary. The singer's task, then, is the synthesis of the inherent elements of sense and style through a purposeful rhythmic freedom. The troubadours' notation gives the singer the freedom to do exactly this, while modern rhythmically specific notations are a serious constraint to it.

Rhythmic Modes

The music of the *ars antiqua* (Notre Dame organa, motets, and conductus of the thirteenth century) is written in rhythmic modes. Its notation does not indicate specific durations, but these can be reliably inferred from context, much like one infers the rhythm of poetry.[8] For this music, transcriptions can generally be accurate, insofar as they translate the durations of the modal rhythms into the closest available modern equivalent. Yet in any translation something is lost. The theory of rhythmic modes is an extrapolation from the theory of poetic meters, using two fundamental durations, long and short, which transcribe easily into quarter and eighth notes. However, the longs and shorts of poetry are not as precisely measured as the durations of our post-mensural "modern" notation, which is heir to the fourteenth century's fascination with measurement and with minute and fine-scaled distinctions. The performer reading from modern notation rarely realizes how crucial the distinction is; but reading the music from the original notation, and thereby inferring both mode and ordo, discovering the rhythmic structure of both measure and phrase from context goes to the root of the style, and thus helps avoid the sing-song monotony which sometimes afflicts performances of this music.

The issue is a fundamental distinction between the attitude toward duration in the thirteenth and in the fourteenth centuries. In the thirteenth century, the concern (in philosophy as well as music theory) was with essences—durations were the contrasting *longitas* and *brevitas*, longness and shortness, and these were only implicit in the notation; in the fourteenth century, durations in great variety were distinguished, just as the speculative grammarians distinguished the varying degrees to which adjectival modification could be made upon the substantive, and the notation explicitly expressed a multiplicity of durations. It is no accident that the tradition of notational theory which developed this variety of durations was called *ars nova*, since the newly received body of the logical treatises of Aristotle, from which these developments proceeded, was called *logica nova* or *ars nova* (in contradistinction to the *ars vetus*, the Aristotelian logical treatises traditionally received).[9] Viewing longs and shorts as essences akin to poetic rhythms suggests a kind of freedom in performance very different from the precision of the musical *ars nova*.

Reading from original modal notation has virtues similar to reading from chant neumes: since the notation is compact, the shape of the phrase is easily seen, not only as a melodic contour, but also as ordo (the rhythmic description of the phrase in music and the line in poetry). Moreover, the implicit groupings of notes suggested by the ligatures give the performer a natural means of articulation that is characteristically French, i.e., it results in groupings across the beat. In the context of this kind of rhythmic freedom, then, the particular rhythm of *organum purum*—a spontaneous free rhythm not tied to specific modes but related to consonance and dissonance[10]—becomes all the more special and remarkable, and it simply cannot be written in fixed note values.

Mensural Music

Mensural notation is the principal notation of the fourteenth and fifteenth centuries, and it is in this repertory that most performers are likely to begin to read from original notation. Its fundamentals can be studied from the basic handbooks.[11] There are a few principles helpful in reading notation, however, which do not emerge from these handbooks, and these are developed here. They concern 1) imperfection and alteration and 2) ligatures.

Imperfection and alteration

Mensural music is founded on the principle that the metric organization of a piece can be either perfect (triple) or imperfect (duple), and this organization can pertain to several levels at once, namely *modus* (division of the long), *tempus* (the breve), and *prolatio* (the semibreve). Duple mensurations are read essentially as modern notation, but triple mensurations involve reading varying durations from a single note, i.e., notes are subject to imperfection and alteration.

The modal rhythms of thirteenth-century music are an excellent school for imperfection and alteration, in that these processes are rooted in modal rhythm, and can be learned there with little difficulty. In reading modal rhythm, a succession of longs and breves is resolved to a triple grouping (a perfection), whether the long alternates with the breve or not. Thus, in the following succession of notes, the performer intuitively groups a breve with the preceding long and sings any long followed by another long as equivalent to three breves:

2 1 3 3 3 2 1 2 1 3

From this the principle of imperfection can be inferred: whenever a long is followed by a breve, the breve "imperfects" the long—it is grouped together with the long to comprise the perfect three beats. Conversely, whenever a long is followed by another long, the first of them is perfect.

Likewise, the principle of alteration can be observed in rhythmic mode three:

3 1 2 3

The second breve is doubled, so that the pattern can be congruent with other triply measured modes, most notably mode five:

mode three:

3 1 2 3

mode five:

3 3 3

These things are so implicit in the system of rhythmic modes that they scarcely need to be defined as principles there. They remained as principles, however, when the patterned rhythms of modal music gave way to the greater freedom and variety of the *ars nova,* including their simultaneous application to all three mensural levels; in this new context they require careful attention. Those who experience them in modal music and make note of how they work will find that their application in mensural music, though necessarily more conscious at first, will seem natural, even logical.

Ligatures

The ligatures of mensural notation might seem too complicated and a hindrance to reading old notation.[12] Their principles are simple, however, and with some practice can be mastered easily. The tables of ligatures found in notation books need never be used, because the shapes are quite logical. Ligatures take the shapes of chant neumes as paradigm; these shapes are then modified to prescribe various durations. Three principles obtain:

1 The basic shapes of the ligatures derive from ascending or descending chant neumes; as the shapes of mensural notation, they are considered with propriety (concerning the beginning of the ligature) and with perfection (concerning the end of the ligature). A two-note ligature in ascent looks like this: ; in descent, like this: . Each has the value of breve-long, deriving from their values in modal notation, where the ending notes of most ligatures are long.

2 Changing either beginning or end of these shapes reverses its value: breve becomes long, long becomes breve. Thus:

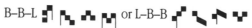

		ascending	*descending*
with propriety & with perfection (the basic shape):	B–L		
without propriety & with perfection:	L–L		
with propriety & without perfection:	B–B		
without propriety & without perfection:	L–B		

Ligatures with more than two notes generally include breves as the internal notes; (rarely a long middle note is indicated by a stem descending to its right); their beginning and ending notes, ascending or descending, are judged exactly as the beginning and ending notes of two-note ligatures:

B–B–L   or L–B–B

3 Opposite propriety, indicated by an ascending stem on the left, conceptually breaks the initial breve of a ligature with propriety into two semibreves, whether the ligature has two or more notes:

S–S–L   S–S–B   S–S

Mensural polyphony, especially the motets of the fourteenth century, potentially involves activity at two or three (or more) levels of metric organization, a hierarchical organization which reflects a hierarchical aesthetic. The process of comprehending this metric ordering through reading imperfect and perfect *modus, tempus,* and *prolatio* instructs in this aesthetic hierarchy, and promises to be an aid in conceiving and projecting the complex ordering of the works.

Ars Subtilior

The style of the late fourteenth century used to be called "mannerist;" more recently the term "ars subtilior"[14] has been proposed, and this term is more appropriate from an aesthetic point of view. The intellectual life of the fourteenth century involved refinement and calculation. It was in this time that the methods for collecting and accounting for ecclesiastical taxes were developed by the papal chancery; clocks could measure time more precisely; adjectives were considered with regard to the varying degree of their application, even in infinitesimal amounts; logicians studied the use of language as it was able to express subtle differences. Precision and subtlety were principal values of the period. The technical virtuosity of the logicians was matched by that of the musicians, and a primary value in the performance of the music is this virtuosity—not a mechanical dexterity, but a virtuosity which plays with the conceptual basis of the music—a virtuosity of subtlety. The mastery of the music is akin to the mastery of sophism, paradox, and conundrum in logic.

The most intricate pieces in the *ars subtilior* style have been the ultimate in the study and transcription of notation, a challenge to the most skilled transcriber; many have thought them so difficult that performance from this notation is beyond the reach of the modern performer; this need not be so. The distinction between performance and sight reading should be recalled: the objective is not instantaneous sight reading, but rather the study of a piece from its notation for performance. Individual performers could well review the notation of their parts first, before the piece is read together. Simpler pieces could be learned first, pieces in which the use of coloration has a simple metrical significance, then pieces which use *traynor,* a kind of metric syncopation indicated by coloration. Gradually, the technique of reading the notation can approach the most difficult pieces; then the performance will reflect its proper aesthetic—the virtuoso display of subtlety.

EDITIONS

Finding good repertory is a crucial part of performance. There are major anthologies presenting pieces chosen for reasons usually not explained. Some of these pieces are real "chestnuts" in the best sense of the word—every performer might well perform them. Others are typical in a less desirable sense, representing the middle level of repertory rather than the peaks. The performer should seek out the peaks, viewing the anthologies as potential sources for music which has stood the test of modern performance, that has been heard by audiences before and is worth hearing again. Just as the Mozart Symphonies can be played repeatedly to the benefit of performers and audiences, so there is a real value in the repeated performance of some of the best works from the Middle Ages; this value is also enhanced when the same work is performed by different performers.

Yet the anthologies cannot be the only source of works. Extensive modern editions now exist, so that much of the polyphonic music of the period is available for study and performance. The resourceful director should read these editions from cover to cover to find pieces suitable to the particular ensemble, voices, instruments, and occasions. The repertories that I perform include a few enduring pieces I have found in collected editions and perform regularly. Every concert contains some works performed before, for which I hope the performers and audience will achieve a deeper appreciation upon repetition. Every concert also presents works I have found searching the monuments and collected editions, in what may be their first performance in modern times. The following lists are not exhaustive, but attempt only to indicate the kinds of edition available. These sets and many other similar ones are available at major research libraries, and richly repay seeking them out.

Among the anthologies, three can serve as examples. Morrocco and Sandin's *Medieval Music*[15] contains, in addition to a large selection of pieces, a whole Mass in the Sarum rite, together with a detailed description of the ceremonies. David Wilson's anthology[16] is particularly good for the range of motets it contains. Denis Stevens's anthology has exclusively sacred music,[17] but it is a shrewdly assembled group of eminently performable pieces, some of them skillfully restored from damaged manuscripts.

Among the comprehensive editions, perhaps the one which stands out the most is *Polyphonic Music of the Fourteenth Century*.[18] This series of twenty-five substantial volumes includes the works of Vitry, Machaut, Landini, and Ciconia, Italian and French secular and sacred music, and English sacred music; it attempts to be a complete collection of these repertories; some volumes include translations of motet texts. Another invaluable collection is *Early Fifteenth-Century Music*.[19] It includes the earliest music of the fifteenth century and complements the previous set. A different kind of scholarly set can be seen in the old edition of the Montpellier Codex;[20] it consists of a manuscript facsimile, modern edition, and extensive commentary on this principal source of the thirteenth-century motet. Many facsimiles of manuscripts are now being published, including, for example, the series *Publications of Mediæval Musical Manuscripts*.[21] Sometimes these facsimile publications are sumptuous and expensive, for example, the *Squarcialupi Codex*;[22] the facsimile attempts to be exact, down to the binding and the lavish use of gold leaf in the initials; the set includes a separate volume of commentary. Another magnificent set, still in progress is the complete edition of Notre Dame organum.[23] Conductus of the Notre Dame school are partly available in Gordon Anderson's edition;[24] although incomplete, it remains a source of many otherwise unpublished pieces. Occasionally a repertory receives separate contrasting editions; this is the case for "Aquitanian polyphony," whose two publications[25] are reviewed by Richard Crocker as examples of radically different editions.[26]

Of the principal monophonic repertories, complete collections have been made for some; the music of the troubadours has two contrasting editions,[27] there is only one for the trouvères.[28] All three of these must be used in connection with an edition of the poetry,[29] since they give only the first stanza to the melody. A somewhat different collection of a complete repertory is the single volume containing the extant musical settings of lyrical poetry in English until about 1400, with complete texts.[30]

Editions of liturgical chant present a unique problem: the most readily available editions were not made for primarily historical reasons, but were prepared for current liturgical use. Thus they must be viewed in light of two rules of thumb for considering liturgical sources: 1) no two liturgical books are alike; and 2) any liturgical book pertains to the customs of its own time and place.[31] The ubiquitous *Liber usualis*[32] was prepared for modern liturgical use before the Second Vatican Council, and contains compositions of the nineteenth and twentieth centuries in numbers that very few suspect, yet it has the virtue of including much of the oldest repertory and showing it in the context of a liturgical day and year in fundamental continuity with the Middle Ages.[33] On the other hand, the recent edition of the *Graduale Romanum*[34] has eliminated most of the neo-Gregorian compositions, giving almost exclusively the medieval pieces, but it has a liturgical arrangement with substantial discontinuities from the medieval liturgy. The only way to be sure a piece is not of recent composition is to verify its presence in a medieval source:

First check to see if the chant has staffless neumes in the *Graduale triplex;* if it does, it dates at least as early as the tenth century. Second, consult the thematic index of chant,[35] which indexes a few representative pitch-specific medieval sources available in facsimile; if a chant is indexed there in one of these sources, then it dates at least as early as that source (11th–13th centuries). Further, consult the increasing body of available manuscript facsimiles of chant sources, or even an extensive collection of sources on microfilm.

The principal series for facsimiles is *Paléographie musicale.*[36] Other series are in the course of publication.[37] A series of editions from historical sources is *Monumenta monodica medii ævi.*[38] A more practical series is devoted to the Sarum Rite (the liturgy of Salisbury), giving extensive rubrics (prescriptions for liturgical actions) in English translation.[39] An additional benefit in searching such sources is, of course, an invaluable cognizance of the medieval repertories and their liturgical contexts.

Every edition must be approached critically, even those which appear to be the finest. The example of Machaut is instructive. Ludwig's old edition[40] used old clefs and was not a particularly attractive production. A subsequent edition by Leo Schrade was included in *Polyphonic Music of the Fourteenth Century.*[41] Its handsome buckram binding and fine watermarked paper conceals problems for performers. Lawrence Earp summarizes the case:

> except for the use of modern clefs and barring to *tempus* in the chansons, making the music vastly easier to read, it is usually inferior to Ludwig's edition. Schrade's text underlay is not trustworthy, and his edition provides far less information on accidentals.[42]

Earp further observes that faults of the edition regularly make their way into recordings, faults as serious as misrepresenting schemes of repetition. The astute performer, thus, needs to develop a sense for the quality of editions and their supporting scholarship. Earp's research guide is an ideal resource for such information concerning Machaut; there is practically no performance of his music that could not benefit from the feast of information and access presented there.

Notes

[1] Willi Apel, *The Notation of Polyphonic Music, 900–1600,* 5th ed. (Cambridge, MA, 1961); David Hiley and Margaret Bent, "Notation, III: History of Western Notation, 1–3," *The New Grove Dictionary of Music and Musicians,* ed. Stanley Sadie (London, 1980), 13, pp. 344–73; Stanley Boorman et al., "Sources, MS," *New Grove* 17, pp. 590–668; the more adventurous should use these secondary sources to lead them to medieval treatises such as those of Anonymous 4, Franco of Cologne, Phillipe de Vitry, Marchetto of Padua, etc.

[2] *Graduale triplex* (Sablé-sur-Sarthe, 1979); this source gives the staffless neumes above the square notation; for the present purposes, the neumes alone should be used; I set the text in large type with a word processor and then draw the neumes above it; there are now "neume processors," computer programs for producing square notation, e.g., *GregEdit* (Fontgombault, France, 1996).

[3] See Christopher Page, ed. and trans., *Summa musicae: A Thirteenth-Century Manual for Singers,* Cambridge Musical Texts and Monographs (Cambridge, 1991), p. 128.

[4] The study of the neumes and their rhythmic signs may be pursued in Eugène Cardine, *Gregorian Semiology,* tr. Robert M. Fowels (Sablé-sur-Sarthe, 1982); for a clear summary of the issues, see David Hiley, *Western Plainchant* (Oxford, 1991), pp. 373–85; for more on this subject, see the chapter on Gregorian chant above.

[5] See Hendrik van der Werf, "Music," in *A Handbook of the Troubadours,* ed. F.R.P. Akehurst and Judith M. Davis (Berkeley, 1996), pp. 121–64.

[6] The recordings of "Can vei la lauzeta mover" and "Baros de mon dan covit" by the Studio der Frühen Musik illustrate such differences; see *Chansons der Troubadours: Lieder und Spielmusik aus dem 12. Jahrhundert,* Das alte Werk (long-playing disk: Telefunken SAWT 9567; compact disk: Teldec 8.35519).

[7] The music of the trouvères contains distinctions of genre which are a good basis for experimentation with rhythm; while the *grand chant courtois* seems to have maintained an improvisatory rhythm, the *virelai* as a dance seems to have had an incisive metric rhythm.

[8] For the basics of modal rhythms, see David Fenwick Wilson, *The Music of the Middle Ages: Style and Structure* (New York, 1990), pp. 193–200, and Ian D. Bent, "Rhythmic Modes," *New Grove* 15, pp. 824–25; for the specifics of modal notation, see Apel, *Notation,* pp. 215–58.

[9] See Bernard G. Dod, "Aristoteles latinus," in Norman Kretzman et al., eds., *The Cambridge History of Later Medieval Philosophy* (Cambridge, 1982), pp. 46–48.

[10] See Jeremy Yudkin, "The Rhythm of Organum Purum," *Journal of Musicology* 2 (1983), 355–76.

[11] A good introduction to the basics of mensural notation, prepared for reading from original parts, is in *Guillaume Dufay, Chansons: Forty-five Settings in Original Notation from Oxford, Bodleian Library, MS Canonici 213,* ed. Ross W. Duffin (Miami, 1983), pp. vi–viii.

[12] See Irving Godt, "Reading Ligatures from their Ground State," *Early Music* 4 (1976), 44–45, and Duffin, *Guillaume Dufay.*

[13] The second shape is an alternative form needed for stepwise ligatures; it amounts to reperfecting the form "without perfection" by adding the downward stem to the right.

[14]   See Ursula Günther, "Das Ende der Ars Nova," *Die Musikforschung* 16 (1963), 105–20.

[15]   W. Thomas Marrocco and Nicholas Sandon, eds., *Medieval Music*, The Oxford Anthology of Music (London, 1977).

[16]   David Fenwick Wilson, ed., *Music of the Middle Ages: An Anthology for Performance and Study* (New York, 1990).

[17]   Denis Stevens, ed., *The Treasury of English Church Music*, vol. 1, *1100–1545* (London, 1965).

[18]   Leo Schrade, Frank Ll. Harrison, and Kurt von Fischer, gen. eds., *Polyphonic Music of the Fourteenth Century*, 25 vols. (Monaco, 1956–91).

[19]   Gilbert Reaney, ed., *Early Fifteenth-Century Music*, 7 vols., Corpus Mensurabilis Musicae 11 (American Institute of Musicology, 1955–1983).

[20]   Yvonne Rokseth, ed., *Motets du XIIIe siècle*, 3 vols. (Paris, 1936).

[21]   *Publications of Mediæval Musical Manuscripts*, 18 vols. (Brooklyn, 1957–).

[22]   F. Alberto Gallo, ed., *Il codice Squarcialupi: Ms. Mediceo Palatino 87, Biblioteca medicea laurenziana di Firenze* (Florence, 1992).

[23]   Edward H. Roesner, ed., *Le Magnus liber organi de Notre-Dame de Paris* (Monaco, 1993–).

[24]   Gordon A. Anderson, ed., *Notre-Dame and Related Conductus: Opera Omnia* (Henryville, 1979–).

[25]   Theodore Karp, ed., *The Polyphony of Saint Martial and Santiago de Compostela* (Berkeley, 1992); Hendrik van der Werf, *The Oldest Extant Part Music and the Origin of Western Polyphony* (Rochester, 1993).

[26]   Richard Crocker, "Two Recent Editions of Aquitanian Polyphony," *Plainsong and Medieval Music* 3 (1994), 57–101; this valuable review article is demonstration that reading reviews of major editions is a good preparation for their use.

[27]   Hendrik van der Werf, ed., and Gerald A. Bond, text ed., *The Extant Troubadour Melodies: Transcriptions and Essays for Performers and Scholars* (Rochester, 1984); Ismael Fernandez de la Cuesta, ed., and Robert Lafont, text ed., *Las Cancons dels Trobadors* (Toulouse, 1979).

[28]   Hendrik van der Werf, ed., *Trouvères-Melodien*, Monumenta monodica medii ævi, vols. 11–12 (Kassel, 1977–1979).

[29]   For example, Thibaut de Champagne, *Lyrics*, ed. and trans. Kathleen J. Brahney, Garland Library of Medieval Literature, A:41 (New York, 1991).

[30]   E. J. Dobson and F. Ll. Harrison, eds., *Medieval English Songs* (London, 1979).

[31]   A third more general rule is "always look in the front and back of the book for indices and supplements," since, though the principal contents of any two books may seem identical, very often printed supplements or even manuscript additions at the back of the book give it a unique identity or usefulness.

[32]   *Liber usualis* (Tournai, 1963); this was the latest edition; there were numerous previous editions, as early as 1896.

[33]   In general, the *Liber usualis* gives medieval pieces for medieval feasts: the cycle of the temporale, i.e., Christmas and Easter, with their dependent feasts and seasons (Sundays of Advent and Lent, after Epiphany, Easter, and Pentecost). However, it also includes feasts of recent origin or revision, for example, Christ the King and the Assumption of Mary. Major saints' days of medieval vintage employ medieval pieces in general, but these are subject to greater complications when they draw from the common of the saints.

[34]   *Graduale Romanum* (Sablé-sur-Sarthe, 1974).

[35]   John R. Bryden and David G. Hughes, eds., *An Index of Gregorian Chant*, 2 vols.

(Cambridge, MA, 1969).

[36] Benedictines of Solesmes, eds., *Paléographie musicale* (Sablé-sur-Sarthe, 1889–1937; 1955–58; 1992– ; Bern, 1968–83; reprint, Bern, 1971–74); a series of less expensive reprints is projected.

[37] *Monumenta palæographica Gregoriana* (Münsterschwarzach, 1984–), and René-Jean Hesbert, ed., *Monumenta musicæ sacræ* (Macon, 1952, 1954; Rouen, 1961, 1970; Paris, 1981).

[38] Bruno Stäblein, David Hiley, et al., eds., *Monumenta monodica medii ævi* (Kassel, 1956–).

[39] Nick Sandon, ed., *The Use of Salisbury* (Newton Abbot, Devon, 1984–)

[40] Guillaume de Machaut, *Musikalische Werke,* ed. Friedrich Ludwig, 4 vols. (Leipzig, 1926–54).

[41] Vols. 2-3 (1956). The critical notes to this edition were distributed separately and have not been made available in subsequent reprints.

[42] Lawrence Earp, *Guillaume de Machaut: A Guide to Research,* Garland Composer Resource Manuals (New York, 1995), pp. 280–81.

40. Tuning

Ross W. Duffin

T uning in the Middle Ages is in one respect a less complex problem than in the Renaissance. Theorists are unanimous in discussing only one size of fifth: the pure fifth, with a harmonic ratio of 3:2. This, then, is the dominant interval in the Middle Ages in the same way that the major third is the dominant interval in the Renaissance. And for the dominant repertory in the Middle Ages, namely Gregorian chant, a tuning system with all pure fifths and high leading tones—what we call Pythagorean tuning—works perfectly well. The difficulties arise when dealing with music with more than one voice and, especially, with more than two voices.

The problem, as anyone who has tried to tune a keyboard by means of pure fifths (or pure fifths and fourths) can tell you, is that Pythagorean tuning does not work as a closed system. The tuning process itself is easy enough, since the pure fifth is one of the easiest intervals to tune; it is just that, having tuned one interval after another, when you should be arriving back on the note you started from, the last note before closing the circle makes too narrow a fifth to the first note by about one quarter of a semitone (approximately 24 cents, or 24/100 of an equal tempered semitone), an uncomfortably dissonant amount.[1] The resultant pseudo-fifth or "wolf," a howling discord, can be moved around in the Pythagorean system depending on where the line of fifths begins, but the one bad fifth cannot be avoided entirely, and that is one of the limitations of Pythagorean tuning on keyboard instruments.

However, music on keyboard instruments plays a much smaller role in medieval music than in Renaissance music—until the late fourteenth century hardly any role at all—so it should not be the focus of a general discussion of tuning in the Middle Ages. Most medieval music is vocal music, so that is where we must begin. Keyboards and other instruments have their own problems that will be addressed later.

The crux of the problem is not whether medieval performers tried to tune their fifths pure. We assume they did so whenever possible. The crux of the problem is whether they were happy with the vertical Pythagorean ditone (408c)—Pythagorean tuning's non-harmonic, wide major third—or whether they preferred to shade it towards the narrower, pure third (386c).[2] (This choice is not open to keyboard players because the tuning of the instrument, once set, cannot be changed during performance.) Actually, the question should probably be not "whether" but "when," since by the end of the Middle Ages there are so many thirds among the vertical sonorities that to perform them all as ditones would be an unpleasant musical experience for everyone. Certainly, the succession of "first-inversion triads" that make up the sound of *fauxbourdon* in the early fifteenth century, and of English music from much earlier, would benefit from purer thirds than those provided by Pythagorean tuning. The roots of the question go back to the writings of Anonymous IV in the late thirteenth century, who says, "...the major and minor third are not reckoned as such [i.e., concords] among some people. Nevertheless amongst the best composers of *organum* and for example in certain lands like in England, in the region which is called Westcuntre, they are called the best concords, since among such people they are greatly used."[3] The English predilection for thirds has been noted by many modern writers; what has not received much attention is the phrase, "amongst the best composers of *organum*." Anonymous IV is thought to have been writing in Paris. That he would make such a statement, unqualified by place, suggests that "good" thirds were not merely an English phenomenon, although it must be said that the writer is thought to have been an expatriate Englishman himself. What this may mean is that, whether the theorists knew it or not, whether they liked it or not, performers were varying from strict Pythagorean tuning, and varying in a way that we would describe as approaching Just intonation, where ideally both fifths and thirds are pure.[4] This is a system that defies easy description, since some notes of the scale are frequently found in different places depending on their vertical context. Little wonder that medieval theorists, even knowing what performers were doing in practical terms, might choose to expound a simpler system that had the weight of a Greek philosopher/mathematician behind it!

Recently, a scholar whose work has helped to shed light on tuning in the Middle Ages read a paper called "Medieval modifications of Pythagorean tuning,"[5] in which he pointed out that, indeed, there are situations where pure thirds would seem to be preferable to Pythagorean ditones. He used the following example, among many others, and here pointed out that a G tuned flat to be pure above the Eb root of the first chord would make an excruciating fifth with the D at the end of the phrase. That is not a "just" solution, however, as I hope the discussion that follows will demonstrate.

Ex. 40.1a. Johannes Ciconia, *Credo*, mm. 68–72.

Just Intonation

Part of the problem with discussions of Just intonation, like those for Pythagorean tuning in the Middle Ages, is that they tend to assume a twelve-note fixed system like the modern keyboard. So while keyboard players may be stuck with a wolf between B and F♯ (really G♭), it is hard to imagine that a singer, faced with a B–F♯ fifth, would choose to sing it as a wolf. And as singers got used to the good pseudo-thirds (384c)—schismatic thirds, as they are called—available in four places even in a keyboard Pythagorean system (D–F♯, A–C♯, E–G♯, and B–D♯ with B–F♯ as the wolf), it seems likely that they would want to sweeten the otherwise excruciating ditones when they occurred in prominent places in the music.[6] Similarly, to limit the choices of the notes in Just intonation to the seven different notes of the C major Just scale is to ignore the flexibility of performers not tied to a fixed system.[7] The counter-argument is that sometimes thirds and sixths were intended as dissonances, and to purify them is to remove the tension that makes the fifths and octaves that much more tranquil. This is an important point and it requires that performers are able to make judgements about the role of the thirds among the sonorities in any given piece or repertoire. Basically, performers must decide whether thirds are used as predominant sonorities or at points of repose. If they are, then Just intonation may be a better choice than Pythagorean.

The way Just intonation works in practice in medieval music is something that has never really been fully addressed before. Writers have talked about it in terms of tonality or in terms of a single mode. But medieval music is not tonal, and its modal unity is frequently broken with excursions to other modes within a piece, in the same way that tonal music touches different key areas within a single movement. The excursions might take one or two measures, they might take about eight measures, or they might take half the piece. The departure from the mode of the final is significant because the Just scale depends on the current mode. Mixing in another mode—commixture, as they called it—requires the adjustment of one to three notes in the diatonic scale, depending on how far away the visited mode is.

Polyphonic music from the late medieval period is written with finals on F, C, G, D, A, and E.[8] (The A final appears mostly in 3rd or 4th mode, that is, with a B♭ creating Phrygian cadences.) Some of those modes occur with a variety of signatures. All of them favor excursions to certain modes more than others, some predominantly so, as shown in Figure 40.1. And although there are some slight variations in preference according to the signature, these tendencies seem to be true for these modal finals no matter what the signature.[9]

Fig. 40.1. Modal finals, signatures, and excursions.

Modal Final	Signatures	Predominant Modal Excursions	Others
F	—, ♭, ♭♭		C, G, A
C	—, ♭, ♭♭	G, F	D
G	—, ♭, ♭♭	C, D	
D	—, ♭		A, G
A	—, (♭)	D	C
E	—	C	D

547

Figure 40.2 gives the most commonly used placement of the notes in each of the modes with the most frequent alternatives given in parentheses. It looks complicated, but will make sense if you keep in mind the following:

1.   Notes a fourth or a fifth apart that are pure to one another have the same annotation, mostly $_{-1}$, $_0$, $_{+1}$, and rarely $_{-2}$. So, for example, C_{+1} and G_{+1} are pure to each other, 498c (4th) or 702c (5th) apart.[10]

2.   Notes a major third apart that are pure to one another are narrow by one unit, either $_{+1}$ up to $_0$, or $_0$ up to $_{-1}$, while notes a pure minor third apart will be wide by the same amount. Thus, C_0–E_{-1}–G_0 or C_{+1}–E_0–G_{+1} form pure "major" triads. The C–E from each of those triads, combined with an A having the same annotation as the E, form pure "minor" triads.

The "unit" by which the notes vary is the syntonic comma (approximately 22 cents), so different placements of each note will be separated by increments of that amount.[11] Thus, a D_0, by virtue of being two pure fifths minus a pure octave away from C_0, is found at 204 cents: 702c + 702c – 1200c = 204c. D_{-1} is 22c lower than that at 182c. The reason that more than one version of some notes is required is because the notes appear in more than one harmonic context. For example, in the C mode, A must frequently shift back and forth between A_0 and A_{-1}: A_0 because it must sometimes make a pure fifth to D_0; A_{-1} because it must sometimes make a pure major third to F_0 or a pure fifth to E_{-1}.

You may notice that some of the numbers are "transposed" from other Just scales you may have seen: This is because I have put each modal final at $_0$, rather than keeping C at C_0.

Fig. 40.2. Just tuning by mode.

F mode:

	(-1)									
	-2	+1			-1	-2		+1		
	C♯	**E♭**			**F♯**	**G♯**		**B♭**		
C	**D**		**E**	**F**	**G**		**A**		**B**	**C**
0	0		-1	0	0		-1		-1	0
	(-1)						(0)			

Cents:

C	D		E	F	G		A		B	C
0	70	204	316	386	498	590	702	772	884	1018	1088	1200
	(92)	(182)							(906)			

548

C mode:

	C	C#	D	Eb	E	F	F#	G	G#	A	Bb	B	C
		(-2)							(-1)				
		-1		+1			-1		-2		+1		
accidental		C#		Eb			F#		G#		Bb		
natural	C		D		E	F		G		A		B	C
deviation	0		0		-1	0 (+1)		0		0 (-1)		-1	0
Cents:	0	92 (70)	204	316	386	498 (520)	590	702	772 (794)	906 (884)	1018	1088	1200

G mode:

	C	C#	D	Eb	E	F	F#	G	G#	A	Bb	B	C
		-1		+1			-1		-1		+1		
accidental		C#		Eb			F#		G#		Bb		
natural	C		D		E	F		G		A		B	C
deviation	0 (+1)		0		0 (-1)	+1 (0)		0		0		-1	0 (+1)
Cents:	0 (22)	92	204	316	408 (386)	520 (498)	590	702	794	906	1018	1088	1200 (1222)

D mode:

	C	C#	D	Eb	E	F	F#	G	G#	A	Bb	B	C
		-1		+1			-1		-1		+1		
accidental		C#		Eb			F#		G#		Bb		
natural	C		D		E	F		G		A		B	C
deviation	+1		0		0	+1		0 (+1)		0		0 (-1)	+1
Cents:	22	92	204	316	408	520	590	702 (724)	794	906	1018	1110 (1088)	1222

A mode:

	C	C#	D	Eb	E	F	F#	G	G#	A	Bb	B	C
							(0)						
		-1		+1			-1		-1		+1		
accidental		C#		Eb			F#		G#		Bb		
natural	C		D		E	F		G		A		B	C
deviation	+1		0 (+1)		0	+1		0 (+1)		0		0	+1
Cents:	22	92	204 (226)	316	408	520	590 (612)	702 (724)	794	906	1018	1110	1222

E mode:

						(0)						
-1		+1				-1		-1		+1		
C#		Eb				F#		G#		Bb		
C		D		E	F		G		A		B	C
+1		0		0	+1		+1		0		0	+1
		(+1)										

Cents:

22	92	204	316	408	520	590	724	794	906	1018	1110	1222
		(226)				(612)						

This is a lot of information to digest. But it should immediately begin to suggest solutions to the puzzle presented by the Ciconia example above: Since the phrase is in the G mode, it is the Eb and Bb that are high, not the G that must be low to make a pure triad. The G is thus still able to make a pure fifth with the D at the cadence, even without having to adjust within the phrase.

Ex. 40.1b. Johannes Ciconia, *Credo*, mm. 68–72.

You may have noticed in Figure 40.2 that the modes in succession are a fifth apart and that, from mode to mode through that sequence, notes sometimes become unstable, then gradually settle in their new position. Just about every note is transformed in this way with, interestingly enough, Eb, F#, and Bb being the most stable in terms of absolute position.

The next step is to look at and compare the degrees of the individual scales (see Figure 40.3). This shows that there is much more similarity among the modes than is apparent in Figure 40.2. In particular, the instability is concentrated around the sixth degree of the scale (as is apparent by the many alternatives given there) and to a lesser extent at the fourth degree. That the fourth degree should be unstable is a little odd since it ought to make a pure fourth with the final but, in fact, it is frequently needed to make a pure major third to the higher form of the sixth degree and a pure minor third to the second degree.

What you also see in Figure 40.3 are indications of the different sizes of semitones, which are then extracted below in Figure 40.4. There are four different sizes of semitone in Just intonation, which have been assigned the abbreviations given here:[12]

$$MM \quad = \quad 134c \quad (133.24c) \quad \text{e.g., } A_{-1}\text{–}Bb_{+1}$$

$$M \quad = \quad 112c \quad (111.73c) \quad \text{e.g., } E_{-1}\text{–}F_0$$

$$m \quad = \quad 92c \quad (92.18c) \quad \text{e.g., } C_0\text{–}C\#_{-1}$$

$$n \quad = \quad 70c \quad (70.67c) \quad \text{e.g., } Eb_{+1}\text{–}E_{-1}$$

Fig. 40.3. Degrees and semitones by modal octave.

F mode scale:

0	92	204	274	386 (408)	520	590	702	772 (794)	906 (884)	1018	1088	1200
	m	M	n	M	MM	n	M	n	MM	M	n	M

C mode scale:

0	92 (70)	204	316	386	498 (520)	590	702	772 (794)	906 (884)	1018	1088	1200
	m	M	M	n	M	m	M	n	MM	M	n	M

G mode scale:

0	92	204	316	386	498 (520)	590	702	794	906 (884)	1018 (996)	1088	1200
	m	M	M	n	M	m	M	m	M	M	n	M

D mode scale:

0	112	204	316	386	498 (520)	590	702	794	906 (884)	1018	1088	1200
M	m	M	n	M	m	M	m	M	M	n	M	

A mode scale:

0	112	204	316	386	498 (520)	610	702	814	884 (906)	996 (1018)	1088	1200
M	m	M	n	M	M	m	M	n	M	m	M	

E mode scale:

0	112	182 (204)	316	386	498	610	702	814	884	996 (1018)	1108	1200
M	n	MM	n	M	M	m	M	n	M	M	m	

For the most part, however, the sizes of the *whole tone* are limited to just two within each mode: major (204c representing m-M or MM-n), and minor (182c representing M-n).[13] For diatonic semitones, the 112c variety is the most common within each mode, although when shifts of mode occur, it is often necessary to use either the 70c or 134c varieties, both of which are melodically less elegant. Melodic inelegance is also necessary sometimes without a mode shift when vertical perfection demands the sacrifice of some melodic interval. Typically, this involves an alternate version of one of the less stable notes of the scale. The awkward interval created is frequently a semitone, as in Ex. 40.2a, but it could be another interval instead—often a fourth, as in Ex. 40.2b. In fact, Fig. 40.3 shows that the wide fourth (520c) above the modal final is a common alternative in several modes.

Ex. 40.2a. Gilles Binchois, *Dueil angoisseus*, mm. 31–34.

Ex. 40.2b. Guillaume Du Fay, *Je me complains*, mm. 1–4.

Fig. 40.4. Sizes of semitones by mode.

F:	m	M	n	M	MM	n	M	n	MM	M	n	M
C:	m	M	M	n	M	m	M	n	MM	M	n	M
G:	m	M	M	n	M	m	M	m	M	M	n	M
D:	M	m	M	n	M	m	M	m	M	M	n	M
A:	M	m	M	n	M	M	m	M	n	M	m	M
E:	M	n	MM	n	M	M	m	M	n	M	M	m

One other thing of interest in Figure 40.4 is the apparent similarity between adjacent modes. In fact, if you were to draw boxes around identical adjacent semitone patterns, you would see that the portions of the scales that correspond most closely are the shared species of diatonic fourth and fifth (See Figure 40.5 and Chapter 36: "Gamut, Solmization, & Modes").

Fig. 40.5. Species of 5ths and 4ths.

5ths

1st		204	316		498		702
	0	0	+1		0		0

2nd	112		316		498		702
	0	+1	+1		0		0

3rd		204	386		590	702	
	0	0	-1		-1	0	

4th		204	386	498		702	
	0	0	-1	0		0	

4ths

1st		204	316		498
	0	0	+1		0

2nd	112		316		498
	0	+1	+1		0

3rd		204	386	498
	0	0	-1	0

Thus, the top parts of the F and C modes correspond (3rd species of fourth), but not the bottom parts which are of different species; the bottom parts of the C and G modes correspond (4th species of fifth); the top parts of the G and D modes correspond (1st species of fourth); the bottom parts of D and A modes correspond (1st species of fifth); the central portions of A and E modes correspond. The latter species fail to correspond more closely because the F♯ in the E mode tends to be lower than the B in the A mode, and the E♭ in the E mode higher than the G♯ in the A mode.[14] Nevertheless, the A and E diatonic scales match perfectly (treating the A mode as Phrygian) and emphasize the value of consistency within a certain species (see Example 40.3).

Ex. 40.3. Basic diatonic Just modal scales.

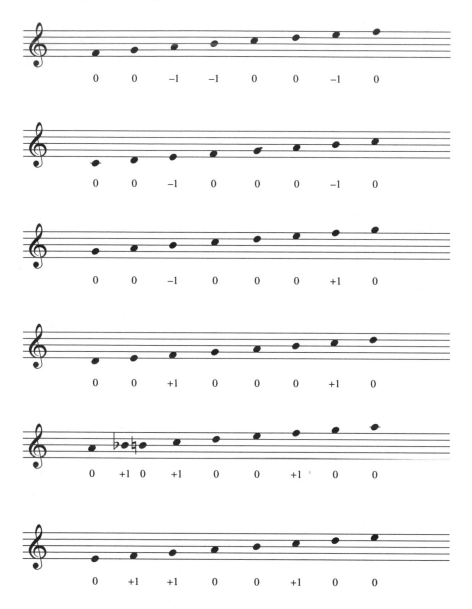

It is important, therefore, to be able to identify melodic species in the individual parts and to make deductions, based on that, about the current or imminent mode.[15] Once you have an idea of that, perhaps by starting with the probable excursions for each mode given above in Figure 40.1, the next step is to decide what specific changes to make in shifting from one mode to another. The way to prepare for that is to know, in going from one mode to each of the others, which notes are likely to need adjusting and in which direction. Table 40.1 shows the simplest way to get from one mode to another in Just intonation. Notice that the simplest way (i.e., changing the fewest notes) sometimes results in a comma transposition from the values shown in Figure 40.2. Where such transposition occurs is marked with an * in Table 40.1.

Table 40.1. Note adjustments in Just tuning.

From To:	F	C	G	D	A	E
F mode		A ↑	A,E,F ↑	D,G ↓ *	D,G ↓ *	D ↓ *
C mode	A ↓		E,F ↑	A,D,G ↓ *	A,D,G ↓ *	A,D ↓ *
G mode	A,E,F ↓	E,F ↓		B,C ↑	B,C ↑	G,B,C ↑
D mode	D,G ↑ *	A,D,G ↑ *	B,C ↓			G ↑
A mode	D,G ↑ *	A,D,G ↑ *	B,C ↓			G ↑
E mode	D ↑ *	A,D ↑ *	G,B,C ↓	G ↓	G ↓	

So, how does this work? Let us take the example of a piece in C mode that visits F and G before returning to C. Starting with the C mode scale from Figure 40.2, as the F mode is introduced, the A_0 of the C mode must begin to change to A_{-1}. Going then from F mode to G mode, A_{-1}, E_{-1}, and F_0 must move up a comma, and at the return to the C mode, the E_0 and F_{+1} move back down to E_{-1} and F_0.

To take a more complex example, the F mode sometimes goes to the C, G, and A modes. If it were to do that in order and then return to F, the first shift would once again be the A, moving from A_{-1} to A_0. Next, as the G mode is introduced, the E_{-1} and F_0 must move up to E_0 and F_{+1}. Then, as the A mode appears, B_{-1} and C_0 must move up to B_0 and C_{+1}. Lastly, to get back to F mode from A, the easiest way is by raising D_0 and G_0 to D_{+1} and G_{+1}. This works perfectly well as a way of preserving Just intonation from mode to mode but would, in this instance, cause the piece to end one comma higher than it began, perhaps confusing or offending people with absolute pitch. We will never know whether such a migration offended the sensibilities of medieval musicians, but for unaccompanied vocal music, it is entirely conceivable that this is what occurred if they were attempting to use Just intonation. The same is true for instruments with some pitch flexibility, like winds and unfretted strings, either by themselves or combined with voices.[16] For instruments of less pitch flexibility, however, the choice was Pythagorean tuning with whatever *ad hoc* modifications could be made to make the music sound better. And indeed, for some repertoires, the choice may have been Pythagorean for singers as well.

Pythagorean Tuning

Wherever thirds and sixths are not used as consonances, but rather, as dissonances that resolve to pure fifths or octaves, Pythagorean tuning is the first choice. Moreover, for instruments of fixed pitch, like harp, organ, psaltery, and lute, it may be the only choice. It is achieved by tuning pure fifths in series until all of the notes have been tuned, but leaving, as mentioned earlier, a dissonant wolf fifth between the first and last notes tuned. The difficulties with Pythagorean tuning are: how to decide where to put the wolf, and how to achieve Pythagorean tuning on a fretted instrument.

The way polyphony works up to the early fourteenth century suggests that Pythagorean tuning was probably set according to the names of the notes most commonly used today, that is, with E♭ being at the bottom of a line of fifths that spirals up to G♯, leaving the wolf between G♯ and E♭. Later in the Middle Ages, theoretical and musical evidence both suggest that the wolf was placed elsewhere, frequently between the B and the F♯ (G♭).[17] This is accomplished by tuning the line of fifths downward to G♭. Obviously, this will not work if the B–F♯ fifth occurs prominently in a piece, but while the diatonic notes remain unaffected, this method does have the advantage of putting the four schismatic thirds of Pythagorean tuning in useful places: D–F♯(G♭), A–C♯(D♭), E–G♯(A♭), and B–D♯(E♭). These are more useful in 3-voice polyphony than the schismatic thirds in regular Pythagorean (B–E♭, F♯–B♭, C♯–F, and G♯–C) because they make possible double leading-tone cadence approaches to D, G, and A that are virtually Just.[18] The fact that this was seen as desirable is more evidence that late-medieval performers were attempting to "justify" the tuning, even in a fixed system.

Fig. 40.6. "Standard" Pythagorean tunings.

G♯–E♭ wolf Pythagorean:

C♯		E♭			F♯		G♯		B♭		
C	D		E	F		G		A		B	C

Cents:
0	114	204	294	408	498	612	702	816	906	996	1110	1200
M		m		m	M		m	M		m		m	M		m

B–F♯ wolf Pythagorean:

C♯		E♭			F♯		G♯		B♭		
C	D		E	F		G		A		B	C

Cents:
0	90	204	294	408	498	588	702	792	906	996	1110	1200
m		M		m	M		m		m	M		m	M		m	M		m

But how does a performer decide, for any piece, where the wolf should go? The "G♭" method works very well in G mode pieces, especially if there is a flat in the signature, since B–F♯ virtually never appears. It also works well in many D mode pieces where it has the added advantage of making an almost pure third above the final. Where it does not work—and this is something not sufficiently emphasized by modern writers—is in C mode pieces, and not very well in F mode pieces. In the C mode, it actually puts the wolf in the double leading-tone cadence to the final; in F, it does not serve to justify the final cadence approach and, of course, creates problems in cadences to C. One thing to try in such cases is to tune the line of fifths down to the leading tone: B in the C mode and E in the F mode.[19] If that does not work because of a triad on the 3rd degree of the scale (which is more likely to happen in F than C), then try tuning fifths at the top of the line until the piece works. (It will have to be at least two fifths to begin with.) Thus, F mode might indeed wind up with a B–F♯ wolf, but only if there are no double leading-tone cadences to C.

It is also conceivable that the line of fifths could be tuned down to the (major) third degree of the mode, as it already is using the "G♭" method in the D mode. This works very well in the A mode because it is so similar to D, but it does not do anything for the Phrygian cadence on A which is left with a ditone between B♭ and D. In fact, it is difficult to find a version of Pythagorean that justifies final cadences in Phrygian mode on either A or E. To do so means tuning up the line of fifths at least to the semitone above the final of the mode, i.e., to D♭ or F. This works, but it means that cadences to C and D, which occur frequently in both those modes, are left unjustified. One other possibility in the E mode is to tune the line of fifths up to the (minor) third, i.e., to G. Interestingly, G–D (ostensibly an inscrutable choice for a wolf) is where Ramos de Pareja puts it in his recommendations for tuning, published in 1482, although he does not mention Phrygian mode specifically. Like the leading-tone method mentioned above, it will not work well if there is a triad on the third degree of the scale and, unfortunately, the few Phrygian pieces in the medieval keyboard repertoire make it hard to generalize. *Des Klaffers neyden* from Paumann's *Fundamentum* of 1452 (in Phrygian on A) seems to work best with the wolf between B♭ and F.[20] It does not work with the wolf between C and G, which would be the equivalent of the G–D wolf in the E mode. The B♭–F wolf is recommended by one theorist, Giorgio Anselmi, around 1434, and it is possible that he had Phrygian mode on A in mind.

One speculative method would be to combine elements of the G♭ method and the B♭–F wolf method. Once the instrument is entirely tuned using the G♭ method, creating good schismatic major thirds for all the sharp notes, one F♯ could be retuned pure to B, one C♯ to that F♯, and so on up to Bb. Then the detuned F♯, C♯, and G♯ could be retuned to their respective octaves, and the new B♭ and E♭ could be tuned throughout to create good schismatic thirds with D and G.[21] This creates three wolf fifths, B–F♯, G♯–E♭, and B♭–F, but it does provide schismatic major thirds in five useful places rather than three and is worth experimenting with.[22] Of course, the impulse to search for more good thirds eventually led to the third-based meantone system, and there is evidence that it may have arisen in practice before it is discussed by theorists. Certainly, a number of works from the Buxheim Organ Book (ca.1460), including even some arrangements of early fifteenth-century works, seem better suited to meantone than any form of Pythagorean.[23]

Fig. 40.7. Other Pythagorean tunings.

A–E wolf Pythagorean:

C	C#	D	Eb	E	F	F#	G	G#	A	Bb	B	C
Cents:												
0	90	204	294	384	498	588	702	792	906	996	1086	1200
m	M	m	m	M	m	M	m	M	m	m	M	

E–B wolf Pythagorean:

C	C#	D	Eb	E	F	F#	G	G#	A	Bb	B	C
Cents:												
0	90	204	294	408	498	588	702	792	906	996	1086	1200
m	M	m	M	m	m	M	m	M	m	m	M	

F#–C# wolf Pythagorean:

C	C#	D	Eb	E	F	F#	G	G#	A	Bb	B	C
Cents:												
0	90	204	294	408	498	612	702	792	906	996	1110	1200
m	M	m	M	m	M	m	m	M	m	M	m	

G–D wolf Pythagorean:

C	C#	D	Eb	E	F	F#	G	G#	A	Bb	B	C
Cents:												
0	90	180	294	384	498	588	702	792	882	996	1086	1200
m	m	M	m	M	m	M	m	m	M	m	M	

F–C wolf Pythagorean

C	C#	D	Eb	E	F	F#	G	G#	A	Bb	B	C
Cents:												
0	114	204	318	408	522	612	702	816	906	1020	1110	1200
M	m	M	m	M	m	m	M	m	M	m	m	

Bb–F wolf Pythagorean:

	C#		Eb				F#		G#		Bb		
C		D		E	F		G		A			B	C

Cents:

0	114	204	318	408	498	612	702	816	906	1020	1110	1200
	M	m	M	m	m	M	m	M	m	M	m	m

B–F# / G#–Eb / Bb–F wolf Pythagorean:

	C#		Eb				F#		G#		Bb		
C		D		E	F		G		A			B	C

Cents:

0	90	204	318	408	498	588	702	792	906	1020	1110	1200
	m	M	M	m	m	m	M	m	M	M	m	m

Naturally, these mode-enhancing varieties are possible when the instrument can be retuned easily. This is true of a harp, psaltery, dulcimer, and harpsichord certainly, but less so of an organ. For organ, it is necessary to find one version that will work in the greatest number of modes, and that is likely to be the Gb method. The harpsichord will find the most use for the varieties given above, while the other instruments will be concerned mostly with the diatonic notes which, as you can see from Figure 40.7, are fairly stable, even when there is a great discrepancy in the placement of the wolf.

Finally, fretted instruments can achieve a form of Pythagorean tuning using instructions for fret placement given by Oronce Fine in 1530.[24] In order to use the ratios given in Figure 40.8, measure the overall string length of the instrument from the nut to the bridge and put a fret at the each of the places indicated as a fraction of that amount. This will result in something fairly close to the B–F# wolf tuning when the open strings are tuned in pure fifths and fourths and any open thirds are left wide as ditones. Once the frets are set according to their correct theoretical placement, it is usually necessary to make minute adjustments by ear.

Fig. 40.8. Pythagorean vs. Equal fretting Ratios.

Fret	Pythagorean	Equal
1	.0508	.0561
2	.1112	.1091
3	.1563	.1591
4	.2100	.2063
5	.2500	.2508
6	.2881	.2929
7	.3333	.3326
8	.3672	.3700
9	.4075	.4054
10	.4375	.4388
11	.4661	.4703
12	.5000	.5000

The central questions concerning tuning in the Middle Ages revolve around how the major third was perceived. As that interval appeared more and more in the music, did performers want to shade the wide and dissonant ditone towards the pure third even though the ratio for the pure third, 5:4, was not recognized in theoretical writings until the Renaissance? Did they prefer to justify the third when it was used as a cadence approach, most prominently between the second and fourth degrees of the mode? Did they prefer to justify the third when it was used as a point of arrival or repose in the music, for example, at the resolution of a cadence? Using Pythagorean tuning, it is rarely possible to satisfy all of these desires simultaneously. As long as the Pythagorean ditone is recognized as an unstable interval that needs to resolve outward to a fifth, the G♯–E♭ wolf version of Pythagorean works perfectly well. As soon as the major third appears as a stable harmonic interval and some shading is sought, the other varieties of Pythagorean may be used to provide some relief. The alternative, for voices and some instruments, is Just intonation. For instruments of fixed pitch, the ultimate alternative—for music in the shadow of the Renaissance—is meantone.[25]

Notes

1   This discrepancy is known as the "Pythagorean comma." It is more precisely given as 23.46 cents and, although the integer creates a roundoff error, 24c will be used for the discussion here with more exact values given for definitions.

2   More precise values for these intervals are 407.82c and 386.31c.

3   *The Music Treatise of Anonymous IV: A New Translation*, Musicological Studies and Documents 4, trans. Jeremy Yudkin (Stuttgart, ca.1985), p. 69. The original Latin reads: "...ditonus et semiditonus apud aliquos non sic reputantur. Tamen apud organistos optimos et prout in quibusdam terris sicut in Anglia in patria, quae dicitur Westcuntre, optimae concordantiae dicuntur, quoniam apud talis magis sunt in usu." See *Der Musiktraktat des Anonymous 4*, ed. Fritz Reckow, Beihefte zum Archiv für Musikwissenschaft 4 (Wiesbaden, 1967), pp. 77-78.

4   There is one primary witness to the *ad hoc* justification of thirds: the Englishman, Walter Odington, who says that singers modify their major and minor thirds to 5:4 and 6:5 respectively in spite of Pythagorean theory. See *Summa de speculatione musicae*, ed. Frederick F. Hammond (Rome, 1970), part 2, chap. 10. The passage is discussed in Hugo Riemann's *History of Music Theory*, trans. Raymond H. Haggh (Lincoln, 1962), pp. 280-82, 392.

5   Jan Herlinger, American Musicological Society Annual Meeting, Montréal, November 6, 1993.

6   More precisely 384.36c. Compared to 386.31c for the acoustically pure major third, this comes much closer than the Pythagorean ditone at 407.82c. The schisma (1.95c) is the difference between the pure third and this pseudo-pure, schismatic third of the Pythagorean system.

7   I disagree, therefore, with this statement: "The initial conclusion to be drawn is that the notion of the Dorian mode as a scale of just intervals is impossible." See Rogers Covey-Crump, "Vocal Consort Style and Tunings," *Companion to Contemporary Musical Thought*, ed. John Paynter *et al.* (London, 1992), p. 1043. Covey-Crump goes on to explain how the system can be modified to work in Dorian mode, suggesting that his "initial

conclusion" was merely a provocative starting point for his discussion. He does limit the additional notes of the just scale to "one or two," however, calling for Pythagorean tuning if more are needed. See p. 1046. See also Covey-Crump's "Pythagoras at the Forge: Tuning in Early Music," in *Companion to Medieval and Renaissance Music*, ed. Tess Knighton and David Fallows (New York: Schirmer, 1992), pp. 317-26.

[8] An exception to this is found in Machaut, who occasionally used a B♭ final, especially in his early works.

[9] I emphasize that these are tendencies: C mode might occasionally go to E, for example. The information in Figure 40.1 is extracted from the unpublished article, "The rhetorical use of mode in the chansons of Guillaume Dufay," by William P. Mahrt.

[10] More precise values for the pure fourth and fifth are 498.04c and 701.96c.

[11] This represents the difference between a Pythagorean ditone and a pure major third (407.82c – 386.31c = 21.51c).

[12] This is in contrast to the two different sizes of semitone found in Pythagorean tuning, 114c (113.69c) and 90c (90.23c).

[13] The whole tone sizes in Pythagorean are similar at 204c (203.91c) and 180c (180.45c), although the minor tone rarely appears in practice. The whole tone in quarter comma meantone is 193c, which is an average of the two sizes in Just tuning.

[14] This is because of the difference in cadence requirements in the two modes: $G\sharp_{-1}$–B_0 in the A mode is sometimes used to make a cadence to A_0, the final in the A mode, but E♭–F♯ never serves that purpose in the E mode. There, the E♭ is needed high and the F♯ is needed low.

[15] Solmization can help in determining tuning (which may be why it was used by singers in learning music) but it seems not to be sufficient by itself without the context of the species.

[16] It is possible that some singers and instrumentalists found a way to "cheat" back to the original pitch.

[17] The evidence for this is summarized in Mark Lindley, "Pythagorean intonation," *The New Grove Dictionary of Music and Musicians* 15, 485-87.

[18] Equally important though little regarded in the making of cadences are the schismatic minor thirds created by this transposition. This is due to the "difference tone" generated when two notes sound together with a minimum of vibrato (it is equal to the difference in their frequencies). While the Pythagorean minor third or semiditone (294c) in the G♯– E♭ Pythagorean tuning gives a colorful and consonant difference tone two octaves and a fourth below the lower note, its inversion as a major sixth creates a difference tone an excruciating quarter tone below that. This would make an uncomfortable harmonic underpinning for an A–C♯–F♯ cadence approach to G, since the A–F♯ sixth would have a difference tone a quarter tone below the sounding C♯. This is pointed out by Bob Marvin in *The Courant* 1, No. 3, p. 29, in a response to Edward C. Pepe, "Pythagorean Tuning and Its Implications for Music of the Middle Ages," *The Courant* 1, No.2, 3-16. The A–F♯ sixth in B–F♯ wolf Pythagorean gives a difference tone very close to D and, although A–C♯–F♯ as a cadential approach to G does not include D, the difference tone may be heard as enhancing the "dominant" function of the approach. The other schismatic minor thirds/major sixths in B–F♯ wolf Pythagorean are C♯–E and G♯–B which can help justify cadences to D and A respectively.

[19] The A–E wolf Pythagorean is essentially that described in the late fifteenth-century Erlangen monochord.

[20] For an edition, see *Keyboard Music of the Fourteenth and Fifteenth Centuries* (Corpus of Early Keyboard Music 1), American Institute of Musicology, 1963, No. 47.

21 A quicker way would be to tune pure thirds at B♭–D and E♭–G, but they would be a schisma wider than the pure fifth method. Tuning exclusively by pure fifths also has the virtue of being more consistent with Pythagorean tuning in general, even though the reason for doing this is to remake some of the sonorities according to pseudo-just ratios. Indeed, this scale approximates Just tuning in the D mode almost to the point of being a "schismatic Just" scale. There is some later theoretical evidence for solutions that combine different methods. Henricus Grammateus in 1518 took the same two methods used here, B–F♯ and B♭–F, but he averaged out the differences between them. Salomon de Caus in 1615 described a method with three wolf fifths, as here, although including two different places: B–F♯/D♯–B♭/G–D.

22 The five schismatic major thirds are D–F♯, E♭–G, E–G♯, A–C♯, and B♭–D. The schismatic minor thirds/major sixths are C–E♭, C♯–E, F♯–A, G–B♭, and G♯–B, making good leading tone approaches to D, G, and A, as well as good Phrygian approaches to D and A.

23 The same could even be said for some of Paumann's works which, even though based on music from around 1400, use many more thirds and sixths than their models, and thus sound less good in Pythagorean than do the vocal originals. See *Keyboard Music of the Fourteenth and Fifteenth Centuries* for editions of Paumann's works.

24 Oronce Fine, *Epithoma musice instrumentalis* (Paris, 1530), facs. in D. Heartz, ed. *Preludes, Chansons and Dances for Lute* (Neuilly-sur-Seine: Société de Musique d'Autrefois, 1964).

25 For a discussion of meantone tuning with practical instructions, see my Chapter, "Tuning and Temperament," in *A Performer's Guide to Renaissance Music*, edited by Jeffery Kite-Powell (New York, 1994).

Select Discography

1. Chant

Gregorian chants for Advent and Christmas. Münsterschwarzach Abbey, dir. Godehard Joppich. Christophorus 77567 (1979; reissued 1991).

Deus, Deus meus: Gregorian chant. Schola Cantorum Gregoriana Essen, dir. Godehard Joppich. Novalis 150 009-2 (1986).

Laudes Mariae: Cantiones ad honorem Beatae Mariae Virgine. Scola Gregoriana, Bruges Cathedral, dir. Roger Deruwe. Talent DPM 291010 (1979, reissued 1987).

Easter Mass (Pre-Vatican II). Choeur des moines de l'Abbaye Saint-Pierre de Solesmes, dir. Joseph Gajard. Accord 221602 (1988).

Sarum chant: Missa in gallicantu. The Tallis Scholars, dir. Peter Phillips. Gimell CDGIM 017 (1988).

Music for Holy Week, Vol. II. Schola Antiqua, dir. R. John Blackley. Oiseau-Lyre 425 114-2 (1989). Chant sung in proportional rhythm.

Palm Sunday Mass (Pre-Vatican II). Choeur des moines de l'Abbaye Saint-Pierre de Solesmes, dir. Joseph Gajard. Accord 201472 (1991).

The Tradition of Gregorian Chant. Various choirs and conductors: Coro des monjes de la abadia de Montserrat, Gregori Estrada, director; Choralschola des Klosters Maria Einsiedeln, Roman Bannwart, director; Choralschola der Abtei Münsterschwarzach, Godehard Joppich, director; Choeur des moines de l'abbaye Notre-Dame de Fontgombault, G. Duchène, director; Coro de monjes de la abadia de Santo Domingo de Silos, Ismael Fernandez de la Cuesta, director; Cappella musicale del Duomo di Milano, Luciano Migliavacca, director. Archiv Produktion 435 032-2 (4 discs originally released as analog discs, 1969-1978, reissued 1991).

Gregorian Chant Gaudete: a selection from the Liturgical Year. Benedictine Nuns of St. Cecilia's Abbey. Herald HAVPCD 157 Calig (1992.)

Like the Sun in his Orb: 13th-century chant from Salisbury Cathedral. Schola Gregoriana of Cambridge, dir. Mary Berry. Herald HAVPCD 148 (1992).

Chants de l'Église de Rome: Vêpres du jour de Pâques. Ensemble Organum, dir. Marcel Pérès. Harmonia Mundi France HMC 901604 (1996).

2. Organum

Österspiel, Östermesse aus Notre Dame de Paris. Schola Cantorum Basiliensis, dir. Thomas Binkley. EMI Deutsche Harmonia Mundi, 1C 165-99 925/26 T (1981).

Leonin: École Notre-Dame: Messe du Jour de Nöel. Ensemble Organum, dir. Marcel Pérès. Harmonia Mundi France HMC 401148 (1985).

Le Chant des Cathédrales: organum, conduits, motets: École de Notre Dame de Paris, 1163-1245. Ensemble Gilles Binchois, dir. Dominique Vellard. Harmonic Records H/CD 8611 (1986).

Polyphonie Aquitaine du XIIe siècle (St-Martial de Limoges). Ensemble Organum, dir. Marcel Pérès. Harmonia Mundi France HMC 901134 (1984, reissued 1987).

Perotin. The Hilliard Ensemble, dir. Paul Hillier. ECM 1385 (1989).

École Notre-Dame: Messe du Jour de Nöel. Ensemble Organum, dir. Marcel Pérès. Harmonia Mundi France HMA 1901148 (1989).

Donnersöhne / Sons of thunder. Vox Iberica 1. Ensemble Sequentia. Deutsche Harmonia Mundi 05472-77199-2 (1992). 12th century chant and polyphony from music for St. James the Apostle in the Codex Calixtinus (Santiago de Compostela).

Le Graduel d'Aliénor de Bretagne: plain-chant et polyphonie des XIIIe & XIVe siècles. Ensemble Organum, dir. Marcel Pérès. Harmonia Mundi France HMC 901403 (1993).

Beyond plainsong: tropes and polyphony in the medieval church. Pro Arte Singers, dir. Thomas Binkley. Focus 943 (1994).

Miracles of Sant'iago: music from the Codex Calixtinus. Anonymous 4. Harmonia Mundi France HMU 907156 (1995).

École de Notre-Dame de Paris: Messe de la nativité de la Vierge. Ensemble Organum, dir. Marcel Pérès. Harmonia Mundi France HMC 901538 (1995).

Les Premierès Polyphonies Françaises: Organa et Tropes du XIe siècle. Ensemble Gilles Binchois, dir. Dominique Vellard. Virgin Veritas VC 5 45135 2 (1996).

Shining light: music from Aquitanian monasteries—12th century. Ensemble Sequentia. Deutsche Harmonia Mundi 05472 77370 2 (1996).
The Age of Cathedrals. Theatre of Voices, dir. Paul Hillier. Harmonia Mundi USA 90157 (1996).
Vox Sonora: Conductus of the Notre Dame School. Diabolus in Musica, dir. Antoine Guerber. Studio SM D2673 (1998).
Sacred Music from 12th-century Paris. Red Byrd, Capella Amsterdam. Hyperion CDA 66944 (1997).
Mystery of Notre Dame chant & polyphony. Orlando Consort. Archiv 453 487-2 (1997).
Aquitania: Christmas music from Aquitanian monasteries—12th century. Ensemble Sequentia. Deutsche Harmonia Mundi 05472-77383-2 (1997).

3. Motet & Cantilena

Multi-century anthologies
Music of the Gothic Era. Early Music Consort of London, dir. David Munrow. Archiv 415 292-2 AH (1976; reissued 1985; reissued as MHS 524643f, 1997). Includes continental motets and hockets of the thirteenth and fourteenth Centuries.
The Service of Venus and Mars: Music for the Knights of the Garter, 1340-1440. Gothic Voices, dir. Christopher Page. Hyperion CDA 66238 (1987). Includes a motet by Philippe de Vitry, and fourteenth and 15th-century English cantilenas.
The Medieval Romantics: French Songs and Motets 1340-1440. Gothic Voices, dir. Christopher Page. Hyperion CDA 66463 (1991). Includes several fourteenth-century motets and one early fifteenth-century double-discantus motet.

13th century
Vox Humana; Vokalmusik aus dem Mittelalter. Studio der frühen Musik. EMI CDM 7 63148 2 (1976, reissued 1989). Includes two motets by Petrus de Cruce.
Medieval Music: Ars Antiqua Polyphony. The Oxford Anthology of Music. Pro Cantione Antiqua, dir. Edgar Fleet. Peters International PLE 115 (Oxford University Press OUP 164) (1978). Music taken from the volume *The Oxford Anthology of Music: Medieval Music* (examples 37-57).
Österspiel, Östermesse aus Notre Dame de Paris. Schola Cantorum Basiliensis, dir. Thomas Binkley. EMI Deutsche Harmonia Mundi, 1C 165-99 925/26 T (1981). Includes motets inserted into an organal setting of the Gradual Haec dies.
Trouvères. Courtly Love Songs from Northern France. Sequentia. Deutsche Harmonia Mundi. RD77155 (1982, reissued 1984). Includes some thirteenth-century motets; the Petronian motets are especially good.
Le Chant des Cathédrales: organum, conduits, motets: École de Notre Dame de Paris, 1163-1245. Ensemble Gilles Binchois, dir. Dominique Vellard. Harmonic Records H/CD 8611 (1986).
The marriage of Heaven and Hell: motets and songs from 13th-century France. Gothic Voices, dir. Christopher Page. Hyperion CDA 66423 (1990).
Codex Las Huelgas: Music from the royal convent of Las Huelgas de Burgos: 13th-14th centuries. Vox Iberica 2. Sequentia. Deutsche Harmonia Mundi 05472-77238-2 (1992).
Codex Las Huelgas. Huelgas Ensemble, dir. Paul van Nevel. Sony Classical SK 53341 (1993).
Love's Illusion: Music from the Montpellier Codex, 13th-Century. Anonymous 4. Harmonia Mundi France HMU 907109 (1994).
The Spirits of England and France I. Music of the Later Middle Ages for Court and Church. Gothic Voices, dir. Christopher Page. Hyperion CD A66739 (1994).

14th century
Le Roman de Fauvel. Clemencic Consort. Harmonia Mundi HMC 90994 (1976, reissued 1992).
Roman de Fauvel. Studio der frühen Musik, dir. Thomas Binkley. EMI Reflexe 1 C 063-30 103 (1972).
Guillaume de Machaut: Chansons, Vol. 2 (polyphony). Studio der frühen Musik, dir. Thomas Binkley. EMI Reflexe CDM 7 63424 2 (1973, reissued 1990). Includes 3 motets and the Hoquetus David.
The Mirror of Narcissus: Songs by Guillaume de Machaut (1300-1377). Gothic Voices, dir. Christopher Page. Hyperion. CDA 66087 (1983, reissued 1987). Includes 2 motets.
Philippe de Vitry: Motets and Chansons. Sequentia, dir. Benjamin Bagby and Barbara Thornton. Deutsche Harmonia Mundi RD 77095 (1988).
Philippe de Vitry and the Ars Nova. 14th-Century Motets. The Orlando Consort. Amon Ra, CD-SAR 49 (1990; reissued as MHS 514429Y, 1997).

Cypriot advent antiphons, Anonymus, c. 1390. Huelgas Ensemble, dir. Paul van Nevel. Deutsche Harmonia Mundi 7977-2-RC (1990).

The study of love: French songs and motets of the 14th century. Gothic Voices, dir. Christopher Page. Hyperion CDA 66619 (1992).

Le Roman de Fauvel. Boston Camerata; Ensemble Project Ars Nova, conceived and dir. Joel Cohen. Erato 4509-96392-2 (1995).

Suso in Italia bella. La Reverdie. Arcana A38 (1995).

English

The Worcester Fragments. Accademia Monteverdiana, dir. Denis Stevens. Nonesuch H-71308 (1975).

Medieval English Music: Anonymes des XIVe et XVe siècles. Hilliard Ensemble. Harmonia Mundi France HMA 901106 (1983).

Sumer is icumen in: chants médiévaux anglais. Hilliard Ensemble, dir. Paul Hillier. Harmonia Mundi France HMC 901154 (1985).

Lancaster and Valois: French and English music, 1350-1420. Gothic Voices, dir. Christopher Page. Hyperion CDA 66588 (1992).

An English ladymass: 13th- and 14th-century chant and polyphony in honor of the Virgin Mary. Anonymous 4. Harmonia Mundi France HMU 907080 (1992).

On Yoolis night: medieval carols & motets. Anonymous 4. Harmonia Mundi France HMU 907099 (1993).

The lily & the lamb: chant & polyphony from medieval England. Anonymous 4. Harmonia Mundi France HMU 907125 (1995).

A Lammas Ladymass. Anonymous 4. Harmonia Mundi USA HMU 907222 (1998).

Hoquetus. Theatre of Voices, dir. Paul Hillier. Harmonia Mundi France HMU 907185 (1999).

15th century

Johannes Ciconia: L'Oeuvre integral. Huelgas Ensemble, dir. Paul van Nevel. Musique en Wallonie, MW 80040-80044 (5 LPs) (1982; reissued as Pavane ADW 7345-47, 1997).

Dunstable: Motets. The Hilliard Ensemble, dir. Paul Hillier. EMI Reflexe CDC 7 49002 2 (1984, reissued as Virgin Classics 7243 5 61342 25, 1997).

Dufay: Missa L'homme armé, Nuper rosarum flores, Ecclesiae militantis, Alma redemptoris mater, O sancte Sebastiane, Salve flos Tuscae gentis. The Hilliard Ensemble, dir. Paul Hillier. EMI Reflexe. CDC 7 47628 2 (1987).

Power: Masses and Motets. The Hilliard Ensemble, dir. Paul Hillier. EMI Reflexe. CDM 7 63064 2 (1982, reissued as Virgin Classics 5 61345 2, 1997).

The Old Hall Manuscript. The Hilliard Ensemble. EMI Reflexe: CDC 7 54111 2 (1986, reissued 1991).

The Island of St. Hylarion. Music of Cyprus 1413-1422. Ensemble Project Ars Nova. New Albion Records NA 038 (1991). Includes anonymous motets from Cyprus, similar to French fourteenth-century motets.

Ave Regina Coelorum. Marienantiphonen in Vertönungen des 15. Jahrhunderts. Isaak Ensemble Heidelberg and Frankfurter Renaissance Ensemble, dir. Eva Lebhertz-Valentin. Conception: Matthias Schneider. Bayer Records BR 100 082 CD (1991).

Homage to Johannes Ciconia. Ensemble Project Ars Nova. New Albion Records, NA 048 (1992).

Guillaume de Machaut: 7 Isorhythmische geistliche Motetten; Guillaume Dufay: Saemtliche Isorhythmischen Motetten, 7 Cantilenen-Motetten. Helga Weber, director. 3 CDs. Renaissance der Renaissance IHW 3.108 I-III (1993).

Venice, Splendour of the World: Music for Popes and Doges from 15th-century Italy. Dufay Consort, dir. Gary Cooper. Dervorguilla DRVCD 105 (1994). Motets by Du Fay, Ciconia, and contemporaries.

Popes & Antipopes. Orlando Consort. Metronome MET CD 1008 (1994).

Dunstaple. Orlando Consort. Metronome MET CD 1009 (1995).

Guillaume Dufay: Music for St. Anthony of Padua. The Binchois Consort, dir. Andrew Kirkman. Hyperion CDA 66854 (1996).

Missa Veterem hominem and other fifteenth-century English music. Gothic Voices, dir. Christopher Page. Hyperion CDA 66919 (1997).

Dufay: The Virgin and the Temple: chant and motets. Pomerium, dir. Alexander Blachly. Archiv 447 773-2 (1997).

A Musical book of hours. Pomerium, dir. Alexander Blachly. Archiv 289 457 586-2 (1997).

Sidus preclarum: complete motets of Johannes Ciconia. Mala Punica, dir. Pedro Memelsdorff. Erato 3984-21661-2 (1998).

4. Polyphonic Mass Ordinary

Guillaume de Machaut: Messe de Nostre Dame. The Taverner Choir, dir. Andrew Parrot. EMI Reflexe CDC 7 47949 2 (1984; reissued 1987).

Dufay: Missa L'homme armé, Nuper rosarum flores, Ecclesiae militantis, Alma redemptoris mater, O sancte Sebastiane, Salve flos Tuscae gentis. The Hilliard Ensemble, dir. Paul Hiller. EMI Reflexe. CDC 7 47628 2 (1987).

Guillaume de Machaut: Messe de Notre Dame / Le Lai de la Fonteinne / Ma fin est mon commencement. The Hilliard Ensemble, dir. Paul Hillier. hyperion CDA 66358 (1989).

Power: Masses and Motets. The Hilliard Ensemble, dir. Paul Hillier. EMI Reflexe. CDM 7 63064 2 (1982, reissued as Virgin Classics 5 61345 2, 1997).

Guillaume de Machaut: Messe de Notre-Dame: Propre Grégorien de la Messe de l'Assomption de la Bienheureuse Viège Marie. Ensemble Gilles Binchois, dir. Dominique Vellard. Harmonic Records H/CD 8931 (1990; reissued as Cantus C 9624, 1998).

Messe de Tournai (XIVe siècle). Ensemble Organum, dir. Marcel Pérès. Harmonia Mundi France HMC 901353 (1991).

Lancaster and Valois: French and English music, 1350-1420. Gothic Voices, dir. Christopher Page. Hyperion CDA 66588 (1992).

Guillaume Dufay: Missa Se la face ay pale: a complete nuptial mass. Pro Arte Singers, dir. Thomas Binkley. Focus 934 (1993).

Guillaume Dufay: Missa Se la face ay pale, Chansons, Missa Sancti Jacobi, Rite maiorem, Ecclesiae militantis. Capella Cordina, dir. Alejandro Planchart. Lyrichord Discs LEMS 8013 (1994). The *Sancti Jacobi* Mass is a *missa plena* with polyphonic Propers.

Guillaume Dufay: Missa ecce ancilla: the Annunciation of the Blessed Virgin Mary. Pro Arte Singers, dir. Thomas Binkley. Focus 941 (1994).

French sacred music of the 14th century. Vol. 1: Mass settings from the Papal Chapel at Avignon. Schola Discantus, dir. Kevin Moll. Lyrichord LEMS 8012 (1994).

Guillaume Dufay: Missa Ecce ancilla Domini: Proprium De angelis Dei officium: a 15th-century Mass from the Cathedral of Cambrai. Ensemble Gilles Binchois, dir. Dominique Vellard. Virgin Classics CDC 5 45050 2 (1994).

Barcelona Mass: Song of the Sybil. Obsidienne, dir. Emmanuel Bonnardot. Opus 111 OPS 30-130 (1995).

Guillaume Dufay: Music for St. Anthony of Padua. The Binchois Consort, dir. Andrew Kirkman. Hyperion CDA 66854 (1996).

Guillaume Dufay: The Missa Caput. Gothic Voices, dir. Christopher Page. Hyperion CDA 66857 (1996).

Guillaume Dufay: Mass for St. Anthony of Padua. Pomerium, dir. Alexander Blachly. Archiv 447 772-2 (1996).

Echoes of Jeanne d'Arc: Missa de Beata Virgine of Reginaldus Liebert. Schola Discantus, dir. Kevin Moll. Lyrichord LEMS 8025 (1996). This Mass is a *missa plena* with polyphonic Propers.

Missa cantilena: Liturgical parody in Italy, 1380-1410. Mala Punica, dir. Pedro Memelsdorff. Erato 0630-17069-2 (1997).

Missa Veterem hominem and other fifteenth-century English music. Gothic Voices, dir. Christopher Page. Hyperion CDA 66919 (1997).

A Florentine Annunciation mass for the feast of the Annunciation. Les Six. Move MD 3094 (1997).

Guillaume Dufay: Music for St. James the Greater. The Binchois Consort, dir. Andrew Kirkman. Hyperion CDA 66997 (1998).

6. Latin Monophony

Carmina burana. Studio der frühen Musik. Teldec 4509-95521-2 (1964, reissued 1994). Includes both monophonic and polyphonic settings of poems from this famous collection.

Carmina burana: Version originale. Clemencic Consort, Rene Clemencic. Harmonia Mundi France HMA 190336.38 (1975/1976/1978).

Spielmann und Kleriker um 1200. Sequentia. EMI Deutsche Harmonia Mundi CDC 7 49704-2 (1981). Includes two anonymous Latin songs: *Olim sudor Herculis* and *Samson dux fortissime.*

Troubadour Songs and Medieval Lyrics. Paul Hillier, Stephen Stubbs, Lena-Liis Kiesel. Hyperion CDA 66094 (1984). Includes Peter Abelard's *Planctus David* and the anonymous *Ex te lux oritur, o dulcis scocia*.

École de Notre Dame de Paris 1163-1245. Ensemble Gilles Binchois. Harmonic Records H/CD 8611 (1986). Includes Perotin's *Beata viscera*, the rondellus *O summi regis mater inclita*, and *Dum medium silentium*.

Carmina burana. New London Consort, Philip Pickett. Vol. I: L'Oiseau-Lyre 417 373-2 (1987); Vol. II: L'Oiseau-Lyre 421 062-2 (1988); Vols. III and IV: L'Oiseau-Lyre 425 117-2 (1989). Includes both monophonic and polyphonic settings of poems from this famous collection.

Nova cantica: Latin Songs of the High Middle Ages. Dominique Vellard and Emmanuel Bonnardot. Deutsche Harmonia Mundi 77196-2-RC (1990). Includes the following five anonymous Latin monophonic songs: *Da laudis homo, Letamini plebs hodie fidelis, Natali regis glorie, Ex Ade vitio, Natus est, Alto consilio*.

Philip the Chancellor: School of Notre-Dame. Ensemble Sequentia. Deutsche Harmonia Mundi 77035-2-RC (1990). Conductus, lai, sequence, and rondellus for voices and instruments. Includes the following songs to texts by Philip the Chancellor, *Sol oritur in sydere, Si vis vera frui luce, Veritas equitas*, and *Luto carens et latere*.

The Feast of Fools, New London Consort, Philip Pickett. L'Oiseau-Lyre 433 194-2 (1992).

Llibre vermell: Pilgrim songs & dances. New London Consort, Philip Pickett. L'Oiseau-Lyre 433 186-2 (1992).

Visions from the book. Ensemble Sequentia. Deutsche Harmonia Mundi 05472-77347-2 (1996).

The Fire and the Rose. Heliotrope. Koch 3-7356-2H1 (1998).

Monastic Song: 12ʰ century monophonic chant. Theatre of Voices, dir. Paul Hillier. Harmonia Mundi France HMU 907209 (1997).

7. Occitan Monophony

Troubadours & Trouvères. Studio der frühen Musik, dir. Thomas Binkley. Teldec 8.35519 (1974; reissued as 4509-95073-2, 1994).

Cansos de trobairitz. Hesperion XX, dir. Jordi Savall. EMI Electrola 1C 065-30 941 (1978; reissued as Virgin Veritas 7243 5 61310 2 6, 1996).

Troubadours et Trouvères. Gérard le Vot, director. Studio SM 12 21.75 (1980, reissued 1993).

Troubadour Songs and Medieval Lyrics. Paul Hillier, Stephen Stubbs, and Lena-Liis Kiesel. Hyperion CDA 66094 (1984).

Vox Humana; Vokalmusik aus dem Mittelalter. Studio der frühen Musik. EMI CDM 7 63148 2 (1976, reissued 1989).

Gaucelm Faidit Songs: Troubadour Music from the 12th-13th Centuries. Kecskés Ensemble. Hungaroton HCD 12584-2 (1986).

The Testament of Tristan: Songs of Berbart de Ventadorn (1125-1195). Martin Best. Hyperion CDA 66211 (1986).

Domna. Esther Lamandier. Aliénor AL 1019 (1987).

Proensa. Theatre of Voices, dir. Paul Hillier. ECM 1368 (837 369-2[Y]) (1988).

Bella Domna: The Medieval Woman: Lover, Poet, Patroness and Saint. Sinfonye, dir. Stevie Wishart. Hyperion CDA 66283 (1988).

The Courts of Love: music from the time of Eleanor of Aquitaine. Sinfonye, dir. Stevie Wishart. Hyperion CDA 66367 (1990).

A chantar: Lieder der Frauen-Minne im Mittlealter. Estampie. Christophorus CD 74583 (1990).

Lo gai saber; Troubadours et Jongleurs 1100-1300. Camerata Mediterranea, dir. Joel Cohen. Erato 2292-45647-2 (DDD) (1990).

Manuscrit du Roi: Trouvères et Troubadours. Ensemble Perceval, dir. Guy Robert. Arion ARN 68225 (1993).

The Sweet Look and the Loving Manner: trobairitz love lyrics and chansons de femme from Medieval France. Sinfonye, dir. Stevie Wishart. Hyperion CDA 66625 (1993).

Bernatz de Ventadorn: Le Fou sur le Pont. Camerata Mediterranea, dir. Joel Cohen. Erato 4509-94825-2 (DDD) (1994).

Dante and the Troubadours. Ensemble Sequentia. Harmonia Mundi 05472-77227-2 (1995).

Songs of the troubadours & trouveres: Music and poetry from medieval France. Peter Becker. Bard DDCD 1-9711 (1997).

Sweet is the Song: Music of the Troubadours and Trouvères. Catherine Bott. L'Oiseau-Lyre CD 448 999-2 (1997).

En chantan m'aven a membrar: Troubadours & Minnesänger. Ensemble Lucidarium. Empreinte Digitale (1998).

8. French Monophony

Troubadours & Trouvères. Studio der frühen Musik, dir. Thomas Binkley. Teldec 8.35519 (1974; reissued as 4509-95073-2, 1994).

Troubadours et Trouvères. Gérard Le Vot, director. Studio SM 12 21.75 (1980).

Chansons de toile. Esther Lamandier. Aliénor AL 1011 (1983).

Trouvères: Courtly Love Songs from Northern France. Ensemble Sequentia. Deutsche Harmonia Mundi RD77155-2-RC (1984; reissued as 77155-2-RC, 1990).

Chanson des Rois et des Princes du Moyen Age. Ensemble Perceval, dir. Guy Robert. Arion ARN 68031 (1987).

Tristan et Iseult: A medieval romance in music and poetry. The Boston Camerata, dir. Joel Cohen. Erato 2292-45348-2 (1989). Medieval songs related to the Tristan legend in Old French, Middle High German, and Provencal, connected with readings from Gottfried von Strassburg's Tristan and that of Thomas de Bretagne.

Music for the Lion-Hearted King. Gothic Voices, dir. Christopher Page. Hyperion CDA 66336 (1989).

The Courts of Love: music from the time of Eleanor of Aquitaine. Sinfonye, dir. Stevie Wishart. Hyperion CDA 66367 (1990).

The Marriage of Heaven and Hell: Motets and Songs from Thirteenth-Century France. Gothic Voices, dir. Christopher Page. Hyperion CDA 666423 (1990).

Guinevere, Yseut, Melusine: the Heritage of Celtic Womanhood in the Middle Ages. Reverdie. Giulia GS 201007 (1991).

Le jeu de Robin et Marion. Schola Cantorum Basiliensis, dir. Thomas Binkley. Focus 913 (1991).

Le Manuscrit du Roi (vers 1250). Trouvères et Troubadours. Ensemble Perceval. Arion ARN 68225 (1992).

Manuscrit du Roi: Trouvères et Troubadours. Ensemble Perceval, dir. Guy Robert. Arion ARN 68225 (1993).

The Sweet Look and the Loving Manner: trobairitz love lyrics and chansons de femme from Medieval France. Sinfonye, dir. Stevie Wishart. Hyperion CDA 66625 (1993).

La Chanson d'Ami: Chansons de Femme au XIIe et XIIIe siècles. Katia Care, voice, Ensemble Perceval, dir. Guy Robert. Arion ARN 68290 (1994).

The Spirits of England and France 2: Songs of the Trouvères. Gothic Voices, dir. Christopher Page. Hyperion CDA 66773 (1995).

Gautier de Coinci: Les Miracles Nostre Dame. Alla Francesca. Opus 111 OPS 30-146 (1995).

Richard Coeur de Lion. Alla Francesca. OPUS 111, OPS 30-170 (1996).

Chansons de trouvères. Paul Hillier. Harmonia Mundi France HMU 907184 (1996).

Songs of the troubadours & trouveres: Music and poetry from medieval France. Peter Becker. Bard DDCD 1-9711 (1997).

Sweet is the Song: Music of the Troubadours and Trouvères. Catherine Bott. L'Oiseau-Lyre CD 448 999-2 (1997).

Le jeu d'amour. Anne Azema. Erato 0630-170722 (1997).

On the banks of the Seine: music of the trouvères. Dufay Collective. Chandos 9544 (1997).

La chambre des dames: Trouvere songs and polyphonies (12th and 13th centuries). Diabolus in Musica, dir. Antoine Guerber. Studio SM D2604 (1997).

9. Iberian Monophony

Les Cantigas de Santa Maria. Clemencic Consort. Harmonia Mundi France HM 977-979 (1976).

Llibre vermell de Montserrat. Hesperion XX, dir. Jordi Savall. EMI CDM 7 63071 2 (1979, reissued 1989).

Chanson des Rois et des Princes du Moyen Age. Ensemble Perceval, dir. Guy Robert. Arion ARN 68031 (1987).

Cantigas of Santa Maria of Alfonso X. The Martin Best Ensemble. Nimbus NI 5081 (1984, reissued 1987).

Cantigas de Santa Maria. Esther Lamandier. Astrée E 7707 (1986).

Visions and Miracles: Gallician and Latin sacred songs from 13th-century Spain. Ensemble Alcatraz.Elektra/Nonesuch 79180-1 (1988).
Cantigas de Santa Maria. Ensemble Micrologus, Civitas Musicae. Quadrivium SCA 014 (1990).
The pilgrimage to Santiago. New London Consort, dir. Philip Pickett. L'Oiseau-lyre 433 148-2 (1991).
Songs for King Alfonso X (the Learned) of Castile and Leon. Ensemble Sequentia. Deutsche Harmonia Mundi 05472-77173-2 (1992).
Cantigas de Santa Maria. Hesperion XX, dir. Jordi Savall. Astrée E 8508(1993).
Wanderers' Voices: Medieval Cantigas & Minnesang. Newberry Consort, dir. Mary Springfels. Harmonia Mundi France HMU 907082 (1993).
Poder a Santa Maria: Andalucia en las Cantigas de Santa Maria. Sinfonye, dir. Stevie Wishart. Almaviva DS 0110 (1994).
Llibre vermell: la route des pèlerins de Montserrat. Ensemble Anonymus, dir. Claude Bernatchez. Analekta AN 2 8001 (1994).
Llibre vermell de Montserrat; Cantigas de Santa Maria. Alla Francesca. OPUS 111, OPS 30-131 (1995).
Cantigas from the Court of Dom Dinis. Paul Hillier with Margriet Tindemans. Harmonia-Mundi France HMU 907129 (1995).
Miracles: Thirteenth-century Spanish songs in praise of the Virgin Mary. Dufay Collective. Chandos 9513 (1997).
Echoes of Spain. Sonus. Dorian DIS -80154 (1997).
Iberian garden: Jewish, Christian and Muslim music in medieval Spain. Vol. 1-2. Altramar. Dorian DIS-80151, 80158 (1997, 1998).
As Melodias de Martin Codax. Vozes Alfonsinas. Included in the book, *Johán de Cangas. Martin Codax. Meendinho: Lírica Medieval, 1200-1350.* Vigo: Edicións Xerais de Galicia, 1998.
Madre de deus: Cantigas de Santa Maria. Ensemble Micrologus. Opus 111, OPS 30-225 (1998).

10. Sephardic Song

Musikalische Volkskunst Spaniens, Cruz Anna Sofardica, L.b. Abinun, DGG Archiv 198460 (1968).
Chants Judéo-Espagnols de la Méditarannée Orientale, Berta Aguado, (Bienvenida) and Dora (Loretta) Gerassy, Inédit (1994).
Chants Judéo-espagnols, Henriette Azen, notes H-V Sephiha, Vouvray, Disques JAM 0782/VL031 (1982).
Romances históricos de España de mi madre, Henriette Azen, Paris, Voxigrave VKST7325 (1988).
Desde el nacimiento hasta la muerte, Azen, Henriette, Sacem/Vidas Largas SC703 (1991).
Cantos judeo-españoles de Marruecos, Comunidad Israelita de Madrid, Tecnosaga SEC511 (1984).

GERINELDO:
Chansons traditionnelles judéo-espagnoles, Montreal, Education Resource Centre (1983).
De Fiestas y Alegrías, Montreal ERC (1985).
Me Vaya Kappará, Montreal (1988).
En medio de aquel camino, Montréal (1994).
Ya Hasrá: Qué Tiempos Aquellos, by Solly Lévy, 90 minute VHS video, Montreal, Université du Québec à Montréal (1987).

JAGODA, Flory:
Kantikas de mi Nona, New York, Global Village (1982)
Memories of Sarajevo, Global Village (1983)
La Nona Kanta, Global Village (1992).
Kantes Djudeo-Espanyoles, Kol Israel Radio, Jerusalem (1989).
Los Pasharos Sefardíes, Vol. I, II, III, Istanbul, n/d.

Recuerdos Sefardíes, Vol. I, II, III. Esther Roffé, Caracas (1974, 1977, 1984).
Greek-Jewish Musical Traditions. Amnon Shiloah, ed. New York, Folkways 4205 (1978).
Sephardi Songs of the Balkans. Shoshana Weich-Shahaq, ed. Jerusalem, Hebrew University AMTI8001 (1980).
Judeo-Spanish Moroccan Songs for the Life Cycle. Shoshana Weich-Shahaq, ed. book and cassette, Jerusalem, Jewish Music Research Centre (1989).
Romances tradicionales sefardíes de Shoshana Weich-Shahaq, ed. Madrid, Tecnosaga (1992).

Ballads, Wedding Songs and Piyyutim of the Jews of Tetuan and Tangier, Morocco. Henrietta Yurchenco, ed. Folkways FE4208 (1983).

Alegrias y Duelas de la Novia : Songs and Ballads of the Moroccan Jews as sung by the women of Tetuan, Morocco. Henrietta Yurchenco, ed. Global Village Music CD 148 (1994).

Canciones judeo-espanyoles de Tesalonica, Oriente. David Saltiel. RIEN CD14 (1998).

11. Italian Monophony

O Cieco Mondo: die Italienische Lauda. Huelgas Ensemble, dir. Paul van Nevel. Deutsche Harmonia Mundi 7865-2-RC (1989).

Laude: Medieval Italian Songs. Indiana University Early Music Institute, dir. Thomas Binkley. Focus 912 (1991). Four laude from Florence and Cortona Mss. including numerous strophes; texts, translations, essay.

Laude di Sancta Maria: Veillée de chants de dévotion dans l'Italie des Communes. La Reverdie. Arcana A34 (1994). Compelling performances of 14 laude from the Florence and Cortona Mss.; texts, translations, essay.

Suso in Italia bella. La Reverdie. Arcana A38 (1995). Includes the lament on the death of Erico of Fruili, written in 799.

Laudario di Cortona (XIIIe siècle). Ensemble Organum, dir. Marcel Pérès. Harmonia Mundi France HMC 901582 (1996). Laude arranged in a sequence of scenes from the life of Christ.

Nova stella: a medieval Italian Christmas. Altramar. Dorian DIS-80142 (1996).

Saint Francis and the minstrels of God. Altramar. Dorian DIS-80143 (1996). [performances of laude from the oldest layers of the tradition]

12. German Monophony

Minnesänger und Spielleute. Studio der frühen Musik, dir. Thomas Binkley. Teldec 8.44015 ZS (1966-82; reissued1988).

Oswald von Wolkenstein: Lieder. Studio der frühen Musik, dir. Thomas Binkley. EMI Reflexe CDM 7 63069 2 (1972; reissued 1989).

Spruchdichtung des 13. Jahrhunderts. Ensemble Sequentia. Deutsche Harmonia Mundi 1C 069 1999941 (1983).

Codex Engelberg 314. Documenta (Schola Cantorum Basiliensis). Deutsche Harmonia Mundi 77185-2-RC (1986, reissued 1991).

Tristan et Iseult: A medieval romance in music and poetry. The Boston Camerata, dir. Joel Cohen. Erato 2292-45348-2 (1989). Medieval songs related to the Tristan legend in Old French, Middle High German, and Provencal, connected with readings from Gottfried von Strassburg's Tristan and that of Thomas de Bretagne.

Wanderers' Voices: Medieval Cantigas & Minnesang. Newberry Consort, dir. Mary Springfels. Harmonia Mundi France HMU 907082 (1993).

Oswald von Wolkenstein: Lieder. Ensemble Sequentia. Deutsche Harmonia Mundi 05472-77302-2 (1993).

Knightly Passions: The Songs of Oswald von Wolkenstein. New London Consort, dir. Philip Pickett. L'Oiseau-Lyre CD 444 173-2 (1996).

En chantan m'aven a membrar: Troubadours & Minnesänger. Ensemble Lucidarium. Empreinte Digitale (1998).

13. English Monophony

Miri it is: English Medieval Music from the 13th and 14th Centuries. Philip Astle and Paul Williamson, with Paul Hillier. Plant Life PLR-043 (1982).

Sumer is icumen in: chants médiévaux anglais. Hilliard Ensemble, dir. Paul Hillier. Harmonia Mundi France HMC 901154 (1985).

Worldes Blis: English songs of the middle ages. Ensemble Sequentia. EMI Deutsche Harmonia Mundi CDC 7 49192 2 (1988; reissued as MHS 514451M, 1997).

Miri it is: songs and instrumental music from medieval England. Dufay Collective. Chandos CHAN 9396 (1995).

World's Bliss. John Fleagle with Shira Kammen. Archetype 60103 (1996).

14. French Ars Nova

The Service of Venus and Mars: Music for the Knights of the Garter, 1340-1440. Gothic Voices, dir. Christopher Page. Hyperion A66238 (1987). [attempts to use Pythagorean tuning in French items]

The Medieval Romantics: French Songs and Motets, 1340-1440. Gothic Voices, dir. Christopher Page. Hyperion CDA 66463 (1991).

Philippe de Vitry: Motets & Chansons. Ensemble Sequentia. Deutsche Harmonia Mundi 77095-2-RC (1991).

The Study of Love: French Songs and Motets of the 14th Century. Gothic Voices, dir. Christopher Page. Hyperion CDA 66619 (1992).

Lancaster and Valois: French and English Music, 1350-1420. Gothic Voices, dir. Christopher Page. Hyperion CDA 66588 (1992).

The study of love: French songs and motets of the 14th century. Gothic Voices, dir. Christopher Page. Hyperion CDA 66619 (1992).

Machaut and his time: 14th-Century French Ars Nova. Ensemble Alba Musica Kyo. Channel Classics CCS 7094 (1994).

Jehan de Lescurel: Fontaine de Grace: Ballades, Virelais, et Rondeaux. Ensemble Gilles Binchois, dir. Dominique Vellard. Virgin Veritas VC 5 45066 2 (1996).

Guillaume de Machaut

Chansons, Vol. 1 (monophony). Studio der frühen Musik, dir. Thomas Binkley. EMI Reflexe CDM 7 63142 2 (1972; reissued 1989).

Chansons, Vol. 2 (polyphony). Studio der frühen Musik, dir. Thomas Binkley. EMI Reflexe CDM 7 63424 2 (1973; reissued 1990).

The Art of Courtly Love, Vol. 1: Guillaume de Machaut and His Age. David Munrow, Early Music Consort of London. EMI (1973; reissued as Virgin Veritas ZDMB 7243 5 6128402 2, 1996).

Guillaume de Machaut: Le Remède de Fortune. Ensemble Perceval, dir. Guy Robert. Adès 14.077-2 (1977, reissued 1987).

Guillaume de Machaut: Je ne cesse de prier. 2 polyphonic lais. Medieval Ensemble of London. L'Oiseau-Lyre DSDL 705 (1983).

Guillaume de Machaut: Le lay de la fonteinne, Un lay de consolation. Medieval Ensemble of London. L'Oiseau-Lyre DSDL 705 (1983).

The Mirror of Narcissus: Songs by Guillaume de Machaut. Gothic Voices, dir. Christopher Page. Hyperion CDA 66087 (1987).

Le vray remède d'amour: Ballades, Rondeaux, Virelais, Motets et Textes dits. Ensemble Gilles Binchois. Harmonic Records H/CD 8825 (1988; reissued as Cantus C 9625, 1998).

Guillaume de Machaut: Messe de Notre Dame / Le Lai de la Fonteinne / Ma fin est mon commencement. The Hilliard Ensemble, dir. Paul Hillier. hyperion CDA 66358 (1989).

Machault. Little Consort Amsterdam. Channel Classics CCS 0390 (1990).

Music from the 'Remède de Fortune' (ca.1340) and other works of Guillaume de Machaut. Ensemble Project Ars Nova. New Albion NA068CD (1994).

Ay mi! Lais et virelais. Emmanuel Bonnardot. Opus 111 OPS 30-171 (1996).

Codex Reina: ballades, virelais, et rondeaux. Continens Paradisi. Symphonia SY 97155 (1998).

Guillaume de Machaut: Le Jugement du Roi de Navarre. Ensemble Gilles Binchois, dir. Dominique Vellard. Cantus C 9626, 1998).

Guillaume de Machaut: Dreams in the Pleasure Garden. Orlando Consort. Archiv 457 618-2 (1999).

15. Italian Ars Nova

Francesco Landini. Studio der frühen Musik, dir. thomas Binkley. EMA Reflexe 1C 063-30 113 (1973).

Songs and Dances of Fourteenth-Century Italy. Landini Consort. UEA 78001 (1978).

Jacopo da Bologna: Italienische Madrigale des 14. Jahrhunderts. Ensemble Project Ars Nova. Deutsche Harmonia Mundi HM 738 (1985).

Decameron: ballate monodiques de l'Ars Nova florentine. Esther Lamandier. Astrée E 7706 (1986).

Two gentlemen of Verona: Jacopo da Bologna & Giovanni da Firenze. Ensemble of the Fourteenth Century. Move MD 3091 (1997).

A song for Francesca: Music in Italy, 1330-1430. Gothic Voices, dir. Christopher Page. Hyperion CDA 66286 (1988).

Codex Faenza. Ensemble Organum, dir. Marcel Pérès, clavicytherium. Harmonia Mundi France HMC 901354 (1991).
Gherardello da Firenze: Madrigali, cacce, ballate. Ensemble Modo antiquo. Nuova Era 7151 (1992).
Landini and Italian Ars nova. Alla Francesca. Opus 111 OPS 60-9206 (1992).
Il solazzo: music for a medieval banquet. Newberry Consort, dir. Mary Springfels. Harmonia Mundi France HMU 907038 (1993). Vocal and instrumental selections based on a list of pieces assembled by Simone Prudenzani for use in his allergorical works *Il solazzo* and *Il saporetto.*
Amor mi fa cantar. Ensemble Micrologus. Quadrivium SCA 004 (1993).
Landini and His Contemporaries. Ensemble Micrologus. Opus 111, OPS 30-112 (1994).
D'Amor cantando. Ensemble Micrologus. Opus 111, OPS 30-141 (1995).
Suso in Italia bella. La Reverdie. Arcana A38 (1995).
I am Music: Works by Francesco Landini. Ensemble of the Fourteenth Century, dir. John Griffiths and John Stinson. Move MD 3093 (1997).
Armes Amours. Alla Francesca and Alta. OPUS 111, OPS 30-221 (1998).

16. Ars Subtilior

Matteo da Perugia: Secular works. Medieval Ensemble of London. L'Oiseau-Lyre DSLO 577 1980.
Ce diabolic chant. Medieval Ensemble of London. L'Oiseau-Lyre DSDL 704 (1983).
Codex Chantilly: Airs de Cour du XIVe siècle. Ensemble Organum, dir. Marcel Pérès. Harmonia Mundi France HMC 901252 (1987).
Ars magis subtiliter: secular music of the Chantilly Codex. Ensemble Project Ars Nova. New Albion Records NA 021 CD (1989).
Fébus avant!: Music at the court of Gaston Fébus. Huelgas Ensemble, dir. Paul van Nevel. Sony Classical SK 48195 (1992).
Homage to Johannes Ciconia. Ensemble Project Ars Nova. New Albion Records NA 048 CD (1992).
Il solazzo: music for a medieval banquet. Newberry Consort, dir. Mary Springfels. Harmonia Mundi France HMU 907038 (1993). Vocal and instrumental selections based on a list of pieces assembled by Simone Prudenzani for use in his allergorical works *Il solazzo* and *Il saporetto.*
Music from the court of King Janus at Nicosia (1374-1432). Huelgas Ensemble, dir. Paul van Nevel. Sony Classical SK 53976 (1994).
Johannes Ciconia: Motets, virelais, ballate, madrigals. Alla Francesca; Alta. Opus 111 OPS 30-101 (1994).
Ars subtilis ytalica: polyphonie pseudo française en Italie 1380-1410. Mala Punica, dir. Pedro Memelsdorff. Arcana A 21 (1994).
D'amor ragionando ballades du neo-stilnovo en Italie, 1380-1415. Mala Punica, dir. Pedro Memelsdorff. Arcana A 22 (1995).
Balades a iii chans de Johan Robert "Trebor" & al. Ferrara Ensemble, dir. Crawford Young. Arcana A 32 (1995).
Zachara: cantore dell'antipapa. Ensemble Sine Nomine. Quadrivium SCA 027 (1996).
En attendant: l'art de la citation dans l'Italie des Visconti, 1380-1410, 1380-1415. Mala Punica, dir. Pedro Memelsdorff. Arcana A 23 (1996).
En seumeillant. Trio Subtilior. Ars Harmonica AH025 (1997).
Beauté parfaite: Chansons des XIVe et XVe siècles. Alla Francesca. OPUS 111, OPS 30-173 (1997).
Codex Reina: ballades, virelais, et rondeaux. Continens Paradisi. Symphonia SY 97155 (1998).
Perusio: Virelais, Ballades, Caccia. Huelgas Ensemble, dir. Paul van Nevel. Sony Vivarte SK 62928 (1998).

17. Early Du Fay

Guillaume Dufay: Adieu m'amour. Studio der frühen Musik, dir. Thomas Binkley. EMI Electrola (1974; reissued as CDM 7 63426 2 1990).
Guillaume Dufay: Fifteen Songs. Musica mundana, dir. David Fallows. (1974; reissued as MHS 4557 1982).
Dufay: Complete Secular Music. Medieval Ensemble of London, dir. Peter and Timothy Davies. L'Oiseau Lyre 237D1-6 (1981).
Garden of Zephirus. Gothic Voices, dir. Christopher Page. Hyperion CD 66144 (1985).
Castle of Fair Welcome. Gothic Voices, dir. Christopher Page. Hyperion CD 66194 (1986).

Triste plaisir et douleureuse joye. Ensemble Gilles Binchois, dir. Dominique Vellard. Harmonic Records CD 8719 (1987).

A song for Francesca: Music in Italy, 1330-1430. Gothic Voices, dir. Christopher Page. Hyperion CDA 66286 (1988).

La Cour du Roi René: Chansons & Danses. Ensemble Perceval, dir. Guy Robert. Arion ARN 68104 (1989).

The Medieval Romantics. Gothic Voices, dir. Christopher Page. Hyperion CD 66463 (1991).

The island of St. Hylarion: music of Cyprus, 1413-1422. Ensemble Project Ars Nova. New Albion Records NA 038 CD (1991).

Le banquet du voeu 1454. Ensemble Gilles Binchois, dir. Dominique Vellard. Virgin Veritas VC 7 59043 2 (1991; reissued 1998).

Binchois and his contemporaries: The spirits of England and France 3. Gothic Voices, dir. Christopher Page. Hyperion CDA 66783 (1995).

Guillaume Dufay: Chansons. Ensemble Unicorn, dir. Michael Posch, with Bernhard Landauer, countertenor. HNH International: Naxos 8.553458 (1996).

Sweet love, sweet hope: music from a 15th-century Bodleian manuscript. The Hilliard Ensemble. Isis CD 030 (1998).

Mon souverain désir: Gilles Binchois chansons. Ensemble Gilles Binchois, dir. Dominique Vellard. Virgin Veritas 7243 5 45285 21 (1998).

18. Liturgical Drama

Österspiel, Östermesse aus Notre Dame de Paris. Schola Cantorum Basiliensis, dir. Thomas Binkley. EMI Deutsche Harmonia Mundi, 1C 165-99 925/26 T (1981).

Hildegard von Bingen: Ordo virtutum. Ensemble Sequentia. EMI Deutsche Harmonia Mundi CDS 7 49249 8 (1982, reissued 1990).

The Play of St. Nicholas. New York Ensemble for Early Music, dir. Frederick Renz. Musicmasters MM 20049-50 (1982).

Daniel and the lions (Ludus Danielis). Ensemble for Early Music, dir. Frederick Renz. Fone 88 F 09-29 (1987).

Le Jeu de Daniel: Drame Liturgique du XIIe siècle. Lamentations de Jeremie: Robert White. Clerkes of Oxenford, dir. David Wulstan. Calliope CAL 9848 (1988).

The Greater Passion play: Ludus Paschalis sive de Passione Domini. Singers and instrumentalists of the Early Music Institute, dir. Thomas Binkley. Musical Heritage Society MHS 522539T (1990).

Carmina Burana: le grand mystère de la Passion. Ensemble Organum, dir. Marcel Pérès. Harmonia Mundi France HMC 901323-IIMC 901324 (1990).

Le Jeu des Pèlerins d'Emmaus: Drame Liturgique du XIIe siècle. Ensemble Organum, dir. Marcel Pérès. Harmonia Mundi France HMC 901347 (1990).

Ludus Danielis: Mysterienspiel aus dem 13. Jahrhundert. Estampie, Münchner Ensemble für frühe Musik, dir. Michael Popp. Christophorus CHR 77144 (1994).

Historia Sancti Eadmundi. La Reverdie. Arcana A43 (1998).

Hildegard von Bingen: Ordo virtutum. Ensemble Sequentia [second recording]. EMI Deutsche Harmonia Mundi 05472-77394-2 (1998).

Medieval Spirit—The Play of Daniel. Ensemble Venance Fortunat, dir. Anne-Marie Deschamps. L'Empreinte Digitale 13095 (1999).

19. Vernacular Drama

Roman de Fauvel. Studio der frühen Musik, dir. Thomas Binkley. EMI Reflexe 1 C 063-30 103 (1972).

Le Roman de Fauvel. Clemencic Consort. Harmonia Mundi HMC 90994 (1976, reissued 1992).

Adam de La Halle: Le jeu de Robin et Marion. Ensemble Perceval, dir. Guy Robert. Arion ARN 68162 (1980, reissued 1991).

Adam de la Halle: Le jeu de Robin et Marion Schola Cantorum Basiliensis, dir. Thomas Binkley. Focus 913 (1991).

Le Roman de Fauvel. Boston Camerata; Ensemble Project Ars Nova, conceived and dir. Joel Cohen. Erato 4509-96392-2 (1995).

El Misteri d'Elx. Ensemble Gilles Binchois, dir. Dominique Vellard. Virgin Veritas VCD 5 45239 2 (1997).

20. Voice

Spielmann und Kleriker um 1200. Sequentia. EMI Deutsche Harmonia Mundi CDC 7 49704-2 (1981).

Hildegard von Bingen: Ordo virtutum. Ensemble Sequentia. EMI Deutsche Harmonia Mundi CDS 7 49249 8 (1982, reissued 1990).

Spruchdichtung des 13. Jahrhunderts. Ensemble Sequentia. Deutsche Harmonia Mundi 1C 069 1999941 (1983).

Trouvères: Courtly Love Songs from Northern France. Ensemble Sequentia. Deutsche Harmonia Mundi RD77155-2-RC (1984).

Worldes Blis: English songs of the middle ages. Ensemble Sequentia. EMI Deutsche Harmonia Mundi CDC 7 49192 2 (1988).

Hildegard von Bingen: Symphoniae. Ensemble Sequentia. Deutsche Harmonia Mundi 77020-2-RG (1989).

Philip the Chancellor: School of Notre-Dame. Ensemble Sequentia. Deutsche Harmonia Mundi 77035-2-RC (1990). Conductus, lai, sequence, and rondellus for voices and instruments.

Philippe de Vitry: Motets & Chansons. Ensemble Sequentia. Deutsche Harmonia Mundi 77095-2-RC (1991).

Donnersohne / Sons of thunder. Vox Iberica 1. Ensemble Sequentia. Deutsche Harmonia Mundi 05472-77199-2 (1992).

Songs for King Alfonso X (the Learned) of Castile and Leon. Ensemble Sequentia. Deutsche Harmonia Mundi 05472-77173-2 (1992).

Codex Las Huelgas: Music from the royal convent of Las Huelgas de Burgos: 13th-14th centuries. Vox Iberica 2. Sequentia. Deutsche Harmonia Mundi 05472-77238-2 (1992).

Oswald von Wolkenstein: Lieder. Ensemble Sequentia. Deutsche Harmonia Mundi 05472-77302-2 (1993).

Hildegard von Bingen: Canticles of ecstasy. Ensemble Sequentia. Deutsche Harmonia Mundi 05472-77320-2 (1994).

Hildegard von Bingen: Voice of the blood. Ensemble Sequentia. Deutsche Harmonia Mundi 05472 77346 2 (1995).

Dante and the Troubadours. Ensemble Sequentia. Harmonia Mundi 05472-77227-2 (1995).

Shining light: music from Aquitanian monasteries—12th century. Ensemble Sequentia. Deutsche Harmonia Mundi 05472 77370 2 (1996).

Visions from the book. Ensemble Sequentia. Deutsche Harmonia Mundi 05472-77347-2 (1996).

Hildegard von Bingen: O Jerusalem. Ensemble Sequentia. Deutsche Harmonia Mundi 05472-77353-2 (1997).

Hildegard von Bingen: Saints. Ensemble Sequentia. Deutsche Harmonia Mundi 05472 77378 2 (1998).

Edda: An Icelandic Saga—Myths from Medieval Iceland. Ensemble Sequentia. Deutsche Harmonia Mundi 05472 77381 (1999).

21. Vielle

a. Before 1300

Musik der Spielleute. Studio der frühen Musik, dir. Thomas Binkley. Teldec CD 8.44015 ZS (1974, reissued 1988).

Spielmann und Kleriker um 1200. Sequentia. EMI Deutsche Harmonia Mundi CDC 7 49704-2 (1981).

Improvisation in der Instrumentalmusik des Mittelalters. Das Mittelalter-Ensemble der Schola Cantorum Basiliensis. Deutsche Harmonia Mundi HM 624 (1983).

Trouvères: Courtly Love Songs from Northern France. Ensemble Sequentia. Deutsche Harmonia Mundi RD77155-2-RC (1984).

Worldes Blis: English songs of the middle ages. Ensemble Sequentia. EMI Deutsche Harmonia Mundi CDC 7 49192 2 (1988).

Hildegard von Bingen: Symphoniae. Ensemble Sequentia. Deutsche Harmonia Mundi 77020-2-RG (1989).

Danse royale. Ensemble Alcatraz. Elektra Nonesuch 79240-2 (1990).

A dance in the garden of mirth. Dufay Collective. Chandos CHAN 9320 (1994).

Cantigas from the Court of Dom Dinis. Paul Hillier with Margriet Tindemans. Harmonia Mundi France HMU 907129 (1995).

La lira d'Esperia. Jordi Savall, lyra, rebab, vielle. Astrée E 8547 (1996).

b. After 1300

Il solazzo: music for a medieval banquet. Newberry Consort, dir. Mary Springfels. Harmonia Mundi France HMU 907038 (1993). Vocal and instrumental selections based on a list of pieces assembled by Simone Prudenzani for use in his allergorical works *Il solazzo* and *Il saporetto.*

Ay mi! Lais et virelais. Emmanuel Bonnardot. Opus 111 OPS 30-171 (1996).

22. Rebec

Chansons der Troubadours. Studio der frühen Musik, dir. Thomas Binkley. Teldec CD 8.35519 ZA (1970, reissued 1985). With lira: *Baron de mon dan covit, Saltarello* I. With rebec: *Saltarello* II

Chansons der Trouvères. Studio der frühen Musik, dir. Thomas Binkley. Teldec CD 8.35519 ZA.(1974, reissued 1985). The same pieces are also on a Teldec CD entitled *Chanterai por mon coraige.* Teldec 4509-95073-2 (1994) With lira: *Retrowange novelle, Lasse, pour quoi refusai.* With rebec: *Trop est mes maris jalos.* With rebec and lira: *Li joli temps d'estey*

Carmina Burana I. Studio der frühen Musik, dir. Thomas Binkley. Teldec CD 8.43775 ZS (1964, reissued 1987). With rebec: *Iove cum Mercurio, Chramer gip*

Carmina Burana II. Studio der frühen Musik, dir. Thomas Binkley. Teldec CD 8.440 12 ZS (1967, reissued 1988). With rebec: *Homo quo vigeas, Vite perdite, Axe Phebus aureo, Tempus est iocundum.* With lira: *Licet eger cum egrotis, Nu gruonet aver diu heide*

Minnesang und Spruchdichtung um 1200-1320. Studio der frühen Musik, dir. Thomas Binkley. Teldec 8.44015 ZS (1988). With lira: *Mir hat her Gerhart Atze ein pfert, Nu alrest lebe ich mir werde* (Palästinalied), *Blozen wir den anger ligen sahen, Fürste Friderich, Chanconetta Tedescha* I, II, *Der kuninc Rodolp minnet got*

Oswald von Wolkenstein. Studio der frühen Musik, dir. Thomas Binkley. EMI Electrola CD CDM 7 63069 2.(1972, reissued 1989). With lira: *Es fuegt sich*

Cantigas de Santa Maria. Deutsche Harmonia Mundi GD77242 (1980, reissued 1992). With rebec: *Dized' ai, trobadores!— Quena festa e o dia*

Guillaume de Machaut, Chansons I. Studio der frühen Musik, dir. Thomas Binkley. EMI Electrola CD CDM 7 63142 2 (1972, reissued 1989). With lira: *Ay mi!*

Guillaume de Machaut, Chansons II. Studio der frühen Musik, dir. Thomas Binkley. EMI Electrola CD CDM 7 63424 2 (1973, reissued 1990). With rebec: *Hoquetus David.* With lira: *Quant en moy—Amour et biauté parfaite*

Musik der Spielleute. Studio der frühen Musik, dir. Thomas Binkley. Teldec CD 8.44015 ZS (1974, reissued 1988). With rebec and lira: Estampie (Oxford, Bod. Lib. Douce 139)

Guillaume Dufay. Studio der frühen Musik, dir. Thomas Binkley. EMI Electrola CD CDM 7 63426 2 (1974, reissued 1990). With rebec: *Pour l'amour de ma doulce amye*

Minnesänger und Meistersinger, Lieder um Konrad von Würzburg, Songs around Konrad von Würzburg. Christophonus CD 74542 (1988). With rebec: *Willekomen, sumerweter süeze!* With lira: *Aspis-Ton*

Vox Humana; Vokalmusik aus dem Mittelalter. Studio der frühen Musik. EMI CDM 7 63148 2 (1976, reissued 1989). With lira: *Mout m'a fait cruieus assaut*

Elegien des 12.bis 14. Jahrhunderts. Contact P.G.Adam, Zum Park 73, 32130 Enger, Germany. CD no: WKCD 1872 (1993). With rebec: *Planctus David super Saul et Ionatha* (Abaelard).

La lira d'Esperia. Jordi Savall, lyra, rebab, vielle. Astrée E 8547 (1996).

23. Symphonia

Spruchdichtung des 13. Jahrhunderts. Ensemble Sequentia. Deutsche Harmonia Mundi 1C 069 1999941 (1983).

A Feather on the Breath of God. Sequences and Hymns by Abbess Hildegard of Bingen. The Gothic Voices with Emma Kirkby, dir. Christopher Page. Hyperion CDA 66039 (1986). (Contains four selections accompanied by Doreen Muskett, *symphonia.*)

Ensemble Tre Fontane, Vol. 1. Estampies italiennes. Virelais de Guillaume de Machaut. TRFC 0187 (1987). (Pascal Lefeuvre uses medieval materials as a basis for creative improvisations on a modern hurdy-gurdy.)

Mandel Quartet. Hungaroton HCD 31138 (1988). (Contains a selection of medieval dances played on a modern hurdy-gurdy and a set of chants played on *symphonia* by Robert Handel.)

Bella Domna: The Medieval Woman: Lover, Poet, Patroness and Saint. Sinfonye, dir. Stevie Wishart. Hyperion CDA 66283 (1988).

The Courts of Love: music from the time of Eleanor of Aquitaine. Sinfonye, dir. Stevie Wishart. Hyperion CDA 66367 (1990).

The Pilgrimage to Santiago. New London Consort, dir. Philip Pickett. L'Oiseau Lyre 433 148-2 (1991). (Demonstrates the way the ensemble depicted on the door of Santiago de Compostela might have sounded.)

24. Harp

b. Early Medieval

Trouvères: Courtly Love Songs from Northern France. Ensemble Sequentia. Deutsche Harmonia · Mundi RD77155-2-RC (1984). See especially *Onques maiz nus hom ne chanta.*

Worldes Blis: English songs of the middle ages. Ensemble Sequentia. EMI Deutsche Harmonia Mundi CDC 7 49192 2 (1988).

Oswald von Wolkenstein: Lieder. Ensemble Sequentia. Deutsche Harmonia Mundi 05472-77302-2 (1993).

Visions from the book. Ensemble Sequentia. Deutsche Harmonia Mundi 05472-77347-2 (1996). See Abelard's lament.

The Soul of Mbira: Music of the Shona people of Zimbabwe. Recorded in Zimbabwe by Paul Berliner. Nonesuch 9 72054-2 (1973, reissued 1995).

N.B. Examples of a harp style based more on mbira playing will be heard on "Old Icelandic Edda" and *Beowulf* recordings yet to be released by Ensemble Sequentia.

c. Late Medieval

The Service of Venus and Mars: Music for the Knights of the Garter, 1340-1440. Gothic Voices, dir. Christopher Page. Hyperion A66238 (1987).

A song for Francesca: Music in Italy, 1330-1430. Gothic Voices, dir. Christopher Page. Hyperion CDA 66286 (1988).

Harp collection: on original instruments. Frances Kelly, harps. Amon Ra CD-SAR 36 (1989).

Ars magis subtiliter: secular music of the Chantilly Codex. Ensemble Project Ars Nova. New Albion Records NA 021 CD (1989).

Forse che sí, forse che no: musique de danse du quattrocento. Ferrara Ensemble, dir. Crawford Young. Fonti Musicali Atelier Danse fmd 182 (1989). Track 11, *Giove,* features a bray pin harp played by Debra Gomez.

The Island of St. Hylarion. Music of Cyprus 1413-1422. Ensemble Project Ars Nova. New Albion Records NA 038 (1991).

Homage to Johannes Ciconia. Ensemble Project Ars Nova. New Albion Records NA 048 CD (1992).

Balades a iii chans de Johan Robert "Trebor" & al. Ferrara Ensemble, dir. Crawford Young. Arcana A 32 (1995).

25. Lutes

Francesco Landini. Studio der frühen Musik, dir. thomas Binkley. EMA Reflexe 1C 063-30 113 (1973).

Spielmann und Kleriker um 1200. Sequentia. EMI Deutsche Harmonia Mundi CDC 7 49704-2 (1981).

Improvisation in der Instrumentalmusik des Mittelalters. Das Mittelalter-Ensemble der Schola Cantorum Basiliensis. Deutsche Harmonia Mundi HM 624 (1983).

Chansons der Troubadours. Studio der frühen Musik, dir. Thomas Binkley. Teldec CD 8.35519 ZA (1985).

Jacopo da Bologna: Italienische Madrigale des 14. Jahrhunderts. Ensemble Project Ars Nova. Deutsche Harmonia Mundi HM 738 (1985).

Minnesanger und Spielleute. Studio der frühen Musik, dir. Thomas Binkley. Teldec 8.44015 ZS (1988).

Ars magis subtiliter: secular music of the Chantilly Codex. Ensemble Project Ars Nova. New Albion Records NA 021 CD (1989).

Forse che sí, forse che no: musique de danse du quattrocento. Ferrara Ensemble, dir. Crawford Young. Fonti Musicali Atelier Danse fmd 182 (1989).

Bassadanze, balli e canzoni: "a la ferrarese" Italienische Instrumentalmusik der Fruhrenaissance. Alta Capella und Citharedi der Schola Cantorum Basiliensis. Deutsche Harmonia Mundi GD77243 (1984, reissued 1991).

Homage to Johannes Ciconia. Ensemble Project Ars Nova. New Albion Records NA 048 CD (1992).

Hildebrandston: Chansonniers allemands du XVe siècle. Ferrara Ensemble, dir. Crawford Young. Arcana A 35 (1995).
Balades a iii chans de Johan Robert "Trebor" & al. Ferrara Ensemble, dir. Crawford Young. Arcana A 32 (1995).
Fleurs de Vertus. Ferrara Ensemble, dir. Crawford Young. Arcana A 40 (1996).
Intabulations. Crawford Young, lute. Lantefana CD 94101 (1996).

26. Flutes

Spruchdichtung des 13. Jahrhunderts. Ensemble Sequentia. Deutsche Harmonia Mundi 1C 069 1999941 (1983).
Trouvères: Courtly Love Songs from Northern France. Ensemble Sequentia. Deutsche Harmonia Mundi RD77155-2-RC (1984).
Forse che sí, forse che no: musique de danse du quattrocento. Ferrara Ensemble, dir. Crawford Young. Fonti Musicali Atelier Danse fmd 182 (1989).
The Carol Album: Seven Centuries of Christmas Music. Taverner Consort, Choir and Players, dir. Andrew Parrot. EMI Classics CDC 7 498092 2 (1990). Pipe and string drum (played by Shelley Gruskin) can be heard on track 5. Track 24 includes a short appearance of the fife (again played by Gruskin) and side drum.
Ars subtilis ytalica: polyphonie pseudo française en Italie 1380-1410. Mala Punica, dir. Pedro Memelsdorff. Arcana A 21 (1994).
D'amor ragionando ballades du neo-stilnovo en Italie, 1380-1415. Mala Punica, dir. Pedro Memelsdorff. Arcana A 22 (1995).
En seumeillant. Trio Subtilior. Ars Harmonica AH025 (1997).

27. Reeds & Brass

Bassadanze, balli e canzoni: "a la ferrarese" italienische Instrumentalmusik der Fruhrenaissance. Alta Capella und Citharedi der Schola Cantorum Basiliensis. Deutsche Harmonia Mundi GD77243 (1984, reissued 1991).
Forse che sí, forse che no: musique de danse du quattrocento. Ferrara Ensemble, dir. Crawford Young. Fonti Musicali Atelier Danse fmd 182 (1989).
Johannes Ciconia: Motets, virelais, ballate, madrigals. Alla Francesca; Alta. Opus 111 OPS 30-101 (1994).
Gothic Winds. Les Haulz et les Bas. Christophorus CHR 77193 (1996).

28. Bagpipe

Istanpitta: 14th Century Dances. Ensemble for Early Music. Lyrichord Discs LEMS 8016 (1995).
Istanpitta 2: Medieval Dances. Ensemble for Early Music. Lyrichord Discs LEMS 8022 (1996).
Landini and Italian Ars nova. Alla Francesca. Opus 111 OPS 60-9206 (1992).
Canzone e Danze. Piffaro. Deutsche Grammophon 445 883-2 (1994).
Rue des Jongleurs. Ensemble Anonymous. Analekta AN 28002.
The Ace and Deuce of Pipering 1906-1947. Heritage Label HTCD 21.
A Celebration of Pipes in Europe Cornemuses d'Europe en Cornuaille, Festival de Cornuaille 1990, Keltia Musique KMCD 18 (1991).
Gothic Winds. Les Haulz et les Bas. Christophorus CHR 77193 (1996).

29. Organ

Die Spätgotische Orgelkunst: Harald Vogel spielt an der Orgel zu Rysum (1457). Harald Vogel, playing an organ built by Meister Harmannus in 1457. Organa ORA3001 (1982).
Buxheimer Orgelbuch. Ton Koopman, at the Triforium organ, Cathedral of Metz. Astrée Auvidis, E7743 (1983, reissued 1988).
The 1794 Giovanni Bruna organ of Magnano (Piemonte). Bernard Brauchli, organ. Titanic Ti-196 (1990).
Das Buxheimer Orgelbuch: Chanson and Basse Danse Intabulations Vol. 2. Joseph Payne, organ. Naxos 8.553467 (1995).

30. String Keyboards

Philippe Chanel, clavicorde. Gallo CD-545 (1988).
Codex Faenza. Ensemble Organum, dir. Marcel Pérès, clavicytherium. Harmonia Mundi France HMC 901354 (1991).

31. Psaltery & Dulcimer

Miri it is: English Medieval Music from the 13th and 14th Centuries. Paul Williamson, psaltery. Plant Life PLR-043 (1982).
Forse che sí, forse che no: musique de danse du quattrocento. Ferrara Ensemble, dir. Crawford Young. Fonti Musicali Atelier Danse fmd 182 (1989).

32. Percussion

The Art of Courtly Love, Vol. I: Guillaume de Machaut and His Age. David Munrow, Early Music Consort of London. EMI (1973; reissued as Virgin Veritas ZDMB 7243 5 6128402 2, 1996).
Musik der Spielleute. Studio der frühen Musik, dir. Thomas Binkley. Teldec CD 8.44015 ZS (1974, reissued 1988).
Weltliche Musik im christlichen und judischen Spanien 1450-1550. Ensemble Hesperion XX, dir. Jordi Savall. EMI Reflexe CDM 7 63432 2 (1976, reissued in 1991)
Musique Arabo-Andalouse. Atrium Musicae de Madrid, dir. Gregorio Paniagua. Harmonia Mundi HM 389 (1977).
Cansos de trobairitz. Hesperion XX, dir. Jordi Savall. EMI Electrola 1C 065-30 941 (1978; reissued as Virgin Veritas 7243 5 61310 2 6, 1996).
Cantigas of Santa Maria of Alfonso X. The Martin Best Ensemble. Nimbus NI 5081 (1984, reissued 1987).
Bella Domna: The Medieval Woman: Lover, Poet, Patroness and Saint. Sinfonye, dir. Stevie Wishart. Hyperion CDA 66283 (1988).
Visions and Miracles: Gallician and Latin sacred songs from 13th-century Spain. Ensemble Alcatraz. Elektra/Nonesuch 79180-1 (1988).
Diversions. Calliope, a Renaissance Band. Summit Records DCD 112 (1990).
Danse royale. Ensemble Alcatraz. Elektra Nonesuch 79240-2 (1990).
A l'estampida. Dufay Collective. Continuum CCD 1042 (1991).
Monodia cortesana medieval (S. XII-XIII) y musica Arabigo-Andaluza (S. XIII). Dir. Gregorio Paniagua. Hispavox CDM 5 65331 2 (1994)
The Splendour of Al-Andalus. Calamus. MA Recordings M026A (1994).
Istanpitta: 14th Century Dances. Ensemble for Early Music with Glen Velez. Lyrichord Discs LEMS 8016 (1995).
Istanpitta 2: Medieval Dances. Ensemble for Early Music. Lyrichord Discs LEMS 8022 (1996).
La lira d'Esperia. Jordi Savall, lyra, rebab, vielle. Astrée E 8547 (1996).
Amor de lonh. The Martin Best Consort. Nimbus NI 5544 (1998).
Listen also to the use of percussion in other music traditions, particularly European folk music, as well as folk and classical music from North Africa and the Middle East.

33. Untexted Repertoire

Musik der Spielleute. Studio der frühen Musik, dir. Thomas Binkley.Teldec CD 8.44015 ZS (1974, reissued 1988).
Bella Domna: The Medieval Woman: Lover, Poet, Patroness and Saint. Sinfonye, dir. Stevie Wishart. Hyperion CDA 66283 (1988).
Forse che sí, forse che no: musique de danse du quattrocento. Ferrara Ensemble, dir. Crawford Young. Fonti Musicali Atelier Danse fmd 182 (1989).
La Cour du Roi René: Chansons & Danses. Ensemble Perceval, dir. Guy Robert. Arion ARN 68104 (1989).
Danse royale. Ensemble Alcatraz. Elektra Nonesuch 79240-2 (1990).
Bassadanze, balli e canzoni: "a la ferrarese" Italienische Instrumentalmusik der Frührenaissance. Alta Capella und Citharedi der Schola Cantorum Basiliensis. Deutsche Harmonia Mundi GD77243 (1984, reissued 1991).

A l'estampida. Dufay Collective. Continuum CCD 1042 (1991).
Il solazzo: music for a medieval banquet. Newberry Consort, dir. Mary Springfels. Harmonia Mundi France HMU 907038 (1993). Vocal and instrumental selections based on a list of pieces assembled by Simone Prudenzani for use in his allergorical works *Il solazzo* and *Il saporetto*.
A dance in the garden of mirth. Dufay Collective. Chandos CHAN 9320 (1994).
Miri it is: songs and instrumental music from medieval England. Dufay Collective. Chandos CHAN 9396 (1995).
La lira d'Esperia. Jordi Savall, lyra, rebab, vielle. Astrée E 8547 (1996).
Red iris Lirio rojo. Sinfonye, dir. Stevie Wishart. Glossa Nouvelle Vision GCD 920701 (1997).

34. Improvisation & Accompaniment before 1300

Troubadours & Trouvères. Studio der frühen Musik, dir. Thomas Binkley. Teldec 8.35519 (1974; reissued as 4509-95073-2, 1994).
Minnesanger und Spielleute. Studio der frühen Musik, dir. Thomas Binkley. Teldec 8.44015 ZS (1988).
Spielmann und Kleriker um 1200. Sequentia. EMI Deutsche Harmonia Mundi CDC 7 49704-2 (1981).
Improvisation in der Instrumentalmusik des Mittelalters. Das Mittelalter-Ensemble der Schola Cantorum Basiliensis. Deutsche Harmonia Mundi HM 624 (1983).
Trouvères: Courtly Love Songs from Northern France. Ensemble Sequentia. Deutsche Harmonia Mundi RD77155-2-RC (1984).
Worldes Blis: English songs of the middle ages. Ensemble Sequentia. EMI Deutsche Harmonia Mundi CDC 7 49 192 2 (1988).
Visions and Miracles: Gallician and Latin sacred songs from 13th-century Spain. Ensemble Alcatraz. Elektra/Nonesuch 79180-1 (1988).
Bella Domna: The Medieval Woman: Lover, Poet, Patroness and Saint. Sinfonye, dir. Stevie Wishart. Hyperion CDA 66283 (1988).
Philip the Chancellor: School of Notre-Dame. Ensemble Sequentia. Deutsche Harmonia Mundi 77035-2-RC (1990).
Danse royale. Ensemble Alcatraz. Elektra Nonesuch 79240-2 (1990).
Wanderers' Voices: Medieval Cantigas & Minnesang. Newberry Consort, dir. Mary Springfels. Harmonia Mundi France HMU 907082 (1993).
Cantigas from the Court of Dom Dinis. Paul Hillier with Margriet Tindemans. Harmonia-Mundi France HMU 907129 (1995).

35. Ornamentation & Improvisation after 1300

Ensemble Tre Fontane, Vol. 1. Estampies italiennes. Virelais de Guillaume de Machaut. TRFC 0187 (1987). (Pascal Lefeuvre uses medieval materials as a basis for creative improvisations on a modern hurdy-gurdy.)
Bassadanza, balli e canzoni: "a la ferrarese" Italienische Instrumentalmusik der Frührenaissance. Alta Capella und Citharedi der Schola Cantorum Basiliensis. Deutsche Harmonia Mundi GD77243 (1984, reissued 1991).
Forse che sí, forse che no: musique de danse du quattrocento. Ferrara Ensemble, dir. Crawford Young. Fonti Musicali Atelier Danse fmd 182 (1989).
Codex Faenza. Ensemble Organum, Marcel Pérès, director, clavicytherium. Harmonia Mundi France HMC 901354 (1991).
Ars subtilis ytalica: polyphonie pseudo française en Italie 1380-1410. Mala Punica, dir. Pedro Memelsdorff. Arcana A 21 (1994).
D'amor ragionando ballades du neo-stilnovo en Italie, 1380-1415. Mala Punica, dir. Pedro Memelsdorff. Arcana A 22 (1995).
Das Buxheimer Orgelbuch: Chanson and Basse Danse Intabulations. Joseph Payne, organ. Naxos 8.553466-68 (1995-96).
Hildebrandston: Chansonniers allemands du XVe siècle. Ferrara Ensemble, dir. Crawford Young. Arcana A 35 (1995).
En attendant: l'art de la citation dans l'Italie des Visconti, 1380-1410, 1380-1415. Mala Punica, dir. Pedro Memelsdorff. Arcana A 23 (1996).
Intabulations. Crawford Young, lute. Lantefana CD 94101 (1996).
Codex Faenza: instrumental music of the early XVth century. Ensemble Unicorn, dir. Michael Posch. Naxos 8.553618 (1998).

40. Tuning

Miri it is: English Medieval Music from the 13th and 14th Centuries. Alan Wilson, Pythagorean-tuned organ. Plant Life PLR-043 (1982).

The Service of Venus and Mars: Music for the Knights of the Garter, 1340-1440. Gothic Voices, dir. Christopher Page. Attempts to use Pythagorean tuning in French items. Hyperion A66238 (1987).

Buxheimer Orgelbuch. Ton Koopman, at the Triforium organ, Cathedral of Metz. Meantone temperament on intabulations of late medieval works. Astrée Auvidis, E7743 (1983, reissued 1988).

A dance in the garden of mirth. Dufay Collective. Peter Skuce, Pythagorean-tuned organ. Chandos CHAN 9320 (1994).

Balades a iii chans de Johan Robert "Trebor" & al. Ferrara Ensemble, dir. Crawford Young. Just intonation in late medieval secular works. Arcana A 32 (1995).

Select Bibliography

AGRICOLA, MARTIN *Musica Instrumentalis Deudsch*. Wittenberg, 1528/R New York: Broude Bros., 1966; Hildesheim: Georg Olms, 1985. See Hettrick.

ALTON, JEANNINE and BRIAN JEFFERY. *Bele buche e bele parleure*. London: Tecla, 1976.

ANDERSON, GORDON ATHOL. "Notre-Dame and Related Conductus: A Catalogue Raisonné," *Miscellanea Musicologica* (Adelaide) VI (1972), 153-229; VII (1975), 1-81.

―――. "The Rhythm of the Monophonic Conductus in the Florence Manuscript as Indicated in Parallel Sources in Mensural Notation," *Journal of the American Musicological Society* 31 (1978), 480-89.

ANGEL, MARC. *La America: The Sephardic Experience in the United States*, Philadelphia, Jewish Publication Society of America, 1983.

ANGLÉS, HIGINIO. *La Música de las Cantigas de Santa María del Rey Alfonso El Sabio*, Barcelona: Biblioteca Central, 3 vols., 1943-64.

APEL, WILLI, ed. *Keyboard Music of the Fourteenth and Fifteenth Centuries* (Corpus of Early Keyboard Music 1), American Institute of Musicology, 1963.

―――. *The Notation of Polyphonic Music 900-1600*. The Mediaeval Academy of America Publication 38. Fifth edition. Cambridge, MA: The Mediaeval Academy of America, 1953.

ARLT, WULF. "Einstimmige Lieder des 12. Jahrhunderts und Mehrstimmigkeit in französischen Handschriften des 16. Jahrhunderts aus Le Puy," *Schweizer Beiträge zur Musikwissenschaft* 3 (1978), 7-47.

ARMISTEAD, SAMUEL G., et al., *El romancero judeo-español en el Archivo Menéndez-Pidal (Catálogo-Índice de romances y canciones)*, Madrid, Catedra Seminario Menéndez-Pidal, 3 v., 1978.

―――, and JOSEPH A. SILVERMAN. "Sephardic Folk Literature and Eastern Mediterranean Oral Tradition," *Musica Judaica* 6/1 (1983-84), 38-54.

AUBREY, ELIZABETH. "References to Music in Old Occitan Literature," *Acta Musicologica* 61 (1989), 110-49.

―――. "Genre as a Determinant of Melody in the Songs of the Troubadours and Trouvères," *Historicizing Genre in Medieval Lyric*, ed. William D. Paden, forthcoming.

―――. *The Music of the Troubadours*. Bloomington: Indiana University Press, 1996.

AUBRY, PIERRE, ed. *Le chansonnier de l'Arsenal* (trouvères du XIIIe-XIIIe siècle); reproduction phototypique du manuscrit 5198 de la Bibliothèque de l'Arsenal. Paris, 1909.

AUGUSTINE OF HIPPO. *De Musica*, trans. R. Taliaferro. New-York: CIMA Publishing Co., 1948.

BACHMANN, WERNER. *The Origins of Bowing*. London, New York, Toronto: Oxford University Press, 1969.

BAER, YITZHAK. *A History of the Jews in Christian Spain*, Philadelphia, 1961-66.

BAINES, ANTHONY. *Bagpipes*. Oxford: Oxford University Press, 1960.

―――. *European and American Musical Instruments*. New York: Viking, 1966.

―――. "Fifteenth-Century Instruments in Tinctoris's *De Usu et Inventione Musicae*," *Galpin Society Journal* 3 (1950), 19-26.

―――. *Woodwind Instruments and Their History*, Rev. ed. New York: Norton, 1963, Chapter 9 "Medieval Wind Music," 209-36.

―――. "Bagpipe," *The New Grove Dictionary of Musical Instruments*, vol. 1, 99-111. London: Macmillan, 1984.

BALTZER, R., T. CABLE, and J. WIMSATT, eds. *The Union of Words and Music in Medieval Poetry (with cassette by Sequentia)*. Austin: University of Texas Press, 1991.

BARR, CYRILLA. *The Monophonic Lauda and the Lay Religious Confraternities of Tuscany and Umbria in the Late Middle Ages*. Kalamazoo, MI: Medieval Institute Publications, 1988.

BEC, PIERRE. *La lyrique française au moyen âge (XIIe-XIIIe siècle): contribution à une typologie des genres poétiques médiévaux*, 2 vols. Paris, 1977.

BECK, JEAN-BAPTISTE, ed. *Le chansonnier Cangé; manuscrit français No. 846 de la Bibliothèque Nationale de Paris*, 2 vols. Paris, 1927.

―――. *Le manuscrit du Roi; fonds français No. 844 de la Bibliothèque Nationale*, 2 vols. London, 1938.

―――. *Die Melodien der Troubadours und Trouvères*. Strassbourg, 1908.

BECK, NORA M. "Singing in the Garden: An Examination of Music in Trecento Painting and Boccaccio's 'Decameron'" (Ph.D. diss., Columbia University, 1993).

BEDBROOK, GERALD S. "The Problem of Instrumental Combination in the Middle Ages," *Revue Belge de Musicologie* 25 (1971), 53-67.

BEHN, FR. "Die Laute im Altertum und frühen Mittelalter," *Zeitschrift für Musikwissenschaft*, 1 (1918).

BENOLIEL, JOSÉ, *Dialecto judeo-hispano-marroquí o haketía*, Madrid, Castalia, 1977 (1927-52).

BENT, MARGARET. "*Musica Recta* and *Musica Ficta*," *Musica disciplina* 26 (1972), 73-100.

———. "*The Early Use of the Sign Ø*," *Early Music* 24 (1996), 199-225.

———. "Musica Recta and Musica Ficta," *Musica Disciplina* 26 (1972), 72-100.

———, Review of *The Lucca Codex*, ed. J. Nádas and A. Ziino; *Il Codice Rossi 215*, ed. N. Pirrotta; *Il Codice Torino T.III.2*, ed. A. Ziino; *Il Codice Squarcialupi*, ed. F.A. Gallo in *Early Music History* 15 (1996), 251-69.

BERGER, KAROL. "Musica ficta," in *Performance Practice: Music before 1600*, ed. Howard Mayer Brown and Stanley Sadie. London: Macmillan, 1989, 107-25.

———. *Musica Ficta: Theories of Accidental Inflections in Vocal Polyphony from Marchetto da Padova to Gioseffo Zarlino*. Cambridge: Cambridge University Press, 1987.

BERLINER, PAUL F. *The Soul of Mbira: Music and Traditions of the Shona People of Zimbabwe*. Berkeley, 1978.

BESSARABOFF, NICHOLAS. *Ancient European Musical Instruments*. New York: October House, Inc., 1941, 1964.

BEVINGTON, DAVID, ed. *Medieval Drama*, Boston: Houghton Mifflin, 1975.

BLACKWOOD, EASLEY. *The Structure of Recognizable Diatonic Tunings*. Princeton: Princeton University Press, 1985.

BLADES, JAMES. "Percussion Instruments of the Middle Ages and Renaissance," *Early Music* 1 (1973), 11-18.

——— and JEREMY MONTAGU. "Capriol's Revenge," *Early Music* 1 (1973), 84-92.

———. *Early Percussion Instruments from the Middle Ages to the Baroque*. London: Oxford University Press, 1976.

———. *Percussion Instruments and Their History*. New York: Praeger, 1970.

BOGIN, MEG. *The Women Troubadours*. New York: Paddington Press, 1976.

BOONE, GRAEME M. "Dufay's Early Chansons: Chronology and Style in the Manuscript Oxford, Bodleian Library, Canonici misc. 213," Ph.D. diss., Harvard University, 1987.

BOONE, HUBERT. *La Cornemuse. Instruments de Musique Populaire en Belgique et au Pays-Bas*. Brussels: Éditions La Renaissance du Livre, 1983.

BOWLES, EDMUND A. "Eastern Influences on the use of Trumpets and Drums during the Middle Ages," *Anuario Musical* 26 (1972).

———. "Haut and Bas: The Grouping of Musical Instruments in the Middle Ages," *Musica Disciplina* 8 (1954), 115-40.

———. *La Pratique Musicale au Moyen Age / Musical Performance in the Late Middle Ages*. Genève: Minkoff & Lattes, 1983.

———. *Musikleben im 15. Jahrhundert*. Leipzig: VEB Deutscher Verlag für Musik, 1977.

BOYDEN, DAVID D. *The History of Violin Playing from Its Origins to 1761*. London: Oxford University Press, 1965; repr. 1967.

BRAINARD, INGRID. *The Art of Courtly Dancing in the Early Renaissance*. First preliminary edition. West Newton, Mass.: 1981. A new edition is in preparation as of this writing.

BRAUN, JOACHIM. "Musical Instruments in Byzantine Illuminated Manuscripts," *Early Music* 8 (1980), 312-27.

BREWER, CHARLES E. "A Fourteenth-Century Polyphonic Manuscript Rediscovered," *Studia Musicologica* 24 (1982), 5-19.

BRIFFAULT, ROBERT. *The Troubadours*. Bloomington: Indiana University Press, 1965.

BROWN, HOWARD MAYER. "Instruments and Voices in the Fifteenth-Century Chanson," *Current Thought in Musicology*, ed. John W. Grubbs. Austin, 1976, 89-137.

———. "On the Performance of Fifteenth-Century Chansons," *Early Music* 1 (1973), 2-10.

———. "St. Augustine, Lady Music and the Gittern," *Musica Disciplina* 38 (1984).

———. "The Trecento Harp," in *Studies in the Performance of Late Mediæval Music*, ed. Stanley Boorman. Cambridge: Cambridge University Press, 1983, 35-73.

———. "The Trecento Fiddle and its Bridges," *Early Music* 17 (1989), 311-29.

———. "[Renaissance] Introduction" *Performance practice 1: Music before 1600*, ed. Howard Mayer Brown and Stanley Sadie. London: Macmillan, 1989, 147-66

———. "Instruments," in *The New Grove Handbooks in Music, Performance Practice, Music before 1600*, ed. Howard Mayer Brown and Stanley Sadie. London: Macmillan, 1989, 15-36.

———. *Performance Practice: Music before 1600*. London: Macmillan, 1989.

———. "Catalogus. A Corpus of Trecento Pictures with Musical Subject Matter," *Imago Musicae* 1 (1984), 189-244; *Imago Musicae* 2 (1985), 179-282; *Imago Musicae* 3 (1986), 103-87; and *Imago Musicae* 5 (1986), 167-242.

———. "Iconography of Music," *The New Grove Dictionary of Music and Musicians*, ed. Stanley Sadie. London: Macmillan, 1980.

———. "The Trecento Harp," in *Studies in the Performance of Late Mediæval Music*, ed. Stanley Boorman. Cambridge: Cambridge University Press, 1983, 35-73.

BUKOFZER, MANFRED F. *Studies in Medieval and Renaissance Music*. New York: W.W. Norton, 1950.

BULLARD, BETH, trans. and ed. *Musica getutscht: A Treatise on Musical Instruments (1511) by Sebastian Virdung*. Cambridge: Cambridge University Press, 1993.

BUNIS, DAVID. *Sephardic Studies: A Research Bibliography*. New York: Garland, 1981.

BURGWINKLE, WILLIAM E., trans. *Razos and Troubadour Songs*. New York: Garland, 1990.

Carmina Burana, 4 vols., ed. A. Hilka, O. Schumann, and B. Bischoff. Heidelberg: Carl Winter Universitätsverlag, 1930-70.

CARRUTHERS, MARY. *The Book of Memory*. Cambridge: Clarendon Press, 1990.

CATTIN, GIULIO. "Le melodie cortonesi," in Varanini, et al. *Laude cortonesi*, I², 481-516.

CHAMBERS, FRANK M. *An Introduction to Old Provençal Versification*. Philadelphia: American Philosophical Society, 1985.

CICERO. *Rhetorica ad Herrenium*, trans. H. Caplan. 1954; repr. Cambridge, MA: Harvard University Press, 1977, 1981.

COHEN, JUDITH R. "1492-1992 Revisited: The Sephardic Song 'Revival'," *Musicworks* 54 (1992), 36-42.

———. "Sonography of Judeo-Spanish Song, with Commentary," *Jewish Folklore and Ethnology Review* 15/2 (1993), 49-55.

———. *Judeo-Spanish Songs in the Sephardic Communities of Montreal and Toronto: Survival, Function and Change*, Ph.D. diss., University Microfilms #8918229, 1989.

COLDWELL, MARIA V. "Jougleresses and Trobairitz," in *Women Making Music*, ed. Jane Bowers and Judith Tick, University of Illinois Press, Urbana, 1986.

COLEMAN, JANET. *Ancient and Medieval Momories*. Cambridge: Clarendon Press, 1992.

COLLINS JR., FLETCHER, ed. *Medieval Church Music-Drama*. Charlottesville: University Press of Virginia, 1976.

———. *The Production of Medieval Church Music-Drama*. Charlottesville: University Press of Virginia, 1972.

COLLINSON, FRANCES. *The Bagpipe: The History of a Musical Instrument*. London and Boston: Routledge and Kegan Paul, 1975.

COOK, S. RON. "The Presence and Use of Brays on Gut-Strung Harp through the 17th Century. A Survey and Consideration of the Evidence," *Historical Harp Society Bulletin* 8 (1998), 2-39.

COPEMAN, HAROLD. *Singing in Latin*, rev. ed. Oxford: author, 1992.

COVEY-CRUMP, ROGERS. "Pythagoras at the Forge: Tuning in Early Music," in *Companion to Medieval and Renaissance Music*, ed. Tess Knighton and David Fallows. New York: Schirmer, 1992, 317-26.

———. "Vocal Consort Style and Tunings," *Companion to Contemporary Musical Thought*, ed. John Paynter et al. London: Routledge, 1992, 1020-50.

CRANE, FREDERICK. *Materials for the Study of the Fifteenth Century Basse Dance*. Brooklyn: Institute of Mediaeval Music, 1968.

———. *Extant Medieval Musical Instruments: A Provisional Catalogue by Types*. Iowa City (1972).

CUMMING, JULIE E. *The Motet in the Age of Du Fay*. Cambridge: Cambridge University Press, 1999.

CURTIUS, ERNST ROBERT. *European Literature and the Latin Middle Ages*, trans. Willard R. Trask. German 1st ed. Bern: 1948; English 1st ed. 1953; 3rd ed. Princeton: Bollingen Series 36, 1973.

DA CUNHA, CELSO FERREIRA. *O Cancioneiro de Martin Codax*, Rio de Janeiro, 1956.

DANNER, PETER. "Before Petrucci: the Lute in the Fifteenth Century," *Journal of the Lute Society of America* 5 (1972), 4-17.

DAVIS, RUTH. "Arab-Andalusian Music in Tunisia," *Early Music* 24 (1996), 423-37.

DAVISON, ARCHIBALD T., AND WILLI APEL. *Historical Anthology of Music*. Cambridge: Harvard University Press, 1949, # 102a.

DEL POPOLO, CONCETTO. *Il Laudario della Compagnia de San Gilio*, in *Laude Fiorentine*, I¹·². Florence: Olschki, 1990 [critical ed. of the texts of Mgl²].

DESCHAMPS, EUSTACHE. *L'Art de dictier*, ed. and trans. Deborah M. Sinnreich-Levi. Medieval Texts and Studies 13. East Lansing: Colleagues Press, 1994.

DeVale, Sue Carole. "African Harps: Construction, Decoration and Sound," in *Sounding Forms: African Musical Instruments*, ed. Marie-Therese Brincard (exhibition catalogue). American Federation of the Arts. New York, 1989.

Díaz Más, Paloma, *Los Sefardíes*, Barcelona, Riopedras, 1986. English edition 1990, trans. George Zucker.

Dimock, J.F., ed. *Girardi Cambrensis Topographia Hibernica*, Rolls Series 21:5. London, 1867.

Disertori, Benvenuto. "L'unica composizione sicuramente strumentale nei codici tridentini," *Collectanea historiae musicae* 2 (1957), 135-45.

———. "Tyling musico inglese nei codici tridentini," *Studi trentini di scienze storiche* 36 (1957), 10-13.

———. "Un primitivo esempio di variazione nei codici musicali tridentini," *Studi trentini di scienze storiche* 35 (1956), 1-7.

Dorfmüller, Kurt. *Studien zur Lautenmusik in der ersten Hälfte des 16. Jahrhunderts*. Tutzing, 1967.

Dragonetti, Roger. *La technique poétique des trouvères dans la chanson courtoise: contribution à l'étude de la rhétorique médiévale*. Bruges: De Tempel, 1960.

Dronke, Pete. "Medieval Rhetoric," in *The Medieval World*, ed. David Daiches and Anthony Thorlby. London: Aldus Books, 1973.

———. *Medieval Latin and the Rise of the European Love-Lyric*, 2 vols. 2nd ed. rev., Oxford: Clarendon Press, 1968.

———. "The Lyrical Compositions of Philip the Chancellor," *Studi Medievali*, ser. 3, 28 (1987), 563-92.

———. *The Medieval Lyric*, 2nd ed. London: Hutchinson, 1978.

———. *The Medieval Poet and His World*. Roma: Edizioni di Storia e Letteratura, 1984.

Droysen, Dagmar. *Die Saiteninstrumente des frühen Mittelalters*. Diss. Hamburg 1959.

Duffin, Ross W. "Tuning and Temperament," in *A Performer's Guide to Renaissance Music*. New York: Schirmer Books, 1994, 238-47.

———. *Guillaume Dufay—Chansons: Forty-Five Settings in Original Notation*. Miami: Ogni Sorte, 1983.

Dürrer, Martin. *Altitalienische Laudenmelodie: Das einstimmige Repertoire der Handschriften Cortona und Florenz*, 2 vols. Kassel: Bärenreiter, 1996 [diplomatic transcriptions, commentary, and analysis. No emendations of Mgl^1 melodies undertaken--on this, see Wilson, "Indagine" and *The Florence Laudario*, below].

Dutka, Joanna. *Music in the English Mystery Plays: Early Drama, Art, and Music, Reference Series 2*. Kalamazoo, MI: The Medieval Institute, 1980.

Earp, Lawrence M. "Lyrics for Reading and Lyrics for Singing in Late Medieval France: The Development of the Dance Lyric from Adam de la Halle to Guillaume de Machaut," in *The Union of Words and Music*, ed. Rebecca Baltzer et al. Austin: University of Texas Press, 1991, 101-31.

———. "Scribal Practice, Manuscript Production and the Transmission of Music in Late Medieval France," Ph.D. diss., Princeton University, 1983.

———. "Texting in 15th-Century French Chanson: A Look Ahead from the 14th Century," *Early Music* 19 (1991), 194-210.

———. *Guillaume de Machaut: A Guide to Research*. New York: Garland, 1995.

Edwards, Robert. *Ratio and Invention*, Nashville, TN: Vanderbilt University Press, 1989.

Egan, Margarita, trans. *The Vidas of the Troubadours*. New York, 1984.

Ellingson, Te. "Drums," in Milcea Eliade, ed., *Encyclopedia of Religion*. New York: Macmillan 1987, 4: 494-502.

Ellinwood, Leonard. *The Works of Francesco Landini*. Cambridge, Massachusetts: The Mediaeval Academy of America, 1939.

Etzion, Judith, and Shoshana Weich-Shahaq. "The Music of the Judeo-Spanish Romancero: Stylistic Features," *Anuario Musical* 43 (1988b), 221-55.

———. "The Spanish and Sephardic Romances: Musical Links," *Ethnomusicology* 32/2 (1988a), 1-38.

Everist, Mark. *Polyphonic Music in Thirteenth-Century France; Aspects of Sources and Distribution*. New York: Garland, 1989.

Fallows, David. *Dufay*. London: Dent, 1982.

———. "15th-Century Tablatures for Plucked Instruments: A Summary, a Revision and a Suggestion," *Lute Society Journal*, 19 (1977), 7-33.

———. "Secular Polyphony in the Fifteenth Century," *Performance Practice 1: Music before 1600*, ed. Howard Mayer Brown and Stanley Sadie. London: Macmillan, 1989, 201-21.

———. *Songs and Musicians of the Fifteenth Century*. Aldershot, Brookfield: Variorum, 1996.

———. "Specific Information on the Ensembles for Composed Polyphony, 1400-1474," in *Studies in the Performance of Late Mediæval Music*, ed. Stanley Boorman. Cambridge: Cambridge University Press, 1983, 109-59.

――――. "The Gresley Dance Collection, c. 1500," *Research Chronicle of the Royal Musical Association* 29 (1996), 1-20.

FARMER, HENRY G. "Rebab," in *Die Musik in Geschichte und Gegenwart*, vol. 11. Kassel: Bärenreiter, 1960, 79-83.

FERNÁNDEZ DE LA CUESTA, ISMAEL, ed. *Las Cançons dels Trobadors. Tèxtes establits per Robert Lafont amb una revirada alemanda, anglesa, castelhana, e francesa*. Toulouse, 1979.

FERREIRA, MANUEL PEDRO. "A música das cantigas galego-portuguesas: balanço de duas décadas de investigaçao (1977-1997)," in Derek W. Flitter and Patricia O. Baubeta, eds., *Ondas do Mar de Vigo*. Birmingham: Seminario de Estudios Galegos, 1998, 58-71.

――――. "Andalusian Music and the *Cantigas de Santa Maria*," in Stephen Parkinson, ed., *Cobras e Som. Papers from a Colloquium on Text, Music and Manuscripts of the Cantigas de Santa Maria*. Oxford: Legenda, forthcoming.

――――. *Aspectos da Música Medieval no Ocidente Peninsular* (forthcoming).

――――. "Bases for Transcription: Gregorian Chant and the Notation of the *Cantigas de Santa Maria*," in *Los instrumentos del Pórtico de la Gloria. Su reconstrucción y la música de su tiempo*. La Coruña: Fundación Pedro Barrié de la Maza, 1993, vol. 2, 595-621.

――――. *Cantus Coronatus — Seven Cantigas de Amor by Dom Dinis, King of Portugal and the Algarve*, vol. 1 (bilingual critical edition of the Sharrer MS, with facsimiles; forthcoming).

――――. *The Sound of Martin Codax—On the Musical Dimension of the Galician-Portuguese Lyric / O Som de Martin Codax—Sobre a dimensão musical da lírica galego-portuguesa*. Lisbon: IN-CM, 1986 [bilingual ed. with color facs.].

――――. "The Stemma of the Marian Cantigas: Philological and Musical Evidence," in *Cantigueiros* 6 (1994), 58-98.

FISCHER, KURT VON. "On the Technique, Origin, and Evolution of Italian Trecento Polyphony," *Musical Quarterly* 47 (1961), 41-57.

FOLEY, JOHN. *Oral Tradition in Literature*. Columbia: University of Missouri Press, 1986.

FRANK, ISTVÁN. *Répertoire métrique de la poésie des troubadours*, 2 vols. Paris, 1966.

FULLER, SARAH. "Aquitanian Polyphony of the Eleventh and Twelfth Centuries," 3 vols. Ph.D. diss., University of California at Berkeley, 1969.

――――. "On Sonority in Fourteenth-Century Polyphony: Some Preliminary Reflections," *Journal of Music Theory* 30 (1986), 35-70.

GALLO, F. ALBERTO. "Critica della tradizione e storia del testo. Seminario su un madrigale trecentesco," *Acta musicologica* LIX/1 (1987).

GEIRINGER, KARL. "Der Instrumentenname 'Quinterne' und die mittelalterlichen Bezeichnungen der Gitarre, Mandola und des Colascione," *Archiv für Musikwissenschaft* 6 (1924).

――――. "Vorgeschichte und Geschichte der europäischen Laute bis zu Beginn der Neuzeit," *Zeitschrift für Musikwissenschaft* 10 (1927/28).

――――. *Die Flankenwirbelinstrumente in der bildenden Kunst des 14.-16. Jahrhunderts*, Diss. Vienna, 1923.

GEISER, BRIGITTE. *Studien zur Frühgeschichte der Violine*. Bern and Stuttgart: Paul Haupt, 1974.

GENNRICH, FRIEDRICH, ed. *Der musikalische Nachlaß der Troubadours*, 3 vols. Summa Musicae Medii Aevi, 3, 4, 15. Darmstadt, 1958-65.

――――, ed. *Rondeaux, Virelais und Balladen aus dem Ende des XII., dem XIII. und dem ersten Drittel des XIV. Jahrhunderts, mit den überlieferten Melodien*, 2 vols. Dresden, 1921.

GILLINGHAM, BRYAN. "A New Etiology and Etymology for the Conductus," *Musical Quarterly* 75 (1991), 59-73.

――――. *Saint-Martial Polyphony*. Musicological Studies and Documents 44. Henryville, PA: Institute of Medieval Music, 1984.

GODEFROY, FRÉDÉRIC. *Lexique de l'ancien français*. Paris, 1976.

――――. *Lexique de l'ancien français*. Paris, 1976.

GODWIN, JOSCELY. "'Main divers acors': Some Instrument Collections of the Ars Nova Period," *Early Music* 5 (1977), 148-59.

GÖLLNER, THEODOR. "Notationsfragmente aus einer Organistenwerkstatt des 15. Jahrhunderts," *Archiv für Musikwissenschaft* 24 (1967), Abb. 2.

GOTTFRIED VON STRASSBURG. *Tristan*. Nach dem Text von Friedrich Ranke. Stuttgart, 1980 (English translations by Benjamin Bagby).

GRAME, THEODORE, and GENICHI TSUG. "The Horse and the Fiddle: Steed Symbolism on Eurasian Stringed Instruments," *Musical Quarterly* 58 (1972), 57-66.

GREENBERG, NOAH, and WILLIAM L. SMOLDON, eds. *The Play of Herod*. Oxford: Oxford University Press, 1965.

GREENE, GORDON K. "The Schools of Minstrelsy and the Choir School Tradition," *Studies in Music* 2, Western Ontario (1977), 31-40.

GROSSI, JOHN HENRY. "The Fourteenth Century Florentine Laudario Magliabechiano II. I. 122 (B.R. 18): A Transcription and Study," Ph.D. diss., Catholic University of America, 1979.

GUARNIERI, ANNA MARIA, ed. *Laudario di Cortona*, Biblioteca del centro per il collegamento degli studi medievali e umanistici nell'Università di Perugia, 7 (Spoleto: Centro Italiano di Studi sull'alto Medioevo, 1991) [affordable one-volume critical edition of the Cortona texts]

GUILLAUME DE LORRIS and JEAN DE MEUN. *The Romance of the Rose*, trans. Charles Dahlberg. Princeton, NJ: Princeton University Press, 1971.

HAGOPIAN, VIOLA L. *Italian Ars Nova Music: A Bibliographic Guide to Modern Editions and Related Literature*. Second Edition. Berkeley: University of California Press, 1973.

HAMM, CHARLES. "A Group of Anonymous English Pieces in Trent 87," *Music and Letters* 41 (1960), 211-15

HAMMERSTEIN, REINHOLD. *Diabolus in Musica: Studien zur Ikonographie der Musik im Mittelalter*, Bern and Munich: Francke Verlag, 1974

HARDEN, BETTIE JEAN. "Sharps, Flats, and Scribes: *Musica Ficta* in the Machaut Manuscripts," Ph.D. diss., Cornell University, 1983.

HARMS, BEN. "Percussion Instruments," in Jeffery T. Kite-Powell, ed. *A Performer's Guide to Renaissance Music*. New York: Schirmer Books, 1994, 161-71.

HASSELMAN, MARGARET, and THOMAS WALKER. "More Hidden Polyphony in a Machaut Manuscript," *Musica Disciplina* 24 (1970), 7-16.

HERLINGER, JAN. "Marchetto's Division of the Whole Tone," *Journal of the American Musicological Society* 34 (1981), 193-216.

———. *The Lucidarium of Marchetto of Padua: A Critical Edition, Translation, and Commentary*. Chicago: University of Chicago Press, 1985.

———. "What Trecento Music Theory Tells Us," in *Explorations in Music, the Arts, and Ideas: Essays in Honor of Leonard B. Meyer*, ed. Eugene Narmour and Ruth A. Solie. Stuyvesant: Pendragon Press, 1988.

———. *Prosdocimo de' Beldomandi: Contrapunctus: A New Critical Text and Translation*, Greek and Latin Music Theory, vol. 1. Lincoln, Nebraska, and London: University of Nebraska Press, 1984.

HETTRICK, WILLIAM E., trans. and ed. *The 'Musica instrumentalis deudsch' of Martin Agricola: A treatise on Musical Instruments, 1529 and 1545.* Cambridge: Cambridge University Press, 1994.

HIGGINS, PAULA. "Parisian Nobles, a Scottish Princess, and the Women's Voice in Late Medieval Song," *Early Music History* 10 (1991), 145-200.

HIRSHBERG, JEHOASH. "Hexachordal and Modal Structure in Machaut's Polyphonic Chansons," in *Studies in Musicology in Honor of Otto E. Albrecht*, ed. John Walter Hill. Kassel: Bärenreiter, 1980: 19-42.

HOLMAN, PETER. "Viols and bridges," *Musical Times* 126 (1985), 452.

———. *Four and Twenty Fiddlers: The Violin at the English Court, 1540-1690.* Oxford: Clarendon Press, 1994.

HOLSCHNEIDER, ANDREAS. *Die Organa von Winchester. Studien zum ältesten Repertoire polyphoner Musik.* Hildesheim: G. Olms, 1968.

HOPPIN, RICHARD H. "An Unrecognized Polyphonic Lai of Machaut," *Musica Disciplina* 12 (1958), 93-104.

HUBER, JOSEPH. *Altportugiesisches Elementarbuch.* Heidelberg: Carl Winters, 1933 (Portuguese translation: *Gramática do Português Antigo.* Lisboa: Gulbenkian, 1986).

HUGHES, ANDREW. *Manuscript Accidentals: Ficta in Focus, 1350-1450.* Musicological Studies and Documents 27. Neuhausen-Stuttgart: Hänssler Verlag / American Institute of Musicology, 1972.

HUOT, SYLVIA. *From Song to Book: The Poetics of Writing in Old French Lyric and Lyrical Narrative Poetry.* Ithaca, NY: Cornell University Press, 1987.

———. *Allegorical Play in the Old French Motet: The Sacred and the Profane in Thirteenth-Century Polyphony.* Stanford: Stanford University Press, 1997.

JACKMAN, H., ed. *Fifteenth Century Basse Dances.* The Wellesley Edition, vol. 6. Wellesley: Wellesley College, 1964.

JACKSON, ANTHONY. "Sound and Ritual," *Man* 3 (1968), 293-99.

JACOBUS LEODIENSIS (OF LIÈGE). *Speculum musicæ*, ed. Roger Bragard. Corpus Scriptorum de Musica III, 7 vols. American Institute of Musicology, 1955-1973.

JAMES MCKINNON, ed. *Man & Music: Antiquity and the Middle Ages.* London: Macmillan, 1990, chapter 8.

JEAN DE GERSON. *Oeuvres complètes*, ed. Mgr. Glorieux. 10 vols. in 11. Tournai: Desclée & Cie, 1960-73.

JEANROY, ALFRED, ed. *Le chansonnier d'Arras;* reproduction en phototypie. Paris, 1925.

——, LOUIS BRANDIN, and PIERRE AUBRY, eds. *Lais et descorts français du XIIIe siècle; texte et musique.* Paris, 1901.

——. *La Poésie lyrique des troubadours*, 2 vols. Toulouse, 1934.

JEFFERY, PETER. "A Four-Part *In Seculum* Hocket and a Mensural Sequence in an Unknown Fragment," *JAMS* 37 (1984), 16-19.

KARP, THEODORE. "Editing the Cortona Laudario," *Journal of Musicology* 11 (1993), 73-105.

——. "Interrelations between Poetic and Musical Form in Trouvère Song," *A Musical Offering: In Honor of Martin Bernstein.* New York: Pendragon, 1977, 137-62.

——. "Modal Variants in Medieval Secular Monophony," in *The Commonwealth of Music: In Honor of Curt Sachs.* New York: Free Press, 1965, 118-29.

——. *The Polyphony of Saint Martial and Santiago de Compostela.* 2 vols. Berkeley: University of California Press, 1992.

KATZ, ISRAEL JOSEPH. "The 'Myth' of the Sephardic Musical Legacy from Spain," *Fifth World Congress of Jewish Studies, IV.* Jerusalem, 1973.

——. "The Musical Legacy of the Judeo-Spanish *Romancero*," in *Hispania Judaica II*, ed. J. M. Solá-Solé et al. Barcelona: Puvill, 1982, 47-58.

——. "The Traditional Folk Music of Spain: Explorations and Perspectives," *Yearbook of the International Folk Music Council* 6 (1974), 64-85.

KEITEL, ELIZABETH ANN. "A Chronology of the Compositions of Guillaume de Machaut Based on a Study of Fascicle Manuscript Structure in the Larger Manuscripts," Ph.D. diss., Cornell University, 1976.

KELLY, DOUGLAS. *Medieval Imagination: Rhetoric and the Poetry of Courtly Love.* Madison: University of Wisconsin Press, 1978.

KENYON DE PASCUAL, BERYL. "Two Contributions to Dulcian Iconography," *Early Music* 25 (1997), 412-26.

KIBLER, WILLIAM W. *An Introduction to Old French.* New York: Modern Language Association of America, 1984.

KINKELDEY, OTTO. "Dance Tunes of the Fifteenth Century," in *Instrumental Music*, ed. David Hughes. Cambridge: Harvard University Press, 1959; repr. New York: Da Capo, 1972.

KISBY, FIONA. "Royal minstrels in the city and suburbs of early Tudor London: professional activities and private interests," *Early Music* 25 (1997), 199-219.

KNAPP, JANET. "Musical Declamation and Poetic Rhythm in Notre Dame Conductus," *Journal of the American Musicological Society* 32 (1979), 383-407.

KNAUFT, BRUCE M. "On Percussion and Metaphor," *Current Anthropology* 20 (1979), 189-91.

KÖRTE, OSWALD. *Laute und Lautenmusik bis zur Mitte des 16. Jahrhunderts*, Leipzig, 1901.

KREITNER, KENNETH. "Very low ranges in the sacred music of Ockeghem and Tinctoris," *Early Music* 14 (1986), 467-79.

KÜHN, HELMUT. *Die Harmonik der Ars Nova.* Berliner Musikwissenschaftliche Arbeiten 5. Munich, 1973.

LANCIANI, GIULIA, and GIUSEPPE TAVANI, eds. *Dicionário da Literatura Medieval Galega e Portuguesa.* Lisboa: Caminho, 1993.

LANGLAND, WILLIAM. *Piers Plowman.* A.V.C. Schmidt, ed. London and New York: J.M. Dent and E.P. Dutton, 1978.

LAPA, MANUEL RODRIGUES. *Lições de Literatura Portuguesa: Época Medieval*, 10th ed. Coimbra: Coimbra Editora, 1981.

LE MACON, ANTOINE JEAN. *Le Decameron de Boccace.* Originally published Lyon: Guillaume Rouille, 1551; Paris: I. Liseux, 1879.

LECLERQ, JEAN. *Monks and Love in Twelfth-Century France.* Oxford: Oxford University Press, 1979.

LEECH-WILKINSON, DANIEL. "Machaut's *Rose, lis* and the Problem of Early Music Analysis," *Music Analysis* 3 (1984), 9-28.

——. *Compositional Techniques in the Four-Part Isorythmic Motets of Philippe de Vitry and His Contemporaries.* New York: Garland, 1989.

LEFFERTS, PETER M. *The Motet in England in the Fourteenth Century.* Studies in Musicology 94. Ann Arbor, MI: UMI Research Press, 1986.

LEVY, EMIL. *Petit dictionnaire Provençal-Français*, 5th ed. Heidelberg, 1973.

LINDLEY, MARK. "Pythagorean Intonation," *The New Grove Dictionary of Music and Musicians*, ed. Stanley Sadie. London: Macmillian, 1980, 15: 485-87.

LINKER, ROBERT. *A Bibliography of Old French Lyrics*. University, MS, 1979.

LIPPHARDT, WALTHER. "Einige unbekannte Weisen zu den *Carmina Burana* aus der zweiten Hälfte des 12. Jahrhunderts," *Festschrift Heinrich Besseler zum 60. Geburtstag*. Leipzig, 1961, 101-25.

LIPPHARDT, WALTHER. "Unbekannte Weisen zu den *Carmina Burana*," *Archiv für Musikwissenschaft* 12 (1955), 122-42.

LIU, BENJAMIN, and JAMES T. MONROE. *Ten Hispano-Arabic Strophic Songs in the Modern Oral Tradition*. University of California Publications in Modern Philology, V. 125. Berkeley: University of California Press, 1989.

LIUZZI, FERNANDO. *La lauda e i primordi della melodia italiana*, 2 vols. Rome: Libreria dello Stato, 1934/5.

LOCKWOOD, LEWIS. "Pietrobono and the Instrumental Tradition at Ferrara," *Rivista Italiana di musicologica* 10 (1975), 115-33.

———. *Music in Renaissance Ferrara 1400–1505*. Oxford: Clarendon Press, 1984.

LORD, ALBERT BATES. *Epic Singers and Oral Tradition*. Ithaca: Cornell University Press, 1991.

———. *The Singer of Tales*, 1st ed. Harvard University Press; 8th ed. New York: Atheneum, 1978.

MACHAUT, GUILLAUME DE. *La Louange des Dames*, ed. Nigel Wilkins. New York: Barnes & Noble Books, 1973.

———. *Le Jugement du roy de Behaigne and Remede de Fortune*, ed. James I. Wimsatt, William W. Kibler, and Rebecca A. Baltzer. The Chaucer Library. Athens: The University of Georgia Press, 1988.

———. *Le Livre du Voir-Dit*, ed. Paulin Paris. Paris: Société des Bibliophiles François, 1875.

———. *The Fountain of Love (La Fonteinne Amoureuse) and Two Other Love Vision Poems*, ed. and trans. by R. Barton Palmer. Garland Library of Medieval Literature, Series A, vol. 54. New York: Garland Publishing, Inc., 1993.

MAHRT, WILLIAM P. "The rhetorical use of mode in the chansons of Guillaume Dufay," unpublished article.

MAIA, CLARINDA DE AZEVEDO. *História do Galego-Português*, Coimbra: INIC, 1986.

MAILLARD, JEAN H., ed. *Anthologie de chants de trouvères*. Paris, 1967.

———. *Évolution et esthétique du lai lyrique; des origins à la fin du XIVe siècle*. Paris, 1961.

MARCUSE, SIBYL. *Musical Instruments: A Comprehensive Dictionary*, corrected ed. New York: Norton, 1975.

MARROCCO, W. THOMAS, and NICHOLAS SANDON. *Medieval Music*. London: Oxford University Press, 1977.

MARSHALL, KIMBERLY. "Innovations in Organbuilding: 1250-1500," in *Music in Performance and Society: Essays in Honor of Roland Jackson*, Malcolm Cole and John Koegel, eds. Warren, MI: Harmonie Park Press, 1997, 97-98.

MARVIN, BOB. Response to EDWARD C. PEPE. "Pythagorean Tuning and its Implications for Music of the Middle Ages," *q.v.*, in *The Courant* 1/3 (1983), 29.

MCGEE, TIMOTHY J. "Singing without Text," *Performance Practice Review* 6 (1993), 1-32.

———. *Medieval Instrumental Dances*, Bloomington: Indiana University Press, 1989.

———. *Medieval and Renaissance Music: A Performer's Guide*. Toronto: University of Toronto Press, 1985.

———, with A. G. Rigg and David N. Klausner, eds. *Singing early music* Bloomington: Indiana University Press, 1996.

———, ed. *Medieval Instrumental Dances*. Bloomington: Indiana University Press, 1989.

MCKINNON, JAMES. "Iconography," in D. Kern Holoman and Claude Palisca, eds., *Musicology in the 1980s*. New York: Da Capo Press, 1982, 79-93.

———. "Cymbalum," in *The New Grove Dictionary of Music and Musicians*, ed. Stanley Sadie. London: Macmillan, 1980, 5: 116.

MCMAHON, JAMES V. *The Music of Early Minnesang*. Studies in German Literature, Linguistics, and Culture 41. Columbia, SC: Camden House, 1990.

MERSENNE, MARIN. *Harmonie Universelle*. Paris, 1636; repr. The Hague: Martinus Nijhoff, 1957.

METTMANN, WALTER, ed. *Alfonso X, el Sabio: Cantigas de Santa María*, 3 vols., 2nd ed. Madrid: Castalia, 1986-89.

MEYER, PAUL, and GASTON RAYNAUD, eds. *Le chansonnier français de Saint-Germain-des Prés*. Bibliothèque Nationale fr. 20050; reproduction phototypique, 2 vols. Paris, 1891; vol. I repr. New York, 1968.

MINAMOTO, H. "Conrad Paumann and the evolution of solo lute practice in the fifteenth century," *Journal of Musicological Research* 6 (1986), 291-310.

BIBLIOGRAPHY

MÖLK, ULRICH, and FRIEDRICH WOLFZETTEL. *Répertoire métrique de la poésie lyrique française des origines à 1500.* Munich, 1972.

MOLLER, HARTMUT, and RUDOLF STEPHAN. *Die Musik des Mittelalters.* Wiesbaden: Laaber, 1991.

MONTAGU, JEREMY. "The Restored Chapter House Wall Paintings in Westminster Abbey," *Early Music* 14 (1988), 239-49.

――――. *The World of Medieval and Renaissance Musical Instruments.* Woodstock, NY: Overlook Press, 1976.

MORETTI, CORRADO. *L'Organo Italiano,* 2nd ed. Milan: Casa Musicale Eco, 1973.

MUNROW, DAVID. "The Art of Courtly Love," *Early Music* I (1973), 195-99.

――――. *Instruments of the Middle Ages and Renaissance.* London: Oxford University Press, 1976.

MURPHY, JAMES J. *Rhetoric in the Middle Ages.* Berkeley: University of California Press, 1957.

――――. *Three Medieval Rhetorical Arts.* Berkeley: University of California Press, 1971.

MYNETT, ALA. "On the Reconstruction of a Medieval Tabor," *Early Music* 1 (1973), 223-27.

NÁDAS, JOHN. "Song Collections in Late-Medieval Florence," *Atti del XIV congresso della Società Internazionale di Musicologia.* Bologna, 1987, vol. I, 126-35.

NEEDHAM, RODNEY. "Percussion and Transition," *Man* 2 (1967), 606-14.

ODINGTON, WALTER. *Summa de speculatione musicae,* ed. Frederick F. Hammond. Rome, 1970.

PAGE, CHRISTOPHER. "An Aspect of Medieval Fiddle Construction," *Early Music* 2 (1984), 166-67.

――――. "An English Motet of the 14th Century in Performance: Two Contemporary Images," *Early Music* 25 (1997), 7-32.

――――. "Fourteenth-Century Instruments and Tunings: A Treatise by Jean Vaillant? (Berkeley, MS 744)," *Galpin Society Journal* 33 (1980), 17-35.

――――. "Going Beyond the Limits: Experiments with Vocalization in the French Chanson, 1340-1440," *Early Music* 20 (1992), 446-59.

――――. "Machaut's 'Pupil' Deschamps on the Performance of Music: Voices or Instruments in the 14th-Century Chanson," *Early Music* 5 (1977), 484-91.

――――. *Music and Instruments of the Middle Ages. Studies on Texts and Performance.* Aldershot: Variorum, 1997.

――――. "Polyphony before 1400," in *Performance Practice, Music before 1600,* ed. Howard Mayer Brown and Stanley Sadie. London: Macmillan, 1989, 79-104.

――――. "The 15th-Century Lute: New and Neglected Sources," *Early Music* 9 (1981), 11-21.

――――. *The Owl and the Nightingale: Musical Life and Ideas in France 1100-1300,* Berkeley: University of California Press, 1989.

――――. "The Performance of Ars Antiqua Motets," *Early Music* 16 (1988), 147-64.

――――. "The Performance of Songs in Late Medieval France: A New Source," *Early Music* 10 (1982), 441-50.

――――. *Voices and Instruments of the Middle Ages: Instrumental Practice and Songs in France 1100-1300.* Berkeley and Los Angeles: University of California Press, 1987.

PALMER, R. BARTON, ed. and trans. *Jugement deu roy de Navarre by Guillaume de Machaut.* New York: Garland, 1988.

――――. *Jugement dou roy de Behaingne by Guillaume de Machaut.* New York: Garland, 1984.

PARKER, IAN. "The Performance of Troubadour and Trouvere Songs: Some facts and conjectures," *Early Music* 5 (1977), 184-207.

PATERSON, LINDA M. *Troubadours and Eloquence.* Oxford: Oxford University Press, 1975.

PAYNE II, THOMAS BLACKBURN. "Poetry, Politics, and Polyphony: Philip the Chancellor's Contribution to the Music of the Notre Dame School," 2 vols. Ph.D. diss., University of Chicago, 1991.

PELLEGRINI, SILVIO, and GIOVANNA MARRONI. *Nuovo Repertorio Bibliografico della prima lirica galego-portoghese (1814-1977),* L'Aquila: Japadre, 1981 (regularly updated by the *Boletín Bibliográfico de la Asociación Hispánica de Literatura Medieval*).

PENSOM, ROGER. "Performing the Medieval Lyric: A Metrical-Accentual Approach," *Performance Practice Review* 10 (1997), 212-23.

PEPE, EDWARD C. "Pythagorean Tuning and Its Implications for Music of the Middle Ages," *The Courant* 1/2 (1983), 3-16.

PHILLIPS, ELIZABETH V., and JOHN-PAUL CHRISTOPHER JACKSON. *Performing Medieval and Renaissance Music.* New York: Schirmer Books, ca.1986.

PILLET, ALFRED and HENRY CARSTENS. *Bibliographie des troubadours.* Halle, 1933.

PIRROTTA, NINO. *Music and Culture in Italy from the Middle Ages to the Baroque.* Cambridge, MA: Harvard University Press, 1984.

PLANCHART, ALEJANDRO ENRIQUE. "The Early Career of Guillaume Du Fay" *JAMS* (1993), 341-68.

――――. *The Repertory of Tropes at Winchester,* 2 vols. Princeton: Princeton University Press, 1977.

————. "Tempo and Proportions," in *Performance Practice: Music before 1600*, ed. Howard Mayer Brown and Stanley Sadie. London: Macmillan, 1989, 126-44.

PLUMLEY, YOLANDA. *The Grammar of 14th Century Melody: Tonal Organization and Compositional Process in the Chansons of Guillaume de Machaut and the Ars Subtilior.* New York: Garland, 1996.

PODNOS, THEODOR. *Bagpipes and Tunings.* Detroit Monographs in Musicology 3. Detroit: Detroit Information Coordinators, 1974.

POLK, KEITH. *German Instrumental Music of the Late Middle Ages.* Cambridge: Cambridge University Press, 1992.

————. "Vedel and Geige—Fiddle and Viol: German String Traditions in the Fifteenth Century," *JAMS* 42 (1989), 484-526.

————. "Voices and Instruments: Soloists and Ensembles in the 15th Century," *Early Music* 18 (1990), 179-98.

PORTER, LAMBERT C. *La Fatrasie et le fatras: Essai sur la poésie irrationnelle en France au Moyen Age.* Paris: Minard, 1960.

PRICE, PERCIVAL. "Bell," in *The New Grove Dictionary of Music and Musicians*, ed. Stanley Sadie. London: Macmillan, 1980, 2: 424-36.

————. "Chimes," in *The New Grove Dictionary of Music and Musicians*, ed. Stanley Sadie. London: Macmillan, 1980, 4: 242-45.

PRIZER, WILLIAM. "The frottola and the unwritten tradition," *Studii Musicali* 15 (1986), 3-37.

RABY, F.J.E. *A History of Secular Latin Poetry in the Middle Ages*, 2 vols. 2nd ed. Oxford: Clarendon Press, 1957.

RANKIN, SUSAN. "Liturgical Drama," in *New Oxford History of Music*, vol. 2, new edition, ed., Richard Crocker and David Hiley. Oxford: Oxford University Press, 1990, 310-56.

RASTALL, RICHARD. "Music in the Cycle Plays," in *Contexts for Early English Drama*, ed. Marianne Briscoe and John Coldewey. Bloomington: Indiana University Press, 1989, 192-218.

————. *The Heaven Singing: Music in Early English Religious Drama.* Cambridge, Rochester: D. S. Brewer, 1996.

RAVENEL, BERNARD. "Rebec und Fiedel--Ikonographie und Spielweise," *Basler Jahrbuch für Historische Musikpraxis.* 8 (1984), 105-30.

REANEY, GILBERT. "Machaut, Guillaume de," in *The New Grove Dictionary of Music and Musicians*, ed. Stanley Sadie. London: Macmillan, 1980, 11: 428-36.

————. "The Part Played by Instruments in the Music of Guillaume de Machaut," *Studi Musicali* 6 (1977), 3-11.

————. "Voices and Instruments in the Music of Guillaume de Machaut," *Revue Belge de Musicologie* 10 (1956), 3-17 and 93-104.

————. *Guillaume de Machaut.* Oxford Studies of Composers 9. London: Oxford University Press, 1974.

REESE, GUSTAVE. *Music in the Middle Ages.* New York: Norton, 1940.

REMNANT, MARY. *English Bowed Instruments from Anglo-Saxon to Tudor Times.* Oxford: Clarendon Press, 1986.

————. *Musical Instruments of the West.* London: B.T. Batsford, Ltd., 1981.

————. *Musical Instruments: An Illustrated History from Antiquity to the Present.* London: B. T. Batsford Ltd., 1989.

————. "Rebec," in *The New Grove Dictionary of Music and Musicians*, ed. Stanley Sadie. London: Macmillan, 1980, 15: 635-38.

————. "The Diversity of Medieval Fiddles," *Early Music* 3 (1975), 47-51.

————. "The Use of Frets on Rebecs and Mediaeval Fiddles," *Galpin Society Journal* 21 (1968), 146-51.

RIEMANN, HUGO. *History of Music Theory*, trans. Raymond H. Haggh. Lincoln, 1962.

RITTMEYER-JSELIN, DORA. "Das Rebec," *Festschrift Karl Nef zum 60 Geburtstag.* Zurich, 1933.

ROESNER, EDWARD, general editor. *Le Magnus Liber Organi of Notre Dame de Paris*, 7 vols. [planned] Monaco: Éditions Oiseau-Lyre, 1993– .

RUIZ, JUAN. *Libro de buen amor.* Raymond S. Willis, ed. Princeton: Princeton University Press, 1972.

SALMEN, WALTER. *Der Spielmann im Mittelalter.* Innsbruck: Edition Helbling, 1983.

SÁNCHEZ, MIGUEL, ed. *Es razón de alabar, Música tradicional sefardí.* Comunidad de Madrid, 1996.

SANDERS, ERNEST H. "Consonance and Rhythm in the Organum of the Twelfth and Thirteenth Centuries," *Journal of the American Musicological Society* 33 (1980), 264-86.

SAWA, GEORG. "The Survival of Some Aspects of Medieval Arabic Performance Practice," *Ethnomusicology* 25 (1981), 173-86.

SCHNEIDER, WALTER C. "Percussion Instruments of the Middle Ages," *Percussionist* 15 (1978), 106-17.

SCHRADE, LEO. "Music in the Philosophy of Boethius," *Musical Quarterly* 33 (1947), 188.

SCHUELLER, HERBERT M. *The Idea of Music: An Introduction to Musical Aesthetics in Antiquity and the Middle Ages.* Kalamazoo: Medieval Institute Publications, 1988.

SEEBASS, TILMAN. "The Visualisation of Music through Pictorial Imagery and Notation in Late Medieval France," in *Studies in the Performance of Late Mediæval Music,* ed. Stanley Boorman. Cambridge: Cambridge University Press, 1983, 19-33.

SEPHIHA, HAÍM VIDAL *Le Judéo-Espagnol.* Paris: Éditions Entente, 1986.

SEROUSSI, EDWIN. "The Growth of the Judeo-Spanish Folksong Repertory in the 20th Century," *Proceedings of the 10th World Congress of Jewish Studies* II:D173-80. Jerusalem, 1989b.

———. *Mizimrat Qedem, The Life and Music of R. Isaac Algazi of Turkey,* with cassette. Jerusalem, Renanot, 1989.

SESINI, UGO. "Le Melodie Trobadoriche nel Canzoniere Provenzale della Biblioteca Ambrosiana (R. 71 sup.)," *Studi Medievali,* nuova serie, 12 (1939), 1-101; 13 (1940), 1-107; 14 (1941), 31-105.

SILVER, ISIDORE. *"Fatras,"* in *Princeton Encyclopedia of Poetry and Poetics, Enlarged Edition,* ed. Alex Preminger. Princeton: Princeton University Press, 1974, 272.

SLAVIN, DENNIS. "In Support of 'Heresy': Manuscript Evidence for the *a cappella* Performance of Early 15th-Century Songs," *Early Music* 19 (1991), 178-90.

SMITH, NATHANIEL B., and THOMAS G. BERGIN. *An Old Provençal Primer.* New York, 1984.

SMOLDON, W. L., ed. *Visitatio Sepulchri.* Oxford University Press, 1964.

———. *The Play of Daniel,* revised ed. by David Wulstan. Surrey: The Plainsong and Medieval Music Society, 1976.

SOUTHWORTH, JOHN. *The English Medieval Minstrel.* London: The Boydell Press, 1989.

SPANKE, HANS. *G. Raynauds Bibliographie des altfranzösischen Liedes, neu bearbeitet und ergänzt, erster Teil.* Leiden, 1955.

STAUDER, WILHELM. "Zur Entwicklung der Cister," *Festschrift Helmuth Osthoff zum 80. Geburtstag.* Tutzing (1979), 223-55.

———. *Alte Musikinstrumente in ihrer vieltausendjährigen Entwicklung und Geschichte.* Braunschweig: Klinkhardt and Biermann, 1973.

STEVENS, JOHN. "The 'Music' of the Lyric: Machaut, Deschamps, Chaucer," in *Medieval and Pseudo-Medieval Literature,* ed. P. Boitani and A. Torti. Cambridge: Brewer, 1984, 109-29.

———. *Words and Music in the Middle Ages.* Cambridge: Cambridge University Press, 1986.

STOCKMAN, E. "Diffusion of Musical Instruments," *Yearbook of the International Folk Music Society* 3 (1971), 128-37.

STROHM, REINHARD. "Filippotto da Caserta, or, The French in Lombardy," in *In cantu et sermone: For Nino Pirrotta on his 80th Birthday.* Florence: Olschki, 1989, 65-74.

———. *Music in Late Medieval Bruges.* Oxford: Oxford University Press, 1985.

———. *The Rise of European Music 1380-1500.* Cambridge: Cambridge University Press, 1993.

STRUNK, OLIVER. *Source Readings in Music History: Antiquity and the Middle Ages.* New York: Norton, 1965.

SUSAN RANKIN. "Liturgical Drama," in *New Oxford History of Music* vol. 2, new edition, ed. Richard Crocker and David Hiley. Oxford: Oxford University Press, 1990, 310-56.

SWITTEN, MARGARET L. *Music and Poetry in the Middle Ages: A Guide to Research on French and Occitan Song, 1100-1400.* New York: Garland, 1995.

TAVANI, GIUSEPPE. *La poesia lirica galego-portoghese,* in *Grundriß der romanischen Literaturen des Mittelalters,* vol. 2: *Les genres lyriques,* tome 1, fasc. 6, 8. Heidelberg: Carl Winter Universitätsverlag, 1980-83; Portuguese trans.: *A Poesia Lírica Galego-Portuguesa.* Lisboa: Comunicação, 1990.

TAVANI, GIUSEPPE. *Repertorio Metrico della lirica galego-portoghese.* Roma: Edizioni dell'Ateneo, 1967.

TAYLOR, RONALD J., ed. *The Art of the Minnesinger.* 2 vols. Cardiff: University of Wales Press, 1968.

TERNI, CLEMENTE, ed. *Laudario di Cortona.* Florence: La nuova Italia, 1988. Quaderni del "Centro per il collegamento degli Studi medievali e umanistici nell'Università di Perugia" 20 [Introductory study, transcriptions; not readily available outside Italy].

TEYSSIER, PAUL. *Histoire de la Langue Portugaise.* Paris: P.U.F., 1980; Portuguese trans.: *História da Língua Portuguesa.* Lisboa: Sá da Costa, 1982.

THORNTON, BARBARA. "The Singers View," *Early Music* 12 (1984), 523-29.

———. "Hildegard von Bingen aus der Sicht des Interpreten," *Concerto — Das Magazin für alte Musik* 2 (1984), 48-55.

———. "Hildegard von Bingens *Ordo Virtutum.* Die Rekonstruktion eines Mysterien-Dramas aus dem 12. Jahrhundert," *Ansätze zur Musik der Gegenwart Jahrbuch* 4 (1983/84), 171-86.

———. "Vokale und Gesangstechnik: Das Stimmideal der Aquitanischen Polyphonie," *Basler Jahrbuch für Historische Musikpraxis* 4 (1980), 133-50.

TISCHLER, HANS, and SAMUEL N. ROSENBERG, eds. *Chanter M'estuet: Songs of the trouvères.* Bloomington: Indiana University Press, 1981.

TOLIVER, BROOKS. "Improvisation in the Madrigals of the *Rossi Codex,*" *Acta Musicologica* 64 (1992), 165-76.

TOPSFIELD, L.T. *Troubadours and Love.* Cambridge: Clarendon Press, 1975.

TREITLER, LEO. "Homer and Gregory: The Transmission of Epic Poetry and Plainchant," *Musical Quarterly* 9 (1974), 333-72.

———. "'Improvised' and 'Composed' Music in the Medieval West," *Improvisation in Music,* ed. Leonard B. Meyer and E. Zonis. Chicago, 1973.

———. "Musical Syntax in the Middle Ages," *Perspectives of New Music* 4/1 (1965), 75.

TYDEMAN, WILLIAM. *The Theatre in the Middle Ages,* Cambridge: Cambridge University Press, 1978.

UHL, PATRICE. "La Poésie du 'non-sens' en français aux XIIIe et XIVe siècles. Diversité et solidarité des formes," *Perspectives Médiévales* 14 (1988), 65-70.

VAN DEN BOOGAARD, Nico H.J. *Rondeaux et refrains du XIIe siècle au début du XIVe.* Paris, 1969.

VAN DER MEER, JOHN HENRY. "Sackpfeife," in *Die Musik in Geschichte und Gegenwart,* 16 Supplement. Kassel: Bärenreiter, 1979, 1609-28.

VAN DER WERF, HENDRIK, ed. *The Extant Troubadour Melodies: Transcriptions and Essays for Performers and Scholars.* Rochester, 1984.

———. *Trouvère-Melodien,* 2 vols. Monumenta monodica medii aevi, 11 and 12. Kassel: Bärenreiter, 1977-79.

———. *The Chansons of the Troubadours and Trouvère: A Study of the Melodies and their Relation to the Poems.* Utrecht: Oosthoek, 1972.

VAN SCHAIJK, MARTIN. *The Harp in the Middle Ages: The Symbolism of a Musical Instrument.* Amsterdam and Atlanta, 1992.

VAN VLECK, AMELIA E. *Memory and Re-creation in Troubadour Lyric.* Berkeley: University of California Press, 1991.

VARANINI, GIORGIO, LUIGI BANFI, and ANNA CERUTI, eds. *Laude cortonesi dal secolo XIII al XV,* 4 vols. Florence: Leo Olschki, 1981-85.

VASCONCELLOS, CAROLINA MICHAËLIS DE. *Lições de Filologia Portuguesa, seguidas das Lições Práticas de Português Arcaico.* Lisboa: Dinalivro, n. d.

VIRDUNG, SEBASTIAN. *Musica Getutscht.* Basel, 1511; repr. New York: Broude Bros., 1966.

VON FISCHER, KURT. *Studien zur italienischen Musik des Trecento und frühen Quattrocento.* Bern, 1956.

WEISS, PIERO. *Letters of Composers through Six Centuries.* Philadelphia: Chilton Book Company, 1967.

WILKINS, NIGEL. "Music in the Fourteenth-Century Miracles de Nostre Dame," *Musica disciplina* 28 (1974), 39-75.

WILLIAMS, EDWIN. *From Latin to Portuguese. Historical Phonology and Morphology of the Portuguese Language,* 2nd. ed. Philadelphia, 1953; Portuguese trans.: *Do Latim ao Português.* 3rd. ed. Rio de Janeiro, 1975.

WILLIAMS, SARAH JANE. "Vocal Scoring in the Chansons of Machaut," *Journal of the American Musicological Society* 21 (1968), 251-57.

WILSON, BLAKE, ed. *The Florence Laudario: An Edition of Florence, Biblioteca Nazionale, Banco Rari 18,* with texts edited and translated Nello Barbieri. Recent Researches in the Music of the Middle Ages and Early Renaissance, vols. 29-30. Madison, WI: A-R Editions, 1995.

———. "Indagine sul *Laudario Fiorentino* (Firenze, Biblioteca Nazionale, Banco rari 18)," *Rivista Italiana di Musicologia* 31 (1996), 243-80.

———. "Madrigal, Lauda, and Local Style in Trecento Florence," *Journal of Musicology* 15 (1997), 137-77 [A discussion of links between Florentine laudesi and polyphonic traditions].

———. *Music and Merchants: The Laudesi Companies of Republican Florence.* Oxford: Clarendon Press, 1992.

WINTERNITZ, EMANUEL. "The Iconology of Music: Potentials and Pitfalls," in Barry Brook, Edward Downes, Sherman Van Solkema, eds., *Perspectives in Musicology.* New York: Norton, 1972.

———. *Musical Instruments and Their Symbolism in Western Art.* New Haven: Yale University Press, 1979.

WOODFIELD, IAN. *The Early History of the Viol.* Cambridge: Cambridge University Press, 1984.

WRIGHT, CRAIG. *Music and Ceremony at Notre Dame of Paris, 500-1500.* Cambridge: Cambridge University Press, 1989.

———. *Music at the Court of Burgundy, 1364-1419: A Documentary History.* Musicological Studies 28. Henryville, PA: Institute of Medieval Music, 1979.

————. "Voices and Instruments in the Art Music of Northern France during the 15th Century: A Conspectus," *Report of the Twelfth [IMS] Congress, Berkeley 1977.* Kassel: Bärenreiter, 1981, 643-49.

WRIGHT, LAURENCE. "The Medieval Gittern and Citole: A Case of Mistaken Identity," *Galpin Society Journal* 30 (1977), 8-42.

YOUNG, CRAWFORD. "On the Trail of Ensemble Music in the Fifteenth Century," *Companion to Medieval and Renaissance Music,* ed. Tess Knighton and David Fallows. New York: Schirmer Books, 1992, 143-45.

————. "Zur Klassifikation und ikonographische Interpretation mittelalterlicher Zupfinstrumente," *Basler Jahrbuch für historische Musikpraxis* 8 (1984), 67-103.

YOUNG, KARL. "The *Dit de la harpe* of Guillaume Machaut," *Essays in Honor of Albert Feuillerat.* New Haven: Yale University Press, 1943, 1-20.

————. *The Drama of the Medieval Church,* 2 vols. Oxford: Oxford University Press, 1933, repr. 1967.

YUDKIN, JEREMY, trans. *The music treatise of Anonymous IV: A New Translation.* Musicological Studies and Documents 4. Stuttgart, ca.1985.

ZIINO, AGOSTINO. "Laudi e miniature fiorentine del primo trecento," *Studi Musicali* 7 (1978), 653-69 [Facsimiles and transcriptions from fragmentary trecento laudari].

ZIOLKOWSKI, JAN M., ed. and trans. *The Cambridge Songs (Carmina Cantabrigiensia). Garland Library of Medieval Literature* 66, A. New York: Garland Publishing, 1994.

ZUMTHOR, PAUL. *Introduction a la poesie orale.* Paris: Éditions du Seuil, 1983.

————. *La Lettre et la Voix.* Paris: Éditions du Seuil, 1987.

————. *Toward a Medieval Poetics,* trans. Philip Bennett. French 1st ed. Paris, 1972. English 1st ed. Minneapolis: University of Minnesota Press, 1979.

Index